NEW FEDERATIONS
EXPERIMENTS IN THE
COMMONWEALTH

NEW FEDERATIONS

EXPERIMENTS IN THE COMMONWEALTH

BY

R. L. WATTS

PROFESSOR OF POLITICAL STUDIES
QUEEN'S UNIVERSITY, KINGSTON
ONTARIO

OXFORD
AT THE CLARENDON PRESS
1966

Oxford University Press, Ely House, London W. 1

GLASGOW NEW YORK TORONTO MELBOURNE WELLINGTON
CAPE TOWN SALISBURY IBADAN NAIROBI LUSAKA ADDIS ABABA
BOMBAY CALCUTTA MADRAS KARACHI LAHORE DACCA
KUALA LUMPUR HONG KONG

© *Oxford University Press 1966*

PRINTED IN GREAT BRITAIN
AT THE UNIVERSITY PRESS, OXFORD
BY VIVIAN RIDLER
PRINTER TO THE UNIVERSITY

PREFACE

THERE has already grown a considerable body of literature comparing the federal political systems in North America, Europe, and Australia, but as yet no similar intensive comparative study has been made of the many federations which have sprung up in Asia, Africa, and the Caribbean since 1945. In this work, therefore, I have set out to make a comparative analysis of six of these new federal experiments within the Commonwealth: India, Pakistan, Malaya and Malaysia, Nigeria, Rhodesia and Nyasaland, and the West Indies. I have attempted to examine the reasons why federal political institutions were established in these countries, and also the subsequent working of these federal systems. Consequently, I have focused my attention not only upon federal governments but also upon the societies on which they have rested.

A study of this ambitious scope has unavoidably faced a number of limitations. For instance, the brevity of the period during which these new federal systems have operated and the frequent modifications and even transformations which federal institutions in these countries have already undergone during their brief history have added to the difficulties. Nevertheless, some significant patterns among these federations have been discernible, and because the early years of these experiments have been crucial ones, a study of them seemed worth undertaking. If this book assists in the preliminary mapping out of a large field in which there remains scope for much more research to be done, it will have served its purpose.

Politics in the developing countries has been characterized by fluidity and rapid change. It has been necessary, therefore, in order to avoid finding myself on a treadmill continually rewriting simply in order to include references to the latest events, to fix arbitrarily upon a terminal date. For this reason, I have taken the end of 1963 as the final date for most purposes, although where particularly significant later developments are referred to. By 1963 the Nehru era in India was coming to a close, Pakistan had put into operation a new constitution with some federal features, Malaya had been expanded into Malaysia, and Nigeria had founded its federal system upon a new autochthonous republican constitution. By then, too, the initial federal experiments in the West Indies and in Central Africa had disintegrated completely.

Many have contributed to the making of this book, although the responsibility for its failings must remain solely mine. I am indebted to the Principal and my colleagues at Queen's University who made it possible for me to take two full years and several summers of study leave during which this work was prepared; to the Warden and Fellows of Nuffield College, Oxford, who provided me with the congenial haven in which most of the work was done; the

Canada Council and the Rhodes Scholarship Trust whose financial assistance made the travel and study possible.

Both at Oxford and at Queen's I have benefited from the advice and assistance of several persons to whom I am especially grateful. The writing and seminars of K. C. Wheare first inspired my enthusiasm for the study of federal government, and the doctoral thesis for Oxford University upon which this volume is based was prepared under his perceptive and always encouraging guidance. A. F. McC. Madden first directed my attention to the new federations, and subsequently provided indispensable counsel, assistance, and unfailing friendship at every stage of this work to its completion. F. G. Carnell, whose own essay on the new federations contained so many illuminating suggestions, read the entire draft and made many valuable suggestions for its improvement. His recent untimely death I count a heavy personal loss. I should also like to thank J. E. Hodgetts, G. Marshall, D. J. Murray, and B. E. Nelson for reading all or portions of the earlier drafts and offering me their discerning comments and criticisms, and G. P. Browne, B. T. G. Chidzero, K. B. Sayeed, and A. M. Taylor for the valuable assistance and advice they have given me. Furthermore, I am grateful to the many politicians and civil servants who in interviews and conversations supplied so much information and insight, but who almost invariably asked that their names remain anonymous. But above all my greatest debt is to my wife who endured it all and continued throughout to encourage me with her persistent enthusiasm.

R. L. W.

Queen's University
Kingston, Ontario, Canada

CONTENTS

PART THREE
FEDERAL POLITICAL SYSTEMS

CONTENTS

LIST OF TABLES

LIST OF MAPS

(at end)

PART ONE

INTRODUCTION

1

FEDERAL EXPERIMENTS

1. *The popularity of the federal solution*

As a means to political unity, the federal solution would seem to be more popular today than at any time in the last 150 years. A remarkable array of new governments has been created since 1945, and more are now in the process of construction, that claim the designation 'federal'.

In Europe, for instance, West Germany and Yugoslavia have adopted constitutions that purport to be federal and the European Common Market appears to be considered by some of its members as the foundation for a European Federation. In South America, where the federal structure of the United States has often been imitated, at least in form, the constitutions of Brazil (1946), Venezuela (1947), and the Argentine (1949) were federal in appearance, although operated in a unitary manner. The federal solution has enjoyed its greatest popularity during this period, however, among the developing countries of Asia, Africa, the Middle East, and the Caribbean.[1] With the breaking up of the colonial empires in these areas, the urgent need to create viable political units has resulted in many new federal governments and in the consideration of proposals for many more.

In some cases the new federal governments have started life as colonial federations, either imposed by the imperial power or developed by a process of negotiation between nationalists and the imperial government. Of the imperial nations, Britain has been the most prolific creator of colonial federations. The attempt to build an All-India federation collapsed in 1947, but federations were established subsequently in Malaya (1948), Rhodesia and Nyasaland (1953), Nigeria (1954), the West Indies (1958), and South Arabia (1959). In addition, a functional confederation, the East Africa High Commission (1947), was devised to administer common services in the British territories in that region.[2] The French, too, attempted to set up colonial federations in Asia and Africa: one in Indochina, one in French West Africa (A.O.F.), and one in French Equatorial Africa (A.E.F.). The Dutch imposed a federal constitution on Indonesia in 1949.

Imperial governments have not been alone, however, in resorting to the

---

[1] For a survey of the new unions and federations in these areas, see F. G. Carnell, 'Political Implications of Federalism in New States', in U. K. Hicks and others, *Federalism and Economic Growth in Underdeveloped Countries* (1961), pp. 25–37.

[2] Now titled the East African Common Services Organization. See Col. nos. 191/1945, 210/1947; and Cmnd. 1279 and 1433/1961.

federal solution. A number of federations have been created in the former colonial areas by self-governing nationalists. The Constituent Assemblies of India and Pakistan each devised constitutions which claimed to be federal. The constitution of Burma (1947) was sometimes also so described because it provided for autonomy for the minorities, although in intent it was clearly unitary. After the French colonial federations in Africa disintegrated, they were succeeded later by the Mali Federation (1959) and the Union of Central African Republics (1960), both short-lived themselves. The Cameroun Republic in 1961 became the first African state federating a former French and a former British territory. In the Arab world, the Arab Federation of Jordan and Iraq (1958), which lasted only a few months, was created to balance the United Arab Republic (1958), a unitary state combining Egypt and Syria, and to which Yemen was federated until the union collapsed in 1961.

The federal political systems established in the developing areas have not, however, always proved stable or successful. Some have disintegrated; others have been converted into unitary political unions. Many of the colonial federations, for instance, have shattered at the critical time just before or after the withdrawal of the imperial power, as did the British experiments attempting a Hindu–Muslim All-India federation, an inter-island federation in the West Indies, and a federal racial partnership in the Rhodesias and Nyasaland. Similarly the French federations in Indochina, French West Africa, and French Equatorial Africa failed to prove durable. Nor were the federations established by the imperial powers the only ones to crumble quickly: the Arab Federation of Jordan and Iraq, the Mali Federation, and the Union of Central African Republics splintered almost as soon as they had been agreed upon. On the other hand, some of the new federations have instead been transformed after only a brief existence into unitary political systems. Indonesia, for example, as soon as independence was gained, substituted a unitary state for the Dutch-imposed federal structure. In three other cases a federal system lasted for about a decade before succumbing to pressures for a unitary constitutional pattern. In Pakistan the collapse of constitutional government and its replacement by military rule in 1958 marked the end of a decade of troubled federal government. The cumbersome Libyan federal structure created in 1951 was recast into a unitary one in 1963, and Eritrea, federated with Ethiopia in 1952, lost its autonomous status in 1962.

Nor has the federal solution always been accepted as the appropriate one to begin with. In Ghana, Ceylon, Sudan, and the Belgian Congo, despite the urgent advocacy of a federal political structure by certain groups, unitary government was chosen right at the outset.

Viewed against the broad background of the general character of politics in the new states, the failure of many of these federations and the rejection of federal government in other instances is not surprising. Indeed the apparently predominant trend against liberal democratic institutions, the propensity for active presidential forms of government, one-party systems and military rule, the emphasis upon rapid economic growth and upon national solidarity, and the shortage of trained civil servants to manage complex systems of administration would appear to provide a generally unfavourable climate for federal systems of government.

But despite these trends, the popularity of the federal solution appears undiminished. Projects for new federations continue to be advanced. Pakistan, after a period of martial law, in 1962 promulgated a new constitution combining active presidential government with some federal features, and in 1963 agreement was reached upon the expansion of the Federation of Malaya into a Malaysian Federation including Singapore and two of the British territories in Borneo. After the collapse of the West Indies Federation the remnants left by the withdrawal of Jamaica and Trinidad almost immediately began considering a smaller and more cohesive East Caribbean Federation. In East Africa the solution to the problem of the position of the Baganda within a united Uganda was found in 1961 in federalization; to accommodate tribal fears within Kenya a measure of regionalization was adopted in 1963; and in 1963 formal negotiations were begun for a federation of Kenya, Uganda, Tanganyika, and Zanzibar to replace the confederal East African Common Services Organization. Elsewhere in Africa, a federal constitution was proposed for the Congo late in 1962 as a means to reunification, and the former British and French territories of Gambia and Senegal in 1962 began exploring the possibilities of some form of political association. Meanwhile in the Middle East the number of states joining the Federation of South Arabia doubled within its first four years, and Aden Colony itself was added in 1963 despite sharp local opposition. In the same year, for a brief period, a new federal United Arab Republic was projected as the basis for an eventual Pan-Arab federation. In spite of setbacks the federal solution has clearly continued to appeal powerfully to nation-builders in the developing countries.

This popularity of the federal form of government is perhaps surprising when we consider that before 1945 such a development was unexpected. Indeed, writing in 1939, Harold Laski, in an article entitled 'The Obsolescence of Federalism', declared: 'I infer in a word that the epoch of federalism is over.'[1] Federal government in its traditional form, with its compartmenting of functions, rigidity, and inherent conservatism was, he suggested, unable to keep pace with the tempo of life that giant capitalism had evolved. Based on an outmoded economic philosophy, it was a handicap in an era when positive government action was required. Decentralized unitary government was, he therefore concluded, more appropriate in the new conditions of the mid-twentieth century. Even Professor Wheare, much more sympathetic to the potentialities of federal government, conceded in 1945, in the Preface to his study, *Federal Government*, that 'it may be accepted as certain that much of

[1] H. J. Laski, *The New Republic*, xcviii (1939), p. 367.

what I have written may soon be out of date . . . because under the impact of war federal government was undergoing such strenuous testing, and such radical adaptation'. Professor Wheare rejected the view that federal government was out of date, and that it would disappear, but he recognized the trend in existing federations, under pressure of economic crises and war, towards a concentration of central powers sufficient in some cases to threaten the federal principle.[1] In 1945 the federal idea appeared to be on the defensive; yet only eight years later Professor Beloff was able to assert that it was enjoying 'a widespread popularity such as it had never known before'.[2]

This popularity of the federal form of government has stemmed from the conditions accompanying the break-up of the colonial empires. The units of colonial government were often merely the product of historical accident, of the scramble for empire, or of administrative convenience. As a result the colonial political boundaries rarely coincided with the distribution of the racial, linguistic, or religious communities, or with the locus of economic, geographic, and historical interests. In some cases, widely dissimilar peoples and tribes were grouped under a single administrative system and set of communications. In others, people and tribes were split between different imperial powers or administrative provinces. Consequently, with the end of colonial rule there were pressures for the erection of new political units that would represent more closely the economic, historical, and cultural affinities and diversities of the peoples of these areas.

But the creators of these new states have been faced with conflicting demands for both territorial integration and balkanization. They have had to reconcile the need, on the one hand, for relatively large economic and political units (in order to facilitate rapid economic development and to sustain genuine political independence), with the desire, on the other hand, to retain the authority of the smaller political units (associated with traditional allegiances and with the racial, linguistic, and religious communities). These opposing pressures were reinforced by the legacy of colonial rule, which created within the artificial units of colonial administration new loyalties and interests cutting across those of the cultural and traditional communities. Thus the focal issue in nation-building became the conflicting demands for unification and separation. The tension between these pressures appeared in both nationalist movements and in systems of colonial administration. With the prospect of political independence, nationalism divided peoples as well as united them. As a multi-ethnic demand for independent self-government, nationalism was an integrative force, but as a regional, provincial, communal, and tribal urge it was also a divisive force. Likewise, colonial administrators,

---

[1] K. C. Wheare, *Federal Government* (1st ed., 1946), ch. 12. All subsequent page references are to the fourth edition, 1963.

[2] M. Beloff, 'The "Federal Solution" in its Application to Europe, Asia, and Africa', *Political Studies*, i (1953), p. 114.

faced with culturally heterogeneous societies, were torn between the alternative advantages of large or small administrative units, and of direct or indirect rule.

In such situations, where the forces for integration and for separatism have been at odds with each other, the federal solution has proved a popular formula. It makes possible the large political and economic unit composed of varied peoples and cultures in which these smaller groups are assured some autonomy. Thus it provides the common ground between the centralizer and the provincialist. In an age when the prevalence of democratic slogans has made the use of force for the unification of diverse groups difficult to justify as a permanent solution, federal government presents a constitutional way of winning support for political and economic integration from a heterogeneous population.

2. *The scope of this study*

In the case of the classic examples of orthodox federal government, particularly the United States, Switzerland, Canada, and Australia, a considerable number of comparative studies have been made. There has as yet, however, been relatively little systematic writing comparing the more recent federations which have sprung up in the developing areas of the world since 1945. The aim of this study, therefore, is to undertake a comparative analysis of six of these experiments in federal government within the Commonwealth since 1945: India, Pakistan, Malaya, Nigeria, Rhodesia and Nyasaland, and the West Indies. I shall be concerned both with the reasons why federal institutions were established and with the structure and working of these federal systems up to the end of 1963. Occasionally, where it is particularly relevant, references will be made to the even later federal developments within the Commonwealth in South Arabia,[1] Uganda,[2] Kenya,[3] and the East Caribbean,[4] but because it is too early to reach firm judgements about them, these examples will not be examined in detail.

At first sight the six federations selected for this study would appear to be so widely varied as to have little in common. To begin with they have been located in different geographical areas and have had diverse cultural traditions: three are in Asia, two in Africa, and one in the Caribbean. As nations they have varied in size from India with a population of over 435 millions, to the West Indies, including Jamaica, with just over 3 millions.[5] Most of these federations united geographically contiguous territories, but the two regions of Pakistan are separated by 1,000 miles of hostile territory, the West

[1] Cmnd. 665/1959, 1814/1962; S.I. 1963, no. 82.
[2] Cmnd. 1523/1961, 1778/1962; S.I. 1962, no. 2175.
[3] Cmnd. 1700/1962, 1970 and 2156/1963; S.I. 1963, no. 791 and 1968.
[4] Cmnd. 1746/1962.
[5] See Table 1, p. 361. The largest Indian state, Uttar Pradesh, contains twenty times the total population of the West Indies Federation, including Jamaica.

Indies was a federation of scattered islands, and the Borneo states of Malaysia are separated from Malaya by sea. In some the major social diversities have been concentrated territorially, while in others, notably Malaya and Central Africa, the basic racial cleavages seemed to run through each of the constituent territories. A number of these federations, such as the West Indies, Malaya, and Rhodesia and Nyasaland, were formed by the aggregation of separate and distinct states or colonies; others, such as India, Pakistan, and Nigeria, by contrast, appear to have been federalized by devolution from former unitary colonial structures. In some of these federal systems, particularly the Asian examples, political power has been concentrated in the central government to such a degree as to raise frequently the question whether they are really federal at all; in the West Indies, on the other hand, the central government was entrusted with less power than in most confederacies. Three of these federations, India, Nigeria, and Malaya, have proved relatively and even surprisingly stable, but the other three have not. In Pakistan federal government was replaced for a period by military rule, and both the West Indies Federation and the Federation of Rhodesia and Nyasaland have disintegrated. There might, then, seem little ground for comparison of these federations.

Yet these six federations have possessed significant common features. All of them were recent federations, formed since 1947. All adopted constitutions that claim to be federal in the orthodox sense of the term. All were, or had been at one time, British dependencies, and had been strongly influenced by British political traditions. All have attempted to combine parliamentary cabinet government with a federal political system. All were relatively undeveloped economically and sought rapid economic and social development. All were socially diverse and contained significant minorities wishing to preserve their individuality.

Thus, in spite of the considerable variations in social and political traditions and situations, these six federations have sufficient in common to provide a basis for comparison. Indeed, the fact that they possessed certain features in common, yet varied widely in others makes them a particularly suitable group for comparative analysis. The study of these examples should help to illuminate not only their similarities but also their differences. The comparison may help to give us some insight into the interaction in each case between social structure, constitution, and political practice: into how similar federal institutions have worked when superimposed on different social foundations, and how similar social forces have reshaped varied federal institutions.

It must be borne in mind that such a study inevitably faces a number of difficulties and limitations. To begin with, there has been only a brief period of federal government in these countries on which to base conclusions. Thus it is not possible to get the long historical perspective that scholars writing about the older federations have been able to achieve. Moreover, because of this brief existence, there have been few detailed and scholarly monographs on these federal systems, except in the case of India. This has meant that, before any comparison was possible, considerable research into each of the individual federations was necessary. A further difficulty has been that during their brief existence the history of these federations has been one of fluidity and change. In the short period before 1963 most of them had already operated at least two distinct federal constitutions, all of them had undergone frequent modifications, federal government had been suspended for a period in Pakistan, and had suffered severe and in the end fatal strains in the West Indies and in Rhodesia and Nyasaland. At best, therefore, one can at this stage arrive at only tentative conclusions.

Nevertheless, despite difficulties that have placed limitations upon the comparative analysis, it is possible to discern some general patterns of significant similarities and differences among these new federations. Moreover, because the early years in their federal existence have been crucial formative ones, an examination of them is of particular interest and importance. The main value of the study will lie, perhaps, in mapping out a large field in which there is scope for much research to be done.

3. *The federal concept*

The term 'federal' has generally been used loosely in political discussions. A preliminary discussion of the meaning of the term is necessary, therefore, in any study of the operation of federal government in the developing countries. As a rule the adjective 'federal' has been applied to constitutions and to forms of government, although some writers, notably Harold Laski and W. S. Livingston, have also talked of 'federal societies'.[1] Most of those who have spoken of 'federal government' have had in mind at least a form of political association in which two or more states constitute a political unity with a common government, but in which these member states retain a measure of internal autonomy. Within this loose general meaning, however, there have been a wide variety of more specific uses of the term 'federal'.[2]

Perhaps the oldest meaning of the expression 'federal government' appears in its use to refer to the loose linking together by treaty of sovereign states for specific military or economic purposes. In this sense the term 'federal' is synonymous with 'confederal'. Indeed, etymologically there is little to distinguish between 'federal' and 'confederal', or between 'federation' and 'confederation' or 'confederacy'. Each of these words implies a covenant, compact, or treaty among independent states. Examples of federation in this form

---

[1] H. J. Laski, *A Grammar of Politics* (1925), p. 59; W. S. Livingston, *Federalism and Constitutional Change* (1956), ch. 1.

[2] For a study of the history of ideas of federalism see S. Mogi, *The Problem of Federalism, A Study in the History of Political Theory* (1931), 2 vols.

can be found as far back in history as the confederacies of ancient Greece.[1] Other prominent examples were the Swiss Confederation before 1848, the United Provinces of the Netherlands 1579–1795, the United States of America before 1787 and the German Empire 1871–1918.[2] This usage is still current in contemporary Europe, where the various European supra-national agencies designed to secure co-operation between nations have sometimes been referred to as 'federal'.

In other cases 'federal government' has been taken to be equivalent to decentralized government. Many of the governments of South America, which purport to be federal, have in practice combined devolution of power to regional governments with an overriding authority exercised by the central government.[3] This would appear also to be the nature of federal government in the U.S.S.R. and Yugoslavia, and in Germany under both the Weimar Constitution and the Constitution of the Federal Republic of Germany 1949.[4] The federal relationship of the overseas territories to the metropolitan country in the French Union, while it lasted, was also clearly this type of decentralization.

Political theorists, students of political institutions, and constitutional lawyers, in attempting to make the term 'federal' more precise, have usually fixed it exclusively on a form of government midway between these two extremes.[5] To distinguish 'federal government' from both 'confederal government' on the one hand and 'decentralized unitary government' on the other, it has often been defined as a particular form of government in which, following the model of the United States Constitution of 1787, general and regional governments, neither subordinate to the other, exist within a single country. By contrast, in a confederal form of government the central government would be subordinate to the regional governments,[6] and in a unitary system the regional governments would be subordinate to the central government. The fundamental and distinguishing characteristic of a federal system is that neither the central nor the regional governments are subordinate to each other, but are instead co-ordinate.

From this definition of the federal concept, as involving two co-ordinate levels of sovereignty within a single country, the widely accepted theory of

---

[1] E. A. Freeman, *History of Federal Government in Greece and Italy* (2nd ed., 1893).

[2] Wheare, *Federal Government*, chs. 1, 2.   [3] Ibid., pp. 21–22.

[4] Ibid., pp. 23–26. E. Plischke, *Contemporary Government of Germany* (1961), pp. 63–66, disagrees with Wheare, however, and argues that the Federal Republic of Germany is federal in the sense that national and state governments are co-ordinate.

[5] Among scholars, particularly in Germany, the distinctions between the various forms of confederation and federation have been worked at most meticulously. There is an extensive technical literature on the subject in which such terms as 'staatenbund', 'bundesstaat', and 'staatenstaat' are dealt with and defined. See W. Anderson, *Federalism and Intergovernmental Relations* (1946), pp. 6–7; Mogi, op. cit., 2 vols.

[6] For a different view see C. J. Hughes, *Confederacies* (1963). He argues that the differentiating characteristic is that a confederacy is a form of union in which the federal link is more strongly political than legal.

'dual federalism' has been developed. It was assumed that the dual sovereignties—general and regional—must exist side by side, each separate and virtually independent of the other in its own sphere.[1] A number of implications have generally been taken to follow. The general and regional governments must each act directly on the people. There must be an explicit constitutional demarcation of powers and functions between the general and regional governments. Governments at both levels must each be limited to their own sphere of action and must each be independent within their own sphere. Generally, although not necessarily, the division of authority must be specified in a written constitution, and an independent judiciary must be created to interpret the supreme constitution and to act as guardian of the constitutional division of powers.

The classic examples of such federations usually cited are the United States prototype of 1787 and the later Swiss, Canadian, and Australian federations, although there are some significant variations among these. Indeed they differ sufficiently for scholars to raise the question whether some of them are truly 'federal' or are instead only 'quasi-federal' in character.[2] The issue is further confused by the fact that the founders of these federations did not use the term 'federal' with such precision. Indeed, the creators of the American model described as 'federal' both the Articles of Confederation of 1777 and the constitution of 1787, advocating the latter simply as a more efficient federal structure.[3] Nor was the term 'federal' included anywhere in the latter constitution. In the Swiss and Canadian cases the founders of these federations often referred to the structures they created as 'confederations', apparently making no precise differentiation between 'federations' and 'confederations'. Nevertheless, it has been generally believed that a distinctive characteristic common to the United States, Switzerland, Canada, and Australia is that the general and regional governments were intended to act as separate—and separated—sovereigns, operating in distinct spheres of activity.

Recent developments in the American, Canadian, and Australian federations have resulted in a new concept of 'co-operative federalism'.[4] In these federations the extension of nationwide commercial enterprise, the development of an interdependent economy, and the growth of national sentiment, have resulted, particularly under the pressures of economic crises and of war, in extensive inter-governmental administrative co-operation and at least partial financial dependence of the regional governments upon the general

---

[1] Wheare, *Federal Government*, chs. 1 and 2, esp. pp. 10, 14.

[2] Ibid., ch. 2. [3] Ibid., pp. 10–11.

[4] Jane P. Clark, *The Rise of a New Federalism* (1938); *Iowa Law Review*, xxiii (1938), pp. 455–616, 'A Symposium on Co-operative Federalism'; G. C. Benson, *The New Centralization* (1941), esp. chs. 4, 6, 10, 11; A. H. Birch, *Federalism, Finance and Social Legislation in Canada, Australia and the United States* (1955), pp. 304–6; J. A. Corry, 'Constitutional Trends and Federalism', in A. R. M. Lower and others, *Evolving Canadian Federalism* (1958), pp. 92–125.

governments. The trend to 'co-operative federalism' has been described in the following terms:[1]

It has arisen because several separate governments share a divided responsibility for regulating a single economic and social structure. It is most unlikely that any constitution could be devised which would enable each to perform its specific functions adequately without impinging seriously on the others. So their activities are inevitably mingled and co-operative arrangements must be worked out. In the result, formal powers are not co-terminous with operating responsibilities; the two levels of government as well as the several state and provincial governments interpenetrate one another in many places and ways. Under the heat and pressure generated by social and economic change in the twentieth century, the distinct strata of the older federalism have begun to melt and flow into one another.

It is clear that the concept of 'dual federalism', of separate general and regional governments acting, with only minor exceptions, in distinct watertight compartments each independent of the other, is not applicable in the developed federations today. Interdependence and co-operation between the two levels of government are instead their characteristic features.

The first writers to advance the theory of 'co-operative federalism' usually considered this as a recent development, which represented a radical departure from the traditional practices within these federations during the nineteenth century. Two recent students of the American federal system, M. J. C. Vile and D. J. Elazar, however, have gone even further in the rejection of 'dual federalism'.[2] They suggest that the traditional conception of federalism as requiring a sharp demarcation of responsibilities between two independent sets of sovereignties has never worked in practice in the United States, and that in the nineteenth century, as in the twentieth century, administrative co-operation and political interdependence between federal and state governments was a dominant characteristic of the American federal system, despite formal legal pronouncements to the contrary.

In the study of the new federations one of the questions we shall be concerned with is the degree to which these experiments represent examples of 'dual federalism' or of 'co-operative federalism'. We shall find that the statesmen creating the six federations were much influenced by and often used the language of 'dual federalism'. But we shall also find that, as in the older federations, 'dual federalism' proved a practical impossibility and a large degree of interdependence between general and regional governments has proved unavoidable.[3]

It should be made clear at the outset that while the theories of 'dual federalism' and 'co-operative federalism' appear to represent sharply contrasting positions, both are derived from the same basic idea. The notion at the root

---

[1] Corry, op. cit., pp. 121–2.

[2] M. J. C. Vile, *The Structure of American Federalism* (1961), ch. x; D. J. Elazar, *The American Partnership* (1962), ch. i.

[3] See Chapters 10 and 14.

of each is that within a federal system the general and regional governments should be co-ordinate in the sense that neither is subordinate to the other. This was considered traditionally in the theory of 'dual federalism' to require that the general and regional governments be independent of each other, operating in separate and distinct spheres. This conclusion rested on the assumption that the dependence of one level of government upon another would in effect mean subordination, and thus a violation of the federal principle. As long as the dependence of one government upon another is one-sided this presupposition is valid enough. If, however, both levels of government are dependent upon each other—interdependent—then dependence does not necessarily imply the subordination of one to the other.[1] In such a case, where each level is to some degree dependent on the other, there would be a balance of power between general and regional governments. Thus, neither tier of government would be independent, but the authority of neither would be subordinate. This in fact is the contemporary situation in the older federations. The regional governments have become increasingly dependent upon the central governments for their finances, and the central governments have had to rely more and more on the administrative co-operation of the regional governments for the implementation of national policies. The activities of central governments have expanded dramatically, but so also have those of regional governments. The difference between the two versions of the federal concept is chiefly one of emphasis: 'dual federalism' views the two sets of government primarily as equal rivals, 'co-operative federalism' views them as equal partners. What lies at the root of both theories is the premise that in a federation neither level of government is subordinate to the other.

By the federal concept then I mean the principle of organization whereby a compromise is achieved between concurrent demands for union and for territorial diversity within a society, by the establishment of a single political system, within which, general and regional governments are assigned co-ordinate authority such that neither level of government is legally or politically subordinate to the other. Other forms of government may recognize or express elements of both unity and diversity, but make one or other of the levels of government subordinate. Thus in 'confederal government' ultimate supremacy lies with the regional governments, and in 'decentralized unitary government' supreme authority rests with the central government.

Two further points remain concerning this definition of the federal principle. First, it does not provide only one pure federal model, for a whole range of institutional variations implementing the principle of co-ordinate authority is possible. For instance, the manner in which authority is distributed and the actual scope of the functions which are assigned to each tier of government may differ considerably according to the needs of a particular society. The degree to which the two levels of government are either mutually

[1] See Vile, op. cit., pp. 196-7.

independent or interdependent may vary also. Similarly, the institutional arrangements for protecting, amending, and administering the distribution of functions, for organizing central legislation and administration, and for organizing government within the component territorial units may take a variety of forms. As statesmen in the developing countries experiment in new situations, with fresh ways of applying the federal idea, there may well result new forms or adaptations of federal government.

Secondly, this definition provides a general but not an exact test for classifying states as federal or not. When we move away from definitions limited purely to the consideration of constitutional law to definitions encompassing also political and administrative practice and social attitudes as aspects of a political system, inevitably less precision is possible. Moreover, nation-makers, unconcerned with the niceties of theories and more interested in the pragmatic value of institutions, have not been averse to attempting 'mixed solutions' or 'hybrids' in which unitary, federal, and confederal features have been incorporated within a single political system at the same time. But while the dividing line between federal and non-federal governments cannot, therefore, be drawn precisely, we may distinguish individual political systems which are 'predominantly federal', 'predominantly unitary', or 'predominantly confederal'. Some examples may be particularly difficult to classify, for it is conceivable that in some 'mixed solutions' no principle may predominate. An example is the Nigerian constitution of 1951,[1] which was a blend of what are usually considered unitary and confederal institutions. Nevertheless, in most cases it is possible to arrive at some judgement on the degree to which the dependence, independence, or interdependence of general and regional governments is significant.

4. *Federal societies, constitutions, and governments*

When political studies were less an analysis of political and administrative behaviour and more a study of legal and constitutional relations, writers examining federations tended to concentrate primarily on the legal framework within which the general and regional governments carried on their activities. But students of politics have come to recognize that a merely legalistic study of constitutions will not alone explain the political patterns within federal systems. The actual operation and practices within a federation are likely, in response to the play of social and political pressures, to diverge widely from the formal relationships specified in the written legal document.

On the other hand, in the contemporary study of politics, and particularly among those concerned with politics in the new states, excessive legalism has given way to what appears to be a complete preoccupation with group and party behaviour and to the view that the study of institutions, and particularly constitutions, is merely an outmoded absorption with façades. It is significant

[1] S.I. 1951, no. 1172.

for instance that, in spite of the array of new federations created since 1945 in the former colonial areas, there is not a single reference to federalism in the index of G. A. Almond and J. S. Coleman, *The Politics of Developing Areas*, published in 1960. But just as inordinate legalism gives only a one-sided picture, it is a serious mistake, on the other hand, to underrate the role and psychological importance of the constitutional and institutional forms in political behaviour, even in new states. The extensive concern of nationalists themselves in the developing countries with questions of constitutional and institutional forms shows the degree to which these have been considered important and have influenced their activities.

Our study of federal political systems, then, must not be limited either exclusively to questions of institutional structure or merely to patterns of social forces, but rather to the interrelation of the two. It is in the interplay and interaction of the social foundations, the written constitutions and the actual practices and activities of governments, that an understanding of the nature and effectiveness of the recent federal experiments in developing countries is to be found.

Scholars analysing the older federations have been conscious of the importance of the social structure underlying a federal political system. Indeed K. C. Wheare's chapter on 'Some Prerequisites of Federal Government' might be described as in some respects a sociology of federalism.[1] W. S. Livingston has gone as far as to suggest that federalism is a function not of constitutions but of societies. He declares:

> The essential nature of federalism is to be sought for, not in the shadings of legal and constitutional terminology, but in the forces—economic, social, political, cultural—that have made the outward forms of federalism necessary. . . . The essence of federalism lies not in the constitutional or institutional structure but in the society itself. Federal government is a device by which the federal qualities of the society are articulated and protected.[2]

In view of the importance of social forces in moulding federal political institutions, a major part of this study will be concerned with their interplay.

It must be recognized, however, that the causal relation between a federal society and its political institutions is a complex and dynamic one. The pressures within a society may force expression in its political institutions; but these institutions, once created, may themselves shape the pattern of society by determining the channels in which these social pressures will flow. Thus the relationship between a society and its political institutions is not static but one

---

[1] Wheare, *Federal Government*, ch. 3. See also his 'Federalism and the Making of Nations' in A. W. Macmahon (ed.), *Federalism Mature and Emergent* (1955), pp. 28–43; and 'When Federal Government is Justifiable', in G. Sawer (ed.), *Federalism: an Australian Jubilee Study* (1952), pp. 110–17.

[2] W. S. Livingston, *Federalism and Constitutional Change* (1956), pp. 1–2. See also Livingston, 'A Note on the Nature of Federalism', *Political Science Quarterly*, lxvii (1952), p. 81.

of continual interaction. We shall be concerned, therefore, not only with the influence of social forces upon the adoption of federal constitutional structures and upon their subsequent operation,[1] but with the influence of the federal political superstructures upon social loyalties, feelings, and diversities.[2]

A comparative analysis of recent experiments with the 'federal solution' in developing countries is not, therefore, merely a legal and constitutional study, but rather a wider examination of federal societies, federal constitutions, federal governments, and of their interaction. Although in one sense a relatively specialized study, it is thus of interest not only to the constitutional lawyer concerned with the nature of legal frameworks and the student of political institutions occupied with the operation of particular types of political institutions; but also to the sociologist studying phenomena of social integration and diversity, to the economist examining the role of political institutions in fostering or hindering economic growth, to the geographer concerned with the territorial distribution of social interests, to the historian interested in the genesis and evolution of federal societies and institutions, and to the political theorist analysing political concepts and their implications.

[1] Part II (Chapters 3–6).   [2] Chapter 13.

2

THE SIX FEDERATIONS: A SURVEY

1. *India*

THE six federal systems established in the Commonwealth after 1945 had much in common. All represented attempts to combine unity and diversity; in each the federal solution was intended to recognize the claims of minorities and to provide for them within a political union. But in a sense each of these federations was also unique. The particular problems they were designed to cope with varied widely and each constituted a distinct federal experiment.

In India the problem was one of consolidating a country which was as large in population as Europe excluding Russia, and whose regional components in size, resources, and linguistic and cultural distinctiveness could properly be compared to the sovereign nations of Europe. British rule had imposed a strong central authority and had provoked in response a powerful nation-wide movement for independence. But both the imperial administrators and the Congress movement found it necessary to make concessions to the powerful pull of regional interests.

From as early as 1861, and especially after 1919, the history of British India was one of gradual devolution of power to the provinces, as administrators, quite apart from seeking to solve the communal problems, attempted to keep contact with their Indian subjects. By 1935, in the face of the hard realities of the Indian situation, the British Government had committed itself to a federal form of government as the solution to a number of crucial problems facing India. In the first place, it provided a way of yoking together within a single constitutional system the portions of India under indirect rule and those under direct rule. The indirectly controlled princely states, where personal rule prevailed, were scattered throughout India, and together they composed two-fifths of the area and a quarter of the population of continental India. In the British provinces, on the other hand, where representative institutions were evolving, the Congress, hostile to the princes as undemocratic and anti-national, was entrenched. Federation was seen as a way of bringing 'the two Indias' together under a common constitution. Secondly, since the increasing communal antagonism was attributed to the Congress emphasis upon monolithic unity and centralization, and to Muslim fears of Hindu predominance, it was hoped that a federal structure might reconcile the two groups by accommodating Muslim anxieties within a united India. In the event, the Government of India Act, 1935, achieved neither of these aims. The princes, deterred by the undisguised hostility of the Congress, refused to accede to the federation, while Congress insistence upon being the sole and exclusive embodiment of Indian nationalism led to the solidification of Muslim support for a completely separate state of their own. By 1947, in view of the intransigence on both sides, the British Government decided that partition was unavoidable, and two independent Dominions were established on 15 August 1947. The Indian Independence Act, 1947, assigned to the constituent assemblies of India and Pakistan sovereign constitution-making authority, and at the same time provided that the federal scheme of the 1935 Act should serve in each as the interim constitution until the constituent assemblies completed their work.

The Constituent Assembly of India rejected a unitary constitution as 'a retrograde step' in such a vast, populous, and variegated country, but, influenced by the immediate experience of partition, and concerned with the threat of insecurity and disintegration, it insisted that 'the soundest framework for our constitution is a federation with a strong Centre'.[1] The emphasis upon national unity was reflected both in the manner in which the princely states were rapidly integrated into the Indian Union, and in the wide powers invested in the central government under the new constitution.

The Indian Independence Act had terminated the British paramountcy over the princely states and had left them legally independent of both India and Pakistan. But since without the co-operation of these states scattered among its provinces India could not hope to achieve political stability or full economic development, there was a pressing need to incorporate them into the new federation. By a combination of persuasion, cajolery, bribery, and the threat of military power, some 555 states were induced to accede to the Union by 1948. Between 1947 and 1950 the integration of these states into viable units, the democratization and modernization of their administrations, and their subordination constitutionally and financially to the central government, were carried out simultaneously. By 1950 the Ministry of States under the leadership of Sardar Patel had brought the states into an organic unity with the Union and had transformed the map of India.

The new constitution adopted by the Constituent Assembly became operative on 26 January 1950. Its federal features followed closely, indeed might be described as an adaptation of, those of the Government of India Act, 1935. That Act had placed an overriding authority in the hands of the central government, presided over by the British Governor-General in order to provide a check upon the Congress ministries in the provinces. When for quite different reasons the Constituent Assembly, concerned about the strength of the forces for disintegration and disruption, felt the need for a strong central government, it found in the framework of the 1935 Act a ready-made model. Thus, although the Indian Union exhibits the usual characteristics of a federa-

---

[1] *Second Report of Union Powers Committee*, 5 July 1947, in C.A.I., *Reports of Committees* (1st ser., 1947), p. 71.

tion—a dual polity, a distribution of powers between national and state governments, a relatively rigid written constitution, and a supreme court—its salient feature, derived from its forerunner, was a unitary bias. This expressed itself in the wide authority given to the central government in the extensive federal and concurrent lists, in the power to implement treaties, in certain controls over administration in the states, in the power to levy taxes, in controls over public borrowing, and in the procedure for creating new states or altering state boundaries. In addition the Supreme Court and the state High Courts were integrated into a single judiciary, and a common All-India civil service for important posts in both central and state governments was continued. The name itself, 'the Union of India', was deliberately chosen to emphasize the 'indestructible' character of the new federation.[1] In emergencies even more sweeping powers were given to the central government to exercise overriding legislative and executive authority. Indeed, the new constitution was expressly designed to establish a federal system in normal times, but to be easily convertible to a unitary system in cases of war or other emergencies.[2]

In the post-independence period one of the most significant developments has been the popular demand for the reorganization of states on a linguistic basis. The movement for linguistic states had existed long before independence, but until then it had been obscured by the strength of the Hindu–Muslim communal antagonism. The demand arose because the existing provincial boundaries established under British rule were mainly the result of historical accident and administrative convenience, bearing little correspondence to the distribution of the major language groups. As early as 1920 the Congress had accepted the linguistic redistribution of the provinces as a clear objective and had adopted the principle for the purposes of its own internal organization. But after independence, the Congress leadership, fearing that linguistic divisions might have a disrupting effect on the fragile Union, steadily resisted any immediate application of the linguistic principle. Nevertheless, as resentments at differential treatment aroused tensions between different linguistic groups within the multilingual states, the movement for a revision of units gained ground. Under the pressure of public opinion a reluctant Nehru was forced to concede to the demands. First, Andhra was separated from Madras in 1953, and then in 1956 a general reorganization of state boundaries was carried out, making most states unilingual. The result was a substantial simplification and reduction in the number of constituent units within the federation: the existing twenty-nine states and territories in four categories became fourteen states of equal status and five centrally administered territories. Subsequently, under continued pressure, the experiment of a bilingual state in Bombay was abandoned in 1960, when it was divided into the two essentially unilingual states of Maharashtra and Gujarat, and in 1962

[1] C.A.I., *Debates*, vol. vii, p. 43.   [2] Ibid., pp. 34–35.

Nagaland was made a distinct state. Thus only Punjab and Assam, where the territorial mingling of different language groups makes the creation of viable separate linguistic units especially difficult, remain as multilingual states.

The actual working of the Indian federal system since 1950 has reflected the simultaneous development of strong centralizing and decentralizing tendencies. The predominance of the centrally dominated Congress Party in both central and state politics, the long prominence of Nehru's leadership, the dedication to economic and social planning under central direction, the administrative hegemony of the Indian Administrative Service, the willingness of the central government on a number of occasions to invoke its emergency powers, and the emphasis upon national defence in the face of external threats from Pakistan and China, have fortified the authority of the central government. On the other hand, at the same time there have also been evidences of powerful centrifugal tendencies. The central government has clearly been heavily dependent upon the states for a large part of its administration, and the strength of regional linguistic feeling has been strong enough to force a nation-wide reorganization of state boundaries, and to postpone the imposition of a single common national language. Moreover, there has been a shift in the focus of political power and influence from the central government to the states, reflected in the growing importance of state leaders in the counsels of the national leadership. The general effect of the interaction of the two conflicting and highly dynamic forces for integration and regionalism since 1950 has thus been to intensify in practice the federal character of politics in India.

2. *Pakistan*

Pakistan is a country of two large fragments severed from the structure of old India, each of these parts different in every way except one—religion— and separated from each other by a thousand miles of hostile foreign territory. This geographical fact has dominated politics in Pakistan since its creation in 1947, and resulted in a unique federation with only two regional units balancing each other in a state of precarious equilibrium.

Held together only by a fear of Hindu domination and by a desire for an Islamic way of life, the new country has presented its leaders with an almost insurmountable task of unification. The geographic remoteness of the two wings of Pakistan has been sharpened by their linguistic, cultural, and economic disparity. Not only is West Pakistan largely Urdu-speaking and Middle-Eastern in character, while East Pakistan is Bengali-speaking and South-East Asian in outlook, but the widening gap in level of economic prosperity between the rapidly developing west and the backward east has increasingly embittered their relations since independence. With regionalism such a potent force and the sense of unity so frail, the characteristic response of Pakistan's major national leaders—Jinnah, Liaquat, and Ayub—has been to concede the necessity of some form of federal system, but to insist upon centralizing authority at every opportunity in order to counteract the tendencies to disunity. Inevitably, however, at each stage in the tortuous political development of Pakistan, efforts at centralization have provoked stronger feelings of regionalism, thus making necessary concessions from these attempts to concentrate central power.

Between 1947 and 1956 the Government of India Act, 1935, with certain adaptations, served as the working interim federal constitution for Pakistan. The federation was composed of a complex array of units. In the east there was the single province of East Bengal with 55 per cent. of the population; but in the west there were three provinces—the Punjab, Sind, and the North-West Frontier Province—one Chief Commissioner's province, ten acceded princes' states, and a thin strip of Kashmir. The interim constitution possessed the usual features of a federal constitution: central and regional governments, the distribution of authority between them, and a Federal Court to interpret the written constitution. But because the major political leaders felt that the way to counter provincialism was increased central control, the position of the central government was reinforced. From the beginning the central government was assigned extensive legislative and executive authority, and during the period the interim constitution was in operation the central assembly freely used its unilateral power of constitutional amendment to add to its legislative and financial powers. There was also persistent intervention by the central government in provincial affairs through its employment of governors as its agents, its control over the joint higher civil services common to both levels of government, and its frequent resort to emergency powers to suspend provincial governments. Furthermore, until 1954, the party organization of the Muslim League, whereby the central offices closely supervised the provincial branches, further reduced provincial autonomy. This concentration of power in Karachi, and the neglect by the central government of East Bengal in favour of the western provinces, provoked mounting Bengali resentment. In the 1954 provincial election a United Front, held together temporarily by a common demand for autonomy for East Bengal, virtually annihilated the Muslim League in that province. From that time on Bengali demands for greater autonomy were to prove a major recurring theme in Pakistani politics. In 1955, after the Bengali majority in the Constituent Assembly had precipitated a constitutional crisis leading to its dissolution, one of the first acts of the central government in the second Assembly was to push forward the unification of all the units in West Pakistan into a single province in order to counterbalance the potential power of the single large eastern province.

In the meantime the task of reaching agreement on a permanent constitution had proved a protracted one. Contention centred upon the relative representation of the provinces in the central assembly, the degree of provincial autonomy to be permitted, the recognition of Bengali as a national language in addition to Urdu, and the manner in which the political institutions should express Islamic principles. When the new constitution was completed in 1956 it bore a close resemblance to its predecessor, although some modifications were made. The federation was composed of two provinces having parity of representation in a unicameral legislature. Ostensibly, provincial powers were enhanced, but in reality the central government still retained not only virtually all its former legislative and executive powers, but also most of the previous controls by which it might, and frequently did, intervene in provincial affairs.

The adoption of the new constitution did not result in any lessening of the political strife and instability that had characterized government under the interim constitution. In October 1958—when the country's economic condition was rapidly deteriorating; when black marketing, profiteering, and bureaucratic corruption were becoming rampant; when instability in governments at both central and provincial levels was reaching chronic proportions; and when the government was faced with growing defiance of central authority, and a prospect that politics in East Bengal might turn to radical extremes —the army leaders decided that the existing constitutional machinery was not capable of working. In the absence of regular elections the failure of constitutional government could not be attributed to the political incapacity of the voters. Rather it was due to the tragic loss, in the early years, of both Jinnah and Liaquat, the two leaders of national significance, to the subsequent lack of political leaders willing to face up to major domestic problems, and to the unworkable multi-party system that resulted from the factionalism among the West Pakistan landlords and East Pakistan lawyers who predominated in the National Assembly. The new military régime abrogated the constitution, dismissed the central and provincial governments, dissolved all political parties, and proclaimed martial law throughout the country. Under General Ayub Khan as President the structure of government became highly centralized, the powers of government at every level being derived from him. But even he found that for purposes of administration it was convenient to subdivide the country into three areas—the two provinces of East and West Pakistan, and Karachi—and continue much of the structural outline of the previous constitution.[1]

Soon after taking over power President Ayub announced, that, when the immediate problems of stamping out corruption and re-establishing efficient administration had been dealt with, the government would turn to the question of a suitable constitution. His own preference was for an executive presidential system because of its stability, and for strong, if possible unitary, central government in order to restrain the separatist tendencies to which he believed

---

[1] President's Order, no. 1/1958, *The Laws (Continuance in Force) Order, 1958*; *Iftikhar-ud-Din* v. *Muhammad Sarfraz*, P.L.D. 1961, S.C. 585.

the federal principle had given rise.[1] During 1959 the first step was taken when a system of 'basic democracies' was instituted, and a pyramid of four tiers of councils was established within each province. The mixture of nominated and indirectly elected members on these councils was clearly intended to provide a 'controlled democracy'. Then in 1962 a new national constitution was put into force. Under it the executive was separated from the legislature and the primacy and independence of the executive was asserted. At the same time the constitution established 'a form of federation with the Provinces enjoying such autonomy as is consistent with the unity and interest of Pakistan as a whole'.[2] The Constitution Commission reporting in 1961 had recommended a federal system similar to that which had existed previously, but the new constitution as promulgated has differed from that of 1956 in significant respects. On the one hand, there has been a greater devolution of legislative and executive authority, and, in practice, of revenues, to the provinces. But at the same time the central controls over provincial governments have been increased. The governors, now active heads of the provincial executives, are appointed and dismissed by the president and subject to his directions. Conflicts between a governor and a provincial assembly are resolved by the National Assembly. The central legislature may, if it is in 'the national interest' (for the security of Pakistan, for planning a co-ordination, or for achievement of uniformity), legislate within the normally provincial fields. The legalism in federalism has been removed by depriving the courts of power to determine the *vires* of legislation.[3] Despite, or rather because of, these unitary tendencies, separatism has remained a spectre in East Pakistan. The Bengalis, chafing at the continued dominance of the western wing in their political and economic life, and feeling that they have been treated as a colony by the government in Rawalpindi, have wrung some major economic and financial concessions from the central government, but the consolidation of national unity still remains an immense task.

3. *Malaya and Malaysia*

By contrast with the vast federations of India and Pakistan, Malaya and its successor Malaysia, with a population by 1963 of just under 10 million, were extremely small federations.[4] It is not surprising, therefore, that a major characteristic of federal government in Malaya has been its highly centralized form and the weakness of the many tiny states—eleven in Malaya and fourteen in Malaysia—incapable of sustaining the main burdens of modern government. That a federal instead of a unitary form of government has

---

[1] Mohammad Ayub Khan, 'Pakistan Perspective', *Foreign Affairs*, xxxviii (1960), pp. 547–56.　　　　　　　　　　　　　　　　　　　　[2] Constitution, preamble.

[3] The courts have asserted jurisdiction over the *vires* of Presidential orders, but the limitation upon their jurisdiction in cases involving conflicts between central and provincial laws had remained untested up to the end of 1963. See Chapter 12, sections 1–3, esp. p. 283.

[4] See Table 1, p. 361.

prevailed has been due largely to the communal character of its population, and to the insistence of the Malays, and later also the indigenous peoples of Borneo, that their special position be assured.

Both in the peninsula and in Malaysia as a whole, the most significant political feature is the communal character of the population. Each of the states contains a variety of races, although there are regional variations in the relative strengths of the different communities. On the peninsula the major racial groups are the Malays who make up 50 per cent., the Chinese 37 per cent., and the Indians 11 per cent., with the Malays overwhelmingly predominant in the rural north-east and north-west, and all three races forming a mixture along the more developed west coast where most of the Chinese and Indians are concentrated.[1] In the commercial centre of Singapore the same three racial groups are found, but the Chinese form three-quarters of the population. In the less politically mature Borneo states of Sabah and Sarawak a variety of indigenous peoples together constitute majorities, but there are sizeable Chinese and Malay minorities. Thus, in Malaysia as a whole the Chinese comprise 43 per cent., the Malays 40 per cent., the indigenous Borneo peoples 8 per cent., and the Indians 9 per cent. Since the language, religion, and related social customs of each of these communities is distinctive and largely incompatible with the others, communalism colours the entire political scene. Communal resentment has been accentuated because the energetic, tightly knit Chinese have economically far outstripped the rural easy-going Malays, and control most of the economy of the area, while the Malays in turn have tended to reserve the bureaucracy as their special preserve. The adoption of a federal system was aimed, therefore, at reconciling the interests of the two large and several smaller racial communities in such a way as to prevent the most dynamic and still basically alien group—the Chinese—from either dominating or politically undermining the political union.

The history of federalism in Malaya dates back to 1895 when, under British persuasion, four states in central Malaya—Perak, Selangor, Pahang, and Negri Sembilan—were persuaded to form the Federated Malay States.[2] Up to 1941 the general trend was towards greater centralization of authority, although there were efforts in 1909, 1927, and especially after 1932 to reduce the concentration of authority in the central bureaucracy. In the meantime, five other Malay states—Johore, Kelantan, Trengganu, Kedah, and Perlis—came under British protection after 1909, but the rulers of these unfederated states,

---

[1] See Map 4. Source: Census Report, 1957.

[2] On a strict interpretation of the treaty (see Cmd. 4276/1933, p. 6, and Appendix III) the term 'Federation' was a misnomer. The treaty neither established a central government nor attempted a division of powers, beyond stating that the rulers agreed to accept a Resident-General whose advice they would follow in all matters of administration other than those touching the Mohammedan religion. Ostensibly the treaty preserved all the former powers of the rulers in their states, but in practice substantial power became concentrated in the federal secretariat under the Resident-General.

witnessing the effect of the federation upon the sovereignty of their colleagues in the F.M.S., took considerable pains to insist on independence from any form of inter-Malayan federation.

When Malaya was freed from Japanese occupation in 1945 the Colonial Office, considering the pre-war Malayan administration, in which there were ten legislatures in a country scarcely larger than England, as cumbersome, decided that in the interests of efficiency and democratic progress the system of government should be simplified and reformed. Hastily, with little local consultation, the imperial government set about establishing a Malayan Union embracing the nine Malay states and the two British settlements of Penang and Malacca, only Singapore being left separate as an island colony. The result was Malay indignation over the arbitrary imposition of the scheme, over the deprivation of the rulers' historic legal sovereignty, and most of all over the provision of equal citizenship rights for the Chinese and Indians, thus removing the privileged status the indigenous Malays had previously enjoyed under British rule. In the face of effective opposition by the United Malay National Organization and the threat of a mass non-co-operation movement, the British Government bowed to the storm. It agreed to drop the Union proposals and establish instead a federation.

The new federal constitution, embodied in the Federation of Malaya Agreement, 1948, linked together the same states and settlements, and was in fact almost as unitary as the Malayan Union, but Malay support was bought by the British agreement to recognize the identity of the Malay states, by a highly restrictive citizenship law which excluded about half the Chinese and Indians, and by safeguards for the special position of the Malays. Very wide legislative powers were given to the central authorities, who were empowered to legislate on almost all questions other than those touching on Muslim religion and Malay custom. What devolution of authority there was chiefly took the form of a compulsory delegation to the states of executive authority over central laws on a wide number of subjects. The central government was given powerful controls over the state and settlement governments, through the special powers of the High Commissioner to give them directions, the central control of budgets, and a centralized civil service. The 1948 constitution, therefore, represented a hybrid somewhere between unitary and federal government. In actual practice, however, large areas of potential central legislative power remained unexercised, the bulk of administration was left to the states, and the central government did not introduce major legislation or changes of policy without first obtaining the agreement of all the states concerned. Nevertheless, during the nine-year life of this constitution three developments favoured the progressive increase of central authority. The Communist Emergency provided a strong impetus for centralized administration. The advances in elected representation and self-government converted the central institutions into an instrument of, rather than a threat to, Malay nationalism. Finally, the dominance in both tiers of government after 1955 of the Alliance uniting the three communal parties—the United Malay National Organization, the Malayan Chinese Association, and the Malayan Indian Congress—under the leadership of Tunku Abdul Rahman ensured central influence in state politics.

When independence for Malaya in 1957 was agreed upon, the federal system was overhauled. Like its predecessor, the new Federation of Malaya Agreement, 1957, concentrated legislative and financial power in the central government, for the only exclusive state legislative powers of any significance were land, agriculture, forestry, and local government. The federal form was more orthodox, however, for the previous arrangement, whereby in many matters legislative power was conferred on the central government but executive power on the states, was rejected as 'impractical', and legislative and executive authority were now made largely co-extensive. The net effect was to increase slightly the legislative authority of the states, and reduce substantially their executive responsibilities. The predominance of the central government was assured by the sweeping central power to act even in the exclusive state spheres in order to implement treaties, to promote uniformity of state laws, to implement national economic development programmes, and in cases of emergency. In addition, the procedure for amendment of the constitution required, with very few exceptions, only special majorities in the central legislature. During the operation of this constitution between 1957 and 1963, the electoral success and continued dominance of the Alliance in both levels of government was a major factor for political stability and for increasing central authority. Moreover, the tacit acceptance within the Alliance that the central government was essentially a Malay one, in which Chinese and Indians shared, added to Malay confidence in the central institutions. The persistent strength of centripetal forces was evident in the fuller assumption by the central government of its potential powers, and in the passage of a number of constitutional amendments extending central power, although regular consultation of the states preceding central action continued to be characteristic.

An issue which faced the Federation of Malaya soon after independence was the question of its relation to Singapore. Previously Singapore had been expressly excluded, because of its different economic interests as an entrepôt trade centre based on free trade, because the inclusion of its predominantly Chinese population would place the Malays in a minority, and because of Britain's special strategic interests in Singapore. Lee Kuan Yew, the Singapore premier, and the governing People's Action Party, recognizing the inability of Singapore to stand completely on its own, pressed strongly for merger with the federation. For some time Malayan leaders were reluctant, fearing that the addition of a million or more factious Chinese would upset the delicate racial balance within the federation. Moreover, as conservatives, the Malayan leaders distrusted the socialist government and strong radical elements in

Singapore. But when it became apparent that, unless taken under the protective custody of the federation, Singapore might be taken over by the Communists and used as a base for subverting the federation, Tunku Abdul Rahman agreed in 1961 to its accession. At the same time negotiations were begun for the inclusion of the British Borneo territories in order to offset Malay fears of Chinese preponderance within the federation. The Sultan of tiny Brunei, concerned over the future disposal of his oil revenues and over his personal status, decided against acceding, but in the two larger Borneo territories parties supporting Malaysia obtained large majorities in elections which were subsequently endorsed as valid by a United Nations mission. The negotiations came to fruition when Singapore, Sarawak, and Sabah (North Borneo) were joined to the states of Malaya to form the wider Federation of Malaysia on 16 September 1963. In form, the 1957 constitution was retained with modifications that were made to it by the Malaysia Act, 1963. In effect, the changes were so substantial as to create a new federal structure. Most significant was the marked variance in the relation of different states to the central government. The states of the previous federation continued as before, but the new states enjoyed considerably more legislative, executive, and financial autonomy, and their special interests were much more fully safeguarded under the constitution. Born in the face of Indonesian hostility, the new federation found itself immediately under economic and political strains arising from the need to defend itself. Moreover, the internal racial tension generated by the struggle for power between the mainland Malays and the Singapore Chinese erupted in August 1965 in the expulsion of Singapore from the federation.

4. *Nigeria*

In October 1960 Nigeria became the fourth federation in the Commonwealth to achieve independence since 1945, and the only country in Africa to come to independence with a fully operating federal system. Underlying the deliberate choice of a federal form of government was the strength of internal regional forces which could not be ignored. A vast country, stretching from the tropical coast in the south to the Sahara desert in the north, and with a population now of over 55 millions, Nigeria as a political entity was an artificial creation, perhaps the most artificial of all the countries created in the course of the European occupation of Africa. The three regions composing Nigeria in 1960—the Western and Eastern Regions in the south divided by the Niger river, and the vast Northern Region with three-quarters of the country's area and 54 per cent. of its population—were distinguished in every conceivable way: by language, religion, social institutions, geography, history, and even political parties. In the north, culturally and racially distinct from the south, most of the region was dominated by the Hausa language, Muslim belief and law, and the highly organized emirates of the Fulani dynasties. In the south, where Christianity and Animism were the prevailing religions, the culturally conscious Yoruba-speaking peoples predominated in the west, while the rival Ibos were the largest ethnic group in the east. Moreover, the south, penetrated extensively by missionaries and traders, was westernized more rapidly. Consequently, northern leaders have feared that unless there were safeguards they would be overrun by the more advanced southerners. But northern conservatism has in turn been a source of frustration to southern nationalists, fearful that the 'feudal' north might use its overwhelming size to crush the south. A further irritant has been the migration of aggressive, educated Ibos from the over-populated eastern area to both the other regions. Thus, in the decade before independence the development of leadership groups and of political consciousness had a distinctively regional focus which was expressed in the three main parties: the Northern People's Congress drawing its strength solely from the Northern Region, the Action Group based primarily on Yorubaland, and the N.C.N.C. (formerly National Council of Nigeria and the Cameroons, and now the National Convention of Nigerian Citizens) with its centre of support in Iboland.

In view of this diversity and variety within Nigeria, it is perhaps surprising that there is any unity at all, especially since two of the forces in the formation of so many other federations—the strategic need for united defence, and the integrating spirit of a militant struggle for independence—were largely absent. Yet Nigeria has developed a measure of unity. British rule, by creating peace and order, and by imposing a common government, administrative system, jurisprudence, language, educational system, currency, and communications, made possible a feeling of shared Nigerian identity. To this was added a sense of being distinct from the surrounding French territories with their different language and form of administration. Particularly important too has been the leadership of the new élite of men educated in Europe and America and saturated with ideas of democracy, nationalism, and large-scale political organization. Moreover, the desire to play a major role in African affairs, and the vision of the prestige and power of a united Nigeria, have proved a temptingly seductive incentive for unity. Perhaps most influential, however, has been the recognition of economic interdependence. The complementary nature of the regional economies due to differences in climate, soil, and food crops, the dependence of the land-locked north upon the coast for the export of its products, and the advantages of the larger market both for trade and for attracting foreign investment, have weighed heavily whenever regional leaders contemplated separation.

The evolution of federal institutions in Nigeria since 1946 has spanned five different constitutions. Prior to 1946, Nigeria had been amalgamated into a nominally unitary system, but in practice the north and south had been administered by two virtually distinct bureaucracies, the common Governor-General being the only bond of political unity. In 1946 the 'Richards Constitution' extended the sovereign power of the Nigerian Legislative and Executive

Councils to cover the whole of Nigeria, including the north for the first time and thus taking a step towards Nigerian unity. At the same time, by establishing advisory regional councils for the three regions, this constitution set the regional mould within which the federal system subsequently developed. The unitary nature of this constitution, intended to promote Nigerian unity, in practice sharpened inter-regional tensions, for each group feared the central government as a potential instrument for domination by another region. Northern demands for autonomy, intensified Yoruba–Ibo rivalry, and the appearance of political parties primarily motivated by the desire to defend their own regional ethnic interests were the result. The 'Macpherson Constitution' which followed in 1951, a curious blend of unitary and confederal features, suffered from the defects of both without gaining the benefits of either. The central concentration of authority continued to excite regional anxieties, while the lack of cohesiveness in the central legislature and executive, both consisting in effect of delegates from the regional assemblies, soon resulted in deadlock, climaxed by the riots of 1953 and northern threats of secession.

The solution agreed upon by the Nigerian leaders and put into operation in 1954 was the adoption of an orthodox federal constitution. The power of the central legislature to override the regional legislatures was ended, and the principle of a dual polity was extended with the provision for the first time of separate regional public services, judiciaries, marketing boards, and governors in the place of lieutenant-governors. A Supreme Court with exclusive jurisdiction to act as an impartial tribunal in disputes between governments was also created. In operation the new federal system, by granting regional autonomy, helped to reduce inter-regional fears and tensions, while at the same time it strengthened the central government by removing its dependence upon the regional governments. Moreover, the federal structure enabled a solution to be reached to the problem causing the greatest hostility between the north and the south—the issue of early self-government, which had been at the base of northern fears and southern frustration. It made possible, within a united Nigeria, the early grant of self-government to the two southern regions that were clamouring for it, while postponing northern and federal self-government to a later date in order to allay northern anxieties. The marked growth of amity and co-operation among the regional leaders after 1954 indicated the degree to which Nigerian unity benefited. There have been two further Nigerian constitutions, but neither altered radically the fundamental features of the federal system established in 1954. The 1960 constitution made a number of adjustments appropriate for independence, including the addition of central emergency powers not unlike those in the Asian federations, and the 1963 constitution converted the federation into a republican form.

The operation of the Nigerian federal system during its first ten years has not been without strains and difficulties. Because the three original regions each contained significant ethnic minorities—the non-Muslim Middle Belt in the north, the non-Yoruba mid-west, and the non-Ibo peoples of the Calabar, Rivers, and Ogoja Provinces in the east—and because of the preponderant size and hence influence of the Northern Region, there have been persistent demands that the existing regions be splintered to form ethnically homogeneous, 'natural' states. Generally these pressures have been resisted, but in 1963 a new Mid-Western Region was carved out of the Western Region. Also a continual source of bitter controversy, because the population of the Northern Region is greater than that of the others combined, and because the parties are largely regional in their bases of support, has been the issue of regional representation in the central executive and legislature. First a unicameral and later a bicameral legislature was established, and the 1962–3 census provoked heated disputes because it was likely to prolong the supremacy of the purely northern N.P.C. in central politics. The distribution of finances, and particularly the application of the principle of derivation in the assignment of revenues to the regions, has been a subject of acrimony also, no less than three fiscal commissions reporting in the ten years before independence. Nor was it long before the central government used its emergency powers. In 1962 when a constitutional crisis occurred in the Western Region central administration was imposed for seven months. This action, followed by the corruption investigations and treason trials, seriously weakened the Action Group as the opposition to the central N.P.C.-N.C.N.C. coalition, and as the dominant party in the Western Region. Consequently, in 1963 the new United People's Party formed the government of the Western Region in coalition with the former regional opposition N.C.N.C., and in 1964 the major elements within this regional coalition were amalgamated into a Nigerian National Democratic Party. Throughout the life of the federation, regionalism has been a particularly potent force. The intensity of regional loyalties, the bargaining power of regional governments due to the small number of regions and their large size, and the regional basis of the major political parties and of the governing élites, have been strong factors accentuating this trend.

But despite some nearly fatal crises there are signs also of growing central strength. The willingness of the central government to exercise its constitutional powers, its use of emergency powers setting a precedent for central intrusion in regional affairs, its key position as the source for the bulk of regional revenue, its leading role both in co-ordinating and financing development planning, the tendency for regional minorities to look to it for protection against regional majority groups, its increased prestige since independence, the movement of some of the major political leaders from regional to central politics in 1959, and the growing pride in Nigerian control of her own defence and foreign policies, have tended to counterbalance regional and separatist inducements. Thus, Nigeria has remained a federation in which under the dynamic impact of centrifugal and centripetal forces there has been a continuous adjustment of the delicate and precarious balance between the regional and central governments.

5. *Rhodesia and Nyasaland*

Intended to shine as a beacon of multi-racial co-operation on a continent dominated elsewhere by intransigent black and white nationalism, the federal experiment in Central Africa proved instead a disastrous failure, unable to reconcile the interests of its black and white populations.

In each of the three territories which the federation sought to link together, the white settlers constituted only a small minority.[1] But there were crucial differences between the territories. In Southern Rhodesia where the settlers were most heavily concentrated, they had experienced more or less complete control over internal affairs since 1923, and had developed a native policy involving a considerable measure of racial discrimination and segregation. On the other hand, Northern Rhodesia, which following the discovery of the rich copperbelt in 1925 had also acquired an increasingly influential settler population, and Nyasaland, where there were by far the fewest white people, had remained under the administration of the Colonial Office, which espoused an overt policy of the paramountcy of African native interests.

From 1915 on, the settlers of the Rhodesias had on various occasions advocated amalgamation. To them a 'Greater Rhodesia' held out not only the prospect of economic benefits from the incorporation of their complementary economies in an enlarged market and from their enhanced credit-worthiness, but also political advantages that might be derived from creating a dominion sufficiently viable for the protectorates to be freed from the Colonial Office and its pro-native policies. For thirty years the settler campaigns for unification made little headway against British Governments committed to the paramountcy of native interests in the two northern territories. But after 1948 British attitudes began to change. Both major political parties in Britain continued to reject amalgamation of the territories in Central Africa as out of the question, but a federal form of union suggested a means by which the desire of the settlers for unification might be reconciled with the desire of the British Government to protect the Africans of Northern Rhodesia and Nyasaland. Moreover, it was hoped in Britain that this concession would help to persuade Southern Rhodesia to a more liberal native policy, and would establish a political unit with the economic viability which was considered a pre-condition for eventual self-government. A Labour Government took the first tentative step by agreeing to a 'purely exploratory' investigation into the possibility of federation. Soon afterwards the British elections of 1951 produced a Conservative Government with a far less cautious outlook to the problem. Stampeded by a belief that the immediate unification of Central Africa was

[1] See Table 15, p. 382.

urgent if the Southern Rhodesian electorate was to be won to a policy of racial partnership and freed from South African influence, and recognizing that in Northern Rhodesia the initiative was already passing to the local settlers there, the British Government quickly pushed through the federation of the three territories in spite of intense African opposition in the two northern protectorates.

The Federation of Rhodesia and Nyasaland, established in September 1953, was in many respects orthodox in form. But because the basic compromise on which the federal system was founded was that the new central government would perform those functions in which the settlers in all three territories were interested, while matters of concern to the Africans in the two northern territories would remain under British protection through continued Colonial Office control of the territorial governments, the new federation was characterized by four distinctive features. First, it united three territories which continued to have sharply differing constitutional status: Northern Rhodesia and Nyasaland remained as British protectorates, with the Colonial Office responsible for their territorial governments, but the settler-controlled Southern Rhodesia was self-governing, although subject to the formal control of the British Government. Secondly, the federal electorate was extremely restricted, constituting a small white oligarchy.[1] Thirdly, the rationale of the distribution of powers was that matters primarily of interest to the settlers, especially economic affairs, were assigned to the central government, while those primarily of interest to the Africans were left in the hands of territorial governments. Indeed, some subjects such as education and agriculture were split between governments on purely racial grounds. Nevertheless, because in the negotiations preceding federation the settlers had continually pressed for increases in the exclusive and concurrent powers of the central government, central authority was quite extensive in the constitution as finally adopted. Thus, in practice many of the fields allotted to the central government proved to be unavoidably multi-racial in scope. Fourthly, the constitution included a number of 'safeguards' designed to ease African anxieties. Among these were the requirement of the assent of the British Government to constitutional amendments, the establishment of a special standing committee of the Federal Assembly, the African Affairs Board, with authority to request that legislation of a 'differentiating' nature be reserved for assent by the British Government, and the stipulation that within ten years the constitution would be reviewed.

The federation was imposed despite the protests of a majority of the articulate Africans in the hope that, once experienced, its benefits would be recognized by them. But instead of advancing peacefully towards a maturing racial partnership, the federation produced exactly the opposite: deteriorating race relations, African discontent, disturbances, and political instability. The central government, dependent on a predominantly white electorate, was

[1] See Table 15.

unable to concentrate upon conciliating the Africans, for it had to protect its own right flank against those who charged it with jeopardizing white supremacy. As a result, the failure to take any significant steps to demonstrate the reality of racial partnership as the basis of federation, the lack of African representation in the central institutions, the dominant role of Southern Rhodesia—apparent in the majority it held in the central cabinet, in the choice of Salisbury as the federal capital, and the choice of the Kariba site for the major hydro-electric development—and the increased flood of European immigration intensified the distrust of the northern Africans. Moreover, the efforts of the settler central government to expand its authority and to influence the negotiations for the revision of territorial constitutions, and the relative slowness of African political progress in the territories, served to confirm the fears of Africans that federation was a barrier rather than a means to their political advancement. As the Monckton Commission observed, 'the opposition to Federation which . . . was strong at the time Federation was introduced . . . gathered further strength by African disappointment in the manner of its operation'.[1] Thus, instead of reconciling the interests of the black and white peoples, the federation accelerated the spread of militant African nationalism and gave it a single unifying goal to work for—the break up of the hated federation with which settler aspirations to political supremacy seemed to be bound up. The hope that white altruism and black patience would jointly make a success of the federation proved illusory.

The federation lasted just eleven years. During the first phase covering the years 1953 to 1958, there was increasing African disillusionment climaxed by the events of 1957–8—the agreement reached between the British and Federal Governments to consider the grant of dominion status at the 1960 review of the constitution, and the passage of the Constitution Amendment Act, 1957, and the Electoral Act, 1958, both of which, although ruled 'differentiating' measures by the African Affairs Board, the British Government refused to veto. These turned the sullen suspicions of the northern Africans about the true purpose of federation into hardened certainty. The federation was now fully discredited among the Africans of the protectorates, and the period between 1958 and 1960 was one of active and sometimes violent opposition inside and outside the federation. The situation deteriorated so rapidly that in 1959 emergencies were declared in each of the three territories, African leaders were arrested, and in Nyasaland a 'police state' was imposed with the aid of federal troops. The fears of the Nyasaland Africans that federation would enable white Southern Rhodesian troops to enforce settler rule had come true, and the baton charges, the bloodshed, the burning of houses, the searching of villages, the collective fines, and the confiscation of implements did not make the people of Nyasaland like the federation any better.

[1] Cmnd. 1148/1960, para. 41.

During the final phase, between 1960 and 1963, the British Government gradually shifted towards a realization that the experiment had failed and should therefore be terminated. The period began with the Monckton Commission reporting that, in spite of the federation's economic achievements, the 'almost pathological' dislike of federation among the Africans in the two northern territories meant that it 'cannot, in our view, be maintained in its present form'.[1] The Commission recommended a drastic revision of the federal structure in order to win African confidence, but as constitutional advances within Nyasaland and Northen Rhodesia brought into power African nationalist leaders committed to secession, the British Government found it had to go even further. Despite a determined rearguard action by the pro-federal settlers, bitter at the gradual withdrawal of British support, the federation was doomed when late in 1962 the imperial government agreed to permit Nyasaland to secede. When Northern Rhodesia likewise insisted upon its own independence, the federation was finally dissolved on 31 December 1963.

6. *The West Indies*

By comparison with the federal experiment in Central Africa, the West Indies Federation took much longer to create and much less time to disintegrate. Whereas the former failed because too much power was concentrated in the central government and its settler leaders were too aggressive, the latter collapsed because the central government was virtually powerless and its leaders were too timid. A salt-water federation attempting to link together islands which were scattered in a 1,500 mile arc across the Caribbean and which had little sense of community with each other, the ineffectual West Indies Federation at no time captured the imagination of the general public except in a few of the smaller islands.

On various occasions from the seventeenth century on there had been efforts to bring together some of the islands in the Caribbean, but none had achieved lasting success. A federation of the Leeward Islands was actually achieved in 1871 and lasted right up to 1956, but the federation was of a very loose order and was the target of much criticism throughout its existence.[2] Proposals for a wider federation of all the British Caribbean colonies were put forward from time to time during the nineteenth and twentieth centuries,[3] and the Moyne Commission, finding in 1939 that the idea of federation was attractive to many politically conscious West Indians, urged that political union be kept in view as the eventual goal.[4] Events during the Second World

---

[1] Cmnd. 1148/1960, paras. 27, 41, 49.

[2] *Leeward Islands Act, 1871* (Imp. Act 34 & 35 Vict. c. 107). See H. Wrong, *Government of the West Indies* (1923), pp. 148–55, and L. Braithwaite, 'Progress Toward Federation 1938–1956', *Social and Economic Studies*, vi (1957), pp. 135, 144.

[3] Braithwaite, op. cit., pp. 133–7.

[4] Cmd. 6607/1945, esp. pp. 326–8.

War fostered the growth of opinion in the West Indies in favour of political federation. The extension of air communications between the isolated islands facilitated contact between local leaders, and the wartime growth of inter-island organizations of one kind and another led to an appreciation of the value of a joint approach for the solution of social and economic problems. At the same time, when the British Government, in response to the post-war tide of nationalism, set out upon a policy of implementing independence for its colonies, it concluded that federation was the only practical way for the small and scattered islands in the Caribbean to stand effectively on their own. It therefore urged West Indian political leaders to consider such a union.

Despite the initial enthusiasm at the Montego Bay conference in 1947, federation-making proved a long drawn out and difficult process. Between 1947 and 1957 four constitutional conferences were held, two standing committees dealt with general proposals, and six commissions were appointed to examine particular aspects. Discussions became involved and troubled as the special interests, ambitions, and fears of each island came to the fore. Not infrequently, decisions made at earlier conferences were reversed at later ones. The disadvantages of remaining minute separate entities under colonial rule were obvious enough, but generally the benefits to be gained from federation attracted far less attention than the price that would have to be paid for them. The mainland territories, British Honduras and British Guiana, soon chose to hold themselves aloof, while elsewhere, without the unifying force of an external danger or a common struggle against a reluctant imperial power, parochialism, grounded deep in generations of isolated history, continued to exert itself. Moreover, trade and communications between the scattered islands were spasmodic, personal contacts between their inhabitants infrequent, and the island economies mainly competitive rather than complementary. A complicating factor was the rapid constitutional progress in the individual islands after 1944. This made many political leaders eager to consolidate their local political gains, and fearful that in a federation they might lose them. Eventually the most contentious issues—the freedom of personal movement between islands which Trinidad feared, and the customs union which posed problems for Jamaica's policy of tariff protection for its developing industries—were resolved by a compromise accepting freedom of movement and customs union in principle, but postponing their implementation for five years after the commencement of the federation. Finally, in January 1958, after thirteen years of negotiations, the West Indies Federation was born.[1]

As implemented, the federation consisted of ten islands or groups of islands with wide variations in size, population, and wealth. Two islands, Jamaica and

[1] The order in council containing the constitution was actually promulgated in the previous year (S.I. 1957, no. 1364).

Trinidad, together possessed more than three-quarters of the total population and total wealth.[1] The chief characteristic of the federation, and one contrasting with the five other new federations, was the niggardly list of legislative and executive powers assigned to the central government. These were restricted primarily to external relations, inter-island communications, the university, and the West India Regiment. The central government's lack of financial resources and its dependence on a mandatory levy upon the territories dramatized its weakness: with one-tenth the revenue of either Jamaica or Trinidad, it was hardly in a position to achieve the hoped-for economic transformation. The West Indies Federation was also unusual among modern federations in commencing without a customs union or a common currency.

Throughout its brief history, the frail federation was undermined both by the weakness of the forces for integration, and by the inadequacies of the federal structure itself. The absence of a sense of common identity except among a few of the educated middle classes, the relative looseness of inter-island organizations and associations, the extremely limited trade between the islands, the growing rather than diminishing differences in economic structure and level of development, and especially the lack of any feeling of urgency inducing collective action in the face of a common danger, prevented the growth of an integrating sense of community. Furthermore, the form of the federal structure itself contributed to its downfall. The scope of central authority was so restricted, its functions so limited, and its budget so minute, that to most West Indians the federation appeared to involve additional expenditure to no effective purpose. It was not surprising, therefore, that the major charismatic leaders in Jamaica and Trinidad, Manley and Williams, chose to remain as premiers in their own islands, thus further emphasizing the relative insignificance of federal politics. The support of the two largest islands, and particularly of Jamaica, was further alienated by their marked under-representation not only in the federal parliament, but also, as a result of the governing Federal Labour Party's failure in the two big islands at the 1958 federal elections, in the central executive. An important factor weakening the prestige of the central government was the rapid constitutional progress within the islands themselves, which left the central government, by comparison, with a less-advanced constitution. This gave the federation the appearance of a brake rather than an aid to full political independence.

The constitution had deferred the implementation of the customs union, the central right to tax incomes and profits, and central control of internal movement, and had also provided for a general review of the constitution within five years. In the ensuing controversies when these issues were reconsidered, Trinidad emerged as the champion of the view that central power should be increased in order to make the federation more effective. On the other hand, Jamaica, apprehensive lest the transfer of wider powers to the central govern-

---

[1] See Table 2, p. 362.

ment should hamper its successful local development programme, stood as the proponent of the view that the central government should have no more power than the minimum necessary for its recognition as an international entity. The dispute came to a head in a long series of inter-government negotiations beginning in 1959 and culminating in the constitutional review conference of 1961. Because it was feared that a federation without Jamaica could not be viable, concessions were made on nearly every issue: Jamaican representation in the House of Representatives was to be increased, the transfer of direct taxation and control over economic development to the central government was in effect to be subject to Jamaican veto, and the introduction of the customs union was to be phased over nine years. Even then the federation failed to hold Jamaica. A referendum, originally conceived as a weapon both to extort concessions for Jamaica in the constitutional bargaining and to undermine the Jamaican critics of federation, suceeded in achieving the former, but backfired in the latter, for when it was held in September 1961 a majority of Jamaicans voted against federation. Faced with this expression of Jamaican opinion, the British Government hastily agreed to permit Jamaica to secede and achieve its own independence. Soon afterwards Trinidad, unwilling to carry alone the cost of all the smaller islands in a federal union, also opted to secede. Handicapped by the failure to give the central government effective power, and by the parochialism of its leaders, the West Indies Federation had been floundering unhappily since its formation. The withdrawal of Jamaica and Trinidad meant that it could no longer be kept afloat, and on 31 May 1962—the date which previously had been set for its independence—the federation was formally dissolved by the British Government. The idea of a Caribbean federation did not die completely, however. Within a few months the remnants had begun negotiations for the formation of an East Caribbean federation composed of the smaller islands, but as with its predecessor, agreement upon its form proved difficult to achieve.

PART TWO

FEDERAL SOCIETIES

3

MOTIVES FOR UNION

1. *Federal Societies*

THE impact of political, social, cultural, economic, geographic, and historical forces upon constitution-making has been apparent in each of the new federations. The prolonged and tortuous negotiations that preceded the adoption of federal constitutions in Pakistan and in the West Indies, the violent controversies in India, first over Hindu–Muslim counter-claims and later over the demand for linguistic provinces, the discord in Rhodesia and Nyasaland due to African opposition to federation, and the failure in both Malaya and Nigeria of the attempts in 1946 to establish unitary governments without regard for regional and cultural diversities, all give evidence of the influence of social pressures upon the creation of political institutions. Both constitution-makers and commentators have recognized the importance of these forces. A member of the Indian Constituent Assembly, for instance, declared: 'Provincial autonomy came to us not as an extraneous proposition, it was directed by the peremptory need of a country composed of various States and Provinces, peopled by various races, whose cultural, economic and political needs could only be met by autonomous rule.'[1] Even Sir Ivor Jennings, who considered federal constitutions undesirable if at all avoidable, concluded of the Indian example that 'it seems doubtful whether India could have avoided it'.[2] The demand for a federal system of government in Pakistan has been described as 'the dictate of language, race, region and history',[3] and similar statements have been made of Nigeria.[4] Likewise, at Montego Bay, the West Indian federation was considered a product of necessity.[5] The importance of the social background was also realized by the officials' conference of 1951 which laid the foundations for the federal structure of Rhodesia and Nyasaland, for it was only after making surveys of the geographical, historical, and economic factors and of the native policies in these three territories that it proceeded to make its recommendations.[6]

---

[1] C.A.I., *Debates*, vol. ii, p. 288.

[2] I. Jennings, *Some Characteristics of the Indian Constitution* (1953), p. 55.

[3] A. K. Sen, 'The New Federalism in Pakistan', S. Bailey (ed.), *Parliamentary Government in the Commonwealth* (1951), p. 152. See also C.A.P. (first), *Debates*, vol. v, p. 5.

[4] See, for instance, O. Awolowo, *Awo* (1960), pp. 163–5, 173–4, and A. T. Balewa, Nigerian House of Representatives, *Debates*, vol. iii, 26 March 1957, col. 1432.

[5] Col. no. 218/1948, p. 58.

[6] Cmd. 8233/1951, chs. i, ii; Cmd. 8234/1951; Cmd. 8235/1951.

Scholars have pointed out that the distinguishing characteristic of the older federal societies, such as the United States, Switzerland, Canada, and Australia, was the existence, at one and the same time, of a desire to be united under a single general government for certain purposes and to be organized under independent regional governments for others.[1] The newer federal systems have also been the outgrowth of ambivalent attitudes to union and regional independence. The tension between these concurrent desires arose because colonial boundaries, established in the scramble for empire, or based on administrative convenience, usually did not coincide with the grouping of the traditional cultural and social communities. Thus there developed the clash between two conflicting sets of historical forces: between narrow nationalisms based on the traditional political, linguistic, racial, and religious loyalties, and the wider nationalism of the westernized élites which had grown within, and wished to inherit, the larger cohesive units created by British rule. Compounding the situation in the developing societies was the clash between, on the one hand, political and economic ambitions for 'viable' political units large enough to sustain genuine political independence and capable of generating rapid economic development, and, on the other, the desire for political units expressing and capable of protecting the cultures and religions of the smaller but cohesive traditional communities.

While this sketch suggests some of the main social pressures leading to the adoption of federal government in the developing countries, the ambivalence between the motives for union and the motives for autonomy in these societies was, however, more complex. A detailed study of the factors involved is therefore necessary. Among the social factors and motives which have been relevant in most of the new federations have been (1) the desire for political independence, (2) the hope of economic advantage, (3) the need for administrative efficiency, (4) the enhancing of the conduct of external relations, both diplomatic and military, (5) a community of outlook based on race, religion, language, or culture, (6) geographical factors, (7) the influence of history, (8) similarities and differences in colonial and indigenous political and social institutions, (9) the character of political leadership, (10) the existence of successful older models of federal union, and (11) the influence of the United Kingdom government in constitution-making. Each of these factors is potentially either unifying or separating. In this chapter these factors will be considered as forces for unity, while the next chapter will consider their influence upon desires for regional autonomy. The order in which these factors are listed is not meant to indicate any order of importance; indeed, these motives and influences have been of varying relative importance in different federations, although most of them have been present to at least some degree in each case.

---

[1] Wheare, *Federal Government*, ch. 3; Livingston, *Federalism and Constitutional Change*, p. 6.

2. *The desire for political independence*

One of the most powerful motives for inter-territorial union has been the desire for political independence and the belief that only through unity could independence be achieved and, once secured, genuinely maintained. Indeed, in all six of the new Commonwealth federations, the experience of a 'common subjection' to a 'common imperial power' led to the advocacy of a 'common revolt' as a means to self-government. The Indian Congress Party, for example, insisted upon an all-inclusive centrally organized nationalist movement in order to advance the common cause against British rule, and the long drawn out struggle solidified Hindu unity. Opposing the Congress, the Muslim League, which sought independence not only from British control but also from the potential Hindu Raj, united peoples as diverse as the Bengalis and the Punjabis. In Malaya it was opposition to centralization imposed by the imperial government which, paradoxically, resulted in the uniting of the Malays to form the U.M.N.O. in 1946, and later it was the promise of 'merdeka' which cemented the unity of the Alliance and through it of the federation during 1954–7. Later still, Singapore, Sarawak, and North Borneo saw in Malaysia a means of achieving full independence within a reasonably large political unit. The desire for independence was also a unifying factor in the non-Asian federations, although the spirit of nationalist revolt was less intense. Nigeria, for instance, received independence without the lengthy militant struggle that had been necessary in India. Nevertheless, political leaders in the south, and later in the north, frequently stressed the importance of unity and made significant concessions in the interests of achieving Nigerian independence. The desire for independence was important in Central Africa too. Federation appealed to the settlers in the two northern territories, particularly the growing number of artisans on the Northern Rhodesian copperbelt, as a way of escaping from Colonial Office control and racial policy, and to those in Southern Rhodesia as an opportunity to hasten dominion status. Such enthusiasm as there was at Montego Bay for a West Indies federation was based on the hopes expressed by most of the delegates that federation would provide 'the opportunity to liquidate once and for all every vestige of Colonialism'.[1] The subsequent Standing Closer Association Committee Report therefore declared, 'We start from the assumption that the main purpose of our task is to seek the shortest path towards a real political independence . . . what is meant in fact by Dominion status.'[2] Nevertheless, this demand for independence through Caribbean unity was to a considerable extent blunted by the success of the larger regional units in obtaining political advances separately, and by the disappointingly slight advances to self-government envisaged in the actual federal proposals.

[1] Col. no. 218/1948, p. 70.
[2] Col. no. 255/1950, para. 9 and see also paras. 8–20, esp. paras. 16–17. Hereafter, this will be referred to as the S.C.A.C. report.

Sometimes the cry for unity as a means to independence was used by the westernizing nationalists in order to draw peasant support away from the traditional local authorities and towards larger modern democratic political institutions. The Indian Congress Party, for instance, played on the hopes of peoples in the princely states for democratic government by suggesting that only through union with the British provinces might the power of the autocratic princes be overthrown. The resulting popular pressure and threat of revolt against the traditional rulers was in turn used by nationalist leaders in India, Malaya, and Nigeria as a lever for persuading the traditional aristocracies themselves to accept the wider unions in order to preserve some vestige of their authority.

Sometimes unity has been encouraged by the knowledge that the British Government looked upon federation as a prerequisite for the granting of independence. This was a factor in Malaya, Nigeria, and the West Indies, and it would appear that many of the settlers of the Rhodesias considered the inclusion of Nyasaland in the Central African federation as the British price for a potentially independent federation.

Unity has often been advocated not merely as a means to the achieving of independence, but also as a necessity if genuine independence, once obtained, was to be sustained. The importance of 'viable' political units has been stressed repeatedly both by nationalist leaders and by the British Government. Nehru put the problem bluntly: 'The inexorable logic of the age presents the country with radically different alternatives: union plus independence or disunion plus dependence.'[1] A Nigerian warned that 'in division we would fall into poor bits, incapable of standing on our own feet; . . . dependent that is to say, on mighty nations that have pooled their resources together and formed strong mighty countries like China, America, Russia'.[2] At Montego Bay, a delegate suggested the metaphor of the bundle of twigs, difficult to break when tied together, and the West Indian S.C.A.C. report began with the promise: 'we are satisfied that sheer force of circumstances of the modern world makes independence on a unit basis a mirage'.[3] Secretaries of State have often advised, as Mr. Creech Jones did at Montego Bay, that 'the continuance of small territorial units is becoming rapidly an anachronism in the modern world and the only way of preventing domination and obtaining security is . . . establishing federation'.[4]

The necessity of large political units for achieving and sustaining self-government has sometimes been questioned by local political leaders and by commentators. The examples of Ghana, Cyprus, Sierra Leone, Gambia, and

[1] J. Nehru, *The Discovery of India* (4th ed., 1956), p. 547. This argument applied with particular force to the many small princely states which could not hope to stand alone as independent states. See V. P. Menon, *The Integration of the Indian States* (1956), pp. 54–55.
[2] G. B. A. Akinyede, *The Political and Constitutional Problems of Nigeria* (1957), p. 87.
[3] Col. no. 218/1948, p. 34; Col. no. 255/1950, para. 9.
[4] Col. no. 218/1948, p. 9.

Somaliland suggest that imperial powers have not been reluctant to grant full independence to small political units, while Luxembourg, Iceland, and Israel have shown that small countries can maintain their independence. Such examples contributed to Jamaica's feeling that it could 'go it alone'. But most of the small colonies which have achieved full independence had not yet done so at the time federations were formed in India, Pakistan, Malaya, Rhodesia and Nyasaland, and Nigeria. Furthermore, although smaller weak independent nations do exist, most of them have not provided very promising precedents. The examples of Newfoundland joining Canada, the Southern Cameroons having to choose between union with Nigeria or the French Cameroons, and Singapore's desire to join the Federation of Malaya, have also helped to emphasize how difficult it is for small political units to achieve and maintain genuine independence.

3. *The hope of economic advantage*

All six of the new Commonwealth federations were at their inception economically underdeveloped, and were the product of demands for political systems capable of achieving rapid economic growth. Nationalism in these countries has, therefore, been 'tempered by the economic urge'.[1] This desire for swift economic advance has been accentuated by three factors. First, in order to achieve any growth in *per capita* wealth, capital formation must be at sufficient speed to exceed the mushrooming population expansion occurring in these areas. Secondly, deficiencies in educational facilities must be expanded if economic growth is to be facilitated. Thirdly, since economic inferiority suggests political inferiority, economic development has often taken on added significance as tangible evidence of nationhood. Consequently, supporters of federation have almost invariably cited the economic advantages of union: the creation of a larger market enabling economies of scale and maximum exploitation of resources, the greater attractiveness for foreign capital, the stronger bargaining power in trade negotiations, the opportunity for poorer territories to be aided by wealthier ones, and the provision of a wider financial base for supporting social services, economic planning, and active monetary and fiscal policies. Most political discussions on the economic merits of political integration have, however, been surprisingly superficial in nature. Thorough professional analyses of the economic benefits of union were undertaken before federation only in the West Indies, although in Central Africa the subject was intensively examined later at the time of the constitutional review.[2] Generally, then, it has been the *assumed* economic advantages

---

[1] J. Nehru, *The Unity of India* (1941), p. 19.

[2] Regarding the West Indies see Cmd. 7291/1948, pp. 17–20; Col. no. 255/1950, paras. 12–16, 19, 33, Appendix 4; Col. no. 268/1951, paras. 10–13, 20, 135–6; Development and Welfare Org. in W.I., *Financial Aspects of Federation*, Report (Seel), (1953); W.I. 1/58, *Report of the Trade and Tariffs Commission* (Croft), paras. 23–25, 30, 36, 47–50; Office of Premier of Trinidad, *The Economics of Nationhood* (1959). Regarding Central Africa, see A. Hazlewood

that have convinced statesmen of the desirability of federation. Nevertheless, these assumed economic benefits have been among the most influential motives for union.

The economic arguments for federation can be divided into two kinds: first, those which presuppose only a neutral public economic policy, and second, those which presuppose the desirability of an active public policy aimed at economic development and social welfare.[1] In the federations created in the eighteenth and nineteenth centuries, economic justification was primarily of the former type, but in the new federations both types of arguments have usually been advanced. The distinction is important because the form of political integration which is appropriate may vary with the type of economic policy expected.

The economic arguments for union which do not presuppose a positive economic role for government are based primarily on the alleged economies of scale that may be achieved in a larger economic territory. The private sector of the economy, it has been argued, would benefit from the larger free market enabling free movement of goods, labour, and capital, lower costs of production, regional specialization, industrialization, and the attraction of foreign investors. A common monetary system would remove restrictions on inter-territorial transactions, and also make it easier to obtain external credits. The larger area would, in addition, usually lead to a diversification in exports, making the economy less vulnerable to fluctuations in the international market than in the case of smaller territories dependent on one or a few major exports. The public sector of the economy would also stand to gain from a wider union. In the co-ordination and joint operation of common services economies of scale may be achieved. The diplomatic bargaining power in international trade negotiations is likely to be enhanced. The increased credit-worthiness of the larger unit would improve opportunities for government borrowing and give governments greater choice between taxing and borrowing, although this advantage may be lost if the larger unit proves politically unstable. A single larger unit would also make easier the task of preventing tax evasion.

The validity of these claims has on occasion been questioned.[2] In the

and P. D. Henderson, *Nyasaland, Economics of Federation* (1960), pp. 17–19, 30; Cmd. 8234/1951, Part III and Appendixes; C. Leys and C. Pratt (eds.), *A New Deal in Central Africa* (1960), pp. 48–49, 59–97; C. H. Thompson and H. W. Woodruff, *Economic Development in Rhodesia and Nyasaland* (1954), ch. 10; C. Fed. 132/1960, *Report on an Economic Survey of Nyasaland 1958–9* (Jack); Cmnd. 1148/1960, ch. 4; S. Williams, *Central Africa: The Economics of Inequality* (1960). Regarding Malaysia see International Bank for Reconstruction and Development, *Report on the Economic Aspects of Malaysia* (Rueff), (1963).

[1] For an analysis of these arguments see U. K. Hicks and others, *Federalism and Economic Growth in Underdeveloped Countries* (1961), especially chs. 3 and 4.

[2] See, for instance, Hazlewood and Henderson, op. cit., ch. 2 and p. 88; W. J. Barber, 'The Economic Argument' in Leys and Pratt (eds.), op. cit., chs. 7, 8; Cmnd. 1148/1960, pp. 146–7.

first place, size by itself is certainly no panacea, for it is only one factor in economic development. Sweden, Switzerland, and Belgium have achieved considerable prosperity in spite of their relatively small size, and there would seem to be limits to the economies of scale possible in territories with populations of over 50 million.[1] Nevertheless, except for India and Pakistan, the new federations have not been of a size above the point where significant economies might cease to result from integration. Secondly, even where union brings economic gains to an area as a whole, this does not necessarily mean gain to all the units. The removal of monetary friction in inter-unit transactions, and the reduced vulnerability of reserves through diversity of exports, it is true, can be achieved without detriment to the interests of any component territory. But a customs union may have not only 'trade-creation' effects but 'trade-diversion' effects which act adversely on certain territories within the grouping.[2] This is the case particularly in tariff unions between 'advanced' and 'backward' regions. It explains why, in spite of potential economic advantages to the area as a whole, territories like Jamaica, Penang, Nyasaland, Northern Nigeria, and East Pakistan in the new federations, and Western Australia and the Canadian Maritimes, have for economic reasons been reluctant to join federations or have later pressed for secession.[3]

While the economic claims considered so far suggest that, with only a few exceptions, economic unions are generally advantageous, none of these arguments actually requires full political integration. Where no active public economic policy is presupposed, the benefits of economic union could be achieved by institutional co-operation and co-ordination of the type exemplified in the East Africa High Commission, the West Indian Regional Economic Committee, or the Central African Council. It is possible that political unification may achieve further advantages through greater decisiveness; it is not, however, a *necessary* condition for the economic aims considered up to this point.

But the demand for rapid economic development in the former colonial areas has been coupled with an insistence upon an enlarged field of public economic activity. Governments have been expected to provide extensive social services, especially in health and education; to build up public utilities, including road, rail, and air transport; to formulate and administer economic plans; to control the stability and direct the progress of the economy by use of active monetary and fiscal policies. For each of these functions, political organization on an area basis clearly enjoys significant advantages over organization on a small unit basis, and considerable political integration is a prerequisite for the achievement of these benefits.

[1] A. Robinson (ed.), *The Economic Consequences of the Size of Nations* (1960), pp. xv–xix, and chs. 4–8.

[2] J. Viner, *The Customs Union Issue* (1950); Robinson (ed.), op. cit., pp. xx–xxi, 252–7; Hazlewood and Henderson, op. cit., pp. 60–64, 90.

[3] See Chapter 4, section 3 also.

In the provision of social services a larger union enables standardization of services and economies of scale, and creates a wider and more solid financial base on which to support the services. It also makes possible the raising of services in all territories to at least a minimum standard through subsidies to poorer regions such as Nyasaland, the Windward and Leeward Islands, Northern Nigeria, Assam and Orissa, the North-West Frontier Province and Sind, the north-eastern states of Malaya, and the Borneo states of Malaysia. Similar benefits are obtained for the formulation and administration of economic plans involving public expenditure within the larger unit. In addition, the financing of such plans is made easier by the greater credit-worthiness of the common government, provided it remains stable. What is more, the problems of economic planning and development often overrun regional political boundaries and must, therefore, be considered in terms of the economic area as a whole.[1] The employment of 'monetary magic' and active fiscal policies aimed at economic stabilization, forced saving, productive credit expansion, and direction of economic development, can also benefit by union because of the wider and more diversified financial base, the increased availability of foreign investment, and the wider scope for variations in policy.[2] Moreover, where such active public economic policies are desired, institutional or technical co-operation by itself, without a common government, is unlikely to be effective, because the allocation of services and expenditure, and the direction of the economy in the interests of the area as a whole, inevitably require controversial choices over the allocation of services, expenditure, and benefits.[3] Thus there have been positive economic grounds for establishing not mere joint services, but full-fledged political federations.

Here a qualification must be made. Although a federation may be superior to separate independent governments in actively promoting economic development, a federal division of authority may, if the central government is given insufficient power, handicap the effectiveness of a national economic policy. The necessity of strong central powers for economic planning was therefore particularly emphasized in India, and the lack of such central powers has been the cause of some criticism of the Nigerian and especially the West Indian constitutions.[4]

[1] Hicks and others, op. cit., p. 155. In some territories there may, however, be a large potential for economic growth as a result of local efforts at propagating improved agricultural techniques among farmers and simple mechanical skills among villagers in small workshops. See J. R. Hicks, in ibid., pp. 87–88.

[2] W. T. Newlyn in ibid., pp. 93–96, 97–102, 103, 110.

[3] Ibid., pp. 95–96, 100, 103; Hazlewood and Henderson, op. cit., pp. 24–25. Note also Cmd. 9475/1955, *East Africa Royal Commission 1953–5 Report*, pp. 86–89, 93, 95, which points to the shortcomings of the East Africa High Commission in promoting economic development.

[4] *States Finances Inquiry Committee*, Part I (1950), para. 16; *White Paper on Indian States* (rev. ed., 1950), para. 203, p. 101; The Citizens' Committee for Independence (Nigeria), *Independence with Honour* (1958), p. 6; D. Seers, 'The Federation of the B.W.I.: The Economic and Financial Aspects', *Social and Economic Studies*, vi (1957), pp. 197–213.

The force of the general economic arguments for political integration has varied in particular federations because of the influence of such factors as the complementary or competitive nature of the regional economies, the degree of historical economic interdependence, the potential for development existing in the federating regions, the size of the territories federating, and the presence of active economic groups organized across territorial boundaries.

Where the products of the federating territories are complementary, economic union is made particularly appealing by the prospects of an increased inter-regional trade, a more diversified economic base to support monetary reserves and government development and welfare policies, an opportunity for regional specialization and industrialization, and a diversification of exports, reducing vulnerability in the international market. If, on the other hand, the federating territories produce the same goods and therefore possess competing economies, little additional trade is likely to be stimulated, and the economic benefits gained from union are limited largely to tackling common problems in the fields of research and trade negotiations. But this sort of joint action does not necessitate a full federal structure.

The impact of complementary regional economies in encouraging union is illustrated by Nigeria. Regional differences in climate, soil, food crops, and other resources have made possible a thriving internal exchange economy. Furthermore, the need of the interior for an outlet to the coast in order to export its products, the southern dependence on this trade, the desire of the Eastern Region to export its surplus population, and the ambition of the Western Region to exploit its organizational skill in the less-advanced regions, have been major factors in promoting Nigerian unity. Regional specialization encouraging internal trade has also been a feature of the Indian economy. The complementary character of the economies of the Rhodesias and Nyasaland —Northern Rhodesia contributing copper and its export revenues, Southern Rhodesia its coal and secondary industries, and Nyasaland its labour—was frequently cited in favour of federation, sometimes with considerable exaggeration. In Malaya, internal trade among the former Malay States has not been extensive, but the former Settlements have relied for their trade and commerce on the produce and natural resources of the interior, while the interior has depended in turn upon their commercial, trading, marketing, and shipping facilities. Even East and West Pakistan, although separated geographically, were, because of their different climates producing different food crops and exports, to some extent complementary.

In the West Indies, however, once British Guiana and British Honduras decided not to join the federation, the federating territories were economically competitive rather than complementary, because of the similarity of their products. Indeed, the proportion of island exports devoted to inter-island trade was below 5 per cent., and in the case of Jamaica about 1 per cent.[1] Thus

[1] Office of Premier of Trinidad, *The Economics of Nationhood* (1959), Table XXI, pp.

the hopes expressed by some of the advocates of federation that a free market would encourage trade among the islands proved unrealistic.

While the hope for economic advantage from union does not require the existence of historical economic ties, in actual fact the development under British rule of interdependent economies and communications has often helped to encourage the desire for union. The commercial, industrial, and financial links already built up were a unifying force in India and within West Pakistan, and were a major factor in the rapid accession of the princely states to the two independent federations. In Malaya the economic integration of the earlier Federated Malay States and the historical interdependence of the Settlements and the hinterland provided a foundation for further economic unity. Already existing close commercial ties were also a factor encouraging Sarawak and especially Singapore, although not North Borneo, to join Malaya in the Federation of Malaysia. Despite the relatively artificial nature of Nigeria as a unit, its integrated economy and communications were built up under British rule following Lugard's amalgamation, and the establishment of central marketing boards during the Second World War contributed to the process. The resulting economic interdependence was a major factor inducing the regional leaders to preserve Nigerian unity during the crisis of 1953. In Rhodesia and Nyasaland the activities of the Central African Council had forged common links in currency, customs administration, railways, other communications, and research, and for some time before federation Nyasaland Africans had been seeking employment in large numbers in Southern Rhodesia. Similarly in the Caribbean some economic links had been built up between the islands by the wartime work of the Development and Welfare Organization and of the Caribbean Commission, by the establishment of a Currency Board for the eastern Caribbean, by the creation of the Regional Economic Committee as a result of the Montego Bay Conference, and by the activities of regional commodity associations.

The seductive prospects of 'limitless resources waiting to be developed' and of 'potential industrialization', so often envisaged, heightened the appeal of economic union in most of the new federations, as it had earlier in the undeveloped continental expanses of the United States, Canada, and Australia. Initially there had been similar hopes even in the Caribbean. The mainland territories were pictured as a 'frontier' where the surplus population of the islands might be re-located and the extensive potential resources developed. But the refusal of British Guiana and British Honduras to participate robbed the federal project of much of its economic glamour; a federation of paupers held little prospect of prosperity.

Another factor affecting the relative strength of the economic motives for union has been the size of the federating units themselves. The states and

45–46; A. D. Knox, 'Trade and Customs Union in the W.I.' in G. E. Cumper, *The Economy of the West Indies* (1960), pp. 243–55.

settlements of Malaya, the smaller islands in the West Indies, and the territories of Central Africa, were all regarded as far too small to support self-sufficient economies; federation, therefore, appeared an economic necessity. By contrast, the three Nigerian regions, East and West Pakistan, and even Jamaica, were large enough to contemplate standing on their own feet, although not with the strength of a larger federation.

In a number of cases the activites of economic interest groups urging federation has been an important factor in the campaign for union. The union of Federated Malay States in 1895, for instance, was largely the result of demands by commercial, agricultural, and mining interests, and the plan for Malayan Union in 1946 followed closely the Association of British Malaya Memorandum submitted to the Colonial Office in 1944. Commercial and industrial interests, concentrated among the settlers, were also among the strongest advocates of federation in Central Africa. In Nigeria, business groups and expatriate companies operating throughout the area were strong supporters of unity. The few influential Indian business families, who controlled much of modern Indian industry and most of the press, provided the bulk of the Congress Party's financial support, and such all-India organizations as the Federation of Indian Chambers of Commerce and Industry were strong advocates of unity. In the Caribbean the West Indian Chambers of Commerce and the Caribbean producers' organizations supported, although sometimes cautiously, closer economic ties.

Trade unions were not strong enough in Pakistan or Nigeria to be influential, but the Malayan and Indian trade union movements were active in the cause of national unity. It was in Central Africa and the Caribbean, however, that trade unions were a major force. The settler trade unions of the Northern Rhodesian copperbelt saw in Roy Welensky their natural spokesman, and in the West Indies the Caribbean Labour Congress and such men as Bradshaw, Bird, Adams, and Manley, all closely associated with labour, were among the most active supporters of federation.

To summarize, in all the new federations, except Pakistan, where the advocacy of partition from India was itself a denial of the economic motivation for union, the demand for political structures capable of pushing economic growth forward rapidly has played a prominent role in promoting unity. The economic advantages of federal union were proclaimed most loudly in the Caribbean and Central Africa, but, paradoxically, would appear in both cases to have been secondary to political considerations. The economic hopes in the former were undermined by the competitive nature of the island economies, and the weakness of economic motives was apparent in the failure of the West Indies Federation, unique among federations in this respect, to achieve even a customs union. In Rhodesia and Nyasaland the economic arguments had more validity, and it was difficult to imagine how Nyasaland on its own could ever be made economically viable. The result was a federation with a highly centralized economy but, as the later controversies indicated, its economic merit was by no means as obvious as its British and settler supporters often assumed.[1] In Nigeria, Malaya, most of Malaysia, and India, however, regional economic interdependence, reinforced especially in India by the determined desire for national economic planning, was clearly among the most decisive factors leading to political unification.

4. *Administrative efficiency*

Another motive for unity has been the hope of improved administrative convenience and efficiency. In developing areas where trained administrators, indigenous or imperial, have been in short supply this has been a particularly important consideration.

The appeal of economy and increased efficiency through unification of administrative organization has been strongest where the federating units were too small to support efficient administrative systems. For instance, the founders of the West Indies Federation repeatedly pointed to the administrative economies to be gained. Ten foreign services and ten armies for a population of about half that of Ontario would have formed a conception verging on Ruritanian. Similar considerations also weighed heavily in Malaya. The wartime difficulties in defending Malaya because of the cumbersome administrative structure, and a new post-war emphasis on 'planning', were major factors in the British advocacy of a unitary Union when the peninsula was regained. Indeed, taking administrative grounds alone, a unitary structure would have appeared more appropriate than federal institutions in both Malaya and the West Indies, but centrifugal forces were too strong to make that possible. The regional units of the other federations were more extensive in area, but the shortage of trained administrators placed a premium on administrative efficiency. In Nigeria, for instance, Lugard looked upon the amalgamation of Nigeria primarily as a means of enhancing administrative efficiency, made necessary because his administrators were spread so 'thin on the ground', and similar needs influenced Nigerian constitution-making right up to independence.[2] In the Rhodesias and Nyasaland the relatively small size of the settler population and the strictly circumscribed territorial budgets made thrifty and efficient management desirable. Pakistan, as a result of partition, was particularly short of trained and experienced civil servants, but even in India, which was better supplied, any tendency to balkanization was denigrated as administratively harmful. In both Pakistan and India the need for administrative efficiency was later advanced also as a justification for regrouping the smaller units into larger states or provinces.[3]

Apart from the general efficiency and economy resulting from unified administration of certain matters, it was also sometimes suggested that union

---

[1] See footnote 2 on p. 46 above.
[2] Cmd. 468/1920, p. 7.   [3] See Chapter 7, section 2.

with more advanced or larger regions would benefit the weaker or smaller territories which otherwise would be unable to support certain specialized services. Nyasaland, the Windward and Leeward Islands, the princely states acceding to Pakistan and India, and the smaller Malay states such as Perlis, all stood to gain in this way from federation.

5. *The conduct of external relations*

Both for military defence and for diplomatic influence there have usually been benefits to be gained from union. The advantages of common defence have been cited in all the new federations, but the sense of urgency has varied. In Nigeria and the West Indies there was no outside threat or pressure to create insecurity and an urgent feeling of the need for a common defence. Nor were the Rhodesias and Nyasaland faced with any direct military threats, although the growing power of white South Africa on one side, and black East Africa and later the Congo on the other sides, did contribute to a feeling of unease among both Central African settlers and British officials. On the Indian continent, protected by the Himalayas, defence was not a major concern before partition, and this helps to explain why progress to Indian political unity was so slow before 1947. With partition, however, and the absence of any geographical barriers between the two new hostile nations, military insecurity became a force for unity within each. Strategic considerations were, for instance, a major factor in the hasty political integration of the princely states into the Union of India. At the same time, it was primarily military insecurity, particularly fear of India as a result of the Kashmir and Indus waters controversies, that held Pakistan together. In Malaya, the débâcle of 1941-2, the strategic position of Malaya within troubled south-east Asia, the threat to internal security due to the Emergency and the consequent need to concert the operations of the armed forces, the police, the civil departments, and the agencies involved, and the potential external threat of China and her satellites to the north, were factors leading Britain to insist on Malayan unification. Later, similar strategic considerations helped to induce Singapore and the Borneo territories to join Malaysia, while Malayan leaders agreed to accept the merger of Singapore in order to control its internal security and prevent it succumbing to Communism. The Indonesian challenge served further to fortify the shaky Malaysian unity for a time.

The vision of international prestige and greater diplomatic influence in a world dominated by large nations has often also provided an appealing inducement to political leaders. India, united, could look forward to enjoying a significant political role because of its immense size and resources, and Prime Minister Nehru's prestige on the world scene bore out this hope. The necessity of countering India's diplomatic influence has in turn been a factor for unity in Pakistan. The potentiality of Nigeria as a major African state, due to its population and to its diversity of resources, and the desire to overtake the prestige of the much smaller Ghana which had gained independence first, helped to unite Nigerian leaders. The smaller federations—the West Indies, Malaya, and Rhodesia and Nyasaland—could not aspire to such international pretensions, but even there, hopes of being able to raise a more significant voice in international discussions and negotiations, and in some cases a resentment in the small territories at their lack of bargaining power in the outside world, have contributed to support for the larger political unit.

6. *Ethnic and cultural community*

Although none of the new federations, with the possible exception of the West Indies, has contained a homogeneous population, nevertheless, common national, racial, religious, cultural, linguistic, or social ties have often contributed to the unification of political units. Pakistan was perhaps the most striking example, for there it was the Muslim religion which was the *raison d'être* of the new nation and which, coupled with anti-Indian feeling, provided the most vivid basis for national unity in territories which otherwise had little in common. In India, too, variety and diversity leaped to the eye at once, but beneath this there was the common impress of Indian culture, and after partition the dominance of a common religion, moulding a basic community of outlook. By contrast, in the West Indian islands which, apart from Trinidad, were generally as a group homogeneous in race, culture, language, religion, and social structure, because of the geographical isolation of each island, none of these cultural affinities served as a positive emotional unifying force, except perhaps cricket!

In some areas where major communal or other social antagonisms cut across territorial boundaries, ranging through all the federating units, communities or classes have been driven to seek to protect or strengthen their position by inter-territorial union. The most obvious examples were Malaya and Rhodesia and Nyasaland. In the former, the racial, religious, linguistic, social, and economic factors tending to differentiate the Malay community from the others in each state, served to unify the Malays, when threatened by the British proposals for Union in 1946, in support of the U.M.N.O. and of a Malay-dominated federation. Later, it was in order to offset the Chinese preponderance that would result from Singapore's inclusion that Tunku Abdul Rahman advocated the addition of the Borneo states to form a 'Greater Malaysia', and emphasized the ethnic ties between the peninsular Malays and the peoples of the British Borneo territories. Among the settlers in all three of the Central African territories, the desire to protect their supremacy in the face of growing African political consciousness lay at the root of their eagerness first for amalgamation and then for federation. On the other side, some Africans in Southern Rhodesia hoped that federation with territories where Africans were more favourably treated would lead to a liberalizing of native policies in their own territory. Although less prominent, the desires of Negroes in Trinidad and British Guiana to protect their position against the East Indian community, the fears of ethnic groups overlapping regional boundaries in Nigeria, particularly the Ibos, and the loyalties of castes cutting to some extent across provincial political boundaries in India, also encouraged these groups to support wider federal unions.

Sometimes the very existence of different ethnic communities within an area has itself, paradoxically, provided a justification for unity. In Rhodesia and Nyasaland, and also the West Indies, the idealistic proponents of federation argued that a successful federal union, harmonizing different racial groups, would set an example to the world of peaceful racial co-existence or 'partnership'.

Of the different ethnic and cultural factors contributing to unity, racial homogeneity played a part in Nigeria and, with some exceptions, in the West Indies, while shared racial cleavages influenced demands for political union in Malaya, Malaysia, and Rhodesia and Nyasaland. A common religion was a major factor in the internal unity both of Pakistan and of India following 1947. In Malaya Islam was an integrative force among the Malay states, and also to some extent between Malaya and the British Borneo territories. At Montego Bay the prevalence of Christianity was cited in favour of British Caribbean unity.[1] An underlying common culture has also contributed to Indian, Malay, and to a lesser degree Nigerian, unity. In addition, the impact of British rule has often left a distinctly British-flavoured culture. In Nigeria, for instance, the contrast with the different cultures and official languages of the surrounding French territories sharpened Nigerian individuality. Similarly the West Indian islands shared a distinctly Anglo-African culture, which contrasted with the Latin culture of neighbouring countries.

In most of the new federations, however, a common indigenous language which might serve as a unifying force has been missing, although 'bazaar-Malay' in Malaya and Hausa in Nigeria have served some of the functions of a lingua franca. In both Pakistan and India there have been difficulties over attempts to establish Urdu in the former and Hindi in the latter as national languages.[2] The English language has, however, usually been a unifying instrument. In the West Indies, and to some extent Central Africa, it has been a predominant medium of communication, and elsewhere it has served as the common language of the small, but politically influential, educated élite.

7. Geographical contiguity

The geographical neighbourhood of the federating territories was a characteristic common in all the older federations at the time of their formation,[3]

---

[1] Col. no. 218/1948, p. 12.   [2] See Chapter 10, section 4.

[3] But distant British Columbia joined Canada soon after 1867, and more recently the U.S.A. has added Alaska and Hawaii as states. Tasmania in Australia, and Prince Edward Island and Newfoundland in Canada, are separated by water from the federations to which they belong.

and four of the six new Commonwealth federations have been composed of geographically contiguous regions. But Pakistan is unique in having its two major regions separated by a wide expanse of alien territory, while the West Indies Federation was composed of islands scattered across the Caribbean Sea. Even in these federations, geographical neighbourhood was a factor at least in encouraging the unity of the western provinces and states of Pakistan which were eventually unified into a single province, and in encouraging closer bonds among those West Indian islands grouped closer together in the eastern Caribbean.

Geographic influences promoting unity were perhaps strongest in Malaya, India, and Nigeria. The outstanding geographical characteristic of peninsular Malaya, small and compact, with water on three sides and only a narrow land frontier to the north, was unity. Singapore too was close, so close that the Malayan Prime Minister conceded in 1957: 'we are in such proximity that anything that happens in Singapore can happen to the Federation'.[1] The British Borneo territories were more distant, however, being separated by some 500 miles of sea. Although before partition the sub-continent of India had often been described as a natural geographic unit, marked off by the Himalayas, this had not been a powerful enough influence to hold Muslims and Hindus together. Nevertheless, in 1947, 'geographical compulsions' were a major factor in inducing the princely states which were scattered among and interlaced with the provinces of British India to accede rapidly to the newly independent federations.[2] Nigeria, although a geographically artificial entity, was marked off by desert in the north, and unified internally by the lines of communication running north and south.

The effectiveness of linking communications has been a vital factor in the geographical unity of these federations. In some cases such as Nigeria, peninsular Malaya including Singapore, India, and within West Pakistan, the development during British rule of a network of railways, roads, airlines, inland waterways, ports and harbours, and telecommunications linking the colonial units, had encouraged a vital sense of interdependence. In Nigeria, for instance, Lord Hailey concluded: 'If there is anywhere a real tie between the North and the South it lies in a geography that makes the North dependent on the South for its line of communications, and the South dependent on the North for some part of its subsistence and a large part of its export'.[3] On the other hand, in the West Indies, in Rhodesia and Nyasaland, and earlier in the formation of the Federated Malay States, where effective communications were lacking, federal unity was itself desired as a means to improved communications. But in all the new federations, including the West Indies and

---

[1] Quoted in L. A. Mills, *Malaya* (1958), p. 134.

[2] *White Paper on Indian States* (rev. ed. 1950), paras. 74, 272.

[3] Lord Hailey, *An African Survey* (rev. ed. 1956), p. 313. See also A. Bello, *My Life* (1962), pp. 135–6, 138, 228–9.

Pakistan where the communicating links were so tenuous, the development of air travel and of radio made communication between distant regions far less difficult than it had been for the older federations of Canada and Australia at the time of their inception.

8. *Historical political association*

In some of the new federations there have been historical forces for unity going back to well before the days of British rule. Each of the Asian federations, for instance, could look back to periods of past glory associated with political unity, and African leaders have also sought historical foundations for nationhood. The fifteenth-century Malay empire of Malacca, the old Indian empires of the Maurya and Gupta dynasties, and the Muslim Mughal empire have provided the basis for national 'myths' on which unity might be built.

The achievement of unity in the new federations has, however, been even more a reflection of the form and character of the common British government the component territories had experienced. These territories inherited many unifying influences: peaceful co-existence under the Pax Britannica, a common legal code and the tradition of rule of law, basically similar administrative structures and political institutions, a shared lingua franca, standardized educational policies, and interlocked communications and economies. In addition, they had already experienced a kind of common federal authority in the overriding powers of the British Government before independence.

The historical impact of British rule on these territories is apparent in the way most of the imperial frontiers have remained unchanged. With the exception of India's absorption of a few tiny French and Portuguese enclaves, all the federations under study were composed solely of former British territories. Despite the artificial nature of the colonial units, it would appear that strong new groupings of loyalties and interests were created by the experience of imperial rule. Thus, Indians have acknowledged that Britain 'gave political unity to India',[1] and Nigerians have described their nation as 'a political union which has been forged on the anvil of British rule'.[2] The very names 'Nigeria' and 'Malaya' appear to have been coined by Britons.[3]

But, in addition to the community of outlook resulting from a shared history of British rule, federation has usually also been preceded by the experience of actual inter-territorial political association. These have ranged from bonds verging on centralized unitary colonial administration in Nigeria, pre-partition India, and Malaya, to loose inter-territorial conferences, committees, and councils in the West Indies and Central Africa.

Nigeria after 1914, and India until 1935, had already been united under

---

[1] Nehru, *The Unity of India*, p. 19.

[2] N. Azikiwe, *Zik, Selected Speeches of Dr. Nnamdi Azikiwe* (1961), p. 190.

[3] A. H. M. Kirk-Greene, 'Who Coined the Name "Nigeria"?', *West Africa* (22 December 1956), p. 1035; G. L. Peet, *Political Questions of Malaya* (1949), p. 8.

British rule in a form that was ostensibly unitary.[1] Even after 1935 the existence of an All-India civil service, inherited by India at independence, was a powerful unifying force. In Malaya a high degree of co-ordination had in practice been achieved before 1940 through the centralized bureaucracy of the Federated Malay States and the dual role of the Governor of the Straits Settlements who acted also as High Commissioner for the Malay states. But although the British administrations of India, Malaya, and Nigeria were unified, in none of these cases was the unification complete. The legal sovereignty of the Indian princes and the Malay rulers was maintained, and Northern Nigeria was never fully integrated with Southern Nigeria. The cases of Malaya and Nigeria are of special interest. In both, the British Government's attempts in 1946 to impose unitary unions, with little consultation of local opinion, failed.[2] Yet each of these efforts was a significant precursor of federation. The Malayan Union represented the first attempt to join in a single unit the various territories that were to constitute the Federation of Malaya in 1948, and the Richards Constitution, for the first time, extended the membership and the full authority of the Legislative Council to the whole of Nigeria, including the Northern Region.

Even in the federations that were not preceded by a relatively integrated British administration, there had been some prior political association between territories. In the Rhodesias the amalgamation movement among the settlers had resulted in several commissions investigating the issue, in the institution of a Central African Governors' Conference in 1935, and in the formation of the purely consultative Central African Council in 1945.[3] In the West Indies the movement for political association could be traced even further back, the Leeward Islands Federation of 1871 and the looser grouping of the Windward Islands being examples in the nineteenth century.[4] During the Second World War, the co-ordinating activities of the Anglo-American Commission and of the Development and Welfare Organization served as 'a rudimentary federal structure'.[5] The early post-war conferences and committees on closer association in the West Indies also created some functional interterritorial organizations, the Regional Economic Committee being the most notable of these. These looser forms of political association in Central Africa and the Caribbean contributed to the desire for federal unity in two ways. First, they fostered some community of outlook through political contact.

[1] Cmd. 468/1920; J. S. Coleman, *Nigeria: Background to Nationalism* (1958), pp. 44–60; P. N. Masaldan, *Evolution of Provincial Autonomy in India* (1953), pp. 8, 13, 24, 143.

[2] S.R. & O., no. 463/1946, *Malayan Union Order in Council, 1946*; S.R. & O., no. 1370/1946, *The Nigeria (Legislative Council) Order in Council, 1946*.

[3] See Cmd. 8233/1951, paras. 14–16; R. Gray, *The Two Nations* (1960), ch. 5; D. S. Rothchild, *Toward Unity in Africa* (1960), pp. 89–95.

[4] Two articles by L. Braithwaite in *Social and Economic Studies*, vi (1957), 'Progress Toward Federation, 1938–1956', p. 133, and ' "Federal" Associations and Institutions in the British West Indies', p. 286, consider the forms of closer association preceding federation.   [5] Col. no. 218/1948, p. 28.

Secondly, they usually pointed up the shortcomings and relative inadequacy of loose political institutions lacking executive powers.

9. *Similarity of political and social institutions*

Because the federating units in the new federations were all British colonies or former colonies, there has usually been a general similarity in the systems of law, administrative structure, and political institutions, and this has facilitated the uniting of these territories. In the provinces of India and Pakistan, for instance, there already existed uniform constitutions as stipulated by the Government of India Act, 1935. Likewise, the Nigerian regions possessed broadly similar institutions under the Richards and Macpherson constitutions, and the degree of constitutional uniformity among the Federated Malay States was high. Although the territorial constitutions of the West Indies and the Rhodesias and Nyasaland were by no means identical, under the guiding hand of the British Government they were all aiming towards British parliamentary institutions. Thus the broad similarity of political institutions, each sharing a British parliamentary orientation, has provided a common foundation, although this influence was often counteracted by differences in constitutional status and degree of political advancement, by uneven application of the policy of indirect rule, and by contrasts in indigenous institutions.[1]

Inter-territorial uniformities or similarities in social institutions, structure, classes, or castes, have to a limited degree also encouraged unity in many of the new federations. Sometimes the regional social differences may have appeared more obvious, but the system of caste differentiation in India, the kampong as the basis of Malay social institutions, the relation throughout the West Indian islands of class and status to colour shading, and the relatively common pattern of underlying social organization in Nigeria once one gets down to the lineage level and below, are examples of underlying common social institutions. Even in the Rhodesias and Nyasaland, where racial policies appeared to be in sharp variance, the officials' conference of 1951 was more impressed by 'the degree of similarity between the policy and practice of the three Governments rather than the degree of difference'.[2]

Urbanization has often served, as in Kuala Lumpur, Lagos, or the Rhodesian copperbelt, to introduce different groups or tribes to each other, although occasionally such meetings have instead helped to emphasize social differences rather than similarities. The difficult process of transition from indigenous to modern forms of organization, common to most developing areas, has also generally provided the basis for some feeling of shared problems and interests.

[1] See Chapter 4, section 9, below.
[2] Cmd. 8233/1951, para. 18. See also paras. 17, 19, and Cmd. 8235/1951, esp. paras. 4, 20.

10. *Political leadership*

Federations do not simply 'happen' because there are desires for unity. The activating of these desires and the achievement of federal union has in every case depended upon the appearance of dynamic and able leadership or statesmanship at the right time. Where such leadership has lacked vigour or the willingness and ability to compromise, the process of constitution-making has proved more protracted and controversial.

The importance of enterprising and capable leadership has been exemplified by the influence of the Congress Party leadership on Indian nationalism. It has been said: 'Nehru was the voice of the Congress, Patel its organizer and Gandhi its inspiration'.[1] Nehru's constant stress on unity, Patel's organizational ability, both within the party and in the integration of the princely states, and Gandhi's example, were decisive elements in the achievement of Indian unity. In Pakistan it was Mohammad Ali Jinnah, the Quaid-i-Azam, who united the Muslims and, with the assistance of Liaquat Ali Khan, his able lieutenant, brought the new state into being. But Jinnah died in 1948, and Liaquat Ali Khan was assassinated in 1951. Thereafter, the lack of strong and effective national leaders resulted in delays in constitution-making and the gradual evaporation of national unity. The uniting of the Malays and the formation of the U.M.N.O. which preceded the 1948 Federation of Malaya was largely the work of Dato Onn bin Ja'afar. But when he failed to carry the Malays in support of inter-racial unity, it was left to Tunku Abdul Rahman, in association with Henry Hau Shik Lee and Tan Cheng-lock, the leaders of the Malayan Chinese Association, and V. T. Sambantham, the leader of the Malayan Indian Congress, to construct an inter-communal Alliance. Nor, without the initiative and persistence of Lee Kuan Yew and the determination of Tunku Abdul Rahman, would the inclusion of Singapore and the widened Malaysian Federation have been attempted. Of prime importance in the federation of the Rhodesias and Nyasaland was the vigorous leadership of Roy Welensky, who was determined to free Northern Rhodesia from the Colonial Office, and of Premier Huggins in Southern Rhodesia.[2] The characteristically charismatic nature of political leadership in the Asian and African countries, exemplified in the hold upon their peoples of such leaders as Gandhi, Nehru, Jinnah, Dato Onn, and Tunku Abdul Rahman, made these men particularly potent forces for unity.

In Nigeria and the West Indies, on the other hand, there was a relative lack of leaders with a vital national outlook, and it was the regional leaders who generally exerted a charismatic influence over their followers. In Nigeria after

[1] M. Brecher, *Nehru, A Political Biography* (1959), p. 390.

[2] Both Huggins and Welensky began as ardent supporters of amalgamation, but Welensky, upon realizing that only federal union would be acceptable to the British Government, persuaded Huggins to join him in a campaign for federation (D. Taylor, *The Rhodesian* (1955), pp. 104–7); R. Welensky, *4000 Days* (1964), pp. 21–26.

1949 leaders with a predominantly regional outlook dominated the scene, weakening the sense of Nigerian unity. The timidity of the West Indian political leaders resulted during the pre-federal negotiations in a concern for the difficulties, rather than the benefits, that federation might confer, and in a failure to convey the concept of nationhood to the mass of the electorate.[1]

But dynamic and charismatic leadership is not sufficient to create unity. Federal political systems are based on compromises, and these require political leadership capable of being conciliatory. It is in this respect, in reconciling differences, that Jawaharlal Nehru in India, Balewa Abubakar Tafawa in Nigeria, and at times the Tunku in Malaya proved particularly adept. By contrast, leaders who have lacked tact have often hindered the effort to create national unity. Examples were the alienation of African opinion by the pronouncements of both Huggins and Welensky, the failure of Dato Onn to win Malay support for the Independence of Malaya Party, and Bustamente's disdain for the smaller Caribbean islands. Where the authority of the traditional rulers or chiefs was still strong, nationalist leaders such as Tunku Abdul Rahman or the Sardauna of Sokoto, who belonged to these ruling classes and could therefore bridge the gap between the educated western élite and the traditional rulers, played a particularly valuable role in winning the latter over to the cause of national unity.

In most of these countries the emergence of an influential, westernized élite has also contributed towards unity. British and American educated professional and business men, particularly lawyers, saturated with western ideas of democracy, nationalism, and large-scale political organization, have invariably played a leading role in the movements for union. The members of these small, educated élites have been determined to show that they, no less than the British, were capable of running a large modern state holding together the various units taken over from the colonial régime. In Central Africa it was the cohesive settler community which performed the function of such an élite. There was some attempt there to build up a moderate African middle class supporting the Europeans in favouring union, but this class wielded little influence among Africans because of its small size and the tendency of African nationalists to regard its members as settler stooges.

11. *Successful models of federation*

The success of earlier federations has been a factor contributing to the desire for federal unions in the developing areas. In an age when democratic slogans make force as a method of political integration unacceptable, examples like Canada and Switzerland suggested that a peaceful integration of culturally diverse peoples might be possible through federation. Large continental federations like the United States, Australia, and Canada also showed how a union of widespread regions could be achieved by means of federal institutions.

[1] On leadership in the West Indies see A. Etzioni, *Political Unification* (1965), chs. 5, 8.

Moreover, the relative economic prosperity which these older federations displayed in the decade after 1945 added to the magic appeal of the federal solution in regions where rapid economic development was desired.[1] Consequently, these older federations were frequently cited as models to be followed in the search for political and economic progress.[2] To the older examples was added, also, that of India which, because of its size, had so quickly gained international prestige after its independence in 1947.[3] The general effect was that in the decades after the Second World War federal union became a fashionable solution for the problems of developing areas. Indeed, so fashionable did it become that it was applied as a panacea to situations where the federal solution had never been applied before, such as the scattered islands of the West Indies, the combination of self-governing and colonial territories in Central Africa, and the dual provinces of Pakistan widely separated by hostile territory. In these unusual situations, it was not surprising that unity proved so fragile a plant.

12. *British policy*

In all the new Commonwealth federations, except India and Pakistan after 1947, the British Government played a major role in constitution-making. Federal unity was not, therefore, simply the result of negotiations between local representatives of the territories involved. British policies aiming at closer association between colonies were particularly significant, for, as Francis Carnell has pointed out:

> The whole experiment in colonial federation-building is a colossal gamble in the sense that, with the best of motives, the colonial power may be wanting to join together the wrong peoples. [Moreover,] as an interested party, it has powers of persuasion, direction, control or even force at its disposal.[4]

Even before 1945, the British Government had in certain areas, notably India, Nigeria, and Malaya, supported a policy of unification, although in each this had been associated with policies of administrative devolution and of indirect rule, which encouraged local autonomy. But the multiplicity of colonial federations created by Britain since 1945 raises the question whether these were simple *ad hoc* expedients to meet local situations, or were instead the result of a general policy of encouraging territorial political association.

The Colonial Office has usually described its approach to the problems of

---

[1] In pointing to these examples little reference was made, except in the Indian Constituent Assembly, to the difficulties the older federations had faced in coping with the depression decade before 1939.

[2] For details of the influence of older federations upon the form of newer federations, see Chapter 6, section 5.

[3] The partition of India also pointed out the dangers of 'Pakistanism' to which southern Nigerians frequently referred in denouncing threats of secession made by the Muslim Northern Region. See, for instance, Azikiwe, *Zik*, pp. 102, 177–8.

[4] F. G. Carnell, 'Political Implications of Federalism in New States', in U. K. Hicks and others, op. cit., p. 59.

the colonial territories as 'empirical'. Because each area has its own unique problems, it has generally been reluctant to apply constitutions 'off the rack' and has preferred constitutions 'made to measure', tailored to fit the specific needs of the territories involved. Thus the 'federal solution' has been considered as an *ad hoc* expedient to be applied where particular circumstances allowed no alternative. In Malaya unity was insisted upon for administrative and strategic reasons. In the West Indies, on the other hand, the primary motives were the encouragement of economic self-sufficiency and the accommodation of self-government. Unity was promoted in Nigeria, first for administrative convenience, and later as a basis for constitutional reform and to meet economic and defence requirements. The hope that Southern Rhodesia might be won to a more liberal native policy, the realization that real power in Northern Rhodesia was slipping into the settlers' hands, the desire to create a viable multi-racial buffer state between white nationalist South Africa and black nationalist East Africa, and the economic advantages for Nyasaland, led important officials in the Colonial Office to concur in support for a Central African federation, a reversal of earlier policy.

Nevertheless, there is some evidence to suggest that British colonial policy after 1945 was actually characterized by a general policy favouring closer territorial association in the colonial areas, although the application of this policy to particular regions may have been 'empirical'. During the war the future of British colonies was much discussed, and a report by Lord Hailey on British Africa as a whole which circulated within the Colonial Office seems to have made a deep impression.[1] Late in the war, during the tenure of Oliver Stanley as Conservative Secretary of State for the Colonies, schemes for bringing greater unity to Malaya, Nigeria, and the West Indies, and for co-ordinating, but not uniting, the Central African territories, were examined and tentatively started upon.[2] The new Labour Secretary of State, Creech Jones, set as basic principles of British colonial policy: assistance towards self-government and self-reliance, and the creation of conditions for social and economic development. These aims made the encouragement of inter-territorial political association in certain areas, such as Malaya, Nigeria, East Africa, Central Africa, and the West Indies, a desirable policy.[3] 'Viability' became the prerequisite for self-government, and inter-regional unity the means. There ensued the hasty attempts to impose unitary administrations in both Malaya and Nigeria in 1946; the continued insistence, even after the failure of unitary government, upon some form of unity in these countries,

[1] See Lord Hailey, *Native Administration in the British African Territories* (1950), Prefaces to Parts I and IV; Coleman, *Nigeria*, pp. 238, 271–5.

[2] U.K. House of Commons, *Debates*, vol. 420 (8 March 1946), col. 710; B. Bourdillon, *Memoranda on Future Political Development of Nigeria* (1939 and 1942); Cmd. 6599/1945, Governor's Despatch, paras. 1, 3; Cmd. 7120/1947, App. I; Cmd. 7987/1950, para. 146.

[3] See, for instance, Col. no. 218/1948, pp. 6–7; Cmd. 6724/1946, para. 2; U.K. House of Commons, *Debates*, vol. 414, cols. 255–6; vol. 425, cols. 265–7.

culminating in a highly centralized federation in Malaya in 1948 and a 'quasi-federal' constitution in Nigeria in 1951; the vigorous encouragement of a West Indian federation at the Montego Bay Conference in 1948; the establishment of the East Africa High Commission, a functional inter-territorial association, in 1947. Creech Jones did, however, resist Central African settler demands for amalgamation, but when on Stanley's advice Welensky induced the settlers to seek federation, Griffiths, Creech Jones's successor as Secretary of State, agreed to an examination of the possibilities.[1] When the Conservatives came to power in 1951, they quickly pushed ahead the negotiations for a Federation of Rhodesia and Nyasaland, despite African opposition. Elsewhere, Nigerian unity was saved by the adoption in 1954 of an orthodox federal system, and the laborious negotiations over the West Indies Federation were brought to fruition in 1957. Thus, a general policy of encouraging inter-colonial federations was carried forward by both major British political parties.

Furthermore, although the organization of the Colonial Office itself encouraged an insular approach to the problems of each colony, lessons learnt in one territory have not always been ignored in others. For instance, the innovation in Central Africa in 1953, in which the 'federal solution' was applied as a way of uniting territories with different degrees of political advancement, was used soon afterwards to solve the Nigerian crisis, where, ironically, it proved far more successful. Similarly, the federal pattern in Malaya in 1948 and again in 1957 owed much to the examples on the Indian continent.[2] The Colonial Office has also frequently relied on such men as Wheare, Jennings, and Raisman, with a wide experience and understanding of federal problems, to serve as advisers, or to act on constitutional commissions. The pragmatic treatment of problems in each area has not, therefore, been as isolated as has sometimes been intimated.

The impact of British policy has been considerable. The highly centralized form of the Federation of Malaya in 1948 and the preservation of Nigerian unity at the 1953 conference were largely the result of British insistence. Indeed, in the latter case, it was said that 'while Britain strives to unite and rule, Africans try to divide and rule'.[3] The West Indies Federation was to some extent an artificial union urged from outside, critics at Montego Bay complaining that Creech Jones 'has come here with his mind absolutely made up to push something down our throats'.[4] In Central Africa, federation was in the end a bargain between the settlers of the Rhodesias and the British Government acting on behalf of the Africans of the northern protectorates, in spite of

[1] Welensky, *4000 Days*, ch. 1.

[2] *Report of the Working Committee* (1946), para. 105; Col. no. 330/1957, paras. 83, 84, 149. See also Chapter 6, section 5.

[3] M. Perham, *The Times* (17 March 1955), p. 7. See also K. Ezera, *Constitutional Developments in Nigeria* (2nd ed., 1964), pp. 197–9.

[4] Col. no. 218/1948, p. 21.

their opposition.[1] Thus, in all four colonial federations, British policy, aiming at the creation of politically and economically self-sufficient nations, was a major factor in their federal unification.

13. *The major motives*

The factors which have induced desires for political unity within the new Commonwealth federations are clearly many and complex. Most of these pressures were present to some degree in each, but the relative importance of different factors has varied with each federation. In India the dynamic leadership, the force of a common nationalism, the desire for economic planning, historical interdependence, a common religion and basic culture, strategic considerations following partition, and in the princely states 'geographical compulsions', were all potent forces for unity. In Pakistan, on the other hand, by far the most important motives were Islam, the intense fear of a Hindu Raj, the leadership of Jinnah, and to a lesser degree common inherited British traditions. Malayan unity in 1948 was primarily the result of British insistence for strategic, administrative, and economic reasons, but the desire of Malays to protect their communal position consolidated Malay nationalism, and later the demand for 'merdeka' cemented an intercommunal Alliance. Geographic, strategic, and economic factors also drove Malaya and Singapore together, while the common interests the wider Malaysia was designed to serve were chiefly security, a means to independence for the acceding states, a racial balance within the federation, and, to some extent, trade. In Nigeria economic interdependence was the decisive factor in preserving Nigerian unity in 1953–4, while the compromises necessary to achieve independence, the effect of common British rule, and, before independence, the continued British insistence upon unity, were also influential pressures.

By comparison with the other Commonwealth federations the forces for unity in the West Indies were relatively weaker. The major motives were the desire for political independence and the hope of economic advantage, but these were undermined by territorial ambitions for separate achievements in both spheres. Improved communications, the growth of functional associations fostering a British Caribbean outlook, and British encouragement, explain why federation, previously impracticable, became a serious possibility after 1945. In Rhodesia and Nyasaland many settlers first intensely desired amalgamation and later accepted federation, both to gain freedom from British control, and to protect their position in the face of rising African consciousness and the threats of external white and black nationalism. The British Government came to accept federation for the economic benefits it might

---

[1] In Central Africa, British policy was formulated not only by the Colonial Office, responsible for the protectorates, but also by the Commonwealth Relations Office—less used to influencing than to being influenced—which was responsible for Britain's relations with Southern Rhodesia. In 1962 this arrangement was replaced when a new single Central African Office responsible for all affairs of the federation was created.

bring Africans as well as settlers, and as a means to establishing an experiment in racial partnership. The urgency with which the British Government undertook this policy was prompted by the desire to save Southern Rhodesia from following South Africa's example, and by the realization that in Northern Rhodesia *de facto* authority appeared already to be passing into the hands of the settlers.

Certain features distinguish the motivating forces in these new federations from those in their predecessors created in the eighteenth and nineteenth centuries. K. C. Wheare has suggested that in the earlier federations seven factors leading to a desire for union always seemed to be present: (1) military insecurity and the consequent need for common defence; (2) a desire for independence from foreign powers; (3) a hope of economic advantage; (4) some prior loose political association; (5) geographical neighbourhood; (6) similarity of political institutions; (7) leadership or statesmanship at the right time.[1] Of these, the necessity of common defence has been significant only in the Asian federations. Nor have the federated territories always been contiguous. With improved means of communications federations of territories separated by sea or even hostile territory have been attempted in the West Indies, Malaysia, and Pakistan. In so far as all the component territories of each of these federations have been influenced by British traditions, some similarity of political institutions has usually existed. But where the territories had achieved different degrees of political advance, or where a policy of indirect rule had been applied in certain regions, the differences in political and social institutions have been far more obvious than the similarities.

The other factors for unity usually present in the older federations, the desire for independence, the hope of economic advantage, some prior historical association, and dynamic leadership, have, as we have seen, generally been present in the newer federations.[2] But their character has not always been the same. Where economic advantages were conceived in the earlier federations in terms of the benefits that would apply to the private sector of the economy, in most of the new federations the economic arguments for unity have been related to the role of governmental activity in promoting rapid economic development. Generally, too, the form of prior political association has been much tighter, in some cases even possessing unitary characteristics, with the result that federation has often been preceded by considerable political and economic interdependence. Finally, in the older federations many years, even decades, were available for adjustment to new circumstances, but in the new federations the speed at which political, economic, and social changes have been taking place has both accentuated the demands for unity and the strains imposed upon that unity.

[1] Wheare, *Federal Government*, pp. 37–40.
[2] Their present prosperity should not be allowed to obscure the fact that such federations as the United States, Canada, and Australia started life also as economically underdeveloped areas.

4

MOTIVES FOR REGIONAL AUTONOMY

1. *Levels of diversity*

IT has sometimes been argued that only societies in which the social diversities are geographically distributed can properly be called federal.[1] This claim is based on the argument that since the distinguishing characteristic of a federal political system is the distribution of authority between central and regional governments, such a form of government presupposes a society in which diversities are regionally distributed. Implicit in this view is the corollary that where a major diversity, such as race or communalism, instead of being strongly localized in particular regions, cuts through a whole society, it is potentially non-federal.

But while social diversities which are territorially distributed are generally much more likely to result in demands for regional autonomy, they are not, from a purely logical point of view, a necessary prerequisite for federal institutions. Even where there are no regionally localized interests, a territorial distribution of power within a federal structure might be advocated simply as a means to limited government and the prevention of tyranny within a plural society.[2] In developing countries where democratic experience is limited, federal political systems may lessen the risk of political power becoming monopolized, for such institutions provide a number of independent points where the party that is nationally in the minority at a particular time can obtain power or maintain itself while it formulates and demonstrates its policies and capacities. It is perhaps significant that, of the newly independent West African states, Nigeria seems least likely to develop one-party government. Thus even in the largely plural societies of Malaya and Central Africa there was a demand for a federal division of political authority in order to provide some safeguards against potential national dominance by one community.

Nevertheless, generally speaking, it has been territorially located historical, economic, cultural, racial, and social differences which have produced

---

[1] Livingston, *Federalism and Constitutional Change*, pp. 2–3; Carnell, 'Political Implications of Federalism in New States', in U. K. Hicks and others, *Federalism and Economic Growth*, pp. 22–23, 49–53; K. C. Wheare, 'Federalism and the Making of Nations', in A. W. Macmahon (ed.), *Federalism Mature and Emergent* (1955), p. 32.

[2] See, for instance, F. Morley, *Freedom and Federalism* (1959); G. Dietze, *The Federalist: A Classic on Federalism and Free Government* (1960), esp. pp. 336–9; Vile, *The Structure of American Federalism*, pp. 36–39.

demands for regional autonomy. This was clearly the case in India, Pakistan, Nigeria, and the West Indies. By contrast, Malaya and Central Africa were primarily plural societies, in which racial divisions and communalism cut through the whole society. But even in these examples there were important geographical variations. Though relatively small, Malaya was by no means a uniform area. The regional differences in stages of economic development, in cultural tradition, in history, and in communal proportions, gave a real basis for federal government and for the continuance of the various state governments which were manifestations of these variations.[1] Moreover, within Malaysia the regional distinctiveness of Singapore and the Borneo states was even more marked. In Central Africa there were significant regional differences in the outlook of the settlers, as the Victoria Falls Conference of 1949 and the party divisions within the federation indicated. Furthermore, the different territories have been inhabited by different African tribes. When to this is added their distinct historical development, their sharply varying racial policies, and their significantly different proportions of settler population, it can be seen that regional diversities were not inconsiderable in Central Africa.

Although all the new federations have contained sectional groups which were geographically distributed, rarely have these coincided precisely with the regional political units. In the first place, social diversities have not generally been territorially segregated so exactly that regional political boundaries could mark off completely homogeneous units. People just do not arrange themselves like that. Even in such federations as Canada, India, and Nigeria, where the fundamental social groupings appear clearly to be concentrated geographically, there are overlaps at the edges. In Canada, for instance, not all French Canadians live in Quebec. In Nigeria there are a considerable number of Ibos in the other regions, and some Yorubas in the Northern Region. Indeed, commissions investigating the revision of regional political boundaries have concluded, in both Nigeria and India, that it would be impossible to draw boundaries that did not create some minorities within the regional units.[2] The extent to which social diversities are territorially localized would appear, therefore, to be a question of degree. In such federations as Canada, India, Pakistan, Nigeria, and the West Indies, the fundamental social interests were geographically concentrated to a relatively high degree; while in the cases of the United States, Malaya, or Central Africa, they were less precisely localized, certain major racial, economic, or class interests cutting across territorial boundaries.

Secondly, even where social diversities are basically regional in their dis-

---

[1] See, for instance, Map 4, and also T. E. Smith, 'The Malayan Elections of 1959', *Pacific Affairs*, xxxiii (1960), p. 38.

[2] Cmnd. 505/1958, p. 87; C.A.I., *Report of the Linguistic Provinces Commission* (1948), (Dar), paras. 57–68, 69–78, 116, 119, 125, 129; India, *Report of the States Reorganization Commission* (1955), paras. 154, 233.

tribution, the geographical location of historical, racial, cultural, economic, and other social interests may not coincide precisely with each other. Territorial diversities may operate at several different geographical levels: some may coincide fairly closely with the actual regional political units, others may correspond to groups of states or provinces, while still others may represent divisions within individual territories.

In all the new federations, internal diversities have operated in a variety of regional contexts. For instance, in India there was the fundamental division between the Indo-Aryan, Hindi-speaking Ganges heartland in the north and the racially Proto-Mediterranean, Dravidian-speaking Deccan and coastal plains of the south. At the next level there were the five economic regions roughly represented by the Zones into which the states have been grouped. Then there were the political states themselves, representing, before 1956, historical diversities, and, since the reorganization of the state boundaries, the major linguistic regions. Finally, within the states existed important differences of caste, religion, economic class, and, in a few cases still, language.

Similarly, regional diversities have operated in Pakistan at several levels. First there were the differences between East and West Pakistan:

separated by a distance of more than a thousand miles . . . the language, the tradition, the culture, the costume, the custom, the dietary, the calendar, the standard time, practically everything, is different. There is, in fact, nothing common in the two wings, particularly in respect of those which are the *sine qua non* to form a nation.[1]

But among the various provinces and states within West Pakistan there was another level of diversity marked by distinctions of physical feature, language, social structure, and custom. Finally, within the individual political units there were sharp social differences between the big landlords and the urban classes.

Divergent views in Malaya and Malaysia can only be understood in terms of several territorial groupings. There were the sharp racial and economic contrasts between the peninsula and Singapore which resulted in the latter's exclusion from the Union of 1946 and from the Federation of 1948, in Singapore's special status within Malaysia in 1963, and in its secession in 1965. Also sharply distinct from the other states because of their separation by sea and their different racial composition are the two Borneo states of Malaysia, which in turn are differentiated from each other by distinct histories, communal groups, and economic orientation. Within peninsular Malaya itself there were the marked historical and constitutional differences between the settlements and the Malay states, and among the latter between the former Federated and Unfederated Malay States. Differences in economic development and racial composition further distinguished the north-eastern states from those to the south along the west coast. Within these groups of regions, each state was itself characterized by a distinctive historical identity. Then within the states themselves there existed the sharp communal differences:

[1] C.A.P. (second), *Debates*, vol. i, p. 1816.

the Malays living in their kampongs, the Chinese primarily concentrated in the mines and the cities, and the Indians located on the plantations.

The Nigerian picture was equally complex. First, there was the basic distrust between the north and the south due to the differences of religion, social institutions, traditions, degree of westernization, and relative size of population. But within the south itself there was the Yoruba–Ibo rivalry represented by the Western and Eastern Regions. Although each of the original three regions contained a predominant ethnic group, the Hausa–Fulani in the Northern Region, the Yorubas in the Western Region, and the Ibos in the Eastern Region, each of these political units also included within its boundaries considerable minority groups in the northern Middle Belt, the Mid-West, and the eastern Calabar, Ogoja, and Rivers areas.

It might be thought that in the West Indies, the individual islands, marked off by geography, and with their distinctive historic traditions, would represent the location of the major diversities. While this was to a large extent true, even there, regional differences operated at several levels. First there was the distinction between the islands and the mainland territories, sharp enough to result in British Guiana and British Honduras refusing to join the federation. Within the federation, Jamaica, with half the population and located far to the west, considered itself so distinct from the other territories as a group, that in the end it chose to secede. Within the Eastern Caribbean islands, Trinidad, like Jamaica, stood out as a 'big island', while among the 'small islands' there were groupings of outlook among the Leewards and the Windwards. Even within some of the political units, small as they were, diversities were sometimes apparent, as between the two islands of St. Kitts and Nevis, or again in Trinidad between the negro majority and the East Indian community concentrated mostly in their own villages.

In Rhodesia and Nyasaland, apart from regional differences represented by the three territories themselves, the two Rhodesias together were distinct from Nyasaland in their considerably greater proportion of settler population and their potential for economic development, while the two protectorates taken together were in sharp contrast with Southern Rhodesia by virtue of their control by the Colonial Office and their more liberal racial policies. Within Northern Rhodesia itself the settler population was virtually all concentrated along the line of rail and in the copperbelt, whereas large areas of the rest of the protectorate were wholly populated by Africans, who themselves belonged to different tribal groups.

Where the political regional units have coincided fairly closely with the territorial distribution of the most significant social diversities, the demand for local autonomy has generally been strong. But where they have not coincided, there have often been demands for revisions of regional boundaries, either to consolidate existing regional units into larger ones with common interests, or to split existing heterogeneous regions in order that minorities within them might each obtain regional autonomy for themselves. Such pressures were strongest in India and Nigeria where they took the form of movements for linguistic and ethnic regional units, and in Pakistan, where they resulted in the unification of the western provinces.[1]

The social diversities which lead to demands for regional autonomy are thus complex, and operate at many geographical levels.

2. *The prospect of independence*

The approach of self-government has often accentuated inter-group tensions. A common thread running throughout the various debates over federalism has been the fear, on the part of one group, of domination by another once British control was removed. Examples were the Muslim fears of a permanent Hindu majority in an undivided India, the regional groups within the Union of India seeking to safeguard their positions, the increased communal tension in Malaya, especially Malay fears of Chinese domination within the proposed Union, and the apprehensions in the Borneo states that joining Malaysia would place them under Malayan control. Other instances were the inter-regional distrust and general apprehensiveness which dominated the Nigerian constitutional conferences, the apprehensiveness of West Indian island leaders, and the dread of African National Congresses in Nyasaland and Northern Rhodesia that an independent federation would mean domination by Southern Rhodesian settlers. In such situations the checks and balances of a federal system were intended to preclude the seizure and ruthless use of power by a majority or determined minority within the union.

A disparity in the populations and resources of the uniting political territories has invariably exacerbated such fears. The smaller units have usually feared domination and even absorption by the larger regions once British control was removed; the larger territories have sometimes looked upon the smaller ones as economic burdens with which they would be saddled when British aid ended. Examples were the tensions between the smaller states and Uttar Pradesh in India, between the southern and northern regions in Nigeria, between the provinces and states within West Pakistan and Punjab, between all the territories of West Pakistan and East Bengal, between 'the small islands' in the West Indies and Jamaica and Trinidad, and between the settler populations of Northern Rhodesia and Southern Rhodesia. The result has often been not only demands for regional autonomy, but heated disputes over regional representation in the central political institutions, and sometimes even demands that the larger regions be split.[2]

Where individual political regions have contained distinctive majorities and

---

[1] See Chapter 7, section 3.

[2] See Chapter 7, section 2, on demands for regional reorganization and Chapter 11 on controversies over central representation.

minorities within their boundaries, as in India and Nigeria, the apprehensions aroused by the approach of independence have stirred the minorities to demand regional autonomy for themselves through the creation of new states. Sometimes, where this has been impracticable, such minorities have instead demanded special constitutional guarantees limiting the autonomy of the regional majorities. Such pressures occurred, for instance, in Malaya, and also in India and Nigeria. On the other hand, the Hindus of East Bengal and the East Indians of Trinidad were strong advocates of regional autonomy, fearing that in the wider union they would have even less influence than in their own regions.

In territories where Britain had exercised indirect rule, traditional rulers such as the emirs and chiefs of Northern Nigeria, the sultans of Malaya, and the princes of India, fearing that after independence they would be cast aside by modernizing and centralizing nationalists, have usually also been strong supporters of regional autonomy in order to protect their positions.

Frequently, those territories which were more advanced constitutionally had qualms that union would retard their own progress to self-government by forcing them to go at the pace of the more backward territories. In Nigeria it was southern frustration at northern conservatism which sparked the riots and the constitutional crisis of 1953. The federal system adopted in 1954 enabled a compromise by making possible, within a united Nigeria, the grant of self-government in 1957 to the two southern regions that were pressing for it, while postponing northern and federal self-government for several years to allay northern anxieties. In the West Indies the politically advanced islands insisted at Montego Bay upon a resolution demanding an increasing measure of territorial self-government 'as an aim in itself without prejudice and in no way subordinate to progress towards federation'.[1] The anxiety of some Southern Rhodesian settlers that union with the northern protectorates would mean increased Colonial Office control, produced the Rhodesia League demand for dominion status before federation, while in Malaya it was the settlements which had misgivings that their progress to self-government would be retarded by association with the Malay states.

The belief that self-government could be achieved more quickly independently has sometimes resulted even in outright separation. British Guiana and British Honduras advanced such reasons for refusing to join the West Indian Federation. The exclusion of Singapore from Malaya before 1957 and the partition of the Muslim areas from India in 1947 were accepted in Malaya and India because attempts to include them would have delayed political independence. Penang, Jamaica, Trinidad, Nyasaland, and Northern Rhodesia each demanded secession in order to achieve self-government, and except in Penang, Britain granted the request.

Thus, while the desire to achieve and maintain political independence has

[1] Col. no. 218/1948, pp. 97–98, 105–6.

so often been a unifying force, it has frequently also stimulated an opposing force.

3. *Regional economic interests*

Although in most of the new federations economic motives have played a prominent part in the desire for unity, regional economic interests have also been among the important motives for regional separation.

In the first place, even where economic integration promises advantages to an area as a whole, there may be specific economic factors preventing certain territories within the area from sharing in the benefits.[1] The operation of natural market factors may provide unequal benefits for different regions and even increase, rather than reduce, inequalities. Fears and complaints of such effects were expressed in Nyasaland, East Pakistan, Northern Nigeria, and the Leeward Islands, just as they were earlier in Western Australia, the Canadian Maritimes, and the southern U.S.A. Furthermore, the application of active public monetary policies, aiming at the vigorous economic development of an area as a whole, inevitably cannot accommodate every specific regional economic interest at the same time.

Secondly, although the regional economies of India, Nigeria, Malaya, Central Africa, and to a lesser degree Pakistan, were essentially complementary, and so stood to gain from economic union, the very regional differences which made them complementary often fostered strong regional attitudes. Differences in products and therefore problems of production, in types of exports, in sources of foreign capital, and in appropriate policies to promote economic development, resulted in Nigeria, for instance, in the placing of many of the responsibilites for economic development in the hands of regional governments.

Most of the new federations have attempted to unite territories with distinctive economic interests. In Pakistan, although the provinces and states within West Pakistan were economically interdependent, the two major regions of West and East Pakistan possessed distinct economies based on different climates and products. Similarly, each of the Nigerian regions and the Southern Cameroons specialized in different products and exports. Malaya's economy has been described as 'not one but three': the subsistence economy of the northernmost states based on traditional Malay methods of rice-growing and fishing, the wealthy but unstable plantation and mining economy of the west coast plain, and the ebullient, raffish, mercantile economy of Penang and Singapore based on free trade. This was a major factor in the resistance to inclusion and the later noisy secession movement of the Queen's Chinese in Penang, in the original exclusion from Malaya of Singapore for a decade and a half, and in the special terms for its later merger in the federation and the customs union. To these three economic areas the incorporation of the

---

[1] See also Chapter 3, section 3, for a discussion of this point.

Borneo states within Malaysia, added a fourth, largely agricultural and with a trade in the case of Sabah focusing as much on Japan, Hong Kong, and the Far East as upon the other states of the federation. In Central Africa the three territories depended for their wealth on different products and relied upon different sources for their major governmental revenue. The concentration of industrial development in India in the Bihar-Bengal, Bombay, and Kaveri Valley vicinities, and the localization of various plantation and other agricultural products in certain regions, sharpened internal divisions too. In the West Indies the different economic interests of the mainland territories was a factor in their decision not to join the federation, while Jamaicans, with about 1 per cent. of their total exports going to the other islands and with a variety of secondary industries expanding behind their protective tariff, looked upon their own island as a separate economic unit. Even Trinidad, which put more emphasis on the benefits its secondary industries might derive from federation, was so concerned about the effects of free movement of population that a special conference was necessary to deal with the problem.[1] Moreover, the basically competitive character of the Caribbean island economies meant that the distinctness of the territorial economic interests was not moderated, as in the other federations, by the prospect of increased trade within the united area.[2]

Economic regionalism has exerted its strongest influence where the economic map has corresponded closely with the political map. On the other hand, in India, within West Pakistan, and amongst the west coast mainland states of Malaya, where economic regions have not coincided with internal political boundaries, economic factors have been less influential, though by no means irrelevant, in the demands for regional autonomy. In India, for instance, the States Reorganization Commission decided that the pressure of political, cultural, linguistic, and historical loyalties militated against the redrawing of state boundaries on purely economic lines.[3] Nevertheless, the grouping of Indian states into five zones in 1956 was intended to coincide roughly with major economic regions. The pressure for relatively autonomous economic territories has been strongest in such territories as East Pakistan, the three original Nigerian regions, and Jamaica, where their relative size enabled them to contemplate economic self-sufficiency.

Most of the new federations have joined together territories with acute disparities in economic development and wealth, and these regional inequalities have invariably accentuated separatist pressures. The backward and poorer territories like Orissa and Assam in India, East Bengal in Pakistan, the north-eastern states in Malaya, the Borneo states in Malaysia, the Northern Region and the Southern Cameroons in Nigeria, Nyasaland in Central Africa, and the Windward and Leeward Islands in the Caribbean, were afraid

---

[1] Col. no. 315/1955. [2] See Chapter 3, section 3, above.
[3] *Report of the States Reorganization Commission* (1955), pp. 57–59, 255.

of economic domination and exploitation by the more progressive and wealthier regions. On the other hand, the wealthier regions such as the Western Region of Nigeria, Northern Rhodesia, the western Malay states, Singapore, and Jamaica and Trinidad, were reluctant to take on the support of the poorer territories at expense to their own economic development. Later, this was a major factor in Jamaica's secession, and in Trinidad's refusal thereafter to carry alone the burden of the smaller islands. The demand for active public development policies has invariably aggravated separatist pressures where there is a wide disparity in the wealth of the uniting regions, for different fiscal and monetary policies are likely to be appropriate for different stages of economic development. The resulting pressures for regionalization of governmental development policies have been most apparent in Nigeria and the West Indies.[1] Difficulties in reaching agreements on a common tariff policy have also been experienced where relatively wealthy and advanced territories such as Jamaica, Penang, or Singapore have been combined with poorer and less developed units.

Apart from the direct influence of economic factors upon desires for regional autonomy, many separatist movements which were ostensibly social or cultural in motivation have had strong economic undercurrents. The pre-partition separatism of the Muslim middle class in north-west India was at least in part an attempt to protect themselves from a larger and better educated Hindu group. The linguistic regionalism and Dravidian separatism, which burst to the fore in India once independence was achieved, stemmed in some measure from the intensity of the struggle for jobs between different linguistic and caste groups. In Pakistan, the growing demands for regional autonomy in East Bengal and for the recognition of Bengali as a national language were generated by discontent with the economic policies of the central government, which, dominated by the landlords and businessmen of West Pakistan, neglected East Pakistan.[2] The continual demands in Northern and Western Nigeria for regional autonomy, and occasional threats even of secession, owed a good deal to ethnic and religious differences, but accentuating these was the landhunger driving the aggressive Ibos to migrate to the other regions, a factor which has been described as 'the true origin of tribal antagonism'.[3] In Malaya, because of the sharp differences in the economic roles of the three racial communities, communal resentments were closely related to the dominance of the economy by the energetic Chinese. Thus, for instance, it has been the economically backward north-eastern states which have formed the core of Malay communalism. Similarly, in Central Africa, the racial fears

[1] See pp. 125–8.
[2] C.A.P. (first), *Debates*, vol. viii, pp. 183–4; C.A.P. (second), *Debates*, vol. i, pp. 1818–19, 1845–7, 1909–10, 1942, 1998, 2016–17, 2049–50, 2072, 2083, 2100–2, 2119, 2122–3, 2232–6, 2271–2; R. D. Lambert, 'Factors in Bengali Regionalism in Pakistan', *Far Eastern Survey*, xxviii (1959), pp. 53–56.
[3] H. O. Davies, *Nigeria: the Prospects for Democracy* (1961), p. 21.

which divided the settlers of the Rhodesias from the Africans of the protectorates reflected not only racial but economic differences, between the prosperous settlers in Southern Rhodesia and the copperbelt, and the relative poverty of Nyasaland and the predominantly African areas of Northern Rhodesia. Where settlers considered increased light industry and electric power to be primary, the Africans wanted concentration upon more education and the development of peasant agriculture.

In most of these federations, therefore, overtly cultural and political diversities have been strongly coloured by economic factors.

4. *Administrative convenience*

In many cases the regional units composing the new federations were originally created by the British Government because of administrative considerations. For instance, in India during the nineteenth century it soon became apparent that centralized imperialism was administratively impractical, and as a result the gradual devolution of constitutional power took place. The provincial boundaries inherited by both India and Pakistan, therefore, represented in many cases merely 'administrative areas' formed for the sake of administrative convenience.[1] In Nigeria Lord Lugard recognized the benefits of administrative decentralization, and the regional grouping of first, the northern and southern provinces, and much later, the eastern and western provinces, was not based upon ethnic affinities but primarily upon administrative considerations.[2] In areas where the imperial rulers had found it administratively convenient to decentralize, it was hardly surprising that the same factors should have later contributed to the pressures for regional autonomy.

But if, as suggested in the previous chapter, the desire for greater administrative efficiency was often a motive for unification, what are the arguments that support the regionalization of administration? The first point is that decentralized decision-making is likely to be more efficient and quicker in responding to problems in large areas where communications are difficult, as in India, Pakistan, and Nigeria. Secondly, regional administration, by making use of local knowledge, may achieve greater effectiveness and genuine economies. Thirdly, local units of administration may draw forth suitable personnel who, without this opportunity, might have remained undiscovered. Fourthly, regionalized administration, by giving the territorial bureaucracies less scope for disastrous mistakes, spreads the risks of learning how to administer. Fifthly, compact units, with some measure of homogeneity in the population, simplify the tasks of the administrators. Sixthly, in areas, such as

---

[1] *Report of the States Reorganization Commission* (1955), paras. 20, 25; Masaldan, *Evolution of Provincial Autonomy in India*, p. 169. Administrative convenience was one of the factors taken into account by the States Reorganization Commission in its recommendations (para. 234).

[2] Sir F. D. Lugard, *The Dual Mandate in British Tropical Africa* (1922), pp. 96, 101.

the smaller West Indian islands, where all the administration relevant to a territory could be handled by a small unified local staff, the departmentalization of centrally unified services may result in the multiplication of officials at the local level.

Besides the arguments advanced purely in terms of efficiency, there have also been political reasons for administrative decentralization. Regional autonomy, by dividing the bureaucracy, may make possible easier control over civil servants by the political representatives of the electorate. Political reasons of a different sort have also been relevant. The competition for a limited number of prestige posts in the public services amongst different sections of the uprooted, urbanized middle class has resulted in clamours for regional autonomy as a device for keeping local jobs for local people. In India much of the urge towards linguistic states was derived from the struggle for state civil service positions between different linguistic and caste groups.[1] The movement for greater East Bengal autonomy in Pakistan after 1947 was in considerable measure due to the Bengali feeling that the civil service and the armed forces were primarily in the hands of West Pakistanis.[2] In Nigeria it was in order to avoid being overrun by educated southerners that the Muslims of the Northern Region demanded regional autonomy and a programme of 'Northernization' in the regional civil service.[3] Yoruba reactions to Ibo enterprise, and the demands for new states by intra-regional minorities, were similarly motivated. In Malaya the educated Malays were among the strongest opponents of the Union of 1946, because there was no other outlet for them except public administration in the states. Subsequently too, fears in the Borneo territories of an influx of Malay civil servants, who would appropriate the senior posts vacated by British officials, produced an insistence upon regional autonomy and a policy of 'Borneanization' in the state civil services. Indeed, Francis Carnell has complained that: 'Only too often, one of the main purposes of federalism in the new states has been to legitimize a number of local spoils systems however inefficient they may be.'[4]

5. *Conflicting external relations*

Where different regions within an area have alliances or cultural and economic ties with different countries outside the proposed federation, centrifugal tendencies between the federating territories may be reinforced. Just as in Canada Quebec has always sought closer ties with France while English-speaking Canadians have maintained a special connexion with Britain, similar divergencies have made themselves felt in some of the new federations. In Nigeria the conservative Muslim north clung to British ties and was

[1] *Report of S.R.C.* (1955), paras. 123, 158, 786–91.
[2] C.A.P. (second), *Debates*, vol. i, pp. 1845, 1909–10, 1998, 2049–50, 2104, 2122–3; Lambert, op. cit., pp. 53–56.
[3] Bello, *My Life*, pp. 152–3.
[4] Carnell, 'Political Implications of Federalism in New States', op. cit., p. 47.

conscious of its affinity with Arab North Africa. Southerners, on the other hand, have often pressed for support of neutralism and Africanism. Similarly, the Africans of Northern Rhodesia and Nyasaland tended to look upon the nationalists of East Africa as their natural allies, while the settlers of the Rhodesias looked in the other direction towards South Africa. In East Pakistan the inhabitants are for the most part Muslim Bengalis. As Muslims they supported partition and the creation of Pakistan, but as Bengalis they shared strong cultural as well as economic relations with the Bengalis of India. Because of this West Pakistanis, bitterly hostile to all that was Indian, often distrusted the loyalty of the East Pakistanis.

Where a new state must seek foreign economic aid, the conflict of external outlooks is likely to be accentuated. This has been illustrated by the objections raised in Muslim Northern Nigeria over Israeli technical aid in the two southern regions. There were also tensions between the pro-British outlook of the northern leaders and the frankly pro-western and even pro-American outlook of Chief Awolowo, on the one hand, and those who espoused a more neutralist policy in seeking economic aid, on the other.

Nevertheless, diverging outlooks upon external relations have, as a rule, only been an indirect motive for regional autonomy, since rarely is it argued that external relations should be conducted by regional governments. In Pakistan, Nigeria, and Central Africa, however, these differences have at least weakened the general desire for unity. In British Guiana and British Honduras, their links with neighbouring territories and the pull of a 'continental destiny' were strong enough to be crucial in their decision not to join a British Caribbean federation.

6. *Ethnic and cultural diversities*

Nehru once wrote: 'The diversity of India is tremendous; it is obvious; it lies on the surface and anybody can see it.'[1] But this comment might equally well have been made of most of the other new Commonwealth federations. Indeed, several of them have been described as 'mere geographical expressions' or 'artificial creations' bearing no relation to ethnic or cultural realities. In such culturally complex areas as India, Pakistan, Nigeria, Malaysia, and Central Africa, the racial, religious, and ethnic minorities, fearing discrimination at the hands of numerical majorities, yet unable to support their own separate independence, have looked upon regional autonomy as a way of protecting their distinct identity and way of life.

Racial differences have been most prominent in Malaya, Malaysia, and Central Africa. Although in these federations racial groups were not completely segregated into territorial compartments, nevertheless in each there were highly significant regional variations in the racial proportions of the population. In the four northern states of Malaya, the Malays are clearly predomi-

---

[1] Nehru, *The Discovery of India* (4th ed., 1956), p. 48.

nant, forming between 67 and 92 per cent. of the state populations, while in the west-coast states the Chinese are generally the largest racial group and there is also a strong concentration of Indians.[1] It is not surprising, therefore, that Malay nationalism, in the form of U.M.N.O. opposition to the Malayan Union in 1946 and of P.M.I.P. communalism in 1959, should have flourished most in the northern states. The exclusion of Singapore from the Union in 1946 and from the Federation in 1948, and the special citizenship status of its citizens within Malaysia, were designed to allay Malay fears, for the complete merger of Singapore with its predominantly Chinese population would have upset the delicate racial balance in the peninsula.[2] The greater autonomy of Sarawak and Sabah within Malaysia was related to the communal distinctiveness of the indigenous peoples composed of a variety of linguistic groups, which formed the vast majority of their populations.[3] In Central Africa the proportion of Africans to each settler varied from 15 in Southern Rhodesia to 51 in Northern Rhodesia and 587 in Nyasaland.[4] Moreover, these differences were responsible in considerable measure for the contrasting traditions in their racial policies, which were at the base of the African opposition in the northern territories to amalgamation, and which prompted the British Government to insist instead on federation.[5]

Elsewhere in the new federations, because of considerable intermingling, racial differences have not been the primary divisive factor. Nevertheless, differences of physical features between southerners and northerners in India, between Bengalis, Punjabis, and Pathans in Pakistan, and between the southern forest negroes and northern savanna negroes of Nigeria, did contribute to regionalism.[6] In the West Indies the East Indian minority in Trinidad and majority in British Guiana both expressed fears of union, in the latter case rejecting it.

The religious differences within the new federations—between Hindus and Muslims on the Indian continent, Islam and Chinese religions in Malaya, and Muslims, Christians, and Animists in Nigeria—have gone much deeper than

---

[1] See Map 4. Apart from the four northern states, the Malays are the largest racial group only in Pahang (53%) and Malacca (48%). In Selangor there are three times as many Chinese as native Malays and more Indians than native Malays. (These figures are based on the 1947 census.)

[2] One reason for the Malayan desire to include within a Malaysian federation the British Borneo territories, in none of which the Chinese formed more than 30 per cent. of the total population, was the desire to offset the predominantly Chinese population of Singapore.

[3] There were also marked differences between the indigenous peoples of the two Borneo states.

[4] Based on Cmd. 8234/1951, para. 32.

[5] Cmd. 8233/1951, paras. 20, 38. For a comparison of the importance of differences in racial policy as a motive for federalism in both the Federation of Rhodesia and Nyasaland and the United States see Wheare, 'Federalism and the Making of Nations' in Macmahon (ed.), op. cit., pp. 36–40.

[6] There were also sizeable aboriginal populations in India and Pakistan, and smaller ones in Malaya and the West Indies.

those between different Christian denominations in the older federations. The Hindu–Muslim differences proved too fundamental to be contained within an All-India federation, but because these religious groups were not precisely distributed, both India and Pakistan still contained large religious minorities. The 10 million Hindus of East Bengal, fearing the distrust of the West Pakistanis, were advocates of regional autonomy. India after partition still contained the third largest Muslim population in the world. Although Muslims were no longer in a majority in any state except Kashmir, the Muslim League remained an active political force in Madras and Kerala. Another religious group, the Sikhs, concentrated in Punjab, has continually agitated for a separate Sikh state. The Christians were scattered but have been an influential minority in Kerala.[1]

In Malaysia the racial differences between Malays, Chinese, Indians, and other groups have on the whole been reinforced by their distinct religions.[2] The situation has been further complicated, however, by disagreement between Buddhists, Confucianists, and Taoists among the Chinese, between Hindus and Muslims among the Indians, and between pagans and Muslims among the indigenous groups in the Borneo states. In Nigeria, also, religious differences have reinforced the contrasts between the main linguistic groups of the original units. Within the Northern Region the dominance of Muslim belief and law uniting the Fulani, Hausa, Kanuri, and Nupe tribes, is the basis of regional distinctiveness, although most of the tribes of the Middle Belt are pagan. In the Western Region many Yorubas are Muslims, but at least as many are Christians, while the inhabitants of the Eastern Region are Christians or Animists. In Central Africa the settlers belonged to a variety of Christian churches but the vast masses of Africans were still non-Christian, many of them adhering to tribal or animistic beliefs, and half the population of Nyasaland to Islam. The activities of different missionary groups, and particularly the Church of Scotland in Nyasaland, also distinguished the different territories. Even in the West Indies, where religious differences were less to the fore in politics, the formerly French Windward Islands and formerly Spanish Trinidad were more distinctively Roman Catholic than the other islands, and in Trinidad it was the Hindus rather than the Muslim East Indians who were separatists.

Because a language other than one's own mother tongue has a dampening effect on social intercourse, differences in language have proved a particularly powerful divisive force. Indeed, within India, Pakistan, and Nigeria regional loyalties were firstly and above all a matter of language. In India the pressure

---

[1] Other smaller religious minorities are the Parsis, largely concentrated around Bombay, and the Jains, concentrated in Rajasthan and north Bombay (now Gujarat).

[2] Although the majority of natives in the Borneo states are pagans, sizeable groups have been converted to Islam, giving them closer ties with the Malays. See R. O. Tilman, 'Malaysia: Problems of Federation', *The Western Political Quarterly*, xvi (1963), pp. 902–6, for an analysis of religious issues in Malaysia.

of regional linguistic groups was apparent before independence in the internal organization within the Congress Party. After 1947 the divisive impact of language was felt in the tension between north and south, and in the demands of regional linguistic groups for provincial autonomy and for the reorganization of provincial units.[1] The force of language was also apparent in the necessity to recognize in the constitution thirteen regional languages, each spoken by at least 5 million people.[2] In Pakistan, the different languages spoken within West Pakistan—Urdu, Punjabi, Sindhi, and Pushtu—provided the basis for what resistance there was to the unification of the western provinces and states into a single unit, but linguistic regionalism was most prominent in the demands of East Bengal for regional autonomy and for the recognition of Bengali as an official language. In Nigeria 248 different languages are spoken, but the three major linguistic groups—the Hausa in the northern provinces, the Yoruba in the west, and the Ibo in the east—were each in a majority in one of the three original regions. Moreover, it was from linguistic minorities in each of these regions that much of the pressure for separate states came.

In the other three federations, linguistic differences have reinforced the other more fundamental divisive factors. In Malaysia, for instance, the distinct languages of the Malays, Chinese, Indians, and indigenous Borneo peoples have further accentuated the racial differences. In addition, within each of these communities themselves there have been significant regional variations in language and dialect. In Rhodesia and Nyasaland, English served as a lingua franca, but the different principal tribes in the three territories—the Mashona and Matabele of Southern Rhodesia, the Barotse, Bemba and Tonga of Northern Rhodesia, and the Yao, Ngoni and Nyanja of Nyasaland—each had substantially different dialects, customs and outlooks. Only in the West Indies has language been of relatively minor significance as a centrifugal force, and even there differences in dialect and the existence of a French patois in the Windwards contributed to island distinctiveness.

Associated with religion or language have usually gone other cultural differences: differing literary and musical heritages, different kinds of dishes, distinctive forms of dress, festivals of peculiar regional significance, different codes of family and social behaviour, and special attachment to regional heroes and episodes of the past. The relation between language and culture is clear, for 'with a language goes a way of speaking, a way of making jokes, a whole common world of allusions and references so necessary to easy and enjoyable intercourse'.[3]

Further accentuating regionalism in many cases have been differences in

---

[1] See Chapter 7, section 3.

[2] *Constitution of India, 1950*, Eighth Sched.; *Report of the Official Language Commission, 1956* (1957), pp. 27–29. Sanskrit, although spoken by only 555 persons, was included as a fourteenth official language because of its cultural significance. A linguistic survey of India records 179 languages and 544 dialects in all.

[3] W. H. Morris-Jones, *Parliament in India* (1957), pp. 18–19.

degree of cultural westernization. Under colonial rule, modernization and the penetration of western ideas have often been very uneven. Areas where indirect rule had existed, such as Northern Nigeria, the princely states of India and Pakistan, the Unfederated Malay States, and the protectorates in Central Africa, have usually lagged behind. These areas, fearful of being dominated by the more modernized regions, have been strong proponents of regional autonomy. Muslim conservatism, resulting in educational backwardness, has also usually left predominantly Muslim regions, such as the north-western provinces of pre-partition India and the Northern Region of Nigeria, apprehensive of union with more westernized territories. Awareness of differences on the scale of modernity have also reinforced racial distinctions in Central Africa, Malaya, and Malaysia, and linguistic differences within Pakistan and India. Where such uneven modernization has existed, regional autonomy has been advocated as a way in which the less developed regions, protected from exploitation and domination, might have a breathing space during which they might improve their relative position.

In all the new federations, with the exception of the West Indies, racial, religious, or cultural regionalism assumed the proportions of sub-nationalism. Commentators on the Indian scene and government commissions alike have often looked with alarm at the tendency of linguistic regions to take on the character of separate nationalities.[1] In Pakistan delays in constitution-making and the growing Bengali resentment exposed 'the sub-national emotions' as 'the most intense political sentiments within Pakistan'.[2] The tendency of the Chinese and Indians to retain loyalties to external nations provoked a Malay communalism which in 1946 and afterwards took on the force of a nationalist movement. In Nigeria the politicization of the three main culture groups after 1948, which resulted in the regionalization of the nationalist movement and of political parties, made federalism imperative.[3] The hopes of racial partnership in Central Africa were strained by the separate nationalisms of the settlers in the Rhodesias and the regional African Congresses, the latter being best exemplified by Malawi nationalism in Nyasaland. Thus, where the unions planned were multi-national in character, the demands for regional autonomy within these unions were, not surprisingly, extremely potent.

7. *Geographical dispersion*

Sheer size of area or population has often encouraged regional autonomy.[4] In India, with a population consisting of one-seventh of the human race and an area equivalent to two-thirds of Europe without Russia, it was declared in

---

[1] S. S. Harrison, *India, The Most Dangerous Decades* (1960), chs. 1–4, 7; C.A.I., *Report of the Linguistic Provinces Commission* (1948), paras. 127, 128, 143; *Report of the States Reorganization Commission* (1955), paras. 67, 155–8.

[2] K. Callard, *Political Forces in Pakistan, 1947–1959* (1959), p. 16.

[3] Coleman, *Nigeria*, chs. 15–17.

[4] See Table 1, p. 361, for a comparison of total area and population of each federation.

the Constituent Assembly: 'Nobody suggests that this vast country with its size and multiple people can be ruled on a unitary basis. Over-centralization . . . leads to anaemia at the extremities and apoplexy at the centre.'[1] Pakistan and Nigeria also encompassed vast areas and populations. Each had a total area equivalent to France, Belgium, and the United Kingdom combined, and Pakistan contained a population of 75 million, while Nigeria, with 35 million, was the largest country in Africa and the thirteenth most populous in the world.[2] Consequently, in both Pakistan and Nigeria a federal form of unification was regarded as the 'dictate of geography'.[3] In Rhodesia and Nyasaland the population was relatively small, a mere 6 million at the time of federation, but this was spread over a total area larger than either Pakistan or Nigeria, contributing to feelings of remoteness. By contrast with the other federations, both the territories and populations of Malaya and the West Indies were very much smaller. But although the land area of the West Indies Federation was small, the islands were scattered over a vast area, spanning over 1,000 miles of the Caribbean, with the result that an important factor in West Indian life was sheer distance. The 500 miles of sea separating the Borneo states from the rest of Malaysia had a similar significance.

Magnitude and dispersion were not the only geographic factors inducing regionalism. Many areas were marked off into natural zones by the topography. In Malaya, for instance, which at first sight seems so compact on the map, not only were the islands of Penang and Singapore separated from the peninsula by water, but the populations concentrated on the western and eastern coastal plains were divided by the mountainous central backbone and by the trackless jungle and swamp that cover four-fifths of the surface. In a very real sense topography had been responsible for the creation of the little states originally concentrated at the river mouths along the coasts. In India the Deccan Tableland has served as the great middle rampart historically responsible for the cleavage between the Aryan and Dravidian-speaking peoples. Nigeria too consists of contrasting geographical zones: the dry pastoral area of the north and the forest of most of the south. Moreover, until very recently, communications between north and south were restricted by tropical swamp and forest and by the tsetse fly, and between east and west by the Niger river. In Central Africa the Zambesi river divided the two Rhodesias, while Nyasaland was physically a part of the Great Rift Valley system of East Africa, its navigable rivers and lake leading to Tanganyika and Mozambique rather than to the Rhodesias. In the West Indies it was the sea, above all else, which fostered local insularity, even between islands which were relatively close. West Indians have been inclined to think their political geography

---

[1] C.A.I., *Debates*, vol. v, p. 81.

[2] These population figures are approximately those at the time of federation, and are based on census figures obtained in 1951 and 1952.

[3] C.A.P. (first), *Debates*, vol. v, p. 5; Awolowo, *Awo*, p. 163.

unique in this respect, but the examples of Hawaii, Alaska, Puerto Rico, Newfoundland, Vancouver Island, Indonesia, and now Malaysia, suggest that salt-water unions, although difficult, are not necessarily impracticable. In Pakistan it was not topography or the sea but political geography in the form of 1,000 miles of Indian territory dividing East and West Pakistan which, as Liaquat Ali Khan pointed out, made a federal form of union unavoidable.[1]

Distance is as much a matter of technology and communications as it is a matter of geographical remoteness, and it was the inadequacy of inter-territorial communications which often contributed to outlooks that were predominantly regional. Where regions have lacked contiguity, as in Pakistan and the West Indies, it was necessary to rely on sea and air routes, the former slow and infrequent, the latter too costly for most of the populations. It was not surprising that a non-Bengali reporter in East Pakistan should report: 'People here feel cut off.'[2] Even in the other federations, despite improvements under British rule, communications often left much to be desired. Indian railways were of mixed gauges, and for strategic and commercial reasons ran mainly east and west rather than north and south. In Malaya, because of the central mountains and jungles, roads and railways generally ran north and south, and links between the eastern and western coastal plains were few.[3] Nor, because of the difficulty of communications, had there been much contact or trade between Sarawak and North Borneo, despite their relative closeness to each other. In Nigeria the rivers were of only limited value for navigation, inter-regional roads were limited to the few bridges and ferries crossing the Niger river, and there was no direct railway line between the Eastern and Western Regions.[4] In Rhodesia and Nyasaland roads were generally inadequate, and Nyasaland's only rail link with Salisbury was through Mozambique.[5] Thus, geography and the resulting inadequacies in communications contributed in all these federations, but most of all in the West Indies and in Pakistan, to regional feelings of remoteness.

8. *Historical identity*

Generally, where federal institutions have been established, the units initially chosen as regions within the federation had previously been either separate colonies or protectorates, as in the West Indies, Central Africa, the Malay States, and some of the princely states in India and Pakistan, or divisions of provincial and regional administration, as in the Indian and Pakistan provinces, the Nigerian regions, and the Straits Settlements. Previous existence as a distinct political unit has therefore usually been a factor in the desire for regional autonomy.

[1] C.A.P. (first), *Debates*, vol. v, p. 5.
[2] H. Feldman, *A Constitution for Pakistan* (1955), p. 14.
[3] See Map 4.   [4] See Map 5.   [5] See Map 6.

The relative importance of a distinct sense of history in motivating regionalism has depended on a number of conditions. One of the most important of these is the length of the experience of separate political identity. The islands of the West Indies, most of them with separate histories going back to the seventeenth and eighteenth centuries, were highly individualistic and insular in outlook. The constituent units in the other federations had much shorter histories of separate identity. The Malay states, the Indian princely states, and the Nigerian regions could trace some historical connexion with sultanates, chiefdoms, or kingdoms existing before British rule, but most of the regional boundaries were either formalized or drawn during the period of British rule. On the continent of India the process of devolution had continued through the nineteenth and twentieth centuries, but some of the provinces were relatively recent. In West Pakistan, for instance, Sind had enjoyed only ten years of autonomy before Pakistan came into being, and the North-West Frontier Province less than fifty. The political boundaries established within Nigeria and Central Africa under British rule were all less than sixty years old.

The relative strength of the desire for regional autonomy has depended not only on the length but on the degree of autonomy previously experienced. A factor in the virulent separatism of Northern Nigeria was its isolation from the rest of Nigeria under British administration during the period 1922–46. Moreover, the reluctance of Nigerian politicians to allow their own regions to be split showed the importance of the 1946 and 1951 constitutions in setting the regional mould for Nigerian federalism. In India and Pakistan too, the experience of regional autonomy established in 1937 was relatively brief, but was sufficient to encourage acute provincial consciousness and to create groups of provincial politicians with vested interests in continued provincial autonomy. Invariably, where Britain has practised a policy of indirect rule, as in northern and western Nigeria, the Malay states, the princely states of the Indian continent, and the protectorates of Central Africa, a particularly strong historical feeling of local identity has developed. It is not surprising that the Unfederated Malay States, where indirect rule had been more of a reality, especially Johore and Kedah, should have led the agitation against Malayan Union and the extension of equal rights to the immigrant races in 1946, or that the Northern Region in Nigeria should have been the strongest advocate of regional autonomy.

The force of historical political identity in fostering regional consciousness has depended, however, on the degree to which these historical boundaries have coincided with ethnic and cultural communities. Although the territorial units created under British rule often created historical loyalties of their own, these were subsequently submerged by other stronger regional pressures in the cases of the Indian princely states and provinces, and the territories of West Pakistan.

9. *Dissimilarity of political and social institutions*

Although a British pattern of political and social institutions, introduced during the period of colonial rule, was shared by all the regions within the new Commonwealth federations, nevertheless, the federating territories have usually been marked by contrasts in constitutional status, degree of political advance, application of the policy of indirect rule, and nature of indigenous social institutions.

Differences in constitutional status combined with different degrees of progress towards self-government have been conspicuous in every federation. One of the major reasons for the insistence upon regional autonomy instead of amalgamation in Central Africa was the difference between Southern Rhodesia on the one hand, a colony and self-governing since 1923, and Northern Rhodesia and Nyasaland on the other, both protectorates and still under the control of the Colonial Office. Within Nigeria, too, sharp differences in degrees of regional political advancement, especially the backwardness of the Northern Region relative to the southern regions, made full regional autonomy a necessity if Nigerian unity was to be preserved. Furthermore, because of the special status of the Southern Cameroons as a United Nations Trust Territory, it was separated from the Eastern Region to form a new 'quasi-region' when Nigeria became a federation in 1954. In the West Indies, where Jamaica, Trinidad, and Barbados had made greater progress towards self-government, regional autonomy made these territories willing to be linked with less-advanced islands. All three Asian federations also united territories with contrasts in constitutional status.[1] The Government of India Act of 1935 had differentiated Governor's Provinces, Chief Commissioner's Provinces, Excluded and Partially Excluded Tribal Areas, and acceding Indian States.[2] As a result, both India and Pakistan in their early years were composed of several categories of units enjoying different degrees of autonomy. Because, when Malaya was federated in 1948, the Malays insisted upon retaining the legal sovereignty of their states, the nine states in the federation remained as protectorates while the two settlements continued as British colonies.[3] This distinction was removed in the revised constitution of 1957, but when Malaysia was formed, the special status and safeguards for Sarawak and Sabah were considered necessary in view of their relative political immaturity.

In India, Pakistan, Malaya, and Nigeria, the uneven application of the British policy of indirect rule had further increased regional contrasts in political institutions. In India, for instance, it was recognized that it would be easier to unite the 'two Indias'—the British provinces and the princely states, the latter generally characterized by autocratic institutions—within a federal

---

[1] See Chapter 7, section 5, on constitutional details.
[2] *Government of India Act, 1935* (26 Geo. 5, ch. 2), ss. 6, 46–90, 91–92, 94–98.
[3] S.I. 1948, no. 108, ss. 7–54, and Second Sched. cl. 110.

system.[1] Not only did indirect rule differentiate the Malay states from the settlements in pre-war Malaya, but within the Malay states there was a sharp difference between the Federated and the Unfederated Malay States in the degree of British control which had been exercised. In Nigeria too, Lord Lugard's policy of indirect rule had had varying success, becoming the foundation of the political system of the Northern Region, but failing to take root among the more individualistic peoples of the Eastern Region.

Contrasts between dominant political outlooks in different regions—between conservatism and radicalism or socialism—have also been a divisive force. This has been most apparent in the distrust of Singapore's turbulent left-wing politics on the part of Malayan leaders, in the clash between West Pakistan politicians, largely influenced by landowners, bureaucrats, and businessmen, and the more radical representatives of East Bengal, and in the mutual distrust in Nigeria between the conservative north and the southern nationalists.[2]

As important as differences in political institutions and outlooks have been contrasts in indigenous social institutions. The differences in Nigeria between the large, highly organized, autocratic Fulani–Hausa emirates of the north, based on Islamic traditions and law, the sizeable urban-centred Yoruba and Edo kingdoms in the west combining aristocratic and democratic principles, and the atomic structure of the small autonomous or semi-autonomous groups of the Middle Belt and the Eastern Region, particularly the individualism and egalitarianism of the Ibos, sharpened regional contrasts. Similarly, the essentially regional caste structures in India, the differences between East and West Pakistan in urban–rural ratios and in the role of large landowners, the heterogeneity in Malay customs and land laws and the varying degrees of urbanization in the different states, the distinctive policies of Singapore in the fields of labour relations and education, the contrasts in the treatment of Africans in Central Africa, and the varieties of marriage and family law in the West Indies, have contributed enormously to the consciousness of regional identity.

10. *Regional political leadership*

The effectiveness of the demands for regional autonomy has depended upon the quality and strength of its leadership. The forceful stands taken by such men as Fazlul Huq, H. S. Suhrawardy, and Nurul Amin in East Bengal, Abdur Rashid Khan and Qaiyum Khan in the North-West Frontier Province, Dato Onn against Malayan Union, the Sardauna of Sokoto, Chief Awolowo, and Nnamdi Azikiwe, the three towering regional leaders in Nigeria,

---

[1] C.A.I., *Debates*, vol. iii, p. 345; vol. v, pp. 38–39; *White Paper on Indian States* (rev. ed., 1950), paras. 220, 241.

[2] In South Arabia one of the most divisive forces was the clash between the autocratic rulers of the amirates and the radical politicians of Aden.

Bustamente in Jamaica, N. V. Gadgil and Swami Sitaram in India, R. O. Stockil in Southern Rhodesia, and Dr. Hastings Banda for Nyasaland, stirred the regional consciousness of their territories.

Often, the previous existence of regional or territorial governments had created groups of politicians favouring continued regional institutions. The constituent assemblies of India and Pakistan both contained significant proportions of men who had been, or still were, members of provincial legislatures and who saw little in favour of a unitary constitution. In Malaya it was significant that it was the chief ministers of the Malay states, and especially of Johore and Kedah, who dominated the U.M.N.O. in its early period. In Nigeria, despite their overt espousal of the movements for new states, the leadership of the southern regions proved reluctant to weaken the regional bases on which their power rested. The opposition to unification of any sort in the West Indies was often led by politicians with vested interests in the status quo. Furthermore, the views of regional leaders in the new federations were often reinforced by the active campaigns for territorial autonomy carried on by western-minded local élites, anxious to retain or to gain access to regional patronage.

Where, as a result of indirect rule, traditional rulers or chiefs wielded influence, they were usually among the supporters of regional autonomy. The emirs of Northern Nigeria, the Indian princes led by the Nawab of Bhopal, the rulers of Malaya jealous of their sovereignty, and the chiefs of Nyasaland, were active in their opposition to amalgamation and served as particularly influential focal points for regional loyalty.

11. *Models of regional autonomy*

The successful working models of regional autonomy in the older federations have provided precedents for the builders of the new federations. The main lesson learnt from such federations as Switzerland, Canada, and the United States has been that, within a federal system, the absorption of minorities is not the necessary result of political union. In the new federations where racial, religious, linguistic, and other cultural diversities have been so potent, the examples of the earlier multi-national federations attracted much attention. Because of the Soviet Union's success in imposing political and economic union upon a large and culturally heterogeneous mass of peoples, the policy in the U.S.S.R. of recognizing the diverse nationalities has often been cited in the developing countries as a justification for granting regional autonomy to ethnic and cultural groups, although constitutional details have shown little U.S.S.R. influence. The popularity of federal forms of union in other developing countries further encouraged demands for regional autonomy within later unions. For instance, the Government of India Act, 1935, showing that regional autonomy and a high degree of centralization were compatible, was influential in all three Asian federations, while the example of Rhodesia and Nyasaland suggested to Nigerian constitution-framers that if autonomous regional units were established, territories with different degrees of political advancement could be combined.[1]

12. *British policy*

That British insistence has been decisive in some cases in the development of regional autonomy has been clear. The settlers of Central Africa accepted a federal system instead of outright amalgamation in 1953 simply as the price the British Government demanded for a political union.[2] Both major British political parties were opposed to amalgamation, but, with varying emphasis, were willing to consider a federal structure as a means of ensuring continued British trusteeship in the protectorates.[3] It was also the British Government's insistence upon the lapse of its paramountcy over the Indian princely states at the time of independence which made their integration into the new Dominions of India and Pakistan dependent upon negotiation.[4]

There were several reasons why regional autonomy appealed to the British Government as a useful device. First, in areas where policies of indirect rule had been applied to certain regions, a federal system made possible the continued identity of autonomous traditional local administrations within a union having westernized central political institutions.[5] Secondly, federal systems have also proved useful instruments for the gradual devolution of authority towards self-government. In British India, Nigeria, and the West Indies, progress towards regional self-government could be made while Britain retained some control of the central government until the whole country was ready for independence. Furthermore, in Nigeria, Rhodesia and Nyasaland, and the West Indies, regional autonomy enabled progress towards regional self-government at different rates of advance appropriate to each region. Thus, in the variations in constitutional development made possible within a united area, a federal system provided an extremely flexible framework.

Some nationalists have not hesitated to allege that colonial federalism was simply an attempt to curtail nationalism, and to maintain imperial suzerainty by a policy of 'divide and rule'. Such allegations have been made by centralizing Hindu nationalists in British India, the National Independence Party criticizing Nigerian regionalization, the politicians suspecting British strategic motives to be at the base of Singapore's separation from Malaya between 1948

[1] For discussion of the degree to which the form of new federations was influenced by other models of federal government, see Chapter 6, section 5, below.

[2] Cmd. 8753/1953, p. 7; Taylor, *The Rhodesian*, p. 105; A. J. Hanna, *The Story of the Rhodesias and Nyasaland* (1960), pp. 248–52.

[3] In Britain the opposition to federation was led by the Africa Bureau, the Central Africa Committee, Racial Unity, the National Peace Council, the Scottish Council for African Questions, and the Fabian Colonial Bureau.

[4] *White Paper on Indian States* (rev. ed., 1950), paras. 71, 262.

[5] See section 9, above.

and 1963, and the settlers in Central Africa fearing federation as a device meant to enable the Colonial Office to reassert its authority. There is some evidence to suggest that the value of regional autonomy as a brake upon independence movements and as a form of political conservatism may have influenced British policy in some of the colonial federations.[1] But generally such charges have overstated the case. The policy of regionalization in Nigeria, for instance, was supported by Bourdillon and Richards as an integrative policy, and at the 1953 and 1954 conferences it was the Nigerian leaders rather than the Colonial Office officials who insisted upon full regional autonomy.[2] Similarly in India, even after the end of British control, the very nationalists who had condemned provincial autonomy in 1935 spoke of the necessity of a federal system in view of the size and diversity of the population of the Union. As Francis Carnell has suggested:

whatever the verdict in the past, the charge of colonial 'divide and rule' could never be sustained in the twilight of colonial rule in Africa today. It is an intransigent tribalism rather than 'colonialism' which now encourages political balkanization. Departing colonial powers, tired of their political responsibilities, clutch at any political leadership thought capable of negotiating a smooth transfer of power.[3]

Nevertheless, the participation of the imperial government as a third party in the negotiations leading to the creation of colonial federations has sometimes complicated the scene. The administrators and advisors of the retiring imperial power have often been called upon to interpret regional preferences which were imperfectly revealed, and much, therefore, has depended upon their judgements of the relative importance of different pressures. Moreover, as a third party in the negotiations the British Government was frequently used by regional groups as a lever in the bargaining, thus distorting the picture and sometimes making agreement more difficult to reach than it might have been in direct negotiations between the local groups. The imperial power has, therefore, contributed indirectly as well as directly to the force of demands for regional autonomy.

13. *The major motives*

As with the factors leading to desires for political unity, those inducing desires for regional autonomy within the new Commonwealth federations have been complex and have varied in importance in different countries.

In India, because of the vastness of its territory and population, the integration of the princely states with their historic and institutional differences,

---

[1] Brecher, *Nehru*, pp. 156, 264–5; N. D. Varadachariar, *Indian States in the Federation* (1936), pp. 142–3; A. B. Keith, *A Constitutional, History of India, 1600–1935* (1936), pp. 473–4.

[2] Sir B. H. Bourdillon, 'The Nigerian Constitution', *African Affairs*, xlv (1946), p. 92; Cmd. 6599/1945, Governor's Despatch, para. 3; Coleman, *Nigeria*, p. 469; Ezera, *Constitutional Developments in Nigeria*, pp. 197–9; *West Africa* (15 August 1953), p. 745; (5 September 1953), p. 817.

[3] Carnell, 'Political Implications of Federalism in New States', op. cit., p. 59.

and the deep roots of linguistic regionalism, there was little disagreement about the need for a federal rather than a unitary form of constitution.[1] In Pakistan similar cultural and historical differences were at work, but the geographical separation of the eastern and western wings was crucial. Moreover, the mutual fears of domination, caused by East Bengal's large population on the one hand, and the concentration of political and economic power in West Pakistan on the other, accelerated the growing provincial consciousness that accompanied the delays in constitution-making. Similarly in Nigeria, the overwhelming size of the north, and the superior modernization of the south, sharpened regional differences into fears of domination. But the fundamental regional divisions there were both ethnic and religious. The deep cultural and institutional contrasts between the three dominant national groups, the Hausa–Fulani in the north, the Yoruba in the west, and the Ibo in the east, were augmented by the basic religious division between the Muslims dominant in the north and the non-Muslims predominant elsewhere.

In the West Indies, as in Pakistan, geographic separation, and with it problems of communications, were decisive in fostering regional separatism. But rather than deep linguistic and cultural differences, it was the distinct histories and traditions of the islands, the contrasts in degree of political development, inequalities in wealth and size, the non-complementary economies, and the separation by water, which created an insular pride amounting to parochialism.

In both Malaya and Central Africa fears of racial domination were the major factor in the resort to a federal form of union, and these fears were further embittered by the resentment of the indigenous races because the threat of subjection came from immigrant peoples. The basic motives in the Malay rejection of a union in favour of a federation were primarily their apprehensions of Chinese domination, this racial distrust being reinforced by religious, linguistic, and economic differences, and secondly, the Malay revulsion against the deprivation of the rulers' historical sovereignty and the individuality of the states. Racial, economic, and institutional differences were also fundamental in the exclusion of Singapore from the 1948 federation, and in the extended autonomy of Singapore, Sarawak, and Sabah within the Malaysian Federation. In Central Africa British insistence upon territorial autonomy in the protectorates was designed primarily to allay African fears by making possible continued British trusteeship in those units, but was also made necessary by the different constitutional status of the territories. At the same time, among the settlers themselves there were economic, historic, and social reasons why Northern Rhodesians were willing to accept regional autonomy as a protection against Southern Rhodesian domination.

How do these motives for regional self-government compare with those that

[1] C.A.I. *Debates*, vol. iv, p. 579; *Second Report of the Union Powers Committee* (1947), para. 2.

produced the older federations? K. C. Wheare has suggested that the only factors for separation within union common to all the older federations were: (1) a previous existence as distinct colonies or states; (2) a divergence of at least some economic interests; (3) geographic size or barriers isolating regions.[1] As we have seen, each of these factors has also been present in some degree in all the new federations. In the older federations the character of political leadership and the existence of federal models upon which to pattern institutions often contributed also to the adoption of federal structures, and this has likewise been true of the newer samples.

In some of the older federations, most noticeably Switzerland and Canada, differences of nationality, assisted by difference of language, race, religion, and dissimilarities of social and political institutions, were factors in the desire for regional separation within a political union. What distinguishes the new federations from the older ones is that these particular divisive forces have been generally of much greater significance. Ethnic and cultural diversities have been prominent in all the new federations, except the West Indies, and the contrasts have invariably been sharper and deeper. In all the new federations there have also been striking differences in the degree of political development of the uniting territories, creating difficulties in reconciling varied political, administrative, and social systems within a single polity. These factors, especially when accentuated by disparities in the size, wealth, and modernization of the regions, have made fear of domination by other regional groups after independence an especially potent motive in the demand for regional autonomy as a protective device. Finally, another feature that has distinguished the new federations has been the use of federal institutions by the imperial government as an instrument of its policy. By comparison with the process by which the Canadian and Australian federations were created, the British Government has itself generally played a much more prominent role in the negotiations that have produced federal rather than unitary unions.

---

[1] For a discussion of the factors leading to the desire for regional separation within the older federations see Wheare, *Federal Government*, pp. 40–44.

5

THE NATURE OF FEDERAL SOCIETIES

1. *The balance of motives*

THE analysis of the preceding chapters has indicated that the specific motives for union or for separation which were dominant have naturally varied in the different federations. But two features stand out as common to them all. First, there was a geographical distribution, at least to some degree, of the diversities within each of these societies, with the result that demands for political autonomy were made on a regional basis. Secondly, in each of the recent federations, as in the older ones, there existed at one and the same time powerful desires to be united for certain purposes, because of a community of outlook or the expectation of common benefits from union, and deep-rooted desires to be organized under autonomous regional governments for others, because of contrasting ways of life or the desire to protect divergent interests. The result in each was a tension between the conflicting demands for territorial integration and for balkanization.

Are these two criteria sufficient to differentiate federal societies from others? Livingston suggests that they are.[1] If, then, a federal society is characterized simply by the conjunction of demands for unity and for territorial diversity, there may be a whole range of federal societies varying according to the relative strengths of these opposing pressures. Indeed, Livingston suggests that there is a whole 'spectrum' of federal societies, stretching from the nearly wholly integrated to the nearly completely diversified. The value of this account is that it recognizes that there is no precise point at which all societies on one side may be classified as diversified or 'federal', and all those on the other as unitary. On the other hand, the weakness of this definition is that it is too broad. Under this definition, the term 'federal' as applied to societies becomes so broad as to include virtually all societies, thus reducing its value as a term of classification.

But are there any other characteristics common to these federal societies? An examination of the recent federations suggests that, like the older federations, what was distinctive about the social situations which produced them was not merely the duality of demands for union and regional autonomy, but the relative balance or equilibrium in each between the conflicting forces for unity and diversity.[2] In India for instance, the Dar Commission, examining

---

[1] Livingston, *Federalism and Constitutional Change*, pp. 1–7.
[2] Cf. Wheare, *Federal Government*, pp. 35–36, 49.

the pressures for unity and for linguistic provincialism, described these forces as 'engaged in a mortal combat'.[1] Even in the West Indies there was some balance between the two tendencies. The island parochialism was far more shallow than the ethnic and cultural divisions within India, Pakistan, or Nigeria, but at the same time the West Indies also lacked the powerful cohesive force, which in India was derived from the independence movement, the organization of the Congress Party, and the desire for economic planning, which in Pakistan was based on a common religion and a common hostility to India, and which in Nigeria grew from the interdependence of the regional economies. Thus, although the strength of desires for unity or desires for territorial autonomy has varied greatly from federation to federation, it has been the relative balance of the demands for integration and for diversification, as counterweights to each other, which has been significant in creating situations where federal institutions were considered desirable.

This analysis, and the experience of the older federations, might lead one to expect that an important condition for the creation of federations would be the absence of military or economic emergencies necessitating centralized control. Most of the new federations, however, have been born under emergency conditions. There have been economic strains in all of them as a result of their underdevelopment and their desire for immediate economic improvement. In the three Asian federations there have been, in addition, threats to security, such as the crises which followed partition on the Indian continent and the Terrorist Emergency in Malaya. But in the new federations these pressures for centralization have been offset by equally deep racial and cultural diversities. The result is that even the powerful demands for unity stimulated by the emergency conditions have failed to overwhelm the deep-seated internal diversities. By contrast, the absence in the Caribbean of any external threat meant that the desire for union was only temporarily sufficient in the West Indies to overcome the strength of island loyalties.

These examples suggest that instead of applying the term 'federal', as Livingston has recommended, to the whole spectrum of societies ranging from the nearly completely integrated to the nearly disintegrated, it might be more appropriate, and closer to ordinary usage, to restrict the term 'federal' to a segment of the spectrum. It is likely to be misleading to describe as 'federal' societies in which there are elements of both unity and diversity but in which one or other of these is clearly dominant. Where the wider nationalism has been overwhelming, unitary political institutions have usually resulted in spite of internal diversities, and where regional nationalism has been predominant, partition or balkanization has followed in spite of the existence of some desires for unity. It has only been where there was an approximate equilibrium between the wider and narrower nationalisms that federal political institutions have been adopted. But although this narrows the group

[1] C.A.I., *Report of the Linguistic Provinces Commission* (1948), para. 143.

of societies for which the classification 'federal' is appropriate, Livingston's image of a spectrum of societies, ranged in degree of territorial integration, may still be useful. If federal societies are conceived as a *segment* of this spectrum, it may help us to recognize that within the 'colour' representing federal societies, where the pressures for unity and diversity are fairly closely balanced, there could be a range of 'shades' or variations, and that the borders of this range are not distinct but shade on one side into societies in which homogeneity, in varying degrees, predominates, and on the other side into societies in which heterogeneity, in varying degrees, predominates.

2. *The choice of federal institutions*

That federal institutions were conceived primarily as compromises between the conflicting pressures for amalgamation and separation was clear in each of the new Commonwealth federations. The Union Powers Committee of the Indian Constituent Assembly, in recommending that 'the soundest framework for our constitution is a federation', expressly pointed to both the need for a strong central authority and the political and administrative pressures for provincial autonomy.[1] The Pakistan Constituent Assemblies, aware that Pakistan was united by religion but divided by geography, language, culture, and history, was at great pains to steer a course midway between these two conflicting demands by the adoption of ostensibly federal institutions.[2] In Malaya, with its mosaic of Heraclitean opposites, the federal solution of 1948 bought Malay support for a close strategic, economic, and administrative union in the context of the developing emergency, by preserving the historical and legal sovereignty of the states and their rulers and maintaining the special position of the Malays.[3] The later Malayan constitution of 1957 represented an attempt to put in juridical form the compromises which constituted the basis of the Alliance power, and the subsequent amendments made to this constitution for the Malaysian Federation were designed to reconcile the strong central government desired by Malayan political leaders with the safeguards insisted upon by the acceding states for their special interests. In Nigeria the orthodox federal system established in 1954 enabled not only a compromise between the economic and diplomatic motives for unity and the demands of regional ethnic groups for autonomy, but also a compromise on the issue of early self-government between the eager southerners and the conservative northerners. At Montego Bay, both Creech Jones and Adams emphasized that a federal compromise would enable islands to retain autonomy on domestic matters and avoid domination by other territories, while securing benefits through surrendering sovereignty

[1] C.A.I., *Second Report of the Union Powers Committee* (1947), para. 2.
[2] C.A.P. (first), *Debates*, vol. v, p. 5; C.A.P. (second), *Debates*, vol. i, pp. 1816, 2072–3, 2091, 2095–2104, 2227, 2291–2.
[3] Cmd. 7171/1947, esp. para. 3; *Report of the Working Committee* (1946), para. 14.

on certain major issues.[1] Later the Rance Committee was careful to stress that this compromise placed the central government neither 'over', nor 'subordinate' to, territorial governments.[2] Federation in Central Africa was also seen as a compromise solution. Not only did it attempt to reconcile the economic, strategic, administrative, and political desirability of union on the one hand with the recognition of African fears and of the contrasting racial policies and constitutional status of the territories on the other, but it also made possible agreement between the Rhodesian settlers desiring amalgamation and the British Government unwilling to give up its role as protector of African native interests.

In the colonial federations the impact of social pressures on constitution-making has been affected by two temporary factors. The influence of the imperial power as a third party in the constitutional negotiations, and the enthusiastic nationalism generated by the drive to political independence, have meant that political institutions created in these special circumstances have not always accurately reflected the underlying centrifugal and centripetal forces in these societies. As a result the process of working out the appropriate political compromises has sometimes continued long into the period after independence.[3]

But, given conflicting demands for unity and diversity within a society, is a federal solution the only constitutional compromise by which they may be accommodated? At first sight there would seem to have been a wide variety of alternative constitutional systems which might have been applied. Some countries such as the United Kingdom, New Zealand, South Africa, Ceylon, Ghana, and Indonesia, have, in spite of strong internal regional differences, preferred unitary forms of government in which ultimately complete authority is conferred on the central government. Unitary government may take several forms: centralized unitary government as in Ceylon and Ghana, decentralized unitary government, in which some authority is devolved upon subordinate governments, as in South Africa, or unitary government with special minority safeguards, 'entrenched clauses', or a 'bill of rights', as in Ireland and some of the Scandinavian countries. The advantages claimed for a unitary concentration of authority in any of these forms, as opposed to a federal division of authority, are that it provides a strong central focus for political integration and that it is more flexible and adaptable, particularly for economic planning. On the other hand, critics have argued that the concentration of power makes its conversion to autocracy easier, and that therefore it is unlikely to allay minority fears. In this respect the examples of South Africa, Ghana, Ceylon, the Belgian Congo, Burma, and Indonesia are hardly encouraging.

Another alternative to a federal compromise lay in some looser form of political association. A confederal form of government, such as the East African Common Services Organization, the European Economic Com-

[1] Col. no. 218/1948, pp. 9, 40–41.   [2] Col. no. 255/1950, para. 22.   [3] See section 4, below.

munity, and earlier the United States before 1789, provided one possibility. In these an organization to regulate matters of common concern was set up, but regional governments retained to themselves sovereignty and some control over their delegates and over the major policies of the joint organization. Another possibility was an even looser form of political combination simply taking the form of inter-governmental co-operation. The Central African Council and the West Indian Regional Economic Committee were examples of this kind of joint action.[1] These various forms of looser political integration permit a measure of co-operation and interchange of views without the surrender of sovereignty by the component units which is necessary in a federal system. Their weakness, however, apparent in most of the examples mentioned, is that their policies are likely to be limited to those which are unanimously supported by the regional governments. This means that active public development policies, involving adjustments of tariff rates and fiscal and monetary controls, because of their inherently controversial nature are made difficult to implement on an area basis, where economists suggest there are significant advantages to be gained. In the case of advisory inter-governmental councils, the lack of a common executive to carry out decisions further limits the effectiveness of joint action.

Federal government, then, is only one of several possible constitutional solutions, but there would appear to be a prima facie case for arguing that, in reconciling ambivalent demands for unity and diversity, federations possess some advantages over either unitary or confederal systems. As a compromise, a federal system, by distributing authority between central and regional governments, makes possible complete political unity for certain functions and regional autonomy for others. Compared to unitary institutions, regional autonomy within a federal system permits the expression of regional claims which, if resisted, might provoke harsh resentments representing a greater threat to national unity, provides some safeguard to regional groups in the protection of their own special interests, and reduces the risk of the monopoly of power by an autocracy or a bureaucracy. Compared to confederal institutions or to inter-governmental co-operation, federal governments enable positive centralized policies, not dependent on unanimous regional agreement, with regard to those functions assigned to the central government, and in addition are more likely to provide a focus for the development of a common nationality.

But these advantages, it would appear, are bought only at a price. Compared to unitary government, federal government tends to be legalistic, complex, conservative, and rigid.[2] It may be expensive in human and economic

---

[1] Cmd. 7987/1950, paras. 146–53; L. Braithwaite, 'Progress Toward Federation, 1938–1956', *Social and Economic Studies*, vi (1957), pp. 166–77.

[2] See Carnell, 'Political Implications of Federalism in New States', op. cit., p. 18; A. V. Dicey, *Introduction to the Study of the Law of the Constitution* (10th ed., 1959), pp. lxxvii–lxxxii and 138–80; C.A.I. *Debates*, vol. vii, p. 35; C.A.P. (second), *Debates*, vol. i, pp. 2293–4.

resources, due to the dual system of governments required. Moreover, concessions to internal diversities may reinforce and harden them, proving cumulative in effect. Fears that this would be the case were expressed, for instance, in India, Pakistan, and Nigeria. For these reasons, Sir Ivor Jennings has suggested that 'nobody would have a federal constitution if he could possibly avoid it'.[1] On the other hand, compared to confederal organization or joint governmental action, federal government may prove difficult to operate where the sense of common outlook is insufficiently strong or the dissimilarity of political institutions too great.

Why then, in the areas under study, was the federal solution chosen instead of alternative forms of political integration? In most of them, alternative forms were actually considered, and in some even experimented with, but in each of them the constitution-makers came to the conclusion that, in the circumstances, federal institutions were the only practicable solution.

The constitution-makers usually examined comparative studies of other forms of government, prepared for the purpose. In most cases the rejection of alternatives was based also on the experience of non-federal solutions attempted and found unsatisfactory. The most striking examples of this were the rejection of unitary government in Malaya and in Nigeria, after communalism and regionalism had been exacerbated by the attempts to impose a Malayan Union in 1946 and to establish in Nigeria unitary and quasi-unitary constitutions in 1946 and 1951.[2] In India, too, it was the failure of unitary government and of dyarchy that led the British Government to advocate a federal structure in the 1930's, and which later resulted in the Indian Constituent Assembly's Union Powers Committee suggesting that a return to unitary government would be a 'retrograde step'.[3] In the second Constituent Assembly of Pakistan the demand for provincial autonomy was often defended by pointing to the unsatisfactory quasi-unitary features of the Government of India Act, 1935.[4] Later, the Constitution Commission of 1961, reporting after three years of unitary martial law, criticized the proposals of the official delegation for a permanent unitary structure, and instead reported in favour of a federal system.[5] Thus, as in Canada much earlier, dissatisfaction with unitary government, which failed to express internal diversities, was a major reason in Malaya, Nigeria, Pakistan, and India for the adoption of federal institutions.

In a number of cases an unsatisfactory experience with looser unions in-

---

[1] Jennings, *Some Characteristics of the Indian Constitution*, p. 55.

[2] It was ironic that after Governor Richards had warned that 'it would be useless to pretend that unity exists at the present, nor would clumsy attempts to achieve it result in anything but opposition' (Cmd. 6599/1945, Governor's Despatch, para. 25), his own attempt to impose unity should have provoked a virulent regionalism.

[3] C.A.I., *Second Report of the Union Powers Committee* (1947), para. 2.

[4] C.A.P. (second), *Debates*, vol. i, pp. 1793–5, 1985, 2017, 2072–3, 2096–2104, 2130, 2271–2.   [5] *Report*, ch. iv.

fluenced their rejection in favour of a federal system. The shortcomings of the Central African Council as a purely advisory body without executive powers, and the inadequacies in the West Indies of wartime arrangements for inter-island co-operation and of the later Regional Economic Committee, suggested that federal institutions with genuine executive powers were needed. Elsewhere, the isolation of Northern Nigeria within the formally integrated administration of Nigeria before 1945, the hodge-podge of treaties, engagements, and sanads between the Indian princely states and the paramount power, and the complexities of pre-war inter-state co-operation in Malaya, made especially apparent during the Japanese invasion, all pointed to the need for more closely integrated political structures.

The choice of federal institutions in these countries was, therefore, not merely an arbitrary one. It was the result of social pressures which made constitutional alternatives inapplicable. Common to all these cases was the conviction of the constitution-makers that federal institutions were 'unavoidable'—the only possible compromise in the particular circumstances. For example, it was widely accepted in both the Indian and Pakistan constituent assemblies and by the Pakistan Constitution Commission of 1961 that the adoption of federal structures was dictated by peremptory needs.[1] The scrapping of the Malayan Union proposals of 1946 in favour of a federation was made necessary by the violent reaction of the Malays to the earlier scheme. In Nigeria the federal solution was adopted as a last resort when the constitutional crisis of 1953 convinced Nigerian leaders of 'the need for a compromise in order to avert the liquidation of Nigeria as a political entity'.[2] In the Rhodesias and Nyasaland the demands of the settlers for amalgamation made anything looser than federation impractical, while British unwillingness to relinquish its trusteeship for African interests in the protectorates made a closer union impossible. In 1953 Sir Godfrey Huggins wrote:

An economic union has been mooted in Britain, while some people in our country still fancy an outright amalgamation. But for one reason or another, such theoretical alternatives are quite impossible. . . . I believe that this final scheme, if put into effect, will offer the last and only chance of a true partnership developing between Europeans and Africans in Central Africa.[3]

In the West Indies, too, the alternatives were rejected as unacceptable: there was no hope of agreement in support of a unitary structure, and a mere advisory council was regarded as likely to be an ineffective 'glorified debating society'.[4] As Manley observed at Montego Bay, 'Federations are not born of anything else except necessity, economic, social, and moral necessity'.[5]

---

[1] C.A.I., *Debates*, vol. ii, p. 288; vol. iv, p. 579; *Second Report of the Union Powers Committee* (1947), para. 2; C.A.P. (first), *Debates*, vol. v, p. 5; C.A.P. (second), *Debates*, vol. i, pp. 1816, 2091; *Report of the Constitution Commission, Pakistan, 1961* (1962), ch. iv, esp. paras. 63, 68.   [2] Azikiwe, *Zik*, p. 133.
[3] London, *Sunday Times* (8 February 1953).
[4] Col. no. 218/1948, p. 35.   [5] Ibid., p. 58.

The significant point about all these new Commonwealth federations was that the adoption of a 'federal solution' in each was not an arbitrary choice but a last resort, a grudging compromise made necessary by the need to accommodate concurrent pressures for unity and for regional autonomy. Where social diversities were so deep-seated, federal institutions with their inherent complexities were considered the necessary price for the achievement of the benefits of political integration.

3. *The capacity for federal government*

So far we have considered the social pressures which convinced constitution-makers that federal political institutions were the desirable, indeed the only possible, compromise. But we must distinguish between the factors which make communities *desire* federal systems and the factors which give them the *capacity* to support such a form of government.[1] The two, of course, are not isolated, since the desires for union and for regional autonomy may themselves be the most important prerequisites for the ability to operate federal institutions, while the desire for federal union may be substantially discouraged by the knowledge that the capacities to maintain such a constitutional form are lacking. We have already seen that in India, Pakistan, Malaya, Nigeria, Rhodesia and Nyasaland, and the West Indies, at their inception as federations, the dual desires for integration and diversification were present in a relatively balanced, if often precarious, tension. We must now examine in what way the constitution-makers were influenced by assessments of the capacities of these societies to operate federal institutions.[2]

In his study of the prerequisites of federal government, K. C. Wheare pointed to a number of conditions which in his view had made possible the success of the four older federations.[3] The capacity to maintain unity was, he suggested, dependent not only on the existence of a desire for union, but also on a fundamental similarity of regional political and social institutions, and on a general respect for constitutions, the rule of law, and independent judiciaries. Some community of race, language, religion, or nationality was also likely to help states to work together. The capacity to maintain regional autonomy, on the other hand, depended not only on the presence of desires for distinctiveness, but also on the regions having a sufficient previous existence as distinct governments to ensure their stability, and sufficient homogeneity to make them cohesive communities. Finally, the capacity to combine at the same time both unity and regional autonomy depended upon a delicate balance between general and regional loyalties, upon the avoidance of

---

[1] Wheare, *Federal Government*, pp. 36, 44–45, emphasizes this distinction.

[2] We are concerned in this chapter only with the considerations that influenced the constitution-makers in choosing federal institutions. Conclusions based on the subsequent experience of the new federations in operation, concerning the factors necessary for effective federal government, will be discussed in Chapter 13, below.

[3] Wheare, op. cit., pp. 44–52.

excessive disparities in regional size and wealth likely to stimulate struggles for ascendancy, and upon the availability of sufficient economic resources and men with the capacity to govern, in order to operate both general and regional governments.

Constitution-makers in the new federations have taken some of these considerations into account. The desirability of constitutional government and of some fundamental uniformity in the component regions was recognized in a number of cases, leading to constitutional provisions designed to ensure this.[1] Even in Central Africa where the Bledisloe Commission had earlier rejected federation expressly because of contrasts in the constitutional development and racial policies of the territories, a major factor in the report of the officials' conference of 1951 in favour of federation was the conviction that these differences had been sufficiently reduced to make federal government workable.[2]

The dangerous effects of sharp disparities in the size and wealth of regional units has also attracted considerable attention.[3] This concern was an important factor in the reshaping of the Indian states in 1947–50 and 1956, and of West Pakistan in 1955. It also contributed to the controversy over new regions in Nigeria and to suggestions for the regrouping of islands as regions within the West Indies Federation. In Central Africa, too, the question received consideration when the 1951 conference noted that the reduced economic inequality of the territories made federation practicable.[4]

Questions of the cost of federal government—both in finances and in legislators and administrators—were often raised. The significance of this problem was illustrated by the query of an American visitor to Central Africa who asked: 'Would you not do better with more bridges and fewer Governors?'[5] The need to economize on both financial and human resources strongly influenced a number of decisions. Examples were the repudiation of linguistic provinces for India by the Dar Commission, the rejection of small states by the States Reorganization Commission, the avoidance of a three-tier federation in Pakistan, the refusal of the Minorities Commission and the Colonial Secretary to approve the creation of new states in Nigeria, the provision for concurrent membership in legislatures in Malaya, the extensive use of the principle of nomination in the West Indian and Malayan senates, the concentration of central functions in Malaya from 1946 on, and the simplified form of state government under the Malayan and Malaysian constitutions. In Central Africa the advocacy of federation by the officials' conference was based on the assessment that the combined resources of the area were 'fully

---

[1] See Chapter 7, section 5.
[2] Cmd. 8233/1951, para. 17–19, 23.
[3] See Chapter 7, section 2.
[4] Cmd. 8233/1951, para. 24.
[5] P. Mason, 'The Conference and the Minorities Commission', *West Africa* (22 November 1958), p. 1115.

adequate to support a scheme of closer association'.[1] In the West Indies, because the cost of federation exercised so many minds and there were so many exaggerated ideas current, a series of reports, attempting to dispel these qualms and suggesting that most of the costs of the central government represented transfers of expense from the island governments, was prepared.[2] Elsewhere, it was sometimes argued that the extra expense of a federal system might be counteracted by local economies through decentralized administration, and furthermore that in the larger unions, such as India, Pakistan, and Nigeria, some administrative decentralization would be necessary under a unitary government anyway. Nevertheless, the inevitable added expense in men and finances of federal systems was a problem which constitution-makers in developing countries could not ignore.

In some federations the importance of satisfactory inter-regional communications as a prerequisite for effective federal government was also stressed. In the West Indies and Pakistan where the regions were so widely separated, and also in Nigeria and the Rhodesias and Nyasaland where communications were sparse, the importance of rapid development of communications was emphasized as essential to the successful working of federation.

But although the constitution-makers did often take into consideration factors affecting the capacity for working federal institutions, the fact remains, nevertheless, that in most of the new federations many of the conditions suggested by K. C. Wheare as necessary for effective federal government were simply missing. The sense of constitutionalism and legalism rarely had deep roots. This was most apparent in Pakistan, while the Malay states, the Indian princely states, Northern Nigeria, and the settler-dominated Rhodesias and Nyasaland, possessed an oligarchic flavour. In all of these federations there were striking dissimilarities of social and political institutions, and in all, except the West Indies, regional differences of race, language, religion, or nationality were explosive forces making co-operation difficult. In many the historical identity of the regional politicial units was a recent British creation, as in Nigeria, Central Africa, and some of the provinces of India and Pakistan, or began only at the time of federation, as in the consolidated princely states in India and Pakistan. Nor were regional units always homogeneous; the territorial units of India at partition, Pakistan, Malaya, Malaysia, Nigeria, Central Africa, and Trinidad all contained heterogeneous populations. It was not surprising, therefore, that some of these units in India and Pakistan should have lacked stability, or that there were insistent demands in Nigeria for the creation of new regions. Sharp disparities in size and wealth of the regional units were also apparent in all the new federations, but particularly in the

[1] Cmd. 8233/1951, para. 24.
[2] Col. no. 218/1948, pp. 25, 36, 47, 96–99; Col. no. 255/1950, paras. 18, 107–12; Development and Welfare Org. in W.I., *Financial Aspects of Federation of the British West Indies* (Seel), (1953); Cmd. 9618/1955, chs. 3, 4.

West Indies, Pakistan, and Nigeria, in each of which a single territory contained at least half the federal population.[1] Nor were any of these federations,
being relatively underdeveloped areas, wealthy in economic resources or in
trained and experienced legislators and administrators. Nigeria and Pakistan
were especially handicapped in this respect.[2]

But although in the new Commonwealth federations there was often a lack
of the conditions considered desirable for effective federal government, this did
not deter the constitution-makers. It was not that the importance of these was
overlooked, but rather that in the final analysis there appeared to be no option.
Where in particular circumstances the federal compromise was the only alternative to political balkanization, the attempt to work federal government,
whether all the conditions desirable for its effective operation were present
or not, had to be made anyway.

4. *The dynamic character of federal societies*

The conflicting forces and demands that have made the original choice of
federal government necessary have invariably continued to exert pressure and
to influence the operation of these political institutions after their creation.
While this has been apparent in all the new federations, it has been most
obvious where the settlement of certain contentious issues was expressly
postponed in the initial federal compromise. Thus, the provisions for constitutional review in the West Indies, Rhodesia and Nyasaland, and Nigeria,
and for a flexible amendment process for state boundaries in India, provided
opportunities for renewed controversy.[3] In Pakistan where the temporary
character of the federal structure was prolonged for nine years this tendency
was clearest of all.

But the picture is further complicated by the fact that the equilibrium
between the motives for union and for separation within a society rarely
remains constant, particularly in societies undergoing rapid political and
economic development. In such countries the rates of change in the different
sectors of society often vary—economic development, for instance, may outstrip the slower evolution of social institutions—and the result of these
varying speeds is frequently a changing equation within the society. Several
factors have operated in the new Commonwealth federations to affect the
balance of social forces in the early years after their formation.

Where the unity generated by nationalist movements in the drive for
freedom from alien rule was a major element in the original desire for
federal union, as in the Asian federations, the tendency for this nationalism
to evaporate with the achievement of independence may gravely threaten the

---

[1] See Chapter 7, section 2.
[2] G. A. Almond and J. S. Coleman, *The Politics of the Developing Areas* (1960), p. 542,
listing developing countries according to eleven indexes of economic development, ranked
both Nigeria and Pakistan below Angola, the Belgian Congo, Saudi Arabia, or Viet Nam.
[3] See Chapter 12, sections 4 and 5, esp. pp. 303–4, 306–8.

maintenance of national unity. The disintegration of the Muslim League and the growth of provincialism in Pakistan illustrated this danger. Similar tendencies have also been apparent in India and Malaya, but in these two cases the ability of a major political party, through skilful leadership, to remain dominant for a considerable period after federation has helped to contain the shift in the equilibrium of social pressures.

The timing of independence from alien rule may have an important bearing on the play of social forces within a young federation. Where independence virtually coincided with the creation of a new federation, as in India and Pakistan, federal unity faced the danger of early evaporation. One might expect, then, that in a colonial federation, where the drive for independence continued for some time after its formation, federal unity would be enhanced during its critical early years. This was certainly the predominant pattern during the Malayan campaign for 'merdeka', and during the period of inter-regional compromises in Nigeria 1957–60. But this has not always been true. Post-federation movements for self-government have sometimes strained rather than encouraged national unity by arousing regional or minority fears over the situation that would follow independence. The disruptions within the West Indies and Central Africa were prime examples of this tendency, but the agitation of intra-regional minorities in Nigeria which reached a peak during 1957–9, and the controversy within the Malayan Alliance over certain provisions of the independence constitution, show that there too similar anxieties were at work. Moreover, in some instances, the achievement of independence has actually increased, rather than weakened, federal unity by giving the central government greater responsibilities and so enhancing its prestige. This helps to explain in some measure the steady growth in the political influence of the Nigerian Federal Government, the further concentration of central authority in Malaya between 1957 and 1963, and the continued strength of the Indian Union Government.

Continued economic hopes and expectations, and the centralized and co-ordinated planning necessary to fulfil these, have often increased national unity after federation. Most notable in this respect has been the role of centralized planning in India and Pakistan, but the growing realization within Nigeria of economic interdependence, and amongst the settlers in the Rhodesias the economic achievements popularly attributed to federation, were other instances. On the other hand, controversies over economic development have sometimes undermined such tendencies. The East Bengali complaints of economic neglect by Karachi, the dissatisfaction of the north-eastern Malay states, the disputes over Nyasaland's lack of economic benefits from federation, the resentment of Northern Rhodesians at having to subsidize the other territories, the economic and financial disagreements between Union and state governments in India, and the West Indian dissension over customs union and central economic powers, were examples.

Emergency conditions have also tended to rally support for centralized action, especially in the Asian federations. India and Pakistan, for instance, have been faced by both external and internal crises which have contributed to the concentration of central power. Besides the external threats to security arising out of their mutual hostility and from the menace of Chinese encroachment, there have been internal administrative, economic, and constitutional emergencies requiring central initiative at the times of partition, the integration of the princely states, the reorganization of regional units, foreign exchange crises, and political instability in regional governments. In Malaya the terrorist emergency lasting over a decade resulted in the centralization of administration and the encouragement of anti-communist national consciousness. The bellicose Indonesian 'confrontation' of Malaysia after its formation initially helped to close ranks among the territories and racial groups of the new federation, provoked an overwhelming Alliance victory in the 1964 elections, and added to central power by making necessary the declaration of a state of emergency within a year of the federation's birth. Sometimes, however, emergencies have had a dual effect, affecting unity negatively as well as positively. The Central African emergencies of 1959, for instance, resulted in inter-governmental co-operation and fostered settler solidarity, but they also reinforced northern African opposition and awoke the British Government to the strength of the 'winds of change'. The Western Nigerian emergency of 1962 provided a telling demonstration of the potential power of the central government and in so doing strengthened its political influence immensely, but at the same time it provoked increased Yoruba regional consciousness, and resulted eventually in a realignment of the federal alliances among regional political parties. Of the new federations, only in the West Indies was there no comparable emergency affecting the balance of forces after its formation.

Another factor affecting the social equilibrium after federation has been the administration of foreign affairs. Nehru's distinctive foreign policy and his role on the world stage much enhanced Indian unity, and Tunku Abdul Rahman's stand on South Africa's membership in the Commonwealth helped to express the multi-racial unity of Malaya. In some instances, however, notably East Bengali cultural affinity with West Bengal, the clash of Northern Nigeria's sympathy for Britain and for the Islamic Arab world with the desire of radical southerners for neutralist foreign policies, and the Malay affinity for non-communist and hence non-Chinese allies, foreign policy has caused internal dissensions. In the Southern Cameroons and in Nyasaland, growing consciousness of closer affinities with neighbouring external territories even encouraged demands for outright secession.

The degree of inter-territorial contact made possible by the system of internal communications has also affected national unity after federation. Where communications have remained relatively inadequate, as in the West Indies and Pakistan, regional feelings of isolation and remoteness, if anything, gathered strength. By contrast the improvement of communications in Nigeria has contributed noticeably to increased inter-regional contact.

The constant self-assertion of local interests and of demands for regional autonomy has itself often had a cumulative effect. The unremitting campaigns for cultural regionalism in India, East Pakistan, and Nigeria, the Malay stress upon local historical and legal identity in reaction to Chinese influence in central government, the repeated affirmation of African opposition to federation in Nyasaland and Northern Rhodesia, and the continued emphasis upon separate island interests in the West Indies, accentuated regional divisions and even, on occasion, made constitutional revision necessary. The strength of these pressures is illustrated by the frequency with which secession has been advocated. Apart from the actual secessions of the Southern Cameroons in 1961, Jamaica and Trinidad in 1962, Nyasaland and Northern Rhodesia, agreed upon in 1963, and Singapore in 1965, there have been secession movements in Penang in 1949, among the Naga tribes of India since 1954, in southern India over a number of years, in East Bengal in 1954, and in each of the Nigerian regions at different times.[1]

Sometimes, the extremely precarious nature of the original equilibrium of social forces has itself become a new factor contributing to continued unity. In India, Malaya, and Nigeria, where no group could hope to dominate easily, political leaders have in the early years seen the necessity of making compromises in order to preserve unity. By contrast, where one group has been sufficiently strong to impose its own will, federal unity has deteriorated. Jamaica, for instance, was able to contemplate insisting upon her own terms for remaining a member. Northern Nigeria and East Bengal also had preponderant populations, but this was partially offset by relative economic backwardness. In Central Africa, because the Africans formed such an overwhelming proportion of the population, they could think in terms of potential majority rule, and the settlers in turn were induced to think of oligarchy as the only way to preserve their influence.

Constitutions themselves have entered into and become part of the complex pattern of social pressures by generating new loyalties and creating vested interests. There are a few signs, for instance, that the federal constitutions of India, Malaya, and Nigeria, by allaying some of the fears of regional groups and by encouraging inter-regional co-operative machinery and compromises, have each contributed to a sense of common nationality. On the other hand, regional loyalties have often been hardened at the same time by federal constitutions. The artificial regions of Nigeria have proved surprisingly stable, Indian linguistic regionalism has been reinforced by the revision of state boundaries, the provincial consciousness of East Bengal was further enhanced by political autonomy, local particularism has been emphasized in

[1] See Chapter 12, section 5.

Malaya, and a new Malawi nationalism has solidified in Nyasaland. Federal constitutions, it would appear, have themselves tended to encourage both unity and diversity.

The net effect of all these many factors has varied in the different federations since their formation.[1] The strongest pressures for increased centralization have occurred within Malaya where, as a result, by 1962 the concentration of central power verged on the unitary.[2] Local interests continued to express themselves, as indicated by the deference shown to state governments in the operation of the 1948 constitution, and by the local successes of the Pan-Malay Islamic Party in the 1959 elections, but the campaign to stamp out terrorism during the Emergency, the drive for 'merdeka' up to 1957, and the Malay determination to concentrate power at the centre in their own hands, were powerful forces for greater centralization. With the creation of a wider Malaysia, this trend was in some measure offset by the necessity to accommodate the special local interests of Singapore and the Borneo states, but Singapore's secession in 1965 has left the centralizing forces dominant.

In Nigeria too, the trend up to 1963 was towards increased unity, although the divisive forces had not lost their potency. In the period before independence, northern fears of domination by modernized southerners, southern anxiety over the size and conservatism of the Northern Region, and the agitation of intra-regional minorities for their own autonomy, contributed to the spirit of apprehension dominating the 1957–8 conferences. This was evident in the controversies at that time over the control of the police, the creation of new states, the contents of the bill of rights, and the division of financial resources. The continued tension between centrifugal and centripetal tendencies since independence has been apparent in the crises over the central exercise of emergency powers in the Western Region, over the creation of a Mid-Western Region, and over the 1962–3 census results. Nevertheless, between 1954 and 1963 the persistence of regional loyalties, focused in the predominantly regional character of the political parties, was counterbalanced by the compelling economic interdependence, by the pressure for independence, and after 1960 by the increased prestige of the independent central government and its leadership in economic planning.[3] More recently, however, the election crises of 1964–5 have made clear just how fragile Nigerian unity remains.

In India since 1950 two opposite and highly dynamic forces have continued to operate. Linguistic provincialism, reinforced by regional caste lobbies and economic interests, has exerted a constant pressure resulting, despite the reluctance of Congress leaders, in the reorganization of state boundaries.

---

[1] For the actual extent of authority assigned to governments in each federation, see Chapter 8, section 5.

[2] See, for instance, *Constitution Amendment Act, 1960* (F. 10/1960), esp. ss. 12, 28.

[3] The secession of the Southern Cameroons was an exception to this general trend, however.

These regional forces continue to consolidate their strength. They have given rise to a new generation of increasingly influential party leaders rooted primarily in state politics, and there has been a gradual weakening of the grip of the central organs of the Congress Party upon state politics. Thus there has been a shift in the political centre of gravity towards the states. Nevertheless, the desire for unity has remained a continuing and potent aspiration, finding expression in unified economic planning, the continued dominance of the centralized Congress Party in central and state governments, the All-India outlook of the Indian Administrative Service, and the willingness of the central government to use its emergency powers in the states. Moreover, the Chinese invasion of 1962 provoked a renewed emphasis upon national unity, giving further momentum to the forces for centralization and counteracting, at least temporarily, the strong and persistent forces for disunity.

In the other three federations there was a marked shift in the direction of disintegration. In Pakistan, for instance, although Islam, the unremitting hostility to India, and the centralized bureaucracy, had a unifying effect, linguistic provincialism continued to mount, even after the imposition of military rule in 1958. Separatism was strongest in East Pakistan because of its social and cultural distinctiveness, its geographical remoteness, and the resentment of Bengalis at being treated as a colony by the distant central government, first in Karachi and then in Rawalpindi. Thus, in spite of concessions to Bengali feeling in the 1962 constitution, separatism has remained a force in East Pakistan.

In the West Indies the forces for cohesion, unrooted in popular support, proved too weak to sustain the growth of the federation. Island parochialism persisted, particularly in Jamaica because of its relative size, remoteness from the other islands, its lack of influence upon the central government and civil service, and the increasing, rather than decreasing, distinctiveness of the Jamaican economy.[1] Countering the Jamaican views were the demands for a closer and more effective union pressed by leaders in Trinidad and some of the smaller islands. Because the economic issues had been left undecided in the constitution, the tension between these opposite pressures was focused in the early years of the West Indies Federation upon the negotiations for a customs union and upon associated revisions of the constitutional structure. In the controversies that ensued, federal unity proved too fragile to survive.

In Rhodesia and Nyasaland it was the continued intensification of African political consciousness expressly antithetical to federation which made federal government impossible to maintain. The apparent economic expansion within the federation, and the persistent efforts of the settlers to ensure their political

---

[1] For instance, between 1951 and 1957 Jamaica's *per capita* income increased by 98 per cent., while that of Barbados increased by only 37 per cent., and those of the small islands by even less. See A. Etzioni, 'The West Indian Federation: A Constitution Against Reality', *I.P.S.A. Sixth World Congress, Geneva, 1964, Federalism /11*, pp. 10–11.

supremacy by strengthening the central government, were factors for increased centralization. But counter to this ran the 'pathological' abhorrence of any political union on the part of Africans in the two northern territories, a dislike fostered by their frustration at the slowness of the implementation of partnership and by their apprehension at the signs of the dominance of Southern Rhodesian settlers within the federation. The mounting strength of this opposition expressed itself in the developments between 1957 and 1963, erupting in the emergencies of 1959 and culminating in the secessions of Nyasaland and Northern Rhodesia.

Several implications follow from the dynamic character of federal societies. First, it would seem that in societies where such powerful and opposing social forces continue to exert themselves, the quality of leadership, especially in the early years after the achievement of federation, may be crucial. The continued unity of India and Malaya has owed much to such men as Nehru and Tunku Abdul Rahman. In Nigeria no political leader has dominated the scene, and initially unity was hampered by the refusal of major party leaders to participate in central politics, but in the decade after 1954 the co-operation among most of the major regional leaders, and Prime Minister Balewa's skill in sustaining coalition governments in Lagos, fostered Nigerian unity. It is significant that the federations which have suffered the greatest difficulties have been those where strong national leadership failed to develop after federation, as in Pakistan following the deaths of Mohammad Ali Jinnah and Liaquat Ali Khan, and in the West Indies, where the timid reluctance of the major island leaders to enter central politics weakened the popular support and the effectiveness of the federal government. Difficulties have also been stirred where national leaders have failed to recognize the supreme importance of tact and conciliation in federal politics, examples being the provocation of Jamaicans by Grantley Adams on the income-tax issue, and the antagonizing of the Africans of Nyasaland and Northern Rhodesia by settler politicians, especially by the bellicose pronouncements of Roy Welensky.

Secondly, because the pattern of social forces is not static but changing, the timing of federation may be extremely important. If attempted at the moment when the balance of social pressures favours a federal compromise, the federal institutions may go on to generate loyalties sufficient for their maintenance. But if there is a long delay, the right moment may pass. For instance, despite the initial enthusiasm in 1963 for an East African federation uniting Tanganyika, Uganda, and Kenya, as negotiations progressed it soon became apparent that, with the experience of separate independence, the individual territories were less and less willing to sacrifice their sovereignty. In the West Indies the negotiations dragged on for a decade, and by the time federation was finally achieved most of the initial enthusiasm had worn off. On the other hand, in Central Africa federation was rushed because the settlers, fearing a change in British policy towards support of black African nationalism, and the British Government, fearing that Southern Rhodesia might be lost to apartheid, both considered this the last opportunity for a union. The general conviction that 'the sands were running out' resulted in the ignoring of African opposition to the scheme, thus in African eyes discrediting the federation as an imposed solution.[1] These examples illustrate how crucial the timing of the institution of a federal system may be to its success.

Thirdly, the dynamic character and changing economic requirements of federal societies, particularly those in former colonial areas undergoing rapid economic development, point to the need for constitutional flexibility and adaptability. Some rigidity may be necessary to ensure regional confidence in the federal compromise as a safeguard for local interests, but if federal institutions are too inflexible, they may soon cease to reflect the changing degree of political and economic integration within these societies. Adaptability may be especially important where the original political compromises were arrived at under special circumstances: where the imperial power played an influential role in constitution-framing, or where the enthusiasm for independence exaggerated briefly the desires for union. In such instances there may be a need during the early years for adjustment and continued constitution-making. The reorganization of Indian states, the completely revised Malayan constitution of 1957, the widening of Malaya into Malaysia, and the many revisions made to the Nigerian federal system during the period 1954-63, point to the value of federal experiments which can be adjusted on the basis of experience.[2]

[1] P. Mason, *Year of Decision* (1960), pp. 27, 35–36.
[2] See Chapter 12, sections 4–7 below.

6

THE VARIETY OF FEDERAL SOCIETIES

1. *Degrees of integration*

IN the preceding three chapters we examined the social pressures which influenced the adoption of a federal system as distinct from other forms of political organization. But the federal institutions themselves have been far from identical. While the term 'federal' signifies a political system within which neither level of government is permanently subordinate to the other, this classification covers a whole range of compromises, from relatively 'tight' federations within which most of the services and functions are concentrated in the central government, to very 'loose' ones in which only very limited responsibilities are assigned to the central government. In all the new Commonwealth federations, even where federalism itself was accepted with little dispute as the only practicable solution, there have been intense controversies over the precise shape the federal institutions should take, and particularly over the scope of powers to be assigned to each of the tiers of government. Besides the distribution of responsibilities, there has also been room within the general outlines of the federal form of government for variations in the number and size of regional units, the nature of inter-governmental institutions if any, the structure and regional composition of the institutions of central government, the recognition of official languages and religions, special safeguards for minorities, the site and status of capital cities, and the procedures for constitutional amendment. In this chapter, therefore, we shall turn to a study of those factors which have influenced the varying forms which federal institutions have taken in different countries.[1]

One of the most important factors affecting the precise pattern of federal government within a country has been the degree of social integration. To return to the metaphor of the spectrum of societies graded in terms of relative degrees of territorial integration, within that section of the spectrum identifiable as the federal 'colour' because of a general equilibrium between integrating and disintegrating pressures, there is room for a considerable range of 'shades' of social cohesion.[2] Such variations among federal societies have stemmed from differences in the strength and relative significance of particular motives for union or for regional autonomy.

The marked central bias of the Indian constitution, for instance, flowed from

---

[1] For details of the federal institutions themselves see Part III.
[2] See Chapter 5, section 1, above.

a profound and firm experience of unity during British rule, from the common revolt against imperial rule, and from hopes for economic development. In the Federation of Malaya Agreement, 1948, the strong central government and constitutional flexibility, aiming at administrative efficiency, were initially mainly the result of British insistence. The revised federal structure of 1957 was clearly a synthesis of the demands of the various groups composing the Alliance, but reflected the dominant role of the U.M.N.O. which favoured a concentration of central power and the preservation of Malay predominance. Thus a strong central government was maintained but the historic rights of the states were not destroyed, all communities shared rights of citizenship but the special position of the Malays was safeguarded, constitutional amendment was made more rigid but remained by no means inflexible, English was retained as an official language but not Chinese or Indian, and Islam became the state religion although the state remained secular. In Central Africa, where the settlers in the Rhodesias played such a dominant role, their pressure for greater centralization manifested itself in progressive additions to the central powers, and in changes in the form of the African Affairs Board during the period of pre-federal negotiations.

In the other federations the weight of the dominant social forces lay clearly in favour of a greater concentration of functions in the regional governments. This was most evident in the West Indies. The Montego Bay Conference and the Rance Committee, recognizing the impact of geography and of social and economic diversity, recommended a relatively weak central government, but regional misgivings were so intense that in the course of the following negotiations central powers and finances were further reduced. Solutions rejected at Montego Bay and by the Rance Committee as inadequate were adopted, central power over income tax and free movement was postponed, and the customs union issue was left for later settlement.[1] The result was a central government with a revenue of less than 6 per cent. of that of Trinidad, the wealthiest territorial government.[2]

The regional emphasis in Nigeria, although nothing like so extreme in its effect on the distribution of functions, reflected the fears of each region that the central government would be controlled by the other regions. In the 1953 compromise the N.P.C. gave up its programme of virtual secession, the N.C.N.C. gave up its advocacy of a quasi-unitary federation, and the Action Group views, favouring autonomous and powerful regions, prevailed as being midway between the others.

In Pakistan the growing force of Bengali provincialism made itself felt, especially after the 1954 elections. The successive Basic Principles Committee Reports, and the modifications to the draft constitution prepared for the

---

[1] Col. no. 218/1948, p. 99; Cmd. 7291/1948, pp. 15–16; Col. no. 255/1950, paras. 29–30, 33–35; Cmd. 9733/1956, paras. 25–30; Col. no. 315/1955.

[2] See Tables 10A and 10B, p. 375.

second Constituent Assembly, displayed a progressive movement towards greater provincial powers. But national political leaders and bureaucrats, favouring administrative centralization and fearful that any devolution of authority would contribute to the powerful forces for disintegration, proved reluctant to make more than nominal concessions, and consequently the degree of centralization was at least equal to that in India. The 1962 Pakistan constitution continued this trend. In response to continued regional pressures, certain functions were passed to the provinces, and the scope of central powers was reduced by leaving to the provinces all matters formerly on the concurrent legislative list, but at the same time these concessions were potentially nullified by the insertion of a number of unitary features.

Social pressures have also continued to affect the form of federal institutions after their creation. Where the original constitutional compromises failed to reflect accurately the balance of these continuing social forces, or where the precise balance of social forces within a society has itself shifted, there has been a tendency for federal government as practised to diverge from the strict stipulations of the constitution or even for the constitution itself to be altered. The effect of the failure of constitutional structures to express fully the desires and aspirations of the societies on which they were based is illustrated by the reluctance of the Malayan, Nigerian, and West Indian central governments in the early years after federation to exercise their full powers, by the movements for linguistic states in India and Nigeria, by East Bengal's continued demands for greater autonomy, by the resentment of Africans in the Central African protectorates at their lack of political advance after federation, by the disappointment of Trinidad with the anaemic West Indies Federation, and by Jamaica's demands for even greater economic decentralization. These examples suggest that the stability of a federal compromise will depend, in the first place, on how accurately the distribution of authority and the particular institutions initially adopted reflect the desired degree of political and economic integration, and secondly, as already noted in the previous chapter, upon the flexibility of the federal system enabling it to adapt to alterations in the balance of social forces themselves after federation.

One might be tempted to suspect that in the early years 'tight' federations would generally tend to become looser, as exemplified by India, Pakistan until the trend was arrested by military rule, Rhodesia and Nyasaland, and previously Canada, and that 'loose' federations would generally grow tighter, as illustrated by Nigeria and earlier by the United States and Australia. This will not stand as a general rule, however, for Malaya, a 'tight' federation, moved in the direction of increased centralization in practice, while the West Indies, the 'loosest' of the federations, simply disintegrated. Thus it appears that the real key to the particular pattern of evolution in a given federation lies in the dominant forces peculiar to that society.

Variations in federal institutions may be due not only to varying degrees of social integration, however, but also to the way in which diversities have been distributed. The distinction between territorially diverse societies and plural societies has led to the suggestion that among the new federations a contrast can be drawn between territorial federations such as India, Pakistan, Nigeria, and the West Indies, and racial federations such as Malaya and Rhodesia and Nyasaland.[1] Francis Carnell has argued that in the latter, communities being geographically intermingled, the political security of any particular race 'depends on its ability to keep control at the centre over as wide a range of powers as possible'.[2] By contrast with the other federations, Malaya and Rhodesia and Nyasaland, he has noted, have exhibited a high degree of centralization, a more rapid development of central political parties and leaders, and an emphasis on questions of electoral franchise, citizenship rights, and communal representation in central government, rather than on issues of the distribution of powers and finances between governments, federal capital sites, or territorial representation in the central government.

But although the distinction between territorial and racial federations points to some significant characteristics, the contrast is not so clear-cut. In the first place, the difference is not so much one of kind as one of degree. As we noted in Chapter 4, even in Malaya and Central Africa there were very significant territorial differences in racial proportion, as well as in economic, historic, and in Central Africa, tribal interests. Moreover, in the other federations regional political units have rarely coincided, or could coincide precisely, with all the forms of diversity spanning different areas. Furthermore, while Malaya and Rhodesia and Nyasaland both exhibited tendencies to greater centralization, these so-called racial federations each, nevertheless, also experienced the problems supposedly characteristic of territorial federations. In Central Africa there were virile secession movements, controversies over the allocation of revenues and legislative powers, disputes over the site of the federal capital, and differences over territorial representation in the institutions of central government. There have been secession demands and controversies over the allocations of revenues and legislative powers in Malaya and Malaysia too.[3] Moreover, in 1946–8, it was the Malays through U.M.N.O. who, as a safeguard against the danger of a central concentration of authority which might fall into Chinese hands, insisted upon land being left under the control of the states. On the other side, among the territorial federations India and Pakistan displayed a high degree of centralization.

[1] Carnell, 'Political Implications of Federalism in New States', op. cit., pp. 49–53; Rothchild, *Toward Unity in Africa*, pp. 10–12; D. V. Cowen, 'Constitution-making for a Democracy', *Optima* (Supplement), (March 1960), pp. 33–41; S. A. de Smith, *The New Commonwealth and its Constitutions* (1964), pp. 256–9.

[2] Carnell, op. cit., p. 50.

[3] See, for instance, *Secession of Penang and Province Wellesley Petition*, 12 October 1949; *Report of the Committee Appointed to Review the Financial Provisions* (1955); Col. no. 330/1957, paras. 82, 90–96; Cmnd. 210/1957, paras. 26, 28, 35. In the final negotiations for Singapore's accession, the financial arrangements proved the most troublesome issue.

Furthermore, India, Pakistan, and Nigeria have in practice provided representation for non-territorial religious and social groups in the central executive, and there have been disputes over electoral and franchise arrangements in Nigeria and Pakistan.[1] The difference between territorial and racial federations, although by no means insignificant, is more one of degree than of kind.

The comparison among the new federations is drawn better, therefore, if it is made in terms of varying degrees of regional homogeneity. The heterogeneity of regional units has been most marked in the 'racial' federations of Malaya and Rhodesia and Nyasaland, but in other federations, especially certain areas of India, Pakistan, and Nigeria, sectional interests operating concurrently at a variety of levels—some regional, some inter-regional, and some intra-regional—have made the creation of homogeneous units extremely difficult or impossible.[2] Even in the Caribbean, Trinidad itself represented a plural society. The degree of regional heterogeneity does appear generally to have a significant effect upon the form of federal institutions. Where the regional units have been relatively heterogeneous, as in Malaya, Rhodesia and Nyasaland, India before 1956, unified West Pakistan after 1955, and Nigeria, there has been considerable pressure for special safeguards for minorities or communities within the regions, for centralization of power, and even for subordination of the regional governments.[3] Where plausible, there have also been demands for the revision of territorial units to coincide as far as possible with the dominant social interests, although this has often been resisted on the grounds that new intra-regional minorities would be created in the process.[4]

Thus it is clear that the distribution of social diversities as well as the degree of social integration has had a significant influence upon the particular form of federal institutions adopted.

2. *The evolution of federations*

The distinction has sometimes been made between federations formed by 'aggregation' and those formed by 'devolution'.[5] In the former, sometimes considered the orthodox process, federations come into existence through an agreement between a number of states, hitherto separate, transferring some of their functions or services to a new central government. In the latter, unitary political systems are transformed into federations by the surrender of authority to provincial adminstrations in order to accommodate disruptive local loyalties. There is a third possibility: federations may evolve by a complex process of both aggregation and devolution. In considering these

[1] See Chapters 8 and 11, below.
[2] See Chapter 4, section 1, and Chapter 7, section 3.
[3] See Chapter 7, section 3.   [4] See Chapter 7, section 3.
[5] Carnell, 'Political Implications of Federalism in New States', op. cit., pp. 53–55; J. R. Hicks, *Essays in World Economics* (1959), pp. 217–18; Rothchild, *Toward Unity in Africa*, pp. 2–3.

different forms of evolution to federal government it is necessary also to distinguish between social and constitutional processes, for it is possible, as illustrated by the case of Nigeria, for a process of constitutional 'devolution' from a formally unitary colonial administration to coincide with a social 'aggregation' of culturally and historically distinct groups, the two processes meeting in a political federation.

India, Pakistan, and Nigeria have frequently been classified as examples of federation by devolution. Indeed, constitution-makers in these countries have often considered their own federations unique in this respect, overlooking comparable earlier South American experiments.[1] Nevertheless, in the cases of India, Pakistan, and Nigeria, it would be more accurate to say that, like Canada, these federations were the product of both devolution and aggregation. In India and Pakistan the achievement of provincial autonomy in 1935 was the culmination of a long history of increasing decentralization within British India, but in both, the creation of the new independent federations required the accession of legally sovereign princely states, and this was achieved only after considerable negotiation. Thus it was possible for Indians to say: 'As a result of the political unification brought about by integration of Princely States and jurisdictions within the sub-continent of India, the country has attained a degree of political unity never witnessed before for almost a couple of thousand years.'[2] Nigeria too appeared ostensibly to be an example of federation by decentralization, for the constitutions of 1946, 1951, and 1954 progressively devolved authority to the regions until in 1954 they became fully autonomous. But while this description is constitutionally accurate, it is misleading, for despite the earlier unitary amalgamation of Nigeria by Lugard, there had in practice been an almost complete division of administration between north and south until 1945. Indeed, in that year Governor Richards wrote: 'At present no unity exists nor does the constitution encourage its growth.'[3] In terms of social integration, therefore, the Richards Constitution of 1946 represented 'the beginning of the fusion of innumerable small units into three and from these three into one'.[4] In this respect the evolution of Nigerian federal government was comparable to the Malayan experience: in each, for a brief period after 1946, unitary government was imposed by Britain as a means to increased unity but found to be unsatisfactory, only a federal solution proving acceptable. It is fair to say: 'federalism in Nigeria is not a fragmentation of a long-established natural unity, but in some measure a reversion, though with great differences, to the past.'[5]

[1] C.A.I., *Debates*, vol. v, p. 80; A. K. Brohi, *Fundamental Law of Pakistan* (1958), pp. 58–59; Nigeria, *Proceedings of General Conference, Ibadan* (1950), pp. 37, 68, 83.
[2] *Report of the Official Language Commission, 1956* (1957), p. 251.
[3] Cmd. 6599/1945, Governor's Despatch, para. 3.
[4] Sir B. H. Bourdillon, 'The Nigerian Constitution', *African Affairs*, xlv (1946), p. 92.
[5] Nigeria, *Report of the Commission on Revenue Allocation (1951)*, para. 8.

The federations of Rhodesia and Nyasaland, the West Indies, Malaya, and Malaysia were all ostensibly formed by aggregation. This was clearly the case in Central Africa where, with the exception of loose consultative machinery, there had been no previous political or legal links between distinct colonial units. The same could generally be said of the West Indies, although the disbanding of the Leeward Islands Federation, and the return of some powers to its constituent islands at the time the wider but weaker federation was formed, involved an element of devolution.[1] The federations of Malaya and Malaysia were ostensibly formed by aggregation, but were actually the result of a complex process. Up to 1946 the legal sovereignty of the states was always explicitly declared, and it continued to be recognized in the Federation of Malaya Agreements of 1948 and 1957 which both required the assent of the rulers of the federating states.[2] But the abortive Malayan Union scheme of 1946 left its influence upon the federal constitutions which followed. Examples of this devolutionary aspect in the development of federal government in Malaya were the degree of centralization under the Agreement of 1948, the splitting of the former colony into separate settlements in Penang, Malacca, and Singapore, the increased autonomy achieved in 1948 by each of the former Federated Malay States, the reformulation of the distribution of powers in 1957 which was designed to give the states a greater measure of autonomy in limited but important fields, and the grant of equal status to the settlements in 1957.

Of the new federations, then, Rhodesia and Nyasaland and the West Indies may be classified as, basically, examples of federation by aggregation, while the remainder evolved through a combination of devolution and aggregation.

These different processes of federal evolution have influenced the form of each federal system.[3] The impact of the devolutionary process has been apparent in all three Asian federations. It helps to explain the continued concentration of central power, the relative subordination of the regional units, the flexible constitutional amendment procedures, the unitary judicial systems and inter-governmental civil services, and the strength of the national political parties already existing before federalization. The effect of the devolutionary process in Nigeria was not as powerful, but it accounts for the relatively strong central powers assigned by the federal constitutions of Nigeria. It would appear also that the subsequent instability of regional boundaries in India, Pakistan, and Nigeria was related partly to their devolutionary origin and brevity of historical identity.

The process of aggregation has also had distinctive effects. It helps to

---

[1] *Leeward Islands Act, 1956* (4 & 5 Eliz. 2, ch. 23).

[2] *F.M.S., Treaty of Federation, 1895*, conclusion; *F.M.S. Agreement, 1909*, art. 11; *F.M.S. Agreement, 1927*, art. 15; *Fed. of Malaya Agreement, 1948*, preamble; *Fed. of Malaya Agreement, 1957*, preamble.

[3] For constitutional details, see Part III.

explain the weak constitutional powers of the West Indian central government, the regionalism in Nigerian politics which discouraged the central government from exercising its constitutional powers, the rigid amendment processes in these two federations, and the establishment of strictly dual civil services in the West Indian and Central African federations. The process of federating formerly distinct units also accounts for the conjunction of regions with differing constitutional status within Malaya in 1948, Malaysia in 1963, India, especially before 1956, Pakistan before 1955, and Rhodesia and Nyasaland in 1953, and for the general stability of regional boundaries in Malaya, the West Indies, and Central Africa. It was also a contributory factor towards the confederal character of the West Indian political parties. Rhodesia and Nyasaland, although a federation by aggregation, possessed some of the characteristics one would expect of a devolutionary federation. It was relatively centralized and the central political parties developed rapidly. These features would appear to have been due to certain other factors, notably the process of pre-federal negotiation, which was primarily between Southern Rhodesia and the British Government acting on behalf of the other territories, and the oligarchic character of federal politics in Central Africa.[1]

The form of each federation and the scope of central or state powers has also been affected by the particular conditions existing at the time the constitution was framed. In India and Pakistan the communal frenzy and disruption of partition coincided with independence, the threat of balkanization due to the lapse of paramountcy and the attempts of the larger princely states to remain independent, the early hostilities over Kashmir, and the administrative problems associated with the initial period of independence. It meant that both federations were born in a period of political and economic crisis. This was further heightened by the immediate demands for linguistic provinces in India, and by the controversies in Pakistan over the role of Islam in the constitution. The result in each was a quest for stability expressed in the establishment of strong central governments with extensive emergency powers, in the reliance upon the tried constitutional framework of the Government of India Act, 1935, and in early attempts to dampen pressures for linguistic provinces and provincial autonomy.[2] In India, for instance, because of anxiety over the centrifugal forces encouraging disintegration, centralizing constitutional provisions were defended as necessary to prevent imminent balkanization, critics being disarmed by promises that 'normally' many of these central powers would not be used.[3] In Malaya the terrorist emergency delayed the introduction of the elective principle, concerted the operation of the armed forces, police, and certain civil departments and agencies, and led to the inclusion of

---

[1] See sections 3 and 6 of this chapter.

[2] C.A.I., *Second Report of the Union Powers Committee* (1947), para. 2; C.A.I., *Debates*, vol. vii, pp. 34–35; vol. xi, pp. 515, 647; C.A.P. (first), *Debates*, vol. v, p. 5.

[3] C.A.I., *Debates*, vol. iv, pp. 897, 902, 983; vol. v, pp. 169–70; vol. vii, p. 247; vol. viii, pp. 430–2; vol. ix, p. 177; vol. xi, pp. 515, 647.

relatively extensive emergency powers in the 1957 constitution.[1] Thus, common to all three Asian federations was the impact, at the moment of their formation, of major external and internal threats to security, encouraging the concentration of central powers.

In the other federations at the time of their establishment there were no comparable emergency conditions encouraging centralization to such a degree. Nevertheless, in Central Africa the advance of black nationalism to the north and white nationalism to the south, and the potential meeting of these in the Rhodesias, gave urgency to the search for a compromise based on a solid stable federation. In Nigeria the internal crisis culminating in the Kano riots emphasized the deterioration in relations between north and south, and the danger of disintegration, thus inducing the regional leaders to accept the compromises of 1953–4. Significantly, in the West Indies, where at the time of federation there were no external threats, and where with the progressive political advance of the islands there was no feeling of urgency, the pressure for concentrating power in the central government was weakest.

3. *Procedures of constitution-making*

The procedure followed and the groups represented in the preparation of a constitution are likely to have some effect on the form of the federal institutions devised. When we look at the negotiations which preceded the recent federal constitutions we are confronted with a bewildering variety: constituent assemblies, local and Whitehall conferences, inter-governmental committees, independent commissions, constitutional advisers, referenda, and discussions in legislative councils. The main problem in deciding upon a procedure is to determine who should participate and what weight should be given to different groups in the negotiations. The answer is rarely straightforward, for it is precisely questions of representation and relative authority within the constitutional structure that the negotiators themselves will be concerned with deciding. This explains why the issue of constituent assembly procedure led to the final breakdown of the Cabinet Mission Plan in India in 1946, why the Chinese in Malaya complained in 1946–7 of U.M.N.O. predominance on the Working Committee, why Nigerians favouring a unitary structure were critical of the dominant role of the regional political parties in the constitutional conferences in 1953–4, and why Africans in the Central African protectorates resented the imposition of a federation to which they had never consented.

Constituent assemblies were used only in India and Pakistan. In determining at the time of partition whether the representatives of certain regions would remain with the Indian Constituent Assembly or transfer to the Pakistan Constituent Assembly, the decisions were made in several ways: in Bengal and Punjab by the provincial legislators representing Muslim majority

[1] Cmd. 9714/1956, paras. 1, 10; Col. no. 330/1957, paras. 172–5, 187–8.

districts, in Sind by the Provincial Legislative Assembly, in British Baluchistan by a meeting of tribal representatives, and in the North-West Frontier Province and Sylhet in Assam by referenda. Representation in both constituent assemblies was roughly one member for each million of population, members being indirectly elected by the existing provincial legislatures. In both assemblies representation for the princely states was negotiated at the time of their accession. In the Indian Constituent Assembly the representatives of these states formed a sizeable group, 89 out of a total strength of 324, and although the states initially acceded on only a limited list of subjects, their representatives were permitted to take part in all constitution-making.[1] In the first Pakistan Constituent Assembly, of the authorized 79 members, 4 represented acceding states, and 6 (5 for Punjab and 1 for Sind) were additions made to give added representation to areas where the flood of refugees had increased the population.[2] The principle of parity of membership for East and West Pakistan, a source of controversy in the debates of the first Assembly over the proposed central legislature, was applied by the Governor-General's order to the second Constituent Assembly itself.[3]

In the deliberations of these constituent assemblies minority and regional interests gained extensive opportunity for expression. The provisions permitting dual membership in provincial legislatures and constituent assemblies ensured that provincial views were strongly presented. In addition, there were representatives of all the major minority groups present, and the delegates of the princely states played an important role in lobbying for maximum decentralization, especially in India where they constituted over a quarter of the members. In addition, in India the interim central government carried on continual negotiations with the provincial and state governments over the Draft Constitution, and a formal ratification of the Draft Constitution by the governments of the princely states was considered necessary.

But although regional groups played an important part in the preparation of the Indian and Pakistan constitutions, it was the assembly committees and the governing parties who dominated the process. Because the constituent assemblies were busy functioning also as interim legislatures, much of the work of constitutional preparation was delegated to committees. In the Indian Constituent Assembly, the Union Constitution Committee, the Provincial Constitution Committee, the Union Powers Committee, the Advisory Committee on Fundamental Rights, and the Expert Committee on Financial Provisions, were the main committees which established the fundamental principles of the future constitution. Their reports, little changed by the Assembly, were collated and embodied by the Drafting Committee into a

---

[1] C.A.I., *Debates*, vol. v, pp. 338, 358–60; vol. vii, pp. 4–5, 12–15.

[2] See Table 12A. As in India, the representatives of the acceding states were permitted to participate in all constitutional discussions and were not limited merely to those subjects listed in the initial accession. C.A.P. (first), *Debates*, vol. vi, pp. 31–32.

[3] G.G.O. 12/1955. See Table 12A.

Draft Constitution which was considered by the Assembly as a whole, and modified only in details. In Pakistan the main work of preparing the constitution fell in the first Constituent Assembly to the Basic Principles Committee and its three main sub-committees, the Sub-committee on Federal and Provincial Constitutions and Distribution of Powers, the Sub-committee on Franchise, and the Sub-committee on the Judiciary. The recommendations of the Basic Principles Committee raised considerable controversy, however, and reports were presented in 1950, 1952, and 1954 before approval was gained from the Assembly. In the second Assembly the Draft Constitution was actually prepared by the Ministry of Law, taking the B.P.C. Report approved in 1954 as its starting-point.[1]

In both India and Pakistan the governing parties were a dominant force in constitution-making. In the Indian Constituent Assembly the Congress Party never had a majority of less than two-thirds. Thus, although the Congress did try to avoid the appearance of a majoritarian tyranny and encouraged minority representation on committees, the real power of decision-making lay with the party caucus and leadership, most controversial issues being decided off the floor of the Constituent Assembly.[2] Nehru and Patel dominated the main committees and the debates on major issues, and although Ambedkar held the spotlight as chairman of the Drafting Committee, the real decisions were made in the Congress caucus, these being merely translated into constitutional language by the Drafting Committee.[3] Because the Congress had always favoured the centralization of power and had tended to a 'stepmotherly' outlook on the relation of the central government to the provinces, its predominance in the Constituent Assembly resulted in the establishment of a centralized federation with a variety of quasi-unitary central controls over the state governments. Moreover, because federation-n.aking was fundamentally conducted from above by a single dominant party, some of the process of bargaining absent in the formation of the federation was to assume increasing dimensions during the subsequent decade.

In Pakistan during most of the life of the first Constituent Assembly the main discussions were within the Muslim League, and decision-making was dominated by the League oligarchy. The Basic Principles Committee had a strong 'official' flavour, its membership being heavily weighted with central ministers, complemented by the chief ministers of the provinces and the Chief Justice of Pakistan. Despite containing the majority of Pakistan's population, East Bengal was consistently under-represented on the B.P.C. and its

---

[1] C.A.P. (second), *Debates*, vol. i, pp. 1791–2.

[2] See, for instance, C.A.I., *Debates*, vol. ii, pp. 308–27, 335; vol. iv, pp. 809–12; vol. v, pp. 134, 319. Of 7,635 amendments tabled, only 2,473 were actually moved (ibid., vol. xii, p. 972).

[3] Ambedkar, of his role as chairman of the Drafting Committee, later declared: 'I was a hack. I did what I was asked to do. I only carried out the wishes of the majority.' Quoted by Brecher, *Nehru*, p. 423.

sub-committees, a fact which helped to provoke Bengali discontent. Following the collapse of the Muslim League in the East Bengal elections of 1954, the party composition of the second Constituent Assembly was considerably altered. Consequently, it was a coalition of Muslim Leaguers from Punjab, favouring a unified West Pakistan, and United Front members from East Bengal, favouring increased provincial autonomy, that produced the new 1956 constitution.

The constituent assemblies of India and Pakistan were fully sovereign. In India the claim that this sovereignty was not dependent on the Indian Independence Act, 1947, went unchallenged, but in Pakistan, at the time of the Governor-General's dismissal of the first Constituent Assembly, the Federal Court ruled that the authority of the Assembly was derived from the British Act.[1] In either case, an important implication was the claim that the sovereignty of these federations stemmed not from the agreement of pre-existing sovereign units, but from a fully sovereign constituent assembly.[2] This assertion overstated the case, however, for it neglected the prior sovereignty of the princely states, which had made necessary the progressively wider instruments of accession, and the formal ratification of the constitution by them.[3] Nevertheless, it helps to explain the concentration of central power and the inclusion of regional constitutions in both the Indian and Pakistan constitutions, and the choice of the title 'Union' in India.[4]

In the colonial federations, Malaya, Nigeria, the West Indies, and Rhodesia and Nyasaland, the legal power to frame their constitutions rested with the United Kingdom, and these constitutions were originally promulgated by British statutory instruments.[5] But after the dismal failures of the British attempts to impose unitary unions in Malaya and Nigeria in 1946, the British Government was well aware of the need to seek effective compromises acceptable to the local peoples. A wide variety of expedients was resorted to in seeking solutions.

Generally, conferences were employed for the preparation of constitutional settlements. These conferences varied widely in membership and influence.

---

[1] C.A.I., *Debates*, vol. i, pp. 38–40, 49–51, 144, 285, 293; W. I. Jennings, *Constitutional Problems in Pakistan* (1957); K. C. Wheare, *The Constitutional Structure of the Commonwealth* (1960), pp. 95–103; *Federation of Pakistan* v. *Moulvi Tamizuddin Khan*, P.L.D. 1955, F.C. 240.

[2] C.A.I., *Debates*, vol. vii, p. 43; A. K. Brohi, *Fundamental Law of Pakistan* (1958), pp. 50–51. See also *The State of W. Bengal* v. *Union of India*, A.I.R. 1963, S.C. 1241, supporting this view.

[3] *White Paper on Indian States* (rev. ed., 1950), paras. 219, 221–3, App. LIV; Menon, *The Integration of the Indian States*, pp. 468–70; C.A.P. (first), *Debates*, vol. vi, pp. 17–32.

[4] C.A.I., *Debates*, vol. vii, p. 43.

[5] In Malaya, however, the historic legal sovereignty of the rulers in the states continued to be recognized, the federal constitutions of 1948 and 1957 being contained in agreements between Britain and the rulers. These agreements were in turn incorporated in British statutory instruments. The *Malaysia Act, 1963* (F. 26/1963), was also embodied in an intergovernmental agreement between Britain, Malaya, North Borneo, Sarawak, and Singapore (Cmnd. 2094/1963).

Some were local conferences held in the territories involved; many were held in London. Participants on different occasions included representatives of colonial governments, leaders of major colonial political parties, officials of the departments responsible for the territories, delegates indirectly elected, and rulers and chiefs. Sometimes much of the preparation of constitutional frameworks was delegated to important committees.[1]

In all this variety two principles can be discerned. First, the British Government generally attempted to include at these conferences the leaders of the major nationalist political parties in the territories involved, even when they were unrepresented in the local colonial governments, because until they were present to work out compromises amongst themselves, the solutions of the conferences were of little efficacy. Secondly, the British Government has usually tried to create a situation where those involved felt that they were really bargaining, working out a 'social contract', and not merely participating in a talking shop.[2] Significantly, in the one case where these principles were departed from, when during the creation of the Federation of Rhodesia and Nyasaland the British Government itself took the place of the Africans of the northern protectorates at the bargaining table, there resulted a degree of centralization which proved intolerable to the Africans. In the other colonial federations it was the nationalist political parties which shaped the federal systems. The Nigerian federal institutions embodied the inter-regional bargains hammered out by the major regional parties at the conferences in 1953, 1954, 1957, and 1958.[3] The Malayan compromises were largely worked out by the Working Committee in 1948, and by tough bargaining within the Alliance in 1957, both dominated by the U.M.N.O. Similarly, the Inter-Governmental Committee which worked out the constitutional arrangements for Malaysia was composed mostly of representatives of the territories involved. In the Caribbean during the series of constitutional conferences there was continual bargaining between the representatives of the island governments. Thus, with the exception of Rhodesia and Nyasaland, the colonial federations were far from imposed solutions.

Nevertheless, the British Government, as participator in the conferences and negotiations and as ultimate legal sovereign, has influenced the pattern of the federal institutions adopted in its colonies. The personalities of such Colonial

---

[1] Especially important were the Rance (Standing Closer Association Committee) and Standing Federation Committees in the West Indies (Col. no. 255/1950; Cmd. 9733/1956, paras. 50–53), the Working and Consultative Committees (1946–7) and the Working Party (1957) in Malaya (Cmd. 7171/1947, paras. 4–9; Cmnd. 210/1957, paras. 1–2), the Malaysia Solidarity Consultative Committee and the Malaysia Inter-Governmental Committee in Malaysia (Cmnd. 1794/1962, App. F.; Cmnd. 1954/1963).

[2] Hence in all the constitutional conferences, with the exception of the early examples of Montego Bay (1947) and Ibadan (1950), deliberations were not public.

[3] This pattern continued after independence, for the revised Nigerian constitution of 1963 was considered by an All-Party Conference before presentation in the legislatures for ratification. See Sessional Paper 3/1963.

Secretaries as Creech Jones, Griffiths, Lyttelton, and Lennox-Boyd, as chairmen of the negotiations, influenced the constitutional bargaining. In addition, officials of the Colonial Office have usually put their weight on the side of a strong and stable central administration, particularly in Malaya and Nigeria, and have opposed the fragmentation of existing regions, especially in Nigeria and Northern Rhodesia. They have also invariably insisted upon minority safeguards. Moreover, the legal department of the Colonial Office in drafting the actual constitutional instruments has exerted some influence upon the form of certain details. In the case of the Rhodesias and Nyasaland, officials of the Commonwealth Relations Office, responsible for British relations with Southern Rhodesia, played a significant role in devising a federal structure acceptable to the settlers.

In addition to conferences the British Government has resorted to other devices in seeking effective compromises. On troublesome issues the use of Royal or independent commissions, or of 'roaming professors' as independent advisers, has sometimes proved helpful in clarifying possible lines of compromise, in suggesting analogies from experience elsewhere, and in applying expert knowledge to technical problems.[1] The value of such commissions was also realized in India, where the controversial subjects of linguistic states and official languages were turned over to independent commissions for examination,[2] and in Pakistan, where a Constitution Commission was appointed to advise President Ayub Khan on the form a new constitution should take.[3]

Generally, constitutions prepared by conferences have required formal ratification by territorial legislatures in the colonies, but in Nigeria before independence this was not considered necessary, and in Southern Rhodesia, politically more advanced than the other Central African territories, and in the Northern and the Southern Cameroons, because they were United Nations Trust Territories, referenda were employed.

Despite the variety of procedures adopted for constitution-making, it would seem that nationalist political parties have usually played a predominant role. Whether in constituent assemblies or in constitutional conferences, where these political parties have been cohesive, as in India, Malaya, and amongst the settlers of Central Africa, the result has been a constitution concentrating

---

[1] Examples were the Reid Commission in Malaya (Col. no. 330/1957); the Cobbold Commission regarding the accession of North Borneo and Sarawak to Malaysia (Cmnd. 1794/1962); the Minorities and Fiscal Commissions in Nigeria (Cmnd. 505/1958, *Report of the Commission on Revenue Allocation* (1951), Cmd. 9026/1953, Cmnd. 481/1958); the Customs Union, Fiscal, Civil Service, Judicial and Federal Capital Commissions in the West Indies (Col. no. 268/1951, W.I. 1/58, Cmd. 9618/1955, Col. no. 254/1949, Cmd. 9619/1955, Cmd. 9620/1955, Col. no. 328/1958); and in Central Africa the Judicial, Fiscal, and Civil Service Commissions and the Devlin and Monckton Commissions (Cmd. 8671/1952, Cmd. 8672/1952, Cmd. 8673/1953, Cmnd. 814/1959, Cmnd. 1148/1960).

[2] *Report of the Linguistic Provinces Commission* (1948); *Report of the States Reorganization Commission* (1955); *Report of the Official Language Commission, 1956* (1957).

[3] *Report of the Constitution Commission, Pakistan, 1961* (1962).

central power; where political parties have been primarily regionally oriented, as in the Caribbean, Nigeria, and Pakistan between 1954 and 1958, the tendency has been to emphasize regional autonomy.[1]

The preparation of the Pakistan constitution of 1962 was quite unlike that of any of the other federal constitutions. To begin with, it was prepared during a period when constitutional government and political parties had been suspended. Much of the preparatory work was done by an independent Constitution Commission appointed by President Ayub Khan early in 1960. The Commission was directed to examine the causes of the failure of the previous constitution of 1956, and to recommend the form a new constitution should take in order to consolidate national unity and provide a firm and stable system of government. The Commission circulated a questionnaire to various organizations and members of the public and interviewed a wide variety of persons. It also took great pains to dispel any notion that its independence or freedom to make recommendations was limited. Indeed, in its report it criticized a number of the proposals of the official delegation, particularly those in favour of unitary institutions. The Commission itself recommended instead a federal form of constitution, in which the distribution of powers would differ only in minor details from the previous constitution, the central legislature would be bicameral, and the central executive would take an active presidential form.[2] After the report was submitted in May 1961, several Cabinet committees were appointed to examine it from various points of view. Following that, the Cabinet as a whole, in consultation with senior administrative officers, worked out the final scheme, which was then drafted into legal terms by the government's lawyers. When the new constitution finally appeared in March 1962 it was evident that some of the major recommendations of the Constitution Commission had been disregarded, particularly those concerning the form of the distribution of powers, the undesirability of a reserve omnibus of central powers, the value of an upper house, and the advantages of direct election. The 1962 constitution clearly embodied primarily the views of President Ayub Khan's personal régime.[3]

4. The impact of social and economic planning

The form of federal institutions, particularly the economic powers assigned to central governments and the types of inter-governmental institutions devised, is likely to vary according to whether the central government is expected to play a merely neutral economic role or to undertake an active role in economic and social development. But as we have already noted, each of the new Commonwealth federations was confronted with major economic

---

[1] See also Chapter 13, section 2, on the nature of the political parties within these federations.
[2] *Report of the Constitution Commission, Pakistan, 1961* (1962), esp. chs. iii–v.
[3] For sources on President Ayub Khan's own views, see bibliography for Pakistan.

problems which required public planning and action if they were to be solved at all.[1] All these federations have felt the impact of the need for active public economic policy and planning in order to provide social services, especially health and education, to develop public utilities, particularly rail and air communications, to regulate industrial and labour conditions, to make possible balanced industrial development and maximum use of limited agricultural and other resources, to employ both short-run and long-run stability measures, and to manipulate tariffs, regulate trade, or encourage foreign investment so that economic expansion might outstrip population growth. The effect can be seen both in the original constitutional provisions framed, and later in the manner in which the federal institutions have been operated in order to finance, co-ordinate, and implement economic and social planning.

It might be expected that the emphasis upon national planning and hence on central economic powers would vary with the degree to which federation-makers upheld socialist views. While this has been a factor for centralization in some cases, it does not by itself sufficiently explain the differences among the federations. In the Pakistan Constituent Assemblies the large landowners of Punjab were a particularly influential element. The Malayan Alliance, a conservative and non-socialist coalition, was composed of aristocratic and middle-class Malays, English-speaking Chinese plantation-owners and merchants, and the Indian commercial class. The non-socialist agricultural, commercial, and mining interests were particularly influential in the Rhodesias. But these groups all recognized the need for, indeed pressed for, extensive central economic powers as a means to encouraging economic and social development and modernization. By contrast, the West Indian socialists, particularly the Jamaicans, preferred to achieve welfare states on their own insular scale and were hostile to central economic powers of any kind.

Nevertheless, in both Nigeria and India, it was those with socialist views who were the strongest advocates of centralization. In Nigeria virtually all groups accepted the urgency of active public economic policies, but the N.C.N.C. favoured strong central powers, while the commercial western and conservative northern élites emphasized economic development on a regional basis. The result was a compromise in which central and regional governments each possess considerable economic powers.

In India, despite the influential conservative element in the Congress, represented by Prasad, Patel, and Rajagopalachari, who insisted upon the omission of any explicit reference to socialism in the Objectives Resolution, the dominant theme struck by Nehru and embodied in that resolution and subsequently in the Directive Principles was a desire for Fabian socialism and economic planning.[2] Subsequently the Five Year Plans, the Hindu Code Bill, and the Community Projects were examples of attempts to implement these values. One of the consequences of this emphasis by Nehru was the creation

[1] See Chapter 3, section 3, above.   [2] C.A.I., *Debates*, vol. i, pp. 55–62.

of a powerful central government and a resistance, during the period of constitution-making, to divisive linguistic pressures. Since 1950 the appeal of Five Year Plans and the centralized character of the planning has been a continuing major unifying force within the Union.

For federal constitution-makers intent upon economic development and planning (as all those in the new federations have been), whether socialist or not, two alternative approaches lie open. Generally, because of the advantages of applying planning and active monetary and fiscal policies within the larger area, the major responsibility for these functions has been assigned to the central government.[1] This was the path clearly chosen by the constitution-makers in India, Pakistan, Malaya, and Central Africa. Another possibility, however, is for planning and economic development to be carried out on a regional basis, the path chosen in the West Indies. In Nigeria the solution was a compromise between these two alternatives, some important economic powers being assigned to the regional governments and others to the central government. The choice from amongst these possibilities has been conditioned not only by purely economic considerations, but also by regional cultural differences, for regional groups, such as those in Nigeria or Nyasaland, have sometimes feared that economic centralization would undermine their distinctiveness.[2]

Where economic and social planning on a federation-wide scale was taken as the objective, there has generally been a concentration of strong legislative, executive, and financial powers in the central government, and extensive provisions for inter-governmental co-ordination. In the three Asian federations, Rhodesia and Nyasaland, and to a lesser degree Nigeria, the exclusive lists of central powers have included a large number of economic and industrial items, while the concurrent lists have contained such broad fields as 'Economic and Social Planning', 'Labour', and 'Industrial Development'.[3] In addition, the central governments were given powers to levy customs and excise, some sales taxes, corporation income taxes, and, except in Nigeria, personal income taxes.[4] The three Asian federations also provided for special central powers in the event of economic emergencies. Inter-governmental institutions for co-operative planning and for the co-ordination of government borrowing also abound in most of these new federations. Only in the West Indies was the concentration of central economic power and the establishment of institutions aimed at 'co-operative federalism' almost completely absent.[5]

---

[1] See Chapter 8, section 4.

[2] Similarly, French Canadian separatism in the 1960's has in large part been provoked by the growing realization that Canadian economic interdependence was eroding the distinctive French Canadian culture.

[3] See Chapter 8, section 4, below.   [4] See Chapter 9, below, for details.

[5] D. Seers, 'Federation of the B.W.I.: The Economic and Financial Aspects', *Social and Economic Studies*, vi (1957), pp. 197–214.

The economic centralization in most of the new federal constitutions has been subsequently reinforced by the programmes of economic development carried on after federation.[1] In India planning has been highly centralized, indeed virtually unitary, and the central government has exerted leverage through grants and loans, although for the implementation of its plans it has been heavily dependent upon the states.[2] Economic planning also influenced the timing of the reorganization of states due to the desire to complete administrative changes before the commencement of the Second Plan,[3] and it led to the limitation of the Supreme Court's power of judicial review when this proved an obstacle to successful land reform. In Pakistan too a Planning Board was established, economic plans formulated and co-ordinated, and a programme of village A.I.D. undertaken.[4] In Malaya at first the extensive central powers for control and direction of the economy were used sparingly, considerable scope being left in practice to the state governments, but the Economic Development Plan for 1955–60 and the increased central economic powers under the 1957 constitution have fortified the dominance of the central government. The central government in Rhodesia and Nyasaland was also active in encouraging industrialization through taxation and tariff policies, the Industrial Development Corporation, negotiations overseas, and sponsorship of the Kariba Dam, the symbol of the federation's economic progress. In Nigeria there has been a tendency for economic and social planning to be duplicated in 'fours', the central and regional governments each carrying out their own programmes in parallel, with the National Economic Council in its early years attempting only to co-ordinate these and minimize duplication. This tended to strengthen the political stature of the regional governments. Since independence, however, the dominant role of the central government in the planning for the inter-governmental Development Programme 1962–8, and the superior central financial resources, have enhanced the relative power of the central government enormously.[5] In the West Indies, by contrast with the other new federations, the territorial basis of economic development policy so fortified Jamaican insularity that it was a major factor in its secession and the resulting collapse of the federation.

5. The influence of earlier federal models

References to the constitutional details and to the successes and difficulties of earlier federations have appeared time after time in the deliberations of the

[1] See Chapter 10, section 6, below, for inter-governmental planning procedures.
[2] K. Santhanam, *Union-State Relations in India* (1960), ch. 4; W. H. Morris-Jones, *Government and Politics of India* (1964), pp. 141–3; N. D. Palmer, *The Indian Political System* (1961), ch. 8.   [3] *Report of S.R.C.* (1955), paras. 85, 816.
[4] S. M. Akhtar, *Economics of Pakistan* (5th ed., 1961), pp. 412–46; K. B. Sayeed, *Pakistan, The Formative Phase* (1960), pp. 364–70, 379–80.
[5] See J. P. Mackintosh, 'Federalism in Nigeria', *Political Studies*, x (1962), pp. 239–45; T. Cole, 'Federalism in the Commonwealth', *I.P.S.A. Sixth World Congress, Geneva, 1964, Federalism/18*, pp. 26–27.

constitution-makers. Sometimes extensive surveys of other federal models have been prepared. In India, for instance, B. N. Rau compiled for the members of the Constituent Assembly a series of pamphlets entitled 'Constitutional Precedents', which included selections from certain constitutions together with comments and also comparative studies on such issues as linguistic provinces, central-provincial relations, divisions of powers, composition of central executives and legislatures, second chambers, fundamental rights, amendment procedures, and minority safeguards.[1] Subsequently the Report of the Union Constitution Committee and the Draft Constitution of 1948 both contained numerous explanatory notes pointing to comparisons with other federations or to sections borrowed from other constitutions. It was not surprising, therefore, that the debates of the Assembly were filled with references to other federations, and that these examples had considerable influence on the pattern of institutions adopted, although the main framework for the new constitution was derived from the Government of India Act, 1935.

In the preparation of the West Indian constitution, the consideration of federal precedents was nearly as extensive. When in 1947 the Colonial Secretary suggested a conference on closer association, his memorandum included for consideration the details of the divisions of powers in the earlier Commonwealth federations of Canada, Australia, and India (1935).[2] The Montego Bay Conference which followed decided in favour of a federal structure on the Australian model, and as a result the Standing Closer Association Committee Report, which was notable for the extent to which it referred to the experience of the earlier Commonwealth and United States federations, paid particular attention to the Australian example. Subsequently, the reports of the Judicial Commission and the Federal Capital Commission also relied heavily upon Australian, Central African, American, and Indian precedents. Even after federation the recommendations of the Croft Commission for a customs union and the proposals of Trinidad for a revision of the federal constitution were supported by extensive references to both older and recent federations.[3]

In each of the other new federations there was also extensive consideration of federal examples. Nigerian political leaders looked with interest at other federations, especially those uniting different ethnic groups, such as Canada, Switzerland, India, and Malaya, although on the question of the form of the distribution of powers they were influenced most by the examples of the United States and Australia. In addition, the presence at the Nigerian pre-federal negotiations of Colonial Office officials who had participated in the federating of territories at different stages of constitutional progress in Central

---

[1] C.A.I., *Constitutional Precedents* (1st, 2nd, and 3rd ser., 1947).

[2] Cmd. 7120/1947, Appendix 4.

[3] W.I. 1/58, *Report of the Trade and Tariffs Commission*, Part I, paras. 26–30; *Revision of the Federal Constitution* (Trinidad, 1959), esp. p. 38; Office of Premier of Trinidad, *The Economics of Nationhood* (1959), pp. 7–9, 43.

Africa contributed to the compromise by which the achievement of regional self-government was staggered in Nigeria. In the conferences preceding the federation of Rhodesia and Nyasaland, the presence of K. C. Wheare as an adviser meant that the negotiators had available a wide knowledge of federal practice elsewhere. The Constituent Assembly of Pakistan, although predominantly influenced by the provisional constitution, the Government of India Act, 1935, also cast glances at other federations, including the Constitution of India, 1950, from which certain provisions were borrowed.[1] The Working Committee which devised the Malayan federal structure of 1948 relied chiefly on the Government of India Act, 1935, on the pre-war Federated Malay States, and on the Malayan Union scheme of 1946, for guidance, but the Reid Commission which laid the foundation for the revised constitution of 1957 considered a wider range of federal experience, the examples of India and Pakistan being the most influential.[2]

Commissions appointed to advise the constitution-makers on particular problems or subsequently to review the general federal structure have, as a rule, drawn extensively upon experience in other federations in making their recommendations. The reports of the commissioners advising in Rhodesia and Nyasaland, the West Indies, and Nigeria, on fiscal questions, on judicial systems, on federal capitals, on customs union, and on minority safeguards, have not only pointed to relevant experience elsewhere, but have on occasion recommended the adoption of identical arrangements. Sometimes the commissioners have been able to draw on their own personal experience or knowledge of federal systems.[3] The constitutional review commissions for Malaya and Central Africa each included among their members men from other Commonwealth federations, enabling them to draw on the experience of those countries, and the reports of both commissions referred widely to examples elsewhere. This was perhaps a major factor in the recommendation by the Reid Commission in 1957 of more orthodox federal arrangements for the distribution of authority and for the interpretation of the constitution than had existed under the preceding Federation of Malaya Agreement of 1948.[4] The Monckton Commission also considered carefully the examples of other Commonwealth federations before making its recommendations on fundamental rights and the distribution of powers.[5]

Which federations have had the most influence upon their successors, and

---

[1] C.A.P. (second), *Debates*, vol. i, pp. 1828, 1899–1900, 1980, 2084, 2292.

[2] *Report of the Working Committee* (1946), paras. 33, 78, 100, 105, 117, Appendix; Col. no. 330/1957, paras. 2, 29, 80, 82, 123, 125, 126, 127, 161, 170, 178, 187, and pp. 35, 101; *Malayan Constitutional Documents* (2nd ed., 1962), vol. i, pp. 361–5.

[3] Sir Jeremy Raisman, for instance, led Fiscal Commissions in Pakistan (1952), Central Africa (1952, 1957), Nigeria (1958), and East Africa (1961). Sir Ivor Jennings, as a member of the Reid Commission, was able to bring to Malayan affairs a wide knowledge of constitutional affairs including considerable experience of Ceylon, Pakistan, and India.

[4] Col. no. 330/1957, paras. 2, 82, 123.

[5] Cmnd. 1148/1960, paras. 196, 235; Cmnd. 1150/1960, App. II.

what sort of lessons have they provided for the creators of recent federations?

Of the older federations, the Canadian model has perhaps had the most influence upon the form of the Asian federations, while the examples of Australia and the United States have been more closely followed by the African and Caribbean federations. Much of the impact of Canadian federalism on the Asian federations was indirect, being derived through the influence of the Canadian example on the form and phraseology of the Government of India Act, 1935, which in turn was the model most influential upon the constitution-framers in India, Pakistan, and Malaya. This indirect influence, coupled with a direct consideration of Canadian precedents and difficulties, led in all three Asian federations to the enumeration of regional as well as central powers,[1] the constitutional assignment of relatively extensive powers to the central governments, the inclusion of 'quasi-federal' provisions, the appointment of regional governors by the central governments, unitary judicial systems, the assignment of advisory jurisdiction to the supreme courts, special provisions regarding minority languages and education, varied amendment procedures for different parts of the constitutions, the inclusion in the federal documents of the essential features or even complete details of the regional constitutions, the avoidance of the limitations in Canada preventing the central government from implementing treaties, and in India and Malaya (1957) the inclusion of some nominated members in second chambers. The Canadian example was also considered in the other recent federations, although the West Indians, in adopting a nominated second chamber and leaving constitutional amendment to the British Parliament, chose to ignore Canadian difficulties.

In the Caribbean and African federations the Australian and United States models were the most influential. Indeed, the West Indian constitution-makers expressly 'paid particular attention to the experience of the Commonwealth of Australia'.[2] This was most evident in the nature and even wording of certain provisions and particularly in the form of the distribution of authority, which listed only exclusive and concurrent powers, although the content of these lists was made much slighter.[3] The form of the allocation of powers in Nigeria and in the Federation of Rhodesia and Nyasaland also followed the Australian pattern. By contrast with the Asian federations, the other three federations also followed the pattern of Australia and the United States in providing for completely dual administrative and potentially dual judicial systems, as well as in the smaller number of 'quasi-federal' provisions.

[1] The Pakistan constitution, 1962, unlike its predecessor, did not, however, enumerate provincial or concurrent powers.

[2] Col. no. 255/1950, para. 5.

[3] Ibid., paras. 21, 23. The Rance Committee was, however, strangely silent about the Australian example in dismissing directly elected second chambers (ibid., paras. 55–56.)

Australian and American precedents provided other lessons, too, both for these and for the Asian federations. Examples were the setting aside of the national capital as a federal territory in India, Nigeria, the West Indies, and for a time Pakistan; the unlimited central power to implement all treaties in India, Pakistan (1962), Malaya, Central Africa, and the West Indies; the names of the central legislative houses in Malaya, Nigeria, and the West Indies; the emphasis upon the role of the supreme court as guardian of the constitution in each of these federations; and the form of the provisions regarding inter-state trade in India and Rhodesia and Nyasaland. Australian devices for overcoming the rigidity and legalism of federalism were followed and even improved upon in the use of extensive concurrent legislative lists, provision for the delegation of legislative or executive powers between state and central governments, and in the establishment of a wide variety of inter-governmental institutions, commissions, and councils in all the new federations. The influence of the American model was particularly apparent in the fundamental rights and amendment procedures in the constitutions of India, Pakistan, Malaya, and Nigeria, in the concurrent taxing powers on income in the West Indies, and in the separation of the executives from the legislatures and the single list of exclusive central powers in the Pakistan constitution of 1962. The Nigerian provisions regarding the police, and the West Indian rejection of a directly elected second chamber, were, on the other hand, made expressly to avoid American difficulties.

In one respect the recent federations have all alike followed Commonwealth, and particularly United Kingdom, precedents in adopting responsible parliamentary executives. Only in Pakistan was a presidency on the American model seriously contemplated, and there the adoption of a separated executive followed after the failure of an earlier attempt to rely upon a parliamentary form of executive.

Of the older federations, Switzerland had the least influence on the newer Commonwealth federations, although Swiss examples were often cited. The chief impact of the Swiss model was in showing the possibilities of a multilingual federation and the advantages of recognizing the languages of different groups. The possibility of a Swiss type of fixed executive, of small regional units on the scale of the cantons, of a supreme court with only limited authority to interpret the constitution, or of referenda as part of the procedure for constitutional amendment, received only scant attention.

Constitution-makers have also looked at more recent federal models, these being in some respects more appropriate, since they represented attempts to cope with similar problems. Of the newer federal constitutions the most influential by far has been the Government of India Act, 1935, which provided the fundamental framework for the federal constitutions of India (1950), Pakistan (1956), and Malaya (1948). Indeed, approximately 250 articles of the Indian constitution were taken either verbatim or with only minor changes in phraseology from its predecessor. Similarly, the Pakistan constitution of 1956 was described aptly as simply 'a logical continuation of the scheme of government under the Government of India Act'.[1] The influence of the Government of India Act, 1935, upon the constitutions of India and Pakistan was apparent in the use of three legislative lists, the inclusion of extensive emergency powers, the provision of some central directive and coercive authority over the state and provincial governments, the unitary judiciary, the strong central executive, the inclusion of national and state constitutions in the one document, and the adoption of responsible government on the British model for both tiers of government. On the other hand, the new constitutions of these two federations both departed from their predecessor in adopting a republican form, fundamental rights, adult franchise, direct election to the central lower house, general rather than communal electorates, and unitary citizenship. Some critics, notably Sir Ivor Jennings, have suggested that, since the Government of India Act, 1935, was a colonial structure primarily designed for the division of power between Indian and imperial hands, it 'was a bad precedent for the Constitution of an independent country'.[2] Leaders in the Indian Constituent Assembly defended the large-scale borrowing from the 1935 Act on the grounds that, in a period of uncertainty, this would provide a continuity in the working of the administrative structure.[3] Some even defended the 1935 Act as 'a model legislation'.[4] But it was the quest for stability, made acute by the disruption of partition and the insecurity of the early years of independence which, more than anything else, induced leaders in India and Pakistan to rely on a system of which they already had experience. The Federation of Malaya Agreement, 1948, departed further from the Government of India Act, 1935, but the degree to which it influenced the Working Committee was apparent in the comprehensive central powers and quasi-unitary features.[5]

The Indian constitution of 1950 itself in turn influenced both the Pakistan (1956) and Malayan (1957) constitutions. Many provisions in each were modelled on Indian modifications to the Government of India Act, 1935, or on Indian innovations, particularly those relating to inter-governmental relations and institutions and those designed for constitutional flexibility. The Asian federations appear to have had some influence upon the Nigerian and Central African, but not the West Indian, federations in the arrangements for the division of finances, and upon Nigeria in the inclusion of fundamental rights and the provision of some emergency powers. When Nigeria became

---

[1] K. Callard, *Pakistan, A Political Study* (1957), p. 148.

[2] Jennings, *Some Characteristics of the Indian Constitution*, p. 56. See also C.A.I., *Debates*, vol. iv, pp. 924, 989; vol. v, pp. 90, 371–2; C.A.P. (first), *Debates*, vol. viii, p. 181.

[3] C.A.I., *Debates*, vol. vii, p. 337; C.A.I., *Second Report of the Union Powers Committee* (1947), para. 2.

[4] C.A.I., *Debates*, vol. iv, p. 708. See also ibid., vol. v, p. 104; vol. vii, pp. 37–38.

[5] *Report of the Working Committee* (1946), paras. 33, 105.

a republic in 1963, it was the Indian pattern of presidency that was instituted.[1]

Some of the features of the Federation of Rhodesia and Nyasaland, despite its notoriety, have been adopted elsewhere. The use of a distributable pool in the division of finances, and the staggering of regional advancement towards self-government, were adapted to the Nigerian scene following precedents in Central Africa, and some of the recommendations of the Judicial and Fiscal Commissioners in the West Indies with regard to the supreme court, the delegation of executive authority, and the specification of external affairs, were based on provisions in the constitution of Rhodesia and Nyasaland.

Constitution-makers have been influenced by the success or failure of internal as well as external precedents. Sir Ivor Jennings has said, 'all constitutions are the heirs of the past as well as the testators of the future', and this has been apparent in the way the federal constitutions of India, Pakistan, Malaya, Malaysia, Nigeria, and the West Indies have displayed a continuity with their predecessors.[2] We have already noted the influence in India and Pakistan of the Government of India Act, 1935, which had served after 1947 as the interim constitution in both these countries. The Pakistan constitution of 1956 in turn provided the basis for the new 1962 constitution: a number of features such as the dual provinces, the content of the list of exclusive central powers, and the inter-governmental institutions, were retained with little change, while those aspects of the earlier constitution which were considered weaknesses were modified. The executive ministers were no longer dependent on the support of the legislatures, both the concurrent and provincial lists were omitted, thus extending the provincial residual authority, and the potential central controls over provincial governments were strengthened. The centralized Federation of Malaya Agreement, 1948, in many respects bore the imprint of the earlier Federated Malay States and the proposed Malayan Union, while the constitution of 1957 was in turn strongly influenced by its predecessor. When it came to preparing a constitution for Malaysia, the existing Malayan constitution was simply continued, although some substantial amendments were made to meet the requirements of the acceding states. In Nigeria the scope of legislative powers and finances left to the central government, the unicameral central legislature, and the continued regional units in the federal constitution of 1954, were derived from the quasi-unitary constitution of 1951. The 1960 and 1963 Nigerian constitutions, although completely new documents, each retained not only the fundamental federal framework but even the wording of many of the previous provisions. Even the West Indian constitution-framers were at least partially influenced by such Caribbean forerunners as the Leeward Islands Federation, and by the work of the Development and Welfare Organization and of the Regional Economic

[1] Nigeria, Sessional Paper 3/1963, para. 3.
[2] Jennings, *Some Characteristics of the Indian Constitution*, p. 56.

Committee. Later, the early negotiations for an East Caribbean federation were themselves clearly affected by the lessons drawn from the failure of the West Indies Federation.

Constitution-makers have been guided and influenced not only by constitutional precedents and experience but also by the writings of scholars on the subject of federalism. In their deliberations and reports, references to the views of scholars expounding theories of 'dual federalism', and especially to K. C. Wheare's *Federal Government*, have appeared time after time.

Sometimes earlier models have been imperfectly understood by constitution-makers. At the Ibadan Conference in Nigeria, for instance, some representatives insisted that 'any proper federal system' involved equal representation of regions in the central legislature, and most of them considered the system whereby the central legislature delegated power to the regions as providing regional autonomy.[1] Premier Williams's arguments in 1959 for revision of the West Indian constitution were sometimes based on inaccurate information: he was apparently misinformed on the distribution of powers in Central Africa and on the composition of the central legislature in Nigeria.[2] Nor were the models appealed to by Jamaica at that time always apt.[3] In Central Africa some of the settler enthusiasm for, and hence African opposition to, federation was based on a failure to distinguish the real differences between amalgamation and federation.[4]

Sometimes, too, critics have complained that the new proposals or constitutions were unoriginal, insufficiently grounded in indigenous institutions, or a mere hodge-podge of precedents unsuited to local conditions. Such complaints were made in the Indian Constituent Assembly, in the declaration of martial law in Pakistan, by the P.M.I.P. in Malaya, by some Nigerian writers, and by some of the representatives at Montego Bay. Generally, however, there has been agreement upon the value of examining federal experience elsewhere as providing 'all possible information as to various methods of achieving various ends', and 'a guide and warning to us to avoid the difficulties and dangers and the errors that these systems have fallen into in the course of their natural evolution'.[5] Leaders in the Indian Constituent Assembly, for instance, insisted that it was wiser to profit by the experience and mistakes of other federations and to improve upon them, than to make radical new experiments whose success would be questionable.[6]

But, despite the general acceptance of the wisdom of profiting from the lessons of earlier federations, the constitution-makers have usually insisted that proposals should be chosen, not merely as copies of existing constitutions,

[1] *Proceedings of General Conference* (1950), p. 185 and pp. 91, 100, 121, 124, 128, 180–1.
[2] *Revision of the Federal Constitution* (Trinidad, 1959), pp. 19, 37.
[3] Trinidad M. 12/1960, pp. 76–78, 89.
[4] Cmnd. 1148/1960, para. 28.
[5] Col. no. 255/1950, para. 5; Col. no. 218/1948, p. 37.
[6] C.A.I., *Debates*, vol. vii, p. 37.

but to meet the particular needs, aspirations, and circumstances of each community. The examination of precedents has not prevented new federations from incorporating innovations. Indeed, the Indians considered their constitution an advance over all earlier federations in minimizing rigidity and legalism by a variety of devices, many of them adopted later by Pakistan and Malaya.[1] Other federation-makers too have made innovations. Pakistan created a unique federation of two regional units; the 1956 constitution also established provincial Advisory Boards for the Central Post and Telegraphs Department and devised special Islamic provisions;[2] the 1962 constitution included not only some unique arrangements to prevent deadlocks between the separated executives and legislatures, but also a system of indirect election, and advisory Islamic institutions.[3] The Federation of Malaya Agreement, 1948, provided for compulsory delegation of executive powers on a large number of specified central legislative subjects, and established a Conference of Rulers and an *ad hoc* Constitution Interpretation Tribunal.[4] The Constitution of the Federation of Malaya, 1957, created an elective monarchy and an unusual variety of inter-governmental institutions.[5] The Nigerian constitution-makers devised a unique arrangement for regional representation on the executive council 1954–7, agreed upon Advisory Councils for minority areas and a Police Council in 1958, and recognized a right of secession, although limited to the Cameroons only, in 1960.[6] The Federation of Rhodesia and Nyasaland created an African Affairs Board, and was the first federation to establish on more than an interim basis a unicameral legislature.[7] The West Indies was unique in establishing a political federation without a customs union and in assigning the central government postponed authority over certain subjects such as income tax and freedom of movement.[8] In such cases constitution-makers could never be sure in advance how these innovations would turn out. Some, like the Malayan *ad hoc* Interpretation Tribunal and compulsory delegation of executive powers, the Nigerian arrangement for regional representation on the executive council, and the unicameral legislatures in Malaya and Nigeria, were abandoned, and some such as the African Affairs Board in Central Africa, and the postponed solutions for the customs union and central taxing of income in the West Indies, proved disappointing.

[1] C.A.I., *Debates*, vol. vii, pp. 34–37.
[2] Constitution, 1956, arts. 1(2)(a), 197, 198, 200.
[3] Constitution, 1962, arts. 23–30, 40–48, 74–79, 89, 155–73, 199–207.
[4] Cls. 16, 67–76, 86, 110, 153, Second Schedule.
[5] Arts. 32, 38, 91, 108.
[6] Cmd. 8934/1953, para. 15; Cmnd. 569/1958, paras. 8–15, 52–53, 56, 67; Cmnd. 1063/1960, para. 8.
[7] Constitution, arts. 8, 9, 67–77. Malaya had a unicameral central legislature 1948–59, but the Conference of Rulers performed some of the functions of a second chamber.
[8] Col. no. 315/1955, para. 6; Cmd. 9733/1956, paras. 20, 25–29. Subsequently, both in South Arabia and in Malaysia, the West Indian scheme of phased implementation was adopted.

But others, notably the device of the distributable pool suggested first by Raisman, the elective monarchy and the Conference of Rulers in Malaya, and the Indian provisions for flexibility and inter-governmental co-operation, have worked surprisingly well. The new federations, then, have been not mere copies of older models, but genuine 'experiments' in federal institutions.

6. *Islamic and oligarchic federations*

Pakistan, Malaya, and Nigeria are distinct from the other recent Commonwealth federations in that in each Muslims form the largest religious group.[1] Has Islam then had any impact upon the form of the federal systems in these countries?

Historically Islam has been a religion of authority, enjoining obedience to the command of the ruler. As a result, Muslims in the developing areas have often been accused of autocracy, semi-feudalism, and intolerance, characteristics unlikely to be compatible with constitutional government or federal institutions. Fears that such tendencies might be exhibited by the emirates of Northern Nigeria, the large landowners of West Pakistan and especially Punjab, and the Malay state administrations, have been expressed by southern Nigerians, East Bengalis, and the Chinese in Malaya.

But have these federations displayed an Islamic character? In Pakistan, where Islam had provided the focus for anti-Hindu nationalism, the achievement of partition raised for debate the problem of the form a modern Islamic state should take.[2] Although the ulama advocated the adoption of institutions modelled on the early caliphate, the political leaders of Pakistan were men of western education and secular outlook who, although agreeing to an Islamic flavour for the constitution, insisted upon fundamentally secular political institutions based on western models. In the 1956 constitution the Islamic provisions were limited to affirmations in the preamble, the title of the federation, the directive principles, the reservation of the Presidency to Muslims, the creation of an organization for Islamic research, and the establishment of a commission to advise the National and Provincial Assemblies in making laws conform to the injunctions of Islam.[3] The 1962 constitution followed the same general pattern.[4] Thus, as far as the federal features of these constitutions were concerned, Islam had little effect.

In Malaya and Nigeria, where there existed large non-Muslim groups, the influence of Islam on the constitutional structure was even less. In Malaya and

---

[1] Muslim communities existed also in post-partition India, Trinidad, and Nyasaland, but they did not represent the largest religious group in the federal populations.

[2] The lengthy controversy on this issue involved such practical political issues as the place of religious minorities in an Islamic state and the appropriateness of single or communal electorates. On these controversies see Callard, *Pakistan, A Political Study*, chs. 6, 7; G. W. Choudhury, *Constitutional Development in Pakistan* (1959), chs. 4–6, 13; *Report of Constitution Commission Pakistan, 1961* (1962), ch. xii.

[3] Constitution, 1956, preamble, arts. 1, 24, 25, 32(2), 197, 198.

[4] Constitution, 1962, preamble, arts. 6, 8, 10, 199–207.

later Malaysia, at the insistence of the U.M.N.O., a declaration that Islam was the religion of the federation was inserted in the constitution, and certain religious functions were assigned to the Yang di-Pertuan Agong as monarch, although these gave him no authority to interfere in matters over which states were autonomous.[1] In Nigeria no Islamic provisions were included in the constitution at all.

There still remains the question whether in the operation of federal institutions Islam has had any noticeable influence. Although traditionally Islam has emphasized obedience to the ruler, there would appear to be nothing in Islamic thought requiring executive power to be exercised in an autocratic manner. Indeed writers in Pakistan have taken considerable pains to provide Islamic foundations for democratic institutions.[2] Moreover, the Indian empire of the Muslim Mughals had in practice been characterized by a considerable degree of devolution of authority. Undoubtedly, in practice there have been some conservative and even autocratic tendencies in the Native Authorities of Northern Nigeria, in the state and even central governments of Malaya, and in the operation of political parties in Pakistan, but these have been due not so much to the ideology of Islam as to other factors. Educational, social, and economic backwardness, or a history of isolation under indirect rule, were more important in each of these cases. Moreover, the authoritarian tradition of the Muslim League in Pakistan stemmed more from its role as a nationalist movement under Jinnah than from any considerations of Islamic theory.

This leads us to the wider question of the distinction between democratic and oligarchic federations. Federalism, it has been argued, involving a division of authority and hence constitutional limits on both tiers of government, is a form of constitutional government and therefore incompatible with autocracy.[3] It does not follow from this, however, that federal institutions must be democratic. A constitutional division of authority within a regionally diverse oligarchy is conceivable. Indeed, among the new federations we may distinguish between democratic and oligarchic examples.

The Malayan Federation in the early years after 1948 did not embody the elective principle in either the central or state governments, and it was only in 1957 that provisions were inserted in the federal constitution to ensure that the sultans became constitutional rulers in the states. The Pakistan constitution of 1956 was ostensibly democratic, but between 1947 and 1958 the central and provincial governments were in effect run by a small oligarchy. No direct central elections were held during this period, and both constituent assemblies consistently postponed elections, with the result that they were never

---

[1] Cmnd. 210/1957, paras. 57–60; Cmnd. 1954/1963, para. 15. See also R. O. Tilman, 'Malaysia: The Problems of Federation', *The Western Political Quarterly*, xvi (1963), pp. 903–6.

[2] A. K. Brohi, *Fundamental Law of Pakistan* (1958), pp. 747–69, 787–99; Choudhury, op. cit., ch. 5.

[3] Wheare, *Federal Government*, pp. 46–47.

really representative. Moreover, throughout this period, the constituent assemblies displayed a weakness in the face of the executive and the bureaucracy, and were often dominated by the Governor-Generals or the President in the formation of cabinets and policy. Although the 1962 constitution ended autocratic martial law, it was far from democratic in the western sense of the term. Indeed, the continued disbarring from public life of some of the old politicians and the system of indirect election led almost immediately to a considerable opposition movement demanding 'democratization' of the new constitution. But perhaps the most clearly oligarchic federation was that in Central Africa, where the federal electoral rolls between 1953 and 1960 never contained in any territory more than 5 per cent. of the territorial population.[1] Regional differences among the settlers over such issues as the use of copper revenues led to a federalization of politics within the settler oligarchy, but beneath these differences lay a general identity of outlook within the small community of Europeans.

Have these oligarchic federations—Malaya 1948–57, Pakistan 1947–58 and since 1962, and Rhodesia and Nyasaland 1953–63—any distinctive features in common? Perhaps most significant was a common tendency for central and regional politics to be closely interlocked, whether constitutional provisions encouraged this, as in Pakistan and Malaya, or not.[2] In each of the three federations a small group dominated both central and regional politics, central leaders taking an active part in regional issues, and regional leaders participating in central affairs, thus undermining any federal separation of authority.

7. Conclusions

In general terms the new federations might be graded roughly according to the scope of the functions assigned to the different tiers of government,[3] a variety of factors contributing towards their relative tightness or looseness.

The tightest of the new federations has been Malaya. Among the decisive factors there were the intensity of Malay nationalism, the racial heterogeneity within the states, the creation and early evolution of the federation under emergency conditions, the emphasis of the British Government upon a strong central government, the leadership of such men as Dato Onn and Tunku Abdul Rahman, the dominance of the Alliance Party, the influence of the preceding scheme for a Malayan Union and of the Government of India Act, 1935, which served as the chief models, and the oligarchic character of politics in the early years of the federation. In order to induce Singapore and the Borneo states, with their strong local economic and political interests, to join,

---

[1] Cmnd. 1149/1960, p. 11.

[2] Constitutional provisions permitting dual membership in central and regional legislatures and quasi-unitary controls of regional governments encouraged these tendencies under the provisional constitution of Pakistan and in Malaya. See Chapter 11, section 4.

[3] See also Chapter 8, section 5, below, for the actual distribution of functions.

the federation was converted into the more complicated and slightly less centralized Federation of Malaysia, but it retains the strongest central government among the new federations.

Similar influences towards a marked central bias were operative in India and Pakistan, particularly during their early years of independence. Both were characterized by a potent nationalist movement, a considerable degree of heterogeneity within some of the regional units, a strongly devolutionary genesis, a situation of crisis at the time of their creation, a powerful national leadership in men like Nehru, Patel, and Jinnah, a sovereign Constituent Assembly formulating the new constitutions, an emphasis on economic planning, and a dependence upon the model provided by the Government of India Act, 1935. A further influence in the same direction in India was the predominance of the Congress Party, while in Pakistan the oligarchic character of politics reinforced the tendencies to centralization. In both countries, however, certain other factors led to a greater decentralization than in Malaya. In India the relative homogeneity of certain states, especially after 1956, consolidated linguistic regionalism, while in Pakistan of particular importance was the constant and cumulative assertion of provincial interests resentful of overcentralization, especially in East Bengal, and the splintering of the party system with the rise to dominance of regional leaders and parties after 1954. The impact of the regional pressures was to a considerable extent restrained after 1958, however, by the imposition of an authoritarian régime.

The relatively high degree of centralization in the Central African Federation was due principally to the predominance of Huggins and Welensky and of the United Federal Party in settler politics, and to the fundamentally oligarchic character of the electorate in the racially heterogeneous territories. Other contributing factors were the sense of urgency created by the growth of white and black nationalism in adjacent territories, and the emphasis upon creating an integrated and growing economy. On the other hand, these tendencies were in part counterbalanced by the constant assertion of African fears, the aggregationary process by which the federation was formed, and the influence of the Australian model and the theory of 'dual federalism' upon the framers of the constitutional structure.

In Nigeria the devolutionary aspects of its constitutional development, the heterogeneity within the regions, and subsequently the urge for unified economic planning, resulted in some relatively centralized features. A variety of other factors, however, encouraged the concentration of functions in the regional governments. Especially important were the territorial concentration of diversities in the regional heartlands, the absence of military insecurity or emergency conditions, and the dominance of regional political leaders and parties both in the pre-federal negotiations and in the operation of the federal institutions. The net effect was to make Nigeria a federation of powerful regions.

Of the six federal societies the West Indies was the least integrated. It was an aggregation of distinct and internally homogeneous island societies in conditions marked by the absence of military insecurity or any emergency. In these conditions the Australian model proved the most appealing. The emphasis upon island rather than federal social and economic planning, and the loose confederal organization of the West Indian federal parties, reinforced the trend with the result that the West Indies was, in practice, little more than a nominal federation.

PART THREE

FEDERAL POLITICAL SYSTEMS

7

THE CONSTITUENT REGIONS

1. *The units of regional government*

STUDIES of federal government often concentrate upon such questions as the distribution of legislative and executive powers, the allocation of financial resources, regional representation in central government, the procedures for constitutional amendment, and the scope and significance of judicial review. These are certainly fundamental aspects of any federal system, but they all presuppose the existence of stable regional governments as components of a federation. It would seem appropriate, therefore, to begin the analysis of the political structures of the new federations with a consideration of the regional units of government of which they have been composed.

In the creation and development of the new federations, considerable controversy has often arisen over which social groupings the regional units of government should represent. Such questions have, of course, tended to come to the fore more frequently where the regional governments were created by devolution of authority within a formerly centralized political system than in cases where territories, each with an already developed sense of separate historical and political identity, have joined a federal union. But other factors have also had an important bearing on the shape of regional units. Where historical, ethnic, linguistic, religious, economic, or geographical diversities have not coincided with each other in their distribution, as has frequently been the case, there have often been conflicting claims as to which of these sectional interests should serve as the primary basis for the regional units. Such conflicts concerning the appropriate regional boundaries have been particularly frequent where the regional units of British colonial administration were arbitrary and accidental in their origin, bearing little relation to the social groupings within these territories. The result has often been a heritage of administrative regional units containing heterogeneous populations. In such a setting there has usually arisen a demand for the reorganization of regional boundaries in order to create ethnically homogeneous units. But such demands have conflicted with other sectional interests, both economic and political, fostered by the colonial administrative units and cutting across the older traditional divisions.

The appropriate size and number of regional units have also been matters for consideration. The importance of regional economic viability or administrative efficiency has sometimes led to the grouping or splitting of units to form more suitable regions. Moreover, where there have been sharp disparities in the area, population, or wealth of different regions, there has frequently been pressure to divide the larger units or to combine the smaller ones in order to reduce fears that a federation would be dominated by a few populous or wealthy regions. Geography itself has sometimes dictated the number and size of units however, particularly where, as in the West Indies, Pakistan and Malaysia, the territories have not been contiguous.

Debate over the number and shape of the regional units of government has not been unique to the recent federations.[1] Within the older federations such issues also arose, particularly in the two North American federations as they expanded to fill the empty continent. From its original thirteen colonies the United States has enlarged itself to fifty states including the far-flung territories of Alaska and Hawaii, and it has in addition devised its own unique confederal 'commonwealth' relationship for the 'free associated state' of Puerto Rico.[2] Because the addition of new states affected the balance of federal power, their creation out of the dependent territories of the United States often raised difficulties and controversies. Canada too has grown from its original four to ten provinces, three separate colonies being admitted and three new provinces being created out of parts of the Northwestern Territories and of Rupert's Land. Canada and Australia still have large centrally administered territories which, although too thinly populated at the moment, are regarded as areas out of which full-fledged provinces or states may eventually be erected. In addition to the creation of new regional units, there have also been examples in the older federations of regrouping or dividing of states. In both the United States and Australia states have transferred territory to the federal government, and in the United States, Kentucky, Maine, and West Virginia were carved out of other states as a result of local pressure. In Australia movements for the division of existing states developed in Queensland and in New South Wales, but these were eventually appeased by the granting of economic concessions. In Canada there have also been occasional demands for the separation of Northern Ontario. Of the older federations, Switzerland has had the most stable regional structure, but there were considerable controversies over proposals in 1919–22 to add Vorarlberg and more recently to reunify Basle and to divide Berne.

In each of the newer federations, either at their inception or during the early years of their existence, questions of the size, number, and shape of the component regions have aroused debate. Such controversies have been particularly acute in India, Pakistan, and Nigeria. In India there has been a series of major crises over these issues. The landmarks have been the integra-

---

[1] R. R. Bowie and C. J. Friedrich (eds.), *Studies in Federalism* (1954), pp. 758–64.

[2] See G. K. Lewis, *Puerto Rico: A Case Study in the Problems of Contemporary American Federalism* (Trinidad, M. 12/1960).

tion and consolidation of the princely states at the time of their accession in 1947–50, the creation of Andhra as a linguistic state in 1953, the reorganization of most of the state boundaries on primarily linguistic lines in 1956, the division of Bombay in 1960, the provision for a separate Naga State in 1962, and the continued agitation in Assam over linguistic issues and in Punjab for a Sikh State.[1]

After partition Pakistan consisted of a variety of seventeen regional units of government: four Governors' provinces, one Chief Commissioner's province, ten acceding princely states, some frontier tribal areas, and a strip of Kashmir. Soon afterwards, Karachi as the federal capital was detached from Sind, being placed under an Administrator, and in 1952 it became a Chief Commissioner's province. Some of the princely states were soon consolidated, four being merged into the Baluchistan States Union, and four being grouped together with the frontier tribal areas in the North-West Frontier Agencies. In 1955 there was a major revision when the complex array of units in West Pakistan was amalgamated into a single province, thus reducing the federation to two balanced regional units.[2] Disputes over the regional structure continued, and in 1957 the governing Republican Party actually endorsed a redivision of the province in the West Pakistan Assembly, but the central government of the day did not implement the proposal. The 1961 Constitution Commission found public opinion overwhelmingly against breaking up the province of West Pakistan, and the 1962 constitution therefore made no change.[3]

The history of Nigeria under British rule before 1945 was also one of constant modification to the internal units of administration.[4] It is not surprising, therefore, that the regional structure of the Nigerian Federation should have been a matter of continued debate. The Richards Constitution of 1946 established the three basic regions which were to provide the mould for Nigerian federalism. Subsequently the 1951 constitution included Lagos, which had formerly been separate, within the Western Region. The federal constitution of 1954, however, once more separated Lagos despite the protests of the Action Group, and also marked off as a new quasi-federal region the Southern Cameroons, which had formerly been a part of the Eastern Region. In the meantime Nigerian nationalists such as Awolowo and Azikiwe were advocating a variety of regional schemes based on ethnic lines or on smaller administrative units. With the mounting apprehension of regional minorities at the prospect of independence, demands for the division of the existing regions to create new ethnic states came to the fore at the constitutional conferences

---

[1] See bibliography for literature on these developments. See also Maps 1 and 2 (at end).

[2] See Map 3. On the unification of West Pakistan, see especially: C.A.P. (second), *Debates*, vol. i, pp. 256–1472; *The Establishment of West Pakistan Act, 1955*; Callard, *Pakistan, A Political Study*, pp. 183–93; Feldman, *A Constitution for Pakistan*, ch. 10; W. A. Wilcox, *Pakistan, The Consolidation of a Nation* (1963), chs. 10–13.

[3] *Report of the Constitution Commission, Pakistan*, 1961 (1962), paras. 55, 68.

[4] Coleman, *Nigeria*, pp. 41–60.

in 1957–8, but revision was postponed.[1] Nevertheless, the issue remained alive, being hotly disputed in the 1959 federal election. Moreover, in 1962–3 the N.P.C.–N.C.N.C. coalition actually put into motion the machinery for creating a new Mid-West Region,[2] and there was also talk of enlarging the Federal Territory of Lagos at the expense of the Western Region.

In the other three recent federations the delineation of the regional units has not been quite so controversial, yet the issue has not been unimportant. In the West Indies the islands separated by water would appear to be the natural units. Nevertheless, the original proposals of 1945–6 for a federation of the Windward and Leeward Islands envisaged the possibility that this might form one unit in a larger British Caribbean federation. When the federation was created, however, instead the existing Leeward Islands Federation was dissolved and its member islands became separate units in the larger federation.[3] Nevertheless, the small islands of St. Kitts, Nevis, and Anguilla remained linked as a single unit, while the tiny Cayman, Turks, and Caicos Islands were associated with Jamaica in a special relation.[4] Subsequently, before the collapse of the federation there were suggestions that the smaller islands should be grouped into larger units, or that there should be a double federation in which Jamaica would be linked by a confederal relationship with a tightly federated group of Eastern Caribbean islands.[5]

In Central Africa much of the settler advocacy of amalgamation before 1950 had been directed primarily at a union of the two Rhodesias where most of the settler population had been concentrated. There was even a suggestion that, instead of associating the three territories, the copperbelt and line of rail should be detached from the rest of Northern Rhodesia and amalgamated with Southern Rhodesia, the rest of Northern Rhodesia being turned into two separate protectorates, one of which might possibly be absorbed into Nyasaland. The officials' conference of 1951 rejected such a scheme on economic grounds, and the subsequent negotiations for federation took the existing three territories as the regional units.[6] The idea of amalgamating the Northern Rhodesian line of rail with Southern Rhodesia to form a settler Dominion was revived, however, in some of the submissions to the Monckton Commission, when it was suggested that the rest of the two northern protectorates might be divided into a number of wholly African states loosely associated with the Dominion. Such a scheme was criticized by the Commission as both unfair and unacceptable to the Africans of Northern Rhodesia.[7]

---

[1] See Map 5. See also section 3 of this chapter.

[2] *Mid-Western Region Act,1962*(1962, no. 6); *Mid-Western Region* (*Transitional Provisions*) *Act, 1963* (1963, no. 18).

[3] *Leeward Islands Act, 1956*; Col. no. 255/1950, pp. 46, 78. See also L. Braithwaite, 'Progress Toward Federation, 1938–1956', *Social and Economic Studies*, vi (1957), pp. 140, 143–4.   [4] Constitution, arts. 1, 43 (5).

[5] *The West Indian Economist* (April 1960), pp. 10–11; Lewis, *Puerto Rico: A Case Study*, pp. 76–90.

[6] Cmd. 8233/1951, paras. 36–37.   [7] Cmnd. 1148/1960, paras. 77–78.

In Malaya there has been little dispute about the boundaries of states, but the number and status of the components of the federation has been a major question. Most controversial has been the question of the relation of Singapore to the federation. Singapore was originally excluded from both the Malayan Union (1946) and the Malayan Federation (1948), not only for economic reasons but also for fear that it might upset the internal racial and political balance. When, however, Singapore pressed for inclusion the Malayan leaders agreed in 1961 to its admission in order to prevent it from becoming a base for subverting Malaya.[1] At the same time they took up the active advocacy of a wider Malaysian Federation including the British Borneo territories in order to avoid a Chinese majority. But the Malay and Singapore politicians clashed repeatedly and in 1965 Singapore found itself once again outside the federation.

Since the number and shape of the regional units of government has been a question of such concern in all the new federations, we must now turn to an examination of some of the major issues involved: first, the size and number of the component regions, and secondly, the social homogeneity within regional units.

2. *The size and number of regions*

It must be made clear at the outset that in any discussion of the size of regions, their population, area, and financial resources are all relevant. Population is an important criterion because it indicates the magnitude of the administrative problems involved, and also because it usually forms the basis for regional electoral influence in the institutions of central government. But the other two criteria are also important: area serves to suggest how compact or decentralized regional administration itself must be, and financial resources indicate the degree of political as well as economic self-sufficiency likely to be displayed by the regional governments. Bearing these points in mind, in this section I shall focus attention on three aspects of the problem: first, the absolute size of the region; second, the size of the regions relative to each other; third, the actual number of regional governments.

Among the new federations there has been a striking contrast in the absolute size of the component regions, as population figures clearly indicate. Three of the federations have consisted of regions of massive size: all the Indian states after their reorganization in 1956 except Jammu and Kashmir and the Union territories, both provinces of Pakistan after the unification of West Pakistan in 1955, and two of the three original Nigerian regions, each contained populations larger than the total federal populations in Central Africa, Malaya, or the West Indies.[2] By contrast, the populations of eight of the ten West Indian territories and of one of the Malayan states, and the electorates

[1] Lee Kuan Yew, *The Battle for Merger* (1961), Appendix 4, 'Tungku's Merger Speeches in Federal Parliament'.

[2] For comparison with the older Commonwealth federations, it might be noted that eight

of the three Central African territories, were each under 75,000. Thus the range in the absolute size of regions in the different federations has been enormous.

In deciding upon the appropriate size for the regional units, constitution-makers have been influenced by a number of criteria. Some of these have weighed in favour of large regions. There is, for instance, the requirement of sufficient population and resources to maintain effective state government. This justification was cited in the consolidation of the 552 Indian princely states into larger units, in the recommendations of the Indian States Reorganization Commission in favour of larger states, in Pakistan in the grouping together of certain princely states and later in the unification of West Pakistan, in Nigeria by both the Minorities Commission and the British Government in opposing the creation of new regions, in Central Africa by the Monckton Commission in rejecting the Dominion Party scheme for dividing up Northern Rhodesia, and in the West Indies by those advocating the grouping together of the smaller islands in the Eastern Caribbean.[1] The importance of such considerations has been apparent in the difficulties experienced by the smaller units in the West Indies, Pakistan, and Malaya in sustaining effectively full governmental machinery, and in the need in these cases for a simplified structure for regional governments.[2] This problem applies with even more force in the Federation of South Arabia and the contemplated East Caribbean federation, where in both cases the total federal population is under one million. A second argument frequently advanced for large regions is that, by reducing the number of regional units necessary, the duplication of administration is minimized. While there is some strength to such an argument, especially where the regions are as small as some of the Malayan states or the islands of the Eastern Caribbean, the larger regions of India, Pakistan, and Nigeria are sufficiently extensive to require a large degree of internal decentralization within the regions, thus counteracting the economies gained from size. A third justification for large regions is that they are better able to function as economic units, especially for purposes of economic planning. The Indian States Reorganization Commission considered this a relevant, although not the fundamental, consideration, and the subsequent grouping of the states into five zones was based on economic regions.[3] Similar economic

---

of the Indian states (after 1956), both provinces of Pakistan (after 1955), and the Northern Region of Nigeria were each larger than the total populations of either Canada or Australia.

[1] It has been suggested that the African tribal units are too small to become regions within federations and are more appropriate as a basis for local government (see R. C. Pratt, 'The Future of Federalism in British Africa', *Queen's Quarterly*, lxvii (1960), pp. 188–9). Nevertheless, this has not discouraged proposals for the federalization of Uganda and Kenya.

[2] For attempts to simplify the regional institutions, see Col. no. 330/1957, paras. 179–81, 186, 192; Cmnd. 1434/1961, paras. 12, 43–46.

[3] *Report of the States Reorganization Commission* (1955), paras. 197–210; J. V. Bondurant, *Regionalism versus Provincialism* (1958), pp. 55–57, 62–63.

arguments were used elsewhere by advocates of the unification of West Pakistan, the incorporation of Lagos in Western Nigeria, the continued inclusion of the Middle Belt in Northern Nigeria, the amalgamation with Southern Rhodesia of the Northern Rhodesian line of rail, and the scheme for a two-tier West Indian federation, with Jamaica and the Eastern Caribbean as the two economic regions. The importance of regional economic self-sufficiency would appear to be limited, however, since in most of these federations a major motive for federal union was the development of a wider interdependent economy. One other justification that might be advanced in favour of large regional units, but which has not usually been cited, is that there is less danger of regional government competing with local government in the functions performed and so reducing the latter to insignificance.

There have also been arguments in favour of small regions. Critics of the larger regions in India and Nigeria have suggested that there may actually be gains in administrative efficiency in compact units of government. Supporters of strong central government have also often argued, especially in Nigeria, that small and less self-reliant regions would not be as likely to oppose the concentration of central power or to contemplate secession.[1] The examples of the larger regional units of Nigeria, India, Pakistan, and the West Indies, asserting themselves at the expense of the central government, and the willingness of the Malayan states and of the smaller Caribbean islands to accept increasing central power, provide some evidence to support these claims. Finally, if federal institutions are to be justified on the grounds that regional governments provide a means whereby members of the electorate in a large nation may have a closer link with their representatives, then the regional units must be small enough for individuals to be conscious of their influence on regional government. There would appear to be some strength to this argument, judging by the pressures for separate regions from groups aware of their political impotence within the larger regional units. Examples have been the desire of the western districts of Uttar Pradesh to be separated, the fears of the other groups that Punjabis would dominate in an amalgamated West Pakistan, the various schemes for village republics in both India and Pakistan, and the feeling of minorities within the Nigerian regions that they could have political influence only if new regions were created.

But the consideration of regional size also involves questions of the size of regions relative to each other within a federation. Here population is particularly important because it generally governs central voting strength, and wealth is significant because of its effect upon the ability to finance services comparable to those of other regions without a greater dependence on central aid.

Because of historical, ethnic, or geographic factors determining the shape

---

[1] Cmnd. 505/1958, p. 48; Azikiwe, *Zik*, pp. 100, 108–9; Awolowo, *Awo*, p. 190; cf. Bondurant, *Regionalism versus Provincialism*, p. 56.

of their regions, the new federations have all been characterized by sharp disparities in the population, area, and wealth of their regional units.[1] If the ratio between the populations of the largest and of the smallest regions is considered, this has not been significantly greater than in the older federations which also contained regions of vastly contrasting size. But Pakistan, Nigeria, the West Indies, and, if the federal electorate is taken as the basis for comparison, Rhodesia and Nyasaland each have contained a single regional unit with a majority of the total federal population, a situation unparalleled in the United States, Switzerland, Canada, or Australia.[2] India, Malaya, and later Malaysia have been better balanced, but even in these federations a few large regions are in a relatively dominant position. In some of the new federations the preponderant population or electorate of a single or a few larger regions has been reinforced by relative wealth, as in the larger Malyan states, Singapore, and Southern Rhodesia, or by both wealth and expanse of area, as with Jamaica and Trinidad in the Caribbean, Bombay before 1960 in contrast to the smaller Indian states, and the Rhodesias compared to Nyasaland. On the other hand, in some instances the massive population or electorate of certain regions has to some extent been offset by the relatively greater wealth or area of other units. The best example was the balance between East Pakistan, with a majority of the population, and West Pakistan, with most of the wealth and area. Similar effects arose from the concentration of wealth in Western Nigeria, Trinidad, Northern Rhodesia, and Bombay (1950–60) and West Bengal, as compared to Northern Nigeria, Jamaica, Southern Rhodesia, and Uttar Pradesh.

These contrasts in regional size and wealth, and particularly the preponderance of certain regions, have almost invariably accentuated inter-regional tension. Examples have been numerous: the indignation in India of the smaller states, particularly those in the south, at the predominance of Uttar Pradesh and Bombay in central politics; the mutual fears of domination by each other in the two wings of Pakistan; the southern fears in Nigeria of northern political supremacy, and the northern apprehension of economic domination by the southerners; the distrust on the part of the smaller islands of both Jamaica and Trinidad, and the chafing of the two larger islands at having to support the poverty-stricken small islands; the fear of the Africans in the two northern protectorates of Southern Rhodesian control of the federal electorate, the resentment of Northern Rhodesians at having their wealth exploited by Southern Rhodesia, and the vexation of settlers in both Rhodesias at having to support Nyasaland financially; the exasperation of the north-eastern Malay states at their relative poverty. As a result, there have been

---

[1] See Table 2, p. 362.

[2] Of older federations only the German Empire of 1871–1918 was comparable in this respect (see Wheare, *Federal Government*, p. 6). In Rhodesia and Nyasaland the population of the three territories was roughly equal, but there was a sharp disparity in the size of the predominantly European electorates. See Table 15, p. 382.

acute debates over issues of regional representation in the central legislatures and executives, and over the relative importance of such criteria as derivation, population, need, or equalization of services, in the distribution of finances to regions. Attempts have usually been made, therefore, to protect the smaller regions through the use of second chambers or weighted representation in the central legislature, and to compensate the less-wealthy territories by adjusted grants and by special grants in aid.[1]

These difficulties, arising out of the disparities in regional size and wealth, have been a factor in most of the movements for reorganizing the shape of regional units. In India a desire to reduce the contrast in the sizes of states was a major motive in the consolidation of the smaller princely states at the time of their integration, in the recommendations of the States Reorganization Commission for enlarging the smaller states, in some of the demands for the splitting of Uttar Pradesh, and in the advocacy of a consolidation of the southern states in order to carry greater weight against the north.[2] Probably the most important motive in the unification of West Pakistan was the desire to balance East Bengal, for it was the repudiation of the Muslim League by East Bengal in 1954 which triggered off the scheme.[3] The southern Nigerian leaders who advocated the creation of new ethnic regions saw in these a means also of weakening the predominance of the Northern Region by detaching the Middle Belt.[4] Ironically, the first new region established in Nigeria, the Mid-Western Region, was supported by the Northern People's Congress with the intention at least in part of weakening the wealthy Western Region controlled at that time by the Action Group.

In a number of cases the solution for sharp disparities in regional size and wealth has been seen in schemes for zonal federations in which a middle tier of government, grouping regions into roughly equal zones, would be introduced between the levels of central and regional government. Such an arrangement was suggested for pre-partition India by Coupland and by the Cabinet Mission of 1946, for Pakistan before the unification of West Pakistan, in the proposals for West Indian federation in 1945–6, and in some of the proposals for Uganda's inclusion within an East African federation.[5] Under these

---

[1] See Chapters 9 and 11 for details.

[2] *White Paper on Indian States* (rev. ed. 1950), paras. 25–29, 271; *Report of S.R.C.* (1955), pp. 67, 162, 164–7, 244–5, 250–1; B. R. Ambedkar, *Thoughts on Linguistic States* (1955), pp. 7–8, 13, 15, 19–20. But the concession in 1962 of a Nagaland state with a population less than one per cent. that of U. P. widened the disparity among full-fledged states.

[3] C.A.P. (first), *Debates*, vol. xvi, pp. 371–2; C.A.P. (second), *Debates*, vol. i, pp. 489–501, 508–9, 513, 683–7, 1423, 1444–60.

[4] Awolowo, *Awo*, pp. 190, 199–200, 206–7; Bello, *My Life*, pp. 215–16. But the Minorities Commission argued that the proposed new regions would be too small to compete on even terms with the other regions (Cmnd. 505/1958, pp. 33, 87).

[5] R. Coupland, *Report on the Constitutional Problem in India* (1944), part iii, ch. 11; Cmd. 6821/1946, paras. 15, 19; C.A.P. (second), *Debates*, vol. i, pp. 489–90; A. K. Sen, 'The New Federalism in Pakistan', S. D. Bailey (ed.), *Parliamentary Government in the Commonwealth* (1951), pp. 152–7; Cmd. 7120/1947, part i, para. 8; A. W. Macmahon, *The*

schemes autonomous regions would have been grouped into zones with zonal governments, which in turn would be united by a central government. In this way the autonomy of small political units could have been retained within zonal groups of roughly equal size. In the end, however, none of these proposals came to fruition because of the complexity involved. Instead, the various units of West Pakistan were simply amalgamated into a single province, and the small Windward and Leeward Islands joined the West Indies Federation as separate units. In India states were actually grouped into five large zones in 1956, but the zonal councils were consultative inter-governmental bodies rather than a middle tier of government.[1]

A simpler scheme designed to deal with the same problem is the concept of double federation, envisaged by the Government of India Act, 1935, later proposed by Jamaica in 1960, and agreed upon in less drastic form for the Federation of Malaysia. Under such a scheme one group of regions belongs to a relatively centralized federation, while other large or wealthy regions such as Jamaica or Singapore, or states with a different constitutional status, such as the Indian princely states of 1935 or the Malaysian Borneo territories, are less closely tied to the central government and retain autonomy over a greater range of powers.[2]

Finally, we must consider the significance of the number of units of which a federation is composed. Perhaps the most striking feature of the new federations is the small number of regional units in many of them.[3] India, for instance, with a population double that of the United States, has less than a third of the number of autonomous states. The examples of Rhodesia and Nyasaland and Nigeria, with three or four regions, and Pakistan after 1955 with only two, are even more striking, especially in view of the immense populations of the latter two federations. The political significance of having so few regions has been twofold. First, the position of the regional governments has in practice been much strengthened at the expense of central power. This was most apparent in Nigeria, 1954–60, where the real political decisions were taken by the regional premiers and the central government did not exercise to the full its constitutional powers. In Pakistan and in Rhodesia and Nyasaland there was a high degree of constitutional centralization, yet the pressures of regionalism accelerated in each until they reached the breaking-point. Secondly, where there has been a small number of regions, a struggle between regions for federal supremacy has been encouraged. The inter-regional fears of domination in Nigeria and the anxiety over Southern Rhodesian supremacy

Opportunities of Federation, Some Structural Problems, University of East Africa Conference on East African Federation (1963), p. 9.

[1] *The States Reorganization Act, 1956* (xxxvii/1956), part iii. For details see p. 245.

[2] See section 5 of this chapter, and pp. 176–7.

[3] Of the older federations the U.S.A. started with 13 states and now has 50, Canada started with 4 provinces and now has 10, Australia started with and still has 6 states, and Switzerland started in 1848 with and still has 22 states.

in Central Africa have been examples of this. But where as in Pakistan after 1955 there were only two provinces, a situation unique among modern federations, this effect was magnified, for each province was determined not to be subordinate to the other. In the resulting struggle between the two wings for ascendancy, there has never been more than an extremely precarious equilibrium.[1] The tensions and strains within Pakistan, Rhodesia and Nyasaland, and Nigeria, suggest that, where federations have been composed of only a few regions, and particularly where one of these regions has held a majority of the electorate, federal stability has been seriously undermined.

3. *Minorities within regions*

Among the recent federations it has not been unusual for the federating regions to contain within themselves populations that were far from homogeneous. Indeed, differences among the new federations in this respect are mainly a question of varying degrees.

The federations of India, Pakistan, and Nigeria have each contained a large number of regions that were heterogeneous in ethnic and religious composition. In India in 1950, for instance, many of the existing state boundaries, the product of 'administrative convenience', did not coincide with the distribution of linguistic groups, and in the initial haste the princely states had been merged into larger consolidations mainly on grounds of administrative expediency and with only a cursory glance at other considerations. With the reorganization of states on primarily linguistic lines in 1956 and the division of Bombay in 1960, the large majority of states were made unilingual.[2] Nevertheless, there still remain some exceptions, the most notable being Assam and Punjab. In addition, the Sikhs of Punjab and the Muslims and Christians of Kerala and Madras represent significant religious minorities within these states. In Pakistan, East Bengal, although linguistically homogeneous, includes a large Hindu minority, and the unification of West Pakistan created a single province within which Pathans, Sindhis, and Baluchis all fear Punjab domination. The three original regions of Nigeria each contained a numerically preponderant ethnic group together with significant minorities. In the words of Buchanan and Pugh describing Nigeria:

Not one of the existing Regions approaches the ideal of an ethnic or linguistic unit; rather does each present a dual personality, consisting in each case of a 'regional nucleus' occupied more or less compactly by a dominant group—Yoruba in the West, Ibo in the East, Hausa-Fulani in the North—with a peripheral zone occupied by minority groups.[3]

[1] The tensions and difficulties between the two halves of Canada, 1840–67, provide an earlier example of a union of two regions in which each was determined not to be subordinate to the other.

[2] For purposes of definition, the *Report of S.R.C.* (1955), para. 783–4, treated as unilingual areas where one language constituted the speech of 70 per cent. or more of the population.

[3] K. M. Buchanan and J. C. Pugh, *Land and People in Nigeria* (1955), p. 94. See Map 5 (at end). See also Cmnd. 505/1958, esp. maps 5 and 6.

Moreover, as Coleman has pointed out, in each region the dominant group was also characterized by a more advanced degree of economic development.[1]

In Rhodesia and Nyasaland, Malaya, and to a lesser degree the West Indies, the heterogeneity within regions was primarily racial, these differences often being reinforced by those of language and religion. All three territories in Central Africa contained a small but politically influential European minority and a large, but itself tribally diverse, African majority. The western and southern states of Malaya were composed of a mixture of Malays, Chinese, and Indians, forming a fundamentally plural society.[2] Even in the West Indies where the populations of most of the islands were relatively homogeneous, shadings of colour were often socially significant, and in Trinidad there existed a considerable East Indian minority.[3]

There have been a number of reasons why the regional units have themselves so often contained mixed populations. In some instances this has been unavoidable simply because population groups, although concentrated in geographical areas, have rarely been marked off precisely into neat territorial compartments. This was most obvious in the relatively plural societies of Central Africa and Malaya, but it has to some degree been true in all the new federations because of the overlapping between groups in the boundary areas.[4] Often intra-regional diversity was inevitable because different types of sectional interests did not coincide in geographical scope. In Pakistan, for example, East Bengal was linguistically homogeneous but religiously heterogeneous, while the components of West Pakistan were economically interdependent but ethnically diverse. Similarly in many Indian, Malayan, and Nigerian regions, historical, economic, ethnic, religious, racial, and administrative sectional interests did not coincide geographically with one another. Finally, in some cases, the regional units of British colonial administration, established by accident or for administrative convenience, have borne little relation to ethnic, cultural, or other social groupings, even when these were relatively distinct geographically to begin with, as in India and Nigeria.

Thus, in practice, regional units containing diverse groups and interests have frequently been unavoidable. This has affected the shape and operation of federal institutions in several ways.

To begin with, in each of the recent independent federations a list of fundamental rights has been included in the constitution.[5] As a rule these have been

---

[1] Coleman, *Nigeria*, p. 329. [2] See Map 4.

[3] G. W. Roberts, 'Some Demographic Considerations of West Indian Federation', *Social and Economic Studies*, vi (1957), pp. 265–9; M. Ayearst, *The British West Indies* (1960), pp. 14–15, 56–67.

[4] C.A.I., *Report of the Linguistic Provinces Commission* (1948), paras. 116, 119, 125, 129, 131, and Cmnd. 505/1958, p. 87, pointed out that in India and Nigeria, whatever revision was made to regional boundaries, the creation of some minorities was unavoidable.

[5] *Constitution of India, 1950*, arts. 12–35; *Constitution of Pakistan, 1956*, arts. 3–22; *Constitution of Malaya, 1957*, arts. 5–13; *Constitution of Nigeria, 1960*, arts. 17–32 and *1963*, arts. 18–33. Those in the *Constitution of Pakistan, 1962*, arts. 5 and 6, were not justiciable,

aimed as much at protecting minorities within regions against regional governments as at protecting regional majorities against national majorities. In the three Asian federations and Nigeria, all minorities in general were guaranteed certain religious, educational, and cultural rights. On the other hand, the constitutions of the Caribbean and Central African federations did not contain declarations of rights, but some were subsequently included in the territorial constitutions.[1]

Sometimes, in addition to a list of fundamental general rights, elsewhere in the constitution further guarantees have been made to specified groups within regions. In India, for instance, special provisions were made regarding the use in the states of minority languages for official purposes, the redress of grievances, and education.[2] The Malayan constitution of 1957 laid down explicit arrangements on behalf of the Malays for the reservation of land and for quotas for permits and the public services within the states, and these provisions were extended to 'natives' in the Borneo states of the Malaysian Federation.[3]

The existence of minorities within regions has also often affected the organization of regional government. Frequently special provision has been made for representation in regional legislatures: in India for Scheduled Castes and Tribes and for Anglo-Indians; in Pakistan for women members; in Nigeria (1954) for 'special interests or communities', an arrangement continued after independence only in the Northern Region; in Trinidad for the representation of the opposition and minorities in the second chamber; in the Central African protectorates for special African representatives.[4] Because of the fears of smaller groups within West Pakistan, Punjab, with a majority of the population in the united province, was limited for a period to no more than two-fifths of the members of the provincial assembly.[5] Provision has also usually been made for the use in state legislatures of minority languages, or of English for at least a specified period in the interests of minorities. At the time of the reorganization of Indian states, regional committees were established within the state legislatures of Andhra and Punjab and separate regional development boards within Bombay, because these states were still

but an amendment conceding to the courts some power to review legislation was passed in 1963.
    [1] Cmnd. 1123/1960 (Trinidad), para. 11; Cmnd. 1291/1961 (Southern Rhodesia), paras. 5–8; Cmnd. 1295/1961 (Northern Rhodesia), para. 28; Cmnd. 1887/1962 (Nyasaland), paras. 25–28.
    [2] Arts. 345, 347, 350, and art. 350A (added by *Seventh Amendment Act, 1956*, s. 21); *Report of the Official Language Commission, 1956* (1957), pp. 54–55, and Appendix VI.
    [3] Constitution, 1957, arts. 89–90, 153; *Malaysia Act, 1963*, s. 62.
    [4] *Constitution of India, 1950*, arts. 332–4; *Constitution of Pakistan, 1956*, art. 77 (2); *Constitution of Pakistan, 1962*, art. 71 (2); *Constitution of Nigeria, 1954*, ss. 22, 30, 36; *Constitution of N. Nigeria, 1960*, s. 7 (*b*); Cmnd. 1123/1960, para. 13; Cmnd. 1149/1960, pp. 39–40, 43–44, 52–53.
    [5] *The Establishment of West Pakistan Act, 1955*, s. 14; Constitution, 1956, art. 77 (5); Constitution, 1962, art. 239.

multilingual.[1] Somewhat similar in function, but influenced by the British arrangements for Scotland, Northern Ireland, and Wales, were the Ministry of Mid-West Affairs and the advisory Mid-West Council established in Western Nigeria in 1957.[2] The setting up of provincial administrations within Northern and Eastern Nigeria was designed also to allay the fears of minorities within these regions.[3] In most cases there have been constitutional provisions designed to ensure equitable representation of minorities within the regional services,[4] but the representation of minorities or special groups on regional executives has generally been left to convention, except for the specified African representation on the executive councils of the Central African protectorates.[5] Separate electorates for minorities or special groups in regional elections have also generally been avoided, except in Central Africa and in Pakistan.[6]

The central government has sometimes been assigned by the constitution a special role as guardian of the minorities against oppression by regional governments. Often the central government has been given direct responsibility, or powers to give directions to state governments, regarding minorities, as in the cases of Scheduled Areas, Tribes and Castes in India and Pakistan, and aborigines in Malaya.[7] In India the central government has also been given power to direct state governments regarding the establishment of regional legislative committees and development boards, the recognition of minority languages, and the use of minority languages for education.[8] Provision has been made too for a special officer reporting to the central government on the operation of minority safeguards within the states.[9] In Pakistan the specification of joint or separate electorates for elections to provincial assemblies was left for the National Assembly, after consulting the provincial legislatures, to decide.[10] Under the Malayan constitution changes in the reservation of land for Malays required not only a special majority in a state assembly but the approval by special majorities in the central parliament.[11] In Central Africa, however, it was not the central government, but the United Kingdom Government, which took on the function of protector of territorial political minorities against discrimination by regional governments.[12]

[1] Art. 371 as inserted by *Seventh Amendment Act, 1956*, s. 22.
[2] Cmnd. 505/1958, pp. 12, 96.
[3] Cmnd. 569/1958, paras. 54–55; Bello, *My Life*, p. 222.
[4] *Constitution of India, 1950*, arts. 16, 335; *Constitution of Pakistan, 1956*, art. 17, 27; *Constitution of Malaya, 1957*, art. 153 (10), and Eighth Sched. s. 18; *Malaysia Act, 1963*, s. 62; *Constitution of Nigeria, 1960*, s. 27, and *1963*, s. 28.
[5] Cmnd. 1149/1960, pp. 43, 54.
[6] Cmnd. 1149/1960, pp. 33–36, 43–46, 53–54; *Constitution of Pakistan, 1956*, art. 145.
[7] *Constitution of India, 1950*, arts. 244, 275 (1), 337–42, and Fifth and Sixth Scheds.; *Constitution of Pakistan, 1956*, arts. 103–4, 204–7; *Constitution of Pakistan, 1962*, art. 223; *Constitution of Malaya, 1957*, Ninth Sched., List I, item 16.
[8] Art. 347, and *Seventh Amendment Act, 1956*, ss. 21–22, inserting arts. 350A and 371.
[9] Art. 350B inserted by *Seventh Amendment Act, 1956*, s. 21.
[10] Art. 145.   [11] Arts. 88–90.   [12] Cmnd. 1149/1960, pp 30–31, 47–48, 54–55.

In some instances inter-governmental advisory bodies, with representation on both the central and regional governments, have been established with a view to promoting the interests of intra-regional minorities. This was one of the functions envisaged for the Indian Zonal Councils when they were created, and was the primary function of the Councils for Minority Areas in Western and Eastern Nigeria and of the Niger Development Board.[1] In Nigeria the anxieties of minorities over the control of police by regional governments resulted in a unique arrangement whereby a single federal police force was normally administered by a Police Council composed of central and regional ministers.[2]

In order to protect themselves, minorities within regions have sometimes demanded their own regional units of government. In many cases, because of the intermingling of different racial groups or because of overlapping sectional interests, such a solution has had little practical appeal, but where more homogeneous regions could be created by revising regional boundaries, the demand for their own 'linguistic' or 'ethnic' regional units has often captured the imagination of intra-regional minorities. The strongest movements of this type have occurred in India and Nigeria, although the critics of the unification in West Pakistan, and the supporters of the Dominion Party scheme in Central Africa for attaching the Northern Rhodesian settled line of rail to Southern Rhodesia, were also aiming at relatively homogeneous units. Elsewhere, it was the demand for homogeneous regional units that lay at the heart of the dispute in Uganda between Bunyoro and Buganda over the lost counties and of the controversies in Kenya over the regional units to be established.[3]

In India, the movement for linguistic states originated well before 1947, the Congress Party having accepted the linguistic redistribution of provinces as a political objective in 1920. But because of the critical circumstances existing at the time of independence, the primacy of the need for national unity, the importance of economic development, and a reluctance to tamper with the economic *status quo*, the Constituent Assembly postponed the revision of states on linguistic lines.[4] However, when as a result of mounting insistence the Congress leadership gave in to the agitation for the creation of a linguistic Andhra State, which was established in 1953, it proved impossible to resist the tidal wave of demands for a major reorganization of states on linguistic lines, this being carried through in 1956.[5] In the few multilingual states

[1] Bondurant, *Regionalism versus Provincialism*, pp. 56, 62; M. V. Pylee, *Constitutional Government in India* (1960), p. 599; Cmnd. 505/1958, pp. 94–97; Cmnd. 569/1958, paras. 52, 56. In Rhodesia and Nyasaland, the African Affairs Board was empowered to assist territorial governments if they requested. See Constitution, art. 70 (*b*).

[2] See pp. 186–7.

[3] Cmnd. 1717/1962; Cmnd. 1899 and 1900/1962.

[4] *Report of S.R.C.* (1955), paras. 58–67, 76–80; *Report of the Linguistic Provinces Commission* (1948), paras. 8, 15, 140, 147, 151–3; Indian National Congress, *Report of the Linguistic Provinces Committee* (1949), pp. 4, 5, 9, 15; C.A.I., *Debates*, vol. x, p. 319.

[5] *Andhra State Act, 1953* (xxx/1953); *Report of S.R.C.* (1955), esp. paras. 88–90; *The States Reorganization Act, 1956* (xxxvii/1956).

remaining, pressure for revision persisted, and in 1960, as a result, Bombay was finally divided.[1] In the same year the principle of a separate Naga State was conceded and its creation was undertaken in 1962.[2] Meanwhile, spurred on by these events, Punjab, where the members of the militant Sikh organization, the Akali Dal, were agitating for a separate Sikh State, and Assam, torn by linguistic fever, continued to be troubled by disturbances and disorders.

The origin of the movement for ethnic regions in Nigeria was more recent. In 1943 Azikiwe suggested a federal commonwealth composed of eight 'protectorates', primarily administrative units, but roughly following ethnic lines.[3] Subsequently, both Azikiwe and Awolowo criticized the regional pattern established by the Richards Constitution, coming down firmly in support of a federal system based on ethnic units.[4] The issue was raised at the Ibadan Conference in 1950, but there the division of existing regions was rejected for fear that regionalization on ethnic grounds alone would be likely to enthrone tribalism.[5] The demands for new states continued, but at the 1953–4 constitutional conferences the views of the Northern People's Congress and the Action Group in favour of the existing regions, on which their political power was based, prevailed, the only new region being the Southern Cameroons, which was separated from the Eastern Region.[6] This precedent, like that of Andhra in India, spurred on minorities elsewhere. The increasing political consciousness of cultural groups, the anxiety of minorities that the impending self-government would mean perpetual domination by the regional majorities, the new minority political parties demanding new states, the rivalry among the major parties for minority votes by means of promises of new regions, and the desire of southern leaders to split the massive Northern Region, all fanned the flames of ethnic regionalism, making this a major issue at the constitutional conferences of 1957–8. But the firm opposition of the Northern Region and the British Government, the report of the Minorities Commission, and the reluctance of Action Group and N.C.N.C. leaders to weaken their own regions, led in the end to the postponement of any change and to the adoption of an extremely rigid procedure for revising regional boundaries.[7] In the federal elections of 1959 the question of new states was again pressed, but the pattern of voting suggested that only in the Mid-West was there a coherent

---

[1] *Bombay Reorganization Act, 1960* (11/1960).

[2] *State of Nagaland Act, 1962* (27/1962); *Thirteenth Amendment Act, 1962* (effected 1963).

[3] N. Azikiwe, *Political Blueprint of Nigeria* (1943).

[4] Azikiwe, *Zik*, pp. 108–9; O. Awolowo, *Path to Nigerian Freedom* (1947), pp. 48, 53–55; Awolowo, *Awo*, pp. 160–75; Coleman, *Nigeria*, pp. 261–2, 277, 323–5, 347–9, 386–90.

[5] Nigeria, *Proceedings of General Conference* (1950), pp. 60, 88, 98, 110, 151, 162–3, 173, 180, 217, 232–6, 244.

[6] Cmd. 8934/1953, paras. 23–24 and Annex VI; Cmd. 9059/1954, paras. 8–11 and Annex III.

[7] Cmnd. 207/1957, paras. 24 (*d*, *e*), 49, 51, 58; Cmnd. 505/1958, esp. pp. 47, 55, 87; Cmnd. 569/1958, paras. 44–51, 57; Awolowo, *Awo*, pp. 183–212.

electoral demand for a new region.[1] Then, in 1961–2, the N.P.C.–N.C.N.C. coalition, influenced as much by the desire to weaken the Western Region controlled by the opposition Action Group as by the desire to safeguard minority interests, set about carving out a Mid-Western Region.[2] Following a referendum in the area in 1963, in which 89 per cent. of the electorate were in favour, a separate administration was established for the new region.[3] As in India, this precedent appeared to stimulate demands for new ethnic regions elsewhere, most notably among the restive Tiv in the Middle Belt.

The arguments advanced for and against the reorganization of states on linguistic or ethnic lines in India and Nigeria were very much the same.[4] The advocates of homogeneous regional units pointed to a variety of benefits. First of all, the creation of such units would eliminate the frustrations of minorities within the existing heterogeneous regions. Secondly, by relieving tension and establishing internal harmony within regions, national unity would be assisted. Thirdly, a unilingual region would involve less administrative complexity, and therefore administrative efficiency would be enhanced. Fourthly, homogeneous political units would encourage in a region the internal cohesiveness necessary for the operation of democratic government.

Those who opposed the reorganization of regions invariably pointed to the difficulties of drawing boundaries which did not create new minorities. They also feared that homogeneous regions, by sharpening linguistic and regional loyalties and fostering sub-nationalisms and even balkanization, would be a threat to federal unity, especially at the critical time just before or after independence. There were, they pointed out, other factors of importance relevant to regional boundaries besides linguistic or ethnic homogeneity: national security, financial viability, the requirements of economic planning, historical loyalties, geographical factors, communications, and administrative convenience. In addition there were the disruptions associated with changing existing boundaries: the cost of changes, the administrative dislocation, the disorganization of economic planning, the bitterness over demarcation, and the weakening of national stability.

Which arguments has experience vindicated? In India the attempt to resist the reorganization of multilingual states into homogeneous units resulted, especially between 1950 and 1956, in considerable strain upon the federal structure. Minorities complained of discrimination by regional governments,

---

[1] B. P. Prescott, 'The Nigerian Election and the Minorities', *West Africa* (20 February 1960), p. 207.   [2] *Mid-Western Region Act, 1962* (1962, no. 6).

[3] *Mid-Western Region (Transitional Provisions) Act, 1963* (1963, no. 18); *Constitution of the Mid-Western Region Act, 1964.*

[4] See, for instance, C.A.I., *Report of the Linguistic Provinces Commission* (1948); Indian National Congress, *Report of the Linguistic Provinces Committee* (1949); *Report of S.R.C.* (1955); Nigeria, *Proceedings of the General Conference* (1950), pp. 60, 82, 88, 93, 98, 110, 151, 173, 180, 190; Cmnd. 207/1957, para. 24 (*b*); Cmnd. 505/1958; Awolowo, *Awo*, chs. 12, 13; Azikiwe, *Zik*, pp. 108–9; Bello, *My Life* (1962), pp. 215–16; O. Arikpo, 'The Future of Nigerian Federalism', *West Africa* (28 May–2 July 1955), pp. 487, 511, 533, 564, 589, 613.

political parties repeatedly exploited minority anxieties and desires for new states, the effectiveness of regional governments was disrupted by agitation and even violence, and national stability and unity were weakened both by the bitterness of the disputes and by uncertainty over the future regional pattern. As a result the demand for linguistic states proved irresistible. Paradoxically, the concessions to these appeals for regional distinctiveness and homogeneity have strengthened both nationalism and regionalism. On the one hand, the creation of unilingual states has reduced the tensions over language issues and contributed to greater unity and stability. At the same time, these new units have also generally reinforced state loyalties by giving them linguistic solidarity.

In Nigeria, as in India, resistance to the creation of ethnic regions provoked expressions of minority grievances, the concentration of political parties upon minority demands for new states, vigorous and sometimes explosive agitation, and bitterness and national instability over claims and counter-claims. But whether there, too, it will in the end prove impossible to resist the cry for ethnic regions is not yet clear. The movement for creation of a Mid-Western Region persisted until successful, but elsewhere the clamour for new regions faded considerably in the early years after independence. A difference in the Indian and Nigerian situations lay in the constitutional provisions covering the revision of regional boundaries.[1] In India these were made extremely flexible, since eventual reorganization was anticipated.[2] But, at the insistence of the Northern Region and of the British Government, the Nigerian procedures were made much more rigid, and this itself helped to discourage some of the movements for new regions. On the other hand, the very inflexibility of the constitutional restrictions tended to stimulate extra-constitutional action among the Tiv.

4. *Federal capitals*

As a unit within a federation, the federal capital has usually been given a special status. Here, two issues have generally provoked debate: first, the location of the capital, and second, the relative powers to be assigned to the central and the adjoining regional governments with respect to the administration of the national capital.

Among the considerations which have been relevant in the siting of the federal capital have been the desire to establish an inspiring focus for federal unity, the convenience of the location in relation to the extremities of the federation, the adequacy of communications, the availability of services, the cost of establishing and developing the capital, and the character of the local political and social atmosphere.[3] The choice of location has also usually been

[1] For details, see Chapter 12, section 5.

[2] C.A.I., *Debates*, vol. vii, p. 439; vol. x, pp. 211, 319.

[3] See especially Col. no. 328/1956, p. 3 and ch. 2; Cmd. 8934/1953, Annex V; Cmnd. 1148/1960, paras. 263–6.

complicated by regional rivalries, the most extreme example being the difficulty the West Indian leaders had in reaching agreement.[1] One of the questions facing federal constitution-makers has been whether to establish the federal capital in a new city or to use an existing city as a base. Regional rivalry and the need to dissociate the national capital from any particular region have sometimes made a new capital necessary. Instances are the transfer of the capital of India in 1912 from Calcutta to Delhi, the decision in Pakistan in 1959 to establish a new capital of Islamabad near Rawalpindi, and the power given to the central legislature to set up new capitals in both Rhodesia and Nyasaland and the West Indies.[2] But elsewhere, questions of cost and availability of services have been factors encouraging the choice of a well-developed city or even an existing regional capital. Such reasons led to the choice of Lagos, Kuala Lumpur, and, initially, of Karachi. For similar reasons Salisbury and Port-of-Spain were originally selected as temporary federal capitals until a more permanent one could be established some time later. In the cases of Delhi, Kuala Lumpur, and Lagos, precedent was also a factor, for each of these cities had been the capital of a previous political union. Distance from the extremities of the federation is likely to be important in locating a capital, for where regions have been relatively distant from the federal capital, resentment has often been felt in these regions at their lack of influence in national politics. Examples were the feelings of Jamaicans about Port-of-Spain, East Bengalis towards Karachi, Northern Nigerians to Lagos, southern Indians towards Delhi, and Nyasaland Africans regarding Salisbury. Indeed, Salisbury was a particularly unfortunate choice as the federal capital, for the greater restrictions affecting Africans there and its continuance as the capital of Southern Rhodesia undoubtedly contributed to the dissatisfaction and suspicion in the northern territories which eventually proved fatal to the federation.[3] A solution adopted in Pakistan in 1956, to meet the problem of distance, was to rotate the meetings of the National Assembly and the Supreme Court between Karachi, the federal capital, and Dacca.[4] The 1962 constitution went even further, establishing two federal capitals, one in the west, Islamabad, serving as the seat of the central government, and the other in the east, Dacca, becoming the seat of the National Assembly.[5] Arrangements for subsidiary

---

[1] The Rance Committee recommended Trinidad; the 1953 Conference chose Grenada; the 1956 Conference rejected this choice but failed to reach agreement; a Federal Capital Commission recommended in order of preference, Barbados, Jamaica, Trinidad; the Standing Federation Committee, 1957, finally chose Trinidad.

[2] *Report of S.R.C.* (1955), para. 585; *Constitution of Pakistan, 1962*, art. 211; *Constitution of R. and N., 1953*, art. 6 (1); *Constitution of W.I., 1957*, art. 6 (2). In Malaya, instead of creating a new federal capital it was intended that eventually the state capital of Selangor should be moved from Kuala Lumpur to Klang. See *Constitution of Malaya, 1957*, art. 154 (3).

[3] Cmnd. 1148/1960, paras. 263–6; H. Franklin, *Unholy Wedlock* (1963), pp. 101–2.

[4] Constitution, 1956, arts. 50, 155.

[5] Constitution, 1962, art. 211.

capitals have also been advocated, though never implemented, in Central Africa and in India.[1]

Another source of controversy has been the relative roles to be assigned to the central and regional governments in the administration of the federal capital. Indeed, in India, Pakistan, and Nigeria a considerable number of adjustments were subsequently made. Delhi began in 1950 as a Chief Commissioner's province, and from 1951 to 1956 had its own legislature and council of ministers, but in 1956 it became a centrally administered Union territory with its own corporation form of municipal government.[2] Karachi was separated from Sind as a centrally administered territory in 1948, became a Chief Commissioner's province in 1952, and then in 1955 became a centrally administered area within the united province of West Pakistan.[3] Lagos was separated from the Western Region in 1954 to become a centrally administered federal territory, but in 1958 certain responsibilities were transferred from the central government to the Lagos Town Council and certain disabilities were removed.[4] In Malaya, too, an adjustment was made when the proviso limiting the exercise of certain central powers in Kuala Lumpur was removed by the first constitutional amendment in 1960.[5]

These difficulties and frequent adjustments have arisen from a number of conflicting pressures. Because of regional rivalry, and because of the desire that the federal capital should be developed as a focus for national unity, there have often been demands that the capital be freed from the influence of the government of the region in which it stands. On the other hand, where, as in the cases of Lagos and Karachi, there have been close ethnic and economic ties with the adjoining region, attempts at separation have aroused considerable resistance.[6] Moreover, where, for special reasons, regional capital cities were chosen for the federal capital, as in the cases of Kuala Lumpur, Salisbury, and Port-of-Spain, separation from the region was out of the question unless the regional capital was moved. The solutions have generally followed one of two general patterns. In India, Nigeria, and Pakistan (1948–55), the national capital was separated as a distinct, centrally administered 'federal territory', with its own local municipal government.[7] On the other hand, in

---

[1] Cmnd. 1148/1960, para. 266; B. R. Ambedkar, *Thoughts on Linguistic States* (1955), ch. 11.

[2] Constitution, arts. 239–41 and First Sched.; *Government of Part C States Act, 1951* (xlix of 1951), s. 21; *Report of S.R.C.* (1955), paras. 580–94; *Seventh Amendment Act, 1956*, ss. 2, 17; *Delhi Municipal Corporation Act, 1957* (66 of 1957).

[3] G.G.O. 14/1948; *The Establishment of West Pakistan Act, 1955*, s. 2.

[4] Cmnd. 207/1957, paras. 55–56; Cmnd. 569/1958, paras. 22–24.

[5] *Constitution (Amendment) Act, 1960* (F. 10/1960), s. 31.

[6] Cmd. 8934/1953, para. 22 (iv) and Annex V; Action Group, *Lagos Belongs to the West* (n.d.); C.A.P. (first), *Debates*, vol. iii, pp. 73–108.

[7] In India (after 1956) and Nigeria citizens in the federal capital were given control of their own local affairs, only the middle (regional) tier of government being avoided. See J. Harvey Perry, *Report on the Financial and Administrative Arrangements in Capitals of*

Malaya, Rhodesia and Nyasaland, and the West Indies, and in Pakistan after 1962, the federal capitals were not separated from the regions in which they were located. Regional laws applied to these capitals, but the central government was at the same time given special extensive legislative and administrative powers with respect to them.[1] Earlier, when West Pakistan had been unified, an arrangement half-way between these two patterns was adopted as a compromise. Karachi was incorporated within the province of West Pakistan, losing its status as a separate federal territory, but the central government was given exclusive legislative and administrative authority within the capital.[2] The result was the anomalous situation in which Karachi sent representatives to a provincial legislature which was expressely denied authority over the federal capital. This situation ended in 1961, when Karachi ceased to be a federal territory.

5. *The uniformity of regional constitutions*

The first impression one gets in examining the regional constitutions is that each federation is characterized by variety rather than uniformity. The Indian constitution of 1950, for instance, specified four categories of states, marked by differing regional institutions and degrees of autonomy, not to mention the special cases of Jammu and Kashmir and the sub-Himalayan protectorates.[3] At the time of the reorganization of states this diversity was reduced to two main categories: autonomous states, and Union territories; but there were special qualifications to the autonomy of Andhra, Punjab, and Assam, while Jammu and Kashmir retained its special status.[4] Later, when Nagaland was made a full-fledged state, some special provisions applying only to it were included.[5] Pakistan shortly after independence consisted of a varied group of four Governor's provinces, a Chief Commissioner's province, a Federal territory, a number of separate acceded states, a union of acceded states, and some frontier tribal areas.[6] Here too, the variety was

---

Federal Territories (Lagos, 1953), pointing to problems of the relationship between the central government and local citizens in federal capitals.

[1] *Constitution of Malaya, 1957*, art. 154 and Federal List items 6 (*e*), 7 (*h*); *Constitution of R. and N., 1953*, art. 6; *Constitution of W.I., 1957*, art. 6; *Constitution of Pakistan, 1962*, art. 131 (4).

[2] *The Establishment of West Pakistan Act, 1955*, s. 2; *The Government of India (Second Amendment) Act, 1955*, s. 9; *The Constitution of Pakistan, 1956*, arts. 1, 211.

[3] See Map 1. The special status of the State of Jammu and Kashmir was a result of the controversy over its accession. The sub-Himalayan dependencies of Sikkim and Bhutan were protectorates on a treaty basis and outside the framework of the Federation (C. H. Alexandrowicz, *Constitutional Developments in India* (1957), pp. 154–5).

[4] Arts. 152–241, 244 (2), 370, 371, and First Schedule as amended by *Seventh Amendment Act, 1956*, ss. 2, 6–17, 22, 29, and Sched.; *Report of S.C.R.*, paras. 236–87; *The Constitution (Application to Jammu and Kashmir) Order, 1954* (C.O. 48/1954), and later amendments. See also B. R. Sharma, 'The Special Position of Jammu and Kashmir in the Indian Constitution', *Indian Journal of Political Science*, xix (1958), pp. 282–90; M. P. Jain, *Indian Constitutional Law* (1962), pp. 597–600. In 1964 Kashmir's special autonomy was reduced.

[5] *Thirteenth Amendment Act, 1962.*   [6] See Map 3.

subsequently reduced. In 1955 the consolidation of the western units meant that there were simply two provinces, but Azad Kashmir retained its special status, and certain parts of West Pakistan remained excluded areas subject to central direction.[1] Moreover, although the two provinces were given virtually identical constitutions, there was a contrast for a brief period during 1956–7 when there were joint electorates in the east and separate electorates in the west. Under the Federation of Malaya Agreement, 1948, the governments of the settlements differed in many respects and possessed less autonomy than those in the Malay states, and even when they were made equal in status in 1957, the former settlements were differentiated by having governors rather than rulers.[2] The 1957 federal constitution stipulated certain uniform 'essential provisions' for state constitutions, but included an alternative form which might serve as a transitional arrangement where necessary, especially in Perlis because of its small size.[3] The Malaysia Act also allows for some variations in the constitutions of the new states, although as units within the federation they have equal status.[4] Uganda at independence in 1962 consisted of five federal states, ten districts, and one territory.[5] The differences in the regional constitutions of Nigeria, 1954–60, were mainly related to the different paces at which each region was advancing towards self-government. By 1960, the three regions had all achieved self-government and their constitutions were basically uniform, although there were some minor variations in composition of legislatures, in arrangements for provincial administration, and in franchises. In the West Indies there was also a wide variation in territorial constitutions because of the contrasting abilites to sustain different stages of political progress, but there too, with the approach of independence, there was an attempt to make territorial constitutions more uniform.[6] The greatest contrasts in constitutional status existed, however, among the three territories in Central Africa, where Southern Rhodesia had experienced self-government for some time before 1953, while the protectorates were still far removed from its achievement.[7] But even there it was assumed that, with time, as the protectorates advanced, the gap would be closed. The reason for these variations in regional constitutions within each of the new federations is not hard to discern. It lies in the different conditions and stages of progress towards self-government in the regions at the time of federation.

But despite the apparent variety within each federation, the statesmen framing the recent federal constitutions have insisted that there should be a

---

[1] *The Establishment of West Pakistan Act, 1955*, s. 2; Constitution, 1956, arts. 1, 103–4; Constitution, 1962, arts. 1, 221, and 223. See also Wilcox, *Pakistan, The Consolidation of a Nation*, chs. 10–13.
[2] Col. no. 330/1957, paras. 189–95; Constitution, 1957, art. 70.
[3] Art. 71 and Eighth Sched., part ii; Col. no. 330/1957, paras. 180, 186.
[4] S. 12, and Second Sched.
[5] Constitution, 1962, s. 3.　　　　　　　　　　　　　　　　[6] Cmnd. 1434/1961.
[7] Cmd. 8233/1951, paras. 12–13, 23, 48; Cmnd. 1149/1960, ch. 4.

basic uniformity in regional institutions, and that these should soon become, if they were not already, representative and not autocratic.[1] It would appear that the constitution-makers have recognized the point made by K. C. Wheare: 'Not only is it desirable that there should be similarity of political institutions in the majority, at any rate, of the federating units, but it is essential, I believe, that these institutions should not be autocratic or dictatorial.'[2] Looked at from this point of view, the variety in regional constitutions within each new federation has in fact generally been one of detail rather than principle. The importance of this basic conformity has been illustrated by the degree to which regional contrasts in fundamental attitudes towards representative institutions have been a source of excessive strain in Pakistan and to an even greater degree in Rhodesia and Nyasaland.[3]

There are a number of ways in which the uniformity of regional constitutions has been ensured. In many of the new federations, the federal constitution itself has stipulated at least the minimum requirements for the form of regional government. The Indian and Pakistan constitutions went furthest in this respect, for, following the Government of India Act, 1935, the federal documents contained complete provincial constitutions.[4] The Nigerian constitution of 1954 did likewise. At independence the federal and regional constitutions were separated into different schedules of the Nigeria (Constitution) Order in Council, 1960, but any alteration in the fundamental similarity of the regional constitutions requires federal ratification.[5] The federal constitutions of Malaya in both 1948 and 1957, and Malaysia in 1963, did not contain complete state constitutions, but certain required 'essential provisions' were specified.[6] The uniformity of regional constitutions was further assured in these federations by giving the central government special emergency powers to enforce the stipulated provisions.[7] In addition, amendment of the regional constitutions, or of the essential features, was specially entrenched, preventing unilateral amendment by the regional governments.[8] Thus not only was a fundamental uniformity of regional institutions insisted

[1] See, for instance, C.A.I., *Debates*, vol. i, pp. 56, 124–5; vol. ii, p. 300; vol. vii, p. 42; Col. no. 330/1957, paras. 177–95; Azikiwe, *Zik*, p. 124.

[2] Wheare, *Federal Government*, p. 46. See also S. A. de Smith, *The New Commonwealth and Its Constitutions* (1964), pp. 264–6.

[3] The strains caused in India by the existence of an elected Communist Government in Kerala, 1957–9, and in Nigeria by authoritarian tendencies in the Northern Region, would also appear to support this contention. Similar tensions have been apparent in the South Arabian Federation as a result of conflicting attitudes to representative institutions between Aden politicians and the rulers of many of the states.

[4] Uganda and Kenya also followed this pattern.

[5] *Constitution of Nigeria, 1960*, s. 5. In 1963 separate new regional constitutions were approved, but Federal ratification continues to be necessary for major alterations. *Constitution of Nigeria, 1963*, s. 5.

[6] Federation Agreement, 1948, cls. 86–110; Constitution, 1957, art. 71 and Eighth Sched.; *Malaysia Act, 1963*, s. 12 and Second Sched.

[7] See Chapter 12, section 6.

[8] See Chapter 12, section 4.

upon, but an interdependence of federal and regional governments was re-cognized as desirable. Only in Rhodesia and Nyasaland and in the West Indies were regional constitutions established completely independently, but even there, the British Government, as the ultimate constitutional authority, was in a position to ensure basic constitutional similarity, and by convention the central government was usually consulted before alterations to territorial constitutions were made. We may conclude, then, that fundamental similarity in form among regional governments within each federation, reinforced by central responsibilities for minorities within regions and by central emergency powers, has been a usual characteristic of regional government within the recent federations.

8

THE DISTRIBUTION OF POWERS I: LEGIS-
LATIVE AND EXECUTIVE AUTHORITY

1. *The distribution of authority*

THE statesmen creating the new federations have invariably started with the assumption that the foundation of a federal political structure is a division of authority between co-ordinate central and regional governments. Indeed, the speeches in the constituent assemblies of India and Pakistan, the writings of Nigerian nationalists, and the reports of constitutional committees in Malaya, Central Africa, and the Caribbean, have often clearly echoed the traditional dualistic definition of the federal principle. For example, when the Union Powers Committee Report was being introduced in the Indian Constituent Assembly, it was declared: 'one of the essentials of a Federal Constitution is that it must provide for a method of dividing sovereign powers so that the Government at the Centre and the Governments in the Units are each within a defined sphere, co-ordinate and independent.'[1] It is not surprising, therefore, that a careful distribution of functions between central and regional governments has actually been worked out and embodied in each of the new federal constitutions.

In distributing powers between the tiers of government, federal draftsmen have had to keep in mind three interrelated aspects of the problem: the assignment of legislative authority, of executive authority, and of financial resources. Generally, it has been thought desirable that there should be a correspondence in the scope of these three aspects, on the grounds that governments should possess the executive authority and the financial resources to implement the functions within their legislative competence. It is quite possible, however, for the scope of these three aspects not to coincide, and, indeed, in several recent federations this has actually been the case. For purposes of analysis, therefore, these modes of the distribution of powers will be distinguished: this chapter will be concerned primarily with the assignment of legislative and executive authority, and the next chapter with the allocation of financial resources.

2. *The form of the distribution of legislative authority*

Although the new federal constitutions have been alike in assigning to both

[1] C.A.I., *Debates*, vol. v, p. 37. For other statements closely reflecting the traditional definition of the federal principle, see also: Col. no. 255/1950, para. 22; Cmd. 8233/1951, para. 46; Cmnd. 1150/1960, para. 53 (i).

central and regional governments at least some co-ordinate authority, there have been great variations both in the manner in which authority has been apportioned and in the content of the functions assigned to each level of government. Attention will be turned first to the form in which authority has been distributed. This section will deal with the manner in which legislative powers have been assigned—the number of legislative lists, the completeness of these lists, and the significance of the residuary power; the next section will examine the relation between the allocation of executive and legislative responsibilities.

The general form of the distribution of legislative powers has in the new federations taken one of three general patterns. The first of these is found in the constitutions of India (1950), Pakistan (1956), and Malaya (1957), in which, following the example of the Government of India Act, 1935, three exhaustive lists of central, state, and concurrent powers were compiled.[1] Originally, in the Government of India Act, 1935, this arrangement had been adopted because no agreement could be reached over where the residuary legislative power should lie.[2] In the Drafting Committee of the Indian Constituent Assembly there was some debate over whether a three-list division of legislative authority was necessary or desirable, once it had been decided to give to the Union residual legislative power, but as the question was merely one of form the majority of members preferred not to disturb the existing arrangement.[3] The influence of the model of the 1935 Act was also apparent earlier, when the Union Powers Committee submitted for consideration three lists in which most of the entries corresponded to those in the previous constitution. Likewise, in Pakistan, it was the example of the 1935 Act which was decisive in the adoption of a three-list division of legislative powers, although there was some adjustment to the content of the lists.[4] A further argument for the use of three legislative lists advanced in India was the desire to allay regional fears about the actual scope of Union power: 'They were not going to be satisfied by saying that the Centre will have only residuary powers. Just to allay the fears of Provinces and of the Indian States, we had to particularise what is included in the symbolic phrase "residuary powers".'[5] Before copying India and Pakistan, Malaya had previously experimented with a different arrangement in 1948, but in 1957, as an improvement, three legislative lists on the Indian model were drawn up, and this form was continued with only

---

[1] *Government of India Act, 1935*, Seventh Sched.; *Constitution of India, 1950*, Seventh Sched.; *Constitution of Pakistan, 1956*, Fifth Sched.; *Constitution of Malaya, 1957*, Ninth Sched. The *Independence Constitution of Kenya, 1963*, Sched. 1, contained three lists, and Sched. 2 contained a further 30 paragraphs of special provisions relating to the distribution of legislative and executive authority.

[2] *The Government of India Act, 1935*, s. 104, left the Governor-General to empower either level of government to legislate on residual matters.

[3] C.A.I., *Draft Constitution of India* (1948), p. 100.

[4] C.A.P. (second), *Debates*, vol. i, pp. 1805, 1828, 1855, 1870, 2100, 2102–3, 2140, 2236.

[5] C.A.I., *Debates*, vol. ix, pp. 856–7.

minor modifications for the Malaysian Federation.[1] A variation on the three-list assignment of legislative authority is that devised for Buganda within Uganda. There are only two lists containing exclusive central and exclusive Buganda powers, but instead of a third concurrent list all residual subjects were placed under concurrent jurisdiction.[2]

A second and apparently simpler way to divide legislative authority is to draw up a single list of exclusive central powers and to assign all residuary powers to the states. This arrangement was tried for a time in Malaya (1948–1957)[3] and the Federation of Arab Amirates of the South (1959–62),[4] but subsequently was abandoned in both. The recent constitution of Pakistan (1962) also contains only a single legislative list.[5]

In the case of Malaya, the Malayan Working Committee of 1946, like the constitution-framers in India and Pakistan, was strongly influenced by the Government of India Act, 1935, which they took as their guide for the distribution of legislative powers. But when, in the different circumstances of Malaya, it was decided to make exclusively federal nearly all the subjects of both the federal and concurrent lists in the earlier Indian Act, the committee concluded that there would be little useful purpose in drawing up additional lists of concurrent and state subjects.[6] Consequently, all residual legislative powers were simply assigned without enumeration to the states, although sources of revenue and heads of expenditure for the states were itemized in separate schedules.[7] A decade later, however, upon the recommendation of the Reid Commission, it was decided to adopt a three-list distribution of powers after all.[8] This was prompted in part by the need to remove difficulties inherent in the previous arrangement, whereby in a large range of subjects legislative and executive responsibilities did not coincide,[9] and in part by the desire to make more explicit the legislative autonomy of the states.

In Pakistan the Constitution Commission of 1961 had recommended a return to the three-list system by which powers had been distributed in the previous constitution.[10] Nevertheless, the constitution, as promulgated in 1962, contained only a single list of exclusive central powers, its content basically unchanged from that of the 1956 Federal List. The earlier concurrent and provincial lists were omitted, and residual power was assigned to the provinces.[11] This new arrangement gives the appearance of increased provincial

---

[1] *Malaysia Act, 1963*, ss. 35, 36, and Fourth Sched.
[2] Constitution, 1962, s. 74 and Sched. 7. For the other federal states in Uganda, however, there is only a single list of exclusive state subjects (s. 75 and Sched. 8).
[3] *Federation of Malaya Agreement, 1948*, cls. 48, 100, and Second Sched.
[4] Cmnd. 1814/1962, p. 10. A two-list system was adopted in 1962.
[5] Constitution, 1962, Third Sched.
[6] *Report of the Working Committee* (1946), para. 33.
[7] Federation Agreement (1948), cls. 100, 112, 113, Third and Fourth Scheds.
[8] Col. no. 330/1957, paras. 33, 81–82.
[9] See section 3 of this chapter for details.
[10] *Report of the Constitution Commission, Pakistan, 1961* (1962), paras. 71, 74.
[11] Constitution, 1962, arts. 131–2, and Third Sched.

autonomy, but in fact the scope of concurrent jurisdiction is widely extended by a provision giving the central government power to legislate with respect to any matter 'where the national interest of Pakistan in relation to—(a) the security of Pakistan, including the economic and financial stability of Pakistan; (b) planning or co-ordination; or (c) the achievement of uniformity in respect of any matter in different parts of Pakistan, so requires'.[1] In many respects, therefore, the arrangement in the 1962 constitution approximates to a two-list form of specifying the assignment of powers.

The constitutions of Rhodesia and Nyasaland, Nigeria, the West Indies, and, after 1963, the Federation of South Arabia have been alike in following a third pattern for the distribution of legislative authority. In each of these there were two lists—one enumerating exclusive central powers, and the other concurrent powers—leaving the regional governments with exclusive authority over the unspecified residual fields.[2] Here it was the example of the United States and Australia that was influential, although the actual designation of concurrent powers was more reminiscent of the Indian precedent than of these two older models. The intention in setting out the division of powers in this way, with residuary legislative power assigned to the regional governments, was to emphasize the extent of regional autonomy.[3] This was particularly the case in the Nigerian constitution of 1954, which accentuated the achievement of regional autonomy by reversing the arrangement in the preceding constitution whereby regional powers had been specified and the central government had possessed the residual legislative authority.[4] When reviewing the constitution of Rhodesia and Nyasaland, the Monckton Commission did consider whether there would be any advantage in having a third separate list of territorial powers, but rejected such an arrangement in the belief that such a list would be liable to raise considerable problems of specification and definition, and so create more dispute and disagreement than it would remove.[5]

These comments of the Monckton Commission point to the dilemma which has faced the makers of all federal constitutions. On the one hand, there is the desire to base the distribution of functions and responsibilities 'on as clear and precise definitions as possible, in order to reduce the area of uncertainty and, possibly, suspicion'.[6] On the other hand, there is the wish to avoid too rigid a definition and to make the division of authority sufficiently flexible to permit action to be adapted to the needs of changing circumstances and

---

[1] Art. 131 (2). Cf. *Report of the Constitution Commission, Pakistan, 1961* (1962), para. 71.

[2] *Constitution of R. and N., 1953*, art. 29 and Second Sched.; *Nigeria Constitution, 1954*, s. 51 and First Sched.; *Constitution of Nigeria, 1960*, s. 64 and Sched.; *Constitution of Nigeria, 1963*, s. 69 and Sched.; *Constitution of W.I., 1957*, art. 43 and Third Sched.; *Constitution of South Arabia, 1963*, s. 58 and Second and Third Scheds.

[3] Col. no. 255/1950, paras. 21–22; Cmd. 8233/1951, para. 64.

[4] S.I. 1951, no. 1172, ss. 81, 91 and Third Sched.

[5] Cmnd. 1148/1960, para. 128.   [6] Cmnd. 1150/1960, para. 53 (ii).

conditions. Generally speaking, the course which the makers of the recent federal constitutions have followed has been to specify a relatively explicit and detailed definition of powers, leaving flexibility to be achieved by a variety of other special devices.[1] This was particularly true of all three independent Asian federations, in each of which there were not only three extensive legislative lists, but a large number of articles in the body of the constitution dealing with special aspects of the distribution of legislative powers. Even in the constitutions of Rhodesia and Nyasaland, Nigeria, and the West Indies, where only two legislative lists were set out, these were relatively detailed and were supplemented by a considerable number of other sections within the constitutions, elaborating certain aspects of the assignment of legislative powers. Contrary to the expectation of critics, the detailed nature of the lists and articles dealing with the distribution of legislative powers has not as yet been a source of extensive litigation.[2] Indeed, the very precision of the lists has helped to avoid excessive litigation during the critical early years, but this may have been achieved at the expense of rigidity and greater litigation later when conditions and problems unforeseen by the constitution-makers develop.[3]

The location of the residual legislative authority may be an important aspect of the distribution of functions, because this power strengthens with time the government to which it is assigned. In all the new federations except India and more recently Kenya and Uganda, the residual power was assigned to regional governments in order to underline their autonomy.[4] The Indian Constituent Assembly had originally assumed that residual authority would be left with the regional governments, but after the agreement upon partition the Assembly decided that, as part of the general attempt to strengthen central powers, residual authority should go to the central government.[5] The significance of the residual legislative power will of course vary according to the detail and comprehensiveness of the lists and sections setting out the location of functions and responsibilities. The scope of the residual authority was widest in the West Indies where the fewest items were enumerated in the

---

[1] For provisions for flexibility, see Chapter 12.

[2] See Chapter 12, section 3.

[3] See Jennings, *Some Characteristics of the Indian Constitution*, pp. 60–62; P. H. Appleby, *Public Administration in India, Report of a Survey* (1953), p. 56. Cf. Wheare, *Federal Government*, p. 78, regarding the experience in Canada of interpreting more than one list of exclusive powers.

[4] *Constitution of Pakistan, 1956*, art. 109; *Constitution of Pakistan, 1962*, art. 132; *Federation of Malaya Agreement, 1948*, cls. 100, 110; *Constitution of Malaya, 1957*, art. 77; *Nigeria Constitution, 1954*, s. 51 (3); *Constitution of Nigeria, 1960*, s. 64 (5); *Constitution of Nigeria, 1963*, s. 69 (5); *Constitution of W.I., 1957*, art. 43 (4); *Constitution of R. and N., 1953*, art. 29 (4). In Kenya the residual power was assigned to the central government. In Uganda in relation to Buganda the residual powers were concurrent, but in relation to the other Ugandan states they were central.

[5] C.A.I., *Second Report of the Union Powers Committee* (5 July 1947), paras. 2–3; Constitution, art. 248, and Union List, item 97.

legislative lists. In India, Pakistan, and Malaya, on the other hand, where legislative powers were set out with such thoroughness, it was recognized that the residue would be of relatively small significance, relating only to matters unforeseen by the framers of the constitution. The fact that only once under the detailed lists of the Government of India Act, 1935, was it necessary to resort to the residual power suggested that there was some justification for this belief.[1] The way in which the Union Government in India has extended its activities recently in the field of Community Development shows, however, that even where legislative powers have been so carefully enumerated, new unforeseen subjects do open up and may significantly affect the balance between central and regional governments.[2]

Most of the new federal constitutions have included a separate concurrent list of subjects in which both central and regional governments might legislate, with central law normally prevailing in cases of conflict.[3] It may be argued that an additional list of concurrent legislative powers is unnecessarily cumbrous, and that it may leave regional governments in doubt about the extent of their legislative authority, since in addition to being normally excluded from the central list, they may at any time be excluded from the concurrent list as well. Nevertheless, the advantages of such a list have outweighed these considerations. First, such a list enhances flexibility. In a new federation it permits the central government to postpone exercising its authority in a field until such time as the matter has assumed national importance, while not preventing any region which is forward-looking from going ahead and legislating in the meantime on its own account.[4] Secondly, it provides a means whereby, in certain spheres, especially the social services, the central government may legislate to secure a basic national uniformity and to guide regional legislation, while leaving with the regional legislatures the initiative for details and for adaptation to local circumstances. Thirdly, a concurrent subject allows the general government to step into what is normally a regional field of activity, in order to provide remedies for particularly backward regions or for difficulties arising from regional legislation which affects other regions. Fourthly, concurrent lists may facilitate 'co-operative federalism', by encouraging co-operative rather than independent action in these fields.[5] Fifthly, such lists may reduce the necessity for complicated, minute subdivisions of individual functions assigned exclu-

---

[1] D. D. Basu, *Commentary on the Constitution of India* (3rd ed., 1955), vol. ii, p. 279.

[2] P. R. Dubhashi, 'Unitary Trends in a Federal System', *Indian Journal of Public Administration*, vi (1960), pp. 246–7.

[3] On the determination of such conflicts, see L. Brett (ed.), *Constitutional Problems of Federalism in Nigeria* (1961), pp. 31–35, 39–40, 242–3.

[4] In Rhodesia and Nyasaland, as a transitional arrangement, the federal legislative list was also made concurrent in order that territorial legislatures might have power to act in these fields until the central legislature was prepared to do so. See art. 29 (2).

[5] *The Constitution of Malaya, 1957*, art. 79, expressly required inter-governmental consultation before the exercise of concurrent legislative power by either central or state legislatures.

sively to one government or another. Thus, a concurrent list may help to escape the rigidity of detailed exclusive lists and to reduce litigation over central or regional priority in these subjects.[1]

It is not surprising, therefore, that in most new federations a wide range of subjects, including such significant areas as social welfare, economic development, and civil, personal, and criminal law, have been made concurrent. In some cases these concurrent lists have been augmented by special arrangements regarding certain subjects. In India the definition of the scope of certain central powers was left to be determined by central law.[2] Thus, in these 'optional central powers', as with normal concurrent powers, the limits between central and regional legislative competence depend upon central legislation. The Malayan constitution of 1957 extended the field of concurrent jurisdiction by specifically giving the central government power to legislate on subjects in the state list in order to implement national development plans or to promote uniformity,[3] and the Pakistan constitution of 1962 gave the central government similar powers.[4] In Malaya, however, such central legislation imposing uniformity in exclusive state subjects required adoption by state legislatures in order to become operative, except in cases involving development plans or land tenure.

Some overlapping of central and regional legislation is inevitable. All the new federal constitutions have made specific provision, therefore, that if laws made by the central legislature within its competence and laws made by a regional government within its competence are inconsistent, then the central laws, whether passed before or afterwards, should to the extent of the inconsistency normally prevail. An exception to this general rule, in every case but India, has been the power given to regional legislatures to amend or repeal any central law originally made under authority delegated by the regions. A different qualification was the innovation in the Government of India Act, 1935, and continued in the constitutions of India and Pakistan (1956), which permitted provincial laws on matters in the concurrent list to prevail, notwithstanding repugnancy to central legislation, if these provincial laws had received the assent of the Governor-General or President.[5] The central legislature, of course, retained the right to override such an enactment by a later law of its own. This arrangement provides a further element of flexibility, but in practice it has meant in India that states have sent much of

---

[1] The Nigerian Constitutional Conference of 1953, however, aimed at keeping the concurrent list short in the belief that this would minimize the possibility of conflict between the centre and the regions (Cmd. 8934/1953, para. 8).

[2] Union List, entries 7, 23, 24, 27, 32, 52, 53, 54, 56, 62, 63, 64, 67; Concurrent List, entries 40, 41. Cf. *Constitution of Malaya, 1957*, Federal List, item 10 (*a*).

[3] Arts. 76 (1) (*b*), 76 (3), 76 (4), 92. But art. 76 (4) did not apply, and art. 92 required state approval in the case of the Borneo states and Singapore in Malaysia (*Malaysia Act, 1963*, ss. 42, 43, inserting new arts. 95D, 95E).   [4] Art. 131 (2).

[5] *Government of India Act, 1935*, s. 107 (2); *Constitution of India, 1950*, art. 254 (2); *Constitution of Pakistan, 1956*, art. 110 (2).

their legislation dealing with purely state subjects to the President for assent in order to have greater confidence that the validity of their law would not be open to legal dispute.[1]

Sometimes, because a federation has been composed of regions of different constitutional status, the general scheme for the distribution of legislative authority has not been applied uniformly to all regions.[2] In some instances central authority has been extended in certain regions. This was the case, for instance, in the Chief Commissioner's provinces in India and Pakistan under the interim constitution, in the Parts C and D states and territories in India between 1950 and 1956, and in the Union territories in India after 1956. These territories were less advanced politically, and therefore the central legislature was assigned authority to legislate for these areas in the normally regional subjects.[3] In Rhodesia and Nyasaland, however, it was the more advanced territories, initially Southern Rhodesia and later Northern Rhodesia, in which extensions were made to central legislative authority, the reason here being the desire of the settlers in those territories for a more centralized regulation of European agriculture.[4] The regional legislatures of the Southern Cameroons in Nigeria, 1954–60, and the settlements in Malaya, 1948–57, also received special treatment. They possessed the normal scope of regional legislative authority, but because of their special constitutional status all their legislation required the assent of the federal Head of State, thus reducing their position to one of only quasi-autonomy.[5]

In other cases, where certain regions have been particularly jealous of their autonomy, the scope of central legislative authority has been made more limited than under the general scheme for the distribution of functions. A notable example was the scheme in the 1935 Indian Act, whereby acceding princely states would have transferred to the central legislature only those subjects specifically mentioned in their Instruments of Accession.[6] This was in fact the arrangement governing the acceding princely states under the interim constitutions of India and Pakistan. Such variations in the distribution of powers were attacked in the Indian Constituent Assembly on the grounds that: 'So long as the disparity exists, the Centre's authority over All-India matters may lose its efficacy. For, power is no power if it cannot be exercised in all cases and in all places.'[7] Under pressure, the rulers of the princely states signed progressively wider instruments of accession, until in the Indian constitution, 1950, the central and concurrent authority applied virtually uni-

---

[1] K. Santhanam, *Union–State Relations in India* (1960), p. 23.

[2] See also Chapter 7, section 5, regarding regions of differing constitutional status.

[3] *Government of India Act, 1935*, s. 98; *Constitution of India, 1950*, art. 246 (4); *Seventh Amendment Act, 1956*, s. 29 and Sched.

[4] Constitution, Second Sched., Federal Legislative List, items 24–26; *The Non-African Agriculture (Transfer to the Concurrent List) Ordinance, 1955* (N.R. Ordinance 61/1955).

[5] S.I. 1954, no. 1146, s. 51 (4); S.I. 1948, no. 108, s. 36.

[6] *Government of India Act, 1935*, ss. 6 (2), 101.

[7] C.A.I., *Debates*, vol. vii, p. 42.

formly to all states except Jammu and Kashmir.[1] In Pakistan the unification of the various types of units in West Pakistan into a single province in 1955 helped to reduce the variations in the scope of central and regional powers, although the Tribal Areas and Azad Kashmir continued under greater central direction.

But although the general trend in India and Pakistan was towards less variation among the regions in the scope of their legislative authority, the tendencies in the West Indies and Malaya were in the other direction. In the negotiations preceding the West Indian federal review, for instance, the Jamaican Government advocated a special confederal arrangement for itself, giving it greater legislative autonomy than the other islands, but the constitutional conference of 1961 decided against such a scheme. When the entry of Singapore and the British Borneo territories into the wider Federation of Malaysia was being negotiated, special exceptions were conceded in the application of the existing Malayan legislative lists to these new states.[2] Because of Singapore's special labour and education problems it was agreed that Singapore should retain control over these and a number of other subjects which in Malaya still fell within central legislative authority. In the case of the Borneo states, certain central subjects, mainly those concerned with native laws and custom, local commerce and communications, and shipping and fisheries, were placed under state or concurrent authority, while others, such as immigration and development planning, remained central powers, but required the approval of the Borneo states to apply there. In addition, as a transitional arrangement a number of central powers were delegated to the Borneo state governments in order not to disrupt existing administrative arrangements. Elsewhere too, in Uganda, a similar arrangement, but with even greater variation, was adopted, with three classes of territories having sharply different degrees of legislative autonomy.[3]

3. *The distribution of executive authority*

Generally speaking, the allocation of executive authority in the new federations has been made co-extensive with the distribution of legislative responsibilities.[4] There are several reasons why such an arrangement has generally

[1] *White Paper on Indian States* (rev. ed., 1950), paras. 175, 218–21, 244; Constitution, art. 246. A few transitional differences (arts. 259, 278, 291, 306) distinguishing the former princely states were removed by the *Seventh Amendment Act, 1956*, s. 29 and Sched. Under *The Constitution (Application to Jammu and Kashmir) Order, 1954*, ss. 2 (6) (*b*), 2 (22) (*b*), (made under article 370 of the constitution), only the central exclusive list, and not the concurrent list, applied to that state, and residual power remained with the state. The *Thirteenth Amendment Act, 1962*, made the application of certain central laws in Nagaland dependent upon approval by the state legislature.

[2] *Malaysia Act, 1963*, Fourth Sched. See Table 3, pp. 363–6 below. See also Cmnd. 1954/1963, paras. 16, 17, 21–23, and Annex A.

[3] Constitution, 1962, ss. 73–75 and Scheds. 7 and 8.

[4] *Constitution of India, 1950*, arts. 73 (1), 162; *Constitution of Pakistan, 1956*, arts. 39, 73; *Constitution of Pakistan, 1962*, arts. 135–6; *Constitution of Malaya, 1957*, art. 80; *Nigeria*

been favoured. First, it reinforces the autonomy of the legislative bodies. Secondly, it assures to a government the authority to implement and enforce its own legislation which might otherwise prove meaningless. Thirdly, where, as in all the new Commonwealth federations, the principle of parliamentary executives responsible to their legislatures has been adopted at both the central and regional levels, it is only if executive and legislative responsibilities coincide that a legislature can exercise control over the body executing its laws. Nevertheless, for special reasons, there have been variations from the general pattern.

To begin with, all the new federations have included, in the interests of flexibility, provisions for the voluntary delegation of executive authority from one government to another.[1]

Secondly, in the Asian federations the provinces and states were assigned by the constitution the normal administrative responsibility for a considerable extent of central legislation. The arguments advanced in favour of such an arrangement were that it would lead to greater efficiency in the local application of general policy, and that it would reduce the necessity for a duplication of administrative services.

It was to the matters on the concurrent legislative list that this arrangement was applied in India and Pakistan. Following the example of the Government of India Act, 1935, the new constitutions vested normal executive powers over subjects on the concurrent lists in the regional governments.[2] In order to preserve the principle of co-extensive legislative and executive powers, however, the central government was assigned authority to give state or provincial governments directions for the execution of central laws, and the central legislature could, if it explicitly specified, place its own law under the jurisdiction of the central executive. The effect of vesting in the hands of the states normal executive power over central laws on concurrent subjects has been to make administration in India and Pakistan much more decentralized than legislation. In the words of the Appleby Report:

No other large and important national government, I believe, is so dependent as India on theoretically subordinate but actually rather distinct units responsible to a different political control, for so much of the administration of what are recognized as national programmes of great importance to the nation.[3]

In practice, for the administration of its social action programmes, the Indian central government has had to administer largely as a 'staff' organization

---

Constitution, 1954, ss. 83, 85–86; *Constitution of Nigeria, 1960*, ss. 79, 80; *Constitution of Nigeria, 1963*, ss. 85, 86; *Constitution of R. and N., 1953*, art. 36; *Constitution of W.I., 1957*, art. 56.

[1] For details, see Chapter 12, section 6.

[2] *Constitution of India, 1950*, art. 73 (1) proviso, arts. 73 (2), 162, 256; *Constitution of Pakistan, 1956*, art. 39 (2) proviso, art. 73 (2), 126 (1); *Constitution of Pakistan, 1962*, arts. 131 (2), 135 (*b*), 136; *Government of India Act, 1935*, ss. 8 (1) proviso (i), 49 (2).

[3] *Public Administration in India* (1953), p. 22.

co-ordinating the states through conferences, rather than directly admini-stering.[1]

The Federation of Malaya Agreement of 1948 carried this sort of arrange-ment even further. It provided for the compulsory delegation to the states and settlements of executive authority for a large number of items on the exclusive central legislative list.[2] Indeed, the essential feature of the Malayan division of authority in 1948 was that, unlike other federations, the main constitutional division of functions between central and state governments lay in the con-centration of nearly all legislative powers in the former, and of a large number of executive responsibilities in the latter. When the Reid Commission came to make its report, however, it recommended against the continuation of the scheme.[3] The arrangement had, on the one hand, confined severely the legis-lative autonomy of the states, while on the other, it had inhibited the central government from exercising its sweeping legislative powers over subjects administered by the states, except after involved consultations with them. The arrangement had required constant inter-governmental consultation, and had often resulted in delays and difficulties. Moreover, if, as was likely from time to time, the party in power in one or more of the states differed in outlook and policy from the party in power in the central government, then such a division of legislative and executive responsibility 'would probably lead to friction and might well have graver consequences'.[4] In 1957, therefore, the experiment was abandoned. The independence constitution adopted the more orthodox federal practice of placing the basic division of functions within the legis-lative lists and of making legislative and executive responsiblities normally correspond.[5]

Thus, experience in the Asian federations suggests that, as a general rule, it is desirable, in the distribution of functions within federations, for legislative and executive authority to be normally co-extensive, although in certain matters benefits may be gained from exceptions to this principle.

4. *The allocation of functions*

The previous sections of this chapter have been concerned primarily with the forms which the distribution of authority has taken in the new federations,

---

[1] This helps to explain why, despite the apparent concentration of central power in the legislative lists, the allocation of resources to the states has had to be relatively large com-pared to other federations and is increasing. See Table 4A, p. 367.

[2] Cls. 86, 110 (3), and Second Column in Second Sched. A similar arrangement was applied in the *Independence Constitution of Kenya, 1963*, s. 106 and Sched. 1.

[3] Col. no. 330/1957, paras. 25, 33, 82. See also J. M. Gullick, *Malaya* (1963), pp. 110–11.

[4] Col. no. 330/1957, para. 82.

[5] Constitution, art. 80 (1) and Ninth Sched. Thus, although the scope of the legislative autonomy of the states was increased, the executive functions of the states were sufficiently reduced to require a considerably smaller revenue. See Table 7A. There were, however, some exceptions to the general correspondence of legislative and executive authority. See art. 80 (2–6). When Malaysia was created the number of these exceptions was increased.

but in this section attention will be turned to the scope of the actual functions assigned to the different levels of government.

The general principle on which the allocation of responsibilities has usually been based is that whatever concerns the nation as a whole, principally external relations and inter-regional activities, should be placed under the control of the central government, and that all matters which are primarily of regional rather than common interest should remain in the hands of the regional governments. Supplementing this basic criterion have been two subsidiary principles: that responsibilities should be assigned to the governments best able to administer them, and that functions which are normally related to one another should be entrusted, so far as possible, to the same authority. Of course, these principles have been interpreted in various ways in different federations because of differences in the strength and kinds of common and regional interests. Nevertheless, as a general pattern, subjects of clearly national interest, such as external affairs, defence and control of armed forces, currency and foreign exchange, foreign and inter-regional trade, maritime shipping, and inter-regional communications, have been assigned to the central government. On the other hand, subjects of basically regional interest have usually been allotted to regional governments. Falling into this category have usually been agriculture and land, many aspects of education, public health and social services, the administration of local public order and justice, the institutions of municipal government, and local public works. A number of fields where strong national and regional interests coincide have generally been made concurrent matters or have been subdivided between governments. Civil, personal, and criminal law, trade, commerce and industry, and trade unions and industrial disputes have usually been treated in this way. As a group the new federations, with the exception of the West Indies, have concentrated more functions in the central government than was thought necessary at the time the older federations were created.[1] This has been a result of the conditions of the mid-twentieth century world in which the 'passive' state has been succeeded by the 'active' state, technical developments have led to greater international and inter-regional interdependence, international commitments affecting internal legislation have multiplied, and the expense of defence and security has increased. Indeed, these very factors have also affected the older federations to such a degree that today the proportion of total public expenditure in the hands of their regional governments is even less than in the newer federations.[2]

While the general pattern is relatively clear, the allocation of certain subjects has proved particularly troublesome or controversial. For instance, although foreign affairs and the operation of the diplomatic service have been accepted with little question as appropriately central functions, the power to

[1] See Table 3, pp. 363–6, for details of the allocation of functions.
[2] See Table 4A, p. 367.

implement international treaties and agreements has, as in the older federations, raised difficulties. There has often been concern lest a sweeping exclusive authority to implement international obligations might provide the central government with a means for encroaching upon the regional legislative field by negotiating an international agreement on such a matter. On the other hand, in the light of Canadian experience, there was apprehension that if the central government lacked the authority to implement its own treaties, this might place the national government in difficulties or weaken its international bargaining position. This has been all the more important at a time when the scope of international obligations has become so extensive.

Faced with this dilemma, the framers of the new federal constitutions have tackled the problem in different ways. In four of the federations, the three in Asia and the West Indies, the arguments that prevailed were those in favour of giving the central government the capacity to implement international treaties, agreements, and conventions, even when subjects normally within the exclusive regional powers were affected.[1] In Pakistan (1956) and Malaya (1957) a qualification was added requiring the central government to consult the regional governments in such cases, and in the latter this central authority did not extend to Muslim law or the custom of the Malays.[2] Such consultation was in India left instead to be developed by convention.[3] The West Indian constitution attempted to reduce territorial suspicions that the sweeping central treaty authority would be used to interfere in territorial administration by giving the territorial legislatures concurrent power to implement international obligations which affected fields normally within their legislative competence, thus, it was hoped, reducing the necessity for central interference.[4] Nevertheless, the central government was in a position where legally it might implement any treaty or international agreement.

On the other hand, in the constitutions of Rhodesia and Nyasaland and of Nigeria, and in the West Indies proposals of 1961, it was the regional fears of undue central interference in regional subjects that prevailed. In these cases the implementation of treaties and international agreements, in so far as they

[1] *Constitution of India, 1950*, art. 253, and Union List, entries 13, 14; *Constitution of Pakistan, 1956*, art. 108 and Federal List, entry 2; *Constitution of Pakistan, 1962*, Third Sched., item 2; *Federation of Malaya Agreement, 1948*, Second Sched., matter 2 (*a*); *Constitution of Malaya, 1957*, art. 76 (1) (*a*), Federal List, items 1 (*a*), 1 (*b*), 1 (*d*); *Constitution of W.I., 1953*, art. 47 (1). The central power to implement international obligations, while extending to state subjects, did not permit other parts of the constitution, such as Fundamental Rights, to be violated. See *Ajaib Singh* v. *State of Punjab*, A.I.R. 1952, Punjab 309, at 319.
[2] *Constitution of Pakistan, 1956*, art. 108 proviso; *Constitution of Malaya, 1957*, art. 76 (2). In Malaysia, the limitation on central implementation of treaties was extended to cases affecting native law and custom in the Borneo states. *Malaysia Act, 1963*, Sixth Sched.
[3] C.A.I., *Debates*, vol. v, pp. 164–6.
[4] Art. 47 (2). Such an arrangement had existed earlier in Nigeria (1954), s. 53 (2–3), but was discarded in 1960.

affected normally regional subjects, required the consent of the regional governments to become operative.[1]

Another area which has been generally a source of difficulty in the distribution of functions has been the realm of economic affairs, especially the regulation of trade and commerce, industries, labour, and economic planning. This has been because in these fields certain aspects of major national significance and others of special regional interest are closely interconnected. It is rarely easy, for instance, to draw a simple clear line between trade and commerce which is inter-regional and that which is only regional. These difficulties are further complicated by the conflicts of economic interests between regions specializing in different products, between industrial and agricultural areas, between regions dependent on exports and those dependent on home markets, and between territories which would benefit from different fiscal and tariff policies. To these economic differences have often been added fears that national fiscal and economic policies leading to the development of an integrated economy might undermine the cultural distinctiveness of the diverse regional groups. But against these pressures for regional control of trade, commerce, and economic affairs has been the strength of the desire for inter-regional free trade and economic development as a major factor in the original creation of most of these federal unions. Moreover, all of these federations were developing countries where a special emphasis was put upon rapid economic growth through active public development policies and controls. There has therefore been a strong incentive to place economic powers where they would be most effective: under central direction.

Because of these conflicting pressures, complicated arrangements have usually been necessary in order that the responsibilities for economic affairs might be shared between central and regional governments. Sometimes subjects in this field have been made concurrent matters, but often there have been complex subdivisions, spelled out in much detail in the legislative lists, assigning certain aspects exclusively to one level of government and certain aspects to the other. In addition to the legislative lists, the constitutions have generally also contained a number of special articles relevant to the authority of different governments over trade, commerce, and economic affairs.[2] But

---

[1] *Constitution of R. and N., 1953*, art. 34; *Nigeria Constitution, 1954*, s. 53 (1); *Constitution of Nigeria, 1960*, s. 69; *Constitution of Nigeria, 1963*, s. 74; Cmnd. 1417/1961, para. 17. See also, Brett (ed.), *Constitutional Problems of Federalism in Nigeria*, pp. 108–28.

[2] *Constitution of India, 1950*, arts. 257 (2), 262, 263, 301–7, 360; *Constitution of Pakistan, 1956*, arts. 119, 126 (2), 130–2, 194, 199; *Constitution of Pakistan, 1962*, art. 142; *Constitution of Malaya, 1957*, arts. 76, 78, 83–95 and amendments by *Malaysia Act, 1963*, ss. 42–44, and Fourth Sched.; *Nigeria Constitution, 1954*, ss. 54, 56A (inserted by S.I. 1957, no. 1530), 56D and 58A (both inserted by S.I. 1959, no. 368); *Constitution of Nigeria, 1960*, ss. 71–76; *Constitution of Nigeria, 1963*, ss. 77–82; *Constitution of R. and N., 1953*, art. 86; Cmnd. 1417/1961, paras. 20, 26. For discussions of the Indian and Nigerian provisions, see Jennings, *Some Characteristics of the Indian Constitution*, ch. 6; Jain, *Indian Constitutional Law*, pp. 575–88; Brett, op. cit., pp. 84–89, 93–107.

despite the complexity of such provisions for multiple control, there has been an attempt in all the new federations, except the West Indies, which was unusual in lacking a customs union,[1] to assure a large degree of free inter-regional trade, and to give to the central government adequate capacity to promote economic development. The exclusive and concurrent lists, for instance, have generally assigned to the national government broad powers over trade, commerce, industry, labour, sources of energy, scientific and industrial research, and statistics, sufficient for comprehensive plans for economic expansion. Even the looser West Indies constitution gave the central government concurrent jurisdiction over a number of these subjects, although, in the face of Jamaican pressure, they were left largely unused, and were further restricted in the scheme agreed upon in 1961.[2] In the other new federations the net effect of the distribution of economic responsibilities has been to place in the hands of the central government the major means for promoting economic development, but to require at the same time a high degree of reliance upon the co-operation of the regional governments for carrying out development programmes. The role of the central governments has tended, therefore, to be primarily one of co-ordination, although central governments have exerted considerable influence through their predominant role in financing plans.

The allocation of responsibility for education, public health, and other social services has not been straightforward either. There are a number of arguments in favour of central control: the advantages that flow from the greater scale of organization permitting specialization and research, the possibility of establishing uniform and common standards of service throughout a federation, the heavy cost of maintaining social services, the close connexion between economic and social affairs, and the increased facility for co-operation with the World Health Organization in its activities of assistance. But on the other side, there are compelling arguments for placing the social services in the hands of the regional governments: the personal nature of these services, the need to adapt them to local circumstances and problems, and their close relation to other aspects of local administration. Consequently, the social services have been left largely in regional hands, except in Malaya. Even there, in the states added to form the Malaysian Federation, a number of these services fall under state or concurrent rather than exclusive central jurisdiction.[3]

In most of the new federations elementary and secondary education, and

[1] The Federation of South Arabia also began initially without a common market, implementing this later. In Malaysia, a common market was to be established gradually over a number of years (Cmnd. 2094/1963, Annex J; see also the 'Rueff Report', *Report on the Economic Aspects of Malaysia*, 1963).

[2] Constitution, Concurrent List; Cmnd. 1417/1961, para. 20. See D. Seers, 'Federation of the British West Indies: The Economic and Financial Aspects', *Social and Economic Studies*, vi (1957), pp. 197–214, for a criticism of the lack of central economic powers in the West Indian constitution.

[3] *Malaysia Act, 1963*, Fourth Sched. See also Cmnd. 1954/1963, Annex A.

even, to some extent, university education, are organized on a regional basis, an arrangement particularly suitable where differing linguistic and religious outlooks are involved. There have been some exceptions, however. Non-African education in Rhodesia and Nyasaland, and education in general in Malaya and subsequently in Malaysia, except for Singapore, were made central subjects. In the case of Malaya the wish to promote national unity through a common language and education outweighed other considerations, and it was on similar grounds that the governments of Nigeria agreed in 1963 to allow the establishment of federal secondary schools as a means to breaking down regional and tribal barriers.

Medicine and health generally, including hospitals, clinics, public health, and sanitation, have also usually been a regional responsibility. Only the constitutions of Malaya, Malaysia, and Rhodesia and Nyasaland prescribed that these should be central or concurrent subjects.[1] Certain matters, however, where uniformity is essential to efficient control, such as regulation of the medical profession and of poisons and drugs, have more often been made central or concurrent subjects.

The other social services, such as unemployment relief, workmen's compensation, social security, and social welfare services, have been treated less uniformly. Most of these subjects were made exclusively central in Malaya, and concurrent in India and in Pakistan (1956), with the exception of unemployment relief, which was left solely to the states and provinces. In the other three federations, however, these social services, federal old-age pensions in Rhodesia and Nyasaland excepted, were left entirely to the regional governments, differences in local conditions proving more important than the desirability of uniformity. For similar reasons, social security was made a state responsibility in Singapore, although elsewhere in Malaysia the Malayan pattern was continued.

Two other subjects which have sometimes caused difficulties have been citizenship and the inter-regional movement of persons. Where the regional units have had a long historical tradition of distinctive citizenship, as in Malaya, Malaysia, and the West Indies, or the members of certain regions have feared the loss of a special status, as in the cases of the Malays in the Malay states, the Chinese in the Malayan settlements, and the Africans of the Central African protectorates, there have been claims for the retention of a separate regional citizenship, or at least a maintenance of the special citizenship status. On the other hand, the desire to encourage a common nationality for the whole of a federation has often led to insistence upon a single federal citizenship. The latter view prevailed in India, Pakistan, and Nigeria, where there was no provision for a separate regional citizenship.[2] In Malaya, on the other

---

[1] But in Malaysia medicine and health were placed on the state legislative list for Singapore.

[2] *Constitution of India, 1950*, art. 11 and Union List, entry 17; *Constitution of Pakistan,*

hand, between 1952 and 1957, federal citizenship was derived from being a national of one of the states. Subsequently, at the time of independence in 1957, a separate distinct federal citizenship, no longer linked to state nationality, was created.[1] When the Malaysian Federation was being planned, this arrangement of a single federal citizenship was applied to residents of the Borneo states, but in the case of Singapore special arrangements were made for a distinct Singapore citizenship, citizens of Singapore being ineligible to vote or stand for election outside Singapore until they qualified by residence and knowledge of Malay, while Malayans who were not citizens of Singapore were likewise ineligible to vote or stand for election in Singapore.[2] In the West Indies the territories retained, to begin with, the status of separate colonies for purposes of the British Nationality Act, and citizenship and naturalization were made concurrent subjects.[3] The constitution of Rhodesia and Nyasaland gave the central government exclusive power to establish a federal citizenship, but naturalization was made a concurrent subject, and the status of British protected persons was continued in the two northern territories.[4]

It has usually been thought desirable, in the interests of enabling all inhabitants to share in the benefits of federation and of encouraging a sense of federal nationhood, to include constitutional provisions guaranteeing the freedom of the internal migration of persons. Against this have been the fears of certain wealthier regions of an influx of population, and the practical need for certain controls over the inter-regional movement of people in the interests of public health and of public security. In most of the federations the control of the inter-regional movement of persons was therefore made a concurrent subject,[5] but this was qualified in all but the case of Rhodesia and Nyasaland by constitutional provisions normally limiting restrictions on the freedom of inter-regional movement.[6] In the West Indies this issue proved so controversial that a special conference on the subject was required, and there it was

1956, art. 218, Federal List, entry 3; *Constitution of Pakistan, 1962*, Third Sched., entry 4; *Constitution of Nigeria, 1960*, ss. 7–16; *Constitution of Nigeria, 1963*, ss. 7–17.

[1] Constitution, arts. 14–31, and Federal List, item 5.

[2] *Malaysia Act, 1963*, ss. 23–34, and Third Sched. This arrangement was meant to assure the Malays on the peninsula that they would not be swamped politically as a result of the merger with Singapore.

[3] *Constitution of W.I., 1957*, Concurrent List, para. 24; S.I. 1957, No. 1364, s. 4 (4). The 1961 Constitutional Conference did decide to make citizenship an exclusive federal subject (Cmnd. 1417/1961, Appendix E, para. xiv).

[4] *Constitution of R. and N., 1953*, preamble and Federal List, item 6; Concurrent List, item 46; Cmnd. 1149/1960, pp. 27–28.

[5] *The Constitution of India, 1950*, made inter-state migration an exclusive central subject (Union List, entry 81), but enabled states to restrict inter-regional intercourse with the consent of the central government (art. 304).

[6] *Constitution of India, 1950*, arts. 19 (1) (*d–g*), 19 (5, 6), 301, 302, 304; *Constitution of Pakistan, 1956*, art. 11; *Constitution of Pakistan, 1962*, art. 6, principle 5; *Constitution of Malaya, 1957*, art. 9 (2); *Constitution of Nigeria, 1960*, s. 26; *Constitution of Nigeria, 1963*, s. 27; *Constitution of W.I., 1957*, preamble, arts. 49–51.

decided to establish freedom of inter-territorial movement under federal control by stages.[1] The intense anxieties of the Borneo states concerning migration into their territories also made special arrangements necessary for Malaysia, whereby entry from inside or outside the federation into these states required their approval.[2]

In federations approaching independence, the prospective departure of the imperial power has often made the allocation of responsibility for public order and control of the police a contentious subject. Regional majority groups have feared that central control of the police might be used to crush their autonomy. Regional responsiblity for public order and the police has also been justified on the grounds that it would make for 'promptitude in action, and for close adaptation of policy and action to local needs'.[3] On the other hand, a failure to maintain public order or a lack of sufficient police reserves within a region may provoke a wider national emergency. In addition, minorities within regions have sometimes feared, especially in Nigeria, that control of the police by regional majorities would be used to suppress them.[4] The solution has varied. In the vast federations of India and Pakistan, and in the scattered islands of the West Indies, the advantages of regional responsibility for public order and the police prevailed. By contrast, the Malayans, preoccupied by threats to their internal security, placed these functions under central control. But in Rhodesia and Nyasaland, and in Nigeria, positions midway between these were adopted. Responsibility for law and order was left in the former to the territorial governments, but provision was made both for territorial police forces and for central power to create a 'Federal police force for service in the employment of, or use in, any Territory at the request and under the operational control of the Governor of that Territory', thus establishing a reserve force.[5] The Federation of Nigeria, however, leaned more towards a centralization of these functions. The maintenance of public order was made a concurrent subject, and in order 'to avoid the danger of the police coming under the control of a political party', the 1954 constitution made the police an exclusive central subject.[6] The Nigeria police force was divided into regional contingents, but the use and operational control of these were vested in the Governor-General, acting at his discretion either directly or through the regional governors, responsible in this case solely to him.[7] During the constitutional conferences of 1957–8, the question whether there should be separate regional forces was raised again. In the end it was decided that public

---

[1] Col. no. 315/1955, para. 6; *Constitution of W.I., 1957*, arts. 49–51; Cmnd. 1417/1961, para. 21.

[2] Cmnd. 1954/1963, para. 16; Cmnd. 2094/1963, Annex E; *Immigration Act, 1963* (F. 27/1963).

[3] Col. no. 255/1950, para. 25. See also Cmnd. 1150/1960, para. 169.

[4] Cmnd. 505/1958, p. 90.

[5] *Constitution of R. and N., 1953*, Federal List, item 36. See also Cmnd. 1149/1960, ch. 16; Cmnd. 1150/1960, paras. 164–73.

[6] Cmd. 8934/1953, para. 22 (i).   [7] Constitution, 1954, s. 84.

order should remain a concurrent subject, and that there should be a single central police force under the administration of a Police Council consisting of both central and regional ministers.[1] The bulk of the force would be in regional contingents, normally complying with the directions of the regional premier, but ultimately subject to the Prime Minister of Nigeria.

5. *The concentration of functions*

The scope of the functions concentrated in one level of government or the other has, of course, varied from federation to federation because of differences in the strength and the kinds of the motives for unity and for regional autonomy.[2] The effect of these varying influences can be seen both in the lists of responsibilities assigned to each of the tiers of government and in the relative financial resources required by central and regional governments to carry out their functions.[3]

By far the greatest concentration of central authority among these federations occurred in Malaya. The Federation of Malaya Agreement, 1948, assigned virtually all legislative authority, except over Muslim law, Malay custom, and most aspects of land tenure, to the federal Legislative Council, although executive authority was more decentralized, with the states being responsible for the administration of land, agriculture, forestry, local government, education, and public health and medicine.[4] The independence constitution (1957) gave the states exclusive legislative authority over a wider field including not only Muslim law, Malay custom, and land, but also agriculture, local works and services, and local government. At the same time, however, the scope of state executive activities was reduced to correspond to these legislative powers, the net effect being a greater centralization of administration. Moreover, the states have not fully exercised the legislative powers they acquired. They have tended to rely more and more on the specialist staff of the central government, and to permit central incursions into state spheres 'for the purpose only of ensuring uniformity of law and policy'.[5] The first constitutional amendment in 1960, for instance, placed local government, one of

---

[1] Constitution, 1960, ss. 98–103; Constitution, 1963, ss. 105–10. This arrangement was first instituted in 1959 by S.I. 1959, no. 1049. See also Cmnd. 569/1958, paras. 9–17, and J. P. Mackintosh, 'Federalism in Nigeria', *Political Studies*, x (1962), pp. 232, 246–7, for a description of the arrangement and its operation, and Cmnd. 1150/1960, paras. 167–9, for a discussion of the merits and defects of a similar possible arrangement in the Central African context. For variations on the Nigerian pattern see *Independence Constitution of Kenya, 1963*, ss. 157–70; *Constitution of Uganda, 1962*, ss. 77 (2), 80, 81, 113, and Sched. 1, art. 39. The Nigerian Constitutions, 1960, s. 98 (7), and 1963, s. 105 (7), also permitted the establishment of local police maintained by the native authorities or by local government authorities.

[2] See Chapter 6.

[3] See Table 3, pp. 363–6, for a comparison of the distribution of functions, and Table 4A, p. 367, for a comparison of relative central and regional expenditure in the new federations.

[4] *Federation of Malaya Agreement, 1948*, Second Sched.

[5] L. A. Sheridan and others, *Malaya and Singapore* (1961), p. 102. See Constitution, art. 76.

the few exclusive state subjects, within the scope of central influence.[1] Countering this tendency to greater centralization, however, is the greater autonomy given to Singapore and the Borneo states in the course of the creation of a wider Malaysian Federation. This example may lead to pressures for greater decentralization in the older Malayan states. Whether the trend to increased centralization is maintained or reversed will depend largely on whether the Alliance Party is able to continue to dominate both the central and most state governments.

At the other extreme from Malaya was the West Indies Federation. There, with extremely limited central authority, with fewer functions to administer than the East Africa High Commission, with a revenue of less than 3 per cent. of that of its own territorial governments combined, and without a customs union or sufficient legislative powers and finances to promote economic development, the central government was little more than a façade.[2] Moreover, island parochialism and the slimness of the Federal Labour Party's majority in the House of Representatives discouraged the exercise by the central government of some of the few powers assigned to it by the constitution. Because the central government had insufficient authority to perform really significant functions, like an engineless car, it proved largely ineffective. Citizens, therefore, were more aware of the nuisances it caused than of the benefits it provided, and federation consequently became discredited. In view of this experience it was not surprising that in the preliminary negotiations for a successor federation in the East Caribbean stress was placed upon providing 'adequate powers to the central government'.[3]

Between the two extremes of Malaya and the West Indies came the other four federations. In each there was a concentration of major functions in the central government, but also considerable scope for regional action.

India, with lengthy lists of union and concurrent powers in the constitution, was clearly intended to be highly centralized in order that national unity might be consolidated.[4] Nevertheless, the legislative powers assigned to the states were not inconsiderable, including such important exclusive fields as public order, police, education, public health, and agriculture, as well as the opportunity to legislate in the concurrent subjects. In practice there have been two marked tendencies. On the one hand, the extensive use by the central

[1] Art. 95A inserted by *Constitution (Amendment) Act, 1960* (F. 10/1960), s. 12.

[2] See Tables 3 and 10A, pp. 363–6, 375. The East Africa High Commission had real control over the major systems of transport and communications, administered (although it did not set the tariff rates) customs, excise, and income tax, and had an annual current expenditure in 1960–1 greater than that of the West Indian central government. See S. R. & O., 1947, no. 2863, *The East Africa (High Commission) Order in Council*, Third Sched.; Cmnd. 1279/1961, *East Africa, Report of the Economic and Fiscal Commission*, Appendix D.

[3] Cmnd. 1746/1962, para. 6.

[4] C.A.I., *Second Report of the Union Powers Committee* (1947), para. 2; Santhanam, *Union-State Relations in India*, pp. 12–13; K. M. Panikkar, *The Foundations of New India* (1963), pp. 154–6, 168–70; W. H. Morris-Jones, *The Government and Politics of India* (1964), pp. 81–83.

government of the broad grants of power in the union and concurrent lists, the role of the central government in national planning, the extension of central authority under emergency circumstances, and the dominance of the central organization of the Congress Party at both levels of government, have accentuated the centralization of legislative and financial authority.[1] On the other hand, counteracting this, the growing strength of regional political pressures has produced a noticeable shift away from the extensive centralism of the early years after 1950. Even as early as 1953 increased administrative decentralization and state autonomy was apparent. In the words of Paul Appleby:

The administrative trend is evidently to go still further, to give over to the states some financial resource now in the province of the Centre, to minimize in practice some of the marginal or interpretative zones of power, and to retreat before an opposition state minister's charges of 'interference' with the states.[2]

Evidence of this trend can be found in a comparison of central and state expenditures. Not only is the revenue needed to finance the current expenditure of all the states combined greater than that of the Union, but it has been increasing more rapidly.[3] In addition, a large portion of the expenditure involved in the Five Year Plans has been spent on the state Plans.[4] It is significant that state current expenditure as a proportion of total public expenditure has been larger in India than in any of the new federations except the West Indies.[5]

Under the pressure of Bengali regionalism the Pakistan constitution of 1956 ostensibly assigned greater powers to the provincial governments than under the preceding interim constitution or the Indian constitution of 1950.[6] The large number of items on the exclusive provincial list as compared with the exclusive federal list was deceptive, however, for in fact the content of the lists was only slightly modified: many of the federal subjects were consolidated under a smaller number of entries while the provincial subjects were split into a larger number of items.[7] In practice the tendency was towards continued centralization of administration and of expenditure. The resulting resentment and discontent of the East Bengalis at being a colony of Karachi was an important factor contributing to the collapse of constitutional, and with it federal, government in 1958. A concession to these East Pakistani feelings was

[1] Santhanam, op. cit., pp. 58–59, 60–65; Panikkar, op. cit., pp. 172–4, 236–43.

[2] *Public Administration in India* (1953), p. 17. See also pp. 3, 9, 10, 17–19, 22, 56.

[3] See Table 5A, p. 368.

[4] About 70 per cent. of the total expenditure in the First Plan and 65 per cent. in the Second Plan related to matters on the exclusive state legislative list (Santhanam, p. 45). The provision by the Union of the funds for these expenditures served, however, as a central lever by which to influence the states (ibid., ch. 4).

[5] See Table 4A, p. 367.

[6] C.A.P. (second), *Debates*, vol. i, pp. 1805, 1993, 2017, 2069, 2072–3, 2096–104.

[7] C.A.P. (second), *Debates*, vol. i, pp. 2069, 2139–41. By contrast with the *Government of India Act, 1935* (amended to 1956) which contained 61, 55, and 37 entries in the federal, provincial, and concurrent lists respectively, the *Constitution of Pakistan, 1956*, contained 30, 94, and 19 entries in the federal, provincial, and concurrent lists respectively.

made in the 1962 constitution, which appeared to increase the scope of pro-vincial authority by omitting the concurrent list of the previous constitution. But the sweeping central power to legislate on any matter in the 'national interest'[1] means that potentially Pakistan could become as centralized as the Malayan Federation. For the present, however, the continued zeal for regional interests has meant that in practice the provinces exercise considerable legislative and administrative responsibilities.

The Nigerian regions were given considerable authority by the federal constitutions of 1954, 1960 and 1963. Their functions included not only such important areas as education, public health, land, and agriculture, as in India and Pakistan, but a somewhat greater responsibility than the states and provinces in those federations over social services generally. The federal and concurrent lists did, however, assign to the central government quite extensive powers over external affairs, citizenship and immigration, defence, public order, civil and personal law, finance, trade, commerce, industrial development, labour, basic communications, utilities, and public works. With the growing prestige of the central government upon independence and the pressure for rapid economic development, there has also been less tendency to leave some of these powers unexercised.[2] Indeed, proportionate to regional expenditure, the current expenditure of the Nigerian central government has been greater than that of the Indian Union government.[3] As in India, however, there has been in practice a general tendency for the central government in economic affairs to concentrate upon 'co-ordination' of regional action rather than upon direct administration.

The distribution of functions in Central Africa was based on two principles: first, that in order to achieve the advantages of a federal system, the central government must be entrusted from its inception with a wide field of responsibilities, and second, that 'those services which have a specially close relation to the day-to-day life and work of the African peoples should remain the responsibility of the territorial Governments'.[4] At successive pre-federation constitutional conferences there was a tendency, however, to add to the central powers, until the central government possessed a very wide range of potential powers indeed. Public order, labour, many of the social services, land, African education and agriculture, and local government were left as territorial subjects, but powers over finance, economic affairs, and communications were heavily concentrated in the central government. The result in practice was a higher proportion of central expenditure than in any of the new federations except Malaya.[5] The settler desire for centralization and African apprehen-

---

[1] Art. 131 (2).

[2] Mackintosh, 'Federalism in Nigeria', *Political Studies*, x (1962), pp. 238–47; R. O. Tilman and T. Cole (eds.), *The Nigerian Political Scene* (1962), ch. 3; T. Cole, 'Federalism in the Commonwealth', *I.P.S.A. Sixth World Congress, Geneva, 1964, Federalism/18*, p. 29.

[3] See Table 4A, p. 367.

[4] Cmd. 8233/1951, paras. 59, 60.   [5] Table 4A.

sions of central control led to an unusual feature of the distribution of powers in Rhodesia and Nyasaland: the division of certain subjects on racial lines. Education and agriculture, which in most other federations were regional subjects, were divided so that European education and, except in Nyasaland, agriculture were central subjects, while African education and agriculture were territorial matters.[1] Because the standard of services provided by the central government in these fields for Europeans was higher than that provided by the territorial governments for Africans, the Africans were given the impression that federation was for the benefit of Europeans only.[2] This arrangement, together with the generally high degree of economic centralization which unavoidably affected African life, so discredited the federation among Africans in the protectorates that the Monckton Commission concluded that the federation could only survive if African support was won by 'a less racial approach to the division of powers' and by 'a substantial transfer of functions from the Federal to the Territorial Governments'.[3]

The variations in the balance and stability of the distribution of functions in these new federations point to two broad conclusions. First, the principle of assigning matters of common interest to the central government and subjects of primarily regional interest to the unit governments has been expressed in a wide variety of arrangements. Both in the interests of efficient administration and of creating a palatable compromise, it has been necessary to adapt the general principle to the particular circumstances of each federation. Where, despite the attempt to do so, the distribution of responsibilities has failed to reflect accurately the aspirations for unity or autonomy, it has led to a shift in the balance of functions actually exercised by each level of government, as in India and Nigeria, or even to the discrediting and collapse of federal government, as in the over-centralized federations of Pakistan and Rhodesia and Nyasaland or the ineffectual federation of the West Indies. This indicates how important and yet how difficult it is to find the appropriate balance for a given society between adequate central power to provide security and economic development, and sufficient regional autonomy to protect vital local aspirations and interests in order to avoid resentment and discontent. Second, while there is clearly no single ideal pattern for the distribution of functions within federations, the experience of Malaya and the West Indies suggests that there are limits to the scope of functions appropriately assigned to the central government, beyond which over-centralization may reduce legal state autonomy to almost meaninglessness, or inadequate central authority and prestige may make a federation ineffective and encourage its disintegration.

[1] *Constitution of R. and N., 1953*, Federal List, items, 24, 25, 26, 30; Northern Rhodesia, *The Non-African Agriculture (Transfer to the Concurrent List) Ordinance, 1955* (N.R. Ordinance 61/1955); Cmnd. 1149/1960, pp. 380–1.
[2] Cmnd. 1148/1960, para. 35.
[3] Ibid., para. 125.

9

THE DISTRIBUTION OF POWERS
II: FINANCES

1. *The problems and principles of federal finance*

'OF all federal problems, the financial relations between the Centre and the units are the most difficult.'[1] So wrote K. Santhanam, a former participant in the debates of the Indian Constituent Assembly and chairman of the second Indian Finance Commission. His claim is supported not only by the troubled history of federal finance in the older federations, but also by the squabbles and the frequent adjustments that have occurred in the new federations.[2] India since independence is a good example. In addition to the financial negotiations involved in the integration of the princely states and in the drafting of the constitution, there were revisions in the allocation of revenue to the states in 1950, 1952, 1957, and 1962 in order to meet their dissatisfaction. Pakistan is another instance. The central government found it necessary in the early years after partition to appropriate a number of provincial tax sources, but later, in 1952, because of central surpluses and provincial hardships, the provinces were given a share in the proceeds of certain taxes. Nevertheless, the allocation of revenues continued to prove a contentious issue in the second Constituent Assembly and further taxing powers were turned over to the provinces. In 1962 yet a further devolution of financial resources was found necessary, the portion of central tax revenues shared with the provinces being increased following the report of the Finance Commission. In Malaya too, the financial arrangements have required frequent adjustment. The Federation of Malaya Agreement, 1948, as in the earlier Federated Malay States, provided for annual *ad hoc* allocations from the central government to the states, but this arrangement did not prove satisfactory, for every year it provoked disputes between the governments as to the amount of the sums to be granted. Consequently, a new system, stressing the autonomy and responsibility of the states, was put into effect in 1956, and soon afterwards, upon the recommendation of the Reid Commission, even further steps were taken in that direction in the independence constitution. In 1962 a constitutional amendment made another minor adjustment. When it came to the negotiations preceding the Malaysian Federation, it was the financial arrangements, particularly those affected by Brunei's desire to retain her oil revenues in perpetuity and Singapore's adamance over continuing to

---

[1] Santhanam, *Union-State Relations in India*, p. 29.
[2] See bibliography for official reports in each country dealing with federal finance.

control its own wealth, which, when all the other difficulties had been over-come, proved the greatest stumbling blocks. Of federal finance in Nigeria it has been said: 'Few subjects have caused as much acrimony in Nigeria as revenue allocation.'[1] The question was a major issue at the Ibadan Conference and also at most of the subsequent constitutional conferences. So controversial was the problem that revisions in the distribution of finances, following the appointment of fiscal review commissions, were made in 1947, 1951, 1953, and 1958, and in 1964 another commission was appointed. In Rhodesia and Nyasaland too, the assignment of revenues proved a contentious subject. Fiscal commissions dealt with the subject in 1952 and 1957, and at the time of the constitutional review in 1960 there was considerable discussion as to whether Nyasaland was receiving adequate central assistance and whether Southern Rhodesia was being favoured unduly at the expense of Northern Rhodesia. But of all the recent federations it was in the West Indies that questions of revenue allocation pro-voked the most dispute. The control of customs and of income tax by the central government provoked so much opposition that in the constitution a settlement of these issues was postponed, and it was just these questions which led to Ja-maica's insistence upon a loose federation and even ultimately upon secession.

The difficulties in federal financial relations arise from two kinds of con-flicts: first, the clashes of interest between the national government and the regional units, and second, those between the different regions in rivalry with each other. Each of these disputes is complicated by the fact that their settle-ment involves both economic and political considerations. In so far as the constitutional allocation of financial powers affects economic efficiency and sets the framework for economic and fiscal policies, it will determine the extent to which it is possible to achieve a maximum utilization of labour and other resources, to promote economic development in particular regions and throughout the federation, and to maintain economic stability. Since economic aspirations were an important motive in the formation of these federations, and since their resources were too limited to afford waste, the criterion of economic efficiency has been of special relevance. But as an essential part of the political bargain incorporated in the federal constitution, the assignment of revenues may have a crucial bearing upon the whole pattern of political and administrative relations between governments. Nor is there any reason to assume that the economic and political considerations will point in the same direction. For instance, a closely integrated national finan-cial system, which may be highly desirable on economic grounds, may threaten to undermine the regional political and cultural distinctiveness which the federal structure is intended to protect. Clashes of these kinds frequently occur when federal systems are created, and therefore the necessity for compromise is inevitable.

[1] A. Ogunsheye, 'The Place of Federation in West Africa', in Hansard Society, *What are the problems of Parliamentary Government in West Africa?* (1958), p. 133.

The fundamental problem of federal finance is that of ensuring that the division of revenue between central and regional governments corresponds with the distribution of functions, in order that each government may have the financial capacity to carry out its responsibilities as well as possible. This balance may be achieved, of course, by adjusting either side of the equation: on one side, the assignment to governments of functions involving expenditure may be modified; on the other side, the distribution of financial resources may be altered by changes in the assignment of tax or other revenue sources, or by providing for transfers of funds from one level of government to another.

There are both short-run and long-run aspects to the problem of matching revenues and functions. To begin with, there have usually been special problems associated with the initial transitional period when a federation is created. Not only are there the problems of dividing assets and liabilities between the two tiers of government, but the transfer to the central government of revenue sources upon which the regions formerly relied may make temporary expedients necessary until the regions have had time to develop the revenue sources assigned to them by the new constitution. These transitional adjustments generally take the form of grants from the central government to the regions to compensate for particularly severe losses or disruptions of revenue, or to meet immediate budgetary needs.[1] The problem during the initial period of federation is often further complicated by difficulties in predicting precise revenue yields where these are affected by the creation of a new customs union.

The attempt to achieve a long-run equilibrium between the revenues and the responsibilities of each government has proved both complex and difficult. The solution sometimes advocated as the ideal has been the assignment of adequate and completely independent tax sources to each level of government.[2] But while such an arrangement would certainly ensure the financial autonomy of both central and regional governments, it has rarely been practicable because of the difficulty of finding independent tax sources which will match precisely the expenditure assigned to governments. Since for political reasons the degree to which legislative and executive powers have been concentrated in central or regional governments has varied, this has meant that the distribution of financial resources appropriate in 'tight' or 'loose' federations has had to vary accordingly. But in relatively underdeveloped countries, customs and excise duties and income tax form the bulk of the public revenues, and the number of other major tax sources are few. Consequently, the scope for varying the assignment of taxes in order to match exactly the allocation of expenditure is quite limited. This has made it neces-

---

[1] Such arrangements were necessary, for instance, in the early years after the integration of the Indian princely states, when Karachi was separated from Sind in Pakistan, when Lagos was separated from Western Nigeria, and when the Borneo states joined Malaysia.

[2] Cmnd. 481/1958, paras. 23–24. See also Wheare, *Federal Government*, p. 93.

sary to search for alternative ways of ensuring both adequate resources and financial autonomy for the regional governments: generally the solution has involved the use of unconditional transfers of revenue, which are guaranteed in the constitution or determined upon the recommendation of fiscal commissions.[1] But because each government could always carry out the functions assigned to it better if it had more revenue, and because there can only be a limited amount to go around, it has inevitably been difficult, whatever the arrangement, to avoid dissatisfaction with the distribution of finances.

It has been argued on occasion that a basic principle of federal finance 'is the political one that wherever possible the responsibilities for raising and spending money should rest with the same authority'.[2] The idea behind this principle is that governments which have the pleasing job of spending money should also have the unpleasant one of raising it. Taken to its logical extreme, the doctrine of political responsibility would preclude any transfers of finances from one level of government to another. But when transfers have proved necessary, the principle has been used to argue that: 'a government should not surrender all control over the expenditure of money it has raised by taxation. This is to say that federal grants to the states should be accompanied by conditions.'[3] But while it is particularly important in developing countries to avoid the wastage of resources caused by political irresponsibility, conditional grants, which seriously inhibit the freedom of action of regional governments, have rarely proved acceptable as a major source of regional revenues in the situations where social or political diversity was strong enough to necessitate a federal solution. Moreover, it may be argued that the idea of strict financial responsibility, which originated in an age of 'small government' when public activity was comparatively restricted, is less relevant in the present era when the individual, lacking expert knowledge, can have little idea of whether governmental expenditures are wastefully or efficiently administered. It must also be remembered that, whichever level of government spends the money, it is the same citizens who are taxed to support these expenditures. Most important, it can be argued that the idea of strict financial responsibility is no longer really applicable in an age when: 'the strict relationship between income and expenditure had disappeared because of the increasing importance of regulation as a motive for taxation on the one hand, and the wider implications of fiscal policies directed towards economic stabilization on the other'.[4] Finally, where some measure of equalization in the revenues of different regions within a federation is an aim, an exact matching of responsibilities for taxation and expenditure is clearly impossible.

A major difficulty in any long-run solution to the equating of the revenue

[1] See sections 5 and 7, below.
[2] A. H. Birch, 'Intergovernmental Financial Relations in New Federations', in U. K. Hicks and others, *Federalism and Economic Growth*, p. 120.
[3] Ibid.
[4] Hicks and others, op. cit., p. 149.

and expenditure of each level of government is that the financial arrangements must be sufficiently elastic to be adaptable to rapidly changing conditions and responsibilities. Unless flexibility is built into the financial distribution specified in the constitution, there is a danger, as experience in the older federations has sometimes shown, that the federal financial scheme will in time become an obstacle hindering growth and development or restricting effective action in cases of military and economic crises. The difficulty is to achieve such adaptability without undermining the autonomy of either the central or regional governments. The ideal solution would be to arrange the tax and grant structure in such a way as to be self-correcting, so that if a gap between the revenue and expenditure of one government opens up, machinery is quickly set into motion to offset it. But in practice this is exceedingly difficult to arrange, because there are so many possible ways in which an initial financial scheme may be affected. A second possibility is to leave the adjustment of resources in the hands of one level of government or the other. But this would achieve flexibility at the expense of making one level of government financially subordinate to the other, and has therefore usually proved politically unacceptable. The third, and amongst the new federations the most popular, solution has been to make provision for a review of the financial arrangements by an independent commission or an inter-governmental council, summoned either at regular intervals or on an *ad hoc* basis as and when needed.

Next to the basic problem of dividing revenues and expenditures between the two tiers of government, the second major financial problem in federations is the question of how financial resources are to be divided among the various regional units. This problem becomes particularly important where, as in most federations, the insufficient independent sources of regional revenue have necessitated financial transfers from the central to the regional governments on a large scale. Among the conflicting principles advanced for the allocation of these transfers have been those of compensation, derivation, need, and national welfare. *Compensation* as a criterion would relate financial adjustments to the disabilities incurred by each regional government upon joining the federation and as a result of the differential impact of central policy. *Derivation* would involve distribution of transfers in proportion to the regional contribution to central taxes. *Need* as a principle of distribution would lead to allocation of transfers among regions according to their population or their particular budgetary requirements. *National welfare* would involve considerations of economically efficient allocation of resources and maintenance of uniform national minimum standards for services.

What complicates the problem of distributing financial resources among regional governments is their inevitable inequality in economic development and fiscal capacity. There have been, for instance, the contrasts in progress and wealth between the provinces and princely states, and among the provinces themselves in India, between East and West Pakistan, between south-western and north-eastern Malaya, between Singapore and the Borneo states of Malaysia, between Western and Northern Nigeria, between Nyasaland and the two Rhodesias, and between the big and the small islands of the West Indies.[1] The result has been conflicting claims between the wealthy regions, favouring the principles of compensation or derivation, and the poorer units, seeking special assistance on grounds of need.[2]

The extent to which the poorer regional units should receive special assistance involves both economic and political considerations. To some degree differences in economic development and standards of services are inevitable within federations, since one of the political reasons for establishing federations is to permit regional diversity. There may also be economic arguments against any redistribution of regional wealth that would encourage labour and other resources to remain in the poorer areas when their productivity would be higher in other parts of the country. On the other hand, there have usually been strong economic and political arguments in favour of some special financial aid to the poorer regions in the interests of equalizing services and facilities within a federation. It may be argued on economic grounds that building roads and railways and improving services like education, public health, and agricultural extension work in the poorer regions would be to the economic advantage of the nation as a whole. There may also be advantages in uniform standards of social services, which reduce the technical hindrances to people wishing to move from one region to another. The political pressures for equity may be even stronger, especially in the field of social services where citizens expect reasonably similar standards of health services and educational opportunities wherever they live within the country. Moreover, regional ability to maintain common standards is less likely to encourage local resentment and discontent. The poorer regions may also argue that sparsity of population, lack of natural resources, and other factors beyond their control, make the provision of services disproportionately burdensome, even to the point where, as in the smaller West Indian islands, their governments could not maintain the basic services without special aid.[3]

But although such considerations have usually made special financial assistance to the poorer regional governments desirable, there still remains the problem of how their need is to be assessed, and on what conditions the aid should be granted. Varying weight may be put upon different criteria; population; *per capita* income (if adequate statistics are available); standards of services; 'special difficulties' because of geographical factors, sparsity of

[1] See Chapter 7, section 2, and Table 2, p. 362.
[2] See, for instance, India, *Report of the Finance Commission, 1957* (1957), para. 100; C.A.P. (second), *Debates*, vol. i, pp. 1818–19; Malaya, *Report of the Committee Appointed to Review the Financial Provisions* (1955), paras. 16, 17; Malaysia, Cmnd. 1954/1963, para. 24, and Cmnd. 2094/1963, Annex J; Nigeria, *Report of the Commission on Revenue Allocation* (1951), paras. 43–49, 57; Rhodesia and Nyasaland, Cmd. 8672/1952, para. 23.
[3] Col. no. 255/1950, para. 35; Cmd. 9618/1955, para. 120.

population, or age-composition; budgetary deficits. Here, too, the principles of political independence and political responsibility may be raised by questions of who, the central government or an impartial commission, is to make the assessment of need, and whether the grants in aid should have conditions attached or be unconditional.

The complex problems in federal finance of balancing the functions and revenues of governments and of achieving an equitable distribution among regions were, of course, also experienced in the older federations.[1] Nor were the new federations any more backward than their predecessors at the time of their formation. What has made the problem more complex in the new federations, however, is that problems which in the older federations arose over a period of decades, and were dealt with one by one, have arisen together right from the beginning. For instance, the concept of the economic function of government has been much wider than was the case in the older federations during their early years. In the federations still retaining colonial status, programmes of economic aid by the imperial power have also complicated internal federal financial relations because of the tendency of regional governments to look beyond the central government for assistance. On the other hand, the devolutionary aspect of the genesis of some of the new federations has sometimes eased the difficulties, for in such federations citizens were already accustomed to central taxes.

2. *The pattern of federal finance in the new federations*

Despite the complexity and variety of the conflicting interests involved in the federal finance of the new federations, it is possible to discern a common pattern in the way these problems have been resolved. Details have varied, of course, and the West Indies Federation stood out as a clear exception, but the other five federations adopted a fundamentally similar approach. To some extent this may be attributed both to the influence of the Government of India Act, 1935, which served as a model for all three Asian federations, and to the role of Sir Jeremy Raisman, who acted as fiscal adviser in many of the new federations. Having experienced, as a Finance Member, the financial arrangements in pre-partition India, Raisman was subsequently called upon to be chairman of fiscal commissions in Pakistan (1952), Rhodesia and Nyasaland (1952 and 1957), Nigeria (1958), and East Africa (1961).[2] His reports have shown a pragmatic rather than a theoretical approach to the financial problems in each federation, but they have exhibited, nevertheless, a similarity in their general approach on such questions as the assignment of independent tax sources, and the use of distributable pools for adjusting revenues to balance functions. Of some influence also among the new federations was the more

---

[1] Birch, *Federalism, Finance and Social Legislation*, ch. 1.

[2] Pakistan, *Financial Enquiry Regarding Allocation of Revenues* (1952); Cmd. 8672/1952; R. and N., C. Fed. 56/1957; Cmnd. 481/1958; Cmnd. 1279/1961.

theoretical analysis made by the Hicks–Phillipson Commission in Nigeria.[1] This report had some influence not only on subsequent Nigerian financial schemes, but also upon the revised Malayan arrangements of 1956.[2]

The solution to the problem of federal finance in the new federations has been based on a treatment of expenditure, the levying and collection of revenue, and transfers of revenue from one level of government to the other, as three separate, variable components. In the allocation of responsibility for expenditure, administrative efficiency and political considerations have dominated. Thus, for reasons of greater efficiency through local administration and, even more influential, because of regional political pressures, many of the expensive and expansive fields of expenditure have been placed in the hands of the regional governments.[3] But in the assignment of powers to levy and collect taxes and other revenues, the principles of economic efficiency and national welfare have prevailed. Consequently, most of the major sources of revenue have been assigned to the central governments in the interests of efficient and economic levying and collection, minimizing double taxation, avoiding financial barriers to inter-regional trade, encouraging the credit-worthiness of the federation, and, most important, enabling an 'active' national fiscal policy.[4] As a result, it has invariably proved necessary to rely on inter-governmental financial transfers of considerable scale in order to bring into balance the functions and revenues of each government.[5] These transfers have also been used to equalize services and social amenities in the less fortunate regions, and to enable flexibility by means of periodic adjustments. In order to save the principle of financial autonomy, a large portion of these transfers has usually taken the form of unconditional grants or shares of central tax revenues, their size being based upon a constitutionally guaranteed formula or upon the recommendations of an impartial fiscal commission or inter-governmental council. On the whole, the principle that political responsibilities for raising and spending money should rest with the same authority has thus been given relatively little weight. Some attempts have been made, however, to ensure financial responsibility by fixing allocations of grants for specified periods during which the regional governments were left with a responsibility for keeping their expenditure within their income.

The financial arrangements in the constitution of the West Indies represented the major exception to this general pattern in the new federations. The Standing Closer Association Committee had actually recommended a

---

[1] Nigeria, *Report of the Commission on Revenue Allocation* (1951), part of which was reproduced in J. R. Hicks, *Essays in World Economics* (1959), ch. 10.

[2] Mr. E. Himsworth, Financial Secretary in Nigeria at the time of the preparation of the Hicks–Phillipson Report, was subsequently a member of the Malayan Financial Committee of 1955, and the latter report clearly shows the influence of the former.

[3] See Chapter 8, section 4, and section 3 of this chapter.

[4] See section 4 of this chapter.

[5] See Table 4A, p. 367, and section 5 of this chapter.

distribution of finances on lines similar to those of the others,[1] but under the continued pressures against a concentration of central power, the final arrangement reversed the pattern found elsewhere.[2] The major tax sources were left with the territorial governments, the central government having taxing powers even weaker during the initial five years than its limited legislative and executive responsibilities. The imbalance between federal expenditure and revenue was, therefore, made up by a mandatory levy upon the territorial governments. The 1961 constitutional conference agreed to abolish the mandatory levy and to give the central government fully independent taxing power sufficient to enable it to finance its developing obligations,[3] but before the new arrangements could be put into effect, the federation had disintegrated.

3. The allocation of expenditure

Considered from the point of view of the necessity to balance the revenues and expenditure of governments, the assignment of legislative and executive responsibilities is itself a facet of the general question of federal finance. It is true, of course, as we have noted in the previous chapter, that the distribution of functions has usually been made primarily on political or administrative grounds. Nevertheless, financial considerations have also been of some significance in the allocation of legislative and executive authority.

In the first place, adjustments have sometimes been made to the assignment of functions as part of the attempt to balance the functions and revenues within each tier of government. The Malayan Working Committee of 1946, for instance, began by distributing the sources of revenue between central and state and settlement governments, and then, in the light of these decisions, proceeded to allocate the heads of expenditure between them.[4] Later, the Reid Commission recommended that education and medical and health services should become wholly federal subjects because of their expense.[5]

Other economic and financial considerations have influenced the assignment of responsibility for expenditure. For instance, in the case of some functions, not only national welfare but expense or the obvious economy of unified administration have been factors in their allocation to the central government. Defence, for example, is extremely costly, especially under modern conditions. In the Asian federations, this subject alone has represented a major portion of central expenditure.[6] There are certain other subjects, too,

---

[1] Col. no. 255/1950, paras. 29–37.

[2] See Cmd. 9618/1955, ch. 7; Cmd. 9733/1956, paras. 24–34; Constitution, 1957, arts. 91–101, and Fourth and Fifth Scheds.

[3] Cmnd. 1417/1961, para. 27.

[4] Report of the Working Committee (1946), paras. 40, 41.

[5] Col. no. 330/1957, paras. 120, 138.

[6] In Pakistan, 1947–61, defence took between 50 and 70 per cent. of central expenditure. In India defence represented up to 40 per cent. of total central expenditure. In Malaya, where the central government had a large number of other responsibilities, defence was still the largest single item, making up about a quarter of central expenditure between 1956 and

where there are advantages to be gained from the economies of scale and opportunities for specialization within larger organizations. Such arguments have influenced the assignment to the central government in many cases of such expensive activities as establishment and operation of public industries and enterprises, utilities, major systems of transport and communications, programmes of research, and even social services. Some of these activities, such as public industries, utilities, and communications, once established, can normally be self-supporting, but their creation may be particularly expensive on the capital account. In addition, it is often where the population is most sparse, and therefore limited in its own financial resources, that there exists the most potential for development.

But many of the expensive 'developmental' expenditure commitments are most conveniently and efficiently administered by the regional governments. Education and health services, for instance, are expensive and particularly important items in underdeveloped countries which are attempting to undergo rapid advance; except in Malaya, it has nevertheless been thought that there are advantages of efficiency and of encouragement of spontaneous local enthusiasm to be gained from regional administration of these activities. Similar arguments for adaptation to local circumstances have led to the assignment to the regional governments of other expensive social services and of research into peculiarly local problems.

Another consideration arises from the significance of expenditure as a factor related to active public fiscal policy. The growth of the economy and the extent of inflationary pressures may be influenced by the degree and kind of public expenditure undertaken on development projects. If such expenditure is carried on primarily by the regional governments in an unco-ordinated manner, it may be impossible for the central government to maintain economic stability. The allocation of those subjects which involve heavy capital expenditure, especially such fields as communications, utilities, and industrial development, may, therefore, be especially significant. This explains why central governments in the new federations have frequently been assigned quite extensive, although not sole, powers in these areas.

Finally, the need for flexibility applies as much to the realm of spending power as to that of revenues. This has been recognized by the statesmen creating the new federations, for in each of them there has been a special provision enabling the central government to give grants to assist regional expenditure for any purpose, whether that purpose is within the central legislative competence or not.[1] In some cases, notably India, Nigeria (1954), and the West

1960. In the non-Asian federations, where external and internal security threats were less serious, defence has formed a smaller proportion of central expenditure.

[1] *Constitution of India, 1950*, art. 282; *Constitution of Pakistan, 1956*, art. 114; *Constitution of Pakistan, 1962*, art. 138; *Constitution of Malaya, 1957*, arts. 109 (3), 110 (4); *Nigeria Constitution, 1954*, s. 55; *Constitution of Nigeria, 1960*, ss. 64 (2), 68; *Constitution of Nigeria, 1963*, ss. 69 (2),73; *Constitution of R. and N., 1953*, art. 95; *Constitution of W.I., 1957*, art. 46.

Indies, the regional governments were also expressly given power to make grants for purposes outside their own legislative powers, thus making it possible, if it were ever necessary and the regional governments were willing, for them to assist the central government financially.[1]

Financial factors have, then, in most of the new federations except the West Indies, been influential in the allocation to the central governments of a relatively heavy burden of expenditure. Nevertheless, expensive and extensive fields of activity have also been assigned to the regional governments, for reasons of administrative economy as well as of political desirability. Indeed, by comparison with the older federations today, all the new federations except Malaya have placed a higher proportion of total public expenditure in the hands of regional governments.[2]

4. The allocation of revenue sources

The dominant principles in the new federations for the allocation of authority to raise revenues—powers of levying and collecting taxes, or of operating profitable enterprises—have been primarily those of efficient administration and national economic welfare.

The effect of this emphasis has been apparent, to begin with, in the form of the division of authority to levy and collect taxes. A marked feature of most of the new federations has been the attempt to demarcate clearly from each other those powers of taxation belonging to the central government and those belonging to the regional governments. In order to avoid the conflicts and tangles of competing or overlapping tax jurisdiction, the duplication of collection agencies, and clashes of fiscal policy, the concurrent right of taxation has been widely avoided, and tax sources have nearly always been assigned exclusively to one level of government or the other. The West Indies Federation was, as usual, an exception to the general trend, for there the major tax sources, customs and excise duties, and taxes on income and profits, were placed on the concurrent list, although for the first five years the central government was severely limited in these fields.[3] Otherwise, there were very few instances of concurrent taxes in the new federations.[4] In Rhodesia and Nyasaland, however, in the interests of territorial financial autonomy and further flexibility, the territorial governments were given power together with the central government to levy income taxes, but for the sake of simplicity of administra-

[1] *Constitution of India, 1950*, art. 282; *Nigeria Constitution, 1954*, s. 55; *Constitution of W.I., 1957*, art. 46; *Malaysia Act, 1963*, s. 48 (1) (e).

[2] See Table 4A, p. 367.

[3] By placing these taxes on the concurrent list, scope for future expansion of central revenues was intended. Constitution, arts. 94, 95, Third Sched., part i, para. 9, and part ii, paras. 18, 35.

[4] In Nigeria, in order to ensure uniformity of treatment among regions in the personal income tax field, the central government was given power to legislate on certain methods of assessment and administration, but not power to levy such taxes. Constitution, 1960, s. 70; Constitution, 1963, s. 76.

tion this took the form of a territorial surcharge on the central income tax, limited to a maximum of one-fifth of the central rate of tax.[1] Even then, although this system enabled a more economic administration than the separate collection of income taxes by both levels of government, in practice it gave rise to technical problems of assessment in determining the sources of private and corporate income, and placed limitations upon central fiscal policy.[2]

In the effort to mark off clearly the separate fields of taxation, and aware of difficulties experienced in the older federations, the draftsmen creating the new federal constitutions have often included specific provisions designed to avoid ambiguity about the taxation of governmental instrumentalities. The position in India, Pakistan, and Nigeria would appear to be roughly similar. In each the salaries of civil servants were not exempted from taxation by a government other than that which they served, but governments themselves might not be taxed by other governments, although in India and Pakistan public commercial enterprises were not included in this exemption.[3] Under the constitution of Rhodesia and Nyasaland taxation of the property of other governments was permitted, but only if a law expressly so provided.[4] The Malayan and West Indian constitutions were less complete on this question, but the former did exempt central and state property from local rates, providing instead for contributions in lieu of these to be negotiated or determined by the Lands Tribunal.[5] In the West Indies the levying of income tax on central officers was made an exclusive central subject.

Despite these efforts the attempt to achieve a clear bifurcation of sources of revenue has not always been completely successful. For instance, in both India and Pakistan, the tendency of regional governments to impose under various names taxes which in reality were customs or excise duties (neither of which were within their jurisdiction) resulted in the growth of obstructions to inter-regional trade.[6] Consequently, constitutional amendments became necessary, adding inter-state sales tax to the union powers in India, and centralizing all sales tax in Pakistan.[7] There have also been difficulties in distinguishing taxes on professions, poll taxes, and company tax from personal income tax, where the authority to levy these has rested with different

---

[1] Constitution, art. 82.

[2] Cmnd. 1150/1960, paras. 194–200.

[3] *Constitution of India, 1950*, arts. 285, 289; *Constitution of Pakistan, 1956*, arts. 112, 113; *Constitution of Pakistan, 1962*, art. 137; *Constitution of Nigeria, 1960*, s. 70 (6); *Constitution of Nigeria, 1963*, s. 76 (6).   [4] Art. 87.

[5] *Constitution of Malaya, 1957*, art. 156.

[6] Santhanam, *Union-State Relations in India*, p. 38; Pakistan, *Financial Enquiry Regarding Allocation of Revenues* (1952), para. 12. For similar difficulties experienced in Rhodesia and Nyasaland, see Cmnd. 1150/1960, paras. 211–12.

[7] *Constitution of India, 1950*, arts. 269 (1) (*g*), 269 (3) as amended by *Sixth Amendment Act, 1956*, s. 3; *Report of the Finance Commission, 1957*, para. 169. Pakistan: *Government of India (Amendment) Act, 1948*; *Government of India (Fourth Amendment) Act, 1950*; *Government of India (Amendment) Act, 1952*.

governments. Nor has there been an absence of litigation over the taxation of governmental instrumentalities.[1] But in spite of these exceptions, generally speaking, and certainly by contrast with the older federations, there has been a relatively clear division of taxing powers.

When it comes to actual assignment, the general tendency has been to allocate most of the major tax sources to the central government. Here a number of reasons have weighed heavily with the statesmen working out the distribution of taxing powers: the efficiency and economy of the levy and collection of these taxes by a single government; the effect of these taxes upon foreign exchange and the balance of payments; the barriers to inter-regional trade which would arise from regional control; the necessity of a nationally integrated 'active' fiscal policy, for encouraging domestic and especially foreign investment in the private sector of the economy, and for maintaining stability against inflationary pressures. Perhaps the strongest of these has been the desire not only to expand the 'liberal' functions of government such as the provision of communications, health services, and education, but also to enable the effective use of fiscal and monetary tools and of planning in support of more ambitious 'active' public policies aimed at stimulating development and keeping the national economy on a steady course of progress. Except where the regions were relatively large, as in Nigeria, or economically self-contained as in the case of Jamaica, this has usually meant that the appropriate authority for the concentration of taxing powers was the central government.

The major indirect taxes—import and export duties, excise duties, and sales taxes—have normally been assigned to the central government, although there have been some exceptions. The levy and collection of customs duties on both imports and exports by the central government has usually been considered essential in order to ensure freedom of inter-regional trade, to facilitate a national tariff policy, and to protect the balance of payments in a developing economy. In the non-Asian federations and Malaysia, some exceptions have been made to this general pattern, however. Full responsibility for customs duties rests with the central government in Nigeria, but in the special circumstances of that country, where the main items of produce exported by the regions differ and are handled exclusively by regional Marketing Boards, an arrangement has been established through regional control of sales tax on these products, which amounts to regionalization of the more important export duties.[2] In Rhodesia and Nyasaland customs duties were assigned to the central government, but a special exception was made in the case of duties on motor spirit, which were left under territorial control. The reasons for this

---

[1] A major example was *Punjab* v. *Federation of Pakistan*, P.L.D. 1956, F.C. 72.

[2] Cmnd. 481/1958, paras. 42–46; Cmnd. 569/1958, para. 40; Constitution, 1960, s. 133 and Exclusive Legislative List, items 10, 38; Constitution, 1963, s. 139 and Exclusive Legislative List, items 10, 38.

were the sharp differences in the existing rates of duty in the two Rhodesias, making a suitable compromise for the central rate difficult, and the importance of this source of revenue in Southern Rhodesia. The same difficulty of achieving a central compromise between existing customs duties also existed in the West Indies, but on a much wider scale. Jamaica was reluctant to lower its high tariff, which was a part of its economic development programme and which, if reduced, would involve a serious loss of revenue. Moreover, since Jamaica was one of the relatively wealthier islands, compensation for loss of tariff revenue seemed out of the question. Because of the difficulties caused by the sharply differing tariff rates, and because there was relatively little trade between the economically competitive islands anyway, the attempt to establish a customs union was in the end postponed. Consequently, although earlier plans had been based on the expectation that customs duties would be federalized, limits were placed in the constitution upon the central power to levy and retain such duties during the first five years, and most duties were levied and retained by the territories.[1] The imposition of a customs union was also postponed when the Southern Arabian Federation was formed in 1959, customs and excise duties being placed in the hands of the central government at the time of Aden's accession four years later.[2] In Malaysia, too, the establishment of a customs union raised difficulties because of Singapore's desire to secure access to the Malaysian market under favourable terms and, at the same time, to safeguard its entrepôt trade. The solution was an arrangement whereby customs duties were placed under central control, but the central government was required to consult a Tariff Advisory Board, jointly appointed by the central and Singapore governments, and Singapore was given the right to delay for certain periods the imposition of duties prejudicial to its entrepôt trade.[3]

The distribution of authority to levy and collect excise duties on the production or manufacture of goods has normally followed the same pattern as the assignment of customs duties. The reasons for this have been the close relation necessary between such excise duties and the treatment of similar goods for import-duty purposes, the desire to avoid the possibility of multiple taxation, and the importance of their effect upon inter-regional trade and upon the location of investment in industrial projects. But since excise duties do not seriously affect the balance of payments, sometimes the control of a few excise duties, such as those on alcohol and narcotics in India and Pakistan, has been granted to the states.[4]

Because of the shortage of major tax sources available to regional governments, in India, as in Canada and the United States, regional sales taxes have

---

[1] Arts. 94–95 and Fourth Sched.
[2] Cmnd. 1814/1962, pp. 11–14, 18–19.   [3] Cmnd. 2094/1963, Annex J.
[4] The adoption of prohibition by many Indian states denied the value of the duty on alcohol to their revenues, however. See B. R. Misra, *Indian Federal Finance* (3rd ed., 1960), ch. xviii.

been relied upon for significant amounts of regional revenue. But in these federations constitutional difficulties have arisen in connexion with inter-state trade, since in order to make the taxes effective, regional governments were driven to take measures which impeded the freedom of trade. In India there resulted considerable litigation, and a constitutional amendment assigning the central government control of all taxes on sales taking place in the course of inter-state trade had to be adopted.[1] In the later federations, except for the West Indies and the Borneo states acceding to Malaysia,[2] the power to impose general sales taxes was made an exclusively central subject. The importance of these taxes as a device for controlling the economy, and the desire to avoid inter-regional barriers, have thus usually proved decisive considerations. But in Nigeria, although sales taxes generally were made a central subject, provision was made for certain exceptions. The desire to enhance the financial independence of the regions led to the assignment to the regional governments of sales taxes on produce, hides and skins, motor spirit, and diesel oil (with certain qualifications), because the collection of such taxes on these particular products could be regionalized without extensive administrative complications.[3] It was for similar reasons that in Malaysia the states partially isolated on the island of Borneo could be permitted to levy non-discriminatory sales taxes.

The major direct taxes—taxes on corporate profits and on personal income—have also generally been assigned to the central government.[4] This is not surprising in view of the importance of this form of taxation as an especially valuable instrument of economic control, and as a means of influencing both the level of foreign and domestic investment and the extent of personal expenditure. Moreover, a uniform system removes problems of internal double taxation, especially where corporations operate in more than one region, and reduces the likelihood that investment will be directed into the wrong locational patterns by regional inducements.

In following this general pattern the recent non-Asian federations have, however, made some exceptions in the interest of increasing regional financial independence. The territorial governments of Rhodesia and Nyasaland, for instance, were given the right to levy a surcharge of up to one-fifth of the

[1] *Sixth Amendment Act, 1956*, amending Constitution, arts. 269, 286, and Union List, entry 92 (by a new entry 92A), and State List, entry 54. See also *State of Travancore-Cochin* v. *Bombay Co. Ltd.*, A.I.R. 1952, S.C. 366; *Poppatlal Shah* v. *State of Madras*, A.I.R. 1953, S.C. 274; *State of Bombay* v. *United Motors Ltd.*, A.I.R. 1953, S.C. 252; *State of Travancore-Cochin* v. *S.V.C. Factory*, A.I.R. 1953, S.C. 333; *Bengal Immunity Co. Ltd.* v. *State of Bihar*, A.I.R. 1955, S.C. 661.

[2] *Malaysia Act, 1963*, s. 35 (3), and Fifth Sched., part v, s. 7.

[3] Constitutions, 1960 and 1963, Exclusive Legislative List, item 38; Cmnd. 481/1958, paras. 39–65.

[4] Succession duties, because of their effect on inter-regional movement and problems of calculating their regional base, have also usually been assigned to the central government. In underdeveloped countries, however, such duties are rarely a major source of revenue.

central income and profits tax, this being collected on their behalf by the central tax authorities.[1] In Nigeria taxes on company profits have always been a central power.[2] Taxes on personal income were at first divided by a distinction between Africans and expatriates, taxes on the former being levied by the regional, and on the latter by the central, governments. Following the Raisman Report, this division was abandoned. Despite the handicaps that would be placed upon central efforts towards a nationally integrated economic policy, the regional governments were given exclusive authority to levy personal income taxes because of the special circumstances of Nigeria in which taxes on personal income were closely related to local administration.[3] In the West Indies the arguments in favour of central control of corporate and personal income tax on grounds of avoiding the overlapping of territorial jurisdiction were weaker than elsewhere, because the distances between the islands meant that the regional derivation of income and the branch operations of companies were more clearly demarcated. Under the constitution, power to tax income and profits was made concurrent, but for the first five years the central authority was limited to taxing the income of its own officers.[4] Because of the importance of these taxes to Jamaica's own development programme, a declaration by Prime Minister Adams that at the end of the five-year period the central government would levy an income tax, and furthermore that it might be retroactive, raised a storm of protest in Jamaica. The question became a major issue of contention, and, due to Jamaican insistence, the 1961 constitutional conference agreed to extend the prohibition against the central government assuming these powers of taxation.[5]

In allocating sources of revenue most of the recent federations have recognized the possibility that in emergencies the central governments might need special taxing powers more extensive than normal. In the four independent federations, India, Pakistan, Malaya, and Nigeria, and also in the West Indies, the sweeping emergency powers enabling conversion of these federations into unitary states provided ample financial power.[6] The constitutions of India and Pakistan in addition provided for special central powers in 'financial emergencies' which threatened the financial stability of these countries.[7] In such circumstances the central governments could give directions to

---

[1] Constitution, art. 82.

[2] Constitution, 1954, Exclusive Legislative List, item 36; Constitution, 1960, s. 70 (1); Constitution, 1963, s. 76 (1).

[3] Constitution, 1960, s. 70; Constitution, 1963, s. 76. The arrangements proposed for an East Caribbean federation followed a similar pattern, taxes on company incomes being a central subject and taxes on personal income being fixed by Unit Governments (Cmnd. 1746/1962, para. 26).

[4] Exclusive Legislative List, para. 9; Concurrent Legislative List, para. 35. Such a restriction, but without any time limit, was adopted in the Federation of South Arabia (Cmnd. 1814/1962, p. 11).   [5] Cmnd. 1417/1961, para. 20.

[6] For a discussion of these powers, see Chapter 12, section 6.

[7] *Constitution of India, 1950*, art. 360; *Constitution of Pakistan, 1956*, art. 194; *Constitution of Pakistan, 1962*, art. 131 (2) (a).

the regional governments, review regional money-bills, and order the reduction of salaries of central and regional officials. In Rhodesia and Nyasaland the central government was empowered in periods of emergency to levy, solely for its own use, a surcharge on income taxes (of which a portion of the proceeds was normally distributed among the regional governments).[1]

Since all the major sources of both indirect and direct taxation have been assigned, with only a few exceptions, to the central governments, the problem in most of the new federations has been to find sufficient sources of independent revenue for the regional governments. The taxes assigned to the regional governments have usually been those with a distinctively local basis. Examples of such taxes have been taxes on land, local duties such as those on entertainment, licences, and capitation taxes. But while some of these sources have provided the regional governments with some measure of independent revenue, this has had to be shared also with the third tier of government, the local authorities. It was because these regional sources of taxation were so limited that, as we have already noted, it was sometimes found necessary to make exceptions to the general tendency to assign the major direct and indirect taxes to the central government, even at the expense of weakening the central controls over the development of the economy.

In addition to revenue raised by taxation, the regional governments have usually relied heavily on other sources of revenue, such as the profits from public utilities and commercial operations. Indeed, in most of the new federations such sources have been responsible for about one-third of the independent regional revenue before the addition of financial transfers from the central government.[2] But while these non-tax revenues have helped to ease the financial shortages of the regions, the danger is that regional governments may be pressed to set high charges for public utilities simply to raise their income, rather than providing economic services. On the other hand, where such services suffer a loss in their operations, they may become a further drain upon state revenues rather than an assistance.[3]

In summary, it would appear that in all the new federations except the West Indies the bulk of the major sources of revenue have been assigned to the central governments, giving them considerable scope for control of the economy. Thus, apart from the West Indies, central revenues before intergovernmental transfers have generally ranged between 60 and 89 per cent. of the total public revenues (central and regional revenues combined).[4]

---

[1] Constitution, art. 81. In India, too, the central government could levy for its own purposes a surcharge on certain duties and taxes, but this was not limited to emergencies (Constitution, art. 271).

[2] See Tables 5B, 6B, 7B, 9B, 10B, pp. 368–75.

[3] See, for instance, India, *Report of the Finance Commission, 1957*, paras. 75–82.

[4] See Table 4A. For a critique of the lack of central fiscal powers for controlling the West Indian economy see Seers, 'Federation of the B.W.I.: The Economic and Financial Aspects', *Social and Economic Studies*, vi (1957), pp. 197–214.

5. *The adjustment of central and regional revenues*

In all the new federations inter-governmental financial transfers have con-stituted an integral part of the system of federal finance. The significance of these adjustments is indicated in Table 4A, which compares the relative pro-portions of governmental revenues, expenditures, and transfers in the different federations, and in Table 4B, which compares the composition of regional revenues.[1] In most of these federations transfers have accounted for a substantial portion of net regional revenue. For instance, as a proportion of regional revenue, transfers from central sources rose in India from 19 per cent. in 1952–3 to 35 per cent. in 1960–1, in Pakistan accounted for 49 per cent. of provincial revenue by 1962–3, in Rhodesia and Nyasaland regularly repre-sented one-third of territorial revenue, and in Malaya after 1958 constituted between 38 per cent. and 41 per cent. of state revenues. The figures are even more striking in Malaya before 1958, where central grants provided about 60 per cent. of state income, and in Nigeria, where central sources have con-sistently been responsible for about two-thirds of total regional revenue. Normally these transfers have been from the central to the regional govern-ments, but in the West Indies they were in the opposite direction, a large portion of central revenue taking the form of a mandatory levy upon the territories. The Federation of South Arabia was unusual in that there was pro-vision for transfers in both directions. States made annual contributions to the central government of an amount stipulated in the constitution, and the central government paid states a sum fixed in the constitution as compen-sation for the assignment of customs and excise duties to the federation, the two sums being set off against each other.[2]

The reason for such substantial inter-governmental financial transfers has been the tendency, described in the preceding sections, favouring a greater con-centration of revenue sources than of expenditure in the central government. These transfers have therefore proved necessary to correct this imbalance. In addition they have also provided a useful means for compensating for regional inequalities in fiscal capacity and for making periodic adjustments to changing circumstances.

Because of the size and importance of these financial transfers, the question whether they should take the form of conditional grants, designated for specific purposes, or of unallocated transfers has been of both economic and political significance. The economic arguments in favour of conditional specific-purpose grants are that they may be used to encourage regional expenditure upon subjects most in the national economic interest, that they may be employed to maintain desirable minimum standards for certain

---

[1] See pp. 367–75 for tables concerning finances. Tables 5A, 6A, 7A, 8A, 9A, 10A show for each federation the relative proportions of central and regional revenues and transfers. Tables 5B, 6B, 7B, 8B, 9B, 10B give the composition of regional revenues, by federation.

[2] Constitution, 1963, ss. 64–68.

services, especially social services, and that the effectiveness of such grants may be measured by the specific results. Such grants also make possible the application of the political principle of 'financial responsibility', for they leave the government which raises the money by taxation some control over the expenditure of these grants through the conditions it imposes.

But there are also economic arguments against conditional grants. To begin with, specific-purpose grants, especially those with a matching-requirement (intended to encourage financial responsibility), tend to distort regional budgets. By placing a premium upon the aided services, they may encourage poor regions to starve other essential services. Secondly, the application of uniform conditions for grants to different regions may be inequitable where regional needs contrast sharply. But if the conditions are made variable in order to meet this difficulty, there arises the same problem as with unconditional grants of determining suitable criteria for these variations. Thirdly, with specific-purpose grants there is the danger of money being frittered away by the central government on its own fads. Nor do such grants, intended to preserve the principle of 'financial responsibility', necessarily prevent regional extravagance and waste. Indeed, the experience in Malaya was that dependence on *ad hoc* central grants militated against careful forward planning by the states, and subsequently a system of steady unconditional transfers was adopted to stress the financial responsibility of the states for equating expenditure with revenue.[1]

But in the new federations it is the political arguments that have been decisive in the preference for unconditional transfers. Where financial transfers have constituted such a major portion of regional revenues, conditional grants have not been acceptable because of their political implications, involving as they do a measure of central control over regional governments. Thus, despite the alleged failings of unconditional grants—that they encourage regional governments to court popularity by extravagant spending while leaving the central government to provide the uncontrolled funds—the preference has been for unallocated financial transfers. The form and proportions of these transfers as components of regional revenue may be seen from Tables 4B, 5B, 6B, 7B, 8B, 9B, and 10B on which the following discussion is based. It is significant that in all the new federations the largest segment of the revenues transferred has been in the form of unconditional transfers such as proportional shares of central tax proceeds, shares of a distributable pool, or block grants. Malaya was the single exception, for between 1948 and 1956 central grants took the form of annual *ad hoc* allocations coupled with close central supervision of state and settlement budgets.[2] In the interests of in-

[1] *Report of the Committee Appointed to Review the Financial Provisions* (1955), para. 3; Col. no. 330/1957, para. 142. Cf. India, *Report of Finance Commission, 1961* (1962), paras. 73, 89–90.

[2] Federation Agreement, 1948, cls. 112, 114, 115, 117–23.

creasing the financial autonomy of the states, some unconditional shares of central taxes and statutory grants were added in 1956,[1] and the system was completely revised in 1958 so as to depend predominantly on unconditional grants.[2] Elsewhere, unconditional financial transfers have predominated, although in both India and Pakistan there has been considerable use of special-purpose grants to support development projects.

A particularly popular form of unallocated transfer among the new federations has been the sharing of all or part of the proceeds from specified central taxes. This type has, in fact, represented the major form of transfer in India, Pakistan, Rhodesia and Nyasaland, and Nigeria. The proceeds from a wide variety of Union taxes in India have been shared, the most productive for the states being personal income taxes and excise duties.[3] In Pakistan after 1952 the revenue from a considerable number of central taxes was shared with the provinces, including at least half of the proceeds from personal income tax, excises, sales taxes, and in the case of East Pakistan, export duty on jute.[4] Central taxes on income alone were the main adjusting head in Rhodesia and Nyasaland, the proceeds being distributed among the central and the three territorial governments.[5] In Nigeria, following the Raisman Report, various proportions of central import duties on motor spirit and tobacco, export duties, excise duties, and mining royalties and rents, have been distributed among the regions.[6] The sharing of central tax revenues was also instituted in Malaya in 1956 in the case of petrol duty, although there these proceeds constituted only a small proportion of total transfers. Under the 1957 constitution some central tax revenues continued to be shared, but their relative proportion was made even smaller.[7] When Singapore joined Malaysia, however, it was agreed that, instead of receiving block grants as the other states did, Singapore should receive 60 per cent. of nearly all central taxes levied in Singapore.[8]

A variation on this general type of financial transfer is the combined distributable pool, used in Nigeria on the recommendation of the Raisman Commission.[9] Here certain proportions of the proceeds of a number of central

[1] *Report of the Committee Appointed to Review the Financial Provisions* (1955), esp. paras. 3–5, 8 (ii) (iii).　　　　　　　[2] Constitution, 1957, art. 109, and Tenth Sched.

[3] Constitution, arts. 268–70, 272; *Report of the Finance Commission, 1957*, chs. ix, x, and pp. 156–65; *Report of the Finance Commission, 1961*, chs. ii–v.

[4] *Financial Enquiry Regarding Allocation of Revenues* (1952), paras. 6, 8, 9, 10, 11; *Constitution of Pakistan, 1956*, art. 118 (3); *Constitution of Pakistan, 1962*, art. 144 (4, 5).

[5] Constitution, art. 80. Under article 83 export duties were to be shared similarly, but no export duties were levied.

[6] Cmnd. 481/1958, chs. vi, ix: *Constitution of Nigeria, 1960*, ss. 131–4; *Constitution of Nigeria, 1963*, ss. 137–40.　　　　　　　[7] Art. 110.

[8] Cmnd. 2094/1963, Annex J, para. 6. The Borneo states were also assigned the proceeds of a few central taxes. *Malaysia Act, 1963*, s. 46, and Fifth Sched., part v.

[9] In a sense the proceeds of each central tax which are shared with the regional governments might be described as a 'distributable pool' and this term has been so used in India, Pakistan, and Rhodesia and Nyasaland. What particularly distinguishes the Nigerian example is the use of the term in the constitution to apply to the combined proceeds of a

taxes are combined into a single distributable pool to be divided among the regions. The purpose of this arrangement has been to provide a pool of revenue from which adjustments for regional needs and for developing circumstances might be made, thus serving the same purpose for which unconditional grants have been used in India and Pakistan.[1]

The advantages of sharing the proceeds of specified central taxes are several. First, the distribution of revenue may be related to the region from which it has been derived if so desired. Secondly, it gives the regional government a direct financial interest in encouraging the growth of the activities upon which these particular central taxes draw. Thirdly, since the regional proportion of the central tax revenue is specified not as an absolute amount but as a percentage of the tax yield, regional revenue expands correspondingly with central revenue, thus giving elasticity to regional income. But the other side to this coin is the disadvantage that fluctuations, down as well as up, are transmitted directly to the regions, which have less capacity to react to these changes. Furthermore, since regional governments do not control the rates of these taxes, they can never be sure in advance what their share is likely to amount to.

Unconditional grants stipulated by the constitution have the advantage that, because the amounts are fixed, the regional governments have a basis upon which to plan for the future, and can take full responsibility for keeping expenditure within income. For this reason unconditional grants were adopted as the main form of financial transfer from the central government to the states in the Malayan constitution of 1957, and when Malaysia was formed, additional unconditional grants were provided for the Borneo states.[2] The mandatory levy upon the West Indian territorial governments, which constituted the main source of central revenue during the lifetime of the federation, was in effect also a statutory unconditional grant, but in the reverse direction to the usual.[3] Although not the main form of unallocated financial transfer, unconditional grants have been found useful also in India and, on a smaller scale, in Pakistan as a device for meeting the budgetary needs of the states and provinces.[4]

group of central taxes. See Cmnd. 481/1958, ch. xi; Constitution, 1960, ss. 130, 134, 135; Constitution, 1963, ss. 136, 140, 141. The annual grant to Sabah in Malaysia, which is calculated as a percentage of the increases in combined central revenue from that state, although titled as a grant, is close in form to a 'distributable pool'. See *Malaysia Act, 1963,* Fifth Sched., part iv, para. 2 (1).

[1] The distributable pool provided about one-quarter of the central transfers to the regions in Nigeria in 1959–60.

[2] Constitution, 1957, art. 109, and Tenth Sched.; *Malaysia Act, 1963,* ss. 45–47, and Fifth Sched.

[3] *Constitution of W.I., 1957,* arts. 91, 93 and Fifth Sched. See Tables 10A, 10C. The amount of the levy was based on an estimate by the pre-federal Fiscal Commissioner of the yield that might be expected if central customs and excise duties were levied on certain commodities at certain rates (Cmd. 9618/1955, ch. vii).

[4] *Constitution of India, 1950,* arts. 273, 275, 278; *Report of the Finance Commission, 1957,*

In all these forms of unallocated financial transfers, whether as shares of specified taxes or of a distributable pool, or as unconditional grants, problems arise as to the amounts to be transferred and the way these are to be distributed among the regions. As to the first of these questions, the total amount to be transferred, the primary consideration has usually been the need to provide adequate revenues for both levels of government to fulfil their expenditure commitments. In some federations changing patterns of expenditure have resulted in modifications to the proportion of tax proceeds or size of the unconditional grants transferred to the regional governments. The Indian Finance Commissions, for instance, have progressively increased the proportion of central income tax given to the states (50 per cent. in 1952, 60 per cent. in 1957, and 66⅔ per cent. in 1962), widened the range of Union excise duties of which the proceeds are shared, and enlarged the size of grants in aid of revenue. In Pakistan the provinces were assigned shares in certain central taxes in 1952 in order to improve their general financial position,[1] and in 1962, when the provinces were given greater executive and administrative responsibilities, the provincial share of central taxes and duties was enlarged by about 67 per cent.[2] The need to match shifts in the patterns of expenditure led to adjustments also in the amounts of unconditional transfers in Malaya in 1956 and 1958,[3] in Rhodesia and Nyasaland in 1957,[4] and in Nigeria in 1958.[5]

When we turn to the question of the way in which these unallocated transfers have been distributed among regions, we find that a variety of criteria have been applied.[6] Where the proceeds of central taxes are shared the principle of derivation has had considerable appeal, for it makes the returns proportional to the regional contributions to these central taxes, and stresses the extent of regional autonomy. It was for this reason that in Nigeria the financial arrangements in operation between 1954 and 1958 were based primarily on the principle of derivation. But in practice it was found that, in a closely integrated economy, there were difficulties in calculating accurately the regional derivation of central revenue.[7] Upon the recommendations of the Raisman Commission of 1958 the arrangements were, therefore,

chs. vi, viii, xii; *Report of the Finance Commission, 1961*, para. 18 and ch. vi; Pakistan, *Financial Enquiry Regarding Allocation of Revenues* (1952), para. 13.

[1] *Financial Enquiry Regarding Allocation of Revenues* (1952), paras. 5, 6, 8, 9.

[2] *Budget of the Central Government for 1962–3: Speech of the Finance Minister* (1962), pp. 4–5; President's Order 23/1962. Corporation tax was added to the group of taxes shared, half the proceeds of this and of personal income tax being transferred. The portion of sales and excise taxes transferred was raised from 50 to 60 per cent., and the whole, instead of 62·5 per cent., of the export duty on jute and cotton assigned to the provinces. In addition the provinces were to receive the whole of estate and succession duties on agricultural land and of taxes on the capital value of immovable property.

[3] *Report of Committee Appointed to Review the Financial Provisions* (1955), para. 3 and ch. 2; Col. no. 330/1957, para. 138.

[4] C. Fed. 56/1957, paras. 15, 16, 20, 21.   [5] Cmnd. 481/1958, ch. xi.

[6] The actual distribution among regions can be seen in Tables 5c, 6b, 7c, 8b, 9b.

[7] Cmnd. 481/1958, paras. 11–20.

substantially modified so that the proceeds of only some central taxes, for which the imputation of source was easily determined, were distributed according to derivation,[1] the others being placed in the distributable pool. The distributable pool itself, on the other hand, was allocated according to need, the criteria used by the Fiscal Commission being: ability to maintain 'minimum responsibilities' of government, 'continuity' of services, 'population', and 'balanced development' of the federation.[2] Elsewhere, too, because the principle of derivation tended to favour the wealthier regions, and because of the difficulties of imputation, the principle of derivation has been qualified. In India, for instance, in the distribution of income tax, 80 per cent. or more has been distributed according to population, the remainder in each case being shared according to collection.[3] The other major source for transfers in India, the basic central excise duties, were distributed according to population, with some extra weight being given to certain states suffering disabilities, thus stressing the principle of regional need.[4] In Pakistan, with the exception of sales tax distributed according to incidence, and in Rhodesia and Nyasaland, the proportions of central taxes allocated among the regions took the form of an award, no formula being specified, although, in each, reference was made both to source of revenues and to regional need as the primary factors.[5] Later, when the distribution of central tax shares in Pakistan was revised in 1962, much greater weight was placed upon population as a criterion than upon derivation, with the result that of the additional Rs. 25·36 crores transferred, East Pakistan received Rs. 17·26 crores and West Pakistan Rs. 8·10 crores.[6] Thus, in most federations, the allocation of central tax revenue among regions has involved some measure of redistribution of national wealth.

The redistributive effect has been even more marked in the distribution of unconditional grants among regions, where 'need' has usually been the

[1] Constitution, 1960, ss. 131–4; Constitution, 1963, ss. 137–40.

[2] Cmnd. 481/1958, paras. 137–40.

[3] *Report of the Finance Commission, 1961*, paras. 32–38. The first and third Finance Commissions distributed 80 per cent. according to population and the second Commission 90 per cent.

[4] *Report of F.C., 1957*, ch. x; *Report of F.C., 1961*, paras. 46–47. The additional Union excises shared after 1957 to replace state sales taxes were, however, distributed on the basis of consumption, with population applied as a corrective criterion (*Report, 1961*, paras. 49–56). Some of the other less-productive central taxes shared were distributed according to derivation (Constitution, art. 268; *Report, 1957*, paras. 137, 179–82; *Report, 1961*, paras. 22–25).

[5] Pakistan, *Financial Enquiry Regarding Allocation of Revenues* (1952), paras. 6, 8, 9, 11; Cmd. 8672/1952, paras. 23, 29–30; R. and N. C. Fed. 56/1957, paras. 13–22.

[6] *Budget of the Central Government for 1962–3: Speech of the Finance Minister*, pp. 4–5. Where the previous formula distributed income tax and excise duties 55 per cent. to West Pakistan and 45 per cent. to East Pakistan, under the new formula based solely on population the respective figures were 46 per cent. and 54 per cent. Sales tax had formerly been distributed according to derivation, but after 1962, 70 per cent. was assigned on the basis of population and only 30 per cent. according to incidence. Estate and succession duty, and taxes on immovable property, now added to the derived provincial revenues were, however, distributed according to collection.

criterion. In India there are a variety of these grants for various disabilities, the primary principle of allocation being that of 'budgetary need'.[1] In calculating this, some effort was made to allow for the tax effort and administrative economy of different states in order to encourage financial responsibility. Likewise, in Pakistan, 'budgetary need' was the consideration leading to the subvention to the North-West Frontier Province.[2] In Malaya, where the bulk of the financial transfers took the form of constitutionally guaranteed grants, 'need' was measured by two criteria: population, on a sliding scale, and mileage of state roads.[3] The Borneo states when they joined Malaysia also received additional annual balancing and escalating grants intended to meet the existing and expected cost of state services.[4] The West Indian mandatory levy which the territories contributed to the central government was in a sense based on the principle of derivation, for the territorial proportions were calculated from the amount they would contribute if the central government levied certain duties at certain rates.[5] But because this meant that the wealthier units contributed more to the central government than they would if the levy was on a *per capita* basis, in effect it helped to redistribute income within the federation.

Although all the new federations (even including Malaya since 1957) have relied upon unconditional financial transfers as the major means for adjusting revenue to expenditure commitments, in each federation the central government has been empowered to make special conditional grants if it wishes.[6] It would appear that, except in Malaya before 1957, the central power to make specific-purpose grants was considered by the constitution-makers as a device in reserve primarily for dealing with unforeseen contingencies. In practice, however, there has been a tendency to use such grants extensively in national economic plans in order to support regional development projects. Indeed, in India and Pakistan the states and provinces have consequently become increasingly dependent upon discretionary central assistance to a degree

---

[1] *Report of F.C., 1961*, ch. vi. The second Finance Commission (*Report, 1957*, paras. 123–6) had included in the calculation of 'budgetary need' the commitments of the states to development expenditure under the Five Year Plan. The third Commission (*Report, 1961*, paras. 63–73) went further. It suggested that 75 per cent. of the total revenue (including central assistance formerly in the form of conditional grants) needed for the state plans should be included in the unconditional grants in aid of revenues in order to encourage state responsibility and autonomy. This recommendation was not unanimous (pp. 51–59), and was not accepted by the Union Government.

[2] *Financial Enquiry Regarding Allocation of Revenues* (1952), para. 13.

[3] Col. no. 330/1957, para. 144; Constitution, 1957, Tenth Sched. For effect of these criteria, see Table 7c.

[4] *Malaysia Act, 1963*, s. 46, and Fifth Sched. Singapore was also required to make a loan to assist development in the Borneo states (Cmnd. 2094/1963, Annex J, para. 9).

[5] Cmd. 9618/1955, ch. vii. See Table 10c.

[6] *Constitution of India, 1950*, art. 282; *Constitution of Pakistan, 1956*, art. 114; *Constitution of Pakistan, 1962*, art. 138; *Constitution of Malaya, 1957*, art. 109 (3); *Nigeria Constitution, 1954*, s. 55; *Constitution of Nigeria, 1960*, ss. 64 (2), 68; *Constitution of Nigeria, 1963*, ss. 69 (2), 73; *Constitution of R. and N., 1953*, art. 95; *Constitution of W.I., 1957*, art. 46.

seriously threatening their financial autonomy.[1] In India the third Finance Commission was sufficiently concerned to present a majority recommendation that 75 per cent. of the revenue component of state plans be covered by un- conditional grants, but this was rejected by the central government as likely to weaken the machinery ensuring effective co-ordination in the formulation and implementation of plans.[2] The trend has been less marked in the non-Asian federations, but there are signs in the Nigerian National Development Pro- gramme, 1962–8, that because of the extra financial resources of the Federal Government and the inelasticity of regional revenues, increasing use will be made of development grants for the regional programmes.[3] Owing to the importance of development grants, regional rivalry has often been a signifi- cant factor in their allocation, the most extreme example being Pakistan where the central government found it necessary in 1962 to accept as a primary principle the distribution of these grants in a manner ostensibly aiming at producing provincial parity of *per capita* income.[4]

The adjustment of central and regional revenues raises one further question: who is to determine the amounts and distribution of the unconditional financial transfers between governments? Clearly it cannot be the central government, for this would give it an opportunity to control the regional governments through control of their revenue. On the other hand, the embodi- ment of the financial formula in the constitution is likely to make impossible the adaptability in federal finance which experience has shown to be necessary. Here too, therefore, some compromise has been necessary. In India, Pakistan, and, within certain limits, Malaya, the revision of the amount and distribution of unconditional financial transfers has been left to the central government.[5] On the other hand, in Rhodesia and Nyasaland, Nigeria, and the West Indies, modification of the amount and distribution of such transfers requires the normal procedure of constitutional amendment.[6] In Malaysia, alterations in the financial arrangements for Singapore and the Borneo states required agreement between governments, or, failing that, decision by an independent

---

[1] See Tables 5B and 6B. See also Santhanam, *Union-State Relations*, pp. 40–59; P. P. Agarwal, *The System of Grants-in-Aid in India* (1959), chs. iii, vii. Of the total outlay of the states upon their share of the 'Plans', central assistance financed 39 per cent. in the First Plan (1951–6), 52 per cent. in the Second Plan (1956–61), and was expected to account for over 57 per cent. in the Third Plan (1961–6). See R. N. Bhargava, *Indian Public Finances* (1962), p. 234, and *India, 1963*, pp. 164–7.

[2] *Report, 1961*, paras. 63–75, 84–90, 93.

[3] *National Development Plan, 1962–8* (Lagos, 1962), pp. 32–33, 45, 177–8, 326.

[4] Constitution, 1962, art. 145 (4).

[5] *Constitution of India, 1950*, arts. 269 (2), 270 (4), 272, 273 (3), 275; *Constitution of Pakistan, 1956*, art. 118; *Constitution of Pakistan, 1962*, art. 144 (5); *Constitution of Malaya, 1957*, art. 109 (2). Note especially Alexandrowicz, *Constitutional Developments in India*, pp. 197–202; cf. Santhanam, *Union-State Relations in India*, pp. 33–34. Alterations to the authority to levy taxes require constitutional amendment in all these federations, however.

[6] *Constitution of R. and N., 1953*, art. 97; R. and N., *The Constitution Amendment Act, 1958* (Act 13/1958); *Constitution of Nigeria, 1960*, s. 4 (1); *Constitution of Nigeria, 1963*, s. 4 (1); *Constitution of W.I., 1957*, arts. 117–18.

assessor.[1] But in all of these federations provision has been made for fiscal review by either impartial commissions or inter-governmental councils in order to facilitate regular adjustment with a minimum of controversy.[2]

6. *Public borrowing*

A desire to establish one large credit-worthy political unit in the place of a number of separate governments, which would have difficulty attracting loans, has been one of the strong economic motives for federation. The arrangements for public borrowing by both central and regional governments were therefore of considerable importance.

The main problems, as with the distribution of other powers between governments, has been the necessity for a compromise between the desires for regional financial autonomy on the one hand, and the benefits of central control or co-ordination on the other. The Indian Expert Committee on Financial Provisions put it this way:

> The most outstanding advantage of the freedom of borrowing is the sense of financial responsibility it creates; for, there is no more accurate, sensitive and dependable meter of the credit of a borrowing government than the reaction of the securities market. . . . Nevertheless it is necessary to have some machinery which would ensure that borrowing governments do not by their competition upset the capital market.[3]

Although regional governments have been keen to enjoy a measure of independent authority in the field of ways and means, the arguments for central co-ordination or even command of all public borrowing have been strong. In the first place, since the control of credit is an essential element in the curbing of inflation and the maintenance of employment, it has been argued that the central government, aided by central banking institutions, should be able to regulate the exercise of borrowing powers by all public authorities as well as by private persons and limited companies. Reckless borrowing by regional governments might produce adverse monetary and economic consequences for the whole nation by increasing the public debt. A second point is that a single or co-ordinated programme of public borrowing is more efficient. By avoiding governmental competition in the loan market, more favourable terms can usually be obtained.[4] A third argument is that by restraining irresponsible regional borrowing the central government may be saved from the burden of having to rescue regions in difficulty. Otherwise there is the danger that default by one regional government may create a panic in the money market, affecting all the other governments within a federation. A fourth

---

[1] See section 7 below.

[2] There were provisions for fiscal reviews also in Uganda (S.I. 1962, no. 2175, s. 20; Constitution, 1962, Sched. 9, para. 2), South Arabia (Constitution, 1963, s. 68 (2)), and Kenya (Independence Constitution, 1963, s. 156).

[3] C.A.I., *Report of the Expert Committee on the Financial Provisions* (1947), para. 81.

[4] But the larger regions, such as Jamaica, have sometimes found that they can float loans on the London market quite easily on their own.

consideration is the possibility that if regional governments are left entirely independent in their public borrowing, backward regions may be handicapped in their development schemes because of their inability to compete with the more prosperous regions.

But while the general case for central control or co-ordination of all public borrowing is strong, it is particularly compelling with regard to external loans. In underdeveloped countries, because of low incomes, the volume of internal savings is insufficient to finance development projects. Thus the foreign loans become especially important. But foreign loans affect the terms of trade and national credit on foreign loan markets. In the case of external loans, therefore, some central control or co-ordination has usually been considered vital. Consequently, many of the new federations have simply left the field of external borrowing exclusively in the hands of the central government, thus severely limiting the independent regional power to borrow. This has been the case in India, Malaya, and Nigeria (except for short-term borrowing by the regions on the basis of external assets). The Australian solution, in which both the central and the state governments gave up their independent borrowing power to submit to the control of a Loan Council, despite its apparent success, has been followed closely only in Rhodesia and Nyasaland.[1] There the Loan Council was the sole authority for the raising of all external loans. In the other two federations, Pakistan and the West Indies, regional governments were given the right to borrow externally. But in the former this power was subject to restriction by the central government.[2] An interesting feature of the Pakistan constitution of 1956 was the provision of special tribunals to which provinces had recourse if central refusal of provincial applications for external loans was 'unreasonable'.[3] Only in the West Indies, where the territorial power to borrow was on the concurrent list, have the territories possessed a real measure of independence in raising external loans.[4]

As far as internal loans are concerned, greater weight has been placed upon the desirability of regional financial autonomy. Malaya was, however, an exception, for up to 1957 only the central government was entitled to raise loans, and thereafter states were restricted to borrowing from the federation or from banks approved by the central government.[5] In all the other federa-

---

[1] *Constitution of R. and N., 1953*, arts. 88–92.

[2] *Constitution of Pakistan, 1956*, art. 116 (3); *Constitution of Pakistan, 1962*, art. 140.

[3] Arts. 116 (4), 129. Under the 1962 constitution, art. 140 (4), disputes on this question are referred to the National Assembly.

[4] Constitution, Third Sched., Concurrent List, para. 10.

[5] *Federation of Malaya Agreement, 1948*, cl. 111; *Constitution of Malaya, 1957*, art. 111 (2). States could influence the raising of loans, and the allocation of central loans to states, however, through their membership on the National Finance Council which advised the central government on these among other matters after 1957 (art. 108). In Malaysia the Borneo states and Singapore were entitled to raise loans within their own boundaries if they had the approval of the Central Bank, and Singapore might borrow outside the state with the approval of the central government. *Malaysia Act, 1963*, s. 49.

tions, the regional governments were entitled to raise internal loans independently.[1] Nevertheless, in most of these federations in practice, a considerable measure of co-ordination was achieved through both inter-governmental consultation and the exercise by the central governments of their constitutional powers to make loans to the regions. State and provincial powers to raise internal loans were qualified in India and Pakistan by the proviso that if any central loans to these governments were outstanding, then central consent was necessary for the raising of any new loans.[2] Since in practice the provincial and state governments in these federations were heavily indebted to the central governments, the independence of their borrowing power was forfeited. The raising of internal loans, as well as external loans, has in practice also been normally undertaken by the central government in both Nigeria and Rhodesia and Nyasaland.[3] Thus, except in the West Indies, central dominance and co-ordination of internal public borrowing has been the general pattern.[4]

7. *Inter-governmental financial institutions*

Most of the new federations have found it convenient to establish inter-governmental financial institutions. These serve two broad purposes: first, they enable the consultation and co-operation between federal and regional governments which is so necessary, because in financial matters it is no longer possible to draw the sharp dividing lines of classical federalism between fiscal powers exercised by the different levels of government; second, these institutions make possible a regular process of adjustment in the financial arrangements to meet new conditions. The problems with which these inter-governmental financial institutions deal fall into three main groups: tax revenue and grant distribution, loan co-ordination, and settlement of disputes. In most of the new federations there have been a number of institutions responsible for different functions, but sometimes a variety of tasks have come under the jurisdiction of one institution, an example being the National Finance Council in Malaya which has been concerned with the distribution of taxes and grants, with the loan requirements of the central and state governments, and with certain aspects of economic development planning.[5]

In nearly every new federation some sort of review of tax revenue and grant

[1] *The Constitution of Rhodesia and Nyasaland, 1953*, Second Sched., Federal List, item 7, vests in the control of the central government 'banks and banking' (except land banks) and 'control of capital issues'. It has been contended that this item included central control of borrowing by territorial governments, but this was disputed (Cmnd. 1150/1960, para. 216), and would appear not to have been the original intention (Cmd. 8672/1952, paras. 37–38).

[2] *Constitution of India, 1950*, art. 293 (3, 4); *Constitution of Pakistan, 1956*, art. 116 (3, 4); *Constitution of Pakistan, 1962*, art. 140 (2–4). But in Pakistan, as with external loans, central consent could not be 'unreasonably withheld'.

[3] There have been some exceptions such as the internal loans raised by Northern Rhodesia in 1960 and 1963, and by Southern Rhodesia in 1963.

[4] Even in the West Indies the placing of territorial borrowing on the concurrent list gave the central government potential control of internal territorial loans.

[5] Constitution, 1957, art. 108.

allocation has been provided for, the two subjects normally being handled by the same commission or council. Usually these questions have been turned over to an advisory commission of independent experts, whose function is to consider the evidence impartially and to arrive at an agreed recommendation. The Indian constitution, for instance, provides for the appointment every five years of a Finance Commission whose task is to make recommendations concerning the tax revenues shared by the Union and the states, the principles determining grants-in-aid, and any other matters referred to it in the interests of sound finance.[1] The constitution of Rhodesia and Nyasaland also provided for a review at five-year intervals by an independent commission examining the adequacy of the proportions of income and profits taxes, export duties, and external loans distributed among the territories, and the first Fiscal Review Commission reported in 1957.[2] In Malaysia regular financial reviews, quin-quennial for the Borneo states and biennial for Singapore, were specified, but the arrangements were unusual in that only if the governments involved were unable to come to agreement was reference to be made to an independent assessor, and then his decision would be binding.[3] In addition a Tariff Advisory Board, jointly appointed by the central and Singapore governments, was set up to advise, over a period of years, on the establishment and maintenance of protective and revenue customs duties. The arrangements for fiscal review in Nigeria, unlike most of the other new federations, have been left simply on an *ad hoc* basis, to be undertaken as and when needed. Nevertheless, frequent advisory fiscal review commissions have been a regular feature, reporting in 1947, 1951, 1953, and 1958. In 1964 another commission, again consisting of non-Nigerian experts, was appointed to review the allocation of revenue between governments. The Nigerian constitutions of 1960 and 1963 have provided for the establishment 'from time to time' of a commission to review and make recommendations on the provisions governing the allocation among the regions of the distributable pool and of mining royalties and rents.[4] One other fiscal commission of this general type was the *ad hoc* commission appointed in Pakistan in 1952 to inquire into the allocation of revenues between the central and provincial governments.[5]

Because adjustments to the distribution of financial resources may affect the balance of political power between central and regional governments, the chief problem has been to win the confidence of the politicians, especially those from the regions, in the impartiality of these advisory commissions. This was particularly important in the Union of India and in the interim Federation of Pakistan, because, in these cases, the appointment of the commission and the implementation of its recommendations lay solely with the central govern-

---

[1] Constitution, arts. 280–1. The first three Finance Commissions reported in 1952, 1957, and 1962 (appointed 1961).   [2] Art. 96; C. Fed. 56/1957.
[3] *Malaysia Act, 1963*, ss. 47, 48; Cmnd. 2094/1963, Annex J.
[4] Constitution, 1960, s. 153; Constitution, 1963, s. 164.
[5] *Financial Enquiry Regarding Allocation of Revenues* (1952).

ment.[1] But confidence in the independence of fiscal review commissions was essential also in Nigeria and in Rhodesia and Nyasaland, for although regional financial interests were safeguarded by the requirement of constitutional amendment for modifications to the transfers of revenue, unless the recommendations of these commissions received support from both levels of government, the financial provisions were likely to be awkwardly inflexible. To date, it would appear that the tradition of impartiality and independence has been established by the fiscal review commissions in all these federations. In India appointment of the Finance Commission is by the central government, but the first three Finance Commissions have strongly favoured the states in their recommendations, and although it was technically open to the central government not to accept their recommendations, it has become a convention that it should do so where the recommendations are unanimous.[2] In Pakistan, too, the centrally appointed fiscal commission of 1952 strongly favoured the provinces. The constitutions of Rhodesia and Nyasaland, and of independent Nigeria, also placed the appointment of fiscal review commissions in the hands of the central government, but only after consultation with the regional governments, and experience to date indicates that in these federations a similar tradition of accepting commission recommendations has developed. The Malaysian proposals for fiscal review with respect to the Borneo states differ from those in these other federations in two respects: first, the independent assessor is to be appointed jointly by the central government and the state governments concerned, and secondly, his recommendations would be not merely advisory but binding upon each party. Generally in these federations the independent fiscal review commissions have succeeded in winning confidence in their impartiality, and this has made possible a flexibility in the financial relations between governments without endangering the fiscal autonomy of the regions. One drawback which all these commissions in the new federations have shared, however, by contrast with the Australian Commonwealth Grants Commission, has been their lack of continuity, each commission being appointed afresh at the time of each review.[3]

The constitutions of Pakistan (1956, 1962) and Malaya (1957), unlike the other recent federations which relied on independent commissions, assigned

---

[1] *Constitution of India, 1950*, arts. 269 (2), 270 (4), 272, 273 (3), 275, 280; *Indian Independence Act, 1947*, s. 8 (1).

[2] Santhanam, *Union-State Relations in India*, pp. 33–38. All the recommendations of the first two commissions were accepted except the suggestion of the second for fixing a uniform rate of interest for all states irrespective of the purposes of the loans. In 1962, when the report of the third commission included a note of dissent, the Union Government accepted all the unanimous recommendations, but rejected one of the majority recommendations for including within the Finance Commission's scheme of revenue devolution part of the central assistance towards state plans.

[3] Some continuity was gained in Rhodesia and Nyasaland through the continued chairmanship of Sir Jeremy Raisman, but the other members differed in 1957 from those on the 1952 commission.

the function of fiscal review to inter-governmental councils composed of ministers representing the central and regional governments.[1] Thus in these cases decisions were arrived at more by bargaining than by impartial examination. In both countries the regional representatives carried considerable weight, for normally they outnumbered those of the central government. Indeed, the Pakistan Finance Commission of 1962 recommended a very substantial increase in the degree of financial devolution. The main difference between these councils lay in their authority. The Malayan National Finance Council, which meets at least once a year, is merely an advisory body making recommendations to the central government upon the allocation of grants, tax proceeds, and loans to the states, and also upon development planning. The National Finance Commission of Pakistan, as provided for in 1956, was intended to undertake a review every five years of the allocation of tax proceeds and grants, and in the case of the distribution of certain central tax revenues its decision was to be binding.[2] The National Finance Commission provided for by the 1962 constitution was similar in most other respects, but its recommendations to the central government were only advisory.

Problems have sometimes arisen in the new federations over the co-ordination of fiscal reviews with economic planning. In most cases, Malaya being an exception, the two activities have been carried out by different commissions or councils. But inevitably the development programmes of governments have depended upon the financial resources available, while the calculation of the budgetary requirements of regional governments has been influenced by commitments to development expenditure. In India this difficulty caused considerable concern to the second and third Finance Commissions. Both pointed to the need for effective co-ordination in view of the overlapping functions of the Planning and Finance Commissions, and the third Finance Commission even went so far as to suggest that either the functions of the Finance Commission should be enlarged to embrace all central assistance including development grants, or that the Planning Commission should be transformed into the Finance Commission.[3] The Pakistan constitution of 1962, devised with an awareness of such difficulties, included a provision assigning to the National Finance Commission the task of making recommendations on the removal of disparities in economic development, these recommendations being submitted to the National Economic Council for consideration in the formulation of its plans.[4] The Malayan constitution of 1957 went furthest

---

[1] *Constitution of Pakistan, 1956*, art. 118; *Constitution of Pakistan, 1962*, art. 144; *Constitution of Malaya, 1957*, art. 108. The total composition of the Pakistan commissions was, in the last resort, in the hands of the central government, however.

[2] The Commission had not been convened, however, before the suspension of the 1956 constitution. The first Finance Commission under the 1962 constitution reported in 1962.

[3] *Report, 1961*, ch. vii.

[4] Constitution, 1962, art. 144 (6, 7). As a result the two provinces were given virtually equal development grants in 1962.

towards co-ordinating fiscal review and economic planning by placing both functions in the hands of the National Finance Council, and by also requiring that it should be consulted by the National Land Council in the formulation of national land policy.[1]

The institutional arrangements for co-ordinating public borrowing have taken a number of forms. In Pakistan and Malaya, where inter-governmental councils composed of central and regional ministers existed for reviewing the tax and grant structure, these councils were also used to deal with loans policy. Rhodesia and Nyasaland and Nigeria, where fiscal reviews were carried out by independent advisory commissions, followed instead the Australian pattern of separate institutions for the co-ordination of central and regional public borrowing.[2] The Central African Loan Council, composed of one representative from each government, like its Australian forerunner actually controlled central and territorial borrowing, but this was limited to external loans.[3] On the other hand, the Nigerian Loans Advisory Board, consisting of the ministers of finance of each government, was only advisory, but extended its recommendations to internal as well as external loans.[4] The Indian states were not permitted to raise external loans and therefore no co-ordinating body was considered necessary, but questions concerning Union loans to the states were referred to the second Finance Commission.[5]

In some of the new federations special machinery has been provided to deal with central–regional financial disputes which are not appropriate for supreme court jurisdiction. Special tribunals for adjudicating inter-governmental disputes over costs incurred by delegated administration were provided for in all three of the Asian and in the Central African federations.[6] Similar tribunals were also created for the settlement of disputes between governments over 'unreasonable' central restrictions on external borrowing by the provinces in Pakistan (1956),[7] over payments for land in Malaya,[8] and over the use and control of inter-state rivers and river valleys in India.[9]

Although no arrangements for standing inter-governmental financial institutions were embodied in the West Indian constitution, the need for fiscal review was clearly recognized in the wording of the article providing for a

[1] Constitution, 1957, arts. 91 (5), 108 (4).
[2] The West Indian Constitutional Conference of 1956 agreed in principle to the establishment of a Loans Council (Cmd. 9733/1956, para. 34), but this was not implemented. Subsequently the East Caribbean Federation Conference, 1962, also agreed upon the creation of a Loans Council (Cmnd. 1746/1962, para. 27).
[3] *Constitution of R. and N., 1953*, arts. 88–92.
[4] Cmnd. 481/1958, paras. 158, 166.
[5] *Report of F.C., 1957*, para. 4 (*d*), ch. xiv.
[6] *Constitution of India, 1950*, arts. 257 (4), 258 (3); *Constitution of Pakistan, 1956*, art. 129; *Constitution of Malaya, 1957*, art. 80 (6); *Constitution of R. and N., 1953*, art. 31 (3).
[7] *Constitution of Pakistan, 1956*, arts. 116 (4), 129.
[8] *Constitution of Malaya, 1957*, art. 87.
[9] *Constitution of India, 1950*, art. 262.

general review of the constitution within five years.[1] The final constitutional conference in 1956 also agreed 'in principle' to the establishment of a Loans Council and to the setting up of a Trade and Tariffs Commission to consider the problems involved in establishing a customs union.[2] The latter decision culminated in the controversial report of the Croft Commission.[3] After considerable debate an inter-governmental committee was able to recommend a solution on this question which was accepted at the 1961 constitutional review conference,[4] but the disintegration of the federation prevented the implementation of the scheme.

In some of the older federations, particularly Canada, there has in the past been a reluctance to set up permanent inter-governmental boards and commissions on the grounds that they would limit the independence of the provinces and tend to minimize the authority of legislatures.[5] But statesmen in the new federations have clearly believed, because of the economic and financial interpenetration of the different levels of government which is inevitable in contemporary federalism, that inter-governmental institutions, instead of encroaching on the federal principle, may be a necessary means to maintaining effectively the federal financial balance under changing conditions.

[1] *Constitution of W.I., 1957*, art. 118.
[2] Cmd. 9733/1956, paras. 26, 34 (i).
[3] W.I. 1/58, *Report of the Trade and Tariffs Commission.*
[4] Cmnd. 1417/1961, paras. 4, 6, 26.
[5] W. A. Mackintosh, 'Federal Finance', in G. Sawer (ed.), *Federalism, An Australian Jubilee Study* (1952), pp. 84–85, 101.

10

DUALITY AND UNITY

1. *Dual or single polity?*

ACCORDING to the traditional definition of the federal principle, if central and regional governments are to be co-ordinate, then each must act directly on the people, be limited to its own sphere, and, within that sphere, be independent of the others.[1] It follows from this definition, then, that authority —legislative, executive, and financial—should be so divided that each level of government may operate independently of the other. A strict application of this principle would also imply a completely dual polity. Each government should have its own legislative and executive institutions completely un-fettered in performing its own functions, its own civil service to administer its responsibilities, and its own courts to interpret its laws.

But although the ideal of a dual polity of mutually independent govern-ments has often been echoed by the creators of the new federations, rarely has it been possible in practice to achieve this. In the recent federations it has been found necessary to establish many points of contact, both constitutional and conventional, between governments. A number of factors have been respon-sible for this pattern. First and most important, the widening scope of govern-mental activity in general and the integrated nature of economic activity in the twentieth century have meant that it is extremely difficult to divide respon-sibilities into isolated central and regional compartments. Because several separate governments share a divided responsibility for controlling a single economic structure, the functions assigned to the different governments are inevitably interrelated. This, together with the rapidly changing character of the economic and social structure in these developing countries, putting a premium upon flexibility, has made necessary close links between the central and regional governments. A second factor which has discouraged the creation of completely dual polities has been the desire to avoid, wherever possible, an unnecessary duplication of agencies. In developing countries where the shortage of trained personnel has been acute, the tendency has been to favour the sharing of certain institutions, such as courts, election commissions, or even administrative services, if this can be made possible without abandoning political autonomy. A third factor, and not an insignificant one, leading to the rejection of rigid barriers between the activities of the central and regional governments, has been the wish to encourage federal unity during the early

[1] See Chapter 1, section 3.

years when it was fragile. The new federations have therefore generally been characterized by an integrated rather than a dual polity.

2. *The courts*

A dual judiciary would seem to be a logical corollary of the dual polity inherent in the federal principle as traditionally formulated. But a dual system of courts, one set to administer federal law and the other to apply regional law, is not strictly necessary so long as the independence of the judiciary from the influence of the executives and legislatures of both levels of government can be assured. Indeed, of the older federations only the United States came close to establishing a parallel system of courts.[1] The central governments of Australia, Canada, and Switzerland have authority to set up their own courts, but generally they have relied upon regional courts to administer their laws. The appellate jurisdiction conferred on the supreme courts has provided a safeguard for the central governments by imposing some uniformity of interpretation for federal law, and the tradition of judicial independence has reduced the possibility of central laws being interpreted by regional courts in such a way as to favour regional interests.

Most of the new federations, influenced by their predecessors and short of experienced judges, have also avoided the duplication of courts. The actual arrangements for the organization of courts has varied, however, there being three general approaches to this problem.[2]

The first was to establish a single system of centrally organized courts. This was the arrangement adopted in the Federation of Malaya, which has had an almost unitary system of courts.[3] Because all civil and criminal law had been made a central responsibility it was considered appropriate that the establishment and jurisdiction of all courts should come under central law. A special exception was made to this general pattern, however, in the case of Muslim courts, which were placed under state jurisdiction because all matters relating to Muslim law and Malay custom were on the state legislative list.[4] But otherwise, all state as well as central law was applied by the central courts.[5] Within the Malaysian Federation a virtually unitary hierarchy of courts under central jurisdiction was continued with a Federal Court of Malaysia surmounting three High Courts, one for the states of Malaya, one for the Borneo states, and one for Singapore. In order to ensure the disinterestedness of the judiciary, the 1957 Malayan constitution established a Judicial and Legal Service Commission, independent of the executive and legislature and having general jurisdiction over all matters of the judiciary and legal service of the central

---

[1] On courts in the older federations, see Wheare, *Federal Government*, pp. 65–68.

[2] On the special role and jurisdiction of federal supreme courts see Chapter 12, section 2.

[3] Uganda and Kenya at independence also adopted this arrangement.

[4] In Malaysia this exception is extended in the Borneo states to native courts for similar reasons.

[5] For a description of the system of courts, see Sheridan, *Malaya and Singapore*, ch. 6.

government.[1] This Commission was abolished in 1960, however, in order to 'simplify' the administrative structure, and its functions were transferred to ministers and the Public Services Commission, occasioning some fears that the independence of the judges might be weakened.[2]

The courts in India and Pakistan formed a single integrated system, but, unlike Malaya, authority over their organization and jurisdiction was divided between the central and regional governments. In setting up a single set of courts, both federations showed the impact of the unified system of courts that had existed in British India from the beginning of the British régime and which had been so deep-rooted that it had been continued in the 1935 federal scheme. The desire to achieve a uniformity in remedial procedure as an aid to national unity further encouraged the continued reliance upon this pattern. The constitutions of India and Pakistan, therefore, set out in considerable detail the organization and jurisdiction of the two upper tiers of the hierarchy of courts: the central Supreme Courts and the state and provincial High Courts. Included were provisions for transfers of judges from one High Court to another, and in India for common High Courts shared by two or more states.[3] The organization of subordinate courts was left in state or provincial hands, but the integrated nature of the system of courts was assured in both federations by the authority given to the High Courts to superintend all courts and tribunals within their territorial jurisdiction, and in India by certain constitutional provisions governing the subordinate courts.[4] Thus, although authority over the organization of the courts at different levels was divided between central and regional governments, the courts formed a single system. The power to assign jurisdiction to courts within this system was also divided, each government being empowered to do so for any subjects within its own legislative competence.[5]

In the other three federations—Rhodesia and Nyasaland, Nigeria, and the West Indies—the system of courts was potentially dual, for the central government was given power to create its own courts.[6] Few additional central courts have in practice, however, been established, apart from the Income Tax

---

[1] Art. 138.

[2] *Constitution (Amendment) Act, 1960* (F. 10/1960), ss. 15, 16, 21, 22, 26; House of Representatives, *Debates*, vol. ii, no. 3 (22 April 1960), cols. 308–9.

[3] *Constitution of India, 1950*, arts. 222, 230–1; *Constitution of Pakistan, 1956*, art. 172; *Constitution of Pakistan, 1962*, art. 99.

[4] *Constitution of India, 1950*, arts. 227, 233–7; *Constitution of Pakistan, 1956*, Third Sched., para. 5; *Constitution of Pakistan, 1962*, arts. 101–2.

[5] *Constitution of India, 1950*, Union List, entry 95; State List, entry 65; Concurrent List, entry 46; *Constitution of Pakistan, 1956*, Federal List, entry 29; Provincial List, entry 92; Concurrent List, entry 19; *Constitution of Pakistan, 1962*, art. 98 and Federal List, entry 46.

[6] *Constitution of R. and N., 1953*, Federal list, item 37; *Constitution of Nigeria, 1960*, s. 119; *Constitution of Nigeria, 1963*, s. 126; *Constitution of W.I., 1957*, art. 90. The *Constitution of Pakistan, 1962*, art. 129, would appear to give similar potential powers, although otherwise the general organization of the judiciary follows the pattern described in the previous paragraph above.

Special Court, the Tariff Court, the Patents Tribunal, and the Courts-Martial Appeal Court in Rhodesia and Nyasaland, and the courts in the federal territory of Lagos in Nigeria. Otherwise, the courts in these three federations have operated with little duplication, the central government relying normally on the regional courts to apply its laws, and the federal supreme court superimposed on these serving as an appellate court.[1]

The central and regional governments in all the new federations have therefore relied upon the same courts to apply their laws. A number of safeguards have made it possible to do this without undermining the co-ordinate relation between central and regional governments. To begin with, in every federation except Malaya, the power to confer jurisdiction upon courts over a law has rested with the legislature making the law. The role of the supreme courts in all these federations as courts of appeal for a wide range of central laws has, in addition, provided a safeguard and established some uniformity in the interpretation of central laws by regional courts. The power of the central legislature, in Rhodesia and Nyasaland, Nigeria, and the West Indies, to create its own courts also presented an alternative should the central government become convinced that jurisdiction by the regional courts had been unsatisfactory. A further alternative in these three federations, in India, and since 1962 in Pakistan, was provided by the power given to the central governments to confer additional original jurisdiction upon the supreme court as a court for central laws.[2] But perhaps most important has been the tradition of judicial independence, encouraged during British rule and fostered by the local bar, in all these federations.[3] Thus, in practice, the sharing of courts for the interpretation of both central and regional laws in the new federations has not represented a threat to the co-ordinate status of the central and regional governments.

3. The civil services

In the case of the civil services even more than in that of the courts, one might assume that the dual polity inherent in a federal system would require a system of dual services. It is true that the British tradition of civil servants independent from politics was encouraged during the period of imperial rule and fostered by the creation of public service commissions in these federations. Nevertheless, the work of administration is so closely linked with the exercise

---

[1] This pattern is also followed in the Federation of South Arabia (Cmnd. 1814/1962, Annex B, paras. 21–25), and in the plans for an East Caribbean Federation (Cmnd. 1746/1962, paras. 56–57).

[2] *Constitution of India, 1950*, art. 138; *Constitution of R. and N., 1953*, art. 57; *Nigeria Constitution, 1954*, s. 146; *Constitution of Nigeria, 1960*, s. 107 (2); *Constitution of Nigeria, 1963*, s. 114 (2); *Constitution of W.I., 1957*, art. 82; *Constitution of Pakistan, 1962*, art. 60.

[3] The independence of the judiciary in Nigeria was further enhanced for a period by the existence of separate regional Judicial Service Commissions for the regional judiciaries, in addition to the central Judicial Service Commission, but under the 1963 constitutions these commissions were no longer considered necessary.

of executive authority that it might seem reasonable to expect each government within a federation to have its own administrative services.

Yet in many of the new federations, particularly those in Asia and the Caribbean, arguments have been advanced for joint or unified services. A number of advantages have been claimed for shared or common services. For instance, by enlarging the field of recruitment a joint service is able to attract the best men for service under either the regional or central governments, thus enabling high standards in the 'strategic posts' of both levels of government. In this way it would make possible the attainment of at least a minimum uniform standard in administration, even in regions handicapped by the low quality of the local candidates available, and ensure that such staff as were available within the federation were deployed to best advantage. The inter-regional composition of a common service would also, it has been claimed, encourage the development of a national point of view among civil servants. The presence of non-residents in the regional services would encourage a less parochial outlook, while lack of local knowledge might be compensated for by their impartiality, independence, and freedom from pressures of local influence. Joint administrative services may also foster and facilitate inter-governmental co-operation, especially where this is such an important element in development planning. Finally, the sharing of services may help to avoid uneconomic duplication in administrative agencies, an especially important point where, as in Malaya and the Caribbean, the regional units have been too small to support an extensive administrative organization.

On the other side, of course, there has been the inevitable uneasiness that a common administrative service, recruited on a national basis and ultimately under central control, would weaken or even destroy regional autonomy. A further major factor encouraging the establishment of dual services—most evident in Nigeria but also potent elsewhere—has been the desire of majority groups within each region for a regional civil service within which their opportunities for appointment and promotion would be favoured. It was not surprising, therefore, that the three non-Asian federations decided to follow the orthodox pattern, each establishing a dual administrative system.[1] The central and regional governments were given their own public services, constitutionally independent of each other, although arrangements for secondment and transfers were usually made available.

In practice, the dualism of the services has been sharpest in Nigeria. There, in the process of 'Nigerianization', each regional service has recruited almost exclusively from the majority group within its boundaries. The effect has been to encourage a regional spirit and loyalty within these separate services, and to discourage interchanges between them and the smaller central service to

[1] In Kenya at independence, however, central and regional governments shared a joint public service (Constitution, 1963, ss. 186–93).

a degree which has undermined the forces making for unity.[1] An exception, however, was the arrangement devised for the police just before independence.[2] A single Nigerian police force is administered normally by a Police Council, consisting of the premiers or law ministers from the central government and each of the regions and the chairman of the Police Service Commission. To ensure the independence of the members of the force there is also a Police Service Commission, advising on matters of appointment, promotion, and discipline.

Separate and independent civil services for the central and regional governments were also established in each of the three Asian federations.[3] But in addition, in each of them, provision was made for joint services and commissions shared by both levels of government.

Integrated 'All-India' services, serving both central and provincial governments, had been a feature of British rule, even under the federal structure of the Government of India Act, 1935, and after independence the Indian Civil Service (I.C.S.) and the Indian Police (I.P.) were continued in a similar form as All-India or All-Pakistan services.[4] In both federations, when the new constitutions were being drafted, there was some concern among supporters of provincial autonomy over the existence of such services. Nevertheless, when provincial ministers in India were consulted, they expressed 'general unanimity' in favour of maintaining the existing joint services,[5] and in Pakistan the dominance of civil servants in federal politics was a barrier to any reduction in the role of the common services.[6] The constitutions of India and Pakistan, therefore, continued the existence of the successors to the I.C.S. and the I.P.: the Indian Administrative Service (I.A.S.) and the Indian Police Service (I.P.S.), the Civil Service of Pakistan (C.S.P.) and the Police Service of Pakistan (P.S.P.). Provision was also made for the creation by the central governments of new joint services in the future. In India this requires a special two-thirds majority in the Council of States, but under the 1962 constitution of Pakistan it requires only an ordinary central law.[7] The recruitment and general pattern of these services in India and Pakistan are under the control of the central government, but the posting and promotion of an officer while serving in a state or province come within the influence of the regional government. Thus in both these federations, without depriving the states or provinces of their

---

[1] Tilman and Cole (eds.), *The Nigerian Political Scene*, ch. 5; Mackintosh, 'Federalism in Nigeria', *Political Studies*, x (1962), pp. 232, 247.

[2] Cmnd. 569/1958, paras. 8–17. See also pp. 186–7.

[3] In Malaya, however, alterations in the establishments of states, in so far as they increased central liabilities for pensions, required central approval, thus seriously restricting the autonomy of the states. See Constitution, 1957, art. 112.

[4] A. Chanda, *Indian Administration* (1958), pp. 95–99; Callard, *Pakistan, A Political Study*, pp. 284–90; *Government of India Act, 1935*, s. 263.

[5] C.A.I., *Debates*, vol. iv, p. 965.

[6] Sayeed, *Pakistan, The Formative Phase*, pp. 383–90.

[7] *Constitution of India, 1950*, art. 312 (1); *Constitution of Pakistan, 1962*, art. 242.

right to form their own separate civil services, there have existed joint services recruited on a national basis, with common qualifications and a uniform scale of pay, the members of which have filled the strategic posts in both central and regional governments. The Malayan constitution of 1957 followed this example by giving the central Parliament power to establish by law 'joint services, common to the Federation and one or more of the States or, at the request of the States concerned, to two or more States'.[1] Special provision was also made for the secondment of officers from one government to another, and for the continuing of earlier arrangements under which, by an agreement between the central and state governments, certain posts in the state public services were in fact filled by central officers.[2] Quite extensive advantage was taken of these opportunities for seconding officers, and this system has been carried over into the Malaysian Federation.

In addition to these arrangements for joint services, the duplication of agencies was further reduced in all three of the Asian federations, by the establishment of a single Election Commission to handle both central and regional elections, and by making the Auditor-General an officer of the constitution responsible for auditing both central and state accounts. Furthermore, although the regional governments were entitled to create separate Public Service Commissions, they could, if they wished, rely instead upon the central Public Service Commission. Since the independence of these various commissions and of the auditors-general was carefully protected by the constitutional provisions, their joint use did not represent a serious threat to regional autonomy.

The political implications of the joint administrative services in operation have, however, been more controversial. In India, the members of the I.A.S. and the I.P.S. have occupied the highest positions under both the Union and state governments. More than half of all secretaries to state governments, and a majority of district collectors and divisional commissioners, have been selected from the I.A.S. cadre.[3] This has facilitated inter-governmental co-operation and encouraged national unity, as well as helping to maintain a high standard of administration in the states. The States Reorganization Commission, therefore, recommended the creation of more All-India services.[4] But for some time the trend was away from reliance upon the joint services. The state governments resisted attempts to establish new All-India services because of the irksome joint controls and regulations necessary for these services, fears of encroachment upon state autonomy, and the greater expense of administration due to the higher salaries required for the members of these services. The growing influence of the regional élites in the linguistic states,

---

[1] Art. 133. [2] Arts. 134, 179.

[3] M. R. Goodall, 'Organization of Administrative Leadership in the Five Year Plans', in R. L. Park and I. Tinker (eds.), *Leadership and Political Institutions in India* (1959), p. 324.

[4] *Report of the States Reorganization Commission* (1955), para. 856. For a similar view, see Chanda, *Indian Administration*, pp. 100–39.

and the fear that state services would be filled with outsiders if the local candidates failed to compete successfully in the All-India competitions, have been particularly important. Thus, the first Appleby Report pointed out that the All-India services were 'becoming proportionately a smaller and smaller part of the whole personnel' in the civil services of India.[1] To arrest this trend the Council of States in 1961 exercised for the first time its power to authorize the creation of new All-India services when approval was given for the creation of an Indian Service of Engineers, an Indian Forest Service, and an Indian Medical and Health Service.[2]

In Malaya resistance to such joint services has been even stronger. Despite the enabling provision in the 1957 constitution, no joint services were established. Instead, there has been a regular practice of seconding officers from one government to another when their services were needed.

The trend in Pakistan, however, went in the opposite direction.[3] The C.S.P. became 'the pivotal service around which all other administrative groups, central, provincial and local, are organized'.[4] Its members occupied most of the senior positions in the central and provincial secretariats, and this was resented especially in East Bengal where at one time there was not a single Bengali in the whole of the Bengal secretariat. The C.S.P. was considerably more centralized than its predecessor, the I.C.S. Where the members of the I.C.S. had been assigned to a provincial cadre, leaving it only to serve at the centre, in the C.S.P. there was one central cadre. In the interests of promoting national unity, members were regularly transferred from one province to another, with the unfortunate result that these civil servants gave the impression that they were not interested in the welfare of the province in which they were working. Moreover, much of the time, 'the civil servants effectively controlled the entire administration in the Provinces and the politicians there were kept in power subject to their willingness to obey Central Government directives'.[5] In effect, it was the C.S.P. which, in a country plagued with political instability and intense provincialism, played a major stabilizing and unifying role. But it exercised this function to such a degree that provincial autonomy was to all intents negated, thus in the end provoking, instead of diminishing, the force of provincialism in East Pakistan.

An alternative way of reducing the duplication of administrative organization without surrendering any degree of autonomy to the central government is that of sharing joint services between two or more states. The Indian constitution provides joint public service commissions to be shared by states if

---

[1] Appleby, *Public Administration in India* (1953), p. 23.

[2] Rajya Sabha, *Debates*, vol. xxxvi (1961), cols. 1148–1204, 1280–1305. On this occasion the central government promised that it would consult the states on the setting up of these services.

[3] On the operation of joint services in Pakistan, see especially, Sayeed, *Pakistan, the Formative Phase*, ch. 14; Callard, *Pakistan, A Political Study*, ch. 9.

[4] Callard, p. 292.   [5] Sayeed, p. 383. See also pp. 351–8.

they wish,[1] but it has been in the federations with the small regional units—Malaya and the West Indies—that such arrangements have seemed most appropriate. In Malaya, for instance, Kelantan and Trengganu have shared a public service commission, and Perlis has relied upon some of Kedah's specialized services,[2] while in the West Indian Windward and Leeward Islands it was found convenient to share an advisory Police Service Commission, a Judicial and Legal Service Commission, a common audit system, and a number of specialist services. Nevertheless, the very forces which have led to the desire for regional identity within federations have usually limited the degree to which this solution has been acceptable.

4. *Official languages*

Because many of the recent federations have been composed of diverse linguistic communities, the question whether there should be a single or two or more national languages has often arisen. Regional groups have usually pressed for the recognition of their languages as official federal languages, fearing that otherwise they would be handicapped in participating in national affairs. On the other hand, nationalists have frequently stressed the importance of a single national language, both as a *lingua franca* making possible inter-regional communication and administration, and as a focus for national unity. Moreover, although English has normally served as the *lingua franca* during the colonial period and even among the élites of the nationalist movements, there has often been a desire to choose an indigenous national language as a symbol of cultural independence. These opposing points of view have frequently clashed sharply and, because language affects access to national jobs and power, the issue has been particularly explosive.

In the non-Asian federations, where English was already widely accepted as the *lingua franca* in general use, the problem has not been too acute. The constitutions of Rhodesia and Nyasaland, Nigeria, and the West Indies all prescribed English as the single official federal language.

In all three of the Asian federations, however, the question of a national language proved extremely controversial and a serious threat to national unity. For instance, it has been said of Pakistan that 'This single issue aroused more heated feelings than any other.'[3] Before partition Urdu had been regarded as the principal language of Muslim India. Bengali, on the other hand, was the language of a single province, and elsewhere in Pakistan was suspect because of its links with Hindu Bengal. The Bengalis cherished their language, and feared that, if Urdu was made the only national language, they would be placed at a further disadvantage in obtaining positions in the civil

---

[1] Art. 315 (2).

[2] Constitution, 1957, arts. 133, 134, enable joint state action.

[3] Callard, *Pakistan, A Political Study*, p. 182. On this question, see especially ibid., pp. 180–3; Choudhury, *Constitutional Development in Pakistan*, ch. 9; Lambert, 'Factors in Bengali Regionalism in Pakistan', *Far Eastern Survey*, xxviii (1959), pp. 55–56.

service and in playing a part in national affairs. Moreover, since Bengal contained a majority of the population of Pakistan, Bengalis felt entitled to expect the recognition of their language as an official national one.

Both Jinnah and Liaquat Ali Khan began by insisting flatly that, in the interests of national unity, Urdu should be the national language of Pakistan.[1] When this was embodied in the Interim Report of the Basic Principles Committee there was a storm of protest, and consequently, when the subsequent Report of 1952 was published, no mention of any state language was made. The bitter struggle continued until the 1954 Report recognized both Urdu and Bengali, but suggested that 'the State should take all measures for the development and growth of a common language'.[2] Even this hope was abandoned by the 1956 constitution, which recognized both Urdu and Bengali, and also provided for the continued use of English for official purposes for twenty years.[3] The 1962 constitution continued this arrangement, but with the qualification that after ten years a commission should be appointed to report on the replacement of English for official purposes.[4]

In Malaya too, language was one of the issues on which the most extreme positions were taken. The Malays insisted upon Malay as the language indigenous to the peninsula, and were opposed to English because it would favour the immigrant races. On the other hand, many of the citizens of the federation, of Chinese and Indian origin, had had little opportunity to learn to speak Malay fluently, and would clearly be handicapped if Malay were to become the sole national language. The Reid Commission, therefore, recommended that, in addition to Malay as a national language, English should continue to be used for ten years, after which the central Parliament would decide whether to abandon English. These proposals were incorporated in the constitution, but a further suggestion of the Reid Commission that, for a limited period of ten years, the right to speak in Chinese or Indian in the central legislature be recognized, was rejected due to Malay opposition.[5] Since independence the Malayan central government has continued to reiterate its determination to make Malay the country's sole official language by 1967, the first opportunity provided by the constitution. A concession has been made, however, to the new Malaysian states, guaranteeing that in these states English would be used for official federal or state purposes for a period of at least ten years after they join the federation.[6] In any case, the Malayan and Malaysian constitutions did embody a permanent guarantee that no person should be prohibited or prevented from using (otherwise than for official purposes), teaching, or learning any language, and the central and state govern-

[1] C.A.P. (first), *Debates*, vol. ii, p. 17; *Quaid-i-Azam Speaks* (Karachi, n.d.), p. 133.
[2] B.P.C., *Report* (as adopted, 1954), para. 276 (6).
[3] Art. 214.   [4] Art. 215.
[5] Col. no. 330/1957, para. 171; Cmnd. 210/1957, para. 61; Constitution, 1957, art. 152.
[6] *Malaysia Act, 1963*, ss. 61, 67. See also, R. O. Tilman, 'Malaysia: The Problems of Federation', *The Western Political Quarterly*, xvi (1963), pp. 906-7.

ments were given the right to preserve and sustain the use of the language of any community within the federation.[1]

The problem in India was complicated by the large number of regional languages. With eleven languages each spoken by nearly 5 million people or more, not to mention a variety of languages spoken by smaller groups, the solution employed in countries like Canada, Switzerland, and in the end Pakistan, of recognizing all major languages as official, was hardly appropriate. There was a clear need of some common linguistic medium for national affairs and for communication between the linguistic groups. English had served as the *lingua franca* of the westernizing élite which had led the nationalist movement, but there was a desire to replace it by an Indian language which could provide the basis for a national cultural resurgence. Moreover, only slightly more than 1 per cent. of the population was literate in English. Hindi, spoken by 42 per cent. of the Indian population, as the most widely spoken of the Indian languages, seemed, therefore, to be the logical choice. But the southern Dravidian-speaking middle class, which was also more at home in English, feared that its opportunities in central affairs would suffer if Hindi replaced English.[2] As a result there was a lengthy and heated debate in the Constituent Assembly on the official language provisions.[3] In the end a compromise was adopted, largely at Nehru's insistence, whereby all fourteen major languages were given equal status as 'languages of India', Hindi became the 'official language' for All-Indian purposes, English was to continue as an official language for fifteen years to mollify the southerners, and official language commissions five and ten years after the commencement of the constitution would advise on the progressive use of Hindi.[4]

Subsequently, when the first Official Language Commission reported strongly in favour of replacing English by Hindi, the long-smouldering discontent and fears of non-Hindi speakers burst forth.[5] Vociferous southern critics bitterly opposed the recommendations of the report, and popular demonstrations and the obliteration of Hindi signs displayed their intense feelings on the subject. The threat at the Congress annual session in 1958 of a split within the party led finally to a compromise solution by which, to satisfy the Hindi zealots, the 'formal' changeover to Hindi would still occur in 1965, but the non-Hindi sections were to be placated by the promise that English might be used as an 'official language' after 1965. The issue remained very much alive, however. The counter-persuasions of the Hindi advocates time after time induced the Union Government to postpone the legal enactment

[1] Art. 152 (1) proviso.
[2] Later, the Official Language Commission did, however, present figures indicating that general literacy in English was no higher in the south (*Report* (1957), pp. 50–51, and App. XII, pp. 468–70).   [3] C.A.I., *Debates*, vol. ix.
[4] Constitution, 1950, arts. 343–9 and Eighth Sched.
[5] *Report of the Official Language Commission, 1956* (1957), esp. pp. 37, 39–40, 49–51, 261–2, 398–425; Brecher, *Nehru*, p. 491.

of the promised compromise, and this procrastination in turn provoked growing discontent and even active resistance in South India to Hindi and its advocates. When in April 1963 the Official Languages Bill was finally introduced, the Lok Sabha witnessed some of the rowdiest scenes in its history. The bill, allowing for the continued use of English for official purposes without a time limit, but also providing for a committee of Parliament to review in 1975 the progress of Hindi's acceptance as the official language, came under fire both from Hindi zealots, opposed to any continued use of English, and from southerners, who were disappointed in the status and safeguards for English incorporated in the bill. Following a lengthy debate and amendments stipulating that the state governments should be consulted when the question was reviewed in 1975, the bill was passed, but both the protagonists and antagonists of Hindi remained dissatisfied with the compromise embodied in the bill. In the meantime, throughout this controversy, the growing strength of linguistic regionalism has been posing an increasing threat to inter-regional communication and national cohesion.[1]

5. Inter-governmental controls

The difficulty of dividing the functions of central and regional governments into neatly separate and completely independent compartments has led in most of the new federations to the introduction of various arrangements whereby one government may control, or at least influence, the activities of another. Often these inter-governmental checks have been specified in the written constitution, but in other cases they have become established simply by convention.

Examples of such controls are the special conditions which have sometimes limited the exercise by governments of their legislative authority. Where the use of legislative powers by one government is closely related to the activities of other governments, all the new federal constitutions, and most of all that of Malaysia, have frequently required either the central government to obtain the consent of the regional governments affected, or the regional government to have the approval of the central government. Such arrangements have also sometimes become accepted by convention.[2] The requirement of consent safeguards the interests of all the governments involved, but there is the danger that, if the governments find agreement difficult, there may, as for instance has sometimes been the case in Malaya, be serious delays and inflexibility.[3] A less rigid arrangement, frequently specified in constitutions or

---

[1] See particularly S. S. Harrison, 'Leadership and Language Policy in India', in R. L. Park and I. Tinker (eds.), *Leadership and Political Institutions in India* (1959), pp. 151–65; S. S. Harrison, *India, The most Dangerous Decades* (1960), esp. chs. 1, 3, 7.

[2] See, for instance, C.A.I., *Debates*, vol. viii, pp. 430–2; N. Srinivasan, *Democratic Government in India* (1954), p. 292; Santhanam, *Union–State Relations in India*, pp. 22–23; Col. no. 330/1957, para. 33.

[3] See, for instance, Col. no. 330/1957, para. 33.

evolved by convention, is that by which on certain matters the central govern-ment is required to consult, but not necessarily obtain the consent of, regional governments, or regional governments are required to consult the central government. In this way it is ensured that the interests of other governments will at least be taken into account, without at the same time running the risk that action might be prevented. This arrangement does not, on the other hand, provide as strong a protection for the other governments involved.

There are other ways, too, by which one government within a federation has been given control over the exercise of legislative power by another. The lengthy concurrent lists in all the recent federal constitutions, of course, pro-vide central control over regional legislative authority in the fields covered by these lists. Where subjects are made concurrent, the central government may exert a general control while leaving the regional legislatures to fill in the details.[1] Sometimes the central government has, in addition, been given ex-press power, in certain conditions, to override exclusive powers of regional governments without their consent, either in the interests of national welfare such as implementing treaties or development programmes, or in the interests of establishing minimum national standards of uniformity.[2]

A unique, although not strictly inter-governmental, device for controlling the exercise of central legislative authority was the African Affairs Board of Rhodesia and Nyasaland. Originally envisaged as an inter-governmental body, it was established under the constitution as a standing committee of the Federal Assembly.[3] The Board was empowered to cause any central bill which was a 'differentiating measure' to be reserved for assent in Britain. Thus it was intended that the Africans in the protectorates, for which the British Government was responsible, would be protected against discriminatory federal legislation. In practice, however, the unwillingness of the British Government to refuse assent to bills reserved at the request of the Board drained it of any effectiveness.[4]

The exercise of executive and administrative powers by a government may also impinge upon the activities of other governments within a federation. It has, therefore, usually been thought necessary to reduce the possibility of clashes by including constitutional provisions prohibiting the executive action of regional governments from impeding the exercise of central executive authority, the restriction often being backed by the sanction of central emer-gency powers.[5] In addition, there have been a variety of other arrangements

---

[1] See pp. 174–5.   [2] See Chapter 8, sections 2 and 4.
[3] *Constitution of R. and N., 1953*, arts. 67–77; cf. Cmd. 8233/1951, para. 49 and Annex III.
[4] On the operation of the Board see especially Cmnd. 298/1957; Cmnd. 362/1958; Cmnd. 1149/1960, pp. 16–18; Mason, *Year of Decision*, pp. 86–87, 137; T. M. Franck, *Race and Nationalism* (1960), pp. 177, 179–81, 304–7.
[5] *Government of India Act, 1935*, ss. 122, 126; *Constitution of India, 1950*, arts. 257 (1), 365; *Constitution of Pakistan, 1956*, arts. 126, 193; *Constitution of Malaya, 1957*, art. 81; *Nigeria Constitution, 1954*, s. 135, and amendments by S.I. 1957, no. 1530 and S.I. 1959,

aiming at the co-ordination of the executive authority of the central and regional governments. Usually there have been provisions enabling the delegation of executive authority by either level of government to the other, normally, although not always, requiring the consent of the government to which power is delegated.[1] The constitution of Rhodesia and Nyasaland also expressly stipulated: 'The Governments of the Federation and of the Territories shall, in so far as it is practicable, consult together on all matters which are of common interest and concern.'[2] The Asian federations have even gone so far as to give the central governments power to give regional governments directions about the exercise of their executive authority in certain fields. Such directions have usually been intended to ensure compliance with central laws when these were administered by state or provincial governments, to ensure the maintenance of national communications, to protect minorities within regions, and in India to control the operation of the armed forces of the former princely states.[3] In Malaya the executive authority of the central government was further extended to conducting surveys, giving advice and technical assistance to states, and inspecting the work of state departments which dealt with matters which were not exclusively state subjects.[4]

In the Asian federations a further link between the central and regional governments has been provided by the regional governors in their dual role as agents of the central government and as constitutional heads of the regional governments. There was considerable discussion in the Indian Constituent Assembly as to whether state governors should be directly elected, but the idea was rejected for fear of friction between a popular governor and a responsible ministry. In addition it was feared that elections would lead to the choice of party men, involve disproportionate expense, induce dependence upon local men as governors, and encourage provincialism. It was decided that governors should be appointed by and hold office at the pleasure of the central government,[5] although it was assumed from the beginning that appointments would in practice only be made with the consent of the government of the state concerned.[6] Apart from the normal discretionary authority

no. 368; *Constitution of Nigeria, 1960*, ss. 66, 80; *Constitution of Nigeria, 1963*, ss. 71, 86. Such provisions did not appear in the constitutions of Rhodesia and Nyasaland and the West Indies.   [1] For details, see Chapter 12, section 6.

[2] *Constitution of R. and N., 1953*, art. 42 (2).

[3] *Constitution of India, 1950*, arts. 244, 256, 257, 259 (1) (repealed by *Seventh Amendment Act, 1956*, s. 29 and Sched.), 339, 347, 350A and 350B (as added by *Seventh Amendment Act, 1956*, s. 21), 371 (as substituted by ibid., s. 22), and Fifth Sched., para. 3, Sixth Sched., para. 18; *Constitution of Pakistan, 1956*, arts. 103 (2), 104 (3–4), 126; *Constitution of Malaya, 1957*, art. 80 (4).

[4] Constitution, 1957, arts. 93–95. In the Borneo states and Singapore, however, some of these central powers were qualified (*Malaysia Act, 1963*, s. 43).

[5] *Constitution of India, 1950*, arts. 155–6. This does not apply in Jammu and Kashmir (art. 152 as amended by *Seventh Amendment Act, 1956*, s. 29 and Sched.).

[6] C.A.I., *Debates*, vol. viii, pp. 430–2. This has been the normal practice. Another convention which has become fairly well established has been that of appointing residents of

of a parliamentary head of state, the governors were also assigned certain discretionary powers as agents of the central government.[1] This was balanced, however, by the conventions of responsible government which for the most part have predominated, except where situations of parliamentary instability have arisen. By combining the roles of central agent and constitutional head of state, the Indian governors have indeed provided a useful liaison between the Union and state governments, but should there be a clash of will between the central governmenta nd a state government supported by its legislature, the choice facing a governor could be extremely difficult.

In Pakistan it was the role of the governors as agents of the central government which prevailed. Under the interim constitution, provincial ministries were frequently dismissed by governors at the direction of the central government, emergency governor's rule was imposed for considerable periods in many of the provinces, the Public and Representative Offices (Disqualification) Act, 1949, was regularly applied against provincial politicians, and governors exercised considerable control over provincial civil services.[2] As a result of provincial pressures the 1956 constitution weakened the scope for central control through governors by placing limits on their discretionary powers.[3] Nevertheless, the governors appointed by the central government continued to exercise considerable personal power, and emergency administration in the provinces remained a frequent occurrence. The degree of central control through the governors was amply illustrated when, during the constitutional crisis in East Pakistan in March 1958, Governor Fazlul Huq, who had dismissed the ministry of Ataur Rahman Khan, was himself immediately dismissed by the central government and replaced by a governor who promptly reinstated the previous ministry.

The 1962 constitution of Pakistan made the position of provincial governors as agents of the central government completely unequivocal. Governors were appointed by the President and in the performance of their functions were 'subject to the directions of the President'.[4] Paralleling the new central institutions, provincial executives were no longer responsible to the legislature. The effect has been to place within the hands of the central government potential control over all provincial executive action, and also, through the

other states as governors, in order to ensure that they are above the party and group politics of the state.

[1] Constitution, art. 200 (reservation of state bills for consideration by President), art. 356 (reporting on emergency situations), art. 371 as substituted by *Seventh Amendment Act, 1956*, s. 22 (setting up regional committees and boards within states), Fifth and Sixth Scheds. (administration of Scheduled Areas and Tribes). See also C.A.I., *Debates*, vol. viii, pp. 494, 500, 540; Santhanam, *Union–State Relations in India*, pp. 23–24. In the cases of 'emergency rule' by the central government following the breakdown of constitutional machinery, the states have been administered by the governor as an agent of the President.

[2] *Government of India Act, 1935*, ss. 51, 59 (3, 4), 92A. See also Callard, *Pakistan, A Political Study*, pp. 102–5, 159–63; Sayeed, *Pakistan, The Formative Phase*, pp. 342–58.

[3] Constitution, 1956, art. 71 (6, 7).

[4] Art. 66.

requirement of the governor's assent, over most provincial legislation.[1] These provisions, perhaps more than any other, place the provinces in a subordinate position, making the federal character of the 1962 constitution legally little more than a façade.

Under the Federation of Malaya Agreement, 1948, the High Commissioner of the federation was able to exercise considerable influence through the heads of states. In the Malay States these were the hereditary rulers. Since these rulers could overrule their executive and legislative councils, and since the rulers undertook to accept the advice of the High Commissioner on all matters except the Muslim religion and Malay custom, the High Commissioner was in a very strong position.[2] The settlements had even less autonomy, for there the Resident Commissioners were appointed by the High Commissioner and directly responsible to him.[3] Following the recommendations of the Reid Commission, the 1957 constitution eliminated this control of states or settlements through their heads of state. In the Malay States the rulers were now made into 'constitutional rulers';[4] in the former Settlements Resident Commissioners were replaced by governors who were appointed by the federal monarch acting at his discretion after consulting the chief minister of the state, and these governors were not responsible in any way to the central government.[5] Consequently, the position of the constitutional heads of the states came to correspond more closely to the situation in the three non-Asian federations, where governors were not agents of the central government.

The arrangements in these other federations were designed to make it clear that the governor had no special relation to the central government. In the colonial federations of Central Africa, Nigeria, and the West Indies, regional governors were appointed directly by the United Kingdom. In Nigeria after independence the regional governors were appointed by the Queen until 1963, and after that by the President, but in each case the constitutions required the appointments to be made on the advice of the regional premiers, who therefore made the actual choices.[6] Central interests are provided a voice, however, by the requirement that the premiers should consult the central Prime Minister first.

[1] Arts. 74, 77, 80–82, 103–4, 114–19.
[2] Federation of Malaya Agreement, 1948, cls. 8, 96, 101.   [3] S.I. 1948, no. 108, ss. 13, 16.
[4] Constitution, 1957, Eighth Sched., s. 1; Col. no. 330/1957, para. 177.
[5] S.I. 1957, no. 1533, Second Sched., art. 1; Third Sched., art. 1. This arrangement was also extended to the new Malaysian states of Sarawak and Sabah in 1963 (Constitutions of Sabah and Sarawak, 1963, art. 1 (in Cmnd. 2094/1963, Annexes B and C)). The Singapore Head of State within Malaysia was appointed by the federal monarch in consultation with the central Prime Minister (Constitution of Singapore, 1963, art. 1 (in Cmnd. 2094/1963, Annex D)).
[6] Constitutions (1960 and 1963) of each Region, s. 1. On the controversy over the discretionary powers of Nigerian regional governors in dismissing premiers see Akintola v. Aderemi and Adegbenro (F.S.C. 187/1962), and Adegbenro v. Akintola, [1963] 3 W.L.R. 63. On the effect of these judgements upon the validity of the appointment of a new Western Region governor, see West Africa (1 June 1963), pp. 597–8, 615, 621.

A particularly important form of inter-governmental control, which was embodied in the constitutions of the four independent federations and of the West Indies, was the extensive emergency power granted to the central government.[1] These provisions, when brought into play, gave the central government virtually unitary control over the regional governments. In the West Indies the territories could also exercise emergency powers which would prevail over ordinary central legislation. Even in Rhodesia and Nyasaland, and Nigeria (before 1960), where emergency powers were not actually written into the constitutions, the Emergency Powers Orders in Council provided equivalent central and regional emergency powers.

Thus, in all of the new federations there have been a variety of inter-governmental controls. These controls have applied in both directions, although in the Asian federations, where the influence of the Government of India Act, 1935, was strongest, it has been the central controls upon state and provincial government that have been far more prominent.

6. *Machinery for inter-governmental co-operation*

In the preceding chapter we noted the variety of inter-governmental financial institutions that have been developed in the new federations, but the unavoidable interrelation of central and regional fields of legislative and executive activity has led also to a wide variety of other institutions for inter-governmental consultation and co-operation. Some of these have actually been specified in the federal constitutions, but more often they have been established simply by agreement as the need arose.

Perhaps the most important of these inter-governmental institutions are those concerned with planning and co-ordinating economic and social development. These have been a particularly important feature in under-developed federations, where various aspects of economic affairs are the responsibility of different governments and where, therefore, lack of co-ordination could seriously hamper economic progress. Consequently standing machinery for co-operation in the field has been established in most of the new federations.

In India it is the Planning Commission of the Union Government which has collated the plans of the various states, drafted the national Plan, and advised on its implementation.[2] The importance of this commission, the

---

[1] For details of provisions for emergency powers, see Chapter 12, sections 6 and 7.

[2] For discussions on the organization of planning in India, see especially, Santhanam, *Union-State Relations in India*, ch. 4; W. Malenbaum, 'Who Does the Planning?', in Park and Tinker (eds.), *Leadership and Political Institutions in India*, pp. 301–13; Goodall, 'Organization of Administrative Leadership in the Five Year Plans', in Park and Tinker (eds.), op. cit., pp. 314–28; Morris-Jones, *The Government and Politics of India*, pp. 115, 141–3; Planning Commission, *The New India* (1958), esp. ch. v; The Indian Institute of Public Administration, *The Organization of the Government of India* (1958), ch. xxvi; Palmer, *The Indian Political System*, ch. 8; I. Narain and P. C. Mathur, 'Union–State Relations in India: A Case Study in Rajasthan', *Journal of Commonwealth Political Studies*, ii (1964), pp. 120–40.

initiative of the central departments in joint programmes with the state departments, and the dependence of the states upon central 'matching grants' and loans to finance their shares of the Plans, have all contributed to giving the Union Government an almost unitary control for purposes of economic development and financing. Nevertheless, the supreme planning body has been the National Development Council composed of the central cabinet, the members of the Planning Commission, and the chief ministers of all the states. Its function has been to lay down the outline for economic planning and to supervise the Planning Commission. This inter-governmental Council has no constitutional authority, but by convention its decisions have come to be accepted as binding on both the Union and state governments. Santhanam has described the position of the National Development Council as even 'approximate to that of a super-Cabinet of the entire Indian federation, a Cabinet functioning for the Government of India and the Governments of all the States.'[1] In addition to the work of this Council, development planning has also involved extensive inter-governmental bargaining and collaboration, both formal and informal, at many levels. There has been virtually continuous consultation between the Planning Commission and state governments and between central and state departments in the formulation and implementation of the Plans, and the central government has been dependent upon the states for the execution of a large portion of the plans.

The organization of development planning in Pakistan was carried out on similar lines. Here again the central government dominated the process, both because of the role of its Planning Board and because of provincial dependence on central development grants and loans.[2] But the general responsibility for formulating financial, commercial, and economic policies and plans and for aiming at uniform standards of economic development was assigned by the constitution to the advisory National Economic Council, composed of the federal Prime Minister, four other central ministers, and three ministers from each of the two provincial governments.[3] This advisory council has been continued under the 1962 constitution, but central dominance has been assured by making membership at 'the pleasure of the President'.[4]

Economic and social planning in Malaya has inevitably been dominated by the central government because of the concentration of legislative, executive, and financial powers in the central government under the constitution.[5] The central government is required, however, to consult the National Finance

---

[1] Santhanam, op. cit., p. 47.

[2] On planning in Pakistan, see S. M. Akhtar, *Economics of Pakistan* (5th ed., 1961), chs. 16–18.

[3] Constitution, 1956, art. 199. In the Constituent Assembly stress was laid upon the function of the National Economic Council as a means to ensuring a fair distribution of development expenditure between the two provinces. See C.A.P. (second), *Debates*, vol. i, pp. 1806, 2158. The 1962 constitution, art. 145 (4), made this a specific task of the council.

[4] Constitution, 1962, art. 145.

[5] See pp. 187–8 and Chapter 9, sections 3 and 4.

Council, composed of central and state representatives, before putting development plans into operation.[1] The 1957 constitution also established a separate National Land Council, composed of central and state representatives, to formulate a national policy for land utilization which is binding on central and state governments, and to advise on national development plans.[2] A further institution for co-ordinating social and economic development has been the Rural and Industrial Development Authority (R.I.D.A.) created by the central government, and composed of central and state representatives. Its function has been to stimulate and undertake economic and social development projects, especially in the rural areas.

The Nigerian National Economic Council, which included representatives of all governments within the federation, was formed in 1955 on the recommendation of the International Bank Mission as a forum for the discussion of economic matters and to foster co-operation between governments. In 1959 it was strengthened by the addition of a Joint Economic Planning Committee, and in 1962 an agreed single national six-year development plan was published.[3] Other Nigerian inter-governmental bodies concerned with related subjects have been the National Council of Natural Resources, the National Manpower Board, the Niger Dams Council, and the Niger Development Board, the latter concerned with the development of the Niger Delta. As in India, although to a lesser degree, the process of co-operative planning has since independence somewhat strengthened the relative influence of the central government, both because of its role as the co-ordinator of national planning and because of its extra financial resources.

When one turns to the other two federations, Rhodesia and Nyasaland and the West Indies, it is quickly apparent that their economic planning machinery was less adequate. The officials' conference of 1951 on Central African federation had recommended a Development Commission composed of central and territorial representatives, with a Central Planning Staff,[4] but these proposals were never implemented. In 1956 an inter-territorial Development Planning Group was appointed to consider the 1957–61 development plans of all the governments, but it did little more than co-ordinate the presentation of those plans. A number of other consultative committees also existed, but the Monckton Commission was critical of the weakness of the machinery for co-ordinating economic planning.[5] Finally in 1961 the central government agreed to set up an Inter-Governmental Advisory Committee to co-ordinate

[1] Constitution, 1957, arts. 92 (1), 108.

[2] Arts. 91, 92 (1). The states added to form Malaysia are not required, however, to follow the policy formulated by the National Land Council, *Malaysia Act, 1963*, s. 43.

[3] Federation of Nigeria, *National Development Plan, 1962–8* (Lagos, 1962); Sessional Paper No. 1/1962, *Federal Government Development Programme* (Lagos). On the organization of planning in Nigeria, see Mackintosh, 'Federalism in Nigeria', *Political Studies*, x (1962), pp. 239–45; *West Africa* (17 February 1962), p. 170, (7 April 1962), p. 371.

[4] Cmd. 8233/1951, paras. 53–54, 56, 73.

[5] Cmnd. 1148/1960, paras. 206–13.

economic development and an Industrial Consultative Committee to co-ordinate local industrial development, but frequently the central government continued to act either without any consultation or hastily with insufficient time for adequate consultation.

In the West Indies, too, there was a general lack of co-ordination in economic affairs. The Regional Council of Ministers, which the Standing Federation Committee had envisaged as a body for considering economic matters of common interest to the territorial and federal governments, met only twice, once in 1959 and once in 1960. An advisory Regional Natural Resources Council composed of central and territorial ministers was, however, also established to enable consultation over natural resources and agriculture.

In addition to the inter-governmental institutions designed to facilitate general economic co-operation, there have been other councils, commissions, and boards intended to co-ordinate the work of central and regional governments in specific activities of mutual concern. Among these have been the River Boards, the Central Council of Health, the Inter-State Transport Commission, and the Drugs Consultative Committee in India; the provincial Advisory Boards for the central Posts and Telegraphs Department and the National Council of Social Welfare in Pakistan; the National Council for Local Government in Malaya;[1] the Tariff Advisory Board in Malaysia; the Police Council, the National Council on Establishments, the Minority Area Advisory Councils, the Joint Consultative Committee on Education, the Central Bank Advisory Committee, the Central Marketing Board,[2] and the statutory boards of certain central corporations[3] in Nigeria; the variety of inter-governmental committees on labour, agriculture, marketing, education, and specific development projects, and certain territorial and central statutory boards containing representatives of other governments, in Rhodesia and Nyasaland;[4] the Regional Labour Board and the Standing Advisory Committee on Medical Research in the West Indies. In some cases special tribunals have also been set up to deal with particular kinds of inter-governmental disputes for which reference to a supreme court might be unsuitable. Among these have been the inter-state Water Disputes Tribunals in India,[5] the inter-provincial disputes tribunals in Pakistan,[6] and the Lands Tribunals in Malaya.[7]

[1] *Constitution (Amendment) Act, 1960* (F. 10/1960), s. 12, inserting art. 95A.

[2] After 1958, the Nigerian Produce Marketing Co. Ltd.

[3] The regional governments are represented on the statutory boards of the Electricity Corporation of Nigeria, the Nigerian Ports Authority, the Nigerian Railway Corporation, and the Nigerian Broadcasting Corporation. See A. H. Hanson, 'Public Utilities in Nigeria, I, Federal Public Utilities', *Public Administration* (Winter, 1958), p. 371; Tilman and Cole (eds.), *The Nigerian Political Scene*, pp. 59–60, 73; Cole, 'Federalism in the Commonwealth', *I.P.S.A. Sixth World Congress, Geneva, 1964, Federalism/18*, pp. 30–31.

[4] See especially Cmnd. 1149/1960, pp. 120–4.

[5] Constitution, art. 262.

[6] These dealt primarily with financial disputes but were not limited to them. Constitution, 1956, art. 129. The 1962 constitution made no provision for these tribunals.

[7] Constitution, 1957, art. 87.

There have also been provisions sometimes for standing machinery for general consultation among governments. Some of these, such as the Indian Inter-State Council[1] and the Pakistan Inter-Provincial Council,[2] were intended to facilitate consultation and co-ordination among state and provincial governments. Despite the enabling article in the constitution, such a Council has not been formed in India, however. Instead, the Zonal Councils, created under the States Reorganization Act, 1956, have been used to further inter-state co-operation.[3] The Indian states were grouped into five Zones, each with its own Council, consisting of the Union Home Minister, and the chief minister and two other ministers from each state in the Zone. The function of these Councils was to provide a forum for closer consultation among the states, and between the states and the central government, on matters of common interest, especially those connected with economic planning. In addition these Councils have also discussed regional problems within each Zone, such as border disputes, official state and national languages, food distribution, and police reserves. The Zonal Councils were deliberative and advisory bodies, and therefore in no way detracted from the legislative and executive authority of the central or state governments. On the whole, they have helped to co-ordinate economic activity, but their ability to resolve disputes over borders and linguistic minorities has been rather limited except in the case of the Southern Zonal Council.

Since 1961 India has established some other inter-governmental councils of interest. Concern over the threat posed to national cohesion by the growing strength of linguistic regionalism led to the holding in 1961 of a National Integration Conference composed of central cabinet ministers, chief ministers of the states, party leaders, and other prominent men, in order to discuss measures to promote national integration, safeguard the interests of linguistic minorities, and plan the national co-ordination of education. As an outcome of this conference a permanent inter-governmental body, the National Integration Council, was established to review and make recommendations on these matters.[4] In the meantime, a Committee of Zonal Councils for National Integration to discuss problems of common interest in all the Zones was also established. Later, when the emergency of the Chinese invasion arose in 1962, it was met by a similar characteristically Indian response. An inter-governmental National Defence Council to advise the

---

[1] Constitution, art. 263.

[2] Constitution, 1956, art. 130. The 1962 constitution omitted this provision, since with only two widely separated provinces there was little need for it.

[3] On the Zonal Councils, see Bondurant, *Regionalism versus Provincialism*, chs. iii, v, vi; Pylee, *Constitutional Government in India*, ch. 42; B. N. Schoenfeld, *Federalism in India* (1960), pp. 16–18; Alexandrowicz, *Constitutional Developments in India*, pp. 178–9; Morris-Jones, *The Government and Politics of India*, pp. 103, 144.

[4] Its membership includes the Union Prime Minister and Home Minister, the chief ministers of all the states, leaders of political parties, the commissioners for minority groups, and representatives of higher education and research.

central government on military affairs and on the mobilization of public participation in the national defence was quickly formed.[1]

Standing machinery for general inter-governmental consultation has also been established elsewhere. During the operation of the Federation of Malaya Agreement, 1948, the Conference of Federation Executives, consisting of the central ministers and the Mentri Mentri Besar (chief ministers) of the states and the Resident Commissioners of the settlements, met before every meeting of the federal Legislative Council to consider prospective central legislation and policy.[2] Under the 1957 constitution it was provided that the Conference of Rulers, joined by the central Prime Minister and the state chief ministers, might deliberate on questions of national policy.[3] The West Indian Regional Council of Ministers, although primarily intended to consider economic matters, was also meant to facilitate general consultation among the Caribbean territories.

Apart from the standing machinery for consultation between governments, in all the new federations there have been a multitude of conferences, composed of central and regional representatives, for the discussion of both general and specialized subjects. In India, for instance, there have been periodic meetings of state governors, of state chief ministers, of finance ministers, or of state and central ministers or officials. Indeed, a characteristic feature of Indian federalism has been the tendency of the central government to rely upon conferences to influence and co-ordinate state activities, rather than to undertake its own direct administration. An example of this was the instinctive reaction of the central government to respond to the Chinese invasion of 1962 by creating an inter-governmental National Defence Council. The general pattern in Nigeria has been much the same: the central government has in the past largely concentrated upon co-ordinating regional activities, although it is now increasing the proportion of its own direct administration. *Ad hoc* inter-governmental conferences have also been a favourite device in other new federations. In most there have been frequent meetings of the premiers, ministers, or officials of governments. Indeed, the organization of such conferences, particularly on specialized fields of common interest, was in the West Indies one of the major activities of the central government. During their period under colonial rule the new federations also benefited from the frequent constitutional conferences, which provided further occasions for contact between the leaders of different governments.

It is clear, then, that generally speaking the new federations have found a neat separation of central and regional functions impossible, and have therefore come to rely upon a high degree of consultation and co-operation between

---

[1] Its membership includes the central Prime Minister and six major central cabinet ministers, seven chief ministers of states, other major political leaders, the military chiefs of staff, and some officials and technical and scientific advisers.

[2] Col. no. 330/1957, para. 33.

[3] Art. 38 (3).

central and regional governments. The federations of Rhodesia and Nyasa-land and the West Indies have been the weakest in this respect. In the former the arrangements for consultation between governments tended to work un-evenly, and the Monckton Commission was rightly critical of the gaps in the machinery for co-operation.[1] In the West Indies the weakness in the realm of inter-governmental consultation was illustrated most vividly by the infrequent and inconclusive meetings of the West Indies Federal Labour Party itself. It was astonishing, for instance, that in the dispute over the Jamaican position on constitutional revision between the federal Prime Minister and the Premiers of Jamaica and Trinidad, all members of this party, the debate should have taken place 'in the form, not of formal meetings, but of press reports and exchanges of cablegrams, culminating in the announcement of the Jamaican proposals in early 1960 to the Federal electorate via the medium of a Colonial Office memorandum'.[2] Elsewhere, however, it would appear to have been clearly recognized that a federal system involving a completely dual polity of isolated central and state governments is impracticable under modern con-ditions, and that any modern federal structure must be an integrated one in which central and regional governments carry on their activities in close co-operation.

[1] Cmnd. 1148/1960, ch. 10; Cmnd. 1150/1960, ch. 5.
[2] Lewis, *Puerto Rico: A Case Study*, p. 88.

11

THE ORGANIZATION OF CENTRAL
GOVERNMENT

1. *The controversial issues*

ALTHOUGH the basis of the federal solution lies in the constitutional distribution of legislative, executive, and financial powers between central and regional governments, the manner in which the central power is to be controlled has often proved one of the most controversial issues raised during the process of constitution-making. Perhaps the greatest difficulty on this question was experienced in Pakistan, where this problem more than any other delayed agreement upon a constitution, but in each of the other new federations, too, the issue of regional representation in the institutions of central government caused considerable debate.

The reason for these controversies lay in the wide differences in population, area, and wealth between regions within these federations. If the normal democratic principle of representation according to population were adopted, the control of central power was likely to be permanently in the hands of a few more populous regions. This problem has been particularly acute where, as in Nigeria, the West Indies, Pakistan, and Rhodesia and Nyasaland, a single region has possessed over half the total electorate.[1] It is significant that these four federations have been more unstable than India or Malaya. Sometimes the contrasts in regional population have been reinforced by corresponding differences in area and wealth, but where this has not been the case, the less populous regions have sometimes put forth area or revenue as other relevant criteria to be considered in addition to population in determining central representation. For instance in the West Indies, when Jamaica demanded fairer central representation in 1959, Eric Williams, Premier of Trinidad, pointed to his territory's greater *per capita* financial contribution to the federation (Trinidad $4.51, Jamaica $2.62) and declared: 'If Jamaica is going to count heads, we are going to count pockets. . . . If . . . Jamaicans want to say no taxation without representation, Trinidad says no Trinidad taxation for the benefit of Jamaican representation.'[2]

The smaller regions, as a rule, have feared that in central politics their votes would be unheard if representation were based on population, for the few populous regions would be in a position of perpetual preponderance. For

[1] See Chapter 7, section 2, and Table 2, p. 362.
[2] *Revision of the Federal Constitution* (Trinidad, 1959), p. 38.

instance, in Nigeria there have been frequent southern fears of permanent domination by the Northern Region, and these apprehensions have been increased by the monolithic character of voting in the Northern Region. These anxieties were at the base of the advocacy by many southerners of the splitting of the Northern Region, and later of the controversy over the accuracy of the 1962–3 census figures upon which the allocation of seats in the House of Representatives would be based.[1] Elsewhere, too, the concern of the smaller regions has been evident. In Pakistan the fears of the western provinces and states of control by East Bengal was a major factor in their opposition to the distribution of seats in the central legislature according to population, and an important motive in the later unification of West Pakistan to balance East Bengal.[2] In India resentment of the powerful influence of Uttar Pradesh in the Union Parliament and cabinet led to arguments for splitting it in order to reduce its power, and also to the advocacy of a Dakshina Pradesh, a large southern state as a counterweight to Uttar Pradesh.[3] The anxieties of the smaller West Indian territories were clearly in the minds of the members of the Standing Closer Association Committee when it was considering the composition of the central legislature.[4] In Central Africa, Nyasaland bitterness at the Southern Rhodesian domination of the Federal Assembly was a source of the African secessionist movement there.[5]

The larger regions of these federations have, on the other hand, usually resented suggestions that they should get less than their 'fair share' of power, often pointing to the financial support they are required to give to the smaller and poorer regions. Moreover, in both Nigeria and the West Indies, by contrast with the older federation of Canada, it was the largest regions which were most reluctant to enter these federations and were in no mood to make sacrifices in their proportionate representation. Representatives of the Northern Region have argued for representation by population, and have consistently refused to be placed in a minority in the central legislature. The Jamaican drift towards secession did result in 1961 in agreement upon a reduction of her under-representation in the West Indian House of Representatives, but this proved too late.[6] In Pakistan, East Bengal feared that a reduction in her central representation would leave her at the mercy of a united group of smaller western provinces. The Bengalis, apprehensive of economic and military domination by West Pakistan, and inflamed over

---

[1] Awolowo, *Awo*, pp. 199–201, 206–7; *Proceedings of General Conference* (1950), p. 15; *West Africa* (December 1962, November 1963, February and March 1964). See p. 257 below.

[2] C.A.P. (second), *Debates*, vol. i, pp. 317, 489–92, 683–7, 1423, 1444, 1455–7.

[3] Note by K. M. Panikkar in *Report of the States Reorganization Commission* (1955), p. 245, and Harrison, *India, the Most Dangerous Decades*, pp. 306–8.

[4] Col. no. 255/1950, para. 63.

[5] Cmnd. 814/1959, para. 43; Cmnd. 1148/1960, paras. 30, 35, 88, and pp. 155–6.

[6] Cmnd. 1417/1961, para. 11.

central policy on the language issue and by economic neglect under the interim constitution, raised objections to the schemes advanced by the Basic Principles Committee's Reports of 1950 and 1952, because their proportion of members in the central legislature would be reduced.[1] The combination of the parity principle and weightage for the smaller provinces in the latter of these reports was resented also in the Punjab, the second largest province, as an arrangement discriminating particularly against it. In Rhodesia and Nyasaland a good deal of controversy raged between those who argued that Southern Rhodesia's predominant representation was justified by the concentration of the electorate there, and those who argued that the total population, not just the white electorate, should be the basis for assigning seats in the Federal Assembly.[2]

Because of these conflicting fears, compromises in the structure and composition of the central legislature and executive, and in the method of appointment and functions of the Head of State, have usually been necessary. These compromises have been difficult to find, and frequently adjustments, especially in the composition of the legislature, have had to be made after federation. Nigeria and Malaya both added second chambers later; the Federal Assembly of Rhodesia and Nyasaland was enlarged, and its composition modified, in 1957, and the Monckton Commission suggested further revisions in 1960; modifications to the West Indian House of Representatives and Senate were agreed upon in 1961; the regional representation in the second Pakistan Constituent Assembly was modified from that in the first; the reorganization of Indian states in 1956 resulted in alterations to the composition of the two central chambers.[3]

Controversies over the organization of the central legislature have usually turned on three points. First, there has been the issue of regional representation. Smaller regions have invariably opposed the principle of representation according to population, and instead weightage to favour these smaller regions, or even regional equality, has often been proposed as a means of allaying their fears. A further argument, that no single region should be in a position to dominate the central legislature by holding a majority of the seats, has frequently been advanced. A second issue has been the method of election to the central legislature. Since the control of central power was what was at stake, it has sometimes been argued that members of the central legislature should be indirectly elected by the regional legislatures rather than chosen by direct election. Such suggestions stemmed in part from the desire of regional leaders to retain some control over central politics, and in part from traditions

---

[1] C.A.P. (first), *Debates*, vol. viii, pp. 181–4; Callard, *Pakistan, A Political Study*, pp. 172–80.

[2] Cmnd. 1148/1960, para. 106, and pp. 125, 155–6; Cmnd. 1150/1960, paras. 47–48. It could be argued that 2 per cent. of the total population of one territory (Southern Rhodesia) controlled 48 per cent. of the seats in the Federal Assembly (see Table 15, p. 382).

[3] See Tables 11–16, pp. 376–83, for details.

derived from the British colonial policy of indirect rule. The third question has arisen out of attempts to solve the other two. As in earlier federations, the bicameral arrangement has had its appeal: it enables a compromise on the other two issues by making possible the use of different principles of regional composition and methods of election in the two central legislative houses. But the greater demands made by the bicameral solution upon the limited supply of experienced legislators available in these developing countries, and the difficulty of giving a second chamber effective power when the executive is responsible to the popular chamber, have somewhat reduced the appeal of the bicameral solution.

2. *Unicameral central legislatures*

Although in the older federations of the United States, Switzerland, Canada, and Australia, a bicameral central legislature was invariably adopted, this solution has been by no means universal in the newer federations. Indeed, in all the federations under study, except the West Indies, there have been unicameral central legislatures, at least for a time. The Indian Constituent Assembly (1947–50) and the Pakistan Constituent Assemblies (1947–54, 1955–6) served as single-chamber legislatures under the interim federal constitutions,[1] and the subsequent constitutions of Pakistan have continued the unicameral principle in the National Assembly.[2] The Federation of Rhodesia and Nyasaland had a single Federal Assembly, and although a special provision was inserted in the constitution enabling the federal legislature to establish a second chamber, this power was not exercised.[3] Both Nigeria and Malaya experimented with unicameral federal legislatures until senates were added in 1959.[4] Even in the West Indies, proposals for a unicameral central legislature were originally advanced at Montego Bay.[5]

Why should unicameral central legislatures have appeared so frequently in these federations? One point of significance is that, with the exception of Pakistan, these examples have occurred only in either purely interim constitutions where they provided the simplest form of temporary organization, as in India (1947–50) and Pakistan (1947–56), or in colonial federations during the period before independence, as in Malaya, Nigeria, and Rhodesia and Nyasaland. It would appear that the usual British pattern of preparing colonies for self-government by a gradual slide in small stages from a colonial legislative council, composed of a minority of elected members, to a fully elected parliament, has tended to result in a unicameral parliament simply because the

---

[1] *Indian Independence Act, 1947* (10 & 11 Geo. 6, ch. 30), s. 8 (1). See Callard, *Pakistan, A Political Study*, pp. 113–18, for an analysis of the Pakistan Constituent Assembly as a central legislature.

[2] Constitution, 1956, art. 43; Constitution, 1962, art. 19.   [3] Arts. 8, 9, 97 (5).

[4] *Constitution of Nigeria, 1954*, s. 5; *The Federation of Malaya Agreement, 1948*, cl. 36. Note, however, the Conference of Rulers in Malaya (cls. 67–76) which performed some of the functions of a second chamber (see section 3 of this chapter).

[5] Col. no. 218/1948, pp. 40, 97, 122, 126–8.

legislative council from which it evolved was unicameral. Nevertheless, the adoption of unicameral central legisltaures in these cases was not simply the result of following the preceding pattern but was also a clearly deliberate decision, for in Nigeria and in Rhodesia and Nyasaland, bicameral solutions were considered and rejected.[1] In Pakistan the first Constituent Assembly struggled with a variety of complicated bicameral schemes, all of which caused heated controversy over the composition and relative powers of the two chambers.[2] After the unification of West Pakistan had reduced the large variety of provinces and states to only two large provinces, the second Constituent Assembly decided upon equal representation of the two provinces in the National Assembly, and rejected a second chamber as superfluous.[3] Furthermore, another unicameral National Assembly was established by the 1962 constitution, in spite of the recommendations of the Constitution Commission in favour of a bicameral central legislature.[4]

Various reasons have been given for the rejection of second chambers in these cases. An important argument, since these federations were all developing countries with only limited numbers of educated and experienced legislators, was that a second chamber would increase the demand for legislators, already made acute by the two tiers of government involved in a federal structure. Furthermore, a single chamber would be less costly and result in less delay in legislation. Some West Indians also looked upon a second chamber, limiting the power of a popularly elected house, as an undemocratic feature.[5] A major factor in both Pakistan and Nigeria, where one region possessed a majority of the federal population, was the unwillingness of that region to accept a minority position in a second chamber, and the preference of that region for a single chamber in which its representation was reduced, but not below 50 per cent.[6] In the case of Pakistan, the example of New Zealand abolishing its Upper House was also cited as an argument against a second chamber.[7]

The decision in favour of a unicameral legislature has invariably necessitated compromises over regional representation within the single assembly. Only

[1] See Nigeria, *Proceedings of General Conference* (1950), pp. 218, 221, 236; Cmd. 8934/ 1953, paras. 10–12; Cmd. 8233/1951, para. 89.

[2] B.P.C., *Interim Report* (1950), paras. 30–39; B.P.C., Franchise sub-committee, *Report* (1952), pp. 1, 4; B.P.C., *Report* (1952), paras. 36–80; B.P.C., *Report* (as adopted, 1954), paras. 39–87.

[3] Constitution, 1956, art. 43.

[4] Art. 19; *Report of the Constitution Commission, Pakistan, 1966* (1962), ch. v.

[5] Col. no. 218/1948, pp. 40, 120, 126–8; Col. no. 255/1950, para. 53.

[6] See, for instance, Nigeria Legislative Council, *Debates* (16 September 1950), p. 190; Cmd. 8934/1953, paras. 10–12; C.A.P. (first), *Debates*, vol. viii, pp. 181–3; vol. xv, pp. 13–16; C.A.P. (second), *Debates*, vol. i, pp. 1992–3. In the West Indies, however, Jamaica from the beginning accepted a minority position in the Senate, and in 1957 Northern Nigeria finally agreed to do likewise in return for its full representation by population in the House of Representatives.

[7] K. J. Newman, *Essays on the Constitution of Pakistan* (1956), p. 355.

in the Indian Constituent Assembly and in the first Pakistan Constituent Assembly was representation based solely on the criterion of population, and both of these were envisaged only as temporary institutions.[1] Except for the first Pakistan Constituent Assembly, whenever a unicameral legislature has been established in a federation where one region possessed a majority of the population, the representation of that region has been reduced to 50 per cent of the seats or less, in order that it might not by itself control the central legislature.[2] In some of the unicameral legislatures an element of the principle of regional equality was introduced. The Eastern and Western Regions of Nigeria, for instance, were given equal representation in both 1951 and 1954, despite significant differences in population. In Malaya the federal Legislative Council between 1948 and 1959 included the President from each State Council and a representative from each Settlement Council, and until 1955 a second member also from each state and settlement.[3]

Most of these unicameral legislatures have also contained special seats for the representation of minority or special interests as distinguished from simply regional ones.[4] Examples were the seats reserved for religious minorities in the constituent assemblies of India and Pakistan, for communities not otherwise adequately represented in the Nigerian House of Representatives, and for Africans or members elected to represent African interests in the Central African Federal Assembly. In each of these cases, however, these special members formed less than a quarter of the total membership and were therefore insufficient by themselves to block any constitutional amendment. But in the Malayan Legislative Council at its inception, the majority of 'unofficial members' were chosen to represent economic interests and minorities, the allocation being ostensibly non-racial, but carefully calculated to provide a racial balance within the Council. Even when the principle of election was introduced in 1955, a third of the members continued to be appointed to represent these special interests.

Unicameral legislatures have also generally required compromises over the method of electing central representatives, several methods often being combined. The Indian and Pakistan constituent assemblies were indirectly elected by provincial legislatures (themselves based on narrow franchises) in order to avoid delay in their formation, but special arrangements had to be made for provinces or states which lacked legislatures.[5] The Pakistan constitution of 1956, specified direct elections, but the method of representation for the

---

[1] These Assemblies consisted of one representative for each million of population (Cmd. 6821/1946, paras. 18, 19).
[2] See Tables 12A, 12B, 14, 15, pp. 377, 378, 381, 382.
[3] See Table 13A, p. 379.
[4] For details, see Tables 12A, 12B, 13A, 14, 15, pp. 377–82.
[5] Cmd. 6821/1946, paras. 18, 19 (ii); C.A.I., *Debates*, vol. iii, p. 356 and Appendix A, pp. 363–74; C.A.P. (first), *Debates*, vol. vi, Appendix, pp. 17–21, and pp. 23–32; vol. viii, pp. 167–9; Pakistan, *The Constituent Assembly Order, 1955* (G.G.O. 12/1955).

Special Areas was left to be specified by Presidential order.[1] The 1962 Pakistan constitution laid down a uniform method of election to the National Assembly, but, in the hope of encouraging higher standards of ability and responsibility among its members, turned to a form of indirect election in which the Assembly was elected in the first instance by the existing 'basic democracies', and in succeeding elections by a special electoral college, itself elected on an adult franchise.[2] These arrangements came under severe criticism, however, and a Franchise Commission subsequently recommended direct election by universal suffrage to the National Assembly. In Nigeria the method of indirect election by the regional assemblies, which under the 1946 and 1951 constitutions had done so much to regionalize central politics, was abandoned in 1954, the southern members being directly elected and the northern indirectly elected by special electoral colleges.[3] In addition, the principle of nomination by the Governor-General acting at his discretion was retained for the six members representing special and minority interests.[4] In Malaya, to the combination in 1948 of nominated members and state and settlement council representatives among the 'unofficials' there was added in 1955 a majority of directly elected members.[5] While the majority of representatives to the Rhodesia and Nyasaland Federal Assembly were directly elected, the principle of indirect election was adopted for the specially elected African representatives from the two northern territories, and the principle of nomination by the Governor for the Europeans representing African interests from the same territories.[6]

The shortage of experienced legislators has, in many of the unicameral legislatures, led to the creation, initially, of small assemblies. In most, however, the resultant heavy demands placed upon the few legislators have led to an increase in the size of the assembly. The Pakistan constituent assemblies, for instance, each with some eighty members for a country of over 75 millions, were clearly handicapped in the effective execution of their business. Consequently, when another unicameral assembly was decided upon for the 1956 constitution, a membership of 310 was chosen.[7] In Rhodesia and Nyasaland the initial Federal Assembly was also found too small, and was increased in 1957 from 35 to 59 members, in order to give a wider base from which to choose the cabinet and to reduce the size of constituencies.[8] The Nigerian central legislature was progressively increased in size from 45 in 1946 and 149 in 1951 to 193 in 1954, while the Malayan federal Legislative Council, which

[1] Art. 147. Special Areas were the tribal areas and the states of Amb, Chitral, Dir, and Swat (art. 218).

[2] Arts. 155–8, 161–2, 168–9, 229.   [3] Cmd. 8934/1953, paras. 10, 14 proviso.

[4] Constitution, s. 11.   [5] Col. no. 330/1957, para. 32.

[6] Constitution, arts. 9–13, and Cmnd. 1149/1960, pp. 5–10.

[7] Art. 44. This was reduced, however, in 1962 to 156 (art. 20).

[8] Cmnd. 298/1957, p. 7. By 1956 over a quarter of the members of the Assembly were ministers, and before 1957 one constituency had been larger than the whole of England. See C. Leys, *European Politics in Southern Rhodesia* (1959), pp. 60, 199.

started with 75 members in 1948, was increased to 99 in 1955. The necessity to increase the size of these unicameral legislatures suggests that the degree to which the number of legislators may be economized on by a unicameral legislature is limited.

Probably the most significant feature of the experience of those federations that have experimented with unicameral legislatures is that, except in Pakistan and Rhodesia and Nyasaland, second chambers have eventually been added.[1] In view of the failure of parliamentary government in Pakistan and the continued controversies over central representation in Rhodesia and Nyasaland, these two cases serve as poor advertisements for the adoption of unicameral legislatures in federations. Experience elsewhere suggests that, while unicameral legislatures may operate satisfactorily as an interim arrangement, as in India, 1947–50, or in colonial federations before independence, as in Malaya, 1947–57, and Nigeria, 1954–9, such a solution is less suitable as a long-term arrangement for an independent federation. With the prospect of independence, the resulting increase in the scope of central power over such matters as defence and foreign policy, together with the departure of the imperial arbiter, makes the issue of the control of central power much more acute. At the same time the cry for democratic government, usually associated with movements for independence, has meant that at this stage it is more difficult to use nominated or indirectly elected members in order to achieve a regional balance within the single legislature. It is not surprising, therefore, that since 1960 Pakistan has been the only independent federation to have a unicameral central legislature.[1]

3. *Bicameral central legislatures*

Generally the bicameral central legislature has proved the more popular solution in the new federations. The West Indian constitution provided for a Senate from the beginning; only a very few members of the Indian Constituent Assembly opposed altogether the creation of the Council of States; in both Nigeria and Malaya there was virtually unanimous agreement over the addition of senates to their independence constitutions.[2] Even in Pakistan, the first Constituent Assembly considered a series of different schemes for a bicameral central legislature, and it was only after the unification of West Pakistan had simplified the issue by reducing the federation to two large provinces that a unicameral scheme was seriously considered. In Central Africa the Victoria Falls Conference of 1949 apparently assumed that there would be an Upper House to which some Africans might be nominated, and even after the decision in 1953 to set up a single Assembly, the possibility of later adding a second chamber was specifically provided for.[3]

[1] The central legislatures in South Arabia (Constitution, 1963, ss. 17–19), and Uganda (Constitution, 1962, s. 37), however, have been established in unicameral form.
[2] Kenya also had a bicameral legislature (Independence Constitution, 1963, s. 34).
[3] Hanna, *The Story of the Rhodesias and Nyasaland*, p. 251; Constitution, art. 97 (5).

Both federal and non-federal reasons have been advanced for a second chamber. The usual federal argument for a bicameral legislature is that, by enabling different principles of composition and election in the two chambers, the central legislature may represent both the unity and the regional diversity of the federation. The normal practice in the federations under study has been that the first chamber, with seats distributed according to population and members directly elected, represents the people of the federation. The second chamber, with seats distributed to represent the equality of the federating regions, or at least weighted to strengthen the representation of the smaller regions, and with members either indirectly elected by the regional legislatures, or nominated, is considered to represent the several units—states, territories, or regions. In most federations a compromise along these lines has been considered not only desirable but necessary, in order to reassure the smaller regions that central power would not be used solely in the interests of the more populous regions. The example of the older federations, furthermore, served as a model, for none of them had abandoned their second chambers, inducing constitution-makers to conclude that 'the need for a Second Chamber has been felt . . . wherever there are federations of any importance'.[1]

In most cases other 'non-federal' reasons have reinforced the argument for second chambers. The value of a second chamber introducing 'an element of sobriety and second thought' and serving 'as a brake or check on the rashness and impetuous proclivities of the Lower House' has been widely recognized.[2] This justification is made more important where experience in democracy has been brief. It has also been argued that in countries where the number of experienced statesmen and legislators is limited, second chambers provide an opportunity for persons of eminence who do not wish to make their careers in politics to contribute nevertheless to the political life of the country. This was the reason for including at least some places for nominated members in the second chambers of Malaya, India, and Nigeria, and for choosing the principle of nomination for all senators in the West Indies.

If we look at the first chambers in these bicameral legislatures, we find that generally the distribution of seats has been based upon population, thus placing the larger regions in an influential position.[3] In the Indian Lok Sabha (House of the People), the Nigerian House of Representatives after the addition of a Senate in 1959, and the bicameral schemes presented to the Pakistan Constituent Assembly in 1950 and 1954, this principle of representation was

---

[1] C.A.I., *Debates*, vol. iv, pp. 927–8. See also Col. no. 255/1950, para. 53; *Report of the Constitution Commission, Pakistan, 1961* (1962), para. 75.

[2] C.A.I., *Debates*, vol. iv, p. 927, and O. Awolowo, 'The Place of the Second Chamber in West Africa', in *What are the problems of Parliamentary Government in West Africa?* (1958), p. 118. In the West Indies, however, it was also suggested that hastening rather than delaying legislation should be the function of the Senate. G. K. Lewis, 'W.I. Federation: The Constitutional Aspects', *Social and Economic Studies*, vi (1957), p. 227.

[3] For details of composition of bicameral legislatures see Tables 11–16, pp. 367–83.

followed quite strictly, even when it resulted, in the Nigerian and Pakistan cases, in giving one region a majority of the seats. In India the effect was that, in 1950, four states (Uttar Pradesh, Madras, Bombay, and Bihar) of the twenty-seven states controlled 261 of the 498 seats, and in 1963 the five most populous states (U.P., Bihar, Maharashtra, Andhra, and Madras) together held a majority of the seats. The situation in Nigeria, whereby one region consequently elected a majority of members to the House of Representatives, was not regarded as too serious while it was expected that these seats would be divided among a number of parties. Indeed in the 1959 elections, although the N.P.C. emerged with the largest number of seats, all in the north, it was short of an overall majority and therefore joined a coalition with the predominantly southern N.C.N.C. But within two years, with the addition of the Northern Cameroons to the Northern Region, and with a number of opposition members crossing the floor, the N.P.C. had by itself a majority and hence an increasingly dominant position in the coalition. Not surprisingly, therefore, the 1962 and 1963 census results which preserved the dominant position of the Northern Region produced a heated and mounting political controversy leading to the turbulent election crisis of 1964–5.

Less precisely based on population has been the representation in the Malayan House of Representatives, which for the first election was based on the existing rather unequal constituencies.[1] Nevertheless, the three largest of the eleven states (Perak, Selangor, and Johore) controlled 50 of the 104 seats. The constitution originally specified that, at the time of redistribution, constituencies should be made relatively equal in the electorate which they contained, but a constitutional amendment in 1962 preserved the existing distribution for a longer period and provided for heavy weighting in favour of rural constituencies at future redistributions.[2] Moreover, in the negotiations for the Malaysian Federation, the representation of the new Borneo states was heavily weighted to take account of their area, potentialities, and difficulties of internal communications, while populous but compact Singapore by comparison was considerably under-represented, on the grounds that its larger measure of state autonomy entitled it to less central influence.[3]

Under the West Indian constitution and also the 1952 proposals in Pakistan, in order to avoid a single region dominating the assembly, the distribution of seats in the first chamber according to population was seriously modified.[4] In neither case, however, was the largest region ever fully reconciled to such an arrangement. To avoid even the appearance of one territory, Jamaica, with over half the federal population, dominating the Assembly, and to ensure adequate representation for the smallest territories, the West Indian Standing

[1] Art. 171; Col. no. 330/1957, para. 75.
[2] Constitution, arts. 46, 113, 116, and Thirteenth Sched. as amended and inserted by *Constitution (Amendment) Act, 1962* (F. 14/1962), ss. 14 (*b*), 20 (*b*), 22, and 31.
[3] *Malaysia Act, 1963*, s. 9. See Table 13A, p. 379.
[4] See Tables 12B, p. 378, and 16, p. 383.

Closer Association Committee recommended a pragmatic allocation of seats taking into account not only population but economic development, productivity, and financial stability, providing a distribution which 'defies reduction to even the most complicated mathematical formula relating it to population figures'.[1] This scheme, slightly modified by the 1953 conference, left Jamaica holding only 17 of the 45 seats in the House of Representatives and was a source of resentment. When the tariff and income tax issues of 1958–9 made Jamaicans realize that with less than two-fifths of the central legislators they could not prevent the other territories from imposing their will on Jamaica, they turned to a demand for representation according to population. After protracted negotiations, agreement was finally reached on a formula giving each territory one basic seat, plus one seat for every 55,000 of population.[2] This resulted in a substantial increase of representation for Jamaica and Trinidad,[3] but the federation disintegrated before it could go into effect.

The method of election considered appropriate for each of these first chambers has been that of direct popular election. Some exceptions were made in both India and Malaysia, however, for special cases. In India representatives for certain less-advanced territories or states and for special minority groups were indirectly elected or nominated, and in Malaysia indirect election by state assemblies was permitted as a transitional arrangement for the acceding Borneo states and Singapore.[4]

When we look at the composition of second chambers we find that equality of regional representation has been the usual, but not the universal, solution. In the West Indies each territory, from Jamaica with over half the federal population, to Antigua with 1·8 per cent. of the federal population, was entitled to two senators, the only exception being Montserrat, which because of its tiny population (0·5 per cent. of the federal total) was limited to one senator on the grounds that no territory should have more senators than members of the House of Representatives.[5] In Malaya and Malaysia the states have also been equally represented by two senators each.[6] The regions of Nigeria are represented in the Nigerian Senate with twelve members each, but the federal capital territory of Lagos has four senators.[7] In India, on the other hand, states were not given equal representation in the Council of States, although some attempt was made to diminish the dominance of the larger states. The representation specified in the constitution was based on a formula recommended by the Union Constitution Committee of one seat

[1] Col. no. 255/1950, para. 63.
[2] Cmnd. 1417/1961, para. 11. A similar formula was subsequently agreed upon for an East Caribbean federation (Cmnd. 1746/1962, para. 15).
[3] See Table 16, p. 383.   [4] *Malaysia Act, 1963*, ss. 94–96.
[5] Constitution, art. 8 (2); Col. no. 255/1950, para. 68. The removal of even this inequality was agreed in 1961 (Cmnd. 1417/1961, para. 10).
[6] Constitution, art. 45. Parliament could, however, by law increase to three the number of senators from each state.
[7] Constitution, 1960, s. 37; Constitution, 1963, s. 42.

per million of population for the first 5 millions, and one seat for every additional 2 millions or part exceeding 1 million.[1] The recommendation of that committee that there be a maximum of twenty members for any single state was not incorporated, however, and as a result the larger states still hold a relatively strong position in the Council of States.[2] In Pakistan the initial recommendation that provinces should receive equal representation in the House of the Units caused a storm of protest in East Bengal, which felt that this was unfair to a province containing a majority of the federal population, and feared that under this scheme it would be converted into a minority in joint sessions of the two houses.[3] Subsequent bicameral schemes considered by the Constituent Assembly gave East Bengal parity with all the other regions combined, either in the second chamber or at least at joint sittings.[4]

The second chambers of India, Nigeria, and Malaya include, in addition to state and regional representatives, a number of members nominated for their eminence or to represent special interests. In the cases of India and Nigeria these are limited to less than 10 per cent. of the total membership of the chamber. In Malaya and later Malaysia the proportion is significantly larger, making up over 40 per cent. of the senate. In practice, the large number of appointed senators in Malaya, and the tendency for these appointed senators to come from certain states, has nullified the principle of equal state representation. In the first Senate, for instance, two of the eleven states, Perak and Selangor, between them contributed 13 of the total of 38 senators.[5]

For all these federal second chambers the method of direct election was rejected and methods different from that for the first chamber adopted.[6] In India, Nigeria, Malaya, and Malaysia there has been a similar pattern, based on a mixture of indirect election and nomination. The regional representatives in each of these examples, as well as in the schemes debated by the first Pakistan Constituent Assembly, have been indirectly elected by the regional governments. This method of election, by making the Second Chamber representative of regional views, gives it a federal character, even when, as in the Indian Council of States, the principle of state equality in representation has not been applied.[7]

---

[1] Constitution, art. 80 (1, 2) and Fourth Schedule; C.A.I., *Report of the Union Constitution Committee* (1947), part iv, ch. 2, para. 14 (1) (*a*) (ii).

[2] See Table 11, p. 376. In 1963, 5 states (U.P., Bihar, Maharashtra, Andhra, and Madras) held 111 of the 226 seats distributed among 16 states and 5 Union territories.

[3] B.P.C., *Interim Report* (1950), para. 31; Choudhury, *Constitutional Development in Pakistan*, pp. 107–9.

[4] B.P.C., *Report* (1952), paras. 38–39; B.P.C., *Report* (as adopted 1954), paras. 41–42. See Table 12B, p. 378.

[5] See Table 13B, p. 380. This represents the same proportion of seats as those held in the House of Representatives by these two states (see Table 13A, p. 379).

[6] But in Malaya, because the Reid Commission was divided on this question (Col. no. 330/1957, para. 62 and pp. 34–35), the Malayan Parliament was given power to introduce a system of direct election for senators under art. 45 (4) (*b*).

[7] For instance, of 31 new faces in the Indian Council of States in 1954, 5 were persons with

Details vary, however. In India election is by state legislative assemblies, or, in the case of Union territories (and formerly Part C states) where assemblies have not existed, by electoral colleges, using the system of proportional representation by means of the single transferable vote.[1] This ensures the representation of different parties and interests from within each state.[2] The recommendation of the Pakistan Basic Principles Committee for the House of Units envisaged the same method of election.[3] The Nigerian regional senators are nominated by the regional governments, subject to an affirmative vote at a joint sitting of the legislative houses of that region, while of the four senators from Lagos, two were to be local chiefs and two were to be chosen to reflect the state of parties in the Lagos Town Council.[4] As agreed in 1957 the regional governments have made their appointments in such a way that each of the provinces within the Northern and Western Regions was represented by at least one senator, and in the Eastern Region representation has been based on senatorial zones.[5] In 1957 it had also been agreed 'to recognize the desirability of ensuring that Senators should represent not only the Government but also the Opposition of the Region and that they should not consist entirely (or perhaps even mainly) of persons with party political affiliations'.[6] In spite of these hopes the regional representatives in the first Senate were predominantly members of the regional governing party, many of them candidates who had failed in the elections to the House of Representatives. The Malayan constitution provided that the senators representing the states should be elected by the state legislative assemblies, by simple majority ballot, any assembly member being free to make nominations.[7] In practice, the result has been similar to that in Nigeria, the nominees of the governing party in the state invariably being elected.[8] The governing Alliance Party in each of the former Federated Malay States and the former Straits Settlements, where the Chinese population tends to be concentrated, however, did divide the two senatorial seats between one U.M.N.O. and one M.C.A. supporter.[9]

prominent positions in states: 2 ex-Chief Ministers, 2 ex-Ministers, and 1 Pradesh Congress Committee President (Morris-Jones, *Parliament in India*, p. 258, note 2).

[1] Constitution, art. 80 (4).

[2] In the first Council of State elections, 1952, although Congress governments were in power in all the states, only 146 of the 200 indirectly elected members were Congress men (Morris-Jones, op. cit., p. 101). In 1960 Congress held 171 of the 220 elected seats.

[3] B.P.C., *Report* (1952), para. 38 (i, iii, iv, v); B.P.C., *Report* (as adopted, 1954), paras. 41 (3) (*d, e*), (4), (5).

[4] Constitution, 1954, ss. 5A, 5C, as inserted by S.I. 1959, no. 1772; Constitution, 1960, s. 37; Constitution, 1963, s. 42.   [5] Cmnd. 207/1957, para. 30.

[6] Ibid., para. 29.   [7] Art. 45 and Seventh Schedule.

[8] In 1959 only Alliance nominees were elected in the nine states controlled by that party, and only P.M.I.P. nominees from Kelantan and Trengganu which had P.M.I.P. governments.

[9] See Table 13B, p. 380. The fact that each state only had two senators meant that when these were divided between one Malay and one Chinese, no seat remained for an Indian. As a result the M.I.C. was unrepresented among the state senators.

For the additional members to represent special interests in the Indian, Nigerian, Malayan, and Malaysian second chambers, the method of nomination by the central government was adopted. The principle of nomination was defended in the Indian Constituent Assembly on the grounds that it would 'give an opportunity, perhaps, to seasoned people who may not be in the thickest of the political fray, but who might be willing to participate in the debate with an amount of learning and importance we do not ordinarily associate with the House of the People', and the actual appointments have been in keeping with this intention.[1] Similar arguments resulted in the use of the method of nomination as a way of securing eminent persons or representatives of special interests as senators in both Nigeria and Malaya.[2] The four nominated senators in the first Nigerian Senate included two from the field of higher education, a European banker, and a medical doctor, the latter receiving one of the two cabinet posts which initially went to senators. In Malaya, where the nominated members form over two-fifths of the total membership of the Senate, the first sixteen nominated senators were about equally divided between representatives of special economic interests and minority groups on one hand, and political appointments on the other.[3]

Unlike the other new federations, the West Indies rejected the method of indirect election for any of its senators, the chief argument being that for the federal legislature, or any part of it, to derive its authority from territorial legislatures would be inconsistent with the federal principle. Direct election of senators was also rejected in order to prevent the Senate from rivalling the authority of the House of Representatives. Instead, ignoring Canadian experience, a wholly nominated Senate was decided upon, on the grounds that it would enable the federation to cast its net wide for experienced men who might be held back by feelings of modesty or diffidence from participating in elections.[4] Despite some criticisms to the effect that it was an undemocratic and a colonial arrangement, nomination to the Senate was made the responsibility of the Governor-General acting at his discretion after prior consultation with the territorial governors.[5] The first appointments aroused controversy when the Governor-General, in an attempt to avoid an embittered opposition, went to the opposition parties in Jamaica and Trinidad for two of

---

[1] C.A.I., *Debates*, vol. iv, pp. 927–8; Constitution, art. 80 (3). Nomination is by the President, which in effect means by the Prime Minister.

[2] *Constitution of Malaya, 1957*, art. 45 (1) (*b*), 45 (2); *Nigeria Constitution, 1954*, s. 5A (1) (*d*) as inserted by S.I. 1959, no. 1772; *Constitution of Nigeria, 1960*, s. 37 (1) (*c*); *Constitution of Nigeria, 1963*, s. 42 (1) (*c*). In both countries appointment is by the Head of State acting on the Prime Minister's advice, but in Nigeria before independence it was by the Governor-General acting at his discretion.

[3] See Table 13B, p. 380.

[4] Col. no. 255/1950, paras. 57–62. Unlike the Canadian senators, members of the West Indian Senate were appointed for only five-year terms, however.

[5] Constitution, art. 8. For criticisms of this method see M. Ayearst, *The British West Indies* (1960), p. 232; L. Braithwaite, 'Progress Toward Federation, 1938–1956', *Social and Economic Studies*, vi (1957), pp. 148–51.

the senators. The power of the Governor-General to exercise his discretion in making senate appointments was therefore subsequently removed.[1] In effect this placed the nomination of senators in the hands of the territorial executives, an arrangement not dissimilar to that in the other new federations. In composition, the West Indian Senate strongly represented island views: the first nineteen senators included eleven former territorial legislators and six former territorial councillors.[2] One of the two Trinidad senators represented the East Indian community there. Senatorial appointment also served as an avenue for strengthening Jamaican representation in the central executive, made necessary by the success of the opposition party in Jamaica in the elections to the central House of Representatives.[3]

A characteristic feature of these federal second chambers has been that, except for the Indian Council of States with 238 members, the others have all been relatively small, ranging from 56 members in the Nigerian Senate, and 50 in the Malaysian Senate, to 19, the size of a large committee, in the West Indies.[4] A factor determining the size of the Indian Council of States was the desire to keep it under half the size of the House of the People, in order that the elected portion of the legislature might ultimately dominate at joint sittings. In the other examples, clearly the intention was to avoid overtaxing the limited supply of experienced legislators.

All these federal second chambers are relatively weaker in constitutional power than their respective popular chambers, and were clearly intended to be so.[5] In each federation the first chamber has had greater power through ultimate predominance in cases of deadlock over ordinary legislation, through the control of finances, and through the responsibility of the cabinet to it. For example, while ordinary central legislation in these federations may be introduced in either house and normally requires passage in both, in cases of deadlock between the two the first chamber has always been given predominant power. In India deadlocks are resolved by a joint sitting, where the House of the People, with more than double the membership of the Council of States, has a clear advantage.[6] The Nigerian, Malayan, Malaysian, and West Indian Senates were merely given power to delay ordinary legislation for six or twelve months.[7] Where money bills are concerned, the initiation of these

---

[1] *Constitution of the W.I. (Amendment) Order in Council, 1960*, s. 19 (a); Cmnd. 1417/1961, para. 10. The revised arrangement was envisaged for the succeeding East Caribbean federation (Cmnd. 1746/1962, para. 14).

[2] Among these were six who had also represented their islands at the pre-federal conferences.

[3] A. G. Byfield (Jamaica) was one of the three senators appointed to the Council of State.

[4] See Tables 11–16, pp. 376–83. The West Indies Senate was less than double the size of the central executive, and smaller than the Nigerian cabinet of 1960.

[5] The Pakistan schemes of 1950 and 1954 (but not that of 1952) proposed, however, equal powers over ordinary legislation, money bills, and control of the executive for the two central chambers. B.P.C., *Interim Report* (1950), para. 39; B.P.C., *Report* (as adopted, 1954), paras. 33, 64 and 81.   [6] Constitution, art. 108.

[7] *Nigeria Constitution, 1954*, s. 66c as inserted by S.I. 1959, no. 1772; *Constitution of*

has been restricted to the first chambers, and as a rule the second chamber may play only an advisory role. Furthermore, while the second chamber is usually represented in the executive, and all cabinet ministers may face questions in the second chamber, the central executive in each of these federations is ultimately responsible only to the popular house.[1]

How effective, then, are these second chambers as guardians of regional interests? In one realm, that of constitutional amendment, they have been given equal constitutional powers with the popular chambers, the approval of the second chamber, voting as a separate house, being required as a rule.[2] The Indian Council of States was also given the exclusive power, upon a two-thirds majority of those voting, to signify the assent of the states to a temporary central invasion of the state legislative list, or to the creation of All-India services common to the Union and the states.[3]

Furthermore, all the second chambers, except the Nigerian Senate,[4] have gained a measure of stability and independence by being unaffected by the dissolution of the popular house. The Indian and the Malayan and Malaysian second chambers were 'permanent bodies', one-third of the Indian Council of States being elected every two years and one-half of the Malayan and Malaysian Senates every three years.[5] The West Indian Senate had a term of five years which was unaffected by the dissolution of the House of Representatives.[6] On the other hand the political authority of the West Indian Senate was undermined by the fact that all its members were nominated, whereas the method of election by regional legislatures gave the other second chambers greater political authority as guardians of regional interests.

Party discipline within the second chamber may, however, significantly affect its role as the guardian of regional interests. In India, for instance, the dominance of Congress in both Union and state elections during the first decade and a half has meant both that party composition within the two central houses has been similar, and that within the Council of States there has been a tendency for party loya ties to override state loyalties. Nevertheless, this has not prevented bitter and violent hostility between the two chambers on occasions, and the Council of States performed an important role in the debate over states reorganization. Neither the Malayan nor the Nigerian Senates have been operating long enough to enable as yet firm conclusions to be drawn on their effectiveness in practice. The first Malayan

---

Nigeria, 1960, s. 59; *Constitution of Nigeria, 1963*, s. 64; *Constitution of Malaya, 1957*, and *Malaysia, 1963*, art. 68 (2); *Constitution of W.I., 1957*, art. 34.

[1] Only in the West Indies was there no provision enabling ministers in the popular chamber to attend meetings of the second chamber.

[2] See Chapter 12, section 4.

[3] Constitution, arts. 249, 312.

[4] *Constitution of Nigeria, 1960*, s. 63, and *1963*, s. 68.

[5] *Constitution of India, 1950*, arts. 83 (1), 85 (2) (*b*) as amended by *First Amendment Act, 1951*, s. 6; *Constitution of Malaya, 1957*, art. 45 (3), Seventh Schedule: ss. 6–7; *Malaysia Act, 1963*, s. 93.　　　　　　　　　　　　　　　[6] Constitution, art. 12 (1).

Senate was overwhelmingly dominated by the Alliance Party, but the debates have suggested a keenness on the part of opposition members to defend state interests, and this may become the distinctive role of the Senate should the hold of the Alliance weaken.[1] In Nigeria, on the other hand, because the regions have been controlled by different parties, party discipline has tended to reinforce regional views, instead of cutting across them.

In any general assessment of their relative effectiveness, it is clear that, like the Senates of Australia and Canada, none of these second chambers has anything like the power, constitutional or political, of the American Senate.[2] The Indian Council of States, because of its method of election, its permanence, and its special constitutional powers, is perhaps potentially the strongest of these, although the lack of regional equality in membership and the dominance to date of the Congress Party have tended to make it a pale reflection of the Lok Sabha. The Nigerian Senate has the most limited constitutional powers. It is not surprising, therefore, that there is little sign that the politicians, administrators, and public take the Senate very seriously, but the equal representation of the regions, combined with the control of different regions by different parties, has occasionally made it a real forum for regional views.[3] The Malayan Senate, due to the present Alliance Party dominance, is an even weaker guardian of states' interests than its slender constitutional powers and large section of nominated members would suggest, while the West Indian Senate, its political status undermined by its method of appointment, and its powers little more than nominal, has been described as representing the constituent islands merely in a 'symbolic way'.[4] Thus, although most of the new federations have found it desirable to add second chambers, in practice these have functioned not as balancing counterparts to the popular chambers, but merely as advisory houses which present regional views, and are able occasionally to check hasty legislation or to veto constitutional amendments.

A unique and interesting institution, which in some of its functions might be described as an upper house, is the Malaysian Conference of Rulers (Majlis Raja Raja). First instituted in 1948 when the Federation of Malaya had a unicameral legislature, it then consisted of the rulers of the nine Malay states attended by their Malay advisers.[5] Its function was to meet the High Commissioner at least three times a year and to consider draft legislation, salary

---

[1] However, the large proportion of nominated senators gives the central government a means by which the resistance of senators elected by opposition parties in the states can to a considerable degree be overcome.

[2] On the Senates of Australia and Canada, see, for instance, Wheare, *Federal Government*, pp. 87–90; R. A. MacKay, *The Unreformed Senate of Canada* (1926, rev. ed. 1963).

[3] B. J. Dudley, 'Focus on the Nigerian Senate', *West Africa* (21 July 1962), p. 787; J. P. Mackintosh, 'The Nigerian Federal Parliament', *Public Law* (1963), pp. 356–9.

[4] Braithwaite, 'Progress Toward Federation, 1938–1956', *Social and Economic Studies*, vi (1957), p. 151.

[5] *Federation of Malaya Agreement, 1948*, cls. 67–76.

schemes, plans for the creation or reorganization of federal departments and services, major changes in immigration policy, and matters of importance concerning the welfare of the states. A Standing Committee of two rulers signified assent to all central bills on behalf of the rulers. The power of the Conference was limited, for in cases of difference with the High Commissioner the rulers were bound to accept his advice, except on matters of Muslim religion and Malay custom, and on immigration policy.[1] The Conference of Rulers thus served some of the functions of an upper house, as a focus for views of the states on central legislation, and some of the functions of a premiers' conference, as a gathering together of the heads of state governments.

Although a Senate was added to the Malayan central legislature in the independence constitution of 1957, the Conference of Rulers was continued.[2] As revised then and subsequently continued in Malaysia, it operates in four forms. First, as a council of the rulers of the nine Malay states acting at their discretion, it is responsible for the election or removal of the monarch and his deputy, for agreeing upon the extension of religious observances and ceremonies, and for consenting to laws affecting the privileges and position of the rulers. Second, as a council of the nine rulers together with the governors of those states not possessing hereditary rulers,[3] acting at their discretion, it is responsible for giving or withholding assent to laws altering state boundaries and for advising on certain appointments. Third, with the same members acting on the advice of their executive councils, the Conference of Rulers gives or withholds consent to laws affecting the special position of the Malays and to certain constitutional amendments. Fourth, as a conference expanded to include the federal Prime Minister and state chief ministers, it may deliberate on matters of national policy and any other matter that it thinks fit. That the Conference of Rulers should continue to play the role, partly of an upper house and partly of a conference of premiers, has been due largely to the weakness of the Senate and to the Malay insistence upon this safeguard of their position.[4]

4. *Dual membership in legislatures*

The traditional statement of the dualistic federal principle, that each government should act directly upon the people and be independent of the other level of government, and the recognition that membership in legislatures at both levels involves a member in conflicting loyalties and responsibilities which militate against his effectiveness in either sphere, have led the United

---

[1] Cl. 8. In cases of disagreement over immigration policy, reference was to be made to the federal Legislative Council. See cl. 72 (3). This gave the Malays a check on immigration policy.

[2] Constitution, art. 38, and Fifth Schedule.

[3] There were governors in Malacca and Penang, and in all three of the new states which joined Malaysia in 1963.   [4] Cmnd. 210/1957, paras. 16–17.

States and the older Commonwealth federations to prohibit dual membership. In the newer federations this example has not always been followed. Under the interim constitutions of India (1947–50) and Pakistan (1947–56) concurrent membership in both provincial and central legislatures was permitted.[1] In Pakistan, for instance, leading political figures performed in both levels of government, and many of the important provincial ministers participated actively in central affairs.[2] In the pre-federal Nigerian constitutions of 1946 and 1951 most of the members were elected by the regional assemblies from among their midst.[3] The Malayan federal Legislative Council (1947–59) included as a special group of members the presidents of the state councils of the nine Malay states and a representative from each of the two settlement councils.[4] In addition, provision was also specifically made to enable Malay officials in the states to serve as unofficial members of the federal legislature.[5] The Malayan independence constitution followed the recommendations of the majority of the Reid Commission in permitting double membership in the federal and state legislatures, although a provision was added requiring a member of a state legislative assembly to resign from that assembly before becoming a central minister.[6] The issue was also a matter of controversy in the West Indies. The S.C.A.C. Report recommended the prohibition of dual membership in federal and territorial legislatures, the 1953 London Conference suggested that it be permitted for the first five years, and in the end the 1956 Conference reverted to the S.C.A.C. proposals.[7]

There were a number of reasons why the permission of dual membership was contemplated or adopted in these cases. A major argument was that in a developing country the prohibition of dual membership might deprive regional legislatures of members with suitable experience. A second argument often advanced was that dual membership would provide useful contacts between federal and regional legislatures and minimize conflict between the two levels of government. Furthermore, in India and Pakistan the arrangement was strictly an interim one, designed to ensure that the central legislature in its capacity as a constituent assembly should be fully representative of regional views.

Despite the arguments advanced in its favour, experience in federations

[1] The *Constitution of Pakistan, 1956*, art. 79 (1), prohibited dual membership, but except in the case of provincial governors (art. 70 (5)), this did not apply before the first election (art. 225 (4)), and therefore had not gone into effect before the end of constitutional government in 1958.

[2] In the first Constituent Assembly, three out of the four provincial chief ministers, as well as a number of lesser provincial ministers, were members of the Assembly. The rulers of Las Bela and Swat were also MCA's. The second Constituent Assembly at its first meeting included 2 governors, 9 provincial ministers, 2 rulers of states, and 1 minister of state government.

[3] S.I. 1946, no. 1370, s. 8; S.I. 1951, no. 1172, ss. 71–73.

[4] Federation Agreement, 1948, cls. 38, 42 (3) (*i*) (*j*).   [5] Cl. 40 proviso.

[6] Art. 43 (8); Col. no. 330/1957, para. 61, and p. 35. This arrangement continues in Malaysia.   [7] Constitution, arts. 11, 12 (*c*, *d*), 22, 23 (*c*, *d*).

permitting dual membership has generally indicated that this arrangement is unsatisfactory. Indeed in India, Pakistan, and Nigeria it was abandoned, and the arrangement continues only in Malaysia.[1] In Pakistan, where dual membership was permitted for eleven years, its unfortunate effects were clearest. Provincial and central political life became closely entangled, and this resulted in chronic instability of governments at both levels. The presence of provincial ministers in the central assembly meant that a high proportion of its members found themselves with public interests which took precedence over their loyalty to and attendance at the House, and this in Callard's view was 'undoubtedly one of the reasons for the weakness of the Constituent Assembly'.[2] In Nigeria too, dual membership strengthened regional partisanship in the central legislature, leading critics to argue that only by ending this arrangement would they 'avoid the possibility of conflicting loyalties amongst members of the central legislature'.[3] The chronic lack of cohesiveness in the central legislature under the Macpherson constitution led in 1954 to the abandonment not only of the method of indirect election but of dual membership.[4] In both Pakistan and Nigeria, where the regional units and the federations were large, double membership placed a particularly heavy load on legislators, but in the much smaller states of Malaya and Malaysia double membership has not imposed so heavy a burden. Although the territorial units in the West Indies were small, dual membership was rejected on the grounds that it would have violated the fundamental federal principle, so unequivocally advocated in the S.C.A.C. Report, that the central legislature must be independent of the territorial legislatures.[5] West Indian commentators have supported this decision on the grounds that dual membership would have weakened the federal structure further by dividing the loyalties of central legislators, and have argued that the prohibition of dual membership enhanced the prestige of the central legislature by making membership a fulltime activity.[6]

The experiences of those federations experimenting with dual membership indicate that its effects have usually been highly undesirable, but it must be recognized that the cure, the prohibition of dual membership, can only be obtained at a price. In both the West Indian and Rhodesian cases the

---

[1] *Constitution of India, 1950,* art. 101 (2); *Constitution of Pakistan, 1956,* art. 79; *Constitution of Pakistan, 1962,* art. 105; *Nigeria Constitution, 1954,* ss. 10 (1) (*f*) (*g*), 14 (*d*); *Constitution of Nigeria, 1960,* ss. 44 (1) (*a*) (*d*), 81 (5), and *1963,* ss. 49 (1) (*a*) (*d*), 87 (5). Even in Malaysia, central ministers, the President of the Senate, and the Speaker of the House of Representatives must give up their membership in state legislatures. Constitution, 1957, art. 43 (8), and *Constitution (Amendment) Act, 1960* (F. 10/1960), ss. 6, 8, 9.

[2] Callard, *Pakistan, A Political Study,* p. 83.

[3] *Proceedings of General Conference* (1950), p. 174.

[4] Constitution, 1954, ss. 10 (1) (*f*) (*g*), 14 (*d*).

[5] Col. no. 255/1950, para. 49.

[6] Braithwaite, 'Progress Toward Federation, 1938–1956', op. cit., p. 154; Lewis, 'W.I. Federation: The Constitutional Aspects', op. cit., pp. 223–4.

prohibition did in fact deprive some of the legislatures of their most promising parliamentarians by forcing them to choose between legislatures. In the West Indies the able men in the larger islands were unwilling to give up island politics for central politics, while the smaller territories, on the other hand, lost many of their best men, both trends adding a further strain to the fragile federation.[1] In Rhodesia and Nyasaland the eagerness of politicians to 'go federal' left Southern Rhodesia without a single cabinet minister.[2] But in Southern Rhodesia, as in Nigeria, the migration of parliamentarians to the central legislature did not prove disastrous, for it did lead to the discovery of highly suitable replacements. Even in the Caribbean, despite their experience, the planners of a new federation of the small eastern islands decided to prohibit dual membership.[3]

5. The locality rule

Since the strength of regional sentiment was a factor in the creation of federal institutions, there has often been pressure for the restriction of seats to residents of the constituency or region they represent. Nevertheless, such requirements have not usually been specified in constitutions. Of the popular chambers, the Nigerian House of Representatives, 1954–9, was the sole example where candidates were required to be locally registered as electors.[4] When Singapore joined Malaysia the position with regard to the central representatives from that state was similar, however, since Singapore citizenship was a qualification.[5] For most of the other popular chambers, citizenship and a certain age were the only qualifications specified, although in Pakistan under the 1956 constitution, in the West Indies Federation, and in the Federation of Rhodesia and Nyasaland, a period of residence within the federation was also specified.[6] In the case of the second chambers, whcih are meant to represent the regions, it was only in the West Indies, where senators were not elected by territorial legislatures, that it was considered necessary to specify that they should be residents of the territory they represented.[7]

But, although rarely specified in the constitution, the convention that candidates for the central legislature should be local residents has already

---

[1] In the first Senate alone, of 19 senators, 7 had transferred directly from island legislatures, and 4 directly from island executive councils.

[2] Franck, *Race and Nationalism*, p. 315.

[3] Cmnd. 1746/1962, para. 13.

[4] Constitution, 1954, s. 8 (3), until amended by S.I. 1959, no. 1772.

[5] *Malaysia Act, 1963*, s. 31.

[6] *Constitution of Pakistan, 1956*, arts. 45 (1), 143; *Constitution of W.I., 1957*, art. 20 (c); R. and N., Cmnd. 1149/1960, p. 7. Cf. residence requirements in Malaya (1957, art. 47) and Pakistan (1962, arts. 103, 157). The Constitutions of Nigeria, s. 39 (c) in 1960, and s. 44 (b) in 1963, did limit candidates in predominantly Muslim Northern Nigeria to males. In India the *Constitution (Sixteenth Amendment) Act, 1963*, disqualified as candidates advocates of secession. Under the Pakistan constitution of 1962, art. 173, until the passage of the *Political Parties Act* (iii/1962), members of political parties were disqualified.

[7] Constitution, art. 9 (c).

grown quite strong in most of the new federations. In the West Indies, Nigeria, Rhodesia and Nyasaland, and Malaya, successful candidates have normally been local men. In Malaya, for instance, between 1955 and 1960, all except two cabinet ministers represented states in which they had been born and had also spent their careers.[1] Island parochialism was too strong in the West Indies for the territories to be represented by other than their own residents at any time. In the 1958 Rhodesia and Nyasaland elections some candidates ran in seats in which they were not resident and three of these were successful, but only one candidate crossed territorial boundaries to contest the election, and he came at the bottom of the poll.[2] Cabinet ministers all represented their own localities. The Nigerian federal elections of 1959 indicated that it was difficult for candidates to get elected in any except their own locality, except perhaps in cosmopolitan Lagos. There were, however, some cases of outsiders being accepted as candidates provided they ran for the party of the locally dominant tribal group.[3] In India the convention is not quite as strong, although it does exert an influence which is likely to grow with the increasing linguistic consciousness of the states.[4] Examples of ministers who were exceptions to the convention were M. A. K. Azad, originally from Calcutta but who held seats in Uttar Pradesh (1953) and Punjab (1957), and Krishna Menon, a southerner, who held a Bombay seat in 1957 and 1962. In Pakistan during the period from 1947 to the suspension of the constitution in 1958, in spite of strong provincial loyalties, members frequently sat for provinces other than those of their origin. Many of these were refugees from Uttar Pradesh, Bombay, or other parts of Hindu India, but a number held seats in provinces other than their own simply from political expediency.[5] It is significant, however, that in East Bengal such ministers were usually regarded as inadequate champions of regional interests.

6. *The control of franchise and electoral laws*

The question whether electoral laws should be uniform or vary from region to region has arisen in most of these federations. On the one hand, if they are uniform, they may be unsuitable for varying conditions. For instance, regions which are more advanced politically, like the southern Nigerian regions, Jamaica and Trinidad, East Bengal, the former Governor's provinces in

[1] Of the two exceptions, Bahaman bin Samsudin represented Perak 1955 (where he had been District Officer), and Negri Sembilan 1959 (where he was born), and Abdul Aziz bin Ishak, born in Perak, but with a career in Selangor, represented the latter state.

[2] *Central African Examiner* (8 and 22 November 1958).

[3] For instance, John Umolu (Benin) in Port Harcourt, Umoru Altine (Fulani) in Enugu, T. O. S. Benson (Yoruba) in an Ibo Lagos constituency. On the choice of candidates, see K. W. J. Post, *The Nigerian Federal Elections of 1959* (1963), ch. vii, esp. pp. 254–60.

[4] For the effect of regional linguistic consciousness and local caste pressures on national candidates, see Harrison, *India, the Most Dangerous Decades*, chs. 3, 4, 6, 7, esp. pp. 109, 200–4.

[5] Callard, *Pakistan, A Political Study*, pp. 82, 177 note 3, 342–4.

India, the Malayan settlements, and Singapore, have demanded wider and more democratic franchises than were considered appropriate by Northern Nigeria, the smaller West Indian islands, the acceding princely states of India and Pakistan, the northern Malay states, or the Malaysian Borneo territories respectively. Varying social conditions may result in similar conflicts. The Muslims of Northern Nigeria were particularly opposed to women being given the vote; the caste Hindus, concentrated in East Pakistan, opposed separate electorates as designed to discriminate against them; the larger settler population of Southern Rhodesia opposed the election there of any Africans by other than an electoral roll dominated by Europeans; and the northern Malay states were particularly keen to limit the strength of the Chinese vote. In some of these cases, therefore, strong arguments have been mounted in favour either of regional control of central electoral laws, or of central laws specifying non-uniform franchises, at least for a temporary period until the politically less-advanced regions have been able to catch up with the others. The examples of the United States and Canada, which started without uniform electoral laws but progressed to a common central electoral law, served as models in this respect. On the other hand, more radical nationalists have sometimes feared that regional control of central electoral laws might provide an indirect means by which conservative regional governments could control the radical temper of a central government.[1] They have often argued, therefore, that it is undemocratic to count votes differently in different regions, or that it is a violation of 'the federal principle' that an aspect of the central political structure should be under regional control.

In actual practice, franchise and electoral laws for the central legislature have, in the end, usually been placed under central control. Apart from a few constitutional requirements specifying adult franchise for citizens, electoral laws in India and Malaya were simply left to the central Parliament.[2] In Nigeria[3] and Pakistan[4] control of central electoral laws was also given to the central legislature. But in both these countries, because of varying regional conditions, different franchises or electoral systems have been applied to different regions. In the Nigerian federal elections of 1954, members of the House of Representatives were elected in the Eastern Region by universal adult franchise, in the Western Region on a tax suffrage of males, and in the Northern Region by an indirect electoral college system based on a tax suffrage of males. The 1957 constitutional conference agreed upon a universal

---

[1] For instance, the N.C.N.C. demand for uniform federal electoral laws was prompted in large measure by fear that the system of multiple electoral colleges would enable the N.P.C. to keep out radical candidates in Northern Nigeria.

[2] *Constitution of India, 1950*, arts. 326–7; *Constitution of Malaya, 1957*, arts. 113, 119, and also 14–31, and Federal List, items 5, 6 (*a*). The *Malaysia Act, 1963*, s. 31, introduced a separate franchise based on Singapore citizenship, for that state.

[3] Constitution, 1954, s. 8 (1); Constitution, 1960, ss. 46–47; Constitution, 1963, ss. 51–52.

[4] Constitution, 1956, arts. 144–5; Constitution, 1962, art. 157, and Third Sched., item 35.

adult franchise in the south and adult male suffrage in the Northern Region, and this was the arrangement used in the 1959 federal elections.[1] In Pakistan the controversy was over joint or separate electorates, and when the ruling coalition in the Constituent Assembly was unable to reach agreement, the decision was left in 1956 to the National Assembly in consultation with the provincial assemblies.[2] Subsequently, the National Assembly, amidst scenes of riot and confusion, passed in October 1956 an electoral law providing for a joint electorate in East Pakistan and separate electorates in West Pakistan.[3] Later, however, the electoral law was amended in 1957 to provide a joint electorate for the whole country.[4]

Control of central electoral laws and franchise in the West Indies and in Rhodesia and Nyasaland was also assigned to the central legislature, but territorial laws were used for the first central elections.[5] It was argued that otherwise considerable time would be required before the new electoral rolls could be prepared. Moreover, neither of these federations was preceded by a pre-federal central legislature or constituent assembly which could make the necessary laws.

In Rhodesia and Nyasaland central franchise and electoral law has been one of the most controversial issues of all. The use by the central government in 1957–8 of its powers over electoral laws and constitutional amendment to extend an electoral system dominated by Europeans to the election of the newly added 'elected African members' became a major constitutional controversy. Because of the resulting loss of African confidence in the Federal Assembly, the Monckton Commission was led to suggest franchise qualifications varying from territory to territory to avoid disqualifying northern territorial voters from voting in central elections,[6] but by then the damage was irreparable.

7. *The central executive*

Among the older federations there was little uniformity in the organization of the central executives. The American Presidency and the Swiss Federal Council, although otherwise possessing few characteristics in common, are both fixed-term executives, while Canada and Australia have both evolved parliamentary forms of government based upon the responsibility of the executive to the legislature. By comparison with this striking diversity of form, only Pakistan and to a lesser degree Nigeria among the six new federations

---

[1] Cmnd. 207/1957, para. 33.   [2] Constitution, art. 145.
[3] *Electorate Act* (36/1956).   [4] *Electorate (Amendment) Act* (19/1957).
[5] *Constitution of W.I., 1957*, ss. 17–18, 107; the delimitation of territories into constituencies was, however, permanently left to territorial law (s. 19). *Constitution of R. and N., 1953*, arts. 10–12; regulations governing the elections of specially elected African members or the nomination of European members for African interests were made by territorial governors, however (arts. 9, 13).
[6] Cmnd. 1148/1960, paras. 108–10.

seriously considered any other form of executive than parliamentary cabinet government.[1] Although there were advocates in India of a separate and fixed executive on the American or Swiss model, the debates indicated a clear preference in the Constituent Assembly for an executive responsible to the popular legislative house.[2] In Malaya, the West Indies, and Rhodesia and Nyasaland, the eventual establishment of cabinets responsible to the legislature was virtually never questioned. When the Nigerians agreed that a republican form of government should be introduced, opinion divided along two lines: one school of thought favoured a constitutional president acting, as in India, in accordance with the advice of a council of ministers; the other school of thought favoured an executive president modelled on the examples of the United States, France, or Ghana. In the end, however, the former view prevailed, because it 'would involve the minimum amount of change from the existing constitutional framework'.[3] In the different federations there have been variations in the degree to which executive responsibility to the legislature and the Head of State's obligation to follow cabinet advice were either actually written into the constitution or were left to convention, but the general principles of a parliamentary form of executive were adopted in each. Even in Pakistan the second Constituent Assembly decided in favour of a parliamentary executive, and it was not until 1962 that a presidential executive separated from the legislature was formally specified in a constitution.

Why has the model of Britain and the older Commonwealth countries been so consistently followed in the new federations? The simplest explanation is that colonial politicians, educated in British political history, living in the milieu of British institutions, and with the precedent of progress to self-government and independence through the evolution of parliamentary government in the older Commonwealth countries before them, have simply become 'accustomed' to expecting the British type of constitution with which they are familiar. Thus, the chairman of the Drafting Committee of the Indian Constituent Assembly contrasted the criteria of stability and responsibility on which the U.S. and British executives were respectively based, and declared that the Committee had 'preferred more responsibility to more stability'.[4] To colonial politicians there was the further incentive that such a political form was more likely to inspire British confidence and, therefore, willingness to hand over power. Cabinet government has also been justified because of its flexibility, enabling adaptation to varying circumstances, especially with regard to the representation of different elements in plural societies.

---

[1] Before independence there were usually certain limitations upon full responsible cabinet government. These were recognized, however, as transitional stages in the progress towards an executive fully responsible for all actions to the legislature. For a study of colonial executives, see H. V. Wiseman, *The Cabinet in the Commonwealth* (1958).

[2] C.A.I., *Debates*, vol. iv, pp. 632–56, 734, 827, 907–21; vol. vii, pp. 32–33, 956–67, 998, 1185; vol. ix, pp. 1036, 1659; vol. x, p. 269.

[3] Sessional Paper 3/1963, para. 3.   [4] C.A.I., *Debates*, vol. vii, p. 33.

The decision to fit together a British parliamentary system and federal organization has had significant effects on the federal institutions in these countries. Indeed, Patrick Gordon Walker has suggested that this combination in the Commonwealth federations—Canada, Australia, and the new federations—represents a distinctive and radical departure in the theory and practice of federalism.[1] The nature of the second chambers, the role of the supreme courts, and the constitutional relations between the two levels of government have all been affected. The second chambers for instance, while based on a regional composition, are all much weaker than the American Senate because of the emphasis upon executive responsibility to the popular house. There are supreme courts umpiring the federal system, but these, following the British rather than the American tradition, have regarded themselves primarily as courts of law, leaving the legislatures to make the law.[2] The attempt to combine elements of the parliamentary system, which in the British model was based on unitary government, together with federal institutions also helps to explain the presence of many 'quasi-federal'— partly federal and partly unitary—features in these federations which do not fit neatly into either of the traditional norms of unitary or federal government typified by Britain and the United States.[3]

Only in Pakistan was a presidential form of fixed executive adopted, and then only after a decade of unstable parliamentary cabinets. The reports of the Basic Principles Committee in the first Constituent Assembly had envisaged cabinets responsible to one or both of the federal legislative houses, although there was some opposition from those who favoured the presidential system as likely to produce a more stable government, and from those who thought such a form more compatible with a full-fledged Islamic state.[4] After the dissolution of the Assembly the need for strong and stable government led the ruling group to consider 'a Constitution in which the American idea of an executive irremoveable for four years was grafted on to a British system of representation'.[5] The plan was dropped, however, because it could not be assumed that the conventions accepted in the United States for solving conflicts between the executive and the legislature would develop in Pakistan, and because the elections to the second Constituent Assembly resulted in a majority distrusting any concentration of power in the Head of State. Instead, the Assembly insisted that the 1956 constitution should elaborate the functions of the cabinet and make it clear that the President would act usually on cabinet advice.[6] But while the executive was supposedly responsible to the

---

[1] Patrick Gordon Walker, 'Federalism in the Commonwealth', *Journal of the Parliaments of the Commonwealth*, xlii (1961), pp. 351–9.

[2] See Chapter 12, section 3.   [3] See Chapter 10.

[4] B.P.C., *Interim Report* (1950), para. 25; B.P.C., *Report* (1952), paras. 12, 23, 27–35, 59–60; B.P.C., *Report* (as adopted, 1954), paras. 14, 26, 30–38, 64–67.

[5] W. I. Jennings, *The Approach to Self-Government* (1958), p. 18.

[6] *Constitution of Pakistan, 1956*, art. 37 (7).

legislature, in practice through most of the period 1947–58, first because of Jinnah's dominance, and later as a result of the confused multi-party situation, the Governor-Generals and the President often dominated their cabinets. Thus, instead of the legislature controlling the ministry, the legislature often functioned under the guidance of the ministry.[1] Finally, in October 1958, responsible cabinet government disappeared altogether with the suspension of the constitution and the imposition of presidential rule and martial law.

When constitutional government was restored in 1962, it was felt that in the light of Pakistan's previous experience the prime need was for a stable and firm government. A presidential executive separated from the legislative body and in some respects modelled on the American example was therefore established.[2] Ministers were responsible not to the legislature but to the President; they had the right to attend the National Assembly but could not be members of it.[3] In order to reduce the chances of conflict between the Assembly and the President, and to prevent paralysis of the administration, a system of checks and balances together with special legislative and financial procedures to overcome deadlocks was laid down.[4] Nevertheless, during the first year of the new constitution, relations between the President and the National Assembly proved stormy, and the President was forced to make a number of concessions.

When we turn to examine the membership of central executives, we find that, because the role of the central executive is so important, there have been pressures for adequate representation of regional interests there as well as in the legislature. These demands have been present in all the new federations, but they have been most acute where regional voices in the legislature were weakened by the absence of second chambers, as in Nigeria, 1954–9, and Pakistan, 1947–58. Most constitution-makers have recognized and even stressed the importance of balanced regional representation in the executive. Nevertheless, as a rule they have preferred to leave this to convention, in order not to restrict the flexibility implicit in the cabinet system.

Of the six new federations under consideration, only in Nigeria was any attempt made to specify in the constitution itself the regional composition of the executive council, and these provisions were removed in 1957.[5] The 1954

---

[1] See Callard, *Pakistan, A Political Study*, ch. 4; M. Ahmad, *Government and Politics in Pakistan* (1959), chs. 1, 2, 6; Sayeed, *Pakistan, the Formative Phase*, chs. 7–9, 15.

[2] Constitution, 1962, arts. 31–36, 104; *Report of the Constitution Commission, Pakistan, 1961* (1962), chs. iii, vi, viii.

[3] Arts. 25, 104. When the President later tried to make it possible for ministers to be members of the National Assembly by issuing the *Removal of Difficulties (Appointment of Ministers) Order* (Order 34/1962), the Supreme Court ruled the order *ultra vires*. (*Fazlul Quader Chowdhury and others* v. *Muhammad Abdul Haque*, P.L.D. 1963, S.C. 486.)

[4] Constitution, arts. 19, 22–30, 37–48, 209.

[5] *Nigeria Constitution, 1954*, s. 88. Each state in the Federation of South Arabia is con-

constitution stipulated that besides the Governor-General presiding, there were to be ten ministers, three from each of the regions and one from the Southern Cameroons, appointed from the House of Representatives.[1] It was agreed in advance, although not specified in the constitution, that these ministers would be appointed by the Governor-General on the recommendation of the leader of the party with an overall majority in the House, or, if there were no overall majority, on the recommendations of the leaders of the majority parties from each region within the House of Representatives.[2] Since no party succeeded in gaining an overall majority in the federal elections of 1954, the Northern People's Congress nominated the three Northern ministers, and the N.C.N.C., with fewer total members in the House but a majority of the federal seats in each of the two southern regions, gained the right to nominate six ministers. This arrangement fostered regional outlooks within the Council, and hindered the development of a politically homogeneous executive. This weakness was accentuated by the preference of the major party leaders to remain as regional premiers, leaving the central Council of Ministers ineffective and despised, the cats-paw and scapegoat of the regional leaders. Finally in 1957, when the office of Prime Minister with power to nominate his own cabinet was established, the rigidity of constitutional requirements for regional representation in the Council was removed, although the Southern Cameroons was promised at least one minister.[3]

In the other federations, although there have been no constitutional stipulations, in practice some attempt has been made to represent all the major regions and to balance the representation of major areas.[4] The Indian cabinet has fairly consistently included ministers from Uttar Pradesh, Bombay and after 1960 Gujarat and Maharashtra, the south (usually Madras and Mysore), Bihar, Punjab, and West Bengal. In Pakistan the four former Governor's provinces, East Bengal, Punjab, Sind, and the North-West Frontier Province, were always represented in the cabinet, even after the unification of West Pakistan, and considerable attention was paid to the balance betwen East Bengal and the Punjab and between East and West Pakistan. The major Malayan states, Perak, Selangor, Johore, Kedah, and Pahang, have always had members in the cabinet, and there has been a fairly constant ratio between ministers from the former Federated and Unfederated Malay States. Since 1958 the former Straits Settlements have also been represented. In Nigeria after 1957 all the regions and Lagos (and the Southern Cameroons

stitutionally entitled to one minister for every six representatives in the Federal Council. (Constitution, 1963, s. 8 (2)).
    [1] S. 88.   [2] Cmd. 8934/1953, para. 15.
    [3] *Nigeria Constitution, 1954*, s. 88, as amended by S.I. 1957, no. 1530, and S.I. 1959, nos. 1049, 1772; Cmnd. 207/1957, para. 36 (d)(e).
    [4] The following comments on regional representation in executives are based on Tables 11: 7–12, in R. L. Watts, *Recent Experiments in Federalism in Commonwealth Countries, a comparative analysis* (Oxford, D.Phil. thesis, 1962), vol. ii.

while in the federation) have had representatives in the cabinet. Likewise, the Rhodesia and Nyasaland cabinet always included ministers from each of the three territories. In the first West Indies council of ministers, all except three of the ten territories were represented, ministers being distributed among the major areas to give Jamaica two, Trinidad one, Barbados two, the Windwards three, and the Leewards three.

In addition, the central executive has usually been constructed to give minorities within regions representation also. The Indian cabinet, for instance, has consistently contained a Muslim, a member of the Scheduled Castes, a Sikh (from Punjab), and on some occasions a Jain or a Christian as well. The first Pakistan cabinet contained a Hindu, but after his defection to India no Hindus were appointed until, during the second Constituent Assembly, the convention quickly grew that the East Bengal representation in the cabinet should include a Hindu.[1] In Malaya the importance of racial balance in the cabinet has been clear at several levels. The composition of the cabinet as a whole was six Malays, three Chinese, and one Indian between 1955 and 1958, but in 1958 the number of Malays was increased to nine. Cabinet representation for Perak and Selangor, where the Chinese and Indian communities are particularly strong, has been divided quite consistently between the Malayan Chinese Association and the Malayan Indian Congress in Perak, and the M.C.A. and the United Malays National Organization in Selangor. In Nigeria during 1954–60, the Middle Belt and Mid-West were each represented in the cabinet, while the Calabar-Ogoja-Rivers area had ministers for some of that period.[2] The enlarged cabinet of 1960 also enabled ten of the twelve provinces within the Northern Region to be represented in the cabinet.[3] The first West Indian Council of State gave St. Kitts–Nevis, with 1·9 per cent. of the total federal population, two ministers so that St. Kitts and Nevis might be represented by separate ministers, and also gave representation to the French cultural background of St. Lucia. No attempt was made, however, to give the East Indian community of Trinidad representation in the cabinet, since it had largely supported the federal opposition party. In 1958 for the first time an African was made a Parliamentary Secretary in Rhodesia and Nyasaland, but the circumstances of the appointment did little to satisfy the Africans of the northern territories where African separatism was strongest.[4]

Second chambers have sometimes provided a means for representing regions or minority groups within the executive. Nomination to the Nigerian Senate, for example, was used after the 1959 elections to bring defeated candidates

---

[1] In some governments there were two Hindus, one representing the Scheduled Castes and the other the Caste Hindus.

[2] The Middle Belt minister for most of the period was, however, Alhaji Muhammadu Ribadu, a Fulani aristocrat.

[3] The Tiv, who voted solidly for the Action Group, remained unrepresented, however, as also did Kabba Province.

[4] See C. Sanger, *Central African Emergency* (1960), pp. 123–31.

for the House of Representatives into the cabinet to represent the Ibibio-Efik of Calabar in Eastern Nigeria, and Zaria Province in the Northern Region, both otherwise unrepresented in the cabinet. The third senator in the cabinet strengthened its Yoruba membership. In the West Indies senators were used in the first Council of State to strengthen Jamaican representation, because of the opposition's electoral success in Jamaica, and to provide a balanced St. Kitts–Nevis membership. In Malaya in 1959 the M.C.A. proportion in the cabinet as a whole and in the representation of Perak in the cabinet was maintained by the appointment of a nominated senator to the cabinet. The Indian second chamber has provided at various times representatives for Mysore, West Bengal, and Uttar Pradesh, and for the Muslim community.

While an attempt has usually been made to represent a relatively balanced variety of regional interests in these federal executives, nevertheless, with the exception of the West Indies, those regions with the most populous electorates have still tended to predominate, and the smallest regions have often gone unrepresented or under-represented. In India, for instance, the two largest states, Uttar Pradesh and Bombay, have at times held between them a majority of the cabinet seats, while southern India and the former princely states have been relatively under-represented.[1] In Pakistan, Baluchistan and the acceding states received no representation in most cabinets during the whole 1947–58 period. Similarly, between 1955 and 1960 the north-eastern Malayan states, Perlis, and Penang had no ministers in the central cabinet, while the four most populous states, totalling 62 per cent. of the federal population, held amongst them 9 out of 10 and later 10 out of 13 of the cabinet seats.[2]

Federations with single regions containing a majority of the federal electorate create a special problem. In some cases the proportional representation of the largest region has been sharply reduced. Jamaica, with over half the West Indian population and two out of eleven of the Council of State seats, was the most extreme example. Indeed, this was one of the major sources of Jamaican dissatisfaction with the federation.[3] Elsewhere, such regions have eventually insisted upon at least half the ministerial posts. In the first Pakistan Constituent Assembly, East Bengal, despite holding 44 of the 79 Assembly seats, never provided more than one-third of the full cabinet ministers, but in the second Constituent Assembly, because of Bengali resentment at previous under-representation, an attempt, not always effective, was made in most cabinets to apply the principle of parity of membership for East and West

---

[1] See R. C. North, 'The Indian Council of Ministers: A Study of Origins', in R. L. Park and I. Tinker (eds.), *Leadership and Political Institutions in India* (1959), pp. 107–8; Brecher, *Nehru*, p. 450.

[2] The lack of cabinet representation in the north-eastern states after 1959 may in part have been due to the electoral success of the opposition P.M.I.P. in Trengganu and Kelantan, but this was itself in part the result of earlier neglect and under-representation of these states in the central government.

[3] Premier Manley quoted in *The Times* (London, 3 April 1961).

Pakistan.[1] In the Nigerian 'national' government 1957-9, the three regions were more or less equally represented, even though the Northern Region had 54 per cent. of the federal population and 50 per cent. of the House of Representatives seats. After 1959, however, within the N.P.C.–N.C.N.C. coalition cabinet, the members from the Northern Region commanded a bare majority over the N.C.N.C. ministers representing the southern regions and Lagos.[2] In Rhodesia and Nyasaland, unlike the other federations, the territory with the largest electorate, Southern Rhodesia, held the majority of cabinet seats right from the first elections in 1953. But this predominance was a major factor contributing to the distrust of the other territories.

As in Canada and Australia, it was the larger, indeed often the largest, regions that provided the first national prime ministers. For instance, the first prime ministers of India, Pakistan, Nigeria, and Rhodesia and Nyasaland all held constituencies in the largest regions of these federations, while in Malaya, Tunku Abdul Rahman represented Kedah, a major state. In Pakistan, of the seven federal prime ministers between 1947 and 1958, four held East Bengal seats and three Punjab seats, showing the clear ascendancy in central politics of the two largest provinces. It was only in the West Indies that the larger territories failed to provide the early leadership in central politics. Because neither Premier Manley of Jamaica nor Premier Williams of Trinidad were willing to enter federal politics, the mantle of central Prime Minister fell upon Sir Grantley Adams of Barbados. Premier Manley apparently felt that by remaining in Jamaican politics he could best defend the cause of federation against its local critics. The subsequent Jamaican disenchantment with federation suggests that if Manley had taken the risk of going into central politics in order to provide Jamaican leadership there, Jamaicans might have felt they had a stake in the federation, instead of regarding it as an imposition.

8. *The Head of State*

Although the adoption of a parliamentary executive in most of the new federations has meant that the powers of the Heads of State were largely nominal, nevertheless, their role has not been unimportant. In the first place, it has usually been the intention that the Head of State should function as a focus for federal unity. Secondly, the Head of State has usually possessed some discretionary powers in the appointment of the Prime Minister or the dissolution of the central legislature; powers which, as experience in Pakistan has shown, become more important when there is no stable majority in the legislature. Moreover, in India, unlike the other federations, since the binding

[1] For instance, after the formation of the Noon government in December 1957, there were prolonged negotiations in an effort to give East Pakistan parity of membership in the cabinet, resulting in the addition of two East Pakistan members in January and February 1958. See *Dawn* (December 1957–February 1958).

[2] In relation ot the Eastern Region and Lagos, the Western Region was relatively underrepresented because it was the area in which the federal opposition, the Action Group, had had the greatest success.

nature of cabinet advice is left completely to convention, the constitutional powers of the President are potentially considerable.[1] In some of the other federations, the Head of State has also been assigned some additional specific discretionary powers, usually to make 'non-political' appointments.[2] The method of appointment, therefore, is of some significance.

The federations possessing colonial status, Nigeria (1954–60), the West Indies (1957–62), and Rhodesia and Nyasaland (1953–63), had Governor-Generals, or in the case of Malaya (1948–57), a High Commissioner. Appointment in these cases was by the United Kingdom Government, thus placing these officials as external arbiters over central politics. Their authority usually included considerable legislative and executive powers, although the constitutional extent of these and their use varied with the proximity of independence.

Most of the new independent federations have initially had Governor-Generals appointed by the Crown. Under the interim constitutions of India (1947–50) and Pakistan (1947–56) there were Governor-Generals with considerable constitutional power, appointed on the recommendation of the central government.[3] In Pakistan, because of the considerable power of the Governor-General, there grew during the life of the first Constituent Assembly an insistence that, if one of the two top offices of Prime Minister or Governor-General went to East Pakistan, the other should be given to the west. But this emerging convention became inoperative during the life of the second Constituent Assembly when, in spite of Bengali protests, three of the four Prime Ministers held Punjabi seats, as had Iskander Mirza before becoming Governor-General (1955–6) and President (1956–8).[4] The experience of Pakistan, with four Prime Ministers and four Governor-Generals in the period 1947–56, illustrates clearly the difficulties of trying to achieve a division of the two main posts between East and West Pakistanis at a time when changes of ministry were frequent. Nor did this compromise succeed in allaying Bengali fears, for whether as Governor-General or as Prime Minister, the Bengali in each pairing always seemed to emerge as subordinate, first to former U.P. men, 1947–51, and then to Punjabis, 1951–8. In Nigeria, the other independent federation with a Governor-General, he was given much less real political power.[5] Nevertheless, after independence the two positions of Prime Minister and Governor-General were divided between the central

---

[1] See Alexandrowicz, *Constitutional Developments in India*, pp. 127–40; A. Gledhill, *The Republic of India* (1951), pp. 107–9; B. A. V. Sharma and N. M. Valecha, 'The Indian President', *The Political Quarterly*, xxxiii (1962), pp. 59–73; K. L. Panjabi, *Rajendra Prasad, First President of India* (1960), pp. 160–7, 187–91, 203–5.

[2] *Constitution of Pakistan, 1956*, arts. 137, 142, 186; *Constitution of Malaya, 1957*, arts. 40, 122 (3), 139 (4), 140 (2) (c); *Constitution of Nigeria, 1960*, s. 86 (1) (d), and *1963*, s. 93 (1) (d).   [3] *Indian Independence Act, 1947*, ss. 5, 8, 9.

[4] C.A.P. (second), *Debates*, vol. i, pp. 683–5. See *Dawn* (13 August 1955), regarding Mr. Suhrawardy's protest at the first failure to observe the developing convention.

[5] *Constitution of Nigeria, 1960*, s. 86.

leaders of the two parties in the coalition, as part of the political compromise which followed the 1959 federal election. It would seem that the temptation to use the position of Governor-General to obtain a 'political' compromise is difficult to resist.

All three of these independent federations, India in 1950, Pakistan in 1956, and Nigeria in 1963, decided to adopt a republican form in which parliamentary cabinet government was retained, but the Governor-Generals were replaced by elected Presidents. There was considerable discussion in the Indian Constituent Assembly concerning the appropriate method of election for the President. Direct popular election was rejected because of its expense and because of the desire to 'emphasize the ministerial character of the Government', while election by the Union Parliament was opposed as likely to make the President a 'dummy' of the party in power in the Union Parliament.[1] Instead, the President is elected for a five-year term by an electoral college consisting of members of both Houses of the Union Parliament and the elected members of the state legislative assemblies, the votes being weighted by a formula giving the Union and state legislatures parity and making the voting strength of each state legislator proportionate to the population he represents.[2] Some Constituent Assembly members advocated rotating the Presidency between north and south or between former British India and the acceding states in order to promote a harmony of feeling, but the representatives of northern and central India rejected such rotation as likely to encourage centrifugal tendencies.[3] It is significant, however, that in the first elections the Presidency and the Vice-Presidency were divided between a northerner and a southerner. When Dr. Prasad retired he was succeeded as President by Dr. Radhakrishnan, the former Vice-President, thus initiating what may become a convention of rotating the Presidency between men from the north and the south. Significantly, the new Vice-President, Dr. Hussan, was a Muslim northerner.

When Nigeria decided that the Governor-General should be replaced by a President exercising largely the same constitutional powers, a method of election differing somewhat from that in India was adopted. Presidents were to be elected for five-year terms by an electoral college consisting of all the members of both central houses.[4] The smaller regions thus received some weightage through the participation of the Senate, but, unlike India, legislators from the regional houses were not included. On the other hand, since a two-thirds majority on the final ballot was specified in Nigeria, the position of the smaller regional groups was strengthened. In the first election Dr. Azikiwe, the previous Governor-General, was elected, thus preserving the distribution between north and south of the two prestigious central posts.

[1] C.A.I., *Debates*, vol. iv, pp. 734–5; vol. vii, p. 998.
[2] Constitution, arts. 54–56.   [3] C.A.I., *Debates*, vol. iv, pp. 821–2, 828, 835–44.
[4] Constitution, 1963, ss. 34–40; see also Sessional Paper 3/1963, paras. 3, 9–30.

In Pakistan a method similar to that in India, involving election by an electoral college composed of the members of the federal and provincial assemblies, was approved in 1956.[1] The first election in 1956, however, was left to the Constituent Assembly alone, the transition causing no disruption as Iskander Mirza, the last Governor-General under the interim constitution, was elected the first President.[2] Because the central legislature was unicameral, a Vice-President to preside over the second chamber was considered unnecessary, but this made impossible a regional compromise between East and West Pakistan over these appointments along the lines which has proved useful in India. President Ayub, in presenting the 1962 constitution to the nation, attempted to make up for this shortcoming by promising a convention that if the President were from West Pakistan, the Speaker of the National Assembly would be from East Pakistan, and vice versa.[3] Under the new constitution, because of the concentration of real power in the hands of the President, the method of his election became especially important. As promulgated, the 1962 constitution specified that the President should be elected by an electoral college containing an equal number of members from East and West Pakistan.[4] Within a year, however, the Franchise Commission recommended that subsequent presidential elections after that of 1965 should be direct and by universal suffrage.

Malaya and Malaysia are unique in having an elected monarch, the Yang di-Pertuan Agong.[5] The Conference of Rulers, consisting for this purpose of the nine rulers of the former Malay States, elect one of their number, on the basis of seniority, for a five-year term. His role is that of a constitutional monarch, although he is assigned some discretionary powers, not only in the appointment of the Prime Minister and the dissolution of Parliament, but in calling meetings of the Conference of Rulers and in making certain appointments.[6] Of the first three monarchs who were placed on the throne by the process of seniority, one was the ruler of Negri Sembilan and another the ruler of the smallest state, Perlis, thus perhaps compensating these two states for a relative lack of representation in the cabinet.

In spite of the variety in the form of these federal Heads of States, it is clear that in all the independent federations considerations of regional balance have affected their appointment.

[1] Constitution, art. 32, and First Schedule.

[2] Constitution, 1956, art. 222, and Sixth Schedule. See also Ahmad, *Government and Politics in Pakistan*, pp. 19–20, 196–7.

[3] Mohammad Ayub Khan, *The Constitution: The President addresses the Nation* (1962), p. 5.   [4] Arts. 9, 10, 155–8, 165–8, 229.

[5] Constitution, 1957, arts. 32–37. See also R. O. Tilman, 'Malaysia: The Problems of Federation', *The Western Political Quarterly*, xvi (1963), pp. 903–5.

[6] Arts. 39, 40, 122 (3), 139 (4), 140 (2) (c), 143 (1) (a). *The Constitution (Amendment) Act, 1960* (F. 10/1960), ss. 15, 22, 23, modified the discretionary powers of the monarch in making appointments.

12

THE SUPREMACY AND RIGIDITY OF
THE CONSTITUTION

1. *The written constitution and its supremacy*

WRITERS on federal government have usually maintained that a constitution which is both supreme and written is necessary for federal government. As K. C. Wheare puts it:

If the general and regional governments are to be co-ordinate with each other, neither must be in a position to override the terms of their agreement about the powers and status which each is to enjoy. So far as this agreement regulates their relations with each other, it must be supreme. . . . In all that concerns the division of authority between governments, the federal principle requires the supremacy of the constitution.[1]

He goes on to argue that committing the supreme constitution to writing, although not in the same way logically entailed by the federal principle, is nevertheless a practical necessity, because the distribution of functions between governments must be precise in order to provide an adequate standard of action. The practice in the older federations—the United States, Switzerland, Canada, and Australia—would appear to bear out these views, for the federal aspects of their constitutions were put in writing, and the principle of the supremacy of their constitutions, although not always expressly declared, was firmly established.

The pattern in the newer federations has been similar. All have had written constitutions. Furthermore, the constitutions of independent Malaya, Malaysia, and Nigeria actually declared explicitly that the constitution was the supreme law of the land.[2] The constituent assemblies of India and Pakistan considered such declarations superfluous, since all the organs of government derived their powers from the constitution, and certain articles set mandatory limits on these powers. This view has been fully supported by the Indian Supreme Court which declared:

In India, it is the Constitution that is supreme and Parliament as well as State Legislatures must not only act within the limits of their respective legislative spheres as demarcated in the three lists occurring in Schedule Seven to the Constitu-

---

[1] Wheare, *Federal Government*, pp. 53–54. See also Livingston, *Federalism and Constitutional Change*, p. 10.
[2] *Constitutions of Malaya, 1957* and *Malaysia, 1963*, art. 4; *Constitutions of Nigeria, 1960*, and *1963*, s. 1.

tion, but Part III of the Constitution guarantees to the citizens certain fundamental rights which the legislative authority can on no account transgress. A statute law, to be valid must, in all cases be in conformity with the constitutional requirements and it is for the judiciary to decide whether any enactment is unconstitutional or not.[1]

Some provisions of the 1962 constitution of Pakistan would appear, however, to undermine its own supremacy. Particularly significant are the articles leaving to the legislatures themselves 'the responsibility of deciding whether a legislature has power under this Constitution to make a law',[2] and that enabling the President to make adaptations or modifications to the constitution in order to remove difficulties.[3] The Supreme Court, in impugning the President's attempt to use the latter power to introduce a semi-parliamentary form of government, however, has upheld the sanctity of the constitution.[4]

In each of the four colonial federations—Malaya (1948), Rhodesia and Nyasaland (1953), Nigeria (1954), and the West Indies (1957)—the constitutions were contained in United Kingdom Orders in Council (derived in the West Indian and Central African examples from special Acts of the British Parliament), and consequently they prevailed over any laws of the central or regional legislatures which might be repugnant to them.[5] Unlike the others, the Malayan federal structure of 1948 was put in the form of an Agreement between the rulers of the states and 'His Majesty' in order to emphasize the dual sources of legal sovereignty, this Agreement being given British legal authority by a United Kingdom order in council.[6]

As written documents, the constitutions of the new Commonwealth federations have usually been lengthy, and expressed in the language of lawyers. The extreme example was the Indian constitution of 1950, which in its original form contained 395 articles and eight schedules, but the constitutions of the other independent federations have been almost as long and complex. This has been due to a number of factors. The desire to utilize experience gained from the working of all the known constitutions and to avoid all the defects and loopholes that might be anticipated in the light of previous experience has inevitably contributed to the detail and length of these new constitutions. The Government of India Act, 1935, which was such an influential model in the Asian federations, was itself one of the longest and most intricate Acts passed by the United Kingdom Parliament. Often, fear that the lack of democratic experience might result in the perversion of the constitution, unless the details were fully spelt out, has led to the inclusion of special provisions for emergencies and for matters of administrative detail which in other countries might normally be found in statutory rather than constitutional laws. The vastness

---

[1] *Gopalan* v. *State of Madras*, A.I.R. 1950, S.C. 27 at 91. See also *In re Delhi Laws Act, 1912*, (1951) S.C.R. 747 at 758–9, 765, 857, 889, 894, 969.

[2] Art. 133.   [3] Art. 224 (3).

[4] *Fazlul Quader Chowdhury and others* v. *Muhammad Abdul Haque*, P.L.D. 1963, S.C. 486.

[5] *The Colonial Laws Validity Act, 1865* (28 & 29 Vict., ch. 63), s. 2.

[6] S.I. 1948, no. 108, s. 5 and Second Sched.

and diversity of these countries has frequently necessitated special treatment for different areas. Further lengthening these constitutions has been the inclusion of the essential provisions or even complete details of regional constitutions in the federal instrument, and the addition of justiciable fundamental rights and sometimes also of non-justiciable directive principles. A factor also has been the intention of the framers to limit the scope for judicial discretion by making provisions, and especially the assignment of responsibilities, precise and explicit.[1]

With constitutions running to such length and detail, it would seem at first sight that little room has been left in most of these federations for the development of conventions, custom, or usage. Nevertheless, a number of areas, particularly certain aspects of the responsibility of cabinets to legislatures, have often been left undetermined by the written constitution. The Indian Constituent Assembly, consciously following the British example, left to convention the question of whether the President or the cabinet was the real executive.[2] All the other independent federations have written some of the basic requirements for responsible cabinet government into their constitutions, but a considerable scope was, nevertheless, left to convention.[3] In the colonial federations advancing to self-government, reliance on evolving conventions for executive councils has permitted flexibility, although the eagerness of local politicians to display evidence of their progress has sometimes made necessary fairly explicit provisions.

Other areas have also been left to convention in even the longest of these constitutions. In India, for example, the power of appointment of state governors is constitutionally vested in the President, but as expected by the Constituent Assembly the convention has prevailed that the State Council of Ministers should be consulted before an appointment is made.[4] Promises were also made in the Indian Constituent Assembly that states would always be consulted regarding the delegation of administrative powers to states, continued administration by states of certain federal laws, the declaration of major ports by Union law, federal laws affecting extradition between states, and the implementation of treaties.[5] The central emergency powers were like-

---

[1] The three Indian legislative lists, for instance, contained a total of 210 entries.

[2] *Constitution of India, 1950*, arts. 74–75, 78, and in the case of Governors, arts. 163–4, 167. See Alexandrowicz, *Constitutional Developments in India*, ch. 7.

[3] *Constitution of Pakistan, 1956*, art. 37; *Constitution of Malaya, 1957*, art. 43; *Constitution of Nigeria, 1960*, ss. 81–88; *Constitution of Nigeria, 1963*, ss. 87–95. Following the Western Nigeria emergency of 1962, the Judicial Committee of the Privy Council ruled in *Adegbenro* v. *Akintola*, [1963] 3 W.L.R. 63, that the wording of the regional constitution did not prohibit the Governor from removing a premier who had not suffered a prior defeat on the floor of the legislature. A hasty retroactive constitutional amendment was then adopted, making more explicit the conditions in which a premier might be dismissed (*The Constitution of Western Nigeria (Amendment) Law, 1963* (W.N. no. 13/1963)).

[4] C.A.I., *Debates*, vol. viii, pp. 430–2; D. D. Basu, *Commentary on the Constitution of India* (3rd ed., 1955), vol. i, pp. 20–21.

[5] C.A.I., *Debates*, vol. iv, pp. 897, 983; vol. v, pp. 165–6, 169–70, 203–5.

wise defended in the Assembly with the argument that, by convention, they would only be used as a last resort.[1] In the case of the Finance Commissions, it is legally open to the President not to accept their recommendations, but in practice it has become a convention that they should be followed where the Commission is unanimous.

In the other federations, conventions have also grown, especially in the area of inter-governmental co-operation and consultation.[2] The number of inter-governmental institutions, not stipulated by the constitutions, that have arisen in these federations exemplifies this trend.

2. *Supreme Courts*

No matter how detailed or complete the distribution of powers may be, the ambiguity of language, overlapping jurisdiction, and the occurrence of un-foreseen problems are bound to result in disputes about the terms of the constitution. Therefore, some independent agency or institution, not wholly dependent upon one level of government, has usually been considered neces-sary for interpreting the constitution and settling disputes. The new federa-tions have been uniform in assigning this role to supreme judicial bodies on the pattern of the United States, Canadian, and Australian supreme courts.[3] Indeed, framers of the more recent federal constitutions have apparently been unaware of the Swiss procedure, where the federal legislature is the final interpreter of the constitution, subject to a referendum of the electorate. Time and again they have made such declarations as: 'A Supreme Court with juris-diction to decide upon the constitutional validity of acts and laws can be regarded as a necessary implication of any federal scheme.'[4]

The only federations under study in which the function of guarding and interpreting the distribution of powers and the whole constitution was not

---

[1] Ibid., vol. ix, p. 177.   [2] See section 7 of this chapter.

[3] For the organization and jurisdiction of supreme courts, see: *Government of India Act, 1935*, ss. 200–18, 318; *Constitution of India, 1950*, arts. 32, 121, 124–47, 211, 360 (4) (*b*), 374–5, Second Sched., Part D, *Seventh Amendment Act, 1956*, s. 5, s. 29 and Sched., and *Fifteenth Amendment Act, 1963*; *Constitution of Pakistan, 1956*, arts. 22, 129, 148–64, 173–8, 194 (3), Third Sched.; *Constitution of Pakistan, 1962*, arts. 49–65, 123–30, Second, Sched.; *Constitution of Malaya, 1957*, arts. 4 (3), 5 (2), 121–31, 138, 173–4, *Constitution (Amendment) Act, 1960*, ss. 15, 16, 20, 32, *Constitution (Amendment) Act, 1962*, s. 23 and Sched. s. 9, and *Malaysia Act, 1963*, ss. 13–15, 17, 21, 22, 40, 87, 90–92, and Sixth Sched.; *Nigeria Constitution, 1954*, ss. 138–41, 144–51, 219, and amendments 1954–60, esp. S.I. 1958, no. 1958, s. 3, and S.I. 1959, no. 386, s. 27; *Constitution of Nigeria, 1960*, ss. 104–14, 119–22, 127, 149 (2), 151–2; *Constitution of Nigeria, 1963*, ss. 111–21, 126, 128, 133, 153 (2), 162–3; *Constitution of R. and N., 1953*, arts. 45–66; *Constitution of W.I., 1957*, arts. 72–90, 113 (2), and *Constitution of W.I. (Amendment) Order in Council, 1960*, ss. 8–12. See also S. R. Sharma, *The Supreme Court in the Indian Constitution* (1959); E. McWhinney, *Judicial Review in the English-Speaking World* (1956), ch. 7; L. Brett (ed.), *Constitutional Problems of Federalism in Nigeria* (1961), pp. 12–28.

[4] C.A.I., *Report of the Union Constitution Committee* (1947), App. A, 'Report of *Ad Hoc* Committee on Supreme Court', para. 3. Cf. C.A.I., *Debates*, vol. vii, p. 35; Col. no. 330/1957, para. 123; Col. no. 255/1950, para. 94.

entrusted to a supreme court with power to review both central and regional legislation were the Malayan Federation between 1948 and 1957, and Pakistan after 1962. In the former the function of interpreting the Federation Agreement was vested in *ad hoc* Interpretation Tribunals.[1] These tribunals consisted of three members: the Chief Justice of the Supreme Court as chairman, and two other members who were either judges of the Supreme Court or possessed the qualifications required for such judges, one being appointed by the High Commissioner and the other by the rulers of the Malay states when occasion arose. Decisions required the support of a majority in the tribunal. The Reid Commission rejected this general arrangement in favour of that found in the other federations on several grounds: first, the states could not maintain their autonomy unless they were enabled to challenge in the courts as *ultra vires* both legislation and executive acts of the central government; secondly, the insertion of fundamental liberties in the constitution required the establishment of a legal procedure by which breaches of basic liberties could be challenged; thirdly, it seemed desirable that a method of securing rapid decisions on constitutional questions should be provided.[2] Accordingly, in the 1957 Malayan constitution the Supreme Court was given jurisdiction over interpretation of the constitution along the lines adopted earlier in Canada, India, and Pakistan. In Malaysia the Federal Court performs this role for the extended federation.

Appointment and dismissal of supreme courts has usually been in the hands of the central government, but in most cases the constitution-framers have paid particular attention to the importance of ensuring as far as possible the independence of these courts. Typical was the declaration in the report of the Judicial Commissioner for the Caribbean federation:

> ... the Federal Court must be manned by judges who are learned in the law and experienced in its practice, and that whatever be the method of their appointment and the manner of their functioning, they must in fact be, and must also manifestly appear to be, able to perform their duties with strict impartiality to all.[3]

The appointment of supreme court judges has generally followed one of three patterns. In India, Pakistan, Rhodesia and Nyasaland, Malaya (after 1960), Malaysia, and Nigeria (after 1963) the central cabinet has had the last word in the appointment of supreme court judges. But, except in Rhodesia and Nyasaland, the central executive has been required to consult certain bodies before making the appointments, although the advice received is not binding.[4] In Malaya (1957–60), the West Indies (1960–2), and Nigeria (1960–3),

---

[1] *Federation of Malaya Agreement, 1948*, cls. 66, 153. For instances of decisions by an Interpretation Tribunal, see *Gazette*, Notification 1123/1950, and Legal Notification 256/1956.

[2] Col. no. 330/1957, para. 123.   [3] Cmd. 9620/1955, para. 3.

[4] In India, Pakistan, Malaya, and Malaysia the executive is required to consult the Chief Justice (titled Lord President in Malaysia) about appointments of other members of the Supreme Court (called Federal Court in Malaysia), in Malaya and Malaysia to consult in

on the other hand, all supreme court appointments, except in the case of Chief Justices, lay with the Heads of State, who were required to act on the advice of Judicial Service Commissions.[1] In the two colonial federations of Nigeria (1954–60) and the West Indies (1958) there was a third pattern: appointment by the Governor-General in pursuance of instructions of the Secretary of State for the Colonies, this being changed in the West Indies (1958–60) to appointment by the Governor-General at his discretion after consulting the Prime Minister. An interesting feature of the supreme courts of Rhodesia and Nyasaland, of Nigeria (between 1958 and 1963) and of Malaysia was that the chief justices of the regional high courts were included as *ex officio* members of the supreme court in order to provide a large enough panel from which to draw.

To ensure the independence of these supreme courts, all the new federal constitutions have also contained provisions to the effect that judges might be removed only 'on grounds of misbehaviour or of infirmity of body or mind', although there are slight variations in wording. A special procedure for removal was also usually specified: in India, Pakistan (1956), Nigeria (1963), and Rhodesia and Nyasaland an address of the central legislature, requiring in all but the last special majorities; in Pakistan after 1962 an inquiry by a Supreme Judicial Council; in Malaya and Malaysia investigation by a special tribunal; in the West Indies an order in council of the Governor-General after reference to the Judicial Committee of the Privy Council, and in Nigeria between 1959 and 1963 a procedure combining the Malayan and West Indian arrangements.[2]

Other provisions, also designed to enhance the independence of supreme courts, have often been included in the federal constitution. As the Reid Commission put it: 'On the one hand judges should not be immune from criticism; on the other hand they ought to be able to sit "fairly and freely, without favour and without fear", and in particular should not exercise their functions with an eye upon the activities of party politics.'[3] The constitutions have therefore as a rule attempted to ensure that the salaries and terms of office of judges normally might not be varied to their disadvantage. The Asian federations also restricted discussion in the legislatures of the conduct of supreme court judges. In addition, the Indian and Pakistan constitutions expressed in the 'directive principles' or the preamble the aim to establish an independent judicature, and included provisions disqualifying justices from subsequently practising in the courts or accepting certain

addition the Conference of Rulers about all Supreme Court appointments, in India to consult other Supreme Court Justices and the Chief Justices of the High Courts about the appointment of Chief Justices, and in Nigeria to consult a different regional premier for each of four justices.

[1] But Chief Justices were appointed in the West Indies and Nigeria by the Governor-General acting on the advice of the Prime Minister, and in Malaya by the monarch at his discretion after consulting the Conference of Rulers and the Prime Minister.

[2] In most cases there were provisions also for automatic retirement at 65, and for voluntary resignation.   [3] Col. no. 330/1957, para. 125.

appointments in order that judicial decisions might not be influenced by the hope of future advantage.

Although the constitutions have generally been designed to encourage impartiality, there have usually been some constitutional loop-holes. As already noted, in all the independent federations the final decision regarding appointments to the supreme court now lies with the central executive, even though other bodies must be consulted. In addition, in all of these federations the size of the supreme court is left to be determined by ordinary central legislation, although the possibility of using this opportunity to 'pack' a court was minimized in India and Pakistan by the power of the chief justice to determine the quorum for a constitutional bench, and prevented in the West Indies, Nigeria before 1963, and Malaya before 1960 by the role of Judicial Service Commissions in appointments. In spite of the existence of some loop-holes and of the formal dependence of the supreme court on the central government in certain cases, there appears to be little evidence that these courts have failed to show impartiality in their function as guardians of the federal constitutions. In this they have been aided not only by constitutional provisions, but by traditions of the bar and bench safeguarding the integrity and independence of the judges in these countries.

When we turn to the functions exercised by the supreme courts, we find that in all the new Commonwealth federations extensive original and appellate jurisdiction has been conferred upon these courts.

To begin with, all have assigned their supreme courts a key role as guardians of the federal distribution of powers. Except in Pakistan after 1962, where in the case of inter-governmental disputes the Supreme Court might 'pronounce declaratory judgments only',[1] supreme courts have invariably been given ultimate authority to interpret the constitution and to pronounce on the validity of both central and regional laws. In cases of justiciable disputes between central and regional governments, or between regional governments, the usual practice has been to assign original and exclusive jurisdiction to the supreme court. Some administrative and financial disputes, more appropriately dealt with by tribunals, arbitrators, fiscal commissions, or some other procedure, have, however, often been excepted.[2] In addition, unlike the arrangements in Australia and the United States, the original jurisdiction over inter-governmental disputes has not been extended in the new federations to include legal disputes between residents of different territories, such disputes usually coming under the appellate jurisdiction of the supreme courts.[3]

---

[1] Constitution, 1962, art. 57 (2). See also art. 133.

[2] *Constitution of India, 1950*, arts. 258, 262, 280, 290; *Constitution of Pakistan, 1956*, arts. 118, 129; *Constitution of Pakistan, 1962*, arts. 140 (4), 143 (3), 144; *Constitution of Malaya, 1957*, arts. 80 (6), 87, 108, and *Malaysia Act, 1963*, ss. 47 (6), 48 (5); *Constitution of R. and N., 1953*, arts. 88–92, 96; *Nigeria Constitution, 1954*, s. 154; *Constitution of Nigeria, 1960*, s. 153; *Constitution of Nigeria, 1963*, s. 164; *Constitution of W.I., 1957*, art. 101.

[3] *The Constitution of Malaya, 1957*, art. 4 (3), went so far as to stipulate that conflicting

The supreme courts in these federations have also been given in each case a wider role as guardian not only of the federal distribution of authority, but also of the constitution as a whole. This jurisdiction includes the interpretation of regional constitutions in all the new federations except the West Indies, where assignment of this jurisdiction was left to the option of the territorial legislature.[1] In the independent federations where fundamental liberties specified in the federal constitution impose limits on both central and regional governments, the supreme court has usually, through either original or appellate jurisdiction, been made a protector of these also. The importance of supreme courts as general guardians and interpreters of constitutions has already been clearly illustrated in India, Nigeria, and Pakistan. In India, for instance, during 1961 the Supreme Court disposed of 531 petitions for the enforcement of fundamental rights and 357 appeals involving other questions concerning the interpretation of the constitution.[2] During the brief period since independence the Nigerian Supreme Court has checked the central government's attempt to use its 'incidental and supplementary' powers in an extensive manner,[3] and has dealt with a series of cases arising out of the declaration of a state of emergency in the Western Region in 1962.[4] The judgements of the Federal Court of Pakistan over the dissolution of the Constituent Assembly in 1954, and the attempted unification of West Pakistan by administrative decree in 1955, were of particular significance.[5] The Supreme Court proved less courageous in 1958, but in 1963 a Supreme Court ruling defended the non-parliamentary form of executive specified in the new constitution against modification by Presidential order.[6]

In addition to tasks of constitutional interpretation, extensive appellate

central or state laws might be invalidated only in inter-government disputes, but this was altered by the *Malaysia Act, 1963*, s. 40, permitting proceedings for a declaration upon whether a law is *ultra vires* to be commenced by other persons with leave of a Federal Court judge.

[1] In India, Pakistan, and Nigeria (1954), where the regional constitutions were included in the federal document, the jurisdiction over the interpretation of the latter included the former as well, while in Rhodesia and Nyasaland (art. 55) and Nigeria (1960, s. 108, and 1963, s. 115), the jurisdiction to interpret the separate regional constitutions was specifically assigned. Cf. *Constitution of W.I., 1957*, arts. 81–82.

[2] *India, 1962*, p. 61.

[3] *Senator Chief T. Adebayo Doherty* v. *Sir Abubakar Tafawa Balewa and others*, (F.S.C. 326/1961).

[4] *F. R. A. Williams* v. *Dr. M. A. Majekodunmi*, (F.S.C. 166/1962); *Adegbenro* v. *Attorney-General of the Federation of Nigeria and others*, (F.S.C. 170/1962); *Akintola* v. *Aderemi and Adegbenro*, (F.S.C. 187/1962). See also O. I. Odumosu, *The Nigerian Constitution: History and Development* (1963), ch. 9, and S. G. Davies, 'Nigeria—Some Recent Decisions on the Constitution', *International and Comparative Law Quarterly*, xi (1962), pp. 919–36. The last of these cases was overruled by the Judicial Committee of the Privy Council in *Adegbenro* v. *Akintola*, [1963] 3 W.L.R. 63.

[5] See especially W. I. Jennings, *Constitutional Problems in Pakistan* (1957); Callard, *Pakistan, A Political Study*, pp. 30–31, 128, 142–7.

[6] *The State* v. *Dosso*, P.L.D. 1958, S.C. 533; *Fazlul Quader Chowdhury and others* v. *Muhammad Abdul Haque*, P.L.D. 1963, S.C. 486.

jurisdiction in civil cases of high value, in certain criminal cases, and, where the court permits, by special leave, have been assigned to the supreme courts of India, Pakistan, and Nigeria. In Malaya and Malaysia the central Parliament determines the scope of the Federal Court's appellate jurisdiction, but in Rhodesia and Nyasaland and in the West Indies there were provisions enabling territorial legislatures to make the decisions of territorial high courts final on subjects not included in the federal or concurrent lists. Since in the new federations the law declared by the supreme courts was binding on other courts, the appellate jurisdiction made the supreme courts, through their capacity to promote a uniformity of interpretation in these areas, an important force for political integration.

In all the federal constitutions except that of Pakistan (1956), provision was also made for the supreme court to serve as a court for central law, if the central legislature wished to confer original judicial power over its own laws upon it. In Rhodesia and Nyasaland and the West Indies, territorial legislatures were also given the right to confer, with central consent, original jurisdiction for territorial laws, thus providing even more flexibility. The conferring upon the supreme courts of original jurisdiction in matters arising under treaties and in those affecting consuls and other foreign representatives was avoided, however, because it had given rise to difficulties in the older federations.[1]

The constitutions of India, Pakistan, Malaya, and Malaysia have followed the Canadian precedent and the Government of India Act, 1935, in providing for references to the supreme courts for advisory opinions.[2] The advantage of this consultative function is that it provides a method of securing a rapid decision on constitutional questions. Advisory jurisdiction has, however, sometimes been criticized on a number of grounds. It is possible that in references for advisory opinions the issue may not be argued as vigorously as in cases where litigants have an immediate interest in the facts. The consideration of a moot point of law without reference to specific cases may result in misleading decisions which embarrass a court, obliged either to defend its decision or reverse its position when the same measure is considered, not *in vacuo*, but in its application to a concrete set of facts.[3] Finally it has been argued that it 'violates the principle of separation of powers, and prejudices the inde-

---

[1] *Nigeria Constitution, 1954*, s. 144 (*c, d*) was the sole exception.

[2] *The Constitution of Nigeria, 1960*, s. 109 (*1963*, s. 116), enabled the Nigerian Parliament to confer advisory jurisdiction on the Supreme Court, but only regarding the prerogative of mercy.

[3] This had been the case in India under the 1935 Act when the Federal Court was obliged to defend its view in *In re Hindu Women's Rights to Property Act, 1937*, A.I.R. 1941, F.C. 72, later in *Umayal Achi* v. *Lakshmi Achi*, A.I.R. 1945, F.C. 25. The Federal Court also expressed misgivings at being called on to exercise this jurisdiction in *In re Levy of Estate Duty*, A.I.R. 1944, F.C. 73. The C.A.I. 'Report of *Ad Hoc* Committee on Supreme Court', op. cit., Part II, referred to consequent differences of opinion on the desirability of advisory jurisdiction.

pendence of the judiciary by associating it with the executive, compelling it to share responsibility for its policy.'[1] It is not surprising, therefore, that in Rhodesia and Nyasaland, in spite of the recommendations of the Judicial Commission, and in the West Indies following both the Central African and Australian examples, no provision was made for advisory jurisdiction. The constitutions of India and of Pakistan (1956) attempted to protect the independence and integrity of the supreme courts by making the responsibility for giving advisory opinions discretionary, and by ensuring that subsequent decisions were not necessarily bound by these opinions.

In practice, reference for advisory opinions has been made in India and Pakistan on a number of occasions: in India before partition four times; in India since 1950, on the delegation of legislative power, on the extent to which the Kerala Education Bill of 1957 infringed the fundamental rights, and on the constitutionality of the cession of territory to implement the Indo-Pakistan Agreement of 1958; in Pakistan in 1955 over the consequences of the dissolution of the first Constituent Assembly, and in 1957–8 over the Governor's power to dissolve a provincial assembly.[2] The reference of the Kerala Education Bill, 1957, was unusual in that it dealt with the constitutionality of a bill which had been passed by the state legislature of Kerala and had been reserved for assent by the President. Following the Supreme Court's opinion the bill was modified. The value of the consultative jurisdiction was perhaps best exemplified by the advisory judgement of the Pakistan Federal Court, which helped to solve the constitutional crisis in 1955 by suggesting how the Governor-General might proceed. Experience of the use of advisory opinions in India and Pakistan suggests that in reducing litigation they have been valuable and generally beneficial.

As can be seen from the foregoing description, the supreme courts of the new federations have been assigned extensive functions. Nevertheless, in most cases certain limits have been placed on their jurisdiction. Certain types of inter-governmental disputes, particularly those involving administrative or financial relations, have generally been assigned to special tribunals, arbitrators, or fiscal commissions.[3] In addition, the jurisdiction of supreme courts has usually been excluded specifically from inquiries into the operation of certain parts of the constitution. For instance such questions as the advice offered by Ministers to Heads of State, and the validity of proceedings in legislatures or of other specified procedures have often been so exempted.

[1] A. Gledhill, *Pakistan* (1957), p. 119.

[2] *In re Central Provinces and Berar Sale of Motor Spirit and Lubricants Taxation Act, 1938*, A.I.R. 1939, F.C. 1; *In re Hindu Women's Rights to Property Act*, A.I.R. 1941, F.C. 72; *In re Allocation of Lands and Buildings*, A.I.R. 1943, F.C. 13; *In re Levy of Estate Duty*, A.I.R. 1944, F.C. 73; *In re Delhi Laws Act, 1912*, A.I.R. 1951, S.C. 332; *In re Kerala Education Bill, 1957*, A.I.R. 1958, S.C. 956; *In re Berubari Union and Exchange of Enclaves*, A.I.R. 1960, S.C. 845; *Reference by the Governor-General*, P.L.D. 1955, F.C. 435; *Reference by the President of Pakistan*, P.L.D. 1957, S.C. 219.

[3] See discussion above of supreme court jurisdiction over inter-governmental disputes.

In some of the new Commonwealth federations the possibility of appeals from the decisions of their own supreme courts to the Judicial Committee of the Privy Council, was left open within certain limits. The case for such appeals was put by the Reid Commission: 'Not only would it be a valuable link between countries of the Commonwealth but in the present position in the Federation it would, we think, be advantageous if the final decision on constitutional questions lay with a Tribunal which has experience with other federal constitutions.'[1] Sometimes there has also been a feeling that there is an advantage in being able to appeal to an external and therefore clearly impartial body. On the other hand, some critics have considered that such an arrangement continues to carry the stigma of colonialism, while others have pointed out that because of the frequently changing composition of the Judicial Committee its members are often unfamiliar with the law of the country which they handle, the vagaries of the Committee's interpretation of the Canadian constitution often being cited as an example. Generally, the latter view has prevailed, for by 1963 India, Pakistan, and Nigeria had abolished such appeals, leaving only Malaysia permitting them.[2]

3. *The scope of judicial review*

It has sometimes been maintained that the corollary to the constitutional supremacy necessary in a federal system is judicial supremacy. The chairman of the Indian Constituent Assembly Drafting Committee conceded this:

That these faults are inherent in Federalism, there can be no dispute. . . . A Federal Constitution means a division of Sovereignty by no less a sanction than that of the law of the Constitution between the Federal Government and the States, with two necessary consequences: (1) that any invasion by the Federal Government in the field assigned to the States and *vice versa* is a breach of the Constitution and (2) such breach is a justiciable matter to be decided by the Judiciary only. This being the nature of Federalism, a federal Constitution cannot escape the charge of legalism.[3]

But while accepting the unavoidability of 'legalism', most of the federal draftsmen have attempted to reduce the scope for judicial discretion and to avoid making a supreme court into 'a third chamber of the legislature'.

The Indian Constituent Assembly was particularly conscious of this danger.[4] In order to diminish litigation and the opportunity for judicial discretion, a number of devices were adopted. A large concurrent list on the Australian model was expected to reduce litigation because of the overriding Union power in these subjects.[5] A considerable number of articles, especially those con-

---

[1] Col. no. 330/1957, para. 126.

[2] *Constitution of Malaysia, 1963*, art. 131. Uganda, South Arabia, and Kenya still provided for appeals to the Privy Council.　　　　　　　　[3] C.A.I., *Debates*, vol. vii, p. 35.

[4] C.A.I., *Debates*, vol. v, pp. 136–7, 138, 139; vol. vii, pp. 35–36, 359, 999–1001; vol. ix, pp. 1196, 1271.

[5] Sometimes, however, concurrent legislative lists have been regarded instead as a potential source of litigation (Cmd. 8934/1953, para. 8). Nevertheless, as expected by the

cerned with administrative details but also including some of the entries in the legislative lists, were made effective only 'until Parliament otherwise provides', thus reducing the opportunity for courts to rule Parliament *ultra vires*. The constitution, including the distribution of powers, was explicitly defined in detail, enabling the Supreme Court to apply a literal interpretation in most cases and, by contrast with the earlier federations, making unnecessary resort to such doctrines as 'implied powers', 'implied prohibitions', 'due process', 'police power', 'original package', and 'immunity of instrumentalities', and leaving little room for judicial application of the residual legislative power.[1] The scope for discretion in interpretation was further reduced by certain articles containing rules of interpretation or definition, and by the inclusion of a set of Directive Principles guiding the interpretation of less explicit provisions. In addition, certain areas were excepted from the jurisdiction of the Supreme Court.[2] Finally, special provisions for Union legislation on exclusive state subjects in a variety of circumstances, and a relatively flexible amendment process, made reliance upon judicial review as a means to constitutional adaptability unnecessary.[3]

Similar devices have also been used, although not always so extensively, to limit the scope of 'legalism' and judicial discretion in the other new federations. In most cases the draftsmen have tried to make the constitutions as precise and legally complete as possible, avoiding the simple and more inspiring but ambiguous language of the older federal constitutions such as that of the United States. All the new federal constitutions have contained detailed provisions governing the distribution of authority, including relatively extensive lists of concurrent powers. Most have devoted certain sections to rules of interpretation and definitions, as well as specifying some limits on the jurisdiction of supreme courts in particular areas. These federal constitutions have also included a variety of special devices and, with the exception of independent Nigeria, relatively easy amendment procedures for large sections of their constitutions, thus making flexibility possible without reliance upon judicial review.[4]

Nevertheless, some scope for 'legalism' remained in all these constitutions.

Constituent Assembly, the number of cases in India so far concerning this field has not been excessive. Major cases were *Zaverbhai* v. *State of Bombay*, A.I.R. 1954, S.C. 752; *Tika Ramji* v. *State of U.P.*, A.I.R. 1956, S.C. 676; *Deep Chand* v. *State of U.P.*, A.I.R. 1959, S.C. 648.

[1] C.A.I., *Debates*, vol. vii, pp. 35–36, 41; *Ram Krishna Rammath* v. *Secretary, Municipal Committee, Kamptee*, A.I.R. 1950, S.C. 11; *Gopalan* v. *State of Madras*, A.I.R. 1950, S.C. 27 (102); *Charanjit Lal* v. *Union of India*, A.I.R. 1951, S.C. 41 (56); *State of Bombay* v. *Balsara*, A.I.R. 1951, S.C. 318 (323); *State of West Bengal* v. *Union of India*, A.I.R. 1963, S.C. 1241 (1256). See also Basu, op. cit., vol. i, pp. 9–11, vol. ii, pp. 207–10, 217; Alexandrowicz, op. cit., pp. 19, 85–86 n.   [2] See preceding section of this chapter.

[3] C.A.I. *Debates*, vol. v, pp. 136–9; vol. vii, pp. 35–36. See sections 4–7 on flexibility of Indian Constitution, and S. R. Sharma, op. cit., pp. 318–21, for the effect of this flexibility on the actual judgements of the Supreme Court.

[4] See sections 4–6 of this chapter. A system of tabling federal laws in territorial legislatures

Questions as to whether particular acts of central or regional governments are within their legislative competence under the distribution of authority are bound to be a source of litigation, and in spite of the care taken in drafting the recent federal constitutions there have been some areas giving room for judicial discretion. Most of the constitutions, for instance, did include in the concurrent or exclusively central legislative lists such vague items as 'economic and social planning' or 'development of industries', which could possibly in time, if interpreted widely by the courts, cover as wide a scope as given in Canada to 'property and civil rights'.[1] Moreover, the very elaborateness of most of the legislative lists and the attempts, especially in the Asian federations, at exhaustiveness may lead to numerous points of overlap and hence disputes as to valid legislative powers. As one commentator on the Indian constitution put it: 'the interpretation of 395 articles will provide ample occupation for practitioners in the field of constitutional law'.[2] While the detailed nature of the legislative lists has made a number of doctrines of interpretation used elsewhere unnecessary, even the Indian Supreme Court has found some rules useful,[3] such as those of 'colourable legislation',[4] 'avoidance of conflict by harmonious construction',[5] 'pith and substance',[6] 'aspect of legislation',[7] 'severability',[8] 'incidental and ancillary powers',[9] 'presumption of constitutionality',[10] 'eclipse',[11] and 'implied repeal'.[12] Moreover, where sections of the new constitution were borrowed from elsewhere, foreign judicial decisions may be directly relevant.[13] Thus, constitution-makers copying

was suggested in Central Africa to reduce litigation, but later abandoned (Cmd. 8573/1952, pp. 32–33; Cmd. 8753/1953, para. 39).

[1] For examples of such items see: *Constitution of India, 1950*, Seventh Sched., List III, entry 20; *Constitution of Pakistan, 1956*, Fifth Sched., Concurrent List, Entry 9; *Constitution of Pakistan, 1962*, art. 131 (2) (*b*); *Constitution of Malaya, 1957*, Ninth Sched., List 1, item 8, and art. 92 (3); *Constitution of R. and N., 1953*, Second Sched., part ii, item 49; *Constitution of W.I., 1957*, Third Sched., part ii, para. 19; *Constitution of Nigeria, 1960*, Sched., part ii, items 11, 12, and *1963*, Sched., part ii, items 11, 12.

[2] Alexandrowicz, op. cit., p. 38.

[3] See discussion in Basu, op. cit., vol. ii, pp. 217–34. For rules of interpretation applied elsewhere see especially *Md. Ali* v. *Crown*, P.L.D. 1950, F.C. 1; *Md. Yusuf* v. *Crown*, P.L.D. 1956, F.C. 395; *Mutosa and others* v. *Minister of Law*, 1959 (1) R. & N. 251 (F.S.C.).

[4] *State of Bihar* v. *Kameshwar Singh*, A.I.R. 1952, S.C. 252 (276–7, 280); *Gajapati Narayan Deo* v. *State of Orissa*, A.I.R. 1953, S.C. 375 (378–81, 384).

[5] *State of Bombay* v. *Narottamdas*, A.I.R. 1951, S.C. 69 (75–76); *State of Bombay* v. *Balsara*, A.I.R. 1951, S.C. 318 (322).

[6] *State of Bombay* v. *Balsara*, A.I.R. 1951, S.C. 318 (322–3). Cf. *Md. Yusuf* v. *Crown*, P.L.D. 1956, F.C. 395 (399–400).

[7] *State of Bombay* v. *Narottamdas*, A.I.R. 1951, S.C. 69 (77).

[8] *R.M.D.C.* v. *Union of India*, A.I.R. 1957, S.C. 628 (633–7).

[9] *Navinchandra Mafatlal* v. *Commissioner, I.T., Bombay*, A.I.R. 1955, S.C. 58 (61); *I.T. Commissioners* v. *Benoy Kumar*, A.I.R. 1957, S.C. 768 (772).

[10] *Charanjit Lal* v. *Union of India*, A.I.R. 1951, S.C. 41 (45).

[11] *Deep Chand* v. *State of U.P.*, A.I.R. 1959, S.C. 648 (664).

[12] *Zaverbhai* v. *State of Bombay*, A.I.R. 1954, S.C. 752 (758).

[13] *Sundararamier* v. *State of Andhra Pradesh*, A.I.R. 1958, S.C. 468 (495); *Atiabari Tea Co. Ltd.* v. *State of Assam*, A.I.R. 1961, S.C. 232 (257).

provisions from other constitutions where the judicial interpretation was already known could reduce ambiguity. But at the same time, by justifying reference to foreign judicial precedents, they opened the door to greater judicial discretion.

The areas in the federal distribution of powers where the greatest conflicts and difficulties of interpretation might be expected, judging by the experience of the older federations, are the implementation of treaties and international agreements, the sources of taxation, the immunity of governmental instrumentalities from taxation by other governments, and the assignment of powers over trade and commerce. Litigation over these questions has generally been minimized in the newer federations by giving central governments sweeping authority to implement treaties and agreements, by putting the adjustment of financial resources in the hands of special non-judicial bodies, and by spelling out in considerable detail the assignment of taxes, the limits upon the powers of governments to tax each other, and the central and regional powers over trade and commerce.[1] Nevertheless, in India, both the state power to levy sales taxes and the very complexity of the constitutional provisions concerning trade and commerce provoked so much litigation that constitutional amendments were precipitated.[2] Elsewhere too, taxation, and particularly the right of one government to tax another, has required supreme court consideration.[3] One other area in the federal distribution of authority which has attracted particular attention in the courts in India and Nigeria has been the scope of the 'incidental' and 'supplementary' powers associated with the exercise of powers granted to each level of government.[4]

Other aspects of constitutional law are also likely to require judicial interpretation. In most of the new federations some features of the relation between executives and legislatures have been committed to writing while other aspects have been left to convention, with the result that already in Pakistan and Nigeria the courts have been called upon to draw the line between law and custom. In Pakistan in 1957 and in Nigeria during 1962–3 cases arose over the relationship of a governor to the provincial or regional executive and legislature,[5] while in Pakistan under the interim constitution and again under the 1962 constitution there were cases concerning the relation of the Head of

---

[1] See Chapters 8 and 9.

[2] On cases over state sales taxes which led to the *Sixth Amendment Act, 1956*, see p. 206 above. On trade and commerce see Constitution, arts. 301–7; *Saghir Ahmad* v. *State of U.P.*, A.I.R. 1954, S.C. 728 (741–2); *Fourth Amendment Act, 1955*, s. 4; *Atiabari Tea Co. Ltd.* v. *State of Assam*, A.I.R. 1961, S.C. 232; Alexandrowicz, op. cit., pp. 95–102; I. Jennings, *Some Characteristics of the Indian Constitution* (1953), pp. 74–82.

[3] *Punjab* v. *Federation*, P.L.D. 1956, F.C. 72; *Muhammad Amir Khan* v. *Controller of Estate Duty*, P.L.D. 1961, S.C. 119; *Commissioner of Taxes* v. *John Howard & Co.*, 1959 (1) R. & N. 151 (F.S.C.); *Hughes* v. *Income Tax Commissioner*, (1961) 3 W.I.R. 224 (F.S.C.).

[4] *I.T. Commissioners* v. *Benoy Kumar*, A.I.R. 1957, S.C. 768 (772); *Senator Chief T. Adebayo* v. *Sir Abubakar Tafawa Balewa and others*, (Nigeria, F.S.C. 326/1961).

[5] *Reference by the President of Pakistan*, P.L.D. 1957, S.C. 219; *Akintola* v. *Aderemi and Adegbenro* (Nigeria, F.S.C. 187/1962); *Adegbenro* v. *Akintola*, [1963] 3 W.L.R. 63.

State and the executive to the central legislature.[1] The inclusion in the constitutions of the independent federations of justiciable fundamental rights has invariably accentuated the amount of litigation over the validity of legislation. This has been particularly marked in India, where most of the work of the Supreme Court has related to the disposal of cases concerning fundamental rights.[2] Although the new federations have generally avoided vague 'due process' clauses, qualifications such as 'reasonableness' regarding restrictions of liberties, and sometimes regarding other constitutional provisions, have in some instances provided judges with considerable room to exercise their discretion.[3] The first Constituent Assembly of Pakistan even went so far as to consider an arrangement whereby the Supreme Court or a committee of men learned in Islamic law might declare invalid any law repugnant to Islamic principles. Following considerable controversy over the proposal, however, these criteria were excluded from the scope of judicial review, being left instead to the judgement of the legislatures, advised by a special commission or council.[4]

While it is still too early to arrive at firm general conclusions about the significance of judicial review in the new federations, some tentative assessment may be offered. In the colonial period before independence, litigation connected with the federal aspects of the constitutions has been negligible. Indeed, in Malaya and Nigeria before the end of British rule and in the West Indies no central or regional laws were invalidated, nor were the courts called upon to settle any disputes between governments.[5] In the independent federations, on the other hand, judicial review has played a significant role. Only in Malaya among these have no laws been invalidated by the courts, and in each federation there have been some legal disputes between governments which required judicial settlement.[6] Three factors have, however, minimized the

[1] *Federation* v. *M. Tamizuddin Khan*, P.L.D. 1955, F.C. 240; *Usif Patel* v. *Crown*, P.L.D. 1955, F.C. 387; *Reference by the Governor-General*, P.L.D. 1955, F.C. 435; *Fazlul Quader Chowdhury and others* v. *Muhammad Abdul Haque*, P.L.D. 1963, S.C. 486.

[2] S. R. Sharma, op. cit., p. 123. In 1957 the Supreme Court dealt with 228 petitions for the enforcement of fundamental rights, as against 136 appeals turning on interpretation of other parts of the constitution. In 1961 the corresponding figures were 531 and 357.

[3] In India the resulting interpretation of art. 19 by the Supreme Court led to a constitutional amendment reducing the scope for judicial review. See especially *Romesh Thappar* v. *State of Madras*, A.I.R. 1950, S.C. 124; *Brij Bhushan* v. *State of Delhi*, A.I.R. 1950, S.C. 129; *First Amendment Act, 1951*, s. 3.

[4] B.P.C., *Report* (1952), paras. 3, 5, 6; B.P.C., *Report* (as adopted, 1954), paras. 4, 6; Constitution, 1956, art. 198; Constitution, 1962, arts. 199–206.

[5] There were no inter-governmental cases in Rhodesia and Nyasaland, but in *Commisioner of Taxes* v. *John Howard & Co.*, 1959 (1) R. & N. 151 (F.S.C.), a central law was held *ultra vires*. Notable cases of inter-governmental litigation in India before independence were *United Provinces* v. *Gov.-General*, A.I.R. 1939, F.C. 58, and *Gov.-General* v. *Madras*, A.I.R. 1945, P.C. 98.

[6] Examples of inter-governmental litigation have been *State of West Bengal* v. *Union of India*, A.I.R. 1963, S.C. 1241; *Punjab* v. *Federation of Pakistan*, P.L.D. 1956, F.C. 72; *State of Kelantan* v. *Federation of Malaya and Tunku Abdul Rahman*, (1963) 29 M.L.J. 355. In early 1962 the Western Nigeria Government challenged the validity of the central

extent of inter-governmental litigation. First, the explicit detail written into the constitutions has left less room for dispute. Secondly, the existence of a variety of devices designed to foster co-operation and consultation between governments has encouraged the settlement of disputes over administrative and political issues by means of negotiation rather than litigation. Thirdly, in Malaya, India, and Nigeria, the cordiality resulting from the dominance in both levels of government of one party or a coalition of parties has also reduced legal disputes, although it did not prevent West Bengal from challenging the Union Government in India in 1962. Significantly, most of the constitutional cases in Nigeria have arisen in Western Nigeria, when it was controlled by a party outside the central coalition. Generally therefore, while the arbitral function of the supreme courts has been of importance in the independent federations, by far the largest portion of the work of these courts has been in the interpretation of fundamental rights and in their appellate jurisdiction. It is probably fair to say also that the new federations have, on the whole, benefited from avoiding the strains of excessive inter-governmental litigation, at least during the critical early years of their existence.

The judgements of the supreme courts in these federations also indicate that generally the justices have not considered themselves as additional constitution-makers, but rather, simply as bodies to apply express laws. Except in Pakistan, where the constitutional crises of 1954–5 and 1958 forced the Pakistan Federal and Supreme Courts to build a bridge of legality between the actions of the Head of State and the principles of the constitutions, the judges, following the British tradition, have usually restricted themselves to the literal interpretation of the constitutional documents.[1] Thus, in effect, constitutional supremacy would appear to have been achieved without excessive judicial discretion.

4. *The formal constitutional amendment procedures*

Although the necessity for amendments in the institutional structure of government arises in all systems, the problem is of particular significance in federations. In the first place, if a federation is characterized by a supreme constitution distributing authority between co-ordinate governments, then the

---

Mid-Western Region Act, 1962 (1962, no. 6), but when a state of emergency was declared one of the first steps of the Administrator of the Western Region appointed by the central government was to withdraw the action. The Eastern Nigeria Government sought to bring its complaints about the conducting of the 1963 census before the Supreme Court, but the Court held that its jurisdiction did not extend to this issue.

[1] For discussions of the degree to which 'literal' rules of interpretation have prevailed, see especially: McWhinney, *Judicial Review*, ch. 7; Alexandrowicz, op. cit., esp. ch. 1; Jain, *Indian Constitutional Law*, pp. 607–12; Sharma, op. cit., pp. 62–65 and ch. 11; Callard, *Political Forces in Pakistan*, pp. 25–26, 46–48; Sheridan, *Malaya and Singapore*, pp. 34–40; R. H. Hickling, 'The First Five Years of the Federation of Malaya Constitution', *Malaya Law Review*, iv (1962), pp. 198–200; Brett (ed.), *Constitutional Problems of Federalism in Nigeria*, pp. 21–25, 46–47, 58, 71, 89–90, 130–1, 134.

ultimate control will lie with those governments in which the power to amend this constitution is confided. Formal constitutional amendment is not, of course, the only method of altering the federal framework. Judicial review, and customs and conventions, may alter the balance or structure of a federation to a large degree. Nevertheless, the formal amendment process is the supreme form of adjustment, for it transcends and repudiates other forms of amendment: 'it may override any of the others and none of the others may override it'.[1] Consequently, the relative roles in the amendment process to be assigned to the two chambers of the central legislature, to the regional governments, to the populace through referenda, and in the case of colonial federations to the United Kingdom government, are of particular importance.

Conflicting demands for flexibility and rigidity in the constitution raise further problems. On the one hand, the constitution must be made adaptable to changing needs and circumstances, as experience in the older federations has indicated. This is all the more important in federations undergoing rapid economic development. On the other hand, the very regionalism which makes a federal system necessary is likely to encourage the demand for an amendment process sufficiently rigid for the regional governments to be secure to some degree in the functions assigned to them. In the words of the Reid Commission: 'It is important that the method of amending the Constitution should be neither so difficult as to produce frustration nor so easy as to weaken seriously the safeguards which the Constitution provides.'[2]

Usually, in the effort to compromise between flexibility and rigidity, differing amendment procedures have been applied to various sections of a constitution, thus enabling some parts, such as the distribution of powers, to be entrenched, while leaving other portions more flexible. Indeed, in some of the new federations there is an almost bewildering variety of procedures.

In each of the independent federations, India (1950), Pakistan (1956 and 1962), Malaya (1957), Malaysia (1963), and Nigeria (1960 and 1963), the articles of the constitutions were grouped into three main categories with different procedures for constitutional amendment.[3] Generally, the power to initiate amendments of all three types has been limited to the central legislature, both houses possessing this power in the bicameral legislatures,[4] but different requirements have been specified for their approval.

---

[1] Livingston, *Federalism and Constitutional Change*, pp. 13–14. See Sharma, op. cit., ch. 15, for instance, on the way in which constitutional amendments have been used in India to overcome judicial interpretation of the constitution.   [2] Col. no. 330/1957, para. 80.

[3] For formal procedures of constitutional amendment see *Constitution of India, 1950*, art. 368; *Constitution of Pakistan, 1956*, art. 216; *Constitution of Pakistan, 1962*, arts. 208–10; *Constitution of Malaya, 1957*, art. 159, and *Malaysia Act, 1963*, ss. 66, 69; *Constitution of Nigeria, 1960*, and *1963*, s. 4. For comparative analysis, see Table 17B, p. 385.

[4] Sometimes, however, special conditions have to be fulfilled before the central legislature may initiate amendments. See, for instance, *Constitution of India, 1950*, arts. 3, 169, 249, 312, 348 (1), 349; *Constitution of Pakistan, 1956*, art. 145; *Constitution of Nigeria, 1960* and *1963*, s. 4 (3, 4).

First, most of the constitution has usually been entrenched by requiring passage in each house of the central legislature by a special majority: in India and Pakistan (1956) two-thirds of those voting and a majority of members, and in Malaya, Malaysia, Nigeria, and Pakistan after 1962 two-thirds of the members.[1] Assent by the Head of State is also necessary in each case. In this type of amendment procedure the regional units are associated with the process only indirectly, the central second chamber which represents their interests being in a position to block amendments which fail to receive the required special majority. This safeguard for regional interests was, however, non-existent in Pakistan because of the unicameral character of the National Assembly, and was weakened in independent Malaya and Malaysia by the large proportion of nominated senators, and in India by the unequal representation of states in the second chamber.

Secondly, certain parts of these federal constitutions have been further entrenched by requiring, before assent by the Head of State, not only the special majorities in the central legislature, but also ratification by a specified number of regional governments: in India by not less than half the state legislatures, in Pakistan by the legislature of any province affected, in Nigeria before 1963 by at least two regional legislatures, and after 1963 by at least three, and in Malaya and Malaysia by the Conference of Rulers in certain cases and by the legislatures of states affected in some other instances.[2] In this way the amendment of constitutional provisions in this category was placed under more direct regional control, and the right of a single tier of government to alter these sections unilaterally was denied. It is noteworthy that, in the new independent federations, the regional approval of constitutional amendments has been given almost invariably to regional legislatures rather than to the electorates. There are two exceptions. The Nigerian procedure for altering regional boundaries or creating new regions includes arrangements for a referendum.[3] The Pakistan constitution of 1962 provides for a referendum amongst the members of the electoral college in certain cases where the President and the National Assembly fail to agree over a constitutional amendment.[4] Otherwise, there has not been provison for a referendum as part

---

[1] In Malaya, Malaysia, and Nigeria the special majorities were required only on the second and third readings. In Pakistan (1962) an amendment vetoed by the President requires repassage by three-quarters of the members of the Assembly followed by either the assent of the President or a referendum. In independent Kenya (1963) majorities of three-quarters of the members of each central house, and for specially entrenched sections nine-tenths of the members of the upper house were required (ss. 71 and Sched. 4).

[2] Normally only simple majorities in the regional legislatures have been required except in Pakistan (1962) and Uganda (1962), where approval by two-thirds of the members of a provincial or state assembly was stipulated. On the amendment procedure in Uganda, see Constitution, 1962, s. 5, and also S.I. 1962, no. 2175, s. 30. In none of the independent federations has a time limit been set within which ratification by regional legislatures must occur, and therefore the situation may arise in the future when it will not be clear whether an amendment bill is dead.

[3] Constitutions, 1960 and 1963, s. 4 (5) (*b*).　　　　　[4] Constitution, 1962, art. 209.

of the constitutional amendment process, although this has not discouraged the fighting of elections on issues of constitutional amendment or prevented a government from resorting to a referendum on a constitutional issue as a means of politicial leverage.[1]

The proportion of a constitution requiring regional ratification has varied considerably.[2] In the Nigerian constitutions of 1960 and 1963, and in Uganda, a very large portion was protected in this manner. Less of the Indian constitution was placed in this category of maximum rigidity, but most of the 'federal' features such as the distribution of legislative and executive powers, the amendment procedures themselves, the Union and state judiciaries, the representation of states in Parliament, and the election of the President, were safeguarded in this way.[3] The reorganization of state boundaries and the revision of financial resources were, however, made particularly flexible.[4] In the 1956 constitution of Pakistan there was greater protection for provincial boundaries, but otherwise considerably less of the 'federal' provisions required provincial ratification for amendment than in India. For instance, the articles defining the extent of central and provincial authority required provincial approval for amendment, but the legislative lists themselves, the consultation of provinces before the implementation of treaties, and the residuary power of the provinces could be altered by special majorities in the National Assembly alone. The Pakistan constitution of 1962 and the Malayan constitution of 1957 left nearly all the 'federal' aspects amendable by special majorities of the central parliament alone, the only articles requiring ratification by the affected states being those affecting regional boundaries.[5] In Malaya, however, the constitutional provisions governing the composition and functions of the Conference of Rulers, the precedence and privileges of the rulers and governors, and the reservation of quotas in the services and of permits for the Malays, did require the consent of the Conference of Rulers. The Malaysia Act, 1963, extended the number of specially entrenched articles by stipulating that no important amendments affecting the Borneo states or Singapore could be made without the concurrence of the government of the state concerned. In terms of constitutional requirements, it would appear that some aspects of the 'federal' structures in India and Pakistan (1956), and most of the 'federal' system in Malaya and (after 1962) Pakistan, were unprotected against unilateral amendment by the central legislature, so long as the required special central majorities approved. But, if we look beyond the mere

---

[1] The linguistic states issue figured prominently in Indian election campaigns; the demand for new regions has been disputed in Nigerian elections; Premier Manley called a referendum to settle the issue of Jamaica's continued membership in the West Indies Federation.

[2] See Table 17A, p. 384, for a comparative analysis.

[3] Moreover, constitutional amendments apply to the state of Jammu and Kashmir only if the state government concurs. Constitution, art. 370 (1).

[4] See sections 5 and 6 of this chapter.

[5] *Constitution of Malaya, 1957*, art. 2 (*b*); *Constitution of Pakistan, 1962*, art. 210.

legal requirements to the conventions that have grown, we find that under the pressure of political forces it has become customary in these countries for the central government to consult the regional governments before the intro- duction of important constitutional amendments, even in those instances where the regions have possessed no formal powers of ratification. This means that in practice the amendment of the federal structure has rarely been a purely unilateral process. Nevertheless, the fact remains that legally the regional governments are not in some instances in a position to prevent amendments to the federal system.

Thirdly, in addition to the two categories of entrenched provisions, usually certain portions of the constitutions of the independent federations have been left flexible, requiring for amendment only the normal procedure for ordinary central legislation. Articles treated in this way have usually been those dealing with administrative details which in older constitutions were simply omitted. The Indian constitution, however, also made some items on the legislative lists flexible by simply leaving the definition of their scope to be determined by Union law.[1] In a few matters, constitutional amendment by simple majority in the central legislature has required special conditions: a prior resolution supported by two-thirds of those voting in the Council of States in India for temporary invasions of the state legislative powers or for creation of All- India services,[2] the sanction of the President after considering the recommen- dations of a Language Commission before alterations during the first fifteen years concerning the official language for courts and bills in India,[3] prior con- sultation of the legislatures of states affected before revision of their boun- daries in India,[4] prior consultation of provincial legislatures before deciding upon the principle of joint or separate electorates in Pakistan,[5] and the consent of each regional governor before amendment in Nigeria of certain transitional provisions.[6]

When we turn to the procedures for constitutional amendment in the colonial federations, two points stand out.[7] *First*, in most of these federations, as in the independent ones, the constitutions are partly rigid and partly flex- ible. In Malaya the bulk of the Federation Agreement of 1948 could be amended by an ordinary central ordinance, provided 'the prior approval of His Majesty and the Conference of Rulers' had been obtained. But certain parts, including the legislative lists, could be amended only by a proclamation of the High Commissioner 'in terms previously agreed upon by His Majesty

---

[1] See Union List, entries 7, 23, 24, 27, 32, 52–54, 56, 62–64, 67, and Concurrent List, entries 40, 41. There was one such example also in *Constitution of Malaya, 1957*, Federal List, item 10 (*a*).

[2] Arts. 249, 312.   [3] Arts. 348, 349.   [4] Art. 3.
[5] Constitution, 1956, art. 145.   [6] S.I. 1960, no. 1652, ss. 16, 18.

[7] For amendment procedures, see *Federation of Malaya Agreement, 1948*, cl. 6; *Con- stitution of R. and N., 1953*, arts. 10, 97–99; *Nigeria Constitution, 1954*, s. 1 (4); *Constitution of W.I., 1957*, arts. 117–18. See also Table 17B, p. 385.

and the Conference of Rulers', and the schedules of sources of revenue and heads of expenditure could be amended only by a proclamation of the High Commissioner after consultation with the central Legislative Council and the Settlement Councils and with the assent of the rulers after each had consulted his Council of State. The normal procedure for constitutional amendment in Rhodesia and Nyasaland was passage by the unicameral Federal Assembly, with support at the final reading by at least two-thirds of its members, and assent by 'Her Majesty' rather than by the Governor-General.[1] If, however, any territorial legislature objected within sixty days, or the African Affairs Board considered an amendment bill a differentiating measure, then the royal assent was to be signified by order in council, and only after the order had been laid before the British Parliament for forty days without the passage of a negative resolution in either House. Federal electoral bills had to meet similar requirements, except that territorial legislatures were given no opportunity for objection. During the first ten years, provisions relating to the distribution of legislative authority and to the amendment and review of the constitution were further protected by requiring the prior consent of each territorial legislature. In the West Indies, amendment by United Kingdom order in council was the normal procedure for nearly the whole of the constitution, but amendments affecting the relative territorial representation in the central legislature required the consent of the legislatures of the territories affected, and alterations to the amendment procedure itself required approval by all the territorial legislatures.[2] Among the colonial federations the Nigerian constitution of 1954 stood alone, for unlike the others it had but one uniform procedure for the amendment of any section: amendment by United Kingdom order in council.

Secondly, in all the colonial federations the United Kingdom retained some control as the ultimate constitutional authority. In both Nigeria and the West Indies all amendments were by United Kingdom orders in council, although in both federations amendments were preceded by consultation with central and regional political leaders, or by constitutional conferences at which much of the real political bargaining was between central and regional politicians.[3]

---

[1] Nyasaland contributed less than one-third of the members of the Federal Assembly, and the total number of African members and members elected for African interests from all three territories was about one-quarter. The special majority required was not, therefore, a serious obstacle to the settlers of the two Rhodesias, provided they were united. See Table 15, p. 382.

[2] The 1961 West Indian review conference agreed that after independence a distinction should be made between ordinary and entrenched provisions, the latter requiring passage by absolute majorities in each central house and in a majority of the territorial representative houses representing a majority of the federal population, thus giving Jamaica a virtual veto. Moreover, the assumption by the central government of certain powers over economic development, income taxes, customs, and freedom of internal movement would have been subject to special conditions requiring inter-governmental consultation and territorial agreement.

[3] In Nigeria in 1957 it was agreed that central or regional legislatures might, after passage

Even in Malaya and Rhodesia and Nyasaland, where procedures somewhat similar to those in independent federations were specified, requiring passage in certain cases by the central legislature and consent in some of these instances by state rulers or territorial governments, the United Kingdom possessed a veto on every amendment: over its introduction in Malaya, and over the royal assent in Rhodesia and Nyasaland.[1] Moreover in the latter case, as in Nigeria and the West Indies, the British Government retained the right to carry through constitutional amendments unilaterally.[2] The Federation of South Arabia differed from the others in that the British Government did not possess a veto over constitutional amendments: majorities of two-thirds in the Federal Council, or if three states objected, three-quarters, and for specially entrenched sections the prior concurrence of the states, were specified, to be followed in each case by assent by the Supreme Council.[3] Nevertheless, the United Kingdom did retain full legislative power to prevail over federal authority.[4] Thus, in the pre-independent federations it was the United Kingdom Government, instead of the regional governments, which was placed in the position of guardian of the federal balance.

A device peculiar to the colonial federations has been the constitutional review conference for considering what constitutional revisions might be undertaken. The constitutions of both Rhodesia and Nyasaland and the West Indies guaranteed that such conferences composed of representatives of the central, territorial, and British governments, should be held after a specified interval of years.[5] In the other two colonial federations the constitutions did not stipulate the calling of such conferences, but in Nigeria they were promised and subsequently held in 1957–8 and 1960,[6] and in Malaya the revision of the constitution before independence was worked out by a similar conference, aided by a constitutional commission and by the conference's working party.[7] Such a conference has the advantage of providing an

of a resolution, submit proposals for constitutional amendment to the Secretary of State for the Colonies, provided such proposals were also communicated to the other Nigerian governments (Cmnd. 207/1957, para. 7).

[1] In Central Africa, however, the British Government in practice failed to reject any constitutional amendments passed by the Federal Assembly, thus giving the impression that this safeguard was relatively ineffective. Nevertheless, the possibility of a veto always hung over any proposals the Federal Assembly might make to alter the constitution.

[2] Cmnd. 1148/1960, para. 288 (b).

[3] Constitution, 1963, ss. 28, 70–71.

[4] S.I. 1963, no. 82, ss. 4, 9.

[5] Constitution of R. and N., 1953, art. 99; Constitution of W.I., 1957, art. 118. The Central African Constitutional Review Conference which opened in December 1960 was preceded by the Monckton Advisory Constitutional Commission (Cmnd. 1148–51/1960), and the West Indian Constitutional Review Conference in 1961 (Cmnd. 1417/1961) was preceded by an inter-governmental conference in the West Indies, and a series of meetings of its committees. A constitutional review was also guaranteed for South Arabia (Cmnd. 1814/1962, p. 15).

[6] Cmd. 8934/1953, para. 27; Cmnd. 207/1957; Cmnd. 569/1958; Cmnd. 1063/1960.

[7] Cmd. 9714/1956; Col. no. 330/1957; Cmnd. 210/1957, paras. 1–5.

opportunity for a thorough review of a constitution after it has been in operation for sufficient time to reveal its weaknesses. These conferences have also provided occasions when provisions more in keeping with federal independence could be worked out at the appropriate time. On the other hand, the promise of such conferences has often encouraged uncertainty and lack of confidence in the future form, or even continued existence, of these federations. Evidence of this was particularly marked in the intensification of inter-regional disputes and secession movements preceding the West Indian and Central African review conferences in 1960–1, and the swelling demand for new regions in Nigeria which reached a peak in 1957–8.

In their amendment procedures the interim federal constitutions of India (1947–50) and Pakistan (1947–56) were unique among the new federations. Not only was there a single uniform amendment procedure for all sections in each, but since the functions of constituent assembly and central legislature were performed by the same body, no part of the constitution required for its revision more than the usual procedure for central legislation.[1] Indeed, in India, and in Pakistan until the rulings of the Federal Court over the dismissal of the Constituent Assembly in 1954, constitutional amendment was even easier than ordinary legislation, for the Governor-General's assent was considered unnecessary.[2]

The formal amendment of regional constitutions within the new federations has rarely been left in the hands of the regions alone. In the independent federations, regional legislatures have been given the power to amend some minor details of the regional constitutions, but for the amendment of the main features the central legislature has invariably been given a prominent role.[3] In Nigeria, for instance, it was decided that 'since the units of a federal structure are interdependent', those aspects of the regional constitutions which were of general concern should require for amendment the concurrence of two-thirds of the members of each House of the federal legislature.[4] The Indian (1950),

---

[1] *Indian Independence Act, 1947*, s. 8.

[2] See K. C. Wheare, *The Constitutional Structure of the Commonwealth* (1960), pp. 95–103.

[3] Constitution of India, 1950, arts. 2–4, 164 (5), 169, 171 (2), 186, 187 (2, 3), 189 (3), 194 (3), 195, 209, 210, 240 (2), 321, 328, 345, 347, 368, Fifth Sched., para. 7, and Sixth Sched., para. 21; *Constitution of Pakistan, 1956*, arts. 77 (3, 4), 89 (5), 189, 216 (1); *Constitution of Pakistan, 1962*, arts. 208–10; *Constitution of Malaya, 1957*, art. 159, and Eighth Sched., s. 19; *Malaysia Act, 1963*, s. 12; *Constitution of Nigeria, 1960* and *1963*, s. 5. On amendment of state constitutions in Malaya, see also R. H. Hickling in Sheridan, *Malaya and Singapore*, pp. 95–96. Where regional legislatures could make amendments, special majorities of two-thirds of the members were required in Malaya, Malaysia, Nigeria, and Uganda, but not India and Pakistan.

[4] Cmnd. 569/1958, paras. 62–63; Constitutions, 1960 and 1963, s. 5 (4, 6). The West Indian proposals of 1961 (Cmnd. 1417/1961, para. 29), and the Uganda Constitution of 1962 (s. 6) were similar. In Malaya (1957) state legislation affecting Malay reservations required approval by a two-thirds' majority in each House of the central Parliament, in order to prevent the Malays' special interests being diminished in the west coast states where they were in a minority (Constitution, art. 89). The requirement of concurrence by a majority

Pakistan (1956 and 1962), and Malayan (1957) federal constitutions went even further. In India and Pakistan, except for a few details, all of the state and provincial constitutions which were contained in the federal documents, and in Malaya and Malaysia the 'essential provisions' for state constitutions which were contained in the federal constitution, were alterable only by the normal federal amendment procedures. Since the regions had power neither to initiate nor, for most of these provisions, to ratify amendments, uniformity as well as rigidity of state and provincial constitutions was ensured.

In the pre-independent federations, the territorial legislatures in the Malay States and in Southern Rhodesia possessed the power to make some amendments, but otherwise amendment of regional constitutions was simply by United Kingdom order in council after consultation with the regional governments and political leaders.[1] The central government was usually consulted before the British Government exercised this power, and in Central Africa the influence of the Federal Government in such instances was on several occasions a source of controversy.[2]

Thus, whether by constitutional requirement or by convention, it has been usual to recognize in the procedures for amendment of both the federal and the regional constitutions the interdependent relationship between governments.

5. The admission, reorganization, and secession of regions

An important aspect of constitutional amendment in federations, and one often requiring special treatment, is the admission, reorganization, and secession of regions.

The procedure for the admission of new territories has generally been more heavily influenced by the desire not to discourage regions which initially refused to federate from acceding at a later date, than by any fears that the inclusion of new units might affect the balance of power within the federation. Most of the new federations entertained hopes that new territories might accede later: the West Indies looked to British Guiana, British Honduras, and the British Virgin Islands, Nigeria to the Northern and Southern Cameroons, Malaya to Singapore and the British Borneo territories, Pakistan to Kashmir, and India to the French and Portuguese enclaves and even to the reincorporation of Pakistan. Consequently, in each of the Asian federations, it was decided that new regions might be admitted simply by ordinary central law.[3]

in the central parliament was added in Malaysia with respect to substantial amendments of the Singapore Constitution (*Malaysia Act, 1963*, s. 12 (1)).

[1] S.I. 1948, no. 108 (Malaya), s. 54; S.I. 1953, no. 1199 (R. & N.), s. 14; S.I. 1954, no. 1146 (Nigeria), s. 1 (4); S.I. 1957, no. 1364 (W.I.), s. 6. See also Cmnd. 1149/1960, p. 31.

[2] See, for instance, H. Franklin, *Unholy Wedlock* (1963), ch. 17. In spite of the convention that the central governments should be consulted before territorial constitutions were amended, the decision to permit Jamaica and Nyasaland to secede was made by the British Government despite the protests of the central governments affected. See section 5, below.

[3] *Constitution of India, 1950*, arts. 2, 4; *Constitution of Pakistan, 1956*, arts. 1 (2) (*b*), 2,

The same procedure was agreed upon in Nigeria with reference to the Cameroons, although the admission of other new territories would necessitate the normal constitutional amendment process requiring special majorities in the central legislature.[1] In the West Indies Federation, the provision enabling new territories to be added by United Kingdom orders in council was expressly designed to make the joining of British Guiana or British Honduras as easy as possible.[2] The Federation of South Arabia also made express provision for the accession of states, a treaty approved by the United Kingdom being sufficient before 1963, and after that an ordinary federal law.[3] Unlike the other new federal constitutions, that of Rhodesia and Nyasaland made no reference to the accession of territories, and therefore this would have required the normal form of constitutional amendment passed by special majorities in the Federal Assembly and assented to by the Queen.

The appropriate procedure for the reorganization of regional units within a federation has generally proved a much more controversial issue. In the new federations, where the colonial boundaries, often established for administrative or economic reasons, have not coincided with the fundamental social diversities, the demands for the revision of boundaries or for the reorganization of regions have sometimes been intense.[4] But if regional boundaries are made easy to alter, and particularly if the central government is given authority to make such modifications unilaterally, the integrity of the regions as autonomous units of government may be seriously undermined.

The Indian Constituent Assembly decided in favour of flexibility. Anticipating the desirability of eventually reorganizing the states on linguistic lines, once the immediate crises of independence, partition, and the integration of the princely states had been surmounted, the Assembly provided that the Union Parliament might by ordinary law split or join states to form new states, increase or diminish the area and alter the boundaries of any state, or change the name of any state.[5] There is a proviso that such bills may be introduced only on the recommendation of the President, and then only

---

201, 203; *Constitution of Pakistan, 1962*, arts. 1 (2) (*b*), 221; *Constitution of Malaya, 1957*, art. 2 (*a*), and 159 (4) (*bb*) as added by *Constitution (Amendment) Act, 1962* (F. 14/1962), s. 24. *The Federation of Malaya Agreement, 1948*, cl. 3, however, provided for the inclusion of new territories by mutual agreement of 'His Majesty' and the rulers.

[1] S.I. 1960, no. 1652, s. 16; Constitution, 1960, s. 4 (1, 2). The 1954 Constitution, s. 1 (4), would have required the normal amendment procedure (a U.K. order in council) for the admission of any territory.

[2] Constitution, art. 117. The 1961 Constitutional Conference and subsequently the 1962 East Caribbean Federation Conference decided, however, to require the procedure for amending the entrenched articles (Cmnd. 1417/1961, para. 36; Cmnd. 1746/1962, paras. 43, 46).

[3] Cmnd. 665/1959, p. 4; Constitution, 1963, ss. 3–4.   [4] See Chapter 7, above.

[5] Constitution, 1950, arts. 3, 4; C.A.I., *Debates*, vol. iii, p. 462; vol. x, pp. 312, 319. The consent of the Jammu and Kashmir State Legislature is necessary before the introduction in the Union Parliament of any bill altering the name or boundary of that state, however (*The Constitution (Application to Jammu and Kashmir) Order, 1954*, C.O. 48/1954, s. 2 (2)).

after he has ascertained the views of the legislatures of the affected states. A subsequent amendment empowers the President to specify a time limit within which a state legislature must express its views, so removing the threat of a state delaying reorganization by a refusal to express its views.[1] Thus the Indian constitution provides an extremely flexible means of adjusting the territories of the states, the concurrence of the states affected not being required, so long as the period for the expression of their views has expired. Moreover, in practice, this power has frequently been exercised by the Union Parliament, the most notable examples being the creation of Andhra in 1953, the widespread reorganization of states in 1956, and the splitting of Bombay 1960.[2] Commentators have, therefore, often considered this unilateral central power as a violation of the federal principle.[3] It must be recognized, however, that the actual use of the power has nearly always been to meet local demands for unilingual states rather than to impose central solutions on unwilling states. Moreover, in most of these cases, local popular agitation and pressure from state legislatures not only motivated the central action, but in later stages led to modification of proposals. Nevertheless, this wide central power of state reorganization as it stands does represent a potential threat to the very existence and integrity of the states, which thereby are made dependent upon the will of the Union Parliament.

By contrast, apprehension of such central power over the regions has led most of the other new federations to follow the example of the constitutions of the U.S.A.[4] and Australia,[5] where the consent of the affected states is required for boundary revisions. The Pakistan constitutions of 1956 and 1962, for instance, required before alterations to the territories of the existing provinces and states not only a special majority in the National Assembly, but the assent of the provincial assemblies affected.[6] Even under the previous

[1] *Fifth Amendment Act, 1955*, s. 2.

[2] *Andhra State Act* (xxx/1953); *The States Reorganization Act* (xxxvii/1956); *Bihar and W. Bengal (Transfer of Territories) Act* (xl/1956); *Bombay Reorganization Act* (11/1960). Other exercises of this power were: *Chandernagore (Merger) Act* (xxxvi/1954); *Rajasthan and Madhya Pradesh (Transfer of Territories) Act* (47/1959); *Andhra P. and Madras (Alteration of Boundaries) Act* (56/1959); *State of Nagaland Act, 1962* (27/1962). Basu, *Commentary on the Constitution of India* (3rd ed., 1955), vol. i, p. 56, vol. ii, p. 619, classifies *The Assam (Alteration of Boundaries) Act* (xlvii/1951) as an example, but A. C. Banerjee and K. L. Chatterjee, *A Survey of the Indian Constitution* (1957), p. 337, suggest that since no reference was made to the state legislature, it must have been in exercise of the treaty-implementing power under art. 253. In the boundary adjustments with Pakistan in 1960, the merger into existing Indian states of the acquired territories was carried out under article 3 by the *Acquired Territories (Merger) Act* (64/1960), but following a Supreme Court ruling the transfer of territories to Pakistan was made by a full constitutional amendment in the *Ninth Amendment Act, 1960*.

[3] Santhanam, *Union–State Relations in India*, pp. 7, 12; Banerjee and Chatterjee, loc. cit.; Basu, op. cit., vol. i, p. 14; Alexandrowicz, *Constitutional Developments in India*, pp. 157, 172. The Union Parliament cannot, however, abolish all states under these provisions.

[4] Art. IV, s. 3 (2).   [5] Ss. 123–4.

[6] Constitution, 1956, art. 216 (1) first proviso; Constitution, 1962, art. 210. Under the former, support of two-thirds of those voting and a majority of the members was required

interim constitution, where a simple majority of the Constituent Assembly possessed full constitutional sovereignty, it was considered politically necessary at the time of the unification of West Pakistan to obtain the consent of the provincial legislatures.[1] The constitutions of independent Malaya and Malaysia enable state boundaries to be altered by ordinary federal law, but only with the consent both of the legislatures of the states involved and of the Conference of Rulers.[2] The Nigerian constitutions of 1960 and 1963 specified several procedures for changing regional boundaries or creating new regions. Substantial alterations require the approval of the legislatures of the regions concerned, or of a majority of the regional legislatures, and a referendum in the territory involved.[3] These arrangements were intended to protect the existing regions which feared movements to divide them, especially the North. Nigerian constitution-makers, unlike those in India, clearly hoped that by making these provisions so rigid they would discourage the already vociferous demands for new states. The danger, on the other hand, of such constitutional rigidity—one which the Indians clearly wished to avoid—is that the frustration of the movements for regional reorganization may induce extra-constitutional action. Stringent as the Nigerian constitutional provisions seem, the pressures for revising the regional structure have not disappeared, and were so strong that in 1963 the requirements for the establishment of a new Mid-Western Region were met.[4]

Elsewhere too, constitutional proposals for independent federations have envisaged the entrenching of regional boundaries. The 1961 West Indian constitutional conference agreed upon requirements somewhat similar to those in Nigeria, although a referendum was not included.[5] The 1962 scheme for an East Caribbean federation did not specifically refer to the alteration

in the National Assembly, and a simple majority in the provincial assemblies; under the latter, support by two-thirds of the members in both the National Assembly and also the provincial assemblies was required.

[1] C.A.P. (second), *Debates*, vol. i, pp. 1828–9. [2] Art. 2 (*b*).

[3] S. 4 (2–6). Minor changes of regional boundaries, i.e. the transfer of an area of not more than 1,000 sq. miles, with not more than 100,000 inhabitants, may be made by a federal enactment passed with a two-thirds majority in each house, amending the constitution, but cannot come into operation until approved by the legislatures of the affected regions. Otherwise, changes of regional boundaries or the creation of new states require: (i) a resolution supported by two-thirds of the members in each federal house; then (ii) in the case of boundary changes: resolutions of approval, either by each of the legislatures of all the regions affected, or by a majority of the regions including that to which the area is to be transferred; or in the case of the creation of new regions: by resolutions of approval, either by the legislatures of a majority of regions, or by the legislatures of at least two regions including any out of which the new state would be created; then (iii) a federal enactment supported at the second and third readings by two-thirds of the members of each house, except that, when new regions are created, simple majorities suffice; then (iv) ratification by the legislatures of at least two regions; then finally (v) a referendum in the area to be transferred, at which approval of at least 60 per cent. of the inhabitants is obtained.

[4] *Mid-Western Region Act, 1962* (1962, no. 6), was followed by a referendum in July 1963 with a sufficient majority supporting the creation of the new region.

[5] Cmnd. 1417/1961, para. 35.

of regional units, but such changes would have required the procedure protecting the entrenched provisions of the constitution, involving territorial approval.[1] In Africa the independence constitutions of Uganda[2] and Kenya[3] specified a procedure similar to that in the Pakistan constitution of 1962.

In the colonial constitutions of the West Indies (1957), Nigeria (1954), Rhodesia and Nyasaland (1953), and South Arabia (1962) no special provisions for the amendment of territorial boundaries were included. The boundaries were entrenched, however, since alterations would have required the normal process of constitutional amendment: a United Kingdom order in council in the West Indies or Nigeria, a special majority in the Federal Assembly and Her Majesty's assent or an Act of the United Kingdom Parliament for Rhodesia and Nyasaland, a special majority in the Federal Council and repassage by a greater majority if three states object for South Arabia.

In each of the six new federations serious threats of secession have arisen in some regions. For example, the Naga and Dravidasthan separatist movements in India reached critical proportions, while in Pakistan there have been occasional East Bengali demands for independence stimulated by resentment at the supervision of Karachi. In Malaya there was a petition for the secession of Penang in 1949,[4] and two years after joining Malaysia Singapore was separated again. All three original regions of Nigeria have threatened to secede,[5] and when the British Cameroons were given the opportunity to vote on whether to remain within an independent Nigeria, the Southern Cameroons chose to leave. Among the strongest secession movements have been those in Jamaica and Nyasaland, culminating in the disintegration of both the West Indian and Central African federations.

As in the older federations it has often been asserted that an essential requirement of a federal political system is that there should be no right of secession from the federation.[6] Four main arguments have been advanced against the toleration of secession in a federation. First, it has been argued that, if a regional government acting alone is given the right to leave the federation, or if the central government acting alone is given the right to expel a member government, then one tier of government is subordinated to the other, violating the principle of co-ordinate governments. Secondly, the right

---

[1] Cmnd. 1746/1962, para. 43.

[2] Constitution, 1962, s. 5. There were special provisions governing the lost counties (S.I. 1962, no. 2175, ss. 7, 26, 30). See also Cmnd. 1778/1962, paras. 15, 66–69.

[3] Constitution, 1963, ss. 239–45. But only a simple majority was required in each House of the National Assembly. Alternatively, under s. 71 and Sched. 4, regional boundaries may be altered, without regional concurrence, by majorities of 75 per cent. in the central lower house and 90 per cent. in the upper house.

[4] *Secession of the Settlement of Penang and Province Wellesley Petition by Penang and Province Wellesley Secession Committee*, 12 October 1949.

[5] Examples were the threats of secession by both northerners and westerners at the Ibadan Conference 1950, by northerners during the 1953 constitutional crisis, by westerners at the 1954 constitutional conference, and by easterners during the 1964 election.

[6] For a critical discussion of this view see Wheare, *Federal Government*, pp. 85–87.

to secede unilaterally weakens the whole federal system by placing a weapon of political coercion in the hands of regional governments. Thirdly, the possibility of the disintegration of the federation through the unilateral actions of governments introduces an element of uncertainty and lack of confidence, which may seriously handicap efforts to build up national unity and economic development. Finally, the example of the earlier federations of the United States, Switzerland, Canada, and Australia, none of which recognized a unilateral right of secession, has sometimes been cited.

It is hardly surprising, therefore, that none of the new independent federations has permitted *unilateral* regional secession. Although not expressly prohibited in the constitution, the right to secede has been implicitly denied to the regions, for in each of the independent federations the exclusion of a region would require a formal constitutional amendment initiated and approved by the central legislature.[1] The Indian Constituent Assembly, furthermore, deliberately chose the term 'Union' to indicate that the federation was indestructible and that the component units would have no right to secede.[2] In 1963 the Union Government, concerned at the mounting strength of southern separatism, went so far as to introduce an 'anti-secession' constitutional amendment outlawing secessionist activities and giving the central government added powers for the preservation and maintenance of the sovereignty of the Indian Union.[3]

The constitutions of the colonial federations, except for that of South Arabia, have also denied to the regions any right of unilateral secession, for the exclusion of any territory invariably required the assent of the United Kingdom.[4] Requests by Penang in Malaya and by Western Nigeria for the right to secede were in fact rejected by the British Government.[5] But, as the creator of the colonial federations, the imperial government retained the right to dissolve them, and in practice has actually agreed in five instances to the secession of territories.

The first of these was the acceptance of the Muslim League demands for the partition of India in 1947, when it became apparent that a united India could not be imposed except at the cost of a major civil war.

The second was the special case of the Cameroons in Nigeria. Because of

---

[1] *Constitution of India, 1950*, arts. 1 (2), 368; *In re Berubari Union and Exchange of Enclaves*, A.I.R. 1960, S.C. 845; *Constitution of Pakistan, 1956*, arts. 1 (2), 216 (1); *Constitution of Pakistan, 1962*, arts. 1 (2), 208–9; *Constitution of Malaya, 1957*, and *Malaysia, 1963*, arts. 1 (2), 159; *Constitution of Nigeria, 1960* and *1963*, ss. 3, 4. The exclusion of Singapore from Malaysia in 1965 followed this procedure.   [2] C.A.I., *Debates*, vol. vii, p. 43.

[3] *Sixteenth Amendment Act, 1963*. See also Lok Sabha, *Debates*, 3rd ser., vol. xii (21–22 January 1963), cols. 5495, 5759–5841.

[4] See section 4 of this chapter on the procedures for constitutional amendment. In the Federation of South Arabia, Aden is to be permitted to secede after seven years if its interests have been unfairly prejudiced and the central government has failed to take remedial action (Cmnd. 1814/1962, p. 8).

[5] *Reply to Petitioners*, Despatch no. 189 (52928/15/51); Cmd. 9059/1954, para. 48; O. Lyttelton, *The Memoirs of Lord Chandos* (1962), p. 416.

their status as United Nations Trust Territories, they were granted at the time of Nigerian independence the opportunity to choose by referenda between continued association with Nigeria and union with the Cameroun Republic. In 1961 the Northern Cameroons decided to rejoin the Nigerian Federation, but the voters of the Southern Cameroons proceeded to exercise their right to secede from Nigeria.

The third example occurred in 1961 when it was agreed that the tiny Cayman Islands, which had previously neither sent representatives to the Federal Parliament nor contributed financially, would be permitted to withdraw from the West Indies Federation.[1]

More dramatic was the secession of Jamaica and the subsequent collapse of the West Indies Federation in 1962. Although in earlier statements Premier Manley of Jamaica had recognized that there was no legal right of secession, this did not prevent him from planning a referendum on the issue of Jamaica's continued membership in the federation, in an attempt both to rout the anti-federation movement and to extort better terms for Jamaica at the constitutional review conference. But when the referendum resulted in a majority voting against Jamaica remaining in the federation, the territorial Government was forced to seek the withdrawal of Jamaica and the attainment of its own separate independence. The British Government hastily 'accepted the result of the referendum as a final indication of Jamaica's wishes', and agreed to Jamaica's withdrawal from the federation and its own independence.[2] At first the British Government expected the West Indies Federation, with modifications necessary as a result of Jamaica's secession, to continue. But soon afterwards the Government of Trinidad decided, without either raising the issue in the election which had just been held or calling a referendum, to follow Jamaica's example in seeking its own independence. Thereupon, the British Government quickly proceeded to dissolve the federation, ignoring the protests of the West Indies Federal Government, which complained that it had not been consulted.[3] The British recognition of Jamaica's right of secession had in fact resulted in the disintegration of the West Indies Federation.

By contrast, in Rhodesia and Nyasaland, where British interests were more directly involved, the United Kingdom Government was for some time more reluctant to permit territories to secede. In spite of the vigorous opposition to continued membership in the federation on the part of the Nyasaland Africans, who felt that the federal racial partnership was in practice no more than a method for maintaining white settler dominance, the British Government repeatedly emphasized its opposition to the secession of any of the

---

[1] Cmnd. 1417/1962, paras. 33–34.

[2] Cmnd. 1638/1962, para. 2–6; U.K. House of Commons, *Debates*, vol. 653 (6 February 1962), cols. 230–5; vol. 655 (13 March 1962), cols. 1101–3; vol. 656 (26 March 1962), cols. 849–940. See also J. B. Kelly, 'The End of Federation: Some Constitutional Implications', *West Indian Economist*, iv (1962), pp. 11–26.

[3] U.K. House of Commons, *Debates*, vol. 655, cols. 1101–3; vol. 656, cols. 849–940.

territories from the federation. The Monckton Commission of 1960, while agreeing that under the existing constitution no legal right of unilateral secession existed, recommended that a right of secession for a specified period might secure a voluntary willingness on the part of the northern territories to maintain the federation until they were in a position to judge its merits, and so enable the federation to survive.[1] By 1962 the British Government found itself forced to go even further. Despite its earlier reiterations about the permanence of the federal structure, it found the uncompromising insistence upon secession of Dr. Banda's Nyasaland Government impossible to resist, and at the end of 1962 the British Government accepted the principle that Nyasaland should not be kept in the federation against its will. As in the West Indies, this decision was reached despite the heated opposition of the central government, which charged the imperial government with failing to honour its pledges,[2] and also as in the West Indies, the British Government found that once the secession of one territory had been approved, other territories quickly demanded the same privilege, with the result that the federation could not be held together.

The experience of these colonial federations shows the dilemma which regional demands for secession placed before the British Government, because these claims represented local independence movements against federal structures created by the imperial government. While on some occasions secessionist demands have been rejected as in Penang and Nigeria, generally the British Government has been unwilling to impose continued federation if it might result in unrest and even civil war. On the other side, the belief that, as with other movements for self-government, the imperial government might be willing eventually to give such demands a hearing, if they were insistent enough, has encouraged secessionist movements. Furthermore, once the prestigious right of complete independence has been conceded for one region, it has proved difficult to hold together a federation in which the bonds of unity have not yet had time to strengthen. It would appear, therefore, that the independent federations have not been unwise in their denial of any right for regions to secede unilaterally.

6. *Other devices for federal flexibility*

Formal constitution amendment is not the only way of modifying federal constitutions. The constitution-makers in the new federations, aware of the

---

[1] Cmnd. 1148/1960, ch. 16.

[2] On the controversy surrounding the dissolution of the Central African federation, see especially Cmnd. 1948, 2000, 2073, and 2093/1963; C. Fed. 231/1962 and 246/1963; Federal Assembly, *Debates*, 3rd Parl., 1st Session (19 and 20 December 1962), cols. 2033–57, 2170–82, 3rd Parl., 2nd Session (8 April 1963), cols. 11–38; U.K. House of Commons, *Debates*, vol. 660 (31 May 1962), cols. 1587–91; vol. 669 (19 December 1962), cols. 1266–72; vol. 672 (28 February 1963), cols. 1457–1580; vol. 675 (1 April 1963), cols. 32–39; House of Lords, *Debates*, vol. 238 (27 March 1962), cols. 957–8; vol. 245 (19 and 20 December 1962), cols. 1148–1230, 1255–62; R. Welensky, *4000 Days* (1964).

difficulties caused by constitutional rigidity in the older federations, and conscious of the need for constitutional pliability in rapidly developing societies, have turned to a wide variety of special devices by which the federal systems might be made adaptable to changing circumstances.

One popular device for enhancing constitutional flexibility in federations has been the use of an extensive list of concurrent legislative powers. This has enabled the central governments to lay down the general lines of national policy in such areas as social welfare and economic and social planning, while leaving regional governments free to legislate for particular local circumstances in these fields.[1]

Provisions for the delegation of powers, both executive and legislative, from one government to another, have also been common.[2] Such arrangements enable the transfer of authority to meet a particular situation as the need arises. Care has usually been taken, however, to preserve the co-ordinate status of the governments involved, by qualifications requiring the consent of, or financial compensation to, the governments to which power is delegated, and by giving the delegating government power to revoke delegated authority. One notable exception to the usual pattern occurred, however, in Kenya. Because of fears that regions with governments of the same party as the central government might hand over their powers and so nullify the regional system, the constitutional proposals of 1963, contrary to an earlier scheme which would have enabled a region to transfer its power to the central government, precluded regions delegating either their legislative or executive authority.[3]

Where executive powers were concerned, the earlier constitutions, India (1935 and 1950), Malaya (1948), and Pakistan (1956), provided for delegation only from central to regional governments. Most of the later constitutions, Rhodesia and Nyasaland (1953), Nigeria (1954), India (after 1956), Malaya (1957), the West Indies (1957), Nigeria (1960 and 1963), and Malaysia (1963), have included provisions enabling the delegation of executive authority in *either* direction, although Pakistan (1962) permitted delegation only from the central government.[4] Normally the consent of the government to which executive power is to be transferred has been required. In the Asian federations

---

[1] See Chapter 8, section 2, and Table 3, pp. 363–6.

[2] See *Government of India Act, 1935*, ss. 103, 107 (2), 124–5; *Constitution of India, 1950*, arts. 252, 254 (2), 258, and 258A as inserted by *Seventh Amendment Act, 1956*, s. 18; *Constitution of Pakistan, 1956*, arts. 107, 110 (2), 127; *Constitution of Pakistan, 1962*, arts. 131 (3), 135 (*b*), 143; *Federation of Malaya Agreement, 1948*, cls. 18, 49, Second Sched., matter 13; *Constitution of Malaya, 1957*, arts. 76, 80, 110 (4), 157, and *Malaysia Act, 1963*, ss. 30 (7), 37, 38, 48; *Nigeria Constitution, 1954*, ss. 52, 136; *Constitution of Nigeria, 1960*, ss. 67, 92, 93, and *1963*, ss. 72, 99, 100; *Constitution of R. and N., 1953*, arts. 31, 32, 41, 42 (3); *Constitution of W.I., 1957*, arts. 44, 57, 58. See also *Constitution of South Arabia, 1963*, s. 58 (5, 6); *Constitution of Uganda, 1962*, ss. 75 (3), 78–79; *Independence Constitution of Kenya, 1963*, s. 74 (1). [3] Cmnd. 1970/1963, pp. 4–5.

[4] South Arabia (1962), Uganda (1962), and Kenya (1962), however, permitted the delegation of executive authority only from the central government.

delegation is sometimes permitted without such consent, but in all such instances, except in Pakistan after 1962, provision has been made for tribunals to assess compensation for the extra costs of administration incurred.

There have also been a variety of provisions for the delegation of legislative powers. Of the federations under consideration, only in Nigeria (and in Malaya between 1957 and 1963) has there been no provision permitting the central government to delegate power to regional legislatures. The delegation of central legislative authority may take two forms. In Malaya (1948), Rhodesia and Nyasaland (1953), the West Indies (1957), Pakistan (1962), and Malaysia (1963), the central legislature could by act confer its legislative authority upon a regional government. On the other hand, in India (1950) and Pakistan (1956) a similar effect was made possible by a special arrangement derived from the Government of India Act, 1935, whereby a provincial law in the concurrent field might prevail over a central law, if the President assented.[1] Delegation of legislative powers in the opposite direction, by regional to central legislatures, has been provided for in all six federations.[2] Generally, regional legislatures were empowered to delegate their authority individually, but in pre-partition India (1935), independent India (1950), and Malaya (1948), only if two or more states consented might the central legislature legislate for uniformity within those states. The constitutions of independent Malaya and Malaysia included both arrangements. As a rule, governments delegating legislative authority retain the right to revoke the transfer of authority, but in India the repeal of central legislation on behalf of states requires the consent of the central Parliament.

Also designed to enhance flexibility have been the arrangements in Malaya after 1957, and in Pakistan after 1962, enabling the unilateral extension of central power in order to secure uniformity or co-ordination, especially for the promotion of economic development.[3] Because such arrangements are likely to emasculate regional autonomy, they have not been popular elsewhere, and in Malaysia these powers were made largely inapplicable to the Borneo states and Singapore.[4]

In a number of federations, notably those in Asia and in the Caribbean, the grant of sweeping central authority to implement treaties and international agreements has been designed to meet unseen future needs and international commitments.[5] Flexibility was sacrificed in order to provide surer safeguards

---

[1] *Government of India Act, 1935*, s. 107 (2); *Constitution of India, 1950*, art. 254 (2); *Constitution of Pakistan, 1956*, art. 110 (2). On the frequent use of this device in India in order to ensure the validity of state legislation, see Santhanam, *Union–State Relations in India*, pp. 22–23.

[2] But in South Arabia and Uganda delegation of legislative authority was permitted only from the central governments, and in Buganda not at all. The independence constitution of Kenya made no provision for any delegation of legislative powers.

[3] *Constitution of Malaya, 1957*, arts. 76 (4), 91–95; *Constitution of Pakistan, 1962*, art. 131 (2) (*b*, *c*). Cf. similar powers in *Independence Constitution of Kenya, 1963*, s. 119.

[4] *Malaysia Act, 1963*, ss. 42–43.   [5] For details, see Chapter 8, section 4.

for regional authority, however, in pre-partition India, Rhodesia and Nyasaland, and Nigeria, where the free scope of central action was limited by the
requirement of regional assent when the implementation of international
agreements affected exclusive regional powers.[1] A provision in the constitutions of Nigeria (1954) and the West Indies (1957) which aimed at increasing
flexibility was that enabling territorial legislatures to implement international
obligations in matters within their own legislative competence.

The older federal structures have sometimes been criticized because their
inherent legalism and rigidity handicapped their ability to cope with emergency
conditions.[2] A distinctive feature of the recent federal constitutions, therefore,
has been the inclusion of provisions for the extension of central legislative and
executive powers in times of emergency. Fearful of both external and internal
political and economic threats to stability, and of difficulties arising from
inexperience in the operation of representative institutions, the constitution-
makers have specified procedures for coping with a wide variety of potential
emergency conditions.

All the new federal constitutions, except those of Nigeria between 1954 and
1960, Rhodesia and Nyasaland, and Uganda, have made provision for virtually unitary central authority in times of threat to security from external
aggression or internal disturbance;[3] and even in the case of the former two,
the Emergency Powers Orders in Council, 1939 to 1959, gave the Governor-
General in Council power to legislate during a public emergency on any matter
including areas normally outside his legislative competence.[4] The power to
declare emergencies was given in India (1950), Pakistan (1956 and 1962),
Malaya (1957), and Malaysia (1963) to the central executive, but required
approval by the central parliament within a specified period of time, and was
given in the West Indies (1957) and Nigeria (1960) to the central legislature.[5]
In none of these is early action in the face of an imminent threat prevented:
specific references to 'imminent danger' were included in the constitutions of
India and Pakistan, and a mere recitation of the existence of a threat was

---

[1] Independent Kenya followed this pattern.

[2] C.A.I., *Debates*, vol. vii, pp. 34–35; cf. Wheare, *Federal Government*, ch. 10.

[3] *Government of India Act, 1935*, ss. 102, 126A; *Constitution of India, 1950*, arts. 250–1,
352–4, 358–9; *Constitution of Pakistan, 1956*, arts. 191–2; *Constitution of Pakistan, 1962*,
arts. 30, 131 (2) (a); *Federation of Malaya Agreement, 1948*, cls. 4, 19, 52; *Constitution of
Malaya, 1957*, arts. 149, 150, *Constitution (Amendment) Act, 1960*, s. 28, and *Malaysia Act,
1963*, s. 39; *Constitution of Nigeria, 1960*, s. 65, and *1963*, ss. 70, 114 (3, 4); *Constitution of
W.I., 1957*, art. 48. See also *Independence Constitution of Kenya, 1963*, s. 69. The *Constitution
of Rhodesia and Nyasaland, 1953*, art. 81, did include provision for a central emergency tax
in time of war, or when a Proclamation of the Governor-General, made with the consent of
the three territorial Governors, declared the existence of a threat to the security of the
federation as a whole. In South Arabia (Constitution, 1963, s. 36), the central emergency
decree power was limited to matters within the normal central legislative and executive
power.

[4] Cmnd. 569/1958, para. 77; Cmnd. 1150/1960, para. 174.

[5] In the colonial federations of India (1935) and Malaya (1948), declarations of emergency
were made by the Governor-General and the High Commissioner acting at their discretion.

a sufficient condition under the other constitutions. During such periods of emergency the central government was usually given virtually unrestricted authority to cope with the situation: the central legislature was permitted to make laws on any subject, including normally regional ones, and the central government could give executive directions to the regional governments. In the West Indies there was in addition provision for territorial emergencies, during which territorial law would prevail over ordinary, but not emergency, central laws.[1]

A number of the new federal constitutions have also specified special central emergency powers to meet cases of failure in the constitutional machinery of regional governments, or of obstruction to the working of the federal system by regional governments. The Government of India Act, 1935, was the first to include such provisions, and these powers were widely used during the war.[2] This power was much resented, and was therefore removed from the interim constitutions of India and Pakistan in 1947, but in the latter case was inserted again in 1948.[3] The constitutions of both India (1950) and Pakistan (1956) included similar provisions as a safeguard for national stability.[4] Subsequently, some central emergency powers regarding constitutional government within the states were also specified in the independence constitution of Malaya.[5] In the West Indies and in independent Nigeria, breakdowns of constitutional government within the regions could be dealt with under the general central emergency powers, because the circumstances in which these powers might be used were left for the central legislatures to decide.[6] The Nigerian constitutions of 1960 and 1963, in addition, provided specifically for central emergency powers in cases where regional executive authority is so exercised as to 'impede or prejudice the exercise of the executive authority of the Federation'.[7] The right to declare a state of emergency in the operation

---

[1] Constitution, art. 48. In Nigeria and in Rhodesia and Nyasaland regional Governors in Council possessed similar emergency powers, not from the federal constitution but from the Emergency Powers Orders in Council, 1939 to 1959.

[2] *Government of India Act, 1935*, ss. 93, 122, 126.

[3] *Pakistan (Provisional Constitution) Order, 1947* (G.G.O. 22/1947) removed s. 93; *Pakistan (Provisional Constitution) Amendment Order, 1948* (G.G.O. 13/1948) inserted a new s. 92A; *Government of India (Amendment) Act, 1955*, replaced s. 92A with a modified and less autocratic version of these powers in a new s. 93. See C.A.P. (second), *Debates*, vol. i, pp. 1519–1616.

[4] *Constitution of India, 1950*, arts. 256–7, 356–7, 365; *Constitution of Pakistan, 1956*, art. 125, 126, 193. The Pakistan constitution of 1962 omits these provisions, the frequent exercise of which had been much resented in the provinces, but art. 74 gives the National Assembly power to decide on conflicts between provincial governors and assemblies.

[5] *Constitution of Malaya, 1957*, art. 71.

[6] *Constitution of W.I., 1957*, art. 48 (4); *Constitution of Nigeria, 1960*, s. 65 (3), and *1963*, s. 70 (3). The general emergency power was actually used in Nigeria in May 1962 to deal with the breakdown of constitutional government in the Western Region. See section 7 of this chapter.

[7] Constitutions, 1960, ss. 66, 80; 1963, ss. 71, 86. There were similar provisions in the *Independence Constitution of Kenya, 1963*, ss. 70, 106 (2).

of regional government was assigned in India (1950) and Pakistan (1948 and 1956) to the central executive, but in Malaya, the West Indies, and Nigeria, votes by simple majorities in the central parliament were required.[1]

The usual arrangement is that, during such emergencies, regional legislative and executive autonomy is suspended. The Government of India Act, 1935, and the constitutions of independent India and Pakistan (1956) went even further, permitting the suspension of any part of the constitution of a province or state except those relating to the high courts. To prevent a permanent conversion to a unitary state, a constitutional limit has been specified for the duration of this type of emergency power, except where the general emergency powers in Nigeria or the West Indies are employed.

In Malaya (between 1948 and 1957), India (1950), and Pakistan (1956), a third type of central emergency power was separately specified: if the financial stability or credit of the federation or part of it was threatened, the central government, following the proclamation of such an emergency, was entitled to give appropriate directions to state or provincial governments and, in the cases of India and Pakistan, to reduce the salaries of both central and state officials and judges.[2] In India the central government could also require all state money bills to be reserved for Presidential assent. In the other federations specific provisions were not made for this type of emergency, although the unqualified general emergency power was wide enough in scope to be applicable to such situations.

For the sake of flexibility a fourth type of emergency power for less-serious situations was specified in the Indian constitution. The Council of State, by a resolution supported by two-thirds of those voting and declaring 'that it is necessary or expedient in the national interest', may enable the Indian Parliament to legislate for a period of one year with respect to a specified matter in the exclusive state list.[3] Somewhat similarly, the Malayan and Malaysian Parliaments could, without resorting to a general state of emergency, pass an act which might extend beyond normal central powers in order to deal with a threat of subversion.[4]

From these examples it is clear that in the new federations the central

---

[1] Under the Government of India Act, 1935, s. 93, such declarations were made by the Governor at his discretion, but required the concurrence of the Governor-General at his discretion. In Nigeria after 1960 majorities of not less than two-thirds of the members of each central house were required in certain circumstances. See Constitutions, 1960, ss. 65 (3) (c), 66 (1), and 1963, ss. 70 (3) (c), 71 (1).

[2] *Federation of Malaya Agreement, 1948*, cl. 19 (1) (c), 19 (2); *Constitution of India, 1950*, art. 360; *Constitution of Pakistan, 1956*, art. 194. The constitutions of Pakistan (1962), art. 131 (2) (a), and Malaya (1957) and Malaysia (1963), art. 150 (1), included this type of emergency together with threats to national security in the general emergency power.

[3] Art. 249. This power was exercised for instance in 1950–2 during the food crisis in order to control black-marketing.

[4] Constitutions 1957 and 1963, art. 149; *Constitution (Amendment) Act, 1960* (F. 10/1960), s. 28.

governments have generally been endowed with ample emergency powers, powers which quite frequently have not gone unused.[1]

The importance of flexibility in the distribution of financial resources has also been widely recognized, for experience in the older federations had demonstrated the futility of formulating final and unalterable financial relations between the two tiers of government. The normal procedures for constitutional amendment are likely to prove too rigid, but at the same time regional groups have invariably insisted that financial modifications should not threaten the federal balance. Consequently, the actual assignment of taxing powers has usually been protected by the requirement of formal constitutional amendment for any change, but special procedures have been devised for adjusting the transfer of revenues from one level of government to another.[2] In this respect the independent Asian federations stand out as a group, for all three left the frequent adjustment of certain shared revenues and unconditional grants in the hands of the central executive or parliament, advised by an independent finance commission or by an inter-governmental council. This has enabled flexibility, while the convention in India that the unanimous recommendations of the independent finance commission are generally accepted by the central government, and the membership in Pakistan and Malaya of provincial and state ministers on the national finance councils, has reassured regional governments that their views would carry some weight.[3] In the other new federations the arrangements for modifications to the allocation of the distributable pool or other revenues and grants were less flexible. In response to regional fears that their autonomy might be undermined, adjustments have required the normal process of constitutional amendment, but provisions were included for periodic reviews, and, in Rhodesia and Nyasaland and Nigeria, for advisory fiscal commissions on these occasions. In Rhodesia and Nyasaland additional financial flexibility was intended in permitting territorial surcharges on central income tax and a federal emergency tax.[4] All these federations further augmented the flexibility in financial relations by giving the central government, and in India, Nigeria, and the West Indies the regional governments, power to give to other governments grants for any purpose.

Another method by which the rigidity normally inherent in a federal structure has been reduced in the new federations is by the proliferation of a wide variety of inter-governmental institutions.[5] Many of these derive their authority from the constitutions, but in addition many others have grown up as governments quickly appreciated the value of consultation and co-operation. A large number of these bodies have been concerned with financial and econo-

---

[1] See section 7 of this chapter.　　　　　　　　　　[2] See Chapter 9 for details.
[3] For the different arrangements for Singapore and the Borneo states in Malaysia, whereby inter-governmental agreement is required, see pp. 216–17, 221.
[4] See p. 203, however, regarding difficulties arising from the system of territorial surcharges on central taxes.
[5] For details, see Chapter 9, section 7, and Chapter 10, section 6.

mic questions, but many have been concerned with other questions such as administrative co-operation, co-ordination of policy, development of national language and culture, common research, educational programmes, local government, and the operation of the police services. Some of these bodies are composed of ministers or officials from the two tiers of governments, while others are composed of independent members. Some are consultative, attempting to co-ordinate the activities of governments at different levels, others are merely advisory, and still others actually administer joint organizations. But all of them attempt to lessen the rigidity that the compartmentalization of functions between governments might cause.

The initial period in the establishment of a new federation invariably requires many adjustments. Most of the new federal constitutions have therefore included certain transitional provisions. Some of these were designed to stretch out over several years the full application of the new constitution, the most extensive of such arrangements occurring in the West Indies and in Malaysia. Also generally included have been some transitional provisions to enable quick modifications or adaptations in order to remove any difficulties which may arise in bringing a constitution into operation, although this authority, normally assigned to the central government, could not be used to alter the fundamental features of a constitution.[1]

It is apparent, then, that most of the new federations have been equipped with a wide variety of devices by which the federal systems might be adapted to meet changing and developing circumstances. How effective these have been and their relative importance in relation to formal constitutional amendment is the question we must now consider.

7. *Recent federal constitutions: rigid or flexible?*

In the preceding sections of this chapter, we have noted the provisions in the new federal constitutions designed to provide both rigidity and adaptability. But as the history of the older federations warns us, only experience can tell us how rigid or flexible these procedures will actually be in practice. For the new federations it is still early to arrive at firm conclusions, but some trends are already observable.

Considering first the passage of formal constitutional amendments, the early years of the new federations suggest that their constitutions have not been unduly inflexible.

When the Indian constitution (1950) first appeared, critics found fault with the extreme rigidity expected to result from the requirements of the amendment procedure itself and from the restrictively elaborate and detailed nature of the constitution.[2] Ambedkar, the chairman of the Drafting Committee,

[1] *Fazlul Quader Chowdhury and others* v. *Muhammad Abdul Haque*, P.L.D. 1963, S.C. 486.
[2] Jennings, *Some Characteristics of the Indian Constitution*, pp. 9–16, 58–60; N. Srinivasan, *Democratic Government in India* (1954), pp. 376–7; Appleby, *Public Administration in India* (1953), pp. 17, 56.

believed, however, that a facile procedure had been provided and declared: 'one can therefore safely say that the Indian Federation will not suffer from the faults of rigidity or legalism. Its distinguishing feature is that it is a flexible federation.'[1] True to the intention of its framers, the Indian constitution has been frequently amended. During the first fourteen years sixteen constitutional amendments were adopted under the special procedure stipulated in article 368, while an additional fourteen ordinary bills—ten amending or reorganizing state boundaries and four admitting new territories—were passed by the required simple majorities in the central parliament.[2] In addition, the authority of the Rajya Sabha to pass a resolution permitting the creation of new All-India services was exercised in 1961 to enable the establishment of three new services.[3]

Of the sixteen formal amendments to the Indian constitution, nine required only special majorities in the central parliament. The other seven, including the extensive seventh amendment in 1956, were quickly ratified by a majority of the states.[4] The sixteen amendments covered a wide range. Four included clarifications and adjustments to the distribution of legislative and executive powers, the general trend being to increase central authority. Two were aimed at overcoming complications in inter-state trade and commerce. Four were connected with the reorganization of states, and four were related to the acquisition or ceding of territory. Three included greater safeguards for minorities, but three imposed restrictions upon the scope and ambit of the fundamental rights, and four restricted the jurisdiction of the courts or modified their organization. Several of the amendments adjusted state or territorial constitutions: two revised the institutions of the centrally administered territories, and three contained modifications affecting certain state constitutions. Some adjustments were also made to the central institutions: one amendment modified the procedure for electing the President and Vice-President, and three adjusted the size and composition of the central Parliament. It is of particular interest that thirteen of the sixteen amendments included provisions which were intended to overcome judicial pronouncements interpreting the constitution.[5]

Of course, to gauge truly the rigidity of the amendment procedure, one must also consider the number of attempts at amendment which have failed. During the first decade only one constitutional amendment bill introduced by the government was defeated.[6] This occurred when, in spite of a favourable

---

[1] C.A.I., *Debates*, vol. vii, p. 36. See also vol. vii, pp. 43–44; vol. x, p. 975.

[2] See p. 307, above, for a list of the ordinary acts modifying state boundaries, and Chapter 7 for a discussion of the significance of these modifications.

[3] Rajya Sabha, *Debates*, vol. xxxvi (5–6 December 1961), cols. 1148–1204, 1280–1305.

[4] Amendments requiring ratification by a majority of states were the second (1952), third (1954), sixth (1956), seventh (1956), thirteenth (1962), fourteenth (1962), and fifteenth (1963).

[5] On this subject, see S. R. Sharma, *The Supreme Court*, p. 123, ch. 15, and pp. 318–21.

[6] Two government-sponsored bills, the *Constitution (Fifth Amendment) Bill, 1955*, and *Constitution (Sixth Amendment) Bill, 1955*, were dropped when equivalent provisions were

vote of 246–2, the bill failed to obtain the required support of a majority of the Lok Sabha's 499 members.[1] The government managed, however, to persuade the House to suspend its rule against the reintroduction of the same bill in a single session, and a similar bill was passed a month later.[2] Otherwise, although constitutional amendment bills have sometimes been altered while passing through the Lok Sabha, the bills have all been passed unamended by the Rajya Sabha, and where required, have as yet never failed to receive ratification by a majority of states.

From this record it would appear that Ambedkar's claim of flexibility was justified. But this apparent adaptability may be deceptive, for it has in large part been facilitated by the overwhelming majorities of the Congress Party in both Union Houses and in nearly all the state legislatures. Thus the present problem is not whether the Indian constitution is too rigid, but how the federal provisions can be entrenched sufficiently when one party is so dominant.[3] In the long run, however, should the Congress Party disintegrate and therefore fail to dominate the Union Parliament or be faced with many state legislatures controlled by opposing parties, then the forecasts of early critics concerning the rigidity of the Indian constitution may still prove correct. But even should this be the case, the fact remains that the mechanical requirements for constitutional amendments are less stringent than those in the United States, and the diversity of procedures will ensure that many of the articles of the constitution remain relatively flexible.

The constitutions of the other independent federations have operated for shorter periods and it is therefore more difficult to assess their long-term rigidity or flexibility. Indeed, the 1956 Pakistan constitution lasted too briefly for any significant amendment to be made to the entrenched sections of the constitution.[4] During the martial law régime 1958–62 the basic administrative structure of the 1956 Constitution was retained,[5] but this was frequently amended by Presidential orders. The major amending orders were those which established the basic democracies (1959), made the exclusive provincial

---

soon afterwards included in the more comprehensive *Constitution* (*Ninth Amendment*) *Bill, 1956*, which when passed became the *Constitution* (*Seventh Amendment*) *Act, 1956*. During this decade, thirteen private bills for constitutional amendment introduced in the Lok Sabha, and two private attempts in the Rajya Sabha, were all defeated.

[1] The *Constitution* (*Seventh Amendment*) *Bill, 1955*. See Lok Sabha, *Debates*, vol. ix (1955), cols. 788–92, 822–91.

[2] This was the *Constitution* (*Eighth Amendment*) *Bill, 1955*, which on passage became the *Constitution* (*Fifth Amendment*) *Act, 1955*.

[3] See debates in state legislatures and Union Parliament on the *Constitution* (*Third Amendment*) *Bill, 1954*, and also *The Statesman*, 7 September 1963.

[4] But the question of the federal electorate which, although not entrenched, required central consultation of the provinces (art. 145), was a major issue, and three acts were passed: *Electorate Act, 1956* (36/1956), *Electorate* (*Amendment*) *Act, 1957* (19/1957), and *Electorate* (*Second Amendment*) *Act, 1957* (36/1957).

[5] President's Order (Post-Proclamation) no. 1/1958, *The Laws* (*Continuance in Force*) *Order, 1958*. See also *Iftikhar-ud-Din* v. *Muhammad Sarfraz*, P.L.D. 1961, S.C. 585.

powers concurrent (1959), provided for the election of the President (1960), transferred the central capital (1960), and merged Karachi in West Pakistan (1961).[1] The new 1962 constitution ,itself 'enacted by the President', was soon under pressure for amendment. The Political Parties Act (III of 1962) removed the prohibition on political parties, and the Constitution (First Amendment) Act, 1963, restoring justiciable fundamental rights, although held up for some time by a lack of the necessary special majority in support, was passed in the last fortnight of 1963. In addition to these acts twelve Presidential orders were issued during 1962 in exercise of his powers under article 224(3) of the new constitution to remove difficulties. Subsequently, however, one of these which attempted to remove the prohibition upon ministers sitting in the Assemblies was held by the courts to be in excess of the President's powers because it constituted more than a mere 'adaptation'.[2]

Of the independent federations, the Malayan constitution (1957) was the easiest to amend because so few amendments required ratification by the states, and because a sizeable portion of the Senate consisted of nominees of the central government. Moreover, as in India, a single party has been dominant in both levels of government. The central government had little difficulty, therefore, in pushing through five constitutional amendments, three of them very substantial in nature, during the first six years following independence.[3] The first was only a temporary adjustment passed in 1958 to overcome certain transitional difficulties, but two major constitutional amendments were pressed through in 1960 and 1962. The 1960 amendment was an extensive act of thirty-five sections which enhanced central powers for emergencies and for preventive detention, increased central control over local government, changed the procedure for appointing judges, and altered some provisions concerning the public services. The 1962 amendment was equally extensive in scope. Loopholes in the citizenship regulations were tightened, the heavy weightage for rural constituencies was made permanent, central control over mining leases and state royalties on mines was increased, the states were assigned as a *quid pro quo* a portion of the export duties on minerals, and the procedure for amending the constitution when new states were admitted was eased to facilitate the creation of Malaysia. Two further constitutional amendments were approved in 1963. The first was devoted mainly to clarifying a number of clauses in the constitution, including certain matters in the legislative lists. The second, the Malaysia Act, 1963, although in form an

---

[1] President's Orders, nos. 2, 17, 18, 20/1959; nos. 3, 20/1960; no. 9/1961.

[2] President's Order no. 34/1962; *Muhammad Abdul Haque* v. *Fazlul Quader Chowdhury and others*, P.L.D. 1963, Dacca 669; *Fazlul Quader Chowdhury and others* v. *Muhammad Abdul Haque*, P.L.D. 1963, S.C. 486.

[3] *Constitution (Temporary Amendment) Ordinance, 1958* (F. 42/1958); *Constitution (Amendment) Act, 1960* (F. 10/1960); *Constitution (Amendment) Act, 1962* (F. 14/1962); *Constitution (Amendment) Act, 1963* (F. 25/1963); *Malaysia Act, 1963* (F. 26/1963). In addition, by mid-1959, all the states had amended their own constitutions in order to implement the Eighth Schedule of the Federal constitution.

amendment to the Constitution of the Federation of Malaya, in effect created an essentially new constitution for an essentially new federation.[1] Despite the ease with which the governing Alliance, possessing the necessary two-thirds in both houses of the Federal Parliament, has been able to amend the constitution, it is significant that both in 1960 and 1962 the central government considered it prudent to consult the state assemblies and party organizations before passage of these amendments. That such consultation was not required constitutionally was made clear, however, when the objections of the state of Kelantan to the validity of the Malaysia Act were rejected in the Kuala Lumpur High Court.[2] Although a considerable portion of the constitutional amendments during the first six years were devoted to clarification of details, the general trend until 1963 was clearly towards increased centralization. This illustrated the continuing centripetal forces, and emphasized the slender protection accorded the states under the 1957 constitution. With the Malaysia Act of 1963 there was a break in the trend to centralization, although the increased state autonomy applied only to the new territories joining the federation. Since this local autonomy is more firmly entrenched in the Malaysian constitution, the position of the new states appears also to be better protected.

At the time it went into effect, the 1960 constitution of Nigeria appeared likely to be the most rigid among those of the independent federations. Not only were a large number of the provisions of this constitution specially entrenched, but also the party situation, with different political parties in control in each region, was expected to make the required passage by two-thirds of the members of each central house and ratification by the legislatures of at least two of the three regions particularly difficult on controversial issues. Actually, throughout the first four years of independence, the central coalition of the N.P.C. and the N.C.N.C. did command both the necessary central majorities and a sufficient number of regional legislatures to carry through any amendments the coalition could agree upon. This was illustrated by the way in which, in addition to three relatively uncontroversial formal amendments to the constitution between 1960 and 1963,[3] the N.P.C.–N.C.N.C. coalition was able in 1962 to obtain approval for carving a new Mid-Western Region out of the existing Western Region despite the opposition of the Western Region government.[4] Another substantial constitutional amendment

---

[1] The ninety-six sections and six schedules of the new act numbered slightly more than half those of the 1957 constitution, and altered the fundamental structure of the federation.

[2] *State of Kelantan* v. *Federation of Malaya and Tunku Abdul Rahman*, (1963) 29 M.L.J. 355 (K.L.).

[3] The *Nigeria Constitution First Amendment Act, 1961* (1961, no. 24) made provision for the incorporation of the Northern Cameroons; the *Nigeria Constitution Second Amendment Act, 1962* (1962, no. 21) made the Director of Public Prosecutions subject to the directions of the Federal Attorney-General; the *Produce (Constitution Amendment) Act, 1963* (1963, no. 1) defined 'produce' with retrospective effect for taxes on the sale or purchase of produce.

[4] *Mid-Western Region Act, 1962* (1962, no. 6); *Mid-Western Region (Transitional*

was the adoption in 1963 of the new republican constitution. At that time the Governor-General was replaced by a President as nominal head of the executive, the appeals to the Judicial Committee of the Privy Council were abolished, the procedure for the appointment of judges was changed, and a variety of other minor adjustments were made. Although the same fundamental federal framework was retained virtually unchanged,[1] the conversion to a republic was made the occasion for adopting a completely new autochthonous constitution.[2] At the same time, revisions to the regional constitutions in order to bring them into line with the new federal constitution were passed by each region and approved by the federal legislature.[3]

In all, up to the end of 1963 six formal amendments to the Nigerian federal constitution had been approved, an interim constitution for the Mid-Western Region had been adopted, and a number of amendments to regional constitutions had been ratified by the central legislature.[4] Both the federal and regional constitutions of Nigeria have proved far from inflexible, largely because of the dominance of the N.P.C.–N.C.N.C. coalition. But this pattern depended on the ability of the coalition to maintain its sometimes precarious stability and cohesion. The need for compromise was illustrated by the one occasion on which an attempt to amend the constitution of the Northern Region, so that the Grand Kadi might become a member of the regional High Court, was defeated in the Federal Senate. Subsequently, this amendment was passed in the next session, after northern senators had made some concessions on bills in which senators from other regions were interested.[5]

Generally, the early years of the new independent federations have shown the formal procedures for amending their constitutions to be relatively, and perhaps even excessively, flexible. This must be attributed, however, as much to the party situations, in which single national political parties or coalitions

---

Provisions) Act, 1963 (1963, no. 18). Later the *Constitution of Mid-Western Nigeria Act, 1964*, provided a permanent constitution for the new region.

[1] See Sessional Paper no. 3/1963, *Proposals for the Constitution of the Federal Republic of Nigeria.* Of the 166 sections in the new constitution only thirty-two represented new or substantially revised sections.

[2] *The Constitution of the Federal Republic of Nigeria* (1963, no. 20), and *The Constitution (Transitional Provisions) Act, 1963* (1963, no. 21). The latter repealed certain enactments which became spent when the republican constitution came into force. *The Constitution (Interpretation) Act, 1964,* was designed to provide for the construction and interpretation of the new constitution.

[3] *The Constitution of Northern Nigeria Law* (N.N. no. 33/1963); *The Constitution of Eastern Nigeria Law* (E.N. Law no. 8/1963); *The Constitution of Western Nigeria Law* (W.N. no. 26/1963).

[4] The most notable of the amendments to the regional constitutions was *The Constitution of Western Nigeria (Amendment) Law, 1963* (W.N. no. 13/1963), which retroactively validated the continued premiership of Akintola after the Judicial Committee of the Privy Council in *Adegbenro* v. *Akintola*, [1963] 3 W.L.R. 63, had upheld Akintola's dismissal by the Governor in 1962.

[5] See J. P. Mackintosh, 'Federalism in Nigeria', *Political Studies*, x (1962), p. 228.

have dominated both central and regional politics, as to the mechanical requirements for amending these constitutions.

When we turn to the transitional constitutions of the interim and colonial federations, we find that these, as might have been expected, were in practice even more flexible. The interim constitutions of India (1947–50) and Pakistan (1947–56) could be and frequently were altered by the central legislatures alone, acting in their capacity as constituent assemblies.[1] Indeed, the first Pakistan Constituent Assembly amended the interim constitution forty-four times between 1948 and 1954, usually in order to enlarge central powers.[2] The second Constituent Assembly's first task was to validate these amendments, which had been ruled invalid by the Federal Court because they lacked the Governor-General's assent.[3] In addition, before proceeding with the preparation of the new constitution, a major amendment, the unification of West Pakistan, was pushed through by the government,[4] and six other amendments to the interim constitution were enacted.

Similarly, the colonial federal constitutions were frequently modified. Many of these alterations were connected with the progressive advances towards self-government and independence, but others represented adjustments made to these federal systems in the light of experience. In the period 1948–57 the Federation of Malaya Agreement, 1948, was amended twenty-one times.[5] The modifications included changes in citizenship requirements, the inclusion of elected members in the Legislative Council, alterations in the composition of the Executive Council, and adjustments in the distribution of legislative powers, sources of revenue, and heads of expenditure. The Nigerian constitution was also frequently amended before independence. There were twenty-two amendments between 1954 and 1960, including major revisions made as a result of the 1957–8 constitutional conferences. Among the alterations were the grant of self-government to the regions, changes in the structure of the regional legislatures, the development of cabinet government in the central executive, the addition of a senate to the central legislature, adjustments to the distribution of powers, a complete overhaul of the allocation of revenues, the inclusion of fundamental rights, the addition of special provisions concerning the control of the police, and constitutional advances for the Southern

---

[1] *Indian Independence Act, 1947*, s. 8.

[2] Until 1949 constitutional amendments in Pakistan could be made by order of the Governor-General. In all, eleven such orders were issued. The situation between 1958 and 1962 was similar (see pp. 321–2).

[3] *The Validation of Laws Act, 1955*. See C.A.P. (second), *Debates*, vol. i, pp. 67–96, 237–55, 1473–1513.

[4] *The Establishment of West Pakistan Act, 1955.*

[5] Of the 21 amendments made under cl. 6 of the Agreement (not including the amendment establishing the new constitution in 1957): 12 were by federal ordinance; 6 by High Commissioner's proclamation in terms agreed by His Majesty and the Conference of Rulers; 3 by High Commissioner's proclamation after consulting the legislative and settlement councils and with the assent of the rulers of the states. In addition the settlement constitutions were amended twice by United Kingdom orders in council.

Cameroons. There were fewer orders in council amending the West Indies federal constitution.[1] Of the five amendments during the brief four-year life of the federation, the most extensive was concerned with providing for cabinet government in the central executive. Over the same period there were, however, also numerous advances towards self-government in the separate territorial constitutions.

In Rhodesia and Nyasaland where the power of constitutional amendment normally lay with the federal legislature, subject to the ultimate assent of the British Government, four amendment acts were adopted during its ten-year life.[2] The first (1954) resolved an ambiguity concerning the territorial surcharge on the central income tax. The second (1957) increased and altered the composition of the Federal Assembly. The third (1958) implemented the recommendations of the 1957 Fiscal Commission. The fourth (1959) altered the wording of an item on the federal legislative list dealing with professional qualifications. During the decade no amendment bills were defeated either on the floor of the federal legislature or by formal rejection of assent by the British Government, although one bill to amend the constitutional provisions concerning the Auditor-General of the federation was withdrawn after it had received a first reading.[3]

The Constitution Amendment Act, 1957, which altered the composition of the Federal Assembly, aroused particularly fierce controversy. The settlers' representatives, controlling three-quarters of the Assembly seats, had no difficulty, however, in securing the necessary special majority for the amendment enhancing the control of the legislature by the European electorate. Although the African Affairs Board classified the measure as discriminatory, the negative resolution moved by the Opposition in the United Kingdom Parliament was defeated and the bill duly received assent. The following year the federal Electoral Bill, 1958, which although not a formal constitutional amendment required a special procedure, was also reserved by the African Affairs Board but nevertheless received assent in Britain. Despite the apparent special safeguards, the control by the settler electorate of three-quarters of the Federal Assembly seats and the unwillingness of the British Government to

---

[1] These United Kingdom orders in council were unusual in that they were not numbered in the Statutory Instrument series. They were entitled *The Constitution of the West Indies (Amendment) Orders in Council*. One was made in 1959, two in 1960, and two in 1962. In addition, S.I. 1962, no. 1084, *The West Indies (Dissolution and Interim Commissioner) Order in Council, 1962*, made under *The West Indies Act, 1962* (10 & 11 Eliz. 2, ch. 19), dissolved the federation.

[2] *The Constitution Amendment Acts, 1954, 1957, 1958, 1959* (Acts 18/1954, 16/1957, 13/1958, and 27/1959). For certain amendments art. 98 of the constitution required that, during the first ten years of the federation, the prior consent of the territorial legislatures was necessary. The separate territorial constitutions were frequently modified by United Kingdom orders in council. The actual dissolving of the federation was by the United Kingdom, S.I. 1963, no. 2085, *The Federation of Rhodesia and Nyasaland (Dissolution) Order in Council, 1963*, empowered by the *Rhodesia and Nyasaland Act, 1963* (Eliz. 2, 1963, ch. 34). [3] Bill no. 18/1955.

refuse assent meant that in practice the constitution was, if anything, too flexible.

Except in Central Africa the relative ease of amendment for the transitional federal constitutions, interim or colonial, has proved beneficial. In the case of the interim constitutions of India and Pakistan, the emergency conditions following upon the conjunction of independence and partition might have made any inflexible arrangement dangerous. In the colonial federations, progressing towards self-government, benefits were gained from regarding the federal systems as experimental and subject to adjustments to eliminate difficulties. The fact that ultimate control of the amendment procedure lay in these cases with an external arbiter, the United Kingdom Government, may have assured regional groups that such alterations would be impartially undertaken. It was significant that in Central Africa, when the failure of the British Government to support the African Affairs Board in 1957–8 shattered the confidence of the Africans of Nyasaland and Northern Rhodesia in the British Government as a protector of their interests, secession movements in these territories increased sharply in intensity.

The apparent relative facility of constitutional amendment in the new federations has not discouraged the use of the other devices designed to enhance their flexibility. Perhaps most dramatic has been the frequent resort to central emergency powers. Indeed, in Pakistan, where the use of central emergency powers quickly became a normal part of the working of central–provincial relations, provincial autonomy was, as a result, seriously curtailed.[1] Nor in India has the record of the use of central emergency powers to deal with constitutional crises in the states been uniformly reassuring. Of the six occasions between 1950 and 1963 when these powers were invoked, five struck down legislatures which supported non-Congress or coalition ministries, and indisputable evidence of ministerial instability existed in only three of these cases.[2] On the other hand, these powers have for the most part been used with more reluctance than in Pakistan,[3] and only for the brief periods necessary to restore stable state government. Thus this device has proved useful for the recovery of constitutional government in troubled states. The emergency powers for dealing with external threats to security were

[1] Central emergency rule was established in the provinces eight times between 1949 and 1958: in Punjab 1949–51, in Sind 1951–3, in East Bengal in March 1954, in East Bengal 1954–5, in East Pakistan twice briefly in 1956–7, in West Pakistan in 1957, and in East Pakistan in 1958.

[2] Between 1950 and 1963 Presidential rule was invoked in the Indian states for brief periods six times: in Punjab 1951, in P.E.P.S.U. (Patiala and East Punjab States Union) 1953, in Andhra 1954, in Travancore-Cochin 1956, in Kerala after considerable delay 1959, and in Orissa 1961. A seventh occasion occurred in Kerala in 1964. See K. K. Koticha, 'Presidential Intervention under Article 356 of the Constitution of India', *Journal of the Indian Law Institute*, ii (1959), pp. 125–33.

[3] On a number of occasions pressure for use of these powers was resisted by the Union Government. Notable examples were the refusal to impose central rule in Travancore-Cochin in 1953, in Punjab in 1961 and 1963, and in Kashmir in 1963–4.

resorted to in India for the first time in 1962 on the occasion of the Chinese incursion.[1] During the period of the emergency all exclusive state legislative authority was in effect made concurrent, and the central government was empowered to impose duties on state governments concerning any matter, thus making the states legally subordinate.

In Malaya and Malaysia threats to security have made necessary emergency action too. During the decade after 1948, the terrorist emergency was a major factor inducing centralized administration, and even when the emergency was officially declared ended in 1960, the central government retained extensive powers over internal security and preventive detention.[2] Within a year of the formation of Malaysia, it was found necessary to place the federation under a state of emergency because of growing Indonesian hostility and incursions.

Nor have emergency powers remained unused in the two African federations. For instance, territorial emergency powers were resorted to in both Southern Rhodesia and Nyasaland in 1959 in the face of growing African unrest. More recently, the Nigerian central government exercised its emergency powers in 1962, placing the Western Region under a federal Administrator for seven months, when a split within the Action Group and the dismissal of Premier Akintola by the Governor led to a constitutional crisis in that region.[3] Some critics, pointing to evidence of the central coalition's desire to crush the opposition Action Group, have considered this resort to the central emergency powers precipitous. It is true that within seven months a relatively stable regional government had been restored, but the emergency action irreparably altered the central-regional balance, and contributed to southern anxieties by showing that the central government dominated by the N.P.C. had much more strength than most observers had suspected.

Many of the special devices in the new federations intended to make federal relations flexible during normal times have also proved useful. The extensive spheres of concurrent authority have enabled the central governments, especially in Nigeria and in Rhodesia and Nyasaland, to delay exercising their optional powers and to take these up progressively. The provisions enabling delegation of powers have also proved convenient. In all the African

[1] A Presidential proclamation under article 352 (1) of the Constitution was issued on 26 October 1962, and subsequently *The Defence of India Act, 1962* (no. 51/1962) was passed. See also B. N. Schoenfeld, 'Emergency Rule in India', *Pacific Affairs*, xxxvi (1963), pp. 221–37.

[2] The emergency powers under art. 150 of the 1957 and 1963 constitutions were invoked for the first time in September 1964 because of Indonesian landings in Johore. But under art. 162 of the 1957 constitution, *The Emergency Regulations Ordinance, 1948*, had been annually renewed until its repeal in 1960. The *Internal Security Act, 1960* (F. 18/1960) made under art. 149 gave the central government continued extensive powers for preserving internal security.

[3] This was an exercise of the general central emergency powers under s. 65 of the constitution. On the emergency, see O. I. Odumosu, *The Nigerian Constitution: History and Development* (1963), ch. 9, and J. P. Mackintosh, 'Politics in Nigeria: The Action Group Crisis of 1962', *Political Studies*, xi (1963), pp. 126–55.

and Asian federations the delegation of central executive authority to regional governments or officers has been used regularly to avoid duplicating administrative machinery. Indeed, in India the central dependence upon the state administrative systems for implementing national policies became so extensive that in some respects administration was made more cumbersome rather than more flexible.[1] The delegation of legislative powers in the new federations has generally been less extensive and has usually been in the other direction, from the regional to the general governments, the purpose being to achieve greater co-ordination and uniformity.[2]

As already noted in Chapter 9, the special arrangements for adjustments to the allocation of financial resources have also clearly facilitated flexibility. One need point only to important revisions in the distribution of revenues as a result of the work of fiscal or constitutional review commissions in India in 1952, 1957, and 1961–2 in Pakistan in 1952 and 1962, in Malaya in 1955 and 1957, in Nigeria in 1947, 1951, 1953, and 1958, and in Rhodesia and Nyasaland in 1956, to see that the financial relations between governments have been regularly modified.

Important too in increasing the flexibility of the new federal systems without subordinating the regional governments has been the large number of special institutions which have made possible a high degree of consultation and co-operation between governments. Apart from those established by the constitutions, in each federation a vast variety of inter-governmental institutions has rapidly developed, especially in the realm of economic planning.[3]

The effect of conventions upon the adaptability of the federal system must not be overlooked. The conventions that have developed in central–regional relations regarding consultation between governments about legislation in the concurrent fields or in areas of special concern to other governments, and between departments of different governments with common interests, have often been valuable in encouraging co-operation and co-ordination.[4] But often, conventions have grown that governments would not exercise certain constitutional powers without the consent of some other government, or only under special circumstances. Such conventions, especially where central authority under the constitution itself is extensive, have helped to safeguard regional interests, but, of course, at the price of increased rigidity. This has

---

[1] Appleby, *Public Administration in India* (1953), pp. 16–24.

[2] For examples, see *The Estate Duty Act, 1953* (xxxiv/1953) in India following enabling legislation in nine states; *The Rhodes National Gallery Act, 1958* (3/1958) following enabling acts in all three territories of Rhodesia and Nyasaland; *The Non-African Agriculture (Transfer to the Concurrent List) Ordinance, 1955* (N.R. Ordinance 61/1955), passed by the Northern Rhodesian Legislative Council. For an example of delegation of legislative authority in the opposite direction in India, see *The U.P. Sugarcane Cess (Validation) Act, 1961* (4/1961).

[3] See Chapter 9, section 7, and Chapter 10, section 6.

[4] See, for instance, Santhanam, *Union. State Relations in India*, pp. 21–22; Cmnd. 569/1958, para. 11; Cmnd. 1149/1960, pp. 120–4; Col. no. 330/1957, para. 33.

clearly been the case in India, and in Malaya before 1957, where the effect has been to create difficulties in economic planning.[1] On the other hand, the lack of such conventions may also be dangerous. In Pakistan, for instance, the centralized national economic planning took a form which fostered Bengali resentment and separatism.[2]

Perhaps as important as any other single factor in determining the rigidity or flexibility of the procedures for formal constitutional amendment and of the various devices for inter-governmental consultation and co-operation has been the relative strength and dominance of certain political parties in both tiers of government. The strength of the Congress Party in India and the Alliance in Malaya to date, of the Muslim League in Pakistan until 1954, and of the United Federal Party in Rhodesia and Nyasaland, together with the relative centralization and close co-ordination between the central and regional branches of these parties, enabled them to override provisions designed to give the constitutions a degree of rigidity. Even in Nigeria the unexpected stability of the N.P.C.–N.C.N.C. coalition throughout the period 1954–64 made the constitution less inflexible than appeared likely in 1954 or even 1960. On the other hand, in the West Indies, the looseness of the governing Federal Labour Party as a confederation of island parties, and the insular personal rivalries of the politicians, resulted in less effective co-operation between governments than elsewhere.

To sum up, the new federations have generally, both through formal constitutional amendments and through other devices, achieved a relatively high degree of flexibility. Except in Pakistan and Malaya, this has been achieved without seriously sacrificing regional autonomy. If the experience of the older federations is any guide, such a measure of flexibility in the early years of the life of a federation, when frequent adjustments to meet unforeseen difficulties may be desirable, is of considerable value.[3]

A corollary of this constitutional flexibility is that reliance upon judicial review as a primary means for constitutional adaptation has been less prominent than in some of the older federations such as the United States. This is not to say that judicial review has played an insignificant role, for in India, Pakistan, and Nigeria, particularly, a number of major constitutional issues have had to be settled by the courts. Nevertheless, there has been a reluctance on the part of politicians to turn to the courts as the chief avenue for

---

[1] In Malaya after 1957 the situation was reversed, since the states proved reluctant to use the wider legislative powers conferred on them, and willing to accept central incursions into state fields. See Hickling in Sheridan, *Malaya and Singapore*, p. 102.

[2] See, for instance, C.A.P. (second), *Debates*, vol. i, pp. 1985, 1998, 2049, 2158.

[3] In the U.S.A., 10 amendments were made within the first three years, while only 12 were made in the subsequent 165 years; the Swiss federal constitution of 1848 was thoroughly revised in 1874; in Australia, of the four successful amendments in the first 50 years, two were made during the first decade; two substantial amendments were made to the Canadian constitution within the first eight years. See Livingston, *Federalism and Constitutional Change*, pp. 26–27, 118, 185, 201.

constitutional development. At the same time, the courts themselves, reflecting British traditions of legal interpretation, have tended to confine their interpretation to the written word, leaving the function of modifying the federal systems to the legislatures employing the amendment process, and to the governments using the variety of other constitutional devices for co-operation and co-ordination.

PART FOUR

CONCLUSIONS

13

THE EFFECTIVENESS OF THE FEDERAL EXPERIMENTS

1. The variety of federal systems

ANY assessment of the effectiveness and suitability of federal governments in developing countries must begin by distinguishing those effects which are the product of federal systems generally as contrasted to other forms of government, and those effects which are the result of the particular variety of federal institutions erected.

Although the new federations, each expressing a desire for both unity and diversity, have had many common features such as co-existing central and regional governments, a constitutional distribution of powers between them, and a supreme written constitution, nevertheless, as we have seen, there have been great variations in their federal structures. Not only have statesmen been influenced by different models, but, in an attempt to devise institutions appropriate to the special conditions of each country, they have often attempted genuine innovations.[1] Each federation has in a sense been a unique experiment, combining in its own distinctive pragmatic way a particular regional structure, distribution of powers, arrangement for inter-governmental co-operation, organization of central government and protection for the constitution.

The analysis of the political institutions of these federations in Part III has indicated the variations among them. There have been contrasts between the populous federations composed only of a few large regions, like Pakistan (after 1955) and Nigeria, and the small federations composed of many relatively tiny units, like the West Indies and Malaya. There have been wide differences in the distribution of legislative, executive, and financial powers, from the very 'tight' Federation of Malaya at one extreme, with nearly all authority concentrated in the central government, to the 'loose', almost confederal, West Indies at the other, with the central government operating as little more than a common agency. In all federations some degree of inter-governmental consultation has proved necessary, but the scope has varied from the high degree of co-ordination in the Asian federations to the more limited co-operation achieved in the West Indies and in Rhodesia and Nyasaland. The form of the central institutions and the extent to which regional representation in the legislature and executive has given regional groups

---

[1] See Chapter 6, especially section 5.

confidence in the central governments has also differed. While all the constitutions have aimed at a balance between adaptability and rigidity, the
amendment procedures and other devices were made somewhat less flexible
in Nigeria than in the Asian federations. In view of these dissimilarities among
the new federations, it is not surprising that, as a consequence, their effectiveness in facilitating economic development, in aiding the operation of representative institutions, in promoting unity, and in protecting minorities has
also varied.

2. *The role of political parties*

The operation and effectiveness of the new federal systems has depended
not only upon the particular form of federal institutions adopted, but also
upon the pattern of the political parties within each federation.

It is true, of course, that the parties themselves have been influenced in
their organization and activities by the nature of the federal framework within
which they have had to operate. But other factors have also shaped the party
system in each federation. In the colonial federations advancing towards
self-government, for instance, the extent to which responsible cabinet government had been achieved was likely to influence the cohesion of political parties
within the legislatures.[1] Differences in electoral systems may also have been
significant in determining the number and nature of political parties. Generally among the new Commonwealth federations, however, the variations in
electoral systems have not been great, apart from the existence for a time of
separate electorates and later the use of an electoral college system in Pakistan,
the reservation of seats for minorities in India, the restriction of the franchise
to adult males in Northern Nigeria, and the special franchises in Central
Africa.[2] The personalities and stature of political leaders have been particularly
important in the new federations, as the contrast between the continued
strength of the Congress Party in India and the disintegration of the Muslim
League in Pakistan clearly illustrated. The national strength of such parties as
the Malayan Alliance and the Central African United Federal Party owed
much to the character of men like Tunku Abdul Rahman, Sir Godfrey
Huggins, and Sir Roy Welensky. By contrast, the weakness of the West
Indian Federal Labour Party was in considerable measure a result of the
clashes of personality among Sir Grantley Adams, Norman Manley, and Eric
Williams, and this was even more true of the opposition Democratic Labour
Party. One of the most important factors determining the pattern of political
parties in the early years of federation has been the strength and solidarity of
the nationalist movement. The Congress Party during the first decade and a

[1] For a discussion of the relationship between responsible government and the nature of
political parties in advancing colonies, see H. V. Wiseman, *The Cabinet in the Commonwealth*
(1958), pp. 124–50.

[2] See Chapter 11. On electoral systems, see T. E. Smith, *Elections in Developing Countries*
(1960).

half after independence, the Muslim League for a few years in Pakistan, and the Alliance Party in Malaya and Malaysia gained unity and prestige from their role in the campaign for independence, whereas the relatively easier path towards self-government in Nigeria and in the West Indies meant that there was less impetus for the development of strong national parties.

The number of political parties, their relative strength in central and regional politics, and their internal organization and discipline, have often affected the whole manner in which the new federal institutions have been worked. Where a single party has been able to aggregate diverse interests and to dominate both central and regional elections so that it controls most governments at both levels, national cohesion and co-operation between governments have been facilitated. This has been the situation in India, Malaya, and until 1954 Pakistan.

In India, for instance, after the general elections of 1951–2, the Congress Party formed governments not only in the Union Parliament but also in all the states, and maintained them until the second general elections in 1957, except for the brief ministry of the minority Praja Socialist Party in Travancore-Cochin in 1954, and the periods when the Punjab, P.E.P.S.U., Andhra, and Travancore-Cochin were under emergency rule.[1] The Congress Party was again widely successful in the second general elections, maintaining control of the Union Government and of all the reorganized states except Kerala where the largest party, the Communist Party, formed a government with the support of independents.[2] The Communist ministry lasted in Kerala for two years before emergency 'President's rule' was established and fresh elections were called, from which a Congress–Praja Socialist Party coalition emerged as the government of the state. In the 1962 general elections, once again the Congress Party captured a majority in Parliament. In the state assemblies it lost quite heavily, but nowhere so much as to lose power.[3] The general preponderance of the Congress Party at both levels of government has been a powerful force for harmony between the Union and state governments in India. It is significant that inter-governmental friction and resort to central emergency rule have been the usual result in the few cases where opposition or coalition ministries have been formed in the states.[4]

[1] In the states, the Congress Party won majorities in 18 out of the 22 states, and was the largest party in the other 4, where it formed coalition governments with independents.

[2] The Congress Party won an absolute majority in 11 out of 13 states and in addition was the largest party in Orissa where it formed a coalition government. In the elections in Orissa in 1961, which followed the breakdown of this coalition and the imposition of emergency rule, the Congress won a majority.

[3] Of the 12 state assemblies contested the Congress still held majorities in 10 and was the largest group in the other 2 (Madhya Pradesh and Rajasthan), where, with the support of Independents, it formed governments.

[4] Of the six proclamations of emergency rule in the states before 1963, five struck down legislatures which supported opposition or coalition ministries or had unseated a Congress ministry. Indisputable evidence of ministerial instability existed in only three cases and in

On the other hand, in the states where Congress ministries have existed the pattern of organization within the Congress Party has tended to reduce the states to a subordinate status. As a legacy of the integrated nationalist movement before 1947, the provincial Congress committees have been accustomed to look for guidance and take directions from the central Congress committees. It is extremely significant, for instance, that with only a few exceptions, state elections have generally been called at the same time as Union elections, and that in these elections the candidates for the state legislatures were finally selected by the All-India Parliamentary Board of the Party. As recently as 1963 six of the state chief ministers resigned under central direction as part of the Congress Party 'Kamaraj Plan' intended to revitalize the party nationally. There has been a tendency for the state Congress organizations to become 'mere implementing bodies rather than policy-making bodies'.[1] Nor is this approach limited to the Congress Party, for other national parties have tended to be organized on centralized lines also. Thus the domination of the centralized Congress Party in both Union and state governments has meant that in many respects India has functioned as an almost unitary state. Nevertheless, a new and influential group of political leaders more deeply rooted in Indian life has been emerging in the states, and, as a result, the focus of power and influence within the national political parties, including the Congress, has begun to shift from the central organization to those in the states.[2] Moreover, the death of Nehru in 1964 removed one of the most influential restraints upon this tendency, although one must not underestimate the continued impact of the carrots and sticks in the hands of the central government, and the larger ambitions of state politicians themselves.

The picture in Pakistan before 1954 was largely similar to that in India, for the highly centralized Muslim League dominated both central and provincial governments.[3] The successive central prime ministers, as presidents of the Muslim League, had extensive powers of supervision and regulation of provincial party affairs, including the dissolution and reconstitution of provincial Leagues and the expulsion and disqualification of provincial office-holders. The rejection of the Muslim League by East Bengal in 1954 and the demands for genuine provincial autonomy were largely a reaction against the unitary control of the Muslim League. As one member of the second Constituent

two the opposition claimed it had not been given a fair chance. The most controversial case was that of Kerala in 1959, where the Communist Government was dismissed because of popular agitation although it still held a slender but faithful and frequently demonstrated majority in the Assembly. See also p. 327.

[1] See especially Santhanam, *Union–State Relations in India*, p. 63.

[2] See N. D. Palmer, 'Growing Pains of Indian Democracy', *Current History*, xliv (1963), pp. 153–4; W. H. Morris-Jones, 'Stability and Change in Indian Politics', in S. Rose (ed.), *Politics in Southern Asia* (1963), pp. 13–23.

[3] On the organization and operation of the Muslim League during this period, see especially Callard, *Pakistan, A Political Study*, pp. 34–48, 163; Sayeed, *Pakistan, The Formative Phase*, ch. 6.

Assembly put it: 'East Bengal is bleeding from the wounds inflicted by the Muslim League coterie.'[1]

In the third Asian federation, Malaya, a single party has also dominated central and state governments. The Alliance Party had swept the central and state elections in 1955, winning 51 of the 52 central seats contested and forming governments in all the states. It was evident at times during the succeeding years that the Alliance was losing some support because of internal strains and stresses, and because other parties were gradually building up a better electoral organization. Nevertheless, in the next central and state elections in 1959, the Alliance once again emerged as the dominant party in central and state politics.[2] With control of the central government and nine of the eleven state governments, the Alliance was able as a matter of deliberate strategy to strengthen the position of the central government without meeting serious resistance from the states it dominated. Significantly, what friction there was between governments occurred in the north-eastern states, where the Pan-Malayan Islamic Party held the reins of power. Within Malaysia, the extension of the Alliance pattern to encompass coalitions of major local parties in the Borneo states,[3] and the increased Alliance central majority as a result of its victory in the 1964 Malayan general elections, has continued the Alliance domination of both levels of government. But the unwillingness of the Alliance to allow Lee Kuan Yew a partnership in national decision making led to the unsuccessful challenge by the People's Action Party against Malay political predominance and culminated in the separation of Singapore in 1965.

The tendency towards a relatively high degree of centralization in the operation of the Federation of Rhodesia and Nyasaland was also, at least in part, attributable to the preponderance in both central and territorial governments of a single political group. Between 1954 and 1960 the United Federal Party and its territorial affiliates dominated all the governments at both levels,[4] and it was only with the success in the 1961 Nyasaland elections of the Malawi Congress Party, committed to secession, that the situation was altered. Unlike the more monolithic parties of the Asian federations, however, the official connexions between the United Federal Party and the branches in the territories were looser, although the informal ties were actually very close.[5]

In the other two federations—Nigeria and the West Indies—the predominance of regional parties in national politics worked in the opposite direction, tending to weaken the relative power of the central government.

---

[1] C.A.P. (second), *Debates*, vol. i, p. 2119.

[2] T. E. Smith, 'The Malayan Elections of 1959', *Pacific Affairs*, xxxiii (1960), pp. 42–46.

[3] R. O. Tilman, 'The Alliance Pattern in Malaysian Politics: Bornean Variations on a Theme', *South Atlantic Quarterly*, lxiii (1964), pp. 60–74.

[4] For the pattern of party successes in elections, see P. Laundy, 'The Parliaments and Legislative Councils', in W. V. Brelsford (ed.), *Handbook to the Federation of Rhodesia and Nyasaland* (1960), ch. 34.

[5] C. Leys, *European Politics in Southern Rhodesia* (1959), ch. v.

Nigerian politics from 1951 on were dominated by the three major parties, the Northern People's Congress (N.P.C.), the National Council of Nigeria and the Cameroons (N.C.N.C.),[1] and the Action Group (A.G.), each based primarily on a single region. Up to 1962 each of these continuously controlled the government in its own region, and the parties became increasingly enmeshed with the administrative, professional, and commercial structure of their own regions. Moreover, in spite of efforts by both the N.C.N.C. and the A.G. to become national parties, electoral trends up to 1962 showed an increasing regional solidarity in the support for Nigerian parties.[2] Thus the main effect of the party system was 'to provide three powerful organizations intent on maintaining regional rights'.[3]

The party structure in Nigeria, therefore, weakened the central government, especially in the period before 1959. Until then, all the national leaders of the three major parties preferred to remain as regional premiers, leaving central politics to their lieutenants, and this put the central government in a distinctly subordinate position. Moreover, since none of the regional parties could gain a clear majority in the central legislature, the central government consisted of a coalition of the N.P.C. and N.C.N.C., joined also for a time between 1957 and 1959 by the A.G. Dependent upon a coalition of regional parties, the central government naturally tended to be reluctant to exercise its full powers.

After 1959 a number of factors made the Nigerian central government more willing than before to exercise its constitutional authority. The increased prestige of the central government with independence induced the leaders of both the N.C.N.C. and the A.G. to desert their regions for central politics, and also enhanced the public respect for the federal Prime Minister. Nevertheless, this shift of emphasis within the political parties was restricted, for Sir Ahmadu Bello, president of the N.P.C., chose to remain premier of the North, while his vice-president became the federal Prime Minister, and when Dr. Azikiwe became Governor-General he was succeeded as national chairman of the N.C.N.C. by Dr. Okpara, the premier of the Eastern Region, who clearly regarded the N.C.N.C. ministers in the national coalition as his subordinates. It was also significant that the crisis within the Western Region Action Group in mid-1962, and the subsequent creation by Premier Akintola of the United People's Party, arose from the attempts of the national A.G. organization to run the Western Region government by remote control.[4] A

---

[1] Renamed National Convention of Nigerian Citizens after the secession of the Southern Cameroons.

[2] J. P. Mackintosh, 'Electoral Trends and the Tendency to a One Party System in Nigeria', *Journal of Commonwealth Political Studies*, i (1962), pp. 194–210.

[3] J. P. Mackintosh, 'Federalism in Nigeria', *Political Studies*, x (1962), p. 235. See also pp. 233–8.

[4] 'Awolowo versus Akintola', *West Africa* (19 May 1962), p. 550; J. P. Mackintosh, 'Politics in Nigeria: The Action Group Crisis of 1962', *Political Studies*, xi (1963), p. 137.

second factor strengthening the central government has been the ability of the N.P.C. to obtain a majority of the seats in the central House of Representatives, making it less dependent upon its coalition partner the N.C.N.C. Paradoxically, this situation was the result of the increasingly regional character of voting in the Northern Region, which held a majority of seats in the central lower house.[1] A third factor which encouraged the central government to play a stronger role was the fact that the N.P.C.–N.C.N.C. coalition could command the support of an overwhelming majority in the central legislature and in all but one of the regional governments.[2] This gave the coalition sufficient confidence to attempt constitutional amendments, and to impose an emergency administration directed against the government of the third region. Thus in some respects the central coalition found itself in almost as strong a position as the dominant parties in the Asian federations, and this strengthened enormously the power of the Nigerian central government after 1959. The emergency within the Western Region in 1962, the creation of the new Mid-Western Region in 1963, and the controversy over the 1962 and 1963 census results, however, upset the balance between the regional parties, and in the manœuvring preceding the federal elections late in 1964, a realignment of political parties focusing upon the struggle for votes in the Western Region took place—the N.C.N.C. allying itself with the Action Group, and the N.P.C. with Premier Akintola's new Nigerian National Democratic Party.[3] The lengths to which the N.P.C. and the N.N.D.P. went in rigging elections to retain power became in 1964–5 a source of increasing unrest.

In the West Indies, on the face of it, a single party was in a strong position. The West Indies Federal Labour Party held power in the central government, while its affiliates controlled the governments of Jamaica, Trinidad, Barbados, and most of the smaller islands. But several factors weakened the central government. To begin with, both the F.L.P. and its opposition, the Democratic Labour Party, represented electoral alliances of island parties rather than unified parties with island branches.[4] Moreover, the principal leaders of these island parties preferred to hold the fort at home, sending a 'second team' as candidates to contest the central seats. The central government was still further weakened when the F.L.P. alliance, instead of sweeping the central elections as expected, scraped home with a narrow majority based mainly on support from the smaller islands. When to all this was added the clash of personalities among the major central and island leaders of the F.L.P., it was

---

[1] Mackintosh, 'Electoral Trends', op. cit., p. 209.

[2] The creation of the Mid-Western Region, and the election there of an N.C.N.C. government early in 1964, gave the federal coalition the support of three of the four regional governments.

[3] The N.N.D.P. joined Akintola's former United People's Party (formed after the 1962 emergency) with the Southern People's Congress (an ally of the N.P.C.), and some elements of the western branch of the N.C.N.C.

[4] On the West Indian parties, see M. Ayearst, *The British West Indies* (1960), ch. ix. esp. pp. 213–15, 223–5.

hardly surprising that the central government proved even weaker in practice than its limited constitutional powers would have led one to expect.

In Pakistan the national dominance of a single party evaporated when, as a result of the East Bengal elections in 1954, different parties came to dominate the eastern and the western provinces. From 1955 on, central politics became a story of shifting factions and unstable coalitions, and the strength of provincialism continued to grow. But while this weakened the hold of the centralized parties upon their provincial branches, the provincial parties, unlike those in Nigeria and the West Indies, themselves displayed extreme instability. The effect was to leave the centralized bureaucracy virtually in control of both central and provincial administration. With the abrogation of the constitution in 1958 the party strife of the politicians was removed from the scene and replaced by the centralized paternalism of the army and civil service in partnership. Subsequently, when the Constitution Commission of 1961 came to examine the reasons for the failure of constitutional government in Pakistan, it attributed the failure not to the federal constitutional structure, which it considered satisfactory, but rather to the 'lack of leadership resulting in lack of well organized and disciplined parties'.[1] It was this conclusion which led to the attempt in 1962 to combine with some federal institutions an active presidential form of executive which would not be dependent for stability upon the legislature. But although it was President Ayub Khan's intention to guide the country into a political situation without parties,[2] as soon as the new constitution had been promulgated a host of political parties resurrecting old rival groups and regional jealousies appeared on the scene, forcing Ayub to build up the Pakistan Muslim League[3] in order to consolidate his support in the legislature and to give his régime a sense of legitimacy.

The pattern of the political parties has, then, had an enormous influence upon the working and effectiveness of the new federations. But it must be recognized that the federal structures have in turn affected the pattern of the political parties. The constitutions have not been mere façades but have themselves influenced the attitudes, decisions, and organization of the political parties. The extent to which power and prestige were concentrated in the central government has, for instance, affected the degree to which party leaders have been attracted to central politics. The preference for the central arena among politicians in the Asian and Central African federations was a reflection of the authority to which they could aspire, while there was little to tempt the politicians of Jamaica and Trinidad when the central government commanded a budget which was less than 10 per cent. of the budgets of either of these islands. The move of some of the major Nigerian politicians

---

[1] *Report of the Constitution Commission, Pakistan, 1961* (1962), para. 25, and chs. i, iv.

[2] Constitution, 1962, art. 173. The *Political Parties Act* (iii/1962), soon afterwards removed the prohibition on political parties.

[3] At first called the Conventionist Muslim League.

from regional to central politics in 1959 further illustrates the effect that the power and prestige of the central government may have upon political parties. The willingness of politicians to participate in central politics and the inter-relation of central and regional parties has also been affected by the provisions permitting or prohibiting dual membership in central and regional legislatures.[1]

The size, number, and shape of the regional units has been another factor shaping party politics. Where the regional units have been few in number and large in size, as in Nigeria and Pakistan, the tendency to organize parties on a regional basis has been particularly strong. It is significant that the regionalization of party politics in Nigeria followed rather than preceded the constitutional marking off of Nigeria into three regions.[2] Similarly, although Pakistan began life with a single dominant party, within less than a decade the eastern and western provinces supported distinctly regional parties. The relative size of Jamaica and Trinidad within the West Indies may also help to explain the local lack of enthusiasm for any central party that was more than an alliance of island parties. The homogeneity or heterogeneity of regions has also influenced the attitudes and character of political parties. Where regions were heterogeneous as in India (before 1956) and in Nigeria, parties have tended to champion minority interests and claims for boundary revisions in order to gain the votes of minorities. On the other hand, where regional units have been relatively homogeneous, parties have tended to be strongly influenced by regional solidarity. This was apparent in East Pakistan, the north-eastern states of Malaya, and the core areas of the Nigerian regions. Even in India where the Congress Party has been dominant nationally, there has been a growth of local opposition parties, and the Congress Party itself has become more 'federal' in character as the regional linguistic élites have crystallized.

The very existence of regional units has in itself been an encouragement to the growth of opposition parties, for it has often provided them with an arena in which they could operate effectively without having to extend themselves nationally. Thus the regions have provided a base for the operation of opposition parties in Western Nigeria, the eastern states of Malaya, East Pakistan, Nyasaland (in 1961), and in some of the Indian states. It is significant that, in an era when one-party rule has characterized many developing countries, none of the new federations has been without at least some opposition parties. There would, then, appear to be some justification for the claim that a federal system may provide a defence against one-party rule. The extent to which this is true is limited, however, by the existence of emergency powers. The way, for instance, in which the central governments in Pakistan, India, and Nigeria have readily resorted to the use of emergency powers against opposition governments in the regions is not reassuring on this score. These examples illustrate the strains which are likely to arise when different parties are in control of the central and regional governments.

[1] See Chapter 11, section 4.   [2] Coleman, *Nigeria*, chs. 15–17.

Critics have sometimes suggested, therefore, that the encouragement given by federal systems to opposition parties may itself be detrimental. It has been argued, for instance:

The political cohesion won during the struggle for independence may be difficult to maintain as older traditional fears and loyalties reassert themselves. In this situation a highly centralized single party rule may appear to be the only way of holding the country together. Federalism will be a luxury to be foregone.[1]

The experience of Pakistan under multi-party politics would appear to support such a contention. But in the other five federations the value of a single-party system as a means to unity is questionable. It is extremely unlikely that single-party rule would have been a workable way of maintaining unity in Nigeria, the West Indies, or Central Africa. In the other federations—India, Malaya, and later Malaysia—the existence of a federal structure does not appear to have prevented the operation of a relatively stable and effective central government.

3. *The effectiveness of federal governments*

Recognizing that there have been wide variations among these federal structures and that the manner of their working has been strongly influenced by the nature of their party systems, we must now turn to a general assessment of the effectiveness of these six federal experiments. At this stage, when their existence has been relatively brief, any conclusions must necessarily be tentative. Nevertheless, the experience of a decade or more in each of the Asian federations and in Nigeria, and of the difficulties of the West Indian, Central African, and Pakistan federations, has been sufficient to suggest some general patterns. The success of these federations must be judged in the light of what was expected of them. Since it was the desire to combine unity for certain purposes with regional autonomy for others that motivated the adoption of federal institutions, their effectiveness may be assessed by the degree to which they have been able to fulfil both these aims at the same time.

The major motives for federal unity varied, but common to nearly all the new federations was the desire for unity as a means of maintaining genuine political independence and international influence.[2] The international prestige and relative neutrality of the large federations such as India and Nigeria, and the ability of Malaya to sustain its independence, suggest that in practice federation has helped to fulfil such hopes. It is true, of course, that some of the shattered fragments of the West Indian and Central African federations have been able to win their own political independence. Nor have other small territories been prevented from obtaining independence. The examples of Ghana, Cyprus, Sierra Leone, Gambia, and Somaliland make this clear. Ghana, because it set the pace for African self-government, has even exercised

[1] R. C. Pratt, 'The Future of Federalism in British Africa', *Queen's Quarterly*, lxvii (1960), p. 200.   [2] See Chapter 3, sections 2 and 5.

considerable influence on the African continent. But while federal unity may not be necessary for the attainment of formal political independence, the ability of the smaller territories to maintain a genuine independence has been severely limited. It is significant that in former French Africa, where federal institutions have faded away, the individual territories have found themselves in a position of semi-dependence upon France. Nor is it to be overlooked that leaders in Singapore in 1963 considered genuine independence possible only through union with Malaya. Moreover, none of the small independent territories has carried the weight in international affairs that India, Pakistan, and increasingly Nigeria have displayed. The political benefits of federal unity have not, then, been illusory.

But the ability of federations to sustain independence and to exert international influence has varied according to the relative size of the federal unions and the powers given to the central government. India has clearly gained internationally from its vast size, as well as from its relatively powerful and stable central government and the personality of its first prime minister. Both Pakistan and Nigeria have also reaped the political advantages of size. On the other hand, Malaya, Rhodesia and Nyasaland, and the West Indies, even as federations, still remained relatively small, and in the latter case political self-sufficiency and international prestige were little enhanced because of the weakness of the central government.[1] Moreover, where, as in the West Indies, one island had already half the population of the federation as a whole, the gain in size from federal unity was proportionately less for that territory than for the smaller territories. Thus, although experience suggests that there are political benefits to be obtained from federal union, much may depend upon the size and form of the federation.

Politicial self-sufficiency also depends upon economic self-sufficiency. Since all of these countries were relatively under-developed and anxious for rapid social and economic advance, and since in most of them economic aspirations were among the most powerful motives for federal union, we must consider how effective the new federations have been in promoting economic development. Indeed, in view of the rapidly expanding populations of most of these countries, the future internal political stability of these federations may well depend upon their success in achieving rapid economic growth.

Critics have sometimes suggested that federal institutions, involving divisions of power, legalism, rigidities, and technicalities, simply create clumsy obstructions preventing the use of the full resources of the state to increase the productivity of the economy.[2] Taken as a group the new federations

[1] Neither the West Indies nor Rhodesia and Nyasaland had, of course, achieved independence before their disintegration. Indeed, the formal dissolution of the West Indies Federation occurred on the very day independence was to have been achieved.

[2] Pratt, 'The Future of Federalism in British Africa', op. cit., p. 200; Carnell, 'Political Implications of Federalism in New States', op. cit., pp. 18, 55–56.

provide some evidence to support this contention. Even those federations in which the control of economic affairs was highly centralized have found that difficulties have been imposed in the realm of economic planning by their federal structures. The Appleby Report complained, for instance, that India was excessively dependent upon the state governments for the implementation of its social and economic programmes. It was significant that in areas for which state governments were responsible, such as education, health, agriculture, and land reform, the achievements of the Indian Plans have lagged the most.[1] In Malaya too, much of the lack of momentum in the field of economic and social development could be ascribed to the overlapping and delay caused by the need to submit plans to many authorities before they could be proceeded with or completed.[2] The demand for equal expenditure in East and West Pakistan constantly bedevilled attempts there to locate development projects where they were economically most efficient,[3] and in Nigeria there has been a tendency for all planning to be done regionally in parallel.[4] Although the economic advantages were often stressed as the chief motive for a federal union in Central Africa, the Monckton Commission came to the conclusion that 'the planning machinery actually set up was inadequate for the task of full economic development'.[5] Thus, although federation may be economically superior to no union at all, there is little doubt that for purposes of promoting economic development a unitary political system is potentially more efficient, provided that it is politically practicable.

But the degree of economic efficiency has varied enormously among the six federations themselves. The Asian and Central African federations, despite their shortcomings, have been able in fact to sustain very heavy programmes of economic development. The Federation of Malaya, with nearly all economic and fiscal powers assigned to the central government, has been in the strongest position to do so. In Pakistan and to a lesser degree India the central governments have also been quite well endowed for controlling the economy, and the extensive special machinery created for inter-governmental economic and financial co-operation has been a further aid. Thus, the Asian federations have been able to make economic strides by means of their Plans. Rhodesia and Nyasaland lacked the institutions of the Asian federations for co-ordinating the economic activity of governments, but the central government was given considerable control over the economy in the original distribution of functions. In spite of its criticisms the Monckton Commission pointed to the economic progress of the Federation of Rhodesia and Nyasaland as its greatest achievement.[6] Although less centralized, the Nigerian

---

[1] Appleby, *Public Administration in India* (1953), pp. 17–19, 56. See also Santhanam, *Union–State Relations in India*, pp. 56–59.

[2] J. Lowe, *The Malayan Experiment* (1960), p. 12.

[3] C.A.P. (second), *Debates*, vol. i, pp. 1818–19, 2072, 2158. See also Constitution, 1962, art. 145 (4).   [4] See Chapter 6, section 4.

[5] Cmnd. 1148/1960, para. 209.   [6] Ibid., ch. 4.

constitution gave the central government considerable scope for economic action, and the central and regional governments in co-operation undertook in 1962 an integrated six-year development plan.[1] Unlike the other new federations, the West Indian federal structure so shackled the central government that it lacked the capacity to achieve the hoped-for economic transformation.[2] Indeed, the contrast in capacity to promote economic development was far greater among these new federations, and particularly between the West Indies and the Asian federations, than the contrast between the latter group and unitary political systems. Thus, it is not merely the creation of a federal system, but the particular form it takes, which has a vital bearing on the capacity to promote economic development.

Federal institutions were also intended to protect regional diversities. Generally, by comparison with unitary states they would appear to have been relatively successful. As we have already noted, the new federations have, for instance, been less prone to single-party rule than the new unitary states like Ghana. However, the degree to which federal systems have provided minorities with protection has also depended on their precise form. Where the regional units have been internally heterogeneous in population and contained their own diverse majorities and minorities, as in Nigeria, Malaya, and Central Africa, groups within regions have not always been well protected unless special devices were adopted.[3] On the other hand, where regions have been relatively homogeneous, regional autonomy has provided their inhabitants with some protection. The extent of this protection has varied according to the relative centralization of legislative, executive, and financial authority, the scope of the devices for control of regional governments by the central government, especially emergency powers, and the degree to which regional consent was required for constitutional amendment. Thus, in practice, the Bengalis of Pakistan and the Africans in the Central African protectorates had little confidence in the federal institutions as safeguards of their interests. Even in India and Nigeria the use of emergency powers and constitutional amendments in the early years suggested that regional interests could be vulnerable. Lack of central representation has also sometimes weakened the confidence of regional groups. Jamaica, for instance, which otherwise was relatively secure, distrusted central action as likely to be against Jamaican interests because that island was under-represented in the federal legislature and executive.

Finally there remains the question whether the new federations have each been able to preserve the balance between unity and diversity. Here no general answer covering all the federations is possible. All of them have had

---

[1] The relative strength of the central government was illustrated by the fact that, of the projected expenditure in the public sector under this plan, the central government was responsible for 61 per cent. On the dominant role of the central government in Nigerian economic planning see Mackintosh, 'Federalism in Nigeria', op. cit., pp. 239–45.

[2] See Chapter 8, sections 4 and 5.

[3] See Chapter 7, section 3.

their difficulties. On the whole, the Union of India, considering the political and economic problems with which it was confronted, has been the most successful in maintaining a balance between the conflicting tendencies of centralization and regionalization, and in adapting to the changing character of its society.

India, in the fifteen difficult years of crisis following the occurrence of partition and independence at the same time, has stabilized its political institutions, reorganized its states, and undertaken vast programmes of economic development. During this period the federal system has encouraged stability and yet proved adaptable. One of the features of Indian political life since independence has been the simultaneous strengthening of both centralizing and decentralizing tendencies, the former encouraged by the programmes of national social and economic planning and by the predominance of the Congress in both central and state governments, and the latter by the solidifying of regional linguistic groups and the reliance of the central government upon the states for much of its administration. The major problem of the future will be whether this balance can be maintained if the hold of the Congress Party is weakened.[1]

The Federation of Malaya, while still experiencing racial tensions, also displayed remarkable and (in the eyes of many observers) surprising stability. Among the contributory factors were the relative economic prosperity of Malaya and the sheer necessity of racial interdependence and co-operation because none of the communal groups was in a strong enough position to dominate completely. The effectiveness of the central government was aided by the extensive constitutional powers assigned to it, and by the national predominance of the Alliance Party. But this effectiveness of the central government was achieved at the expense of local autonomy; the tendency towards increasing centralization verged by 1963 upon that of a unitary system, and this showed how slender was the constitutional protection of state interests. Within Malaysia this situation continues for the states of Malaya, but the greater political strength of local interests and the special constitutional safeguards in the Borneo states are likely to preserve better the autonomy of these states. The attempt to integrate volatile Singapore failed, however, because the P.A.P.'s desire to play a role in politics outside Singapore became too big a threat to the political balance on which the federal system had rested since 1957. The eviction of Singapore relieved the mounting tension, but the stability of the federation will depend upon how quickly and how widely the economic and social expectations of its diverse peoples are met.

Nigeria, after the troubled decade which almost culminated in disintegration in 1953, did, following the adoption of a full-fledged federal political system, produce a profound transformation of attitudes and a growing

---

[1] See, for instance, Harrison, *India, The Most Dangerous Decades*, chs. 1, 7, 8. Harrison tends, however, to underestimate the continued strength of economic planning as a factor for centralization. See Morris-Jones, *The Government and Politics of India*, p. 207.

sense of inter-regional co-operation. Regional autonomy, by reducing inter-regional fears of domination, has actually encouraged unity, and by channelling political energy away from the central arena helped to make for stability at the centre. As a result, after 1954 the prestige and political power of the central government steadily, if slowly, grew. By 1962 it was able to show that it was strong enough even to impose its will upon the advanced Western Region. Nevertheless, the strength of the central government was still limited by the fact that it rested on a coalition of regional parties. Indeed, the stability of Nigeria has depended on a capacity to overcome successive crises rather than on the absence of political strife. Until 1963 the south accepted the preponderance of the conservative north as a temporary compromise, but when the 1963 census confirmed the permanence of the north's stranglehold on federal politics the basis on which the federal system had rested since 1954 was destroyed. It is clear that despite the protracted negotiations and adjustments over the years, the constitutional balance between the various forces in Nigeria is as yet by no means finally resolved.

The other three federations have been distinctly less effective. The federal institutions of Pakistan were the first to collapse. Despite their federal form, in practice they were worked in a highly centralized and essentially unitary manner. It was not surprising that, in a country composed of two regions over 1,000 miles apart and united by little more than a common religion and a shared fear of Hindu India, such centralization provoked reactions of intense provincialism among regional groups and especially the Bengalis.[1] The resulting conflicts and tensions shattered the frail unity inherited from the nationalist movement and destroyed the dominance of the Muslim League. The politics of Pakistan became a kaleidoscope of shifting coalitions of provincial factions, until in 1958 this was replaced by open military and bureaucratic administration. But even under the new régime provincial pressures continued to exert themsleves, and it was found necessary to incorporate a large number of federal features in the new constitution of 1962.[2]

The West Indies Federation, at the other extreme from the political centralization of Pakistan, also collapsed, simply disintegrating.[3] The effectiveness of the central government was limited by its lack of significant powers, and this contributed to its lack of appeal and prestige in the eyes of both political leaders and electorates. The result was, on the one hand, the frustration felt by the smaller islands at the inability of the central government to act effectively, and on the other hand, the disdain of Jamaica, which saw itself bearing the burdens of federation without receiving any benefits. These conflicting viewpoints clashed in the constitutional negotiations leading up to the

---

[1] *Report of the Constitution Commission, Pakistan, 1961* (1962), paras. 58–62.

[2] Ibid., ch. iv.

[3] On the disintegration of the West Indies Federation see especially the writings of H. W. Springer, E. Wallace, J. H. Proctor, Jr., and A. Etzioni (listed in bibliography on pp. 397–8).

review conference of 1961, were temporarily resolved at that conference, but finally destroyed the federation soon afterwards.

The disintegration of the Federation of Rhodesia and Nyasaland took somewhat longer, in part because the British Government put more effort into its preservation. Nevertheless, by 1960 it was already apparent that the federation would only survive if drastic modifications were made.[1] Within three years the separatist pressures had mounted to the point where finally the British Government itself found it necessary to agree to the dissolution of the federation. The reason for the failure of the Central African federation was that, like Pakistan, it was too centralized for the society on which it was imposed. The federal constitution, worked out as a bargain between the settlers and the British Government, failed to give sufficient expression to the realities of the African anxieties. The imposition of the federation and the manner of its working only served to increase rather than reduce these fears.

If any general lesson is to be drawn from these examples, it would seem to be that the effectiveness of federal institutions may vary according to the particular form they take. Where, as in India, Malaya, and up to 1963 Nigeria, the federal constitutional balance has reflected fairly accurately the balance of forces within the society, and has displayed sufficient flexibility to adapt itself to changes in the pattern of the society, federal institutions have proved remarkably successful. But where, as in Pakistan and Central Africa, a centralized federal structure has failed to give regional interests adequate expression or, as in the West Indies, has been too decentralized to provide any significant benefits from union, the federations have experienced serious difficulties or have even disintegrated.

4. *The suitability of federal institutions*

The conclusions in the preceding section suggest that the suitability of federal institutions in the developing countries will depend upon whether the particular form of federal system constructed gives full expression to the desires of the society in question. Federal government suffered failures in Pakistan, the West Indies, and Rhodesia and Nyasaland, not because a federal system was inappropriate, but because the particular form of federal institutions adopted were unsuitable to the specific situation. The federations of Pakistan and Rhodesia and Nyasaland were too centralized, while at the other extreme that of the West Indies created only an ineffective central government. The tragedy is that, because of the unsuitability of a particular form of federal institutions, federal government of any form has become totally discredited in some of these countries.

But the question still remains whether any federal solution at all was appro-

---

[1] See, for instance, Cmnd. 1148/1960, paras. 49, 71, 75, 84.

priate, or whether other political alternatives might have been better, in the six countries under study.

To begin with, have the advantages of federal institutions outweighed their disadvantages in the developing countries? The examples of India, Malaya and between 1954 and 1963 Nigeria bear out the claims made for the advantages of federal solutions.[1] In these cases, federal institutions have made possible a combination of political unity and diversity, have helped to protect regional groups, and have supplied a framework for reaching a consensus. Especially important, they have provided a bridge between the old and the new political cultures, between the local traditional institutions and the westernized central political institutions. Of course, even in the more successful federations these advantages have been bought only at a price. Compared to a unitary system, federal government has involved at least some legalism and rigidity.[2] Concessions to internal diversities have also, especially in India and Nigeria, reinforced and solidified regional loyalties. Yet on balance these disadvantages do not appear to have overridden the advantages of federal institutions, so long as a realistic and adaptable reconciliation between central and regional interests has been achieved. When one considers the complex diversity and difficult circumstances in which the Indian, Malayan, and Nigerian federal systems have had to operate—far more severe than those faced by the older federations—the remarkable feature is not the stresses and strains they have suffered but rather that they have been able to achieve as much unity and effectiveness as they have.

But even if federal institutions are potentially beneficial, have the six countries under study each had the capacity to operate them effectively? The statesmen creating the new federations usually recognized from the beginning that many of the conditions suggested by K. C. Wheare as necessary for successful federal government were missing.[3] We might expect to be able, then, in the light of the failure of some of the new federations and the success of others, to determine which of these conditions have been in practice crucial to effective federal government. Geographical contiguity was certainly missing in Pakistan, the West Indies, and in terms of communications, between the Rhodesias and Nyasaland. Yet other federations like the United States and Canada have linked distant unconnected territories. There were sharp dissimilarities in the political or social institutions within Rhodesia and Nyasaland, the West Indies, and Pakistan. But equally great dissimilarities, although a source of strain, have not prevented India or Malaya from surviving. The shallowness of the foundation of constitutionalism and legalism and the presence of oligarchic elements was not unique to Pakistan or the settler-dominated Rhodesias. Nor were the unsuccessful federations all more

[1] See Chapter 5, section 2 for the advantages claimed for federal governments.
[2] See Chapter 12.
[3] See Chapter 5, section 3, above.

handicapped by lack of trained and experienced legislators and administrators. Both the West Indies and Rhodesia and Nyasaland were better off than Nigeria in this respect. Disparities in the relative populations and wealth of regions have caused tension in India as well as in those federations that have proved less stable. Thus it would appear that most of these disabilities have been shared by successful as well as unsuccessful new federations. But while no single difficulty can be pointed to as the only decisive factor preventing effective federal government, it has been in the West Indies, Pakistan, Central Africa and Nigeria that the coinciding of many of these handicaps at the same time has had the greatest cumulative effect.

Two factors, moreover, improved the capacity of India and Malaya for operating federal institutions. First, in neither of these was one internal group in so strong a position politically and economically to consider itself able to insist completely upon its own way, as did the Jamaicans or the settlers of Southern Rhodesia. The existence of a relative balance among regional groups in India and Malaya induced a sense of interdependence which in turn fostered a willingness to compromise. In Nigeria before 1963 northern economic dependence on the south produced a similar spirit, but the situation changed after the north began to assert its political dominance. It is most significant that of the new federations, the four that have proved most unstable—Pakistan, the West Indies, Rhodesia and Nyasaland, and Nigeria— have been those in which a single region held a majority of the federal electorate. The second factor which distinguished these federations from the less-successful ones was the quality of their political leadership. A vigorous confidence in national unity combined with a willingness to make concessions differentiated the political leaders of India, Malaya, and for a time Nigeria from those of Pakistan, the West Indies, and Rhodesia and Nyasaland.[1]

But if many of the conditions in the new federations, and particularly in Pakistan, the West Indies, and Central Africa, were unfavourable to satisfactory federal government, what were the alternatives available? In the eyes of the statesmen framing their constitutions, the alternatives were even less satisfactory.[2] Even where federal government has failed, the alternatives which have been adopted, military and bureaucratic administration in Pakistan, separate island independence for Jamaica and Trinidad in the West Indies, and an independent existence for each of the Rhodesias and Nyasaland, are by no means obviously superior as permanent political solutions. It is significant that the Pakistan constitution of 1962 restored a degree of federalism, that the smaller islands of the East Caribbean have found it necessary to consider a new federation, and that there has been talk on various occasions in Zambia and Malawi of joining an East African federation.

[1] See Chapter 5, section 4, esp. p. 106.   [2] See Chapter 5, section 2.

Federal systems are no panacea, but in many developing countries they may be necessary as the only way of combining, through representative institutions, the benefits of both unity and diversity. Experience has shown that federations, both old and new, have been difficult countries to govern. But then, that is why they are federal states.

14

THE NATURE OF THE FEDERAL SOLUTION

AT the beginning of this study we examined a number of views about the federal principle. I suggested there that the fundamental and differentiating characteristic of a federal political system is the co-ordinate status of the governments exercising authority. What distinguishes federal from other forms of government is that neither the central nor the regional government is subordinate to the other as in unitary or confederal political systems. We also noted that theorists have advanced two apparently contradictory variants of this basic principle. Those who have elaborated the theory of 'dual federalism' have argued that in a truly federal system the central and regional governments must each have their own demarcated spheres of activity in which each can operate independently of the other, and that the maintenance of functional separation between the two levels of government is the key to the maintenance of a genuine federal system. On the other hand, those who have developed the theory of co-operative federalism have stressed the necessity in any federal system of co-operation and interaction between central and regional governments. According to this view the key to the successful maintenance of a federal system lies in the mutual interdependence of the two levels of government, thus ensuring their collaboration as partners without rendering either level subordinate.

In this chapter we shall be concerned with considering to what degree the new federations in the Commonwealth have embodied either of these forms of the federal concept, and to what degree they may be described as federal at all.

To begin with, it is clear that the statesmen creating these new federations were much influenced by the theory of 'dual federalism'. If we examine their debates and pronouncements we find frequent echoes of the traditional dualistic view that in a federal system the governments must be co-ordinate and equal, each being limited to its own sphere and independent in that sphere.[1] Moreover, the new federations also appear to possess the basic formal characteristics of orthodox federations: central and regional governments each acting directly on the people; a constitutional distribution of authority between central and regional governments; a supreme written constitution interpreted by a supreme court, and requiring special procedures for amendment.

But if we look more closely it is also apparent that all these federations have contained features which in K. C. Wheare's terminology would require

---

[1] See Chapter 8, section 1, and also Chapter 6, section 5.

us to describe these political systems as only 'quasi-federal'. The founders of these federations, unwilling to allow theoretical ideas to override practical considerations, have invariably set up some central controls over the independence of regional governments in the interests of both stability and flexibility. The various ways in which the independence of one level of government from the other has been limited have been examined in Chapter 10. Limitations upon regional autonomy have also been noted in other chapters: there have been special checks upon regional governments to protect minorities within regions; regional governments have been dependent upon central sources for a significant portion of their revenues; various devices have been created to reduce the rigidity of the constitutions, the most far-reaching of these being the usual inclusion of central emergency powers. These apparently non-federal features have been most prevalent in the Asian federations, but have to some extent been present in all the new federations. Even the almost confederal West Indies Federation gave the central government potential unitary control by the grant of extensive emergency powers. It is clear, therefore, that the dualistic principle of federalism has at most been only imperfectly embodied in these new federations.

This raises then the question whether these new federations represent instead examples of 'interdependent federalism' as opposed to 'dualistic federalism', or whether they are even genuinely federal at all. In making this assessment we must bear in mind three points made in the introductory chapter. First, the federal principle may be expressed in a variety of institutional ways and is not limited to simply one pattern. Second, not only the legal relations but also the political and administrative practice between levels of government must be taken into account in gauging whether the governments are co-ordinate. Third, in any such judgement, less exactitude is possible than when purely legal categories are the sole criterion.

Because the Asian federations have possessed so many unitary features, it has sometimes been argued that they cannot properly be described as federal. In the case of India, there is considerable literature on this subject.[1]

[1] Wheare, *Federal Government*, pp. 26–28; G. P. Srivastava, 'Some Unitary Features of our New Constitution', *Indian Journal of Political Science*, xi (1950), pp. 62–65; A. Gledhill, *The Republic of India* (1951), pp. 91–92; I. Jennings, *Some Characteristics of the Indian Constitution* (1953), pp. 63–67; B. M. Sharma, *Federalism in Theory and Practice* (1953), ii, pp. 740–9; A. K. Ghosal, 'Federalism in the Indian Constitution', *I.J.P.S.*, xiv (1953), pp. 317–32; N. Srinivasan, *Democratic Government in India* (1954), pp. 147–9; K. P. Mukerji, 'Is India a Federation?' *I.J.P.S.* xv (1954), pp. 177–9; C. H. Alexandrowicz, 'Is India a Federation?', *International and Comparative Law Quarterly*, iii (1954), pp. 393–403; C. H. Alexandrowicz, *Constitutional Developments in India* (1957), pp. 155–70, 203–4, 234; D. D. Basu, *Commentary on the Constitution of India* (3rd ed., 1955), i, pp. 12–18; A. C. Banerjee and K. L. Chatterjee, *A Survey of the Indian Constitution* (1957), pp. 336–48; V. G. Ramachandran, 'Is the Constitution of India Federal?', *Supreme Court Journal*, xxii (1959), p. 97; P. R. Dubhashi, 'Unitary Trends in a Federal System', *Indian Journal of Public Administration*, vi (1960), pp. 243–56; K. Santhanam, *Union–State Relations in India* (1960), pp. 7–13; N. D. Palmer, *The Indian Political System* (1961), pp. 94–98; M. P. Jain, *Indian*

Many commentators—using Wheare's terminology—have pointed to the Union Government's extensive emergency powers, its ability to revise state boundaries unilaterally, and certain controls it may exercise over state legislation and administration, as evidence that the whole system of Indian government is essentially 'quasi-federal' in character.[1] Other writers have argued that, although the constitution may contain these provisions, in practice many of them have not been resorted to, and, even when they have been exercised, these powers have not been used by the Union to impose its will upon stable state governments supported by their legislatures. State autonomy, they maintain, has been genuine, and in operation it is the federal characteristics of the constitution that have predominated.[2] The answer would appear to lie somewhere between these two positions. The Indian constitution is clearly neither purely federal nor purely unitary, but a combination of both. It does contain provisions which, whether used or not, represent potential limitations upon state autonomy and make possible the subordination of the states, thus certainly representing exceptions to the dualistic federal principle.[3] Moreover, some of these powers have been exercised by the Union Government.[4] On the other hand, the Constituent Assembly clearly intended the proposed political system to be basically federal in character.[5] The nature of Indian federalism was perhaps best summed up by the chairman of the Drafting Committee: 'The Draft Constitution can be both unitary as well as federal according to the requirements of the time and circumstances. In normal times it is framed to work as a federal system.'[6] In practice, despite the centralizing effect of Congress Party domination in both levels of government, economic planning, and the occasional use of emergency powers, nevertheless, the pressures of linguistic regionalism and the dependence of the Union Government upon the co-operation of the states have emphasized the federal character of Indian politics. India may, therefore, be best described as a predominantly federal state with some unitary features.[7]

Constitutional Law (1962), pp. 329–33; K. M. Panikkar, *The Foundations of New India* (1963), pp. 154–6, 236–43; W. H. Morris-Jones, 'Stability and Change in Indian Politics', in S. Rose (ed.), *Politics in Southern Asia* (1963), pp. 9–32.

[1] Wheare, loc. cit.; Mukerji, loc. cit.; Banerjee and Chatterjee, loc. cit., esp. pp. 336, 348; Panikkar, loc. cit.; Gledhill, loc. cit., and Jennings, loc. cit., would appear to take this view.   [2] Alexandrowicz, loc. cit.; Srinivasan, loc. cit.

[3] The most important examples are: arts. 3–4, 31 (3), 31A (1) (as amended by *First Amendment Act, 1951*, s. 4), 200–1, 249, 256–7, 258 (2), 286, 288 (2), 347, 350A and 350B (as inserted by *Seventh Amendment Act, 1956*, s. 21), 352–60, 371 (both before and after *Seventh Amendment Act, 1956*, s. 22).

[4] See, for instance, Chapter 10, section 5, and Chapter 12, sections 6 and 7.

[5] C.A.I., *Debates*, vol. iv, pp. 885, 896, 902–3, 1008–10; vol. v, pp. 37–38, 57–58; vol. vii, pp. 33–37; vol. ix, pp. 133, 953; C.A.I., *Report of Union Constitution Committee* (1947), pt. i, para. 1; C.A.I., *Second Report of the Union Powers Committee* (1947), para. 2.

[6] C.A.I., *Debates*, vol. vii, pp. 34–35.

[7] This is also the view of Basu, loc. cit., Santhanam, loc. cit., Morris-Jones, loc. cit., and to some degree of Palmer, loc. cit. Santhanam suggests that, since India is a federation in which the paramountcy powers of the British Government were taken over by the Union

The question whether the 1956 constitution of Pakistan was genuinely federal was raised in the second Constituent Assembly when the draft was being debated. Under the interim constitution the provinces had in fact been largely subordinated to the central government, and therefore, in the Constituent Assembly, the Bengali advocates of regional autonomy were extremely critical of the new constitution for what they considered to be its unitary features inherited from the Government of India Act, 1935.[1] Supporters of the new constitution, on the other hand, pointed to what they considered its essentially federal features: the supremacy of the constitution, the distribution of powers between co-ordinate governments, and the supreme judicial authority to settle disputes.[2] The final product, like the Indian constitution, was actually a blend of federal and unitary features, in which the unitary elements represented exceptions to the fundamentally federal structure.[3] In practice, however, because of the dominance of the central bureaucracy, and because the central emergency powers and other controls over provincial governments were so frequently resorted to, the constitution was operated in a considerably more unitary manner than in India.

The Pakistan constitution of 1962 was also ostensibly federal. Indeed, the preamble declared that 'Pakistan should be a form of federation with the Provinces enjoying such autonomy as is consistent with the unity and interest of Pakistan as a whole'. The constitution also appeared to contain the usual federal features: central and provincial governments, a constitutional distribution of legal, executive, and financial powers, a Supreme Court with jurisdiction in any inter-governmental disputes, and a rigid process of constitutional amendment. But certain features, such as the control of provincial governors by the President,[4] the reference to the National Assembly of deadlocks between a governor and a provincial legislature,[5] the sweeping central concurrent powers where in the national interest for security, economic planning, or the achievement of uniformity,[6] and the determination of the validity of laws by the legislatures themselves,[7] placed potent unitary levers in the hands of the central government. These, if fully exercised, could reduce the provincial governments to a completely subordinate position and leave the federal structure a mere façade. To some extent braking this tendency, however, has been the vigour of Bengali separatism, and the consequent need to pay at least some respect to provincial autonomy.

The non-federal constitutional provisions have been almost as extensive in the Federation of Malaya, and in addition greater legislative, executive, and financial responsibilities have been concentrated in the central government

Government and applied to all its units, it might appropriately be labelled a 'Paramount Federation'.

[1] C.A.P. (second), *Debates*, vol. i, pp. 1793–4, 1854–6, 1944, 1963–4, 1984, 2017, 2039, 2043, 2130, 2236, 2271–2.

[2] C.A.P. (second), *Debates*, vol. i, pp. 1793–5, 2095–2100, 2292.

[3] The most important 'quasi-federal' provisions were: arts. 90, 126, 127 (2), 191–6.

[4] Arts. 66, 80.   [5] Arts. 74, 77.   [6] Art. 131.   [7] Art. 133.

than in any of the other Asian federations. This was particularly true of the Federation of Malaya Agreement, 1948. The Agreement gave very wide powers to the central authorities who could, if they so wished, legislate against the wishes of state governments on almost all questions other than those concerning Muslim religion and Malay custom. In addition to legislative and executive controls, the bulk of the state finances was provided by the central government on a year-to-year basis after an examination of state estimates.[1] In practice, however, many of these powers of the central government were left unexercised. The 1957 constitution reduced the scope of the functions for which the states were responsible, but, in order to give the states a fuller measure of autonomy over these very limited fields, patterned the federal system on more orthodox lines. Thus the legislative, executive, and financial powers conferred by the constitution were distributed between the central and state governments, each normally being legally independent within its own sphere. But as with the other Asian federations, there were some significant exceptions to the freedom of states from central control.[2] In addition, although amendment of the 'federal' provisions of the constitution required a special majority in the central legislature, no ratification by state legislatures was required except for the alteration of state boundaries.[3] Some qualifications to these special central powers have been introduced, however, with respect to the new states joining the Federation of Malaysia,[4] and this is likely to reinforce the basically federal character of this political system.

The three non-Asian federations have adhered more closely to the orthodox federal principle, there being fewer potentially unitary exceptions. Nevertheless, there too, as noted in Chapter 10, some apparently non-federal aspects in the constitutional relation between central and regional governments were considered necessary: in all of them, for instance, sweeping emergency powers were available to the central government. In addition there were usually some checks limiting the independence of each level of government from the other,[5] and, except in the West Indies, regional governments depended heavily upon the central governments for their financial resources.[6]

Two characteristics appear, therefore, to be common to all the new federations. First, each of these political systems was designed to be convertible in certain situations. Each was intended to operate under normal conditions in a manner fundamentally federal, but in the interests of both stability and adaptability, provisions were inserted into the constitutions making them temporarily convertible into unitary systems in times of emergency.

---

[1] *Federation of Malaya Agreement, 1948*, cls. 8, 19, 100 (2), 111–23. See also S.I. 1948, no. 108, ss. 7, 16, 33.

[2] The most significant were *Constitution of Malaya, 1957*, arts. 76 (4), 92 (1), 93–95, 149 (1) 150 (4, 5).

[3] Arts. 2, 159. See Chapter 12, section 4.

[4] *Malaysia Act, 1963*, ss. 39, 42, 43, 66, 69.

[5] See Chapter 10, section 5.   [6] See Chapter 9, sections 5 and 6.

Secondly, except under the temporary emergency powers, the dependence of one level of government on the other has not been wholly one-sided. The permanent unitary or 'quasi-federal' features limiting the independence of regional governments have usually been counterbalanced by the inclusion in the constitutions themselves of regional checks or controls on the exercise of central powers.[1] In addition, even in the Asian federations, central governments have tended to be heavily dependent for the implementation of national economic and social programmes upon relatively autonomous ministries and legislatures which were directly responsible to their own electorates. Furthermore, the political force of intense regionalism has in each federation, although with varying intensity, acted as a powerful brake upon central dominance. Both constitutionally and politically, therefore, the situation has in fact been one of mutual dependence of central and regional governments on each other. This interdependence has found expression in the proliferation of institutions and arrangements for consultation and co-operation between governments in a wide variety of fields,[2] and in the special weight given to regional balance within the institutions of the central governments themselves.[3] Thus, by comparison with the older federations, a distinctive characteristic of the new federations has been the degree to which central and regional governments have been made more interdependent and their relations more flexible.

It would seem, then, that the statesmen establishing the new federations have been pragmatic rather than dogmatic in their application of the federal idea. Although they usually started with the traditional dualistic conception of federal organization, they have found themselves forced by social and political realities to introduce qualifications. Invariably, in an era of large-scale economic activities, it has been impossible to demarcate the functions of central and regional governments into two isolated compartments, and in framing and operating the new federal constitutions a measure of interdependence has proved unavoidable. The result has been federal systems in which central and regional governments are each independent in certain fields but must interact in many others.

As already noted in the introductory chapter, the lack of complete independence for central and regional governments is not inconsistent with the basic federal principle, as long as central and regional governments are *mutually* dependent on each other. Although none of the new federations fulfilled completely the conditions required by the dualistic notion of federalism, these political systems have represented in their operation examples of 'interdependent federalism'. Each of the new federations constituted, not a dual polity of absolutely separated central and regional governments, but a single integrated political system in which central and regional governments interlocked and in normal practice were balanced so that neither was totally subordinate to the other.

[1] See Chapter 10, section 5.   [2] See Chapter 10.   [3] See Chapter 11.

A further feature of the new federal systems has been their pragmatic flexibility. By comparison with the older federations, these new constitutions have incorporated not only less rigid formal amendment procedures, but also a wide variety of devices and arrangements intended to facilitate both co-operation between governments and adaptability to changing circumstances.[1] Moreover, although judicial review and constitutional amendments have been far from insignificant, one of the most important channels for adaptation has been through agreements between governments and compromises worked out in the political parties. In some of these federations, this flexible co-operation has been facilitated by the relative strength and dominance of certain political parties in both tiers of government.[2] The clear aim of the statesmen founding and operating the new federations has been to establish, not static political structures, but political systems capable of evolving to meet the changing needs and outlooks of the communities they unite.

The pattern of an integrated flexible federal system containing co-ordinate and interdependent authorities has been implemented in a variety of ways, however. There is no single ideal federal system. To meet their own particular conditions, new federations have varied in the size, number, and shape of their regional units, in the form and distribution of legislative and executive authority, in the allocation of revenue sources and precise manner of financial transfers, in the degree to which the judiciary and civil services are shared, in the machinery devised to facilitate consultation and co-operation between governments, in the shape of the central institutions, in the flexibility or rigidity of formal constitutional amendment, and in the special arrangements designed to permit adaptability. Each of the new federations has combined its particular variations of these institutions into its own unique blend of pragmatic federal government. In so far as their central and regional governments have been co-ordinate and interdependent, these new political systems have properly fallen within the federal 'band' of the spectrum of political structures. But within that 'band', the new federations have varied enormously. At one end of the band, close to the point where centralized federal government shades into decentralized unitary government, have been Malaya and Pakistan with their concentration of powers in the central government and their considerable unitary features. At the other end, bordering on the con-federal, was the West Indies with its extremely weak though co-ordinate central government. The other new federations have fallen between these extremes: India close to the other Asian federations, Rhodesia and Nyasaland highly centralized but with fewer unitary potentialities, and Nigeria a federation of strong regions although its central government is far from impotent. It is when the political balance struck has most fittingly expressed the balance of interests within the particular society upon which it rests that these federal institutions have proved most effective.

[1] See Chapter 12, sections 4, 5, 6, 7.   [2] See Chapter 13, section 2.

APPENDIX · TABLES

For List, see page xi, following Contents

TABLE 1

Area and Population of Federations

Federation	Area in sq. miles	Population
India (1961)	1,261,597	439,072,893
Pakistan (1961) . . .	364,737	93,812,000
Nigeria (1962)	356,669	55,653,821
Malaysia (1963) . . .	128,000	9,900,000
Rhodesia and Nyasaland (1959)	486,109	7,994,000
Malaya (1957)	50,700	6,278,758
The West Indies (1960) . .	8,029	3,115,113
Canada (1958)	3,851,809	17,048,000
Australia (1959) . . .	2,974,581	10,008,665

Sources: census and statistical reports.

TABLE 2

Regions with Preponderance of Population, Area, and Wealth

Federation	Total no.	Largest regions	Percentage of all Regions		
			Pop.	*Area*	*Rev.*
West Indies (1959–60) .	10	Jamaica Trinidad	51·5 ⎱ 78 26·5 ⎰	58 ⎱ 84 26 ⎰	42 ⎱ 84 42 ⎰
Nigeria (1960–1)* . .	3	Northern Region Western Region	55·5 20	79 13	33 37
Pakistan (1957–8) . .	2	East Pakistan West Pakistan	55·4 44·6	15 85	33 67
Rhodesia and Nyasaland (1959–60)	3	Southern Rhodesia Northern Rhodesia	71† 26†	31 61	49 38
Malaya (1957–8) . .	11	Perak, Selangor, and Johore	50	38	54
Malaysia (1958) . .	15	Perak, Selangor, Johore, and Singapore	52	15	54
		Singapore	16	0·2	20
		Sarawak and North Borneo	12	60	7
India (1950) . . .	28	Four largest states (*a*)	54	34	49
India (1956) . . .	20	Four largest states (*b*)	50	37	47
India (1962) . . .	25	Four largest states (*c*)	45	31	39
		Uttar Pradesh	17	9	13

* Excluding Southern Cameroons but including Northern Cameroons.
† Population figures for Rhodesia and Nyasaland are for electorates.
(*a*) Bihar, Bombay, Madras, Uttar Pradesh.
(*b*) Andhra, Bihar, Bombay, Uttar Pradesh.
(*c*) Andhra, Bihar, Maharashtra, Uttar Pradesh.

Sources: *Census of West Indies 1960, Preliminary Report*, 1961; *Colonial Office List, 1961*;
Nigerian Digest of Statistics, 1961; *Census of Pakistan, 1951*; Callard, *Pakistan, A Political Study*, p. 156; Cmnd. 1149/1960; *Census of Malaya, 1957, Preliminary Report*; *Estimates: Federation of Malaya and States*, 1958; Cmnd. 1794/1962; *India, A Reference Annual, 1953, 1956–7, 1962*.

TABLE 3

Distributions of Legislative Authority between Central and
Regional Legislatures

The distribution of legislative authority expressly mentioned in the Constitutions or necessarily implied from them is indicated in the following table by the letters F (Federal), C (Concurrent), and R (Regional). If a subject is not mentioned in the Constitution, either because the power to legislate for it is intentionally assigned to the authority exercising residuary power, or because it is not applicable in that Federation, the space in the table has been left blank; the assignment of the residuary power is, however, shown in the first line of the table. Where a Federal power is more restricted than would be implied by the letter F alone, it is shown as FR to indicate that some aspects of the power are Regional or that Regional consent is required for the exercise of Federal authority in that field. Fr indicates Federal powers which can only be exercised after consulting Regional Governments, but do not require their consent. The content and allocation of some subjects, particularly external affairs, defence, law and procedure, machinery of government, parliamentary privilege and emoluments, taxes and loans, and trade are often more complex than might appear from the table, and reference must be made to the Constitutions themselves for details.

It should be noted that in some federations, the distribution of legislative authority does not apply equally to all autonomous regional governments. In India, some items on the Union List and the whole of the Concurrent List do not apply to the State of Jammu and Kashmir, but no notation of these items has been made in the table. For Rhodesia and Nyasaland, F* signifies Federal in Southern Rhodesia only, and C* represents Concurrent in Northern Rhodesia only (after 1956). Under the Malaysia Constitution (1963), the distribution of legislative authority follows that in the previous Federation of Malaya as shown in the table, but certain exceptions apply solely to the new states of Sabah, Sarawak, or Singapore. Items marked F+ or C+ are those which in some of these Malaysian states came wholly or partially under state control or required state consent for the exercise of Federal authority. Items marked Fˣ became wholly or partially concurrent in the case of some of these same states.

Sources for the table were Cmnd. 1150/1960, Appendix II, and the constitutions of the federations as amended, 1960, except in the case of the Pakistan constitutions which were taken as they stood in 1958 and 1962. The notations regarding Malaysia were based on *The Malaysia Act, 1963*, and associated enactments.

	Canada	Australia	India	Pakistan 1958	Pakistan 1962	Malaya	Nigeria	Rhodesia and Nyasaland	West Indies
Residuary power	F	R	F	R	R	R	R	R	R
Whether regional powers are listed	Yes	No	Yes	Yes	No	Yes	No	No	No
External Affairs		C	F	F	F	F	F	F	
Treaty implementation	FR	C	F	Fr	F	Fr	FR	FR	FC
Citizenship and aliens	F	C	F	F	F	F+	F	FC	C
Immigration:									
into Federation	C	C	F	F	F	F+	F	FC	F
between Regions			F	C		C+	C	C	C
Defence	F	FC	F	F	F	F	F	F	F
Police		C	R	R	R	F	FrR	FCR	
Public order			R	R	F	C			
Prisons	FR		R	R		F	C	C	C
Preventive detention			C	FR	FR	F			
Law and procedure									
Civil	FR	C	C	C		FR	CR	CR	C
Personal	FR	C	C	C		F×+R	FR		CR
Criminal	F		C	C		F			C
Constitution and organization of courts	R		FR	FCR	FR	F+	FR	FCR	FR
Machinery of government									
Public services and pensions	FR	FR	FR	FR	FR	F+R	FR	FR	FR
Elections:									
Federal			F	Fr	F	F	F	F	FR
Regional			FR	Fr	F	F×			
Finance									
Foreign exchange			F	F	F	F	F	F	F
Currency and coinage	F	FC	F	F	F	F	F	F	C
Foreign loans	FR	C	F	FR	FC	F	FR	FR	FC
Internal loans	FR	C	FR	FR	FR	F×	FR	FR	FC
Public debt	F		FR	F	FR	F	F		
Audit			F		F	F	FR	FR	FC
Taxes:									
Customs	F	F	F	F	F	F+	F	FR	CR
Excise	F	F	FR	FR	F	F+	F	FR	CR
Corporation	FR	C	F	F	F	F	F	FR	C
Personal income	FR	C	FR	FR	FR	F+	FR	FR	CF
Sales taxes	FR	C	FR	FR	F	F+	FR	FR	
Other taxes	FR	C	FCR	FR	FR	F+R			RC
Banking	F	CR	F	FC	FR	F×	F	FC	C
Cheques and bills of exchange	F	C	F	F	F	F	F	F	C
Stock exchanges			F	FC	FR	F			
Money lending			R	R		F×			
Trade, commerce, and industry									
External trade	F	C	F	F	F	F×	FR	F	C
Inter-regional trade	F	C	F	F	F	F×	FR	C	C
Intra-regional trade	R		RC	R		F×		FR	
Corporations and companies	FR	CR	FR	FCR	FR	F+	FR	FR	C
Insurance			F	FC	FR	F×	FR	FR	C
Patents, trade marks, copyright	F		F	F	F	F	F	F	C
Weights and measures	F	C	FR	FR	F	F	F	F	C
Industries			FCR	FR	FR	F×	C	C	C
Mines and oilfields			FR	FCR	FR	F	F		
Factories			C	C		F+			
Price control			C	C		F×		F	
Co-operative societies			R	R		F		CR	
Planning									
Economic and social			C	C	F	F+r			
Town and country						C		C	
Shipping and navigation									
Maritime	F		F	FR	FR	F×	F	F	C

	Canada	Australia	India	Pakistan 1958	Pakistan 1962	Malaya	Nigeria	Rhodesia and Nyasaland	West Indies
Shipping and navigation (contd.)									
Inland waterways	FR		FRC	R		F×R	FR	F	
Ports			FC	FR	FR	F+×	FR	F	
Fishing	F	CR	FR	FR	FR	F×R			CR
Communications and transport									
Roads and bridges			FR	R		FR	FR	FC	
Railways	FR	C	F	FR	R	F+	F	F	
Air			F	F	F	F	F	F	C
Regulation of traffic						F+R	CR	C	
Carriage of passengers and goods			F			F×			
Mechanical vehicles			C	R		F			
Posts and telecommunications	FR	FC	F	Fr	F	F	F	F	C
Broadcasting and television			F	F	F	F	FR	C	C
Utilities									
Water			FR	R		F×R	FC	FR	
Electricity			C	R		F×+	CR	C	
Gas			R	R	F	F+	CR		
Nuclear energy			F		F		F	F	C
Education									
Elementary and secondary	R		R	R		F+		FR	
University	R		FR	R		F+	FC	F	F
Teacher training	R		R	R		F+			
Libraries			FR	FR	FR	F+			FR
Museums			FR	FR	FR	F+	F		FR
Archaeology and monuments			FCR	CR	FR	F+	C	FR	
Scholarships	R	C	R	R		C+			C
Medicine and Health									
Hospitals and clinics	R		R	R		F+×		C	
Lunacy	R		C	R		F+×			
Poisons and drugs			FC	CR		F+×	CR		
Liquor			R	R		F+×			
Public health and sanitation			R	R		C		C	
Labour and social services									
Trade unions			C	C		F+	C		C
Industrial disputes		CR	C	C		F+	C		C
Unemployment relief	F		R	R		F+			
Workmen's compensation			C	C		F+			
Social security		C	C	C		F+		F	
Social welfare services		C	C	C		C			
Charities			C	R		F×			
Women and children						C		C	
Vagrancy			C	R		C			
Land									
Tenure	R		R	R		CR			
Prospecting			FR	R		R			
Compulsory acquisition		C	C	R		R			C
Transfer	R		CR	R		R			
Reservations	F		F	F	F	RF			
Agriculture	C		RC	R		R		F*C*R	
Forestry			R	R		R			
Agricultural pests and diseases			RC	R		F×		F*C*R	
Agricultural loans			R	R		R			
Animal husbandry			R	R		C		F*C*R	
Drainage and irrigation			FR	R		C		FR	
Soil erosion						C		F*C*R	
Local government	R		R	R		F+R			
Fire brigades						R			
Burial and cremation grounds			R	R		R			
Pounds and cattle trespass			R	R		R		F*C*R	
Markets and fairs			R	R		R			

	Canada	Australia	India	Pakistan 1958	Pakistan 1962	Malaya	Nigeria	Rhodesia and Nyasaland	West Indies
Miscellaneous									
Survey			F	F	F	F+	C	C	C
Census	F	C	F	F	F	F	C	C	C
Statistics	F	C	C	FRC	FR	F	C	C	C
Meteorology		C	F	F	F	F	F	F	
Aborigines	F		FR	FR	FR	F+			
Professions			C	R		F×	C	FR	
Holidays						FR			
Newspapers and printing . .			C	C		F×		C	
Licensing of films . . .			F	R					
Entertainment and sports .			R	R		F×R			
Wild animals and National Parks .			R	R		C	C	FR	
Lotteries			F	R		F			
Betting and gambling . .			R	R		F			
Research			FCR	FCR	FR	F×	C	C	F

TABLE 4A

Comparison of Central and Regional Revenues and Expenditure

| Federation | Year | Percentages of total public revenues* | | | Regional expenditure as % of total public expenditure |
		Central revenue (before transfers)	Regional revenue (before transfers)	Inter-govt. transfers	
Malaya . . .	1959	89	11	7	17
The U.S.A. . .	1959–60	79	21	5	26
Canada . . .	1959–60	81	19	11	33
Australia . . .	1960–1	80	20	17	37
Rhodesia and Nyasaland	1958–9	70	30	14	43
Pakistan . . .	1962–3	73	27	26	49
Nigeria . . .	1959–60	84	16	37	54
India . . .	1960–1	60	40	20	58
W. Indies . . .	1959–60	1	99	2†	97

* Combined central and regional revenue, excluding municipal revenue.
† Mandatory levy upon territories for transfer to central government.

Sources: Annual Budget Statements, Finance Commission reports, Statistical Abstracts, and Year Books. For details see Tables 5A–10A.

TABLE 4B

Comparison of Composition of Regional Current Revenues

| Federation | Year | Percentages of total regional revenues | | | | |
		Independent revenue	Share of central taxes	Constitutional unconditional grants	Conditional grants	Total transfers
India . .	1951–2	81	13	4	2	19
	1954–5	75	14	4	7	25
	1957–8	71	16	6	7	29
	1960–1	65	19	5	11	35
Pakistan .	1948–9	73	25	2	0·2	27
	1954–5	71	27	2	0·3	29
	1957–8	68	27	2	3	32
	1962–3	51	34	1	14	49
Malaya .	1950	43	..	..	57	57
	1954	38	..	..	62	62
	1956	38	3	6	53	62
	1960	59	2	34	5	41
Nigeria .	1953–4	22	25	44	9	78
	1956–7	32	68	..	0·2	68
	1959–60	28	72	..	0·2	72
Rhodesia and Nyasaland .	1956–7	64	34	..	..	34*
	1959–60	70	30	..	..	30*
W. Indies .	1959–60	98	..	..	2†	2

* Excludes reimbursements for work carried out in Territories on behalf of Federal Government.
† C.D. and W. grants from United Kingdom administered by Federal Government.

Sources: Annual Budget Statements, and Finance Commission and Constitutional Commission Reports. For details see Tables 5B–10B.

TABLE 5A

India—Union and State Current Revenues

In crores of rupees

	Union			All states		
Year	Gross revenue	Less transfers	Net revenue	State sources	Add transfers	Net revenue
1937–8	87·8	7·0	80·8	..	..	85·9
1946–7	377·8	51·6	326·2	..	..	246·3
1948–9	413·5	73·0	340·5	..	..	256·4
1949–50	396·1	78·7	317·4	..	..	289·0
1950–1	458·2	74·5	383·7	316·5	66·4	382·9
1951–2	568·2	85·1	483·1	334·0	78·2	412·2
1952–3	492·1	113·4	378·7	326·2	102·2	428·4
1953–4	473·3	122·7	350·6	339·6	104·0	443·6
1954–5	512·1	144·4	367·7	376·3	127·6	503·9
1955–6	559·4	175·4	384·0	416·3	148·2	564·5
1956–7	642·6	138·0	504·6	439·0	138·0	577·0
1957–8	757·8	190·9	566·9	529·2	220·6	749·8
1958–9	872·3	250·4	621·9	572·0	284·8	856·8
1959–60	948·4	273·2	675·2	625·5	330·0	955·5
1960–1	1,007·0	331·2	675·8	683·9	368·3	1,052·2
1961–2 (B.E.)	1,088·5	373·3	715·2	649·6	371·8	1,021·4

Sources: *Reports of Finance Commissions, 1952, 1957, 1961*; *India, A Reference Annual, 1962.*
Union figures are based on Union accounts, State figures on State accounts. Figures for
1961–2 are Budget estimates.

TABLE 5B

India—Composition of State Current Revenues

Percentage of total state Revenue

Sources	1951–2	1954–5	1957–8	1960–1
Own sources:				
Taxes	56·3	52·1	46·6	41·8
Other revenue	24·7	22·6	24·0	23·2
Total	81·0	74·7	70·6	65·0
Central sources:				
Shared central taxes:				
Income and Estate taxes	12·8	11·1	10·2	10·9
Excises	..	3·0	5·3	7·2
Other taxes	..	..	0·6	1·4
Total	12·8	14·1	16·1	19·5
Unconditional statutory grants	4·3	4·5	6·2	4·7
Total statutory transfers	17·1	18·6	22·3	24·2
Conditional grants	1·9	6·7	7·1	10·8
Total transfers	19·0	25·3	29·4	35·0
Total state revenue	100·0	100·0	100·0	100·0

Sources: *Reports of Finance Commissions, 1957, 1961.*

TABLE 5c

India—Per Capita Revenues of States 1960–1

Amounts in Rs. per capita

State	Own sources	Central tax shares	Central grants in aid	Total transfers	Total revenue
Andhra Pradesh . .	13·73	4·64	4·15	8·79	22·52
Assam . . .	13·86	4·58	11·28	15·86	29·72
Bihar . . .	9·87	3·53	3·56	7·09	16·96
Gujarat . . .	16·35	8·34	2·22	10·56	26·91
Kerala . . .	18·34	4·12	4·31	8·43	26·77
Madhya Pradesh. .	14·33	4·17	3·77	7·94	22·27
Madras . . .	18·28	5·95	3·41	9·36	27·64
Maharashtra . .	22·60	3·79	2·00	5·79	28·39
Mysore . . .	24·30	4·63	5·81	10·44	34·74
Orissa . . .	10·66	4·09	6·09	10·18	20·84
Punjab . . .	22·08	4·78	3·36	8·14	30·22
Rajasthan . . .	13·59	4·22	4·01	8·23	21·82
Uttar Pradesh . .	12·45	4·69	2·59	7·28	19·73
West Bengal . .	17·88	6·14	3·23	9·37	27·25
Jammu and Kashmir .	20·06	5·92	14·89	20·81	40·87
All States . . .	15·86	4·77	3·77	8·54	24·40

Source: *Report of Finance Commission, 1961,* Statistical Appendixes.

TABLE 6A

Pakistan—Federal and Provincial Current Revenues

Amounts in crores of rupees

	Central government			All provinces		
Year	Gross revenue	Less transfers	Net revenue	Provincial sources	Add transfers	Net revenue
1948–9	76·8	11·4	65·4	33·8	11·1	44·9
1949–50	98·1	11·2	86·9	34·7	9·7	44·4
1950–1	141·1	17·4	123·7	39·4	14·8	54·2
1951–2	161·8	27·1	134·7	42·8	18·5	61·3
1952–3	152·4	20·9	131·5	41·3	20·3	61·6
1953–4	128·7	18·9	109·8	45·9	19·6	65·5
1954–5	136·4	24·8	111·6	51·4	20·5	71·9
1955–6	166·4	27·7	138·7	55·0	24·9	79·9
1956–7	158·3	27·5	130·8	59·3	32·4	91·7
1957–8	177·9	29·1	148·8	62·9	29·6	92·5
1958–9*	231·0	39·1	191·9	100·6	39·8	140·4
1959–60	217·9	33·4	184·5	83·6	33·6	117·2
1960–1	247·0	40·2	206·8	86·8	40·3	127·1
1961–2	263·6	46·2	217·4	102·2	61·7	163·9
1962–3 (R.E.)	283·1	76·9	206·2	104·5	100·0	204·5

* 1958–9 was 15-month financial year (1 April 1958–30 June 1959).

Sources: Government of Pakistan, *Budget of Central Government for 1963–4: Explanatory Memorandum* (Rawalpindi, 1963), containing tabulation of central and provincial accounts. Figures for 1962–3 are revised estimates.

TABLE 6B

Pakistan—Composition of Provincial Current Revenues

Amounts in crores of rupees

	1948–9		1954–5		1957–8		1960–1		1962–3 (B.E.)	
Sources	E.P.	W.P.	E.P.	W.P.	E.P.	W.P.	E.P.	W.P.	E.P.	W.P.
Own sources:										
Taxes . . .	7·5	7·2	10·7	10·6	15·4	21·6	22·3	27·2	24·2	26·0
Other revenue .	1·3	17·8	4·5	25·6	4·4	21·5	7·6	29·7	9·4	44·9
Total . .	8·8	25·0	15·2	36·2	19·8	43·1	29·9	56·9	33·6	70·9
Central sources:										
Shared tax revenue	8·1	1·9	9·1	10·0	10·8	14·5	14·5	23·0	35·1	34·8
Subventions .	..	1·0	..	1·2	..	1·2	..	1·2	..	2·3
Sub-total . .	8·1	2·9	9·1	11·2	10·8	15·7	14·5	24·2	35·1	37·1
Special grants .	..	0·1	0·1	0·1	0·8	2·3	0·4	1·2	19·9	7·9
Total . .	8·1	3·0	9·2	11·3	11·6	18·0	14·9	25·4	55·0	45·0
Total current revenue	16·9	28·0	24·4	47·5	31·4	61·1	44·8	82·3	88·6	115·9

Sources: Government of Pakistan, *Budget of Central Government: Explanatory Memoranda for 1962–3 and 1963–4* (Karachi 1962, Rawalpindi 1963). Figures for 1962–3 are Budget estimates.

TABLE 7A

Malaya—Federal and State Current Revenues

Amounts in Malayan $ millions

Year	Federal Government			All states		
	Gross revenue	Less transfers	Net revenue	State sources	Add transfers	Net revenue
1948	223	79	144	54	79	133
1949	345	88	257	48	88	137
1950	443	78	365	59	78	137
1951	735	91	644	75	91	166
1952	725	149	576	84	149	234
1953	620	167	453	93	167	260
1954	622	156	466	95	156	251
1955	797	148	649	104	148	252
1956	802	196	607	111	179	291
1957	801	187	614	112	164	276
1958	762	65	697	116	70	186
1959	868	65	803	109	70	179
1960	874	67	808	110	76	186

Sources: *Estimates* of Federation of Malaya and of States and Settlements. Figures for 1959 are revised estimates and for 1960 Budget estimates. Other figures are actual revenue according to Federation and State accounts to the nearest million.

TABLE 7B

Malaya—Composition of State Current Revenues

Amounts in Malayan $ millions

Sources	1950	1954	1956	1958	1960 (B.E.)
Own sources:					
Tax revenues . . .	31·0	54·7	66·0	70·2	71·1
Other revenues . .	27·6	40·6	45·3	46·2	39·2
Total	58·6	95·3	111·3	116·4	110·3
Central sources:					
Share of central taxes .	..	..	7·4	1·8	3·0
Unconditional grants .	..	..	17·8	64·6*	63·4*
Sub-total . . .	..	..	25·2	66·4	66·4
Ad hoc and special grants	78·3	155·8	154·1	3·6	9·6
Total transfers . .	78·3	155·8	179·3	70·0	76·0
Total state revenue . .	136·9	251·1	290·7	186·4	186·3

* Including State Road Grants stipulated in Constitution.

Sources: *Estimates* of Federation of Malaya and of States and Settlements. Figures for 1960 are Budget estimates.

TABLE 7C

Malaya—Receipts of Central Aid by States, 1958

Amounts in $ Malayan millions

States	Percentage of population 1957	Shared central tax revenue	Statutory grants and subventions	Ad hoc grants	Total federal aid
Perak . . .	19·75	..	11·2	..	11·2
Selangor . . .	16	1·8	8·4	2·4	12·6
Negri Sembilan . .	6	..	5·1	0·3	5·4
Pahang . . .	5	..	3·9	0·3	4·2
Johore . . .	14·75	..	8·0	..	8·0
Kedah . . .	11	..	6·6	1·8	8·4
Kelantan . . .	8	..	4·7	0·2	4·9
Trengganu . . .	4·4	..	3·6	..	3·6
Perlis . . .	1·5	..	1·5	0·3	1·8
Penang . . .	9	..	5·3	0·1	5·4
Malacca . . .	4·6	..	4·4	..	4·4

Sources: *Estimates* of States, 1960.

TABLE 8A

Nigeria—Federal and Regional Current Revenues

Amounts in £ millions

Year	Federal Government			All Regions		
	Gross revenue	Less regional allocations	Net revenue	Regional sources	Add Federal sources	Net revenue
1950–1	33	9	24	..	9	9
1951–2	50	10	40	..	10	10
1952–3	51	14	37	2	17	19
1953–4	59	13	46	4	15	19
1954–5	62	27	35	9	27	36
1955–6	60	26	34	13	25	38
1956–7	71	28	43	16	27	43
1957–8	71	29	42	17	27	44
1958–9	77	31	46	17	30	47
1959–60	89	38	51	16	38	54
1960–1	96	42	54	18	36	54

Sources: Federal and Regional *Annual Estimates*, and *Nigerian Digest of Statistics*, 1961. Figures for 1960–1 are revised estimates and no longer include Southern Cameroons.

TABLE 8B

Nigeria—Composition of Regional Current Revenues

Amounts in £ millions

Sources	1953–4			1956–7			1959–60		
	E.R.	N.R.	W.R.	E.R.	N.R.	W.R.	E.R.	N.R.	W.R.
Population	23%	54%	20%	23%	54%	20%	23%	54%	20%
Own Sources: (Taxes and others)	0·9	1·5	1·7	4·9	3·9	4·1	5·4	5·1	4·2
Central sources: Share of central taxes:									
Specified taxes	1·1	1·2	2·4	6·8	9·6	11·4	6·5	8·6	13·3
Distributable pool	..	..	..	..	..	..	2·8	3·7	2·2
Unconditional grants	2·7	3·1	2·6	..	..	..	..	..	..
Total unconditional transfers	3·8	4·3	5·0	6·8	9·6	11·4	9·3	12·3	15·5
Special grants	0·6	0·5	0·6	..	0·1	..	..	0·1	..
Total transfers	4·4	4·8	5·6	6·8	9·7	11·4	9·3	12·4	15·5
Total regional revenue	5·3	6·3	7·3	11·7	13·6	15·5	14·7	17·5	19·7

Sources: *Annual Estimates* of Regional Governments.

Note: Southern Cameroons is omitted.

TABLE 9A

Rhodesia and Nyasaland—Federal and Territorial Current Revenues

Amounts in £ millions

	Federal government			All territories		
Year	Gross revenue	Less transfers*	Net revenue	Territorial sources	Add transfers*	Net revenue
1953–4	..	..	..	59·5	..	59·5
1954–5	47·7	10·8	36·9	18·7	10·8	29·5
1955–6	53·0	11·0	42·0	24·5	11·0	34·5
1956–7	67·0	14·6	52·4	26·2	14·6	40·8
1957–8	71·0	15·6	55·4	27·3	15·6	42·9
1958–9	63·2	13·1	50·1	27·2	13·1	40·3
1959–60	65·0	11·9	53·1	27·8	11·9	39·7

* Not including reimbursements for inter-governmental services.

Sources: Cmnd. 1149/1960, Tables 126, 129, 137, 142, 147; Hazlewood and Henderson, *Nyasaland, The Economics of Federation*, p. 41. 1959–60 figures are Budget estimates.

TABLE 9B

Rhodesia and Nyasaland—Composition of Territorial Current Revenues

Amounts in £ '000

Sources	1956–7			1959–60		
	S.R.	N.R.	N.	S.R.	N.R.	N.
Percentage of federal pop.	34%	30%	36%	36%	29%	35%
I. Own sources:						
Income tax surcharge .	2,331	5,098	183	3,215	2,410	180
Own taxes . . .	5,823	951	903	7,460	1,516	1,625
Other sources . .	3,850	5,307	1,732	4,386	5,762	1,331
Total . . .	12,004	11,356	2,818	15,061	9,688	3,136
II. Share of federal basic income tax . . .	5,282	6,908	2,445	4,456	5,530	1,866
III. Total (I and II) . .	17,286	18,264	5,263	19,517	15,218	5,002
IV. Other items:						
Reimbursement for inter-governmental services	4,464	1,004	402	2,107	620	421
C.D. and W. grants .	..	..	511	..	..	30
Capital revenue . .	..	31	95	..	..	..
V. Total	21,750	19,299	6,271	21,624	15,838	5,453

Sources: Cmnd. 1149/1960, Tables 137, 142, 147. 1959–60 figures are Budget estimates.

TABLE 10A

West Indies—Federal and Territorial Current Revenues

Amounts in thousands of W.I. $

Year	Federal government			All territories		
	Taxes and other revenue	Add. mandatory levy	Net revenue	Taxes and other revenue	Less mandatory levy	Net revenue
1958–9	790	9,120	9,910	386,076	9,120	376,956
1959–60	3,057	9,120	12,177	405,264	9,120	396,144
1960–1	5,940	9,120	15,060	423,638	9,120	414,518

Sources: The West Indies Federation *Estimates*, 1960; *Colonial Office List, 1961, 1962*. Figures for 1958 are actual, 1959 are revised estimates, 1960 are Budget estimates.

TABLE 10B

West Indies—Composition of Territorial Current Revenues

Amounts in millions of W.I. $

Year 1959 Sources	Jamaica	Trinidad	Barbados	Windwards and Leewards	Total
Income taxes	47·5	57·0	8·0	4·2	116·7
Import taxes	48·5	31·4	8·7	10·2	98·8
Excise duties	21·1	10·6	2·9	1·3	36·0
Export duties	..	..	..	2·4	2·4
Death duties	0·9	0·5	0·4	0·2	2·0
Other revenue	31·6	69·8	1·7	6·4	109·4
Total local revenue	149·6	169·3	21·7	24·7	365·3
U.K. grant in aid*	..	..	..	6·6	6·6
Total current revenue	149·6	169·3	21·7	31·3	371·9

* Administered by Federal Government.

Source: Government of Trinidad and Tobago, *Economics of Nationhood* (M23/1959), Table I.

TABLE 10C

West Indies—Composition of Mandatory Levy

Territory	Percentage of population 1957	Percentage of W.I. territorial revenue 1959	Percentage of mandatory levy
Jamaica	52·5	42·0	43·1119
Trinidad and Tobago	25·0	41·9	38·6252
Barbados	7·6	5·7	8·5562
The Windwards:			
Dominica	2·1	1·5	1·6250
Grenada	3·0	1·9	1·6969
St. Lucia	3·0	1·6	1·7400
St. Vincent	2·6	1·5	1·3086
The Leewards:			
St. Kitts-Nevis	1·9	1·4	1·7256
Antigua	1·8	1·9	1·3374
Montserrat	0·5	0·6	0·2732

Sources: *Constitution of the West Indies, 1957*, Fifth Schedule; *Colonial Office List, 1961*.

TABLE 11

India—Composition of Union Legislature, 1952 and 1963

1952

STATES	Lok Sabha	Rajya Sabha
Part A States:		
Assam	12	6
Bihar	55	21
Bombay	45	17
Madhya Pradesh	29	12
Madras	75	27
Orissa	20	9
Punjab	18	8
Uttar Pradesh	86	31
West Bengal	34	14
Total A States	374	145
Part B States:		
Hyderabad	25	11
Madhya Bharat	11	6
Mysore	11	6
P.E.P.S.U.	5	3
Rajasthan	20	9
Saurashtra	6	4
Travancore-Cochin	12	6
Jammu and Kashmir	6 m	4
Total B States	96	49
Part C States:		
Ajmer	2	} 1 r
Coorg	1	
Bhopal	2	1
Bilaspur	1	} 1
Himachal Pradesh	3	
Delhi	4	1
Kutch	2	1
Manipur	2	} 1 rn
Tripura	2	
Vindhya Pradesh	6	4
Total C States	25	10
Part D Territories:		
Andaman and Nicobar Islands	1 n	..
Total C and D States	26	10
Total States	**496**	**204**
Other Nominated Members:		
For literature, science, art, &c.	..	12 n
Part B Tribal Areas (Assam)	..	..
Anglo-Indians	2 n	..
Total	2	12
TOTAL MEMBERS	498	216

1963

STATES	Lok Sabha	Rajya Sabha
States:		
Andhra Pradesh	43	18
Assam	12	7
Bihar	53	22
Gujarat	22	11
Kerala	18	9
Madhya Pradesh	36	16
Madras	41	18
Maharashtra	44	19
Mysore	26	12
Orissa	20	10
Punjab	22	11
Rajasthan	22	10
Uttar Pradesh	86	34
West Bengal	36	16
Jammu and Kashmir	6 m	4
Nagaland (1962)	1 n	1
Total States	488	218
Union Territories:		
Delhi	5	3
Himachal Pradesh	4	2
Manipur	2	1
Tripura	2	1
Andaman and Nicobar Islands	1 n	..
Laccadive, Minicoy, and Amindivi Islands	1 n	..
Dadra and Nagar Haveli (1961)	1 n	..
Goa, Daman, and Diu (1962)	2 n	..
Pondicherry (1962)	1 n	1
Total Territories	19	8
Total States and Territories	**507**	**226**
Other Nominated Members:		
For literature, science, art, &c.	..	12 n
Part B Tribal Areas (N.E.F.A.)	1 n	..
Anglo-Indians	2 n	..
Total	3	12
TOTAL MEMBERS	510	238

m: Appointed on recommendation of State Legislature.
n: Nominated Representatives.
r: Seat held in rotation by the two states.
Reserved Seats: distributed on basis of population in each state:
    1952:   72 for scheduled castes and 27 for scheduled tribes.
    1957 and 1962: 76 for scheduled castes and 31 for scheduled tribes.

TABLE 12A

Pakistan—Composition of Interim Central Legislatures, 1947-56

Units	1st Constituent Assembly					2nd Constituent Assembly 1955-6		
	1947			1953				
	Muslim	Non-Muslim	Total	Added Muslim	Total	Muslim	Non-Muslim	Total
East Bengal Province	31	13	44	..	44	31	9	40
Punjab Province	12	5*	17*	5†	22*	20	1	21
Sind Province	3	1	4	1	5	4	1	5
N.-W. Frontier Province	3	..	3	..	3	4	..	4
Baluchistan Province	1	..	1	..	1	1	..	1
Baluchistan States Union	..	..	..	1	1	1	..	1
Bahawalpur	..	..	..	1	1	2	..	2
Khairpur	..	..	..	1	1	1	..	1
N.-W. Frontier States	..	..	..	1	1	1	..	1
Tribal Areas	..	..	..	..	..	3	..	3
Karachi	..	..	..	..	..	1	..	1
Total West Pakistan	19	6	25	10	35	38	2	40
Total Assembly	50	19	69	10	79	69	11	80

1. The First Constituent Assembly was originally based on the principle of 1 representative for 1 million of population. By 1953, there had been added 5 Punjab seats and 1 Sind seat to represent refugees who had entered Pakistan after partition, and 4 seats to represent acceded states. In the Second Constituent Assembly the principle of parity of representation for East and West Pakistan was introduced.

2. In both Constituent Assemblies, representatives from Provinces were elected by Provincial Assemblies. In Baluchistan, because there was no provincial legislature, representatives were elected by a special electoral college. Representatives of acceded states were nominated by the rulers and representatives of Tribal Areas by the Tribal Advisory Council. The Karachi representative was elected by Karachi Municipal Corporation.

* Four of these seats, 2 Sikh and 2 General (i.e. Hindu), were left unfilled when their holders resigned or vacated Pakistan. The remaining non-Muslim seat in Punjab was designated after 1949 for representation of non-Hindu minorities.

† The 5 added Punjab seats were filled by co-option by the Constituent Assembly because the Provincial Assembly was dissolved at the time.

TABLE 12B

Pakistan—Proposals for Composition of Central Legislature

Units	Percentage of Federal population 1951	Franchise Sub-Committee Report (1952) (bicameral) House of People	House of Units	Joint sitting	B.P.C. Report (1952) (bicameral) House of People	House of Units	Joint sitting	B.P.C. Report (as adopted 1954) (bicameral) House of People	House of Units	Joint sitting	1956 Constitution (unicameral) National Assembly	1962 Constitution (unicameral) National Assembly
East Bengal	55·4	200	60	260	200	60	260	165†	10	175	155‡	78‡
Punjab	24·9	⎱109	⎱33	⎱142	90	27	117	75	10	85	..	..
Bahawalpur	2·4				13	4	17	7	4	11	..	..
Sind	6·1	⎱34	⎱10	⎱44	30	8	38	19	9	28	..	..
Khairpur	0·4				4	2	6	1	1	2	..	..
N.W.F.P.	4·3	⎱39	⎱11	⎱50	25	6	31	13	⎱10*	⎱33	..	..
N.W.F. Tribal	3·5				17	5	22	11*			..	..
Baluchistan	0·8	⎱8	⎱3	⎱11	5	2	7	3	⎱3	⎱8	..	..
B.S.U.	0·7				5	2	7	2			..	..
Karachi	1·5	10	3	13	11	4	15	4	3	7	..	..
Total W. Pakistan	44·6	200	60	260	200	60	260	135†	40	175	155‡	78‡
Total	100	400	120	520	400	120	520	300	50	350	310	156

In the bicameral schemes, the House of People would have been directly elected, and the House of Units would have been elected by Unit Legislatures or, where these did not exist, by special electoral colleges.

* Including Frontier States.

† Not including additional seats reserved for women for first 10 years: 7 from E. Bengal and 7 distributed among units of W. Pakistan.

‡ Including seats reserved for women: under 1956 Constitution a total of 10, 5 from each Province, for the first 10 years; under 1962 Constitution a total of 6, 3 from each Province.

Malaya and Malaysia—Composition of Central Legislatures

Constituencies	Percentage of federal population		Federal Legislative Council 1955 (unicameral)			Malaya Parliament 1959 (bicameral)		Malaysia Parliament 1963 (bicameral)	
	Malaya (1957)	Malaysia (1963)	Elected	State officials*	Total	Dewan Ra'ayat (H. of R.)	Dewan Negara (Senate)	Dewan Ra'ayat (H. of R.)	Dewan Negara (Senate)
States of Malaya:									
Former F.M.S.:									
Perak	19·8	14·0	10	1	11	20	2	20	2
Selangor	16·0	11·3	7	1	8	14	2	14	2
Negri Sembilan	6·0	4·3	3	1	4	6	2	6	2
Pahang	5·0	3·5	3	1	4	6	2	6	2
Total	46·8	33·1	23	4	27	46	8	46	8
Former U.M.S.:									
Johore	14·7	10·4	8	1	9	16	2	16	2
Kedah	11·0	7·8	6	1	7	12	2	12	2
Perlis	1·5	1·1	1	1	2	2	2	2	2
Kelantan	8·0	5·7	5	1	6	10	2	10	2
Trengganu	4·4	3·1	3	1	4	6	2	6	2
Total	39·6	28·1	23	5	28	46	10	46	10
Former S.S.:									
Malacca	4·6	3·3	2	1	3	4	2	4	2
Penang	9·0	6·4	4	1	5	8	2	8	2
Total	13·6	9·7	6	2	8	12	4	12	4
Totals Malaya:	100·0	70·9	52	11	63	104	22	104	22
New States of Malaysia:									
Singapore	..	16·8	..	..	..	..	..	15	2
Sabah (N. Borneo)	..	4·7	..	..	..	..	..	16§	2
Sarawak	..	7·6	..	..	..	..	..	24§	2
Totals New States	..	29·1	..	..	..	..	..	55	6
Totals of Malaysia	..	100·0	..	..	..	..	..	159	28
Appointed Members:									
For Special Interests and Racial Minorities	..	..	..	..	30†	..	16‡		22
Ex officio Members, Speaker and Officials	..	..	..	..	6	..	..		..
Total	..	..	..	..	36	..	16		22
TOTAL MEMBERS	..	..	..	11	99	104	38	159	50

* Presidents of the State Councils in the Malay States and representatives of the Settlement Councils.

† Including 6 for commerce, 6 for planting, 4 for mining, 2 for agriculture and husbandry, 4 for trade unions, and 1 each for Ceylonese, Eurasians and Aborigines.

‡ For Composition see Table 13B.

§ Elected indirectly by State Legislative Assemblies, but direct election to be introduced within 5 years.

TABLE 13B

Malaya—Distribution of Senate Membership by Races and States, 1959

States	State representatives			Nominated members				Totals				
	Malay	Chinese	Indian	Malay	Chinese	Indian	Others	Malay	Chinese	Indian	Others	Total
Former F.M.S.:												
Perak	1	1			1 (d)		2 (e)	1	2		2	5
Selangor	1	1			3 (d, e)	2 (e)	1 (e)	1	4	2	1	8
Negri Sembilan	1	1				1 (e)		1	1	1		3
Pahang	1	1						1	1			2
	4	4 (b)	0	0	4	3	3	4	8	3	3	18
Former U.M.S.:												
Johore	2							2				2
Kedah	2				1 (d)			2	1			3
Perlis	2							2				2
Kelantan	2 (a)			2 (c)				4				4
Trengganu	2 (a)			1 (c)				3				3
	10	0	0	3	1	0	0	13	1	0	0	14
Former S.S.:												
Malacca	1	1						1	1			2
Penang	1	1				1 (e)	1 (e)	1	1	1	1	4
	2	2 (b)	0	0	0	1	1	2	2	1	1	6
Totals .	16	6	0	3	5	4	4	19	11	4	4	38

Sources: Senate *Debates*, 11 September 1959, vol. 1, no. 1, cols. 7–8, and 5 December 1959, vol. 1, no. 3, col. 35; *Straits Budget*, September 1959; J. V. Morais (ed.), *Leaders of Malaya and Who's Who*, 1957–8.

(a) These Senators were P.M.I.P. members; all other Malay Senators representing States were U.M.N.O. members.

(b) These Senators were all M.C.A. members.

(c) Political appointment of U.M.N.O. members to give these states U.M.N.O. representation because State legislatures sent P.M.I.P. Senators.

(d) Political appointment of M.C.A. members: Perak—1; Selangor—2; Kedah—1. The Perak Senator became Leader of the Senate and a cabinet minister.

(e) Senators appointed to represent special communities and interests: Aborigines—1 (Perak); Eurasian—1 (Penang); Ceylonese—1 (Selangor); Muslim League—1 (Penang); Rubber Industry—3 (Perak—1, Selangor—2); Associated Indian Chambers of Commerce—1 (Negri Sembilan); National Union of Plantation Workers—1 (Selangor).

TABLE 14

Nigeria—Composition of Central Legislatures

Territories	Percentage of federal population 1952–3 Census	1946–51 Legislative Council (unicameral)	1951–4 H. of R. (unicameral)	1954–9 H. of R. (unicameral)	1959–62 H. of R.	1959–62 Senate	1963 H. of R.	1963 Senate	1964 H. of R.*	1964 Senate
Northern Region	54	9	68	92	174†	12	174	12	167	12
Western Region	19½	6	32	42	62	12	47	12	57	12
Mid-Western Region (1963)							15	12	14	12
Eastern Region	23	6	34	42	73	12	73	12	70	12
Southern Cameroons (1946–59)	2¼			6	3	4	··	··	··	··
Lagos	1	4	2‡	2			3	4	4	4
Total	100	25	136	184	312†	40	312	52	312	52
Special nominated representatives	··	3	6	6		4		4		4
Officials	··	17	7	3		··		··		··
Total Legislature	··	45	149	193	312†	44	312	56	312	56

* As revised following 1963 census.

† The Northern Region sent 167 members, making the total membership 305, before inclusion of the Northern Cameroons in the Northern Region in 1961.

‡ In the 1951 Constitution these Lagos representatives were included in the Western Region total and not listed separately.

TABLE 15

Rhodesia and Nyasaland—Proposals for Composition of Federal Assembly

Method of representation	Population distribution (1953)			Schemes for composition of unicameral federal assembly				
	Percentage of federal population	Percentage of federal electorate	Electorate as % of territorial population	Cmd. 8233 (1951)	Cmd. 8573 (1952)	Constitution (1953)	Constitution Amendment (1957)	Monckton majority recommendations (Cmnd. 1148/1960)
Southern Rhodesia								
Elected members (a)	..	..	..	14	14	14	24	17
Elected African members (b)	..	..	..	..	2	2	4	10
Specially elected Africans	..	..	..	..	..	..	..	..
European elected for Africans (b)	..	..	..	3 (e)	1	1	1	..
Total	34%	75%	2%	17	17	17	29	27
Northern Rhodesia								
Elected members (a)	..	..	..	8	8	8	14	10
Elected African members (b)	..	..	..	..	..	..	2	10
Specially elected African (c)	..	..	..	2	2	2	2	..
European appointed for Africans (e)	..	..	..	1	1	1	1	..
Total	30%	23%	0·7%	11	11	11	19	20
Nyasaland								
Elected members (a)	..	..	..	4 (f)	4	4	6	3
Elected African members (b)	..	..	..	..	..	..	2	10
Specially elected African (d)	..	..	..	2	2	2	2	..
European appointed for Africans (e)	..	..	..	1	1	1	1	..
Total	36%	2%	0·04%	7	7	7	11	13
Total in Assembly:	..	..	..	35	35	35	59	60
African representatives				4	6	6	12	30
European representatives				31	29	29	47	30

(a) Elected from single-member constituencies; on general roll 1953–7, and on both rolls 1958–62 (controlled by predominantly European electorate).

(b) Elected from separate constituencies; on general roll 1953–7, and on both rolls 1958–62 (controlled by predominantly European electorate).

(c) Elected by African Representative Council of Northern Rhodesia 1953–7; changed in 1958 to election by special electoral body.

(d) Elected by African Protectorate Council of Nyasaland 1953–7; changed in 1958 to election by present and past members of African Provincial Councils together with Africans registered on the general and special voters' rolls in Nyasaland.

(e) Appointed by the Governor of the Territory.

(f) Nominated from panel selected by the Convention of the Association, the system then in use for the Nyasaland Legislative Council.

Table 16

West Indies Federation—Proposals for Composition of Central Legislature

Territory	Percentage of federal population 1957	C.L.C. proposals* 1947 Unicameral	S.C.A.C. proposals, 1950 (Col. no. 255/1950) House of Assembly	Senate	1953 conference and 1957 constitution House of Representatives	Senate	1961 agreement. (Cmnd. 1417/1961) House of Representatives	Senate
Jamaica	52·5	13 (29%)	16 (38%)	2	17 (38%)	2	31 (48½%)	2
Trinidad	25·0	10 (21%)	9 (21%)	2	10 (22%)	2	15 (23½%)	2
Barbados	7·6	6 (12½%)	4 (10%)	2	5 (12%)	2	5 (8%)	2
The Windwards:								
Dominica	2·1	2	2	2	2	2	2	2
Grenada	3·0	4	2	2	2	2	2	2
St. Lucia	3·0	4	2	2	2	2	2	2
St. Vincent	2·6	4	2	2	2	2	2	2
The Leewards:								
St. Kitts-Nevis	1·9	2	2	2	2	2	2	2
Antigua	1·8	2	2	2	2	2	2	2
Montserrat	0·5	1	1	1	1†	1	1	2
Total Federation	100	48 (100%)	42 (100%)	19	45	19	64	20
British Guiana	16·4	9	6	2	..	..	..	..
British Honduras	2·7	4	2	2	..	..	..	..
Total	119%	61	50	23	..	..	..	..

* These figures are calculated from the formula suggested by the Caribbean Labour Congress in their Draft Scheme presented to the Montego Bay Conference (see Col. no. 218/1948, Appendix 2).

† Provision for an alternate member included.

TABLE 17A

Entrenched Sections of Federal Constitutions

Entrenched subjects	India	Pakistan		Malaya			Nigeria	R. & N.	West Indies	
	1950	1956	1962	1948	1957	1963*	1960 1963	1953	1957	1962†
Distribution of powers										
Legislative powers	SE	SE¹	..	SE²	E	ES	SE	SE	E	SE
Executive powers	SE	SE	..	SE²	E	ES	SE	E	E	SE
Taxation powers	SE	E	..	SE	E	ES	SE	E	E	SE
Allocation of revenues	..	..	..	..	..	ES	SE	E	E	SE
Inter-government institutions	E	SE	E	..	E	E	SE	E	..	..
Control of police	SE	E	..	SE	E	E	SE	SE	E	SE
Amendment process	SE	SE	E	E	E	E	SE	SE	SE	SE
Judiciary										
Supreme Court	SE	E	E	E³	E	E	SE	E	E	SE
Regional High Courts	SE	E	E	E	..	ES	SE	..	E	..
Central legislature										
Regional representation	SE	SE	E	E	E	ES	SE	E	SE	SE⁹
Principle of election	E	..	E	SE	E	E	SE	E⁴	E	SE
Second Chamber	SE	..	..	SE	E	E	SE	E	..	SE
Head of State										
Election or appointment	SE	E⁵	E	SE	E	E	SE	E	E	SE
Powers	..	E	E	SE	E	E	SE	E	E	SE
Central public service	E	E	E	E	E	E	SE	E⁷	E	SE
Regional representation	E⁶	SE	E	..	SE⁶	SE⁶	..	..	..	..
Regions										
Regional boundaries	..	SE	SE	E	SE⁸	SES⁸	SE⁹	E	E	SE⁹
Rep. in legislatures	..	SE	E	..	..	..	SE	..	..	SE
Privileges of rulers	E	E	..	SE¹⁰	SE	SE	..	..	..	..
Fundamental rights	E	E	..	..	E	E	SE	..	..	..
Citizenship	..	..	..	E	E	ES	E	..	..	..
Immigration	..	..	..	SE	..	ES¹¹	..	..	..	..
Minority reservations	E	E	..	..	SE⁹	SES⁹	..	..	..	..
National culture										
Official language	E⁵	E	E	E	E⁵	ES⁵	E	E	E	SE
Religion	..	E	E	..	E	ES	..	..	..	..

For amendment procedures signified by E and SE, see Table 17B.

* Constitution of Malaysia, 1963.
† Constitutional proposals agreed upon for 1962, not implemented (Cmnd. 1417/1961).
¹ Articles concerning division of powers: SE; but lists of powers: E.
² Lists concerning division of powers: SE; but clauses regarding lists: E.
³ Interpretation Tribunal and Supreme Court.
⁴ Not subject to Territorial resolution of objection.
⁵ Partially entrenched only.
⁶ Representation of minorities rather than states.
⁷ Amendment by U.K. Statutory Instrument.
⁸ Only simple majorities required in central legislature, but assent of Conference of Rulers and of Legislature of any State affected is required.
⁹ Special procedures.
¹⁰ Protected by State Agreements.
¹¹ In Borneo States only.

TABLE 17B

Amendment Procedures

E = entrenched:

India: two-thirds of votes and majority of members in central Houses.

Pakistan (1956): two-thirds of votes and majority of members in National Assembly.

Pakistan (1962): votes of two-thirds of members of National Assembly; if vetoed by President, repassage by three-quarters of members + either assent of President or referendum.

Malaya (1948): Federal Ordinance with prior approval of H.M. and Conference of Rulers.

Malaya (1957): votes of two-thirds of members of both central Houses.

Malaysia (1963): votes of two-thirds of members of both central Houses.

Nigeria (1960 & 1963): votes of two-thirds of members of both central Houses.

R. & N. (1953): vote of two-thirds of members of Federal Assembly (subject to Territorial resolution of objection) + assent by H.M.

W.I. (1957): U.K. Order in Council.

SE = specially entrenched:

India: E + ratification by one-half of States.

Pakistan (1956): E + ratification by Provinces affected.

Pakistan (1962): E + prior approval by vote of two-thirds of members of Assembly of Province affected.

Malaya (1948): Proclamation by High Commissioner after prior agreement of H.M. and Conference of Rulers, and in certain cases after consultation with state and settlement councils.

Malaya (1957): E + assent of Conference of Rulers.

Malaysia (1963): SE = E + assent of Conference of Rulers.

ES = E + concurrence of Singapore or Borneo States concerned (amendments bringing Borneo States into line with other states require only simple central majorities plus concurrence of states concerned).

Nigeria (1960): E + ratification by two of the three Regions.

Nigeria (1963): E + ratification by three of the four Regions.

R. & N. (1953): E after resolutions of approval in all Territorial legislatures.

W.I. (1957): E after consent of Territorial legislatures.

W.I. (1962): absolute majorities in central legislature and absolute majorities in a majority of the Territorial representative Houses representing a majority of the federal population. (This procedure was agreed upon for 1962, but not implemented. See Cmnd. 1417/1961.)

SELECT BIBLIOGRAPHY

GENERAL

General or comparative works dealing with the newer federations are few in number. There is, however, a bibliographical commentary, *Federalism in the Commonwealth* (London, 1963), edited by W. S. Livingston, which provides a comprehensive survey of works published in English which touch on the emergence, development, and operation of federal institutions in the countries of the Commonwealth. An extensive bibliography may also be found in my *Recent Experiments in Federalism in Commonwealth Countries, A Comparative Analysis* (Oxford, D.Phil. Thesis, 1962), vol. 2.

Of the general works which consider these federations, the most useful is that by U. K. Hicks and others, *Federalism and Economic Growth in Underdeveloped Countries* (London, 1961), which contains an especially stimulating essay by F. G. Carnell on 'Political Implications of Federalism in New States', as well as articles on the economic and financial aspects of federal government in developing territories. S. A. de Smith, *The New Commonwealth and Its Constitutions* (London, 1964), includes a chapter on the federal experiments in Africa, Malaysia, and the West Indies. D. S. Rothchild, *Toward Unity in Africa* (Washington, 1960), gives a well-documented but primarily chronological account of the attempts at federal unions in East, Central, and West Africa. A critical discussion of the suitability of federal systems for African societies appears in R. C. Pratt, 'The Future of Federalism in British Africa', *Queen's Quarterly*, lxvii (1960), p. 188. In 'Federalism in the Commonwealth', *Journal of the Parliaments of the Commonwealth*, xliii (1961), p. 351, Patrick Gordon Walker suggests that the adaptation of the British parliamentary system to federalism has produced in the Commonwealth federations a distinctive variant from other types of federal systems. Also of interest are the mimeographed papers on various aspects of federalism, old and new, prepared for the International Political Science Association Oxford Round Table Meeting in September 1963 and the Sixth World Congress in Geneva in September 1964.

Public finance in the new federations has been considered not only in *Federalism and Economic Growth* (see above), but by several writers: Peter Robson, 'Patterns of Federal Finance in the Newer Federations', *Finanzarchiv*, xxi (1962), p. 415; A. R. Prest, *Public Finance in Underdeveloped Countries* (London, 1962); J. F. Due, 'Tropical African Contributions to Federal Finance', *The Canadian Journal of Economics and Political Science*, xxx (1964), p. 49.

Of the comparative works treating the older federations, the classic is, of course, K. C. Wheare, *Federal Government* (London), first published in 1946. Indeed, statesmen in the new federations have frequently cited this work as authoritatively defining the proper form of federal organization. The fourth edition (1963) includes brief references to the federal experiments undertaken in the Commonwealth since 1945. Also of considerable use as a reference is R. R. Bowie and C. J. Friedrich (ed.), *Studies in Federalism* (Boston, 1954), with its detailed analysis of specific federal institutions in the United States, Switzerland, Canada, Australia, and Germany.

A. W. Macmahon (ed.), *Federalism Mature and Emergent* (New York, 1955), deals mostly with trends in American federal government and with the project for a supernational union in Western Europe, but also contains an article by K. C. Wheare on the making of new federations. B. M. Sharma, *Federalism in Theory and Practice* (Chandausi, 1951 and 1953, 2 vols.), covers much the same ground as Wheare's earlier book except that a great deal more space is devoted to India. Special aspects of federal government are examined comparatively by A. H. Birch, *Federalism, Finance and Social Legislation in Canada, Australia and the United States* (Oxford, 1955), in which part of the final chapter includes a discussion of the new federations, and W. S. Livingston, *Federalism and Constitutional Change* (Oxford, 1956), the first chapter of which presents an interesting definition of federalism in sociological terms.

On the theory of federalism, the classical definition of the federal principle is formulated in Alexander Hamilton, John Jay, and James Madison, *The Federalist* (written in 1787–8; various editions are available), and has subsequently been expounded by A. V. Dicey, *Introduction to the Study of the Law of the Constitution* (London, first published 1885), and by K. C. Wheare (see above). A rigorous analysis of this definition was recently undertaken by R. Davis, 'The Federal Principle Reconsidered', *Australian Journal of Politics and History*, i (1955–6), pp. 59 and 223. Sobei Mogi, *The Problem of Federalism, A Study in the History of Political Theory* (London, 1931), is a two-volume history of the federal concept. The trend to 'co-operative federalism' in the United States was noted by Jane Clark, *The Rise of a New Federalism* (New York, 1938) and similar trends elsewhere subsequently attracted the attention of A. H. Birch (see above). A. R. M. Lower and others, *Evolving Canadian Federalism* (Durham, N.C., 1958), contains an essay by J. A. Corry discussing the development of co-operative federalism in Canada. Since then, both M. J. C. Vile, *The Structure of American Federalism* (London, 1961), and D. J. Elazar, *The American Partnership* (Chicago, 1962), have re-examined the working of the American federal system, concluding that federal-state co-operation is not a recent development but has always been a feature of American federalism.

INDIA

Of the newer federations more extensive material is available on India than on any other. The main sources on the devising of the federal structure are the Constituent Assembly, *Debates* (New Delhi, 1946–9), running to twelve volumes, and the Constituent Assembly, *Reports of Committees* (New Delhi, 1947–50), compiled in three series. The most important of these reports are those of the Union Powers Committee, the Union Constitution Committee, the Provincial Constitution Committee, the Expert Committee on Financial Provisions, the Linguistic Provinces Commission, and the Drafting Committee. Also of interest are the three series of *Constitutional Precedents* (New Delhi, 1947), prepared for the Assembly by B. N. Rau, to give information on constitutional arrangements elsewhere. Much of this material is now also available in B. N. Rau, *India's Constitution in the Making* (Bombay, 1960). The integration of the princely states into the Union was fully reported in the *White Paper on Indian States* (rev. ed., New Delhi, 1950), and by V. P. Menon, who was Patel's right-hand man in the operation, in *The Story of the Integration of the Indian States* (Bombay, 1956).

For a history of the evolution of provincial autonomy before partition, P. N. Masaldan, *Evolution of Provincial Autonomy in India, 1858–1950* (Bombay, 1953), gives an excellent outline, and Sir Reginald Coupland's three-volume *Report on the Constitutional Problem in India* (London, 1943), goes into much more detail. The *Report of the Indian Statutory Commission* (Simon) (London, Cmd. 3568–9/1930), the *Proceedings of the Round Table Conferences*, three sessions, 1931–2 (London, Cmd. 3778, 3997, 4238/1931–2), and the *Report of the Joint Committee on Indian Constitutional Reform* (London, H.C. 5/1934), give an insight into the problems which led to the federal plan of 1935. The difficulties involved in trying to create an All-India federation after the war are apparent in the statements of the British Cabinet Mission (London, Cmd. 6821, 6829, 6835/1946), and in D. R. Gadgil, *Federating India* (Poona, 1945).

The major constitutional documents are *The Constitution of India, 1950*, the subsequent *Constitution Amendment Acts* numbering sixteen by 1963, *The States Reorganization Act* (xxxvii of 1956), and *The Constitution (Application to Jammu and Kashmir) Order, 1954* (C.O. 48). Kashmir is the only state with a separate constitution and this is published in 'revised' form as *The Constitution of Jammu and Kashmir* (Srinigar, 1957). Of interest is the *Government of India Act, 1935* (26 Geo. 5, ch. 2), both because the 1950 constitution was so closely patterned on it, and because it served as the interim federal constitution between 1947 and 1950. The *Indian Independence Act, 1947* (10 & 11 Geo. 6, ch. 30), established the independent federation in 1947.

Of the legal commentaries on the 1950 constitution, I. Jennings, *Some Characteristics of the Indian Constitution* (Madras, 1953), contains some brief but forthright remarks, D. D. Basu, *Commentary on the Constitution of India* (3rd ed., Calcutta, 1955, 2 vols.), (4th ed., Calcutta, 1961–4, five volumes), goes into extensive detail, M. P. Jain, *Indian Constitutional Law* (Bombay, 1962), is a single volume which nevertheless draws heavily on case-law, and Sirdar D. K. Sen, *A Comparative Study of the Indian Constitution* (Calcutta, 1960, first of three volumes), is comparative in emphasis. S. R. Sharma, *The Supreme Court in the Indian Constitution* (Delhi, 1959), studies the role of the Supreme Court and the pattern of its judgements. Legal cases are reported in the *All India Reporter* (A.I.R.), the *Supreme Court Journal* (S.C.J.), and the *Supreme Court Reports* (S.C.R.).

On the working of federal government in India, there are a number of valuable reports. The most important are *The Report of the States Reorganization Commission, 1955* (New Delhi, 1955), the three separate *Reports of the Finance Commissions, 1952, 1957, 1961* (New Delhi, 1952, 1957, 1962), the two reports by Paul H. Appleby on the administrative system, *Public Administration in India, Report of a Survey* (New Delhi, 1953) and *Re-examination of India's Administrative System* (New Delhi, 1956), and the *Report of the Official Language Commission, 1956* (New Delhi, 1957). Books which deal with the operation of the Indian federal system are *Union–State Relations in India* (Bombay, 1960), by K. Santhanam, who had been a member of the Constituent Assembly and chairman of the second Finance Commission, B. N. Schoenfeld, *Federalism in India* (Washington, 1960), which pays particular attention to inter-governmental institutions, and C. H. Alexandrowicz, *Constitutional Developments in India* (London, 1957), which argues that in practice the Indian Union is genuinely federal. A large number of useful articles on various aspects of Indian federal government appear in the *Indian Journal of Political Science*. Other articles of special interest are P. R. Dubhashi, 'Unitary Trends in a Federal System', *Indian Journal of Public Administration*, vi (1960), p. 243; H. J. Friedman, 'Indian Federalism and Industrial Development', *Far Eastern Survey*, xxvii (1958), p. 33; M. Weiner,

'State Politics in India: Report of a Seminar', *Asian Survey*, i (1961), p. 35; and I. Narain and P. C. Mathur, 'Union–State Relations in India: A Case Study in Rajasthan', *Journal of Commonwealth Political Studies*, ii (1964), p. 120.

The reorganization of states and the significance of linguistic regionalism are analysed by Joan V. Bondurant, *Regionalism versus Provincialism: A study in problems of Indian National Unity* (Berkeley, 1958), and Selig S. Harrison, *India, The Most Dangerous Decades* (Princeton, 1960). Among the many articles dealing with this issue are S. K. Arora, 'The Reorganization of Indian States', *Far Eastern Survey*, xxv (1956), p. 27; D. V. Gundappa, 'Indian States and the Linguistic Problem', *Indian Yearbook of International Affairs*, iii (1954), pt. i, p. 35; A. K. Gupta, 'The Indian Parliament and States Reorganization', *Parliamentary Affairs*, x (1956–7), p. 104; R. W. Stern, 'Maharashtrian Linguistic Provincialism and Indian Nationalism', *Pacific Affairs*, xxxvii (1964), p. 37; two by M. Windmiller, 'Linguistic Regionalism in India', *Pacific Affairs*, xxvii (1954), p. 291, and 'The Politics of States Reorganization in India: the Case of Bombay', *Far Eastern Survey*, xxv (1956), p. 129.

The subject of federal finance has also come in for considerable attention. In addition to the reports of the Finance Commissions, there are R. N. Bhargava, *The Theory and Working of Union Finance in India* (London, 1956); B. R. Misra, *Indian Federal Finance* (3rd ed., Calcutta, 1960); P. P. Agarwal, *The System of Grants-in-Aid in India* (Bombay, 1959); and W. Prest, 'Federal–State Financial Relations in India', *Economic Record*, xxxvi (1960), p. 191.

Among the general books and articles on Indian politics which contain material of interest to the student of federalism are W. H. Morris-Jones, *Parliament in India* (London, 1957), *The Government and Politics of India* (London, 1964) which comments on India's inescapable federalism, and 'Stability and Change in Indian Politics', in S. Rose (ed.), *Politics in Southern Asia* (London, 1963), pp. 9–32; K. M. Panikkar, *Geographical Factors in Indian History* (Bombay, 1955), and *The Foundations of New India* (London, 1963); M. Brecher, *Nehru, A Political Biography* (London, 1959); Norman D. Palmer, *The Indian Political System* (Boston, 1961), and 'Growing Pains of Indian Democracy', *Current History*, xliv (1963), p. 147; R. L. Park and I. Tinker (eds.), *Leadership and Political Institutions in India* (Princeton, 1959); Asok Chanda, *Indian Administration* (London, 1958); Alan Gledhill, *The Republic of India* (London, 1951). Of the numerous textbooks on Indian government the best are N. Srinivasan, *Democratic Government in India* (Calcutta, 1954), and the more recent M. V. Pylee, *Constitutional Government in India* (Bombay, 1960). *India: A Reference Annual*, published each year by the Union Government, is rich in information on the activities of Indian governments.

PAKISTAN

Pakistan has operated under three ostensibly federal constitutions since partition. First, between 1947 and 1956, the working constitution was founded on the *Indian Independence Act, 1947* (10 and 11 Geo. 6, ch. 30), the *Government of India Act, 1935* (26 Geo. 5, ch. 2), the *Pakistan (Provisional Constitution) Order, 1947* (G.G.O. 22/1947), and the numerous amendments to each of these. *The Establishment of West Pakistan Act, 1955*, modified this federal structure by unifying all the western provinces and states into a single province. The second constitution, the *Constitution of the Islamic Republic of Pakistan, 1956*, was intended to establish the permanent federal structure of Pakistan, but the *President's Proclamation, 7 October 1958*, annulled it and imposed martial law. Pakistan was then governed under the *Presidential Order (Post-Proclamation) No. 1, 1958*, and subsequent amendments until 1962. *The Constitution of the Republic of Pakistan, 1962*, was the third constitution claiming to be federal. Supreme Court judgements on the law of these constitutions may be found in either the *All Pakistan Legal Decisions* (P.L.D.), or the *Pakistan Law Reports* (P.L.R.).

On the making of these constitutions there is considerable official material, but not all of it is readily available. The Constituent Assembly Basic Principles Committee, *Reports* (Karachi, 1950, 1952, and 1954), and the *Debates* of the first Constituent Assembly (Karachi, 1947–54, sixteen volumes), and of the second Constituent Assembly (Karachi, 1955–6, one volume), are the most important sources on the devising of the 1956 constitution. The *Financial Enquiry Regarding Allocation of Revenues between the Central and Provincial Governments* (Raisman) (Karachi, 1952), not only adjusted the division of revenues under the interim constitution, but also set the basic pattern for the subsequent constitutions. Among the most valuable official reports is the *Report of the Constitution Commission, Pakistan, 1961* (Karachi, 1962). Although many of its recommendations were disregarded in the 1962 constitution as it emerged, the report analyses the causes of the failure of the preceding constitution, and discusses the desirability for Pakistan of a unitary or federal system of government, and of a parliamentary or presidential form of executive. President Ayub Khan's views on the appropriate constitutional pattern may be found in Mohammad Ayub Khan, 'Pakistan Perspective', *Foreign Affairs*, xxxviii (1960), p. 547, and in a presidential address to the nation, *The Constitution* (Karachi, 1962).

Of books dealing with developments before 1958, by far the most useful is Keith Callard, *Pakistan, A Political Study* (London, 1957), which contains a chapter on 'The Federal Structure', analysing the operation of the interim constitution 1947–56 and the constitution of 1956. K. B. Sayeed in *Pakistan, The Formative Phase* (Karachi, 1960), and 'Federation in Pakistan', *Far Eastern Survey*, xxiv (1954), p. 139, makes an intensive study of central-provincial relations, but concentrates primarily on the early period between 1947 and 1951. Helpful articles are those by K. Callard, 'Pakistan', in G. McT. Kahin (ed.), *Major Governments of Asia* (Ithaca, N.Y., 1958), pp. 377–467; R. D. Lambert, 'Factors in Bengali Regionalism in Pakistan', *Far Eastern Survey*, xxviii (1959), p. 49; A. K. Sen, 'The New Federalism in Pakistan' in S. Bailey (ed.), *Parliamentary Government in the Commonwealth* (London, 1951), p. 149. W. A. Wilcox, *Pakistan, The Consolidation of a Nation* (New York, 1963), is useful on the integration of the princely states in Pakistan. S. M. Akhtar, *Economics of Pakistan* (5th ed., Lahore, 1961), devotes several chapters to central and provincial finances.

Books concerned mainly with the devising of the 1956 constitution are G. W. Choudhury, *Constitutional Development in Pakistan* (Lahore, 1959); H. Feldman, *A Constitution for Pakistan* (Karachi, 1955); and K. J. Newman, *Essays on the Constitution of Pakistan* (Dacca, 1956). The latter includes and compares the draft originally presented to the second Constituent Assembly and the constitution as adopted by it.

On the legal details of the 1956 constitution, A. K. Brohi, *The Fundamental Law of Pakistan* (Karachi, 1958) is of value because its author, as Law Minister, piloted through the first Constituent Assembly the Basic Principles Committee Report which laid the foundations for this constitution. A. Gledhill, *Pakistan* (London,

1957), also examines the structure and development of constitutional law in Pakistan.

Discussions of the disintegration of constitutional government in 1958 may be found in K. Callard, *Political Forces in Pakistan 1947–1959* (New York, 1959); K. B. Sayeed, 'Collapse of Parliamentary Democracy in Pakistan', *Middle East Journal*, xiii (1959), p. 389; and K. J. Newman, 'Pakistan's Preventive Autocracy and its Causes', *Pacific Affairs*, xxxii (1959), p. 18. The political situation under the 1962 constitution is analysed in K. B. Sayeed, 'Pakistan's Constitutional Autocracy', *Pacific Affairs*, xxxvi (1963–4), p. 365, and R. S. Wheeler, 'Pakistan: New Constitution; Old Issues', *Asian Survey*, iii (1963), p. 107.

Useful articles on political developments in Pakistan appear in the *Middle East Journal*, *Pacific Affairs*, and *Asian Survey* (formerly *Far Eastern Survey*).

MALAYA AND MALAYSIA

The nature of government in Malaya before 1940, and particularly the contrast between the Federated and Unfederated Malay States, is portrayed in Rupert Emerson, *Malaysia: A Study in Direct and Indirect Rule* (New York, 1937); L. A. Mills, *British Rule in Eastern Asia* (London, 1942); Sir Frank A. Swettenham, *British Malaya: An Account of the Origin and Progress of British Influence in Malaya* (3rd ed., London, 1948); and *Report on a Visit to Malaya, 1932* (Wilson) (London, Cmd. 4276/1933), which contains the pre-war treaties of federation in appendixes.

On the making of the 1948 federation, the most important material is the *Constitutional Proposals for Malaya, Report of the Working Committee, 1946* (Malayan Union Government Gazette, vol. 1, no. 20, 24 December 1946), supplemented by the *Constitutional Proposals for Malaya, Report of the Consultative Committee together with Proceedings, 1947* (Malayan Union Government, 1947). In addition, the United Kingdom reports (London, Col. no. 194/1946, Cmd. 6724 and 6749/1946, Cmd. 7171/1947), and the House of Commons *Debates*, cover the attempt to establish a Malayan Union and its replacement by a federal system. The actual *Federation of Malaya Agreement, 1948*, may be found in *The Federation of Malaya Order in Council, 1948* (London, S.I. 1948, no. 108), Second Schedule. Amendments to this Agreement appeared in the *Federation of Malaya Gazette: Legislation and Subordinate Legislation* (Kuala Lumpur, 1948–57). The *Report of the Committee Appointed to Review the Financial Provisions of the Federation of Malaya Agreement, 1948* (Kuala Lumpur, 1955), led to a change in the allocation of revenues in 1956.

The single most useful source on Malayan federal government is the *Report of the Federation of Malaya Constitutional Commission, 1957* (Reid) (London, Col. no. 330/1957), for it reviewed the operation of the federal system created in 1948, and prepared the basis for the 1957 constitution. Cmnd. 210/1957 (London), and the House of Commons *Debates*, indicate the reasons for the modifications that were made to the recommendations of the Reid Commission. The *Constitution of the Federation of Malaya, 1957*, may be found in *The Federation of Malaya Independence Order in Council, 1957* (London, S.I. 1957, no. 1533), Annex, First Schedule, and with subsequent amendments in *Malayan Constitutional Documents* (2nd ed., Kuala Lumpur, 1962), two volumes. L. A. Sheridan, *Federation of Malaya Constitution* (Singapore, 1961), provides a commentary on the text of the constitution, and the *Malayan Law Journal* (M.L.J.), serves as the reporter of legal cases.

Of books on Malaya, perhaps the best are L. A. Mills, *Malaya: A Political and Economic Appraisal* (Minneapolis, 1958), and H. H. King, *The New Malayan Nation*

(New York, 1957), both of which contain comments on the federal system, and L. A. Sheridan and others, *Malaya and Singapore, The Borneo Territories: The Development of their Laws and Constitutions* (London, 1961), which is useful on the operation of state governments about which little has been written elsewhere. Other books of interest are N. Ginsburg and C. F. Roberts, *Malaya* (Seattle, 1958); J. M. Gullick, *Malaya* (London, 1963); S. W. Jones, *Public Administration in Malaya* (London, 1953); John Lowe, *The Malayan Experiment* (London, 1960); and T. H. Silcock and U. A. Aziz, *Nationalism in Malaya* (New York, 1950).

The most useful articles are F. G. Carnell, 'British Policy in Malaya', *Political Quarterly*, xxiii (1952), p. 269; C. A. Fisher, 'The Problem of Malayan Unity in its Geographical Setting', in R. W. Steel and C. A. Fisher (eds.), *Geographical Essays on British Tropical Lands* (London, 1956); R. H. Hickling, 'The First Five Years of the Federation of Malaya Constitution', *Malaya Law Review*, iv (1962), p. 183; T. H. Huan, 'The New System of Revenue Allocation to States and Settlements in the Federation of Malaya', *Malayan Economic Review*, ii (1957), p. 79; J. Norman Parmer, 'Malaya and Singapore', in G. McT. Kahin (ed.), *Governments and Politics in Southeast Asia* (Ithaca, N.Y., 1959), p. 241; V. Purcell, 'After Merdeka— the Constitutional Outlook in Malaya', *Parliamentary Affairs*, x (1957), p. 388; and T. E. Smith, 'The Malayan Elections of 1959', *Pacific Affairs*, xxxiii (1960), p. 38.

The major reports on the negotiations for a wider Malaysia are the *Memorandum Setting Out Heads of Agreement for a Merger between the Federation of Malaya and Singapore* (Singapore, Cmd. 33/1961), and the United Kingdom Command Papers presenting commission and committee reports and the inter-governmental agreements concerning the inclusion of the Borneo territories: Cmnd. 1563/1961, 1794/1962, 1954 and 2094/1963 (London). The 'Rueff Report', *Report on the Economic Aspects of Malaysia by a Mission of the International Bank for Reconstruction and Development* (Kuala Lumpur, 1963), makes recommendations concerning customs policy and economic unification. Cmnd. 2094/1963 includes a draft of the *Malaysia Act, 1963*, later passed by the Malayan Parliament as Act F. 26/1963. This act establishes the new federation by extensively revising the Malayan Constitution of 1957. A legal commentary upon the new constitution is given by H. E. Groves, 'The Constitution of Malaysia—the Malaysia Act', *Malaya Law Review*, v (1963), p. 245.

On the creation of the Malaysian federation and its political implications, of interest are Lee Kuan Yew, *The Battle for Merger* (Singapore, 1961); M. Leifer, 'Politics in Singapore', *Journal of Commonwealth Political Studies*, ii (1964), p. 102; G. P. Means, 'Malaysia—A New Federation in Southeast Asia', *Pacific Affairs*, xxxvi (1963), p. 138; T. E. Smith, *The Background to Malaysia* (London, 1963); R. O. Tilman, 'Malaysia: The Problems of Federation', *The Western Political Quarterly*, xvi (1963), p. 897; and 'The Alliance Pattern in Malaysian Politics: Bornean Variations on a Theme', *South Atlantic Quarterly*, lxiii (1964), p. 60; Wang Gungwu (ed.), *Malaysia, A Survey* (London and Dunmow, 1964).

NIGERIA

There have been five constitutional landmarks. The first was *The Nigeria (Legislative Council) Order in Council, 1946* (London, S.R. & O. 1946, no. 1370), popularly known as the 'Richards Constitution'. The second was *The Nigeria (Constitution) Order in Council, 1951* (London, S.I. 1951, no. 1172), usually referred to as the 'Macpherson Constitution'. The third was *The Nigeria (Constitution) Order in*

Council, 1954 (London, S.I. 1954, no. 1146), the first truly federal constitution in Nigeria, which together with amendments 1954–60 was reprinted in *Federation of Nigeria Official Gazette,* vol. xlvii, no. 20 (Lagos, 14 April 1960), supplement, part D. The fourth was the 'independence constitution', entitled *The Constitution of the Federation of Nigeria* and found in the Second Schedule of *The Nigeria (Constitution) Order in Council, 1960* (London, S.I. 1960, no. 1652), made under the *Nigeria Independence Act, 1960* (8 & 9 Eliz. 2, ch. 55). The regional constitutions appeared in the Third, Fourth, and Fifth Schedules of the same order. The fifth landmark was the 1963 republican constitution, *The Constitution of the Federal Republic of Nigeria* (Lagos, 1963, Act no. 20). New regional constitutions were enacted at the same time (Northern Nigeria Law no. 33/1963, Eastern Nigeria Law no. 8/1963, Western Nigeria Law no. 26/1963). The *Federation of Nigeria Official Gazette* and the *Gazettes* of each of the regional governments contain the texts of legislative and administrative instruments.

There are a number of official reports which shed light on the development of Nigerian federalism. The *Proceedings of the General Conference on the Review of the Constitution, Ibadan, 1950* (Lagos, 1950), which preceded the Macpherson Constitution is useful because, unlike later conferences, the discussions are reported in full. The reports of the major conferences preparing the subsequent constitutions appear in United Kingdom Command Papers: Cmd. 8934/1953, Cmd. 9059/1954, Cmnd. 207/1957, Cmnd. 569/1958, and Cmnd. 1063/1960. Reports of two conferences held in Lagos were published by the Nigerian Government: *Report of Ad Hoc Meeting of the Constitutional Conference* (Lagos, 1958) and *Nigerian Citizenship: Report by the Ad Hoc Committee of the Resumed Nigeria Constitutional Conference* (Lagos, 1959). A number of specialized aspects were dealt with by commissions. There were four reports on the allocation of revenues: *Administration and Financial Procedure under the New Constitution* (Phillipson) (Lagos, 1947); *Report of the Commission on Revenue Allocation* (Hicks-Phillipson) (Lagos, 1951), containing some interesting comments on federal finance in general which have been reprinted in J. R. Hicks, *Essays in World Economics* (Oxford, 1959); *Report by the Fiscal Commission on the Financial Effects of the Proposed New Constitutional Arrangements* (Chick) (London, Cmd. 9026/1953); *Nigeria, Report of the Fiscal Commission* (Raisman) (London, Cmnd. 481/1958). The demand for the creation of new regions led to the particularly important *Report of the Commission appointed to enquire into the fears of Minorities and the means of allaying them* (Willink) (London, Cmnd. 505/1958). Other official reports of interest are Governor Richards's original *Proposals for the Revision of the Constitution of Nigeria* (London, Cmd. 6599/1945); *The Role of the Federal Government in Promoting Industrial Development in Nigeria* (Lagos, Fed. of Nigeria Sessional Paper No. 3/1958); *Report into the Relationship between the Federal Government and the Lagos Town Council* (Imrie) (Lagos, 1959); *Incorporation of the Northern Cameroons into the Federation of Nigeria* (London, Cmnd. 1567/1961); the *Federal Government Development Programme, 1962–8* (Lagos, Fed. of Nigeria Sessional Paper no. 1/1962); and *Proposals for The Constitution of the Federal Republic of Nigeria* (Lagos, Fed. of Nigeria Sessional Paper no. 3/1963).

For an insight into the issues discussed at the constitutional conferences and the views of the leading participants there are Nnamdi Azikiwe, *Political Blueprint of Nigeria* (Lagos, 1943), and *Zik, Selected Speeches of Dr. Nnamdi Azikiwe* (Cambridge, 1961); O. Awolowo, *Path to Nigerian Freedom* (London, 1947), and *Awo, the autobiography of Chief Obafemi Awolowo* (Cambridge, 1960); Sir Ahmadu

Bello, *My Life* (Cambridge, 1962); and Oliver Lyttelton, *The Memoirs of Lord Chandos* (London, 1962). Supplementing these are the opinions expressed in the debates of the Nigerian legislatures, and the reports and comments in the Nigerian newspapers and in *West Africa* and *Round Table*.

Several books by political scientists or lawyers devote attention to the evolution of Nigerian federalism: J. S. Coleman, *Nigeria: Background to Nationalism* (Berkeley and Los Angeles, 1958); D. S. Rothchild, *Toward Unity in Africa* (Washington, 1960), chs. 8 and 9; K. Ezera, *Constitutional Developments in Nigeria* (2nd ed., Cambridge, 1964); H. L. Bretton, *Power and Stability: the politics of decolonization* (New York, 1962); O. I. Odumosu, *The Nigerian Constitution: History and Development* (London, 1963); and E. O. Awa, *Federal Government in Nigeria* (Berkeley and Los Angeles, 1964).

A number of interesting articles on Nigerian federalism appeared in the period before independence: O. Arikpo, 'Future of Nigerian Federalism: Parts I–VI', *West Africa* (28 May–2 July 1955), pp. 487, 511, 533, 564, 589, 613, a series written by a former Nigerian central minister; A. Hazlewood, 'The Finances of Federation: Parts I–VII', *West Africa* (27 August–8 October 1955), pp. 803, 829, 847, 876, 893, 925, 942, 'The Regions' Revenues', *West Africa* (11 May 1957), p. 437, and 'Federal Finance in Nigeria', *West Africa* (9 August 1958), p. 731; A. Ogunsheye, 'The Place of Federation in West Africa', in the Hansard Society, *What are the problems of Parliamentary Government in West Africa?* (London, 1958), p. 124; J. R. V. Prescott, 'The Geographic Basis of Nigerian Federation', *Nigerian Geographical Journal*, ii (1958), p. 1.

On the post-independence federal system and its working the best descriptions are John P. Mackintosh, 'Federalism in Nigeria', *Political Studies*, x (1962), p. 223, and the three essays by Taylor Cole, 'Emergent Federalism in Nigeria', 'The Independence Constitution of Federal Nigeria', and 'Bureaucracy in Transition', in R. O. Tilman and Taylor Cole (eds.), *The Nigerian Political Scene* (Durham, N.C., 1962). L. Brett (ed.), *Constitutional Problems of Federalism in Nigeria* (Lagos, 1961), is a collection of papers concentrating for the most part on the legal aspects of the federal structure. *West Africa* and *Africa Digest* contain articles and reports of value to those wishing to follow developments in Nigerian politics.

RHODESIA AND NYASALAND

As with most of the colonial federations, the basic sources on the preparation of the federal constitution are the British Command Papers presenting the reports of the various constitutional conferences and special commissions: Cmd. 5949/1939, Cmd. 8233–5 and 8411/1951, Cmd. 8573 and 8671–3/1952, and Cmd. 8753–4/1953. In addition, the United Kingdom House of Commons, *Debates*, and the pamphlets of such organizations as the Africa Bureau, the Capricorn Society, the Conservative Overseas Bureau, the Fabian Colonial Bureau, the United Central Africa Association, and later also the Bow Group and the Church of Scotland, illustrate the controversies between the pro-federation and anti-federation movements. Useful in this respect as well are W. F. Gutteridge, 'The Debate on Central African Federation in Retrospect', *Parliamentary Affairs*, x (1957), p. 210, and Roy Welensky, 'Development of Central Africa through Federation', *Optima*, ii (1952), p. 5, and 'Towards Federation in Central Africa', *Foreign Affairs*, xxxi (1952), p. 142.

The Constitution of the Federation of Rhodesia and Nyasaland was contained in the Annex of *The Federation of Rhodesia and Nyasaland (Constitution) Order in Council,*

1953 (London, S.I. 1953, no. 1199), empowered by the *Rhodesia and Nyasaland Federation Act, 1953* (1 & 2 Eliz. 2, ch. 30). Comments on *The Constitution Amendment Act, 1957* and *The Federal Electoral Act, 1958* (Salisbury, no. 6/1958), were contained in British Parliamentary Papers, Cmnd. 298/1957 and Cmnd. 362/1958. The division of revenues was adjusted following the *Report of the Fiscal Review Commission, 1957* (Raisman) (Salisbury, C. Fed. 56/1957). Cmnd. 707, 814, 815/1959 (London), refer to the Nyasaland emergency of 1959 and the subsequent inquiry. Judgements of the courts appeared in the *Rhodesia and Nyasaland Law Reports* (R. & N.).

The operation of the Federation of Rhodesia and Nyasaland between 1953 and 1960 is examined intensively by the *Report of the Advisory Commission on the Review of the Constitution of Rhodesia and Nyasaland* (Monckton) (London, Cmnd. 1148/1960), and its extensive Appendixes (London, Cmnd. 1149–51/1960). Particularly useful are *Appendix VI, Survey of Developments since 1953* (Report by Committee of Officials) (Cmnd. 1149), and *Appendix VII, Possible Constitutional Changes* (Report by Committee of Officials) (Cmnd. 1150). The five volumes of evidence presented to the commission, *Appendix VIII, Evidence* (Cmnd. 1151), however, are more limited in value because of boycotts by African nationalists in the two northern Protectorates.

At the time of the federal review in 1960 a flood of books on the Central African Federation appeared, most of them pleading particular cases. Among those critical of the working of the federation were P. Mason, *Year of Decision* (London, 1960); C. Leys and C. Pratt (eds.), *A New Deal in Central Africa* (London, 1960); T. M. Franck, *Race and Nationalism* (London, 1960); T. R. M. Creighton, *The Anatomy of Partnership* (London, 1960); E. Clegg, *Race and Politics* (London, 1960); and C. Sanger, *Central African Emergency* (London, 1960). On the other hand, C. E. Lucas Phillips, *The Vision Splendid, The Future of a Central African Federation* (London, 1960), attempted to present the settler point of view. At the same time, new studies were made of the economic significance of the federal union. A. Hazlewood and P. D. Henderson, *Nyasaland, The Economics of Federation* (Oxford, 1960), is especially good, but the *Report on an Economic Survey of Nyasaland 1958–9* (Jack) (Salisbury, C. Fed. 132/1960); the Monckton Report itself (Cmnd. 1148/1960); W. J. Barber in Leys and Pratt (eds.), *A New Deal in Central Africa*; and S. Williams, *Central Africa: The Economics of Inequality* (London, 1960), also discuss the subject.

Of works not specifically aimed at influencing the federal review in 1960, the most useful are Colin Leys, *European Politics in Southern Rhodesia* (Oxford, 1959), the relevant chapters in D. S. Rothchild, *Toward Unity in Africa* (Washington, 1960), tracing the history and operation of the Federation of Rhodesia and Nyasaland, and D. Taylor, *The Rhodesian* (London, 1955), a biography of Sir Roy Welensky. The *Handbook to the Federation of Rhodesia and Nyasaland* (Salisbury, 1960), edited by W. V. Brelsford, contains much useful data.

The creation and operation of the Central African Federation has occasioned many articles. Of interest in addition to those in *Optima, Round Table,* and *Africa South* are G. H. Baxter and P. W. Hodgens, 'The Constitutional Status of the Federation of Rhodesia and Nyasaland', *International Affairs,* xxxiii (1957), p. 442; B. T. G. Chidzero, 'Nyasaland and the Central African Federation', *Queen's Quarterly,* lxvii (1960), p. 201; E. P. Dvorin, 'Emergent Federalism in Central Africa', in G. M. Carter and W. O. Brown (eds.), *Transition in Africa: Studies in Political Adaptation* (Boston, 1958), p. 62; K. Kirkwood, 'British Central Africa: Politics under Federation', *Annals of the American Academy of Political and Social Science*, ccxcviii (1955), p. 130; C. Leys, 'The Case Against Federation in Central Africa', *Public Law* (Spring, 1960), p.18; P. Mason, 'Prospects and Progress in the Federation of Rhodesia and Nyasaland', *African Affairs*, lxi (1962), p. 17; A. Taylor and E. P. Dvorin, 'Political Development in British Central Africa, 1890–1956, A Select Survey of the Literature and Background Materials', *Race*, i (1959), p. 61; F. M. G. Willson, 'The Rhodesias and Nyasaland', *Current History*, xlvi (1964), p. 148.

The controversy over the secession of Nyasaland and the subsequent dissolution of the federation can be traced in the debates of the United Kingdom and Central African legislatures and in their parliamentary papers, notably Cmnd. 1887/1962, 1948, 2000, 2073, and 2093/1963 (London), and C. Fed. 231/1962 and 246/1963 (Salisbury). Sir Roy Welensky, *4000 Days: The Life and Death of the Federation of Rhodesia and Nyasaland* (London, 1964), presents his view that the federation was betrayed by the British Conservatives. A different view is advanced by H. Franklin, *Unholy Wedlock, The Failure of the Central African Federation* (London, 1963), who considers the federation an act of folly which has finally been redeemed. The issues involved in the break-up of the federation are also discussed in P. Keatley, *The Politics of Partnership* (London, 1963), and G. Jones, *Britain and Nyasaland* (London, 1964). The federation was actually terminated by *The Rhodesia and Nyasaland Act, 1963* (Eliz. 2, 1963, ch. 34), and *The Federation of Rhodesia and Nyasaland (Dissolution) Order in Council, 1963* (London, S.I. 1963, no. 2085).

THE WEST INDIES

On the prolonged negotiations over the establishment of the West Indies Federation there is a long series of United Kingdom Command Papers and Colonial Office Papers. Of these the most important are the Secretary of State's proposals, *Closer Association of the British West Indian Colonies* (London, Cmd. 7120/1947), the *Conference on the Closer Association of British West Indian Colonies. Proceedings* (London, Col. no. 218/1948), this being the only conference of which the actual proceedings rather than only the decisions are reported, the *British Caribbean Standing Closer Association Committee. Report* (Rance) (London, Col. no. 255/1950), which laid the foundations for the form of federal system adopted, and the reports of the 1953 (London, Cmd. 8837 and 8895/1953), 1955 (London, Col. no. 315/1955), and 1956 (London, Cmd. 9733/1956) constitutional conferences showing the subsequent controversies, modifications, and reversals of decisions. In addition, several specialized commissions examined the unification of the public services (London, Col. no. 254/1949 and Cmd. 9619/1955), the establishment of a customs union and the division of finances (London, Col. no. 268/1951 and Cmd. 9618/1955), the structure of the judicial organization (London, Cmd. 9620/1955), and the location of the federal capital (London, Col. no. 328/1956). Comments on the pre-federal negotiations are contained in articles in *Round Table*, and two by J. H. Proctor, Jr., 'The Functional Approach to Political Union: Lessons from the Effort to Federate British Caribbean Territories', *International Organization*, x (1956), p. 35, and 'Britain's Pro-Federation Policy in the Caribbean: an Inquiry into Motivation', *Canadian Journal of Economics and Political Science*, xxii (1956), p. 319. W. A. Domingo, *British West Indian Federation: A Critique* (New York, 1956), presents the view of Jamaicans reluctant to join the federation. Hume Wrong, *Government of the West Indies* (Oxford, 1923), describes earlier attempts at federations and unions in the British Caribbean.

The Constitution of the West Indies was contained in the Annex to *The West Indies* (*Federation*) *Order in Council, 1957* (London, S.I. 1957, no. 1364), empowered by the *British Caribbean Federation Act, 1956* (4 & 5 Eliz. 2, ch. 63). In *Public Law* (1959), S. S. Ramphal, 'The West Indies, Constitutional Background to Federation' (p. 128), and J. C. McPetrie, 'The Constitution of the West Indies' (p. 293), comment on the legal aspects of the federal constitution. Legal cases were reported in *The West Indies Reports* (W.I.R.).

A particularly useful work is the special issue of *Social and Economic Studies*, vi (1957), 'Federation of the West Indies', commemorating the establishment of the Federation. It contains excellent articles by L. Braithwaite on the nego-tiations leading to federation, by D. Seers on the economic and financial aspects, by G. K. Lewis on the constitutional structure, and by Morely Ayearst on its political significance. D. Lowenthal (ed.), *The West Indies Federation, Perspectives on a New Nation* (New York, 1961), is also a symposium of essays. The operation of federal government is given a brief treatment in Morely Ayearst, *The British West Indies, The Search for Self-Government* (London, 1960), his discussion of the nature of West Indian political parties being an important contribution. In addition, the debates of the West Indian legislatures, *The West Indies Federal Review* (Port of Spain, 1960–2), published by the Federal Information Service, and the frequent articles and editorials on the federation in *The West Indian Economist* and in the local island newspapers are helpful in rounding out the picture.

The economic and financial aspects of the West Indian Federation are considered in the *Report of the Trade and Tariffs Commission* (Croft) (Port of Spain, W.I. 1/1958), 2 parts; in a special issue of *Social and Economic Studies*, ix (1960), devoted to discussing this report; in G. E. Cumper (ed.), *The Economy of the West Indies* (Kingston, Jamaica, 1960); and in D. J. Morgan, 'West Indian Finances', *Economic Journal*, lxvii (1957), p. 751.

The controversies arising at the time of the constitutional review led the Trinidad Government to publish several studies examining the effectiveness of the existing West Indian federal system, pointing to experience elsewhere, and arguing for a stronger central government: *Revision of the Federal Constitution* (Trinidad, 1959, a speech by the Premier of Trinidad, Dr. Eric Williams); *The Economics of Nationhood* (Trinidad, M23/1959); G. K. Lewis, *Puerto Rico: A Case Study of the Problems of Contemporary American Federalism* (Trinidad, M. 12/1960); and T. O. Elias, *Federation versus Confederation and the Nigerian Federation* (Trinidad, M. 10/1960). The Jamaican proposals at that time may be found in the *Bulletin of the W.I. Federal Labour Party*, i (1959), the *Ministry Paper on the West Indies Federation* (House of Representatives, Jamaica), reprinted in *The Nation* (Port of Spain, 11 March 1960), and the *Statement by the Jamaican Delegation* (London, January 1960). The tensions over the revision of the federal constitution are considered in 'Federation in the West Indies, its Economic and Financial Sig-nificance', *Round Table*, l (1960), p. 148, and S. W. Washington, 'Crisis in the British West Indies', *Foreign Affairs*, xxxviii (1960), p. 646. *The Report of the West Indies Constitutional Conference, 1961* (London, Cmnd. 1417/1961), sets forth the compro-mises agreed upon for an independent federation. The subsequent secession of Jamaica and the disintegration of the federation are discussed in the *Report of the Jamaica Independence Conference* (London, Cmnd. 1638/1962); the United Kingdom House of Commons, *Debates*, vols. 653, 655 and 656 (1962); H. W. Springer, *Re-flections on the Failure of the First West Indian Federation* (Occasional Paper no. 4,

July, 1962, Harvard Centre for International Affairs); E. Wallace, 'The West Indies Federation: Decline and Fall', *International Journal*, xvii (1962), p. 269; J. H. Proctor, Jr., 'Constitutional Defects and the Collapse of the West Indian Federation', *Public Law* (Summer, 1964), p. 125; A. Etzioni, *Political Unification* (New York, 1965), ch. 5; and a number of articles in the *West Indian Economist*, including J. B. Kelly, 'The End of Federation: Some Constitutional Implications', iv (1962), p. 11. *The West Indies Act, 1962* (10 & 11 Eliz. 2, ch. 19) and *The West Indies (Dissolution and Interim Commissioner) Order in Council, 1962* (London, S.I. 1962, no. 1084), finally terminated the Federation, but the *Report of the East Caribbean Federation Conference, 1962* (London, Cmnd. 1746/1962), and the subsequent commission reports (Cmnd. 1991 and 1992/1963), presented proposals for a new smaller federation.

TABLE OF CASES

INDEX

Abdul Aziz bin Ishak, 269 n.

Adbul Rahman, *see* Tunku Abdul Rahman.

Abdur Rashid Khan, *see* Rashid Khan.

Adams, Grantley H., 51, 95, 109, 207, 278, 336.

Administration: decentralization of, 20, 76–77, 189, 199, 201; educated *élite* as source of administrators, 52, 77, 231–2, 351–2; effect of linguistic differences on, 20, 77, 233; efficiency as a motive for union, 52–53; efficiency as a basis for the allocation of functions, 180, 199–204 *passim*; efficiency as an argument for the reorganization of regional units, 52, 77, 145–6, 150, 151, 161; federalism and demands upon administrative skills, 97–98, 101–2, 103, 225, 229, 232; spoils systems, 77, 88, 229, 231–2; *see also* Civil services.

Admission of regions to federations, 26, 27, 305–6, 320.

Africa Bureau, 89 n.

Agarwal, P. P., 216 n.

Agriculture, jurisdiction over, 32, 180, 182, 187, 188, 190, 191, 346.

Ahmad, M., 274 n., 281 n.

Akali Dal, 160.

Akhtar, S. M., 128, 242 n.

Akintola, S. L., 324 n., 328, 340, 341.

Akinyede, G. B. A., 44 n.

Alexandrowicz, C. H., 165 n., 216 n., 245 n., 279 n., 284 n., 293 n., 294 n., 295 n., 297 n., 307 n., 355 n., 356 n.

Almond, G. A., 15, 103 n.

Altine, Umoru, 269 n.

Amalgamation, as an alternative to federation, *see* Unitary political systems.

Amb, 254 n.

Ambedkar, B. R., 121, 153 n., 164 n., 319.

Amendment of constitutions: amendment acts, 319–27; formal procedures, 131, 132, 167, 263, 297–305, 347; procedures for allocation of finances, 195–6, 199, 201–2, 213, 216–17, 219–24, 300, 318, 325, 326, 329; regional constitutions, 167, 304–5; *see also* Admission of regions, Delegation of authority, Emergency powers, Flexibility of federal systems, Regional units, Rigidity of federal systems, Secession of regions, *and under each federation*.

America, *see* United States of America.

Anderson, W., 10 n.

Andhra Pradesh, 19, 147, 157, 159, 160, 165, 257, 259 n., 307, 327 n., 337.

Andhra State Act, 1953, 159 n., 307 n.

Angola, 103 n.

Anguilla, 148.

Antigua, 258.

Appleby, P. H., 173 n., 178, 189, 232, 319 n., 329 n., 346.

Arab Amirates of the South, *see* South Arabia.

Arab Federation of Jordan and Iraq, 4.

Argentine, 3.

Arikpo, Okoi, 161 n.

Armed forces, jurisdiction over, 180.

Aryan languages in India, 69, 83.

Assam, 20, 48, 74, 120, 147, 155, 165.

Association of British Malaya, 51.

Ataur Rahman Khan, 239.

Australia, Commonwealth of: compared with new federations, 47, 66, 92, 113, 146, 152, 154 n., 180, 198, 202, 221, 251, 264, 266, 271, 273, 278, 288, 330; as a model for new federations, 55 n., 61–62, 129, 131–2, 140, 141, 172, 218, 223, 226, 282, 285, 292, 307, 310; nature of federalism in, 11, 42.

Awolowo, Obafemi, 41 n., 78, 83 n., 87, 147, 151 n., 153 n., 160, 161 n., 249 n., 256 n.

Ayearst, M., 156 n., 261 n., 341 n.

Ayub Khan, Mohammad, 20, 22, 124, 125, 281, 342.

Azad Kashmir (Pakistan), 21, 147, 166, 177.

Azad, Maulana Abul Kalam, 269.

Azikiwe, Nnamdi, 57 n., 62 n., 87, 99 n., 147, 151 n., 160, 161 n., 167 n., 280, 340.

Bahaman bin Samsudin, 269 n.

Balewa, Abubakar Tafawa, 41 n., 61, 109.

Balkanization: examples of, 4, 34, 37; pressures for, 6, 94; *see also* Secession of regions.

Baluchistan, 120, 155, 277.

Baluchistan States Union, 147.

Banda, Hastings, 88, 312.

Banerjee, A. C., 307 n., 355 n., 356 n.

Barbados, 86, 108 n., 163 n., 276, 278, 341.

Barber, W. J., 46 n.

Barotse, 81.

Basu, D. D., 174 n., 284 n., 293 n., 294 n., 307 n., 355 n., 356 n.

Belgium, 47.

Bello, Ahmadu, 56 n., 61, 77 n., 87, 153 n., 158 n., 161 n., 340.

Beloff, M., 6.

D d

MAPS

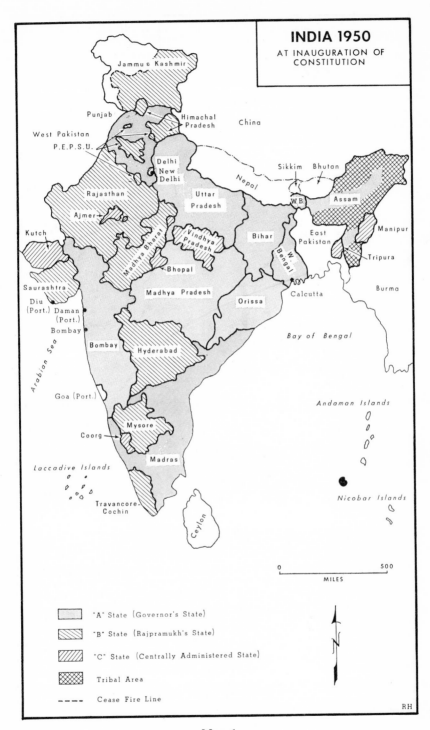

INDIA 1950
AT INAUGURATION OF CONSTITUTION

Jammu & Kashmir

Punjab

Himachal Pradesh

China

West Pakistan

P.E.P.S.U.

Delhi New Delhi

Sikkim   Bhutan

Nepal

Rajasthan

Uttar Pradesh

W.B.

Assam

Ajmer

Manipur

Kutch

Vindhya Pradesh

Bihar

East Pakistan

Tripura

Madhya Bharat

Bhopal

W. Bengal

Saurashtra

Madhya Pradesh

Orissa

Calcutta

Burma

Diu (Port.)   Daman (Port.)

Bombay

Bay of Bengal

Bombay

Hyderabad

Arabian Sea

Goa (Port.)

Andaman Islands

Mysore

Coorg

Laccadive Islands

Madras

Nicobar Islands

Travancore-Cochin

Ceylon

0   500
MILES

"A" State (Governor's State)

"B" State (Rajpramukh's State)

"C" State (Centrally Administered State)

Tribal Area

– – – –   Cease Fire Line

N

RH

MAP 1

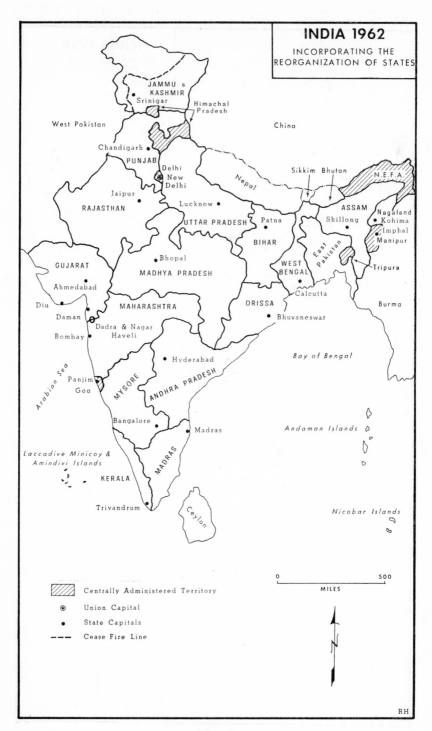

INDIA 1962
INCORPORATING THE
REORGANIZATION OF STATES

West Pakistan

JAMMU &
KASHMIR
Srinigar

Himachal
Pradesh

China

Chandigarh

PUNJAB

Delhi
New
Delhi

Jaipur

RAJASTHAN

Lucknow

UTTAR PRADESH

Nepal

Sikkim Bhutan

N.E.F.A.

ASSAM
Shillong

Nagaland
Kohima
Imphal
Manipur

Patna

BIHAR

East
Pakistan

GUJARAT

Ahmedabad

Diu

Daman

Bombay

Dadra & Nagar
Haveli

Bhopal

MADHYA PRADESH

MAHARASHTRA

WEST
BENGAL

Calcutta

ORISSA

Bhuvaneswar

Tripura

Burma

Arabian Sea

Panjim
Goa

MYSORE

Hyderabad

ANDHRA PRADESH

Bay of Bengal

Andaman Islands

Bangalore

Madras

Laccadive Minicoy &
Amindivi Islands

MADRAS

KERALA

Trivandrum

Ceylon

Nicobar Islands

///// Centrally Administered Territory

⊛ Union Capital

• State Capitals

- - - - Cease Fire Line

0   500
MILES

N

RH

MAP 2

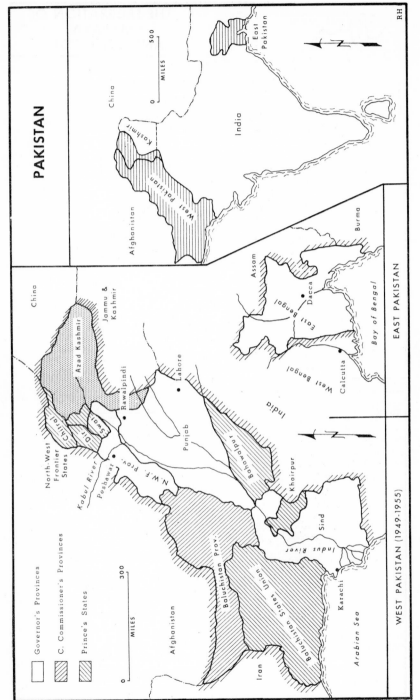

PAKISTAN

West Pakistan

China

Kashmir

Afghanistan

India

East
Pakistan

MILES

0   500

Governor's Provinces

C. Commissioner's Provinces

Prince's States

China

Jammu &
Kashmir

Azad Kashmir

North-West
Frontier States

Dir

Swat

Chitral

Rawalpindi

Kabul River

Peshawar

N.W.F. Prov.

Lahore

Punjab

India

Bahawalpur

Baluchistan Prov.

Khairpur

Sind

Indus River

Baluchistan States Union

Karachi

Afghanistan

Iran

Arabian Sea

Assam

East Bengal

Dacca

West Bengal

Calcutta

Bay of Bengal

Burma

MILES

0   300

EAST PAKISTAN

WEST PAKISTAN (1949-1955)

MAP 3

RH

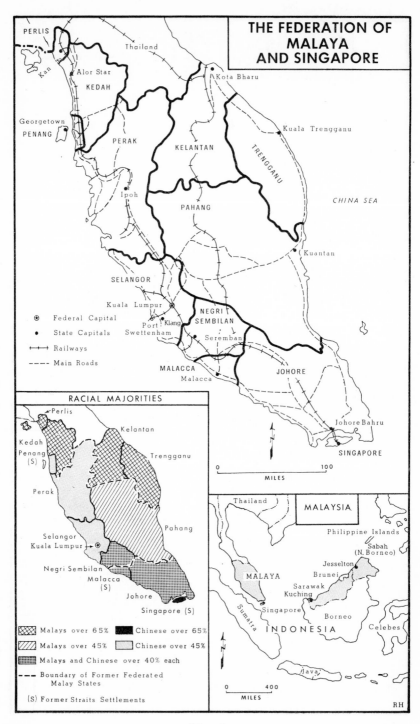

THE FEDERATION OF
MALAYA
AND SINGAPORE

PERLIS

Thailand

Kan

Alor Star

KEDAH

Kota Bharu

Georgetown
PENANG

PERAK

Kuala Trengganu

KELANTAN

TRENGGANU

CHINA SEA

Ipoh

PAHANG

Kuantan

SELANGOR

Kuala Lumpur

⊛   Federal Capital

•   State Capitals

├─┼─┤ Railways

- - -   Main Roads

Port
Swettenham

Klang

NEGRI
SEMBILAN

Seremban

MALACCA
Malacca

JOHORE

Johore Bahru

N

SINGAPORE

0   100
MILES

RACIAL MAJORITIES

Perlis

Kelantan

Kedah
Penang
(S)

Trengganu

Perak

Pahang

Selangor
Kuala Lumpur   ⊛

Negri Sembilan
Malacca
(S)

Johore

Singapore (S)

▨ Malays over 65%   ■ Chinese over 65%

▨ Malays over 45%   ▨ Chinese over 45%

▨ Malays and Chinese over 40% each

- - - Boundary of Former Federated
       Malay States

(S) Former Straits Settlements

N

Thailand

MALAYSIA

Philippine Islands

Sabah
(N. Borneo)

Jesselton

MALAYA

Brunei

Sarawak
Kuching

Sumatra

Singapore

Borneo

INDONESIA

Celebes

Java

0   400
MILES

RH

MAP 4

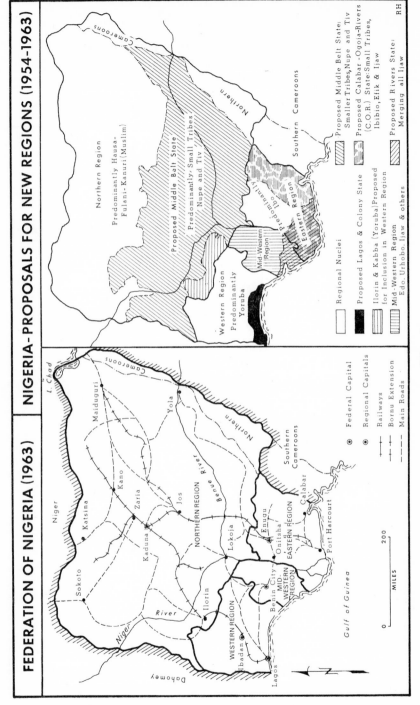

FEDERATION OF NIGERIA (1963) | NIGERIA—PROPOSALS FOR NEW REGIONS (1954–1963)

MAP 5

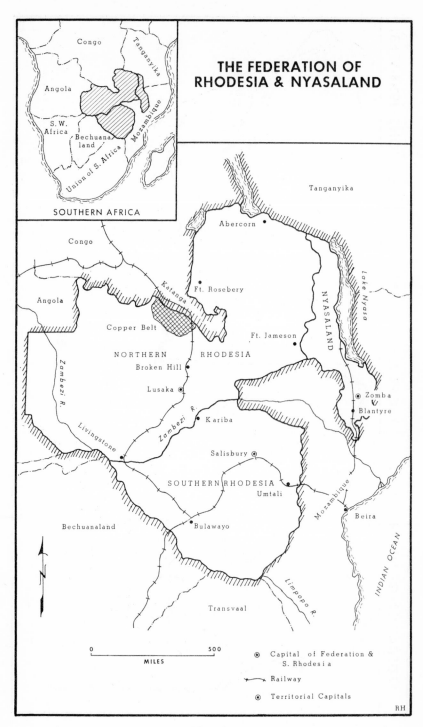

THE FEDERATION OF
RHODESIA & NYASALAND

SOUTHERN AFRICA

Congo

Angola

S.W.
Africa

Bechuana-
land

Tanganyika

Mozambique

Union of S. Africa

Congo

Angola

Tanganyika

Abercorn

Ft. Rosebery

Katanga

Copper Belt

NORTHERN   RHODESIA

Broken Hill

Lusaka

Zambezi R.

Livingstone

Ft. Jameson

NYASALAND

Lake Nyasa

Zomba

Blantyre

Kariba

Zambezi R.

Salisbury

SOUTHERN RHODESIA

Umtali

Mozambique

Beira

INDIAN OCEAN

Bechuanaland

Bulawayo

Limpopo R.

Transvaal

0   500

MILES

⊛   Capital of Federation &
       S. Rhodesia

➤   Railway

⊚   Territorial Capitals

RH

MAP 6

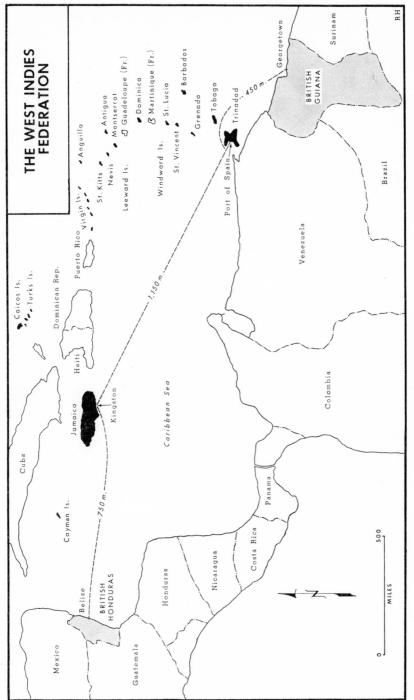

THE WEST INDIES
FEDERATION

Caicos Is.
Turks Is.

Anguilla

Virgin Is.
St. Kitts
Nevis   Antigua
            Montserrat
Leeward Is. ♫ Guadeloupe (Fr.)
            Dominica
Windward Is. ♫ Martinique (Fr.)
            St. Lucia
St. Vincent
            Barbados
Grenada
Tobago

Puerto Rico

Cuba

Cayman Is.

Dominican Rep.

Haiti

Kingston

Jamaica

Caribbean Sea

750 m.

1,150 m.

450 m.

Port of Spain
Trinidad

Georgetown

BRITISH
GUIANA

Surinam

Venezuela

Brazil

Colombia

Mexico

Belize
BRITISH
HONDURAS

Guatemala

Honduras

Nicaragua

Costa Rica

Panama

N

0   500
MILES

MAP 7

RH